International Payments, Debts, and Gold

SECOND EDITION

International Payments, Debts, and Gold

SECOND EDITION

COLLECTED ESSAYS BY

FRITZ MACHLUP

NEW YORK: NEW YORK UNIVERSITY PRESS

1976

ACKNOWLEDGMENTS

Grateful acknowledgment is made to the following for permission to use essays which appeared in their publications:

The London School of Economics and Political Science for articles in the November 1939 and the February 1940 issues of *Economica*. (Chapter I)

Istituto di Economia Internazionale for the article which appeared in *Economia Internazionale*, 1951. (Chapter II)

Royal Economic Society and the Macmillan Company for articles published in the March 1950 and March 1958 issues of *Economic Journal*, and in Allen and Allen, *Foreign Trade and Finance*, copyright 1959, the Macmillan Company. (Chapters III and V)

The Scottish Economic Society for the article appearing in the *Scottish Journal of Political Economy*, Volume I, October 1954. (Chapter IV)

The Journal of Finance for the article appearing in Volume XVI, No. 2, May 1961. (Chapters VI and XI)

American Economic Association for articles appearing in the June 1955 and May 1941 issues of *American Economic Review*. (Chapters VIII and X)

Kyklos for the article appearing in *Kyklos*, 1956. (Chapter IX)

International Finance Section, Princeton University. (Chapter XIV)

Springer-Verlag for the article appearing in *Zeitschrift für Nationalökonomie*, 1930. (Chapter XVII)

Fritz Machlup, for a chapter and portions of another chapter which appeared in *International Trade and the National Income Multiplier* copyright 1943 by the Blakiston Company. (Chapters XVIII and XX)

The Banca Nazionale del Lavoro, Rome, for the article appearing in its *Quarterly Review*, No. 86, September 1968. (Chapter XXI)

I am also grateful to Sidney S. Alexander, Thomas Balogh, Walter Gardner, Gottfried Haberler, and James E. Meade for their courtesy in permitting the appearance of extended quotations of their work in this book.   F. M.

Preface to the Enlarged Second Edition

The first edition of this book was published in 1964 by Charles Scribner's Sons, New York, under the title *International Payments, Debts, and Gold*, and in 1966 by Allen & Unwin, London, under the title *International Monetary Economics*. When the book was out of print at Scribners and the copyright was assigned to me, I arranged for the publication of this enlarged second edition by the New York University Press, which had previously undertaken the republication of three other books of mine.

A good many of the articles which I have published on international monetary problems during the last twelve years seemed suitable for inclusion in this collection. There were several on exchange-rate systems, especially on flexible rates; several on gold and other official reserve assets; several on new proposals for monetary reform; several on Euro-dollars and other xeno-currencies. The final choice fell on my article "The Transfer Gap of the United States," first published in 1968. This paper, which was widely discussed, approvingly and critically in the literature, fitted most appropriately into Part Five on "Capital Movements and the Transfer Problem." It thus could serve as the endpiece of the volume without disturbing the preceding text.

This does not mean that no changes had to be made in the first 464 pages. A few flaws of exposition in various chapters had been brought to my attention by my students, but particularly by Professor Toru Mabuchi, who translated Parts One, Two and Three for a Japanese edition, which Diamondo of Tokyo published in 1974. Readers of this second edition in English will be the beneficiaries of the care with which Professor Mabuchi read and scrutinized my text. Other changes had to be made in the introductions to the five parts in the sections on "earlier versions and records of changes."

In the Preface to the first edition I mentioned that the essays included in Part Five were of rather different vintages: 1928 the oldest and 1963 the newest. Since the essay added to this second edition was written in 1968, the time span has lengthened to forty years. If a kind fate should want it, there might, in a couple of years, be a third edition of this book: I could then add a new essay, which would lengthen the span to fifty years.

The reviewers' reception of the first edition of this book was most gratifying. If I may vent one complaint, it is that with all their praise of my "classical" and "famous" contributions they failed to call attention to an essay that I had not published before: Chapter XIX, "The Transfer Problem Revisited." In this piece I had analyzed a problem that had not been raised before, namely, the problem of unilateral transfer under conditions of growth in both the paying and the receiving countries. My fellow-students of international economics evidently have not noticed that a new contribution was mixed in with a collection of articles they had known so well that they did not think it necessary to examine the book. I cordially invite the reviewers of the second edition to correct this oversight.

FRITZ MACHLUP

New York University
April 1976

Preface to the First Edition

All the essays brought together in this volume are on monetary international economics. Some of them have long been on the reading lists of college and university courses; others are published here for the first time in English; and some have been written especially for this volume in order to achieve a more comprehensive treatment of the subject. To be exact, seven of the twenty chapters have not been previously available in English, and five of these were written only in the last two years.

In a sense, the entire book deals with the "balance of payments," though these words appear only in the title of Part I. Clearly, the effects of devaluation, discussed in Part II, are primarily those upon the balance of payments; the questions of gold and foreign reserves, treated in Part III, arise chiefly in connection with adjustments of the balance of payments; the plans for international monetary reform, reviewed in Part IV, are largely designed to cope with balance-of-payments problems; and the subject of Part V, the transfer problem arising from unilateral payments and capital movements, is again a special aspect of balance-of-payments adjustment.

Both the oldest and the newest essays are in Part V, where two pieces written in 1929 and 1931 are placed between others written in 1962 and 1963. The explanation lies in "history repeating itself": the transfer problem, discusssed 35 years ago in connection with German reparations payments, called for renewed attention in connection with the foreign obligations assumed by the United States.

With regard to my older essays the question arose whether they ought to be revised or reproduced without change, or at least without changes of substance. I chose the latter alternative: to make only a few corrections of errors and some improvements of style. And I decided to furnish a record of alterations: lists of *variora* are presented in the introductions to the five parts. Incidentally, these introductions contain much that would otherwise have to be said in this preface. Each of the introductions gives a quick preview of the chapters, a brief survey of some of the major themes discussed, references to earlier versions published, and the mentioned record of changes.

Decisions had to be made concerning differences in the style of citations, in the format of headings and subheadings, and in the spelling of certain words, used in articles which had originally appeared in different journals in different countries. The style of citations and the format of headings have now been made uniform, but the spelling has been left as it was. This program saved the labor of changing "programme" and "labour" in articles first published in England. For the painstaking work of combing the manuscript for inconsistencies or defects of style and exposition, I want to thank my assistant, Mr. Leon P. Sydor, and the copy editor, Mrs. Thelma F. Grube.

I want to thank also several unnamed colleagues and friends who have encouraged me and the publishers to assume that the collection of my essays on international payments, debts, and gold will serve a good purpose and will be welcomed by teachers and students.

FRITZ MACHLUP

Princeton, New Jersey
January 1964

Contents

LIST OF GRAPHIC ILLUSTRATIONS

LIST OF TABLES

List of Tables (cont.)

LIST OF T-ACCOUNT SETS AND MODELS

International Payments, Debts, and Gold

SECOND EDITION

▪ PART ONE ▪

Foreign Exchange and Balance of Payments

The seven essays brought together in Part One, although written in different periods—from 1938 to 1963—and arranged here in the order in which they were written, form a sequence which looks as if it had been designed for a textbook. The subject is systematically developed, beginning with the market for foreign exchange and the "market balance of payments," proceeding to elasticity considerations, to distinctions between the different, though frequently confounded, concepts of the balance of payments, to a careful interpretation of the meanings of equilibrium and disequilibrium, and concluding with an exposé of the mysterious numbers game that has been going on for many years around the "accounting balance of payments."

PREVIEW OF THE CHAPTERS

Chapter I, "The Theory of Foreign Exchanges," is essentially an analysis of market equilibrium, dissecting both supply and demand in the market for foreign currency, first with flexible, then with fixed, exchange rates.

Chapter II, "Elasticity Pessimism in International Trade," examines the arguments that have raised doubts in many minds about the proposition that higher prices for foreign currency would eliminate an existing excess demand in the foreign-exchange market.

Chapter III, "Three Concepts of the Balance of Payments and the So-called Dollar Shortage," shows that besides the concept of "market balance" there are two other concepts, one of the "program balance" and one of the "accounting balance," which are all too often confused with one another; and how this confusion was responsible for many erroneous views about an alleged dollar shortage in the early 1950's.

Chapter IV, "Dollar Shortage and Disparities in the Growth of Productivity," is a reasoned attack on theories purporting to explain that the dollar shortage has been "chronic" and that this was a necessary consequence of the growth of productivity having been faster in the United States than in the non-dollar countries.

Chapter V, "Equilibrium and Disequilibrium: Misplaced Concreteness and Disguised Politics," is a methodological exposition of the equilibrium concept as an analytical tool in economic theory in general and in international-trade theory in particular.

Chapter VI, "Comments on 'The Balance of Payments,'" offers brief remarks on a few semantic issues in connection with the "balance-of-payments mechanism," "rules of the game," and "balance-of-payments discipline."

Chapter VII, "The Mysterious Numbers Game of Balance-of-Payments Statistics," explains the 57 or more varieties of surpluses or deficits in the accounting balance of payments, and why none of the varieties can reasonably be presented as "the" balance of payments. Perhaps the most striking part of this essay is the story of the U.S. balance of payments for the year 1951, a story which kept changing over the years until the originally reported surplus of five billion dollars was eventually transformed into a deficit of one billion.

Major themes

One major theme to be stated boldly in this introduction can be found as a faint but consistent voice in the background of several issues treated in these essays. It concerns the essential difference between *needs and desires* on the one hand and *demand* on the other. The failure to make a sharp distinction between these notions seriously impedes economic discussion. To be sure, there can be no demand where there is not also need or desire; but there may be *urgent need* and *great desire* with *little or no demand.*

Demand implies preparedness to offer something in exchange for the thing demanded. This is to say, demand for one thing *is* supply of something else, usually money, sometimes goods or services. Persons who have nothing to offer—for example, persons who have not the money to pay for what they need or desire—cannot exercise economic demand. Failure to bear this in mind has made some writers come forth with very naive propositions, attempting, for example, to explain an excess *demand* for foreign exchange by great *needs* for imports. To emphasize the distinction is not to play down the "human element" or to close one's ears and heart to "crying needs"; it is merely to insist on preserving common sense and to avoid confusion.

Closely connected with this distinction is the notion of the "program balance" of payments. It is commonly overlooked that any attempt to forecast the "accounting balance" of payments of future years implies assumptions about a political program. For example, those who try to estimate next year's payments deficit of the United States must judge the political possibility or "impossibility" of reducing foreign aid and military expenditures abroad, and of pursuing expansionary fiscal and monetary policies at home to promote fuller employment. At the same time, they must judge how much of an increase in liquid dollar liabilities the monetary authorities of other countries are willing to absorb. These are political judgments.

Similarly, there are writers who use a concept of "equilibrium" with built-in political objectives. This notion is very different from the purely theoretical concept of equilibrium, designed to probe the mutual consistency of all magnitudes in a fully specified set of economic variables.

A theme of considerable methodological significance will be displayed in connection with the "numbers game" of balance-of-payments statistics. The common phrase about the "stubborn facts of history" will prove to be illusory, if not ironic, when it is shown that "historical" statistics are altered by theories being modified under the pressure of present-day problems. What a shock to empiricists to see their facts being molded by changing theories!

Earlier Versions and Record of Changes

Chapter I: "The Theory of Foreign Exchanges."
Written in 1938.
First published in *Economica*, New Series, Vol. VI (November 1939), pp. 375-397 and (February 1940), pp. 23-49.
Reproduced in American Economic Association, *Readings in the Theory of International Trade*, ed. by Howard S. Ellis and Lloyd A. Metzler (Philadelphia: Blakiston, 1949; Homewood, Ill.: Irwin, 1952), Chapter 5, pp. 104-158.
Spanish translation in *Ensayos sobre Teoria del Comercio Internacional* (Mexico and Buenos Aires: Fondo de Cultura Economica, 1953), Chapter 5, pp. 93-139.
German translation in Klaus Rose, ed., *Theorie der internationalen Wirtschaftsbeziehungen* (Cologne: Kiepenheuer und Witsch, 1965), pp. 169-213.

CHANGES: (1) Throughout the essay, the expression "increase (decrease) in foreign-exchange rates," easily mistaken to refer to the prices of domestic money in terms of foreign currencies, was replaced by the expression "increase (decrease) in the prices of foreign currency." See footnote 4 in Section A, §5.

(2) A paragraph in Section B, §9, was expanded to add a qualification omitted in the earlier versions. Footnote 6 was added.

(3) Related revisions were made in Section B, §§11 and 12; for the same reason, the fifth and sixth paragraphs in §14 of Section C were revised.

(4) Figure 4 in Section D, §20, was slightly redrawn to reduce the distance of the curves from the vertical axis. A slight change was made at the end of the second paragraph.

(5) In Section D, §22, in the enumeration of factors at work, Arabic numbers 1 to 8 were replaced by letters *a* to *h*; qualifications concerning elasticities of supply and demand and their effects were amended.

(6) In the fourth paragraph of Section D, §23, one sentence was changed for stylistic reasons.

(7) In the first sentence of §25, a reference to "existing" Exchange Stabilization Funds was made more specific by stating the years 1934 to 1939. The next sentence was slightly improved in style.

(8) Footnote 20 was added in Section E, §29.

(9) The third paragraph in Section E, §30, was revised to improve the exposition.

(10) In Section E, §31, the first two paragraphs were rewritten for the sake of greater clarity. Here and elsewhere "England" and "English" were replaced by "Britain" and "British."

(11) The first sentence of §32 was somewhat improved.

(12) Footnote 21 was added in Section E, §33.

Chapter II: "Elasticity Pessimism in International Trade."
Written in 1948-1949.
Published in *Economia Internazionale,* Vol. III (1950), pp. 118-137.

CHANGES: A few lines were changed in the paragraph on "The neglect of the elasticities of supply," and a few words, here and there, for stylistic reasons. Fig. II-1 was redrawn.

Chapter III: "Three Concepts of the Balance of Payments and the So-called Dollar Shortage."
Written in 1949.
First published in *The Economic Journal,* Vol. LX (March 1950), pp. 46-68.
Reproduced in William R. Allen and Clark Lee Allen, eds., *Foreign Trade and Finance* (New York: Macmillan, 1959), Chapter 5, pp. 97-123.
Japanese translation in *Chosa Geppo,* Vol. 42 (November 1953), pp. 115-129.

CHANGES: (1) Practically no alterations were made—to be exact: altogether four words were changed—in the first three sections.

(2) In Section D, "Conclusions," four paragraphs were written in 1958 to replace one paragraph in the 1950 version, because Allen and Allen had found the original exposition somewhat cryptic. A footnote marks the insert.

(3) The long footnote 37 was also inserted in the 1959 reproduction of the essay.

Chapter IV: "Dollar Shortage and Disparities in the Growth of Productivity."

Written in 1953-1954.

First published in *Scottish Journal of Political Economy*, Vol. I (1954), pp. 250-267.

Japanese translation in *Chosa Geppo*, Vol. 44 (June 1955), pp. 127-137.

Portuguese translation in *Revista de Ciências Econômicas*, No. 73 (São Paulo. June–September 1955), pp. 3-22.

CHANGES: Aside from the regularization of typographical peculiarities, the only change from the earlier version is the addition of a brief clause, inserted between dashes in a sentence appearing in the fourth paragraph of Section E.

Chapter V: "Equilibrium and Disequilibrium: Misplaced Concreteness and Disguised Politics."

Written in 1955-1957.

First published in *The Economic Journal*, Vol. LXVIII (March 1958), pp. 1-24.

Reproduced in Fritz Machlup, *Essays on Economic Semantics* (Englewood Cliffs, N.J.: Prentice-Hall, 1963), pp. 43-72; paperback edition (New York: Norton, 1967), pp. 43-72; new printing (New York: New York University Press, 1975), pp. 43-72.

Partial reproduction in N.J. Demerath III and Richard A. Peterson, eds., *System, Change and Conflict* (New York: Free Press, 1967), pp. 445-454.

Spanish translation in Fritz Machlup, *Semántica Económica* (Mexico: Siglo Veintiuno, 1974), pp. 49-76.

French translation in Fritz Machlup, *Essais de sémantique économique* (Paris: Calmann-Lévy, 1971), pp. 13-46.

CHANGES: Footnotes 19 and 25 were added.

Chapter VI: "Comments on 'The Balance of Payments'."

Written in 1960.

First published as part of the article "Comments on 'The Balance of Payments' and a Proposal to Reduce the Price of Gold," *The Journal of Finance*, Vol. XVI (May 1961), pp. 186-188.

CHANGES: (1) Only the first three pages of the original paper are reproduced here; the rest is Chapter XI in Part 3 of this volume.

(2) The internal headings were added.

(3) In the third sentence, second paragraph, first section, seven words were inserted which had been omitted from the original article owing to the typist's propensity to skip.

Chapter VII: "The Mysterious Numbers Game of Balance-of-Payments Statistics."

Written in 1962 and first used in a lecture in Geneva, Switzerland, this essay is published here for the first time.

I

The Theory of Foreign Exchanges

A. Sources of Supply and Purposes of Demand ▪ B. Elasticities in Commodity Trade ▪ C. Capital Movements, Unilateral Transfers, and Payments for Services ▪ D. Gold Movements, Gold Standard, and Pegged Exchange Rates ▪ E. Exchange Speculation and Interest Rates

1. Excessive specialisation has led to the disturbing fact that the techniques developed in economic theory are insufficiently employed in the various applied fields. The courses and textbook chapters on Money and Banking, Cycles, International Trade, Transportation, Public Utilities and others—are all cases in point. The beginning student of economics wonders why he had to waste time on the "useless" tools of analysis that were presented to him in Value Theory and which he never afterwards found of service when he came to the applied fields.

One of the objectives of this article is to show how the simple curve analysis can be used to advantage in the theory of foreign exchanges. The presentation here will be an abridged statement of the essentials.[1] An exposition in a textbook or in class would of course have to be less condensed and would have to include numerous illustrations in order to cover the abstractions with realistic dressing.

Another objective of the article is to incorporate into the theory of foreign exchanges relevant results of recent work in monetary economics. New practices of exchange stabilisation funds, on the one hand, new or modernised economic doctrines on the other hand [2]—both developed only

[1] Much of the subject matter presented here is based on Professor Haberler's *International Trade.*

[2] We refer only summarily to the contributions by J. M. Keynes, *The General Theory of Employment, Interest and Money;* Arthur Gayer, *Monetary Policy and Economic Stabilisation;* G. von Haberler, *Prosperity and Depression;* Jacob Viner, *Studies*

7

during the last few years—make it necessary to rewrite foreign-exchange theory in significant parts. An attempt in this direction will be made, especially in the later sections of this article.

Section A will lay out the conceptual scheme and some simplifying assumptions for the demand and supply analysis of the foreign-exchange market. Section B will discuss the factors that determine the elasticities of supply and demand on a foreign-exchange market when transactions result exclusively from commodity trade between two countries with independent currencies. Section C will deal with the effects on foreign exchanges of capital movements, unilateral payments, and payments for services, between countries with independent currencies. Section D will introduce the assumptions of the gold standard in its old and modern forms, and will discuss the causes and effects of gold flows between the countries concerned. Section E will examine the supply and demand conditions on a foreign-exchange market under the influence of private pegging and speculating activities, with special consideration of their effects upon interest rates.

A. Sources of Supply and Purposes of Demand

2.   For the sake of simplicity we shall combine the spot and forward exchange markets, and also the foreign-exchange markets at the domestic place (say New York) and at the foreign place (say Paris), into *one* perfect market. These assumptions might be easily dropped at any stage of the analysis, in order to demonstrate the functioning of speculation in spot and forward exchanges, and of arbitrage between the local and foreign markets. Such demonstrations would prove that the merger of all these partial markets into a single foreign-exchange market with the one currency as the "commodity" and the other currency as "money" assumes little away from the facts of the real world.

It is not difficult, for example, to translate the demand for dollars on the Paris market into a supply of francs on the combined foreign-exchange market, and likewise the supply of dollars on the Paris market into a demand for francs on the combined foreign-exchange market.[3]

---

in the Theory of International Trade; F. A. von Hayek, *Monetary Nationalism and International Stability;* P. Barrett Whale, "International Trade in the Absence of an International Standard," *Economica,* 1936, "The Work of the Pre-war Gold Standard," *Economica,* 1937; F. W. Paish, "Banking Policy and the Balance of International Payments," *Economica,* 1936; Thos. Balogh, "Some Theoretical Aspects of the Gold Problem," *Economica,* 1937.

[3] It is a good undergraduate exercise to practice such a translation: starting from a demand curve for dollars in terms of francs the amounts of dollars are shown by the horizontal axis (x), the amounts of francs offered in exchange for these dollars are shown by the rectangle (x y); this gives a supply curve of francs for dollars where the abscissae correspond to the values of the rectangles in the original demand curve, while the ordinates on the new supply curve, i.e., the prices of francs in terms of dollars, cor-

To simplify further we shall speak of two countries only. The abstraction from the existence of more than two countries could be immediately dropped, if the device were adopted to treat the "rest of the world" as the second country, and some composite of the various currencies as *the* foreign exchange. It is, however, less confusing to discuss matters first with reference to two countries only.

3. In good analytical fashion we shall examine the various sources of supply, and purposes of demand, one by one. Let us thus take commodity trade between the two countries as the first thing to be isolated.

If commodity exports are to be the only source of supply of foreign exchange, and commodity imports the only purpose of demand, we have to abstract from the gold standard in its various forms. Sales of gold constitute a supply of foreign exchange, and gold purchases a demand for foreign exchange. Gold movements will be introduced only at a later stage of the analysis.

If commodity trade is to be the only factor behind supply and demand on the foreign-exchange market, we have to abstract, furthermore, from the supply out of old stocks (foreign balances held by individuals, banks or official funds) and out of new debts (due to foreigners), and from the demand for foreign exchange for purposes of accumulating new stocks of foreign balances and of reducing old debts. In short, foreign lending and borrowing, i.e., the acquisition and diminution of foreign balances and debts, are ruled out at this stage; they will be introduced later.

It goes without saying that foreign long-term investments, unilateral payments, and the exchange of invisible services are all assumed away, if commodity trade is to be studied in isolation.

4. It is clear that the equality of exports and imports follows logically from these assumptions. If foreign lending and borrowing (and the other non-commodity transactions) are ruled out entirely, export surpluses or import surpluses cannot exist even in the shortest run.

It would, of course, appear too unrealistic to assume that the goods imported and exported cross the border at exactly the same moment. And it would be difficult to see how an increase in the demand for imports should make for a *simultaneous* increase of imports and exports, if the timing were thought to refer to the moments at which the goods pass the frontier or the customs house.

This slight difficulty disappears if the time refers to the moment at which the export orders are given and received and if simultaneously with

---

respond to the quotient of the abscissae divided by the values of the rectangles (x/xy) of the original demand curve. The analogous calculation has to be done in order to transform the original supply curve of dollars in terms of francs into a demand curve for francs in terms of dollars. This sounds complicated—yet every sophomore ought to be able to do it, or he has never grasped the meaning of demand and supply curves.

each order the importer buys foreign exchange and the exporter sells foreign exchange. This assumption corresponds, incidentally, to the actual practice of wholesale trade: the importer covers the foreign exchange needed for payment for the orders given, and the exporter sells the foreign exchange expected for the order received, on the forward exchange market, at the time the business is concluded.

If every importer buys the foreign exchange at the time when he gives the order, and if he cannot buy the foreign exchange (directly or indirectly) from anybody but an exporter, it follows that imports cannot exceed, or fall short of, exports, in the sense defined, for even the shortest instants of time.

The volume of imports and exports, however, will depend on the foreign-exchange rate at which the amounts of exchange demanded and supplied are equal.

5. A rise in the price of foreign currency [4] makes imported commodities more expensive in terms of dollars (assumed here to be the domestic currency) and exported commodities cheaper in terms of the foreign currency. A fall in the price of foreign currency makes imported commodities cheaper in terms of dollars and exported commodities more expensive in terms of the foreign currency. This explains why the importers' demand curve for foreign exchange will usually (abstracting from speculative transactions) have a downward slope from the left to the right, and why the exporters' supply curve of foreign exchange will usually have an upward slope from the left to the right. Exceptions will be discussed presently.

Every demand and supply curve must refer to a certain period of time which is allowed for the depicted changes and adjustments to take place. Curves which do not allow any time for market reactions to take place are usually called "instantaneous curves." Apart from these we should for our purposes distinguish at least three sets of curves. The *shortest period* allows only for the effects of the change in foreign-exchange rates upon import and export orders, with domestic prices in the two countries unchanged. These effects are too provisional to be of much analytical value, because changes in the quantities of goods to be ordered will affect, with little or no delay, the prices at which the various producers are willing to sell, or the various distributors are willing to buy.

The *short period* allows, therefore, for both reactions to take place:

[4] In the earlier version of this essay I said "rise in the foreign-exchange rate." By this I meant a rise in the prices of foreign currencies in terms of domestic money. A footnote warned the reader against possible confusion with the opposite meaning, in which many writers, in the British tradition of indirect quotation, use the same expression to refer to a rise in the foreign value of the domestic currency. In the present version I shall remove the possibility of confusion: I shall never speak of increases or decreases in rates without stating that these are prices of foreign currencies in terms of domestic money.

it shows, for example, how the quantities of foreign exchange supplied by exporters will react upon a rise in the price of foreign currency after the export industries have adapted their selling prices in dollars to the increase in business.

In other words, the short-period demand and supply curves of foreign exchange are not drawn on the basis of "given commodity prices" in the two countries, but on the basis of "given demand and supply conditions" in the commodity markets of the two countries. These given conditions are the traditional short-period curves which assume given tastes of consumers and given fixed equipment of producers.

The *long-period* curves on the foreign-exchange market are based on long-period conditions in the commodity markets of the two countries; the main adjustment of supply, for example, which is allowed to take place in the long run is, of course, that of plant capacity. It is understood that an increase in exports which is expected to be lasting may induce producers to expand plant capacity and to supply their products, after this adaptation, in increased quantities or at lower prices. Consequently, the long-period curves of the foreign-exchange market will be more elastic than the short-period curves.

In what follows we shall be concerned, first and foremost, with *short-period* analysis.

6.   The argument that short-run supply implies *some* lapse of time until the reaction to a change in price takes place does not restrict the validity of the statement that, under the enumerated conditions, exports and imports must balance for any interval of time. Assume that DD' and SS' (Fig. I-1) are the short-period curves for the foreign-exchange market. Exports equal imports at the foreign-exchange rate OQ. A sudden change in tastes makes for an increased demand for foreign currency for increased imports. At the given rate, OQ, the amount demanded would be ON, an amount which is, of course, not to be had. Therefore the price of foreign currency will rise. Under the assumption that the short-run reaction of supply takes time but no time is allowed, the price will rise to OT. At this increased rate, the quantity of foreign exchange demanded (OM) will be no greater than before, which is obvious as long as the "instantaneous supply" is assumed to be perfectly inelastic.

It need hardly be mentioned that exports equal imports both in terms of foreign exchange ($OM=OM$) and in terms of dollars ($OMRT=OMRT$). The volume of exports and imports has increased in terms of dollars ($OMRT>OMPQ$) and remained unchanged in terms of the foreign currency ($OM=OM$).

The described situation based on a zero elasticity of the instantaneous supply corresponds to Professor Taussig's "*impact theory*" of foreign-exchange rates under dislocated currencies. (*International Trade*, pp. 344–345.)

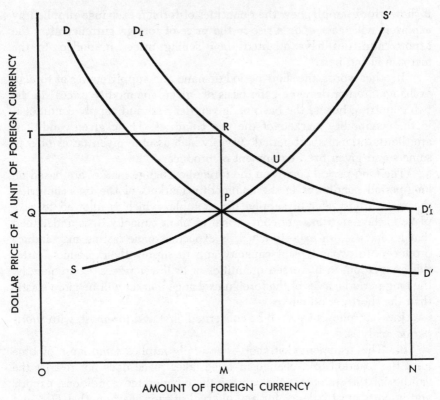

Fig. I-1. Increase in demand, supply perfectly inelastic

It corresponds more to the conditions of reality if we assume that the reactions on the supply side begin to take place after a trivial lapse of time: If it is not "misplaced concreteness" to transform operational time into clock time, one may assume that the reactions on the part of exporters will start after no more than a few minutes—because at the higher prices much money can be made by arbitrage in international commodities. More and more of the short-run elasticity of supply will come into play the more minutes, hours or days we allow to pass. A theory which does not concern itself with minute-by-minute oscillations of the market will neglect the instantaneous inelasticities and proceed to the elasticities of the short period.

B. ELASTICITIES IN COMMODITY TRADE

7. The study of the elasticities of supply and demand is, thus, the core of the theory of foreign-exchange rates. If, under our present assumptions, commodity imports are the substance behind the demand for for-

eign exchange, and commodity exports the substance behind the supply of foreign exchange, we have to turn to the conditions of the domestic demand for, and foreign supply of, our imports and to the conditions of the foreign demand for, and domestic supply of, exports.

Let us begin with the *supply of foreign exchange,* that is, the export of commodities. What determines the increase (or decrease) in exports which is brought about by a certain rise (or fall) in the price of foreign currency?

To be quite modern in the emphasis placed upon regulations, we may list in the first place the foreign restrictions which are directed against an increase in imports. If quotas had been established by foreign nations for all possible import articles and if the quotas had been completely exhausted in all articles, it is clear that a rise in the price of foreign currency cannot bring about any rise in our exports, and hence in the amount of foreign exchange. The elasticity in the foreign demand for our exports, that is to say, the elasticity of supply of foreign exchange, would be zero (or negative) above a certain rate. Below this rate the supply of foreign exchange would not be perfectly inelastic, because our exports can certainly fall below the limit set by quotas; below the critical rate there would then be numerous articles in which the foreign import quotas were not exhausted and, hence, in this range our exports would be allowed to rise and to fall as the price of foreign currency rises or falls.

Tariffs at a given level play a different role. If a certain quantity of goods were sold under the given tariff and at a certain foreign-exchange rate, a larger quantity could be sold if a rise in the price of foreign currency made the goods cheaper for foreign buyers. If a considerable portion of the price paid by the foreign buyer in terms of his currency consists of a specific import duty, a rise (or fall) in the price of his currency will reduce (or raise) the price he pays for the imported good only by a smaller percentage. The foreign demand for our exports will thus become less sensitive to changes in the foreign-exchange rate. The role of the tariff is analogous to the role played by the foreign cost of transportation and distribution. The higher these costs the less sensitive is the demand to exchange-rate fluctuations.

8.   Foreign import restrictions are, as we have seen, factors influencing the elasticity of foreign demand for our exports. No detailed explanation is needed for the statement that *the elasticity of supply of foreign exchange will be higher, the higher the elasticity of the foreign demand for the articles which we export.*

But this is not all. The same or similar products may be produced also in the foreign country. The price of our exports is reduced (raised) for foreign buyers as the price of foreign currency rises (falls). The increase (decrease) in our exports will then depend, in part, on the reduction (increase) in output by the foreign producers. If the foreign supply, which competes with our exports, is very elastic, that is, if their output falls (rises) much as our exports are offered at reduced (increased) prices in terms of their currency, our exports will increase (decrease) by relatively more. We can thus state that *the elasticity of supply of foreign exchange will be higher, the higher the elasticity of supply of foreign products which compete in the foreign market with our exports.*

This second factor is rather important. It is this factor which may be decisive in making the elasticity of supply of foreign exchange a positive value (i.e., in giving the curve an upward slope from the left to the right) in cases where the foreign demand for the articles which we export happens to possess an elasticity smaller than unity. With an elasticity of demand less than unity the quantity of goods demanded would increase as the goods become cheaper, but it would not increase by the same percentage; the amount of foreign money spent on the goods would thus decrease. The elasticity of supply of foreign exchange would then be negative (i.e., the supply curve would be backward-rising from the right to the left). But if the lower price (in terms of foreign currency) at the same time reduces the supply from foreign competitors, enough business might accrue to our exporters to raise the amount of foreign exchange received for our exports. In short, even when the elasticity of demand, on the foreign market, for the *articles* which we export is smaller than unity, the elasticity of demand for *our* exports may be greater than unity if the supply by foreign rival producers is sufficiently elastic.

We must add that in all probability the elasticity of foreign demand for our exports ("our" stands for almost any country) is greater than unity. This is, at least, likely (*a*) where the export industry is in strong competition with foreign production (which would appear to be almost certain if the second country were the rest of the world) and/or (*b*) where goods which had not been exported become exportable at a higher price of foreign currency. This, naturally, means a high elasticity of demand between certain price ranges since, in those articles, sales increase from zero to a positive figure. Such articles are likely to exist everywhere—so that it would be quite mistaken to estimate the elasticity of demand for our exports by confining oneself to the actual export articles and neglecting the potential ones.

9.   In order to export more, the export industry must be capable of increasing the quantities supplied to foreign buyers. This will depend, in part, on the capacity of our export industry to expand its output, and, in part, on the willingness of domestic buyers of the exportable articles to forego the consumption of them as they rise in price. The combined effect which the elasticity of domestic supply of the exportable article and the

elasticity of domestic demand for the exportable article [5] will have upon the supply of foreign exchange from exports cannot be stated without somewhat awkward provisos. For it will depend upon the elasticity of the foreign demand for our exports, that is, on the combined result of the two propositions stated in §8. If this elasticity is absolutely greater than unity, two additional propositions will hold: the third stating that *the elasticity of supply of foreign exchange will be higher, the higher the elasticity of supply of exportable articles,* and the fourth, that *the elasticity of supply of foreign exchange will be higher, the higher the elasticity of our domestic demand for the goods whose surplus production is exported.* If, however, the elasticity of the foreign demand for our exports is (absolutely) smaller than unity, the elasticity of supply of foreign exchange will be negative. In this case *lower* elasticities of domestic supply of the exportable goods, and *lower* elasticities of domestic demand for them, will make the elasticity of supply of foreign exchange received for the exports *less negative* and, therefore, *higher* (this time speaking of its algebraic value). In the extreme case, if the elasticity of supply of exports were converging to zero, the elasticity of supply of foreign exchange would likewise converge to zero.[6]

10.   As we have stated, it is not likely that (barring trade restrictions of a certain type) the elasticity of foreign demand for our exports is smaller than unity; hence, it is not likely that the supply of foreign exchange is of negative elasticity within any "practical" range. (By "practical" I mean under conditions which are likely to be encountered in reality.)

Nevertheless, it is interesting to examine what would be the consequences of such a negatively elastic supply of foreign exchange. Let us compare the effects of an increased demand for imports under conditions of a positively inclined supply curve with those under conditions of a *negatively* inclined supply curve of foreign exchange. This is done in Fig. I-2, where the supply curve SS″ turns backward from a certain point on.[7]

---

[5] To understand better the relationship between the two, let us suppose, for a minute, that the supply of the commodity, part of which is exported, is absolutely inelastic. This means that no more can be produced, however high its price rises. The part bought by domestic consumers, however, will probably diminish as the price rises; it will diminish much upon a modest rise in price, if the elasticity of demand for this product is high. The exports of this commodity may thus increase even if its production cannot be increased.

[6] These provisos had been omitted in the earlier versions of this essay on the tacit assumption that the elasticity of foreign demand is ordinarily above unity. This omission has been noted and criticized by several authors. See, e.g., Paul T. Ellsworth, "Exchange Rates and Exchange Stability," *Review of Economics and Statistics,* Vol. 32 (1950), pp. 1–12.

[7] The curve cannot rise backward more sharply. The slope of the negative inclination must at every point be steeper than that of the rectangular hyperbola passing through that point. This is clear when we consider that, as the price of foreign currency

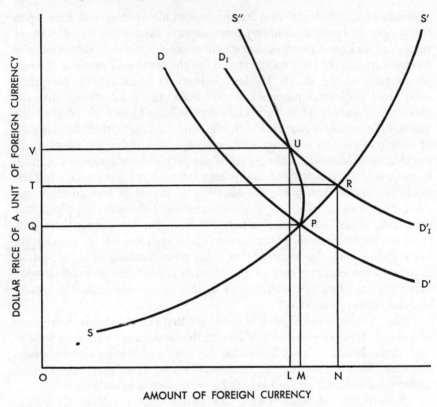

Fig. I-2. Increase in demand, supply positively or negatively elastic

Before the increase in demand for imports the foreign-exchange rate is *OQ;* exports and imports amount to *OM* in terms of foreign exchange, and to *OMPQ* in terms of dollars. If the supply curve is "normal," i.e., positively inclined (*SS'*), the increase in demand (from *DD'* to $D_I D'_I$) raises the price of foreign currency to *OT*, and raises exports and imports both in terms of foreign exchange (from *OM* to *ON*) and in terms of dollars (from *OMPQ* to *ONRT*). If, however, the supply curve is "abnormal," i.e., negatively inclined, the price of foreign currency rises to *OV;* exports and imports fall in terms of foreign exchange (from *OM* to *OL*) and rise in terms of dollars (from *OMPQ* to *OLUV*).

Exports equal imports, of course, whether calculated in terms of dollars or in terms of the foreign currency. But while both exports and imports

rises, the price of our exports is lowered only in terms of foreign currency, but not in terms of dollars. The dollar prices of the exports will rather be higher than before. The increased quantities exported may thus fetch reduced proceeds in terms of foreign exchange while the proceeds in terms of dollars are certainly increased.

rise in terms of dollars, they fall in terms of the foreign currency, if the supply of foreign exchange is of negative elasticity.

11.   In §7 to §10 the conditions of supply of foreign exchange from commodity exports were examined. We turn now to an examination of the conditions of *demand for foreign exchange* for commodity imports. Most of the statements which will have to be made concerning the elasticity of demand for imports will be analogous to those made about the supply side.

The role of quotas is obvious. With quotas for all possible import articles and with all quotas exhausted, the demand for imports, and, thus, the demand for foreign exchange, must become perfectly inelastic below a certain price of foreign currency. Above this price demand will be of elasticities greater than zero in absolute value, i.e., algebraically negative.

The role of tariffs is no different than before. The greater the portion which specific customs duties are of the selling price of imported articles, the less sensitive will demand be to changes in the prices of foreign currencies. Hence the higher the tariffs the less will the quantities of foreign exchange demanded fall as the prices of foreign currencies rise, and *vice versa*.

Four fundamental rules linking supply and demand conditions for the imported articles to the elasticity of demand for foreign exchange can be stated as follows (relating to its absolute, not algebraic value):

(1) *The elasticity of demand for foreign exchange will be higher, the higher the elasticity of the domestic demand for the articles which we import.*

(2) *The elasticity of demand for foreign exchange will be higher, the higher the elasticity of supply of domestic products which compete in the domestic market with our imports.* As, for example, the price of foreign currency falls (because of an increase in the supply of foreign exchange, owing perhaps to an increased foreign demand for our products), foreign products become cheaper in terms of dollars. If competing domestic producers will greatly reduce their output as prices fall, i.e., if their supply is very elastic, imports will rise even if the domestic demand for the articles concerned is (very or perfectly) inelastic. Likewise, even with an inelastic demand for the articles concerned, imports will fall sharply as the price of foreign currency rises, if the domestic rival producers expand output readily as domestic prices rise.

(3) *The elasticity of demand for foreign exchange will be higher, the higher the elasticity of supply by foreign producers of the articles which we import.* If, for example, a fall in the price of foreign currency tends to reduce foreign prices in terms of our currency, imports would not be able to rise, in spite of our elastic demand for them, if foreign supply were perfectly inelastic. The selling prices of these foreign products in terms

of their own currency would rise so much as to offset the price reduction which the lower price of foreign currency would imply for our buyers in terms of our currency. Statement (3) holds only if the elasticity of demand for imports is above unity; it is also qualified by the fourth rule.

(4) *The elasticity of demand for foreign exchange will be higher, the higher the elasticity of the foreign demand for their own products.* If, for example, foreign producers are not capable of expanding their output as our demand rises, and if therefore the prices of their products in terms of foreign currency rise, this may induce foreign domestic buyers to forego the purchase of these goods, thus releasing them for our disposal. Our imports can therefore increase even if foreign production cannot, a fall of foreign consumption providing the goods whose production seems to be fixed. Likewise, even with an inelastic supply by the producers of the articles concerned, imports will fall sharply as the price of foreign currency rises, if foreign home consumption expands readily as prices in their country fall. These statements rest again on the assumption that the elasticity of our demand for imports are above unity.

12. The reader with a sense for symmetry will now expect a digression on the possibility of negative elasticity of demand, i.e., of a backward-falling demand curve. Nothing of this sort is in order, unless we wish to enter into perfectly absurd theorising about imports being sufficiently affected by prestige values of imported luxuries.

The lack of symmetry is only a seeming one, resulting from the properties of our curve analysis. In the case of exports of goods and the *supply* of foreign currency, we have seen that, if the foreign demand for our exports is of smaller than unitary elasticity, this implies that the amounts of *foreign currency* spent for our exports will fall as the exports, owing to a higher price of foreign currency, rise in physical volume. In the case of imports and the *demand* for foreign currency, however, an elasticity of the domestic demand for imports of less than unity means that the amounts of *domestic currency* spent for imports will fall as these imports, owing to a lower price of foreign currency, increase in physical volume. The curves in our graphs show the amounts of foreign currency on the abscissa, but the amounts of domestic currency by the rectangular areas produced by abscissa and ordinate. Hence a decline in the amounts of foreign currency supplied, as the price of foreign currency rises, is shown by a backward-rising supply curve, whereas a decline in the amounts of domestic currency is not shown by any "backward" turn of the demand curve but simply by a slope which is steeper than that of rectangular hyperbolas passing through the same points.

As to the question whether the demand for foreign exchange for import purposes is likely, in reality, to be of an elasticity smaller than unity, we must recall what was said in §8 on the analogous problem. One point which was emphasised there was the degree of competition. Elasticity of demand from the point of view of any particular *seller*, or selling country, is a function of the number of sellers, or selling countries, which compete for higher shares of the market. If the other country is larger than the own country, or, if the other "country" is the rest of the world, then it is highly probable that the share of our exports in the foreign market is small, and, hence, the elasticity of foreign demand for our exports is very high.

These considerations are not applicable to the problem of elasticity of demand from the point of view of any particular *buyer*, or buying country. Whether the domestic demand for an imported article is elastic or inelastic is not a function of the number of sellers; here we are concerned with the total market demand, the elasticity of which depends on "tastes," consumption habits, income, income distribution, etc. Even if the importing country is smaller than the other, or even if the other "country" is the rest of the world, there is nothing which would make us expect our demand for imports to be highly elastic.[8]

The other point used in the argument in favour of a high elasticity of foreign demand for our exports was the existence of potential export articles. This point is valid also in a consideration about the elasticity of our demand for imports. There are undoubtedly a number of goods which at a given exchange rate are not among imported articles but which might become imported articles if the price of foreign currency were lower. Whether or not this circumstance is sufficient to make total demand for imports of an elasticity greater than unity cannot be answered in general theory.

C. Capital movements, unilateral transfers, and payments for services

13.   Commodity trade has been assumed to be the only source of demand and supply of foreign exchange up to this point. Imports of goods have been the substance behind the demand, exports of goods the substance behind the supply. We proceed now to including unilateral payments and long-term capital movements into our analysis. We still rule out invisible services, gold movements, and short-term capital movements.

[8] One might think that the proposition advanced in the text hinges on the definition of "commodity" or "imported article." If these terms were narrowly applied so as to regard special types, brands, qualities, etc., as separate articles, the demand for each "article" would naturally be more elastic the greater the number of near substitutes. This is, however, not the same thing as the elasticity of the market demand as dependent or not dependent on the number of sellers of each "article." Whereas demand as seen by each seller possesses greater elasticity the greater the number of sellers of the article, market demand as the aggregate of the buyers' demand schedules possesses an elasticity which is independent of the number of sellers of the article.

Let us assume that a series of large payments is to be made from our country to the foreign country, so that there emerges a demand for foreign exchange which is not arising from a demand for imports. The purpose of the payments may be investment in the foreign country, or settlement of old debts, or a war tribute, or something of the sort. In order to obtain the aggregate demand for foreign exchange, we have to add the demand for foreign exchange of those who wish to make these payments, to the demand for foreign exchange of those who wish to import commodities. (That the latter demand is not likely to be the same as it would be without the non-trade payments will be discussed later.)

The purpose of the payments will, of course, have a bearing on the elasticity of the demand for foreign exchange. If it concerns the payment of a debt contracted, or a tribute imposed, in terms of our own currency, so that a fixed amount of our currency has to be used for purchasing foreign exchange, then the demand for foreign exchange arising from this payment has an elasticity of one, i.e., the demand curve is a rectangular hyperbola. If it concerns the unpostponable payment of a debt contracted, or a tribute imposed, in terms of foreign exchange, so that a fixed amount of foreign exchange has to be purchased, then the demand for foreign exchange arising from this payment has an elasticity of zero, i.e., the demand curve is a vertical straight line—at least up to some point above which an increase in the price of foreign currency would surpass the good faith or solvency of the payers, in terms of their own currency.

The amount of the payments is not fixed in either terms in case of investments in the foreign country. Apart from changes in expectations due to changes in the foreign-exchange rate, it seems certain that the elasticity of demand for foreign exchange for purposes of long-term foreign investment is more than zero, and it may be also more than unity.

14.   Let us assume provisionally that the emergence of the demand for foreign exchange for purposes of investment abroad ("capital export") leaves demand and supply of foreign exchange arising from demand for imports and supply of exports unchanged. What are the probable changes in exchange rates, in imports, in exports?

For the accompanying graph (Fig. I-3), the exchange rate would be MP or OQ, if demand and supply of foreign exchange were exclusively due to demand for imports and supply of exports ($D_I D'_I$ and $S_E S'_E$); imports, in this case, would equal exports in terms of foreign exchange ($OM=OM$) and in terms of the own currency ($OMPQ=OMPQ$). If now the demand for foreign exchange of "capital exporters" is added to the demand for foreign exchange of the commodity importers, an aggregate demand curve ($D_{I+C} D'_{I+C}$), to the right of and above the first demand curve, would make an exchange rate of OQ impossible: the price of foreign

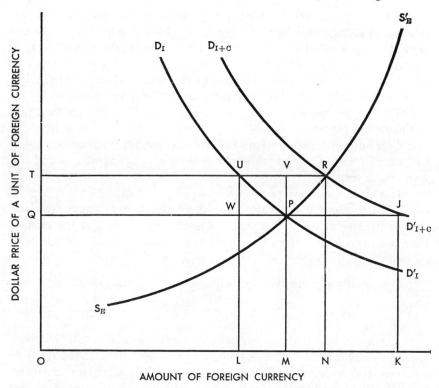

Fig. I-3. Capital exports resulting in reduced commodity imports and increased commodity exports

currency will be driven up to MV or OT, where the quantities demanded and supplied are equal (TR or ON).

At this increased exchange rate capital exporters buy less foreign currency than at the lower rate ($UR < PJ$), commodity importers buy less than at the lower rate ($TU < QP$), and commodity exporters sell more than at the lower rate ($TR > QP$). Who provides the foreign exchange (UR or LN) which the capital exporters take from the market? It is provided through an increase in the amounts supplied by commodity exporters (VR) and through a decrease in the amounts demanded by commodity importers (UV).

We see, then, that the capital export brings with it a decrease in commodity imports and an increase in commodity exports, all calculated in terms of foreign exchange:

Capital export = Fall in commodity imports + Rise in commodity exports, i.e.,

$$LN = LM + MN.$$

If these quantities are calculated in terms of our own currency, instead of in foreign exchange, the result may be different. For, if the demand for imports is of an elasticity smaller than unity, the domestic value of imports will rise, rather than fall, as the price of foreign currency is increased. Accordingly, in our graph, imports in terms of dollars are higher at the higher price of foreign currency than at the lower price ($OLUT >$ $OMPQ$). We are therefore confronted with the fact that in consequence of the capital export, commodity imports may show an increase in terms of dollars but a decrease in terms of foreign currency. Statisticians, trying to "verify" a fall in imports due to increased capital exports, should beware of this trap.

This does not interfere with the development of an export surplus, calculated in domestic currency. The domestic value of exports will be increased more than the domestic value of imports, so that the change from balanced trade to an export surplus is realized in terms of domestic currency as well as in terms of foreign currency:

Commodity exports=Commodity imports+Capital exports

i.e., ON $=$ OL $+$ LN
and $ONRT$ $=$ $OLUT$ $+$ $LNRU.$

The above results follow logically from our assumptions. If there are, among the international transactions, no (invisible) services rendered or received, and if there are no movements of gold or short-term balances, the balance of trade is uniquely determined by the balance of capital movements. A so-called "favourable" trade balance must be equal to a net capital export, and a so-called "adverse" trade balance must be equal to a net capital import.

15.   "Invisible" exports and imports, that is, the balance of services or "current items" other than commodity trade in the balance of international payments, can be introduced into our analysis without any difficulties. Demand and supply of foreign exchange arising from these services received from, or rendered to, residents of foreign countries, can be treated graphically exactly as we have just treated the demand for foreign exchange arising from capital exports.

We can easily imagine a demand curve for foreign exchange for foreign travel. The aggregate demand curve for foreign currency for both visible imports (commodity) and invisible imports (tourists' expenditures abroad) might look exactly like the aggregate demand curve in Fig. I-3. The result of our considerations would, of course, be analogous. For example, if foreign travel were the only service item, the export surplus in the trade balance would be equal to the net "deficit" in the balance of tourist expenditures; or, conversely, the import surplus in the trade balance would be equal to the net "gain" in the balance of tourist expenditures. And again, an increase in the demand for foreign travel would lead to an increase in commodity exports and a decrease in commodity imports in terms of foreign currency; and to an increase in commodity exports and a decrease or increase in commodity imports in terms of our own currency.[9]

It may be mentioned that some of the service items are complementary, while others are competing with exported and imported commodities; furthermore that supply and demand of foreign exchange arising from these current service items may be of all possible elasticities, ranging from less than zero to more than unity.

Some examples may be instructive.

(a) "Immigrants' remittances" to their relatives in foreign countries may be solely dependent on the remitters' budgets, or, on the other hand, solely dependent on the beneficiaries' needs; the respective demand for foreign exchange would be fixed in dollars, that is, of unit elasticity in the former case, and fixed in foreign exchange, that is, of zero elasticity in the latter. The elasticity would be between zero and one, if both factors bore on the size of the remittances.

(b) Interest and dividends received from foreign securities involve a supply of foreign exchange. If the amounts are fixed in foreign money, the respective supply of foreign exchange is perfectly inelastic; if, on the other hand, the amounts are fixed in terms of our own currency (which can be the case with special bonds only), the respective supply of foreign exchange is negatively elastic, that is to say, it is exactly minus one.[10]

(c) Payments for freight and shipping services sometimes bear a complicated relationship to the commodities imported and exported. If it is assumed that the foreign country has no merchant marine and that both exports and imports have to be transported on our boats, the supply of foreign exchange arising from these shipping services must necessarily tend to make our balance of trade "adverse." (Would that we might get rid of these nonsensical terms "adverse" and "favourable"!) If all commodity prices are fixed f.o.b. our ports, every import gives rise to a demand for foreign exchange, in payment for the goods, and a supply of foreign exchange, in payment for their transportation; and every export gives rise to a supply of foreign exchange received for the goods exported and another for their transportation. In deriving a supply curve of the

[9] If the possibility of a backward-rising supply curve of foreign currency is to be accounted for, the last statement should read: "An increase in the demand for foreign travel would lead to an increase or decrease in commodity exports and a decrease in commodity imports in terms of foreign currency; and to an increase in commodity exports and a decrease or increase in commodity imports in terms of our own currency."

[10] In other words, the supply curve would look just like a demand curve of unit elasticity (i.e., a rectangular hyperbola).

foreign exchange which proceeds from shipping services, one is then faced with the difficulty that any change in the exchange rate may increase transportation in one direction but decrease it in the other. The supply of foreign exchange from shipping services is of "normal" elasticity only if the services of our marine compete with those of the other country (or, that is, of the rest of the world). In this case, a rise in the price of foreign currency implies a relative cheapening of the services of our merchant marine in terms of foreign currency, and this would (in the case of competition sufficient to produce an elastic demand for the services of *our* merchant marine) bring our marine sufficiently increased business to secure increased proceeds in terms of foreign exchange, unless competing fleets lowered their prices to American ports.

16.   It is now time to drop our provisional assumption that the emergence of a demand for (or supply of) foreign exchange for purposes other than commodity imports (or exports) leaves the importers' demand and the exporters' supply unchanged. It may be well, however, to warn here against the possible confusion between demand (in the schedule sense), on the one hand, and quantity demanded, on the other.

The fall in commodity imports (in terms of foreign money) which was found above to be the necessary consequence of a new demand for foreign exchange by capital exporters did not constitute a fall in the commodity importers' demand for foreign exchange, but merely a fall in the amount of foreign exchange demanded by commodity importers. The amount of foreign currency demanded by commodity importers diminished because of the rise in the price of foreign currency which was caused by the capital exporters' demand for foreign exchange. This reaction represented a movement *along* the commodity importers' (unchanged) demand curve.

Now, we have to examine whether there may not be also a shift *of* the commodity importers' demand curve (and commodity exporters' supply curve), resulting from a new demand for foreign exchange for payments of any sort—such as capital exports, unilateral remittances, or payments for foreign services bought.

Let us assume an increase in demand for foreign travel. The persons who plan to spend an increased amount for their trip to the foreign country probably plan to spend a decreased amount of their budget for other things. Among these other things may be imported articles. (Instead of consuming imported foodstuffs here, the tourists will consume them abroad; thus less may be demanded to be imported.) What happens then is a shift of demand from imported articles to touring abroad. The increase in the demand for foreign exchange arising from tourists' expenditures abroad may, in this case, be partly offset by a decrease in the demand for foreign exchange arising from commodity imports. The offsetting is only in part, because the consumers' expenditures for the imported articles would have included payments for domestic services of distribution (services of the importers, wholesalers, transporters, retailers). Thus, not all of the amounts spent by the consumers on the goods in question constitute demand for foreign exchange, whereas after the switch of these expenditures over to foreign travel the entire sum goes into purchasing foreign exchange.

Some of the consumers' purchasing power devoted to foreign travel may have been withdrawn from buying goods which are exportable. The diminution of the domestic demand for exportable goods may easily induce the producers to look for more outlets in the foreign market, or, in other words, it may cause the supply of exports, and, under certain conditions, the exporters' supply of foreign exchange to increase. This would constitute a shift of the supply curve to the right and downward.

What has been said of the influence of the tourists' demand upon the importers' demand for, and exporters' supply of, foreign exchange is similarly valid for other sources of demand for foreign exchange. We have to ask from what markets the purchasing power of those who now demand foreign exchange is withdrawn. In the case of capital export, where would the money funds have gone, had their owner not decided in favour of foreign investment? Have the funds come from an increase in voluntary saving, or from the usual flow of voluntary savings, or from disinvestment (omitted replacement) in home industry? Or have they come, perhaps, from idle hoards, or from bank-credit expansion, in which cases no other demand is reduced by the increased capital export? This last possibility shall be ruled out for the moment. Only later shall we allow changes in the monetary circulation to be related to international transactions.

17.   The shifts of the importers' demand and exporters' supply curves due to the increase in tourists' or capital exporters' demand for foreign exchange must not be confused with those famous shifts due to a "transfer of purchasing power" from the paying country to the receiving country. These are different matters which do not come into the picture before we get to international movements of gold and short-term balances. At our stage of the analysis monetary circulation is assumed not to be affected by international transactions. Thus, an increased demand for foreign exchange by tourists does not involve a withdrawal of purchasing power from circulation but merely a change of the flow of purchasing power through the national economic system.[11]

[11] The assumption that monetary circulation is not affected by transactions such as foreign investments is admittedly unrealistic, even if international movements of short-term balances are ruled out. Improved investment opportunities abroad would lead to dishoarding and to increased borrowing from banks. And even apart from this the change in the money flow would most likely involve some slight change in the income velocity of circulation. However, a clean analysis must first abstract from all these complications.

Let us look again at our Fig. I-3 and ask ourselves where the money spent by capital exporters for foreign exchange (*LNRU*) comes from and where it goes. The question "where does it come from" is, however, very loosely expressed; it should not mean the channels through which it has reached the capital exporters, but rather the directions into which it *does not go* because of the switch toward foreign investment. The answer will be different in the case of increased saving, in which the money is diverted from the market of (domestic or imported) consumers' goods; and different in the case of maintained saving, in which the money is diverted from the market of (domestic or imported) producers' goods. The other question, "where does the money go," can be accurately answered: it goes to exporters of commodities.

Without capital export or any other demand for foreign exchange by others than importers, commodity exporters get no more and no less than the amount spent on foreign exchange by commodity importers (*OMPQ* in Fig. I-3). When a demand for foreign exchange by capital exporters becomes effective, a greater part of the total money flow goes to commodity exporters. They get what is spent on foreign exchange by capital exporters plus what is spent on foreign exchange by commodity importers, though the latter amount may be greater or smaller than it was prior to the export of capital.

This reshuffling in the distribution of purchasing power in the national economic system makes it highly improbable that the original importers' demand and exporters' supply curves remain unchanged. The final direction of the shifts cannot be ascertained *a priori*. Although we have argued above that the increase in demand for foreign exchange by tourists or capital exporters or the like *may* lower the demand for foreign exchange by commodity importers, the contrary may be true just the same. The factors of production employed by the busy export industries may be willing to spend much more for imported articles than the tourists or capital exporters would have done—had they not become tourists or capital exporters. Thus the capital export may result in an increase in the commodity importers' demand for foreign exchange, whereas it can, of course, never result in an increase in the amount of foreign exchange demanded by commodity importers.

18. Before we proceed to introduce movements of gold and short-term balances into our analysis, a word on the "purchasing power parity theory" seems to be in order. This theory claims that the foreign-exchange rate is determined by the ratio between the real purchasing power of the two currencies; the price levels in the two countries would thus be the independent variables, the exchange rates the dependent variables of the relationship.

We have avoided a discussion of the concept of "price levels" in our analysis so far, and we shall try to do without it for the rest. We emphasised, however, from the beginning that commodity prices must not be assumed as "given" because they may be affected by the international transactions themselves. Even for the simplest considerations not *actual* prices but *potential* prices, that is to say, supply and demand conditions, served to explain the determination of foreign-exchange rates. And we saw that without "inflation" or "deflation" in any of the countries concerned, the exchange rates between them could be changed through a number of events. The degree of the change, however, is always determined by the potential commodity prices, i.e., by the supply and demand conditions on the two markets.

Nothing is more capable of altering supply and demand conditions, and thus the exchange rate of a country, than inflation. While changes in tastes, changes in productivity, changes in capital movements, etc., can change exchange rates somewhat (or even by substantial percentages), inflation in one of the countries can change the rates by huge multiples. It is for this reason that the explanation of very great changes in the exchange rates has to turn to the increase in monetary circulation, and to the subsequent changes in supply and demand conditions (loosely expressed: to the change in "price level") as the causal factors. There cannot be a minute's doubt that the "balance-of-payments" theory was all wrong and the "inflation" theory essentially correct, when the vast movements on the foreign-exchange markets were discussed in the first part of the 1920's. The greatest possible increase in the demand for imports plus the greatest possible fall in the supply of exports plus the greatest possible flight of capital would not be able to produce the conspicuous exchange depreciations of that period—had it not been for the inflations; for these inflations a measure was devised in the form of "purchasing power parities."

In this historical perspective, the purchasing-power-parity theory must be given full credit. It was important, at the time, to pronounce tersely: "Don't be so ridiculous as to hold the 'need for imports' responsible for the depreciation of the domestic currency, if it is only inflation which can account for the effective demand for these imports." But this must not blind us to the fact that changes in the foreign-exchange market—less conspicuous, but significant enough—may take place without any preceding change in the monetary circulations and purchasing-power parities of the countries concerned.

D. Gold movements, gold standard, and pegged exchange rates

19. As long as commodity trade, exchange of services, long-term investments and unilateral payments are treated as the only sources of

supply of and demand for foreign exchange, as long, therefore, as international movements of gold and short-term balances are excluded, the analysis can be said to deal with "independent currencies."

As soon as international movements of gold (and other monetary metals) and short-term (bank) balances are introduced as sources of supply of and demand for foreign exchange, the analysis proceeds to currency systems whose effective circulation is not independent of international transactions. Inflow and outflow of gold and acquisition and disposal of foreign bank balances may change the effective monetary circulation of the countries concerned. The essence of the gold standard lies in the existence of institutions guaranteeing that gold and foreign bank balances can be bought and sold at fairly fixed prices.

Leaving international movements of bank balances for the last step of our analysis, we introduce first international gold movements, and make the assumption that the monetary authorities of both countries are prepared to buy and sell gold at fixed prices or pairs of prices. This assumption, i.e., the assumption of the gold standard maintained in both countries, implies that at a certain exchange rate the supply of foreign exchange becomes infinitely elastic, and at another (somewhat lower) price of foreign currency, the demand for foreign exchange becomes infinitely elastic.

Under an "orthodox" gold standard system, it is not the monetary authorities themselves who offer to sell or to buy foreign exchange. They buy and sell gold only.[12] On the other hand, the people who wish to make payments abroad are not those who themselves would buy gold from the monetary authorities. The ancient textbook story about the business man who has to make a payment abroad and finds, when the price of foreign currency rises above a certain point, that it is cheaper to buy gold and ship it to the foreign country, is unrealistic without necessity. It is more correct and no less simple to refer to the gold *arbitrageurs* who buy gold from the monetary authority, ship and sell it abroad, and supply the foreign balances thus obtained to the foreign-exchange market. It is, furthermore, easy to understand that this business works under fairly constant marginal cost and that the supply of foreign exchange is infinitely elastic, as soon as the respective rate—the gold export point—is reached, and as long as the monetary authorities in the two countries maintain their preparedness to sell and buy gold at the fixed prices.

For analogous reasons, the gold *arbitrageurs'* demand for foreign exchange is infinitely elastic, as soon as the price of foreign currency falls to the gold import point. They are willing to buy every amount of foreign balances at this price, since they can use them to buy gold in the foreign country and import and sell it to the monetary authority.

[12] In some gold standard countries, the "modern" system of exchange-stabilisation funds was already practiced in the 19th century.

The gold *arbitrageurs* are dealers in gold and foreign balances. In order to postpone movements in foreign balances to the next step of our analysis, we simply assume here that the gold *arbitrageurs* do not change the size of their stocks in foreign exchange. This assumption implies merely that they use any amount of newly obtained foreign balances immediately, either for selling them to final buyers, that is, to people who wish to make foreign payments, or for buying foreign gold to import it. Likewise, they replenish any amount of foreign balances which they have disposed of from their "stock" immediately, either by buying foreign exchange from final sellers, that is, from people who have received payments from abroad, or by buying gold from the monetary authority to export it.

20.   An example of the functioning of the foreign-exchange market in gold standard countries is illustrated in Fig. I-4. It is assumed that initially commodity trade is the only source of international payments. $D_I D'_I$ is the commodity importers' demand for foreign exchange, $S_E S'_E$ the commodity exporters' supply of foreign exchange; OM is the amount of foreign exchange bought and sold at the equilibrium rate MP. Exports amount to

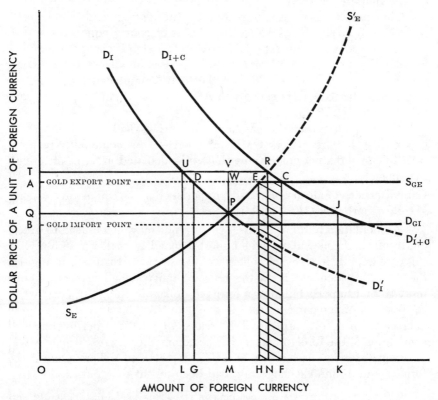

Fig. I-4. Capital exports resulting in gold outflows

OM in terms of foreign currency and to $OMPQ$ in terms of dollars; imports are of course equal to exports.

Capital export appears and increases the demand for foreign exchange to $D_{I+c}D'_{I+c}$. We know from previous considerations that the commodity importers' demand for foreign exchange is likely to be affected by changes in the distribution of the income stream which accompany the capital export. However, since we cannot know *how* the import demand will change, we assume it to be unchanged. (To assume, instead, that the importers' demand would change in a definite way would hardly increase our understanding of the adjustment.)

In absence of the gold standard the price of foreign currency would rise to OT or NR, exports would rise to ON, imports would fall to OL. Under the gold standard the price of foreign currency cannot rise to OT, which is above the gold export point OA. At the exchange rate OA the supply of foreign exchange becomes perfectly elastic, the supply curve sharply turning parallel to the X-axis. The commodity exporters' supply curve breaks off at E and is replaced by the gold exporters' supply curve (S_{GE}) of infinite elasticity.

This supply curve is intersected by the aggregate demand curve ($D_{I+c}D'_{I+c}$) at C. The exchange rate FC is of course equal to OA, the gold export point. At this rate the amount of foreign exchange demanded by capital exporters is DC or GF and the amount demanded by commodity importers is AD or OG. Of the total amount demanded, AC or OF, commodity exporters contribute AE or OH, and gold exporters contribute EC or HF.[13]

We see, thus, that the capital export brings with it a decrease in commodity imports ($OG<OM$), an increase in commodity exports ($OH>OM$) and a net gold export (HF), all calculated in terms of foreign exchange:

Capital export=Fall in commodity imports+Rise in commodity exports +Gold exports, i.e., $GF=GM+MH+HF$.

A calculation in terms of our own currency may, again, lead to different results if the elasticity of the import demand is smaller than unity. In this case imports in terms of dollars would rise rather than fall. In Fig. I-4 the importers' demand is, in the relevant range, of an elasticity above unity so that imports fall also in terms of dollars ($OGDA<OMPQ$) when the price of foreign currency rises from OQ to OA. The change of the trade balance to an export surplus will be realised in terms of our own as well as in terms of the foreign currency. The commodity export surplus is GH in terms of foreign exchange and $GHED$ in terms of dollars. Only if the former equilibrium exchange rate had been just at the gold export point

---

[13] The repercussions which a concomitant reshuffling in the distribution of purchasing power may have on the original supply and demand conditions are neglected here for the reasons given in §17.

would the emergence of a new demand for foreign exchange for capital exports lead not directly to an export surplus but initially merely to gold exports.

For our new situation shown in Fig. I-4 the "balance of payments" can be written as follows:

Commodity exports+Gold exports=Commodity imports+Capital exports, i.e., $OH+HF=OG+GF$ and $OHEA+HFCE=OGDA+GFCD$.

In the absence of the gold standard, commodity exports would be greater (by HN) and commodity imports would be smaller (by LG) than under the gold standard; the export surplus would be equal to capital exports. The gold standard allows this commodity export surplus to develop more slowly. But develop it will, because the equilibrium pictured in Fig. I-4 is distinctively temporary.

21.   The inherent tendency to change in the situation described above is connected with the destiny of the dollars paid to gold exporters. This money goes another way than the money paid to commodity exporters. Commodity exporters pay the proceeds from their sales ($OHEA$ in Fig. I-4) chiefly to the producers of export commodities; and the producers pass the money on to producers of intermediate products and to factors of production, etc. Gold exporters, on the other hand, turn the proceeds from their sales of foreign exchange ($HFCE$ in Fig. I-4 less their commission and transport charges) over to the monetary authorities in payment for gold. Thus most of the money passes out of existence.

Provided no policy of "offsetting" is pursued by the monetary authorities, this contraction of circulation alters not only the distribution but also the total amount of money income in a decided direction: money income falls. The fall in money income, in turn, affects demand and supply of foreign exchange in a definite way: [14] the demand, both by commodity importers and by capital exporters, falls, and the supply by commodity exporters rises. That is to say, the demand curves shift to the left, the supply curve to the right.

This increase in supply and decrease in demand may not be sufficient, at the first stroke, to bring the market price of foreign currency down below the gold export point. Then another dose of gold exports will further reduce domestic circulation. The income deflation, resulting from a gold outflow without offsetting, cannot help eventually leading to a diminution of demand for foreign exchange and to an increase in the supply of foreign exchange. If the shift in demand and supply curves takes place only after a considerable time lag, then a more complete reversion of the situation is likely to occur: the delayed reduction in importers' demand and the increase in exporters' supply may then, when

[14] Subject to qualifications set forth subsequently.

they finally arrive, push the price of foreign currency down to the gold import point, thus causing the gold *arbitrageurs'* infinitely elastic demand for foreign exchange to become effective. Gold *arbitrageurs* would pay out to commodity exporters dollars newly created by the monetary authorities in payment for the imported gold, and domestic circulation would rise again.

While the reduction of demand for foreign exchange cannot fail to take place if incomes fall in consequence of a gold outflow, the increase in supply of foreign exchange may, under rather exceptional circumstances, fail to appear. The same "abnormal" conditions which are capable of making for a negative elasticity of the supply curve (see §8) may, in concurrence with other factors, possibly cause a perverted shift of the supply curve to result from income deflation. To recall shortly, inelasticity of foreign demand for our export articles and inelasticity of foreign supply of substitutes for our export articles are the conditions in point; conditions which cannot be realised if our exports compete heavily with foreign products, and if we produce goods which are not actually but potentially exportable. The perverted shift is, however, still more "extremely unlikely" than the perverted elasticity, if it is assumed that the gold inflow into the foreign country is not offset there by official sterilisation or private hoarding. With the gold inflow allowed to have its effects on foreign money incomes, *price elasticity* of foreign demand for our exports can be ever so small without preventing our commodity exporters' supply of foreign exchange from rising, if only the *income elasticity* of foreign demand for our exports is not negligible. It would be almost absurd to assume that both price elasticity and income elasticity of demand are so small that neither higher incomes of foreign buyers nor lower prices charged by our sellers would lead to increased exports measured in terms of foreign currency.

The shift to the right of the foreign demand for our exports, as is known from the famous controversy about the transfer problem of reparation payments, may result in an increase in the commodity exporters' supply of foreign exchange even without any price reductions on the part of our exporters.

22.   It may be desirable, at this stage, to summarise in a convenient catalogue all the factors which may concur in bringing about an export surplus as the result of an export of capital or of any other payment to the foreign country.

a.   Domestic purchasing power used for making the remittance may have been withdrawn from buying imported goods; hence the demand for foreign exchange for our commodity imports may fall.

b.   Domestic purchasing power used for making the remittance may have been withdrawn from buying exportable goods; hence the supply of foreign exchange from our commodity exports may rise.

c. The price of foreign currency is raised; hence the amount of foreign currency demanded for our commodity imports falls.

d. The price of foreign currency is raised; hence the amount of foreign currency supplied from our commodity exports may rise.

e. Domestic purchasing power used for buying gold is wiped out; hence the demand for foreign exchange for our commodity imports falls.

f. Domestic purchasing power used for buying gold is wiped out; hence the supply of foreign exchange from our commodity exports may rise.

g. Foreign purchasing power is created through the gold purchases by the foreign monetary authorities; hence the prices of foreign products may rise and the demand for foreign exchange for our commodity imports may fall.

h. Foreign purchasing power is created through the gold purchases by the foreign monetary authorities; hence foreign demand for our exports rises and the supply of foreign exchange from our commodity exports rises.

Factors *a, b, c* and *d* can be effective under the gold standard as well as under independent currency systems; factors *e, f, g* and *h* can function only under the gold standard or with pegged exchange rates. Factors *a, b, e, f, g* and *h* represent shifts *of* the supply or demand curves, factors *c* and *d* represent movements *along* the supply and demand curves of the foreign-exchange market. Factors *a* and *b* do not function reliably; factors *e* and *f* can function only if no "offsetting" policy, or dishoarding, is at work in the paying country; factors *g* and *h* can function only if no "sterilisation" policy, or hoarding, is at work in the receiving country; factors *b, d,* and *f* may refuse to function, or may function perversely, if the price elasticities of foreign demand for our exports are (in absolute value) less than unity; finally, factor *g* may refuse to function (or may function perversely) if the elasticity of domestic demand for foreign products is smaller than unity. Under normal market conditions and under normal gold-standard management factors *c, d, e, f, g* and *h* can all be expected to function; the more of these forces that are at work the less will be the disturbances; the fewer of these forces that are at work simultaneously, the heavier will be the disturbances that can be expected to result from a sudden change in the flow of capital or unilateral payments.

It must be noted that the "normal gold-standard management" just mentioned does not imply the necessity of a reinforcing credit expansion in case of gold inflow, or the necessity of a reinforcing credit restriction in case of gold outflow. In other words, it is not necessary for the functioning of the described mechanisms that monetary circulation increases or decreases by some multiple of the gold in- or out-flow. The "automatic" increase in circulation through a gold purchase by monetary authorities (or banks in general) or the "automatic" decrease in circulation through a gold sale by monetary authorities (or banks in general) is all that is needed—and all that is justifiable on grounds of international equilibrium theory.

23. No change in our analysis is required when we substitute the assumption of a more "modern" gold-standard system for the assumption of an orthodox one. We may drop the assumption of legally guaranteed gold sales and purchases by the monetary authorities (to and from gold *arbitrageurs* or the public in general) and substitute the assumption of an Exchange Stabilisation Fund which undertakes to stabilise the foreign-exchange rates within relatively narrow margins.

The infinitely elastic demand for foreign exchange was, under the old system, the demand by gold *arbitrageurs* who bought (at the lower gold point) foreign balances in order to import gold and to sell it to the monetary authorities. Under the new system, there is the infinitely elastic demand for foreign exchange on the part of the Exchange Stabilisation Fund, which buys all foreign balances offered at the low point below which the price of foreign currency or balances is not to be allowed to fall. The infinitely elastic supply of foreign exchange was, under the old system, the supply by gold *arbitrageurs* who sold (at the upper gold point) foreign balances obtained by the export of gold which they bought from the domestic monetary authorities. Under the new system, there is the infinitely elastic supply of foreign exchange by the Exchange Stabilisation Fund, which sells all foreign balances demanded at the upper point above which the price of foreign currency is not to be allowed to rise.

If the Exchange Stabilisation Fund does not carry varying amounts of foreign balances but rather uses all foreign balances acquired to buy gold, and furnishes all foreign balances needed by selling gold, on the foreign gold market, and if, furthermore, the Fund sells the gold it acquires to the central-banking system and buys the gold it needs from the central-banking system—then the Exchange Stabilisation Fund is nothing else but a large-scale gold *arbitrageur,* acting exactly as do the gold *arbitrageurs* in our orthodox gold-standard case above. The legal framework under which all these actions take place is of small significance from a purely theoretical point of view.

The Exchange Stabilisation Fund may, instead of selling gold to and buying gold from the monetary authorities, keep the gold on its own account (on "inactive account"). What we must ask in this case is: where does the domestic money that pays for the foreign balances come from? The Exchange Stabilisation Fund itself is ordinarily not authorised to create money.

The Fund may have been endowed with a sufficient amount of domestic money—so far back in the past that we need not inquire now whence the money came; the Fund then "dishoards" (i.e., pays out idle balances) when it acquires gold, and "hoards" (i.e., sets idle the balances received) when it sells gold. If this is so, the analysis holds as laid out in previous sections. Effective domestic circulation is increased, as foreign balances are offered to the Fund, by dishoarding rather than by creating domestic balances; effective domestic circulation is decreased, as foreign balances are supplied by the Fund, by hoarding rather than by wiping out domestic balances.

The Fund may, on the other hand, not have sufficient working balances in domestic money; it may obtain the domestic balances, which it needs for purchasing foreign balances offered to it, by borrowing from the banks; likewise it may use the domestic balances, which it receives for foreign balances sold, to repay its bank debts. In this case we find that our analysis still holds, provided the banks have enough excess reserves (i.e., such high reserve ratios that the banks' supply of credit is infinitely elastic for a certain range). The expansion of bank loans for the purpose of financing the Fund's purchases of foreign balances, and the liquidation of bank loans by means of the proceeds from the Fund's sales of foreign balances, produce precisely the changes in domestic circulation which would result from the working of the "automatic" gold standard.

24. The situation is different if the Exchange Stabilisation Fund finances its purchases by borrowing from the public rather than from the banks, or by borrowing from banks which have no ample provision of excess reserves; and, as to the converse movement, the situation is different from the analysed ones if the Fund uses its sales proceeds for repaying loans to the public rather than banks, or to banks which have been short of excess reserves. In these cases the purchases and sales of foreign balances by the Exchange Stabilisation Fund will not increase and decrease effective circulation by the full value of the foreign balances bought or sold.

Assume that capital import sets in (Fig. I-5) and that the Exchange Stabilisation Fund buys, as is necessary in view of the adopted policy, *HFCE* dollars' worth of foreign balances (or gold), raising the *HFCE* dollars by borrowing from the public. If the public had just become more thrifty and furnished the *HFCE* dollars out of new voluntary savings, then the balances of the savers would be transferred *via* the Exchange Stabilisation Fund to the sellers of foreign exchange, i.e., to the capital importers. Hence no increase in circulation would result from the capital import and the foreign-exchange purchases of the Fund.

The assumption of an increase in thriftiness simultaneous with the "favourable balance of payments" is, of course, rather arbitrary. Let us assume instead that the Exchange Stabilisation Fund tries to borrow from a public whose propensities to save have not changed. The total demand

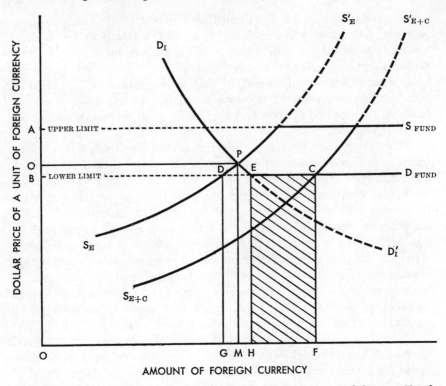

Fig. I-5. Capital imports resulting in purchases by Exchange Stabilization Fund

for loanable funds increases to the extent to which the infinitely elastic demand for foreign exchange on the part of the Exchange Stabilisation Fund becomes effective (i.e., by $HFCE$). In simpler words, the Fund seeks liquid funds to buy foreign balances or gold, and the money market may become stiffer.[15] Increased interest rates will induce some holders of idle balances to dishoard them: so, while the greater part of the money raised by the Fund will be withdrawn from other employments, a portion will come from hitherto inactive balances. Only a small part of the $HFCE$ dollars paid out by the Fund to the sellers of foreign balances will thus constitute an increase in effective circulation. The larger part will constitute active money that merely changes the channels of its flow. That is to say, the gold acquired by the Fund has been "sterilised." [16]

Much the same result will follow if banks participate in financing the

[15] About this (temporary) rise in interest rates due to capital imports see §30 and §31.

[16] It should be recalled that, according to our present assumptions, it makes no difference whether we say that the Fund buys foreign balances or that the Fund buys gold. If the Fund buys foreign balances it is only to use them for gold purchases; if the Fund buys gold it is (indirectly) using foreign balances.

Fund's purchases but have no ample excess reserves. In this case some slight net expansion of bank credit may take place under the inducement of increased interest rates, but the bulk of the loans to the Fund (mostly in the form of purchases of Treasury bills) will be at the expense of other loans and investments. Only if the supply of bank credit is perfectly elastic, can effective circulation be increased by the full amount which the Exchange Stabilisation Fund borrows in order to finance its perfectly elastic demand for foreign exchange. If the elasticity of supply of bank credit is less than infinity, only a part of the amount borrowed by the Fund constitutes an expansion of monetary circulation.

Vice versa, if a capital export leads to sales of gold (or foreign balances) by the Fund, and if the Fund uses the proceeds from these sales to pay off bank debts (i.e., to buy back Treasury bills), the full amount will disappear from circulation only if the banks have ample excess reserves. But if the banks have been nearly loaned up, they will be able to make other loans and investments when their earning assets and demand deposits diminish through the Fund's repayments.[17] Hence only a part of the amount which the Fund received from the capital exporters and returned to the banks will constitute a contraction of monetary circulation.

Let us look back at our graph Fig. I-4 and assume this time that it is the Exchange Stabilisation Fund which provides the amount HF of foreign balances (by selling gold) and receives for them $HFCE$ dollars. Assume, furthermore, that the $HFCE$ dollars are used by the Fund for repaying bank loans, that is to say, for purchasing from the banks $HFCE$ dollars' worth of Treasury bills. The deflationary effect of this transaction depends then chiefly on the elasticity of supply of bank credit. If the banks have been completely loaned up, and their credit supply is of zero elasticity, *none* of the $HFCE$ dollars will be wiped out (except for a negligibly short interval) because the banks have other uses for these funds. (If this implies slightly lower interest rates, a small fraction of the amount might be hoarded under the inducement of the lower interest.) If the banks have had abundant reserves, and their credit supply is of infinite elasticity, *all* of the $HFCE$ dollars will be wiped out. If the supply of bank credit is of more than zero and less than infinite elasticity, the amount of deflation will be between nil and $HFCE$.

It should be mentioned that the effects of capital and gold flows may be completely perverted if capital importers wish to hold inactive bank balances and if capital exporters have been holding inactive bank balances. In these cases, with the supply of bank credit less than perfectly elastic, the inflow of foreign funds may be deflationary and the outflow inflationary.

25. Some of the Exchange Stabilisation Funds in the years 1934 to

[17] Certain qualifications concerning the reverse situation (see §30 and §31) apply also to this case.

1939 avoided carrying large amounts of foreign balances. When they acquired foreign balances they quickly used them for buying gold abroad, and when they needed foreign balances they obtained them by selling gold abroad. It might, however, be otherwise. The Stabilisation Funds might be willing to carry any amount of foreign balances. They might increase their "stocks" of foreign exchange by buying, and decrease them by selling. Movements in foreign balances held would then be substituted for international gold movements.

Let us introduce these assumptions to the situations discussed in connection with our graphs Fig. I-4 and Fig. I-5. No gold is then exported, but the Exchange Stabilisation Fund reduces its holdings in foreign balances by HF (Fig. I-4) when it sells foreign exchange to capital exporters. No gold is imported, but the Exchange Stabilisation Fund increases its holdings in foreign balances by HF (Fig. I-5) when it buys foreign exchange from capital importers. One change in our conclusions which is certainly called for by the change in assumptions concerns the balance of international payments.

In §20 we stated that the capital export (GF of Fig. I-4) was equal to a fall in commodity imports (GM) plus a rise in commodity exports (MH) plus a net export of gold (HF), all calculated in terms of foreign currency. Now, under the changed assumptions, we have to state that the capital export (GF) is equal to a fall in commodity imports (GM) plus a rise in commodity exports (MH) plus a net reduction in foreign short-term balances (HF). A reduction of balances due from foreign banks is, of course, a repayment of debts by foreigners, and thus, in technical language, a movement of short-term capital from the foreign country to our country. We arrive therefore at this restatement regarding the changes in international transactions:

Long-term capital export=Fall in commodity imports+Rise in commodity exports+Short-term capital import, i.e., $GF=GM+MH+HF$.

The balance of payments for the period during which the curves remain unchanged as in Fig. I-4 reads now as follows:

Commodity exports+Short-term capital import=Commodity imports+ Long-term capital export, i.e., $OH+HF=OG+GF$, and $OHEA+HFCE= OGDA+GFCD$.

That this cannot be a position of ultimate equilibrium is clear. It is not necessary to prove this by referring to the fact that the stocks of foreign short-term balances must be exhausted sooner or later, just as it was not necessary to prove the instability of the gold export situation by referring to the limited gold stock. What makes for the instability of this temporary equilibrium is the deflationary effect of the "short-term capital import." This short-term capital import is a not very descriptive term for the underlying phenomenon: the disposal of balances held with foreign banks by the Exchange Stabilisation Fund.

The extent of the deflationary effect depends, as shown before, on the use which the Fund makes of the proceeds from the sale of foreign exchange. The deflationary effect causes eventually the supply curve of foreign exchange to shift to the right and the demand curves to shift to the left. The ultimate equilibrium [18] of the balance of international payments will then show (increased) commodity exports equal to (decreased) commodity imports plus (decreased) long-term capital exports.

The discussion of the converse case, that of long-term capital imports, can be brief. The provisional change in the balance of payments as shown in Fig. I-5 would be this:

Long-term capital import=Fall in commodity exports+Rise in commodity imports+Short-term capital export, i.e., $GF=GM+MH+HF$.

The "short-term capital export" of this balance is, of course, nothing else but the purchase of foreign exchange or, more concretely, of foreign bank balances by the Exchange Stabilisation Fund. By acquiring claims against foreign banks the Fund "exports" short-term capital which takes up a part of the import of long-term capital. "Export of short-term capital" is again not a very descriptive term for the phenomenon designated, i.e., for the purchase by the Fund of balances with foreign banks.

This transaction has an inflationary effect, the extent of which will depend on the methods employed in financing the Fund's purchases of foreign exchange. The inflationary effect will cause a decline in the supply of foreign exchange, both from commodity exports and capital imports, and an increase in the demand for foreign exchange for commodity imports. The result of these shifts will be a final equilibrium with (increased) commodity imports equal to (decreased) commodity exports plus (decreased) long-term capital imports.

E. EXCHANGE SPECULATION AND INTEREST RATES

26. In all the preceding sections, since we dropped the assumption of independent currency systems, we have carried on our analysis on the assumption of organised exchange-rate stabilisation. This stabilisation of foreign-exchange rates was first (§19-§22) the result of an "orthodox" gold-standard system with legally guaranteed gold sales and purchases; later (§23-§25) it was the result of a "modern" gold-standard system with sales and purchases of gold or foreign balances by an Exchange Stabilisation Fund.

[18] "Ultimate" describes this equilibrium position only if the capital export is regarded as a *datum* for our problem. From another point of view the incentive to export capital diminishes, of course, as the cumulative sums exported grow.

To drop the assumption of organised exchange stabilisation is not equivalent to returning to the assumption of flexible exchange rates or, still less, to returning to the assumption of independent currencies. Exchange stabilisation, firstly, may be the result of persistent pegging by commercial banks and foreign-exchange dealers. Secondly, movements in foreign short-term balances, whether the exchange rate is fixed or flexible, ordinarily involve changes in the monetary circulation, thus removing the criterion of an "independent" currency.

Persistent pegging by commercial banks and foreign-exchange dealers could be motivated by open or tacit agreements among them, or by their general belief in the permanence of the value of the currencies, or, most plausibly, by their confidence in the existence of some organised stabilisation scheme or in some latent stabilisation policy of the monetary authorities. The last of these motives may render it possible that the actual stabilisation of the exchange rates is achieved through the stabilising purchases and sales of foreign balances by commercial banks and dealers without the existing (or only imagined) official stabilisation machinery ever being put into operation.

The range over which the demand for foreign exchange at a certain low rate, and the supply of foreign exchange at a certain high rate, are perfectly elastic is, of course, smaller if this demand and supply are thus based solely on the voluntary pegging activities of commercial banks and dealers. If the monetary authorities stand behind the voluntary pegging in that they offer their ever ready organised stabilisation machinery (orthodox or modern), then we may interpret the infinite elasticities of demand and supply of foreign exchange as resulting, for a certain range, from private pegging and, for another range, from official stabilising. In the absence of effective organised stabilisation the supply curve would resume its usual upward direction, and the demand curve would resume its usual downward direction, once the readiness or the forces of private pegging are exhausted. Private pegging would have exhausted its power to supply foreign exchange, when all the holdings in foreign balances had been disposed of and new foreign credit could be had only at increased cost. Private pegging would have exhausted its power to demand foreign exchange, when the institutional limits of credit expansion had been reached and domestic funds could be raised only at increased cost. Fig. I-6 depicts this situation.[19]

[19] Fig. I-6 shows that dealers would be willing to sell an amount EV of foreign exchange before the price of foreign currency could rise above OA, and that dealers would be willing to buy an amount RT (or $R'T'$) of foreign exchange before the price of foreign currency could fall below OB. The combined demand curve (of importers and dealers) is $D_1RTUD'_1$, the combined supply curve (of exporters and dealers) is $S_EEVWS'_E$.

If the appearance of a demand for foreign exchange for purposes of capital export

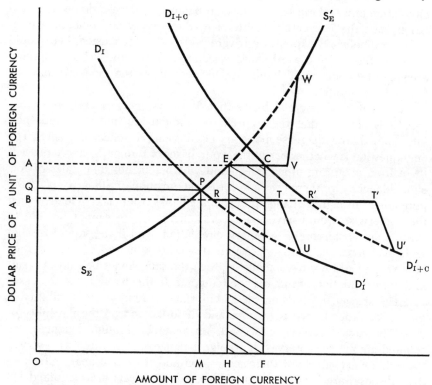

Fig. I-6. Capital exports resulting in sales from exchange dealers' holdings

It is, however, quite possible that the range over which private pegging can effectively secure perfect elasticities of supply and demand at a pair of exchange rates is large enough for most practical situations. (In Fig. I-6 the supply by dealers is sufficient to meet the increase in demand.) This will be more probable the more inflationary and deflationary are the effects of foreign-exchange purchases and sales by the pegging banks and dealers. For, if these purchases of foreign balances increase domestic

---

raises the aggregate demand for foreign exchange from $D_I D'_I$ to $D_{I+C} D'_{I+C}$, the price of foreign currency rises from OQ to OA and dealers sell EC from their holdings of foreign balances. They receive $HFCE$ dollars from the capital exporters.

The graph is, however, open to objections on methodological grounds. Firstly, the assumptions concerning expectations of future exchange-rate changes are of one type in the case of the exporters' and importers' supply and demand, and of a totally different type in the case of the dealers' supply and demand. This problem will be alluded to later on in §33. Secondly, the exporters' and importers' supply and demand refer to a *flow* of foreign exchange (e.g., exporters sell AE per month) whereas the dealers' supply and demand refer to a *stock* of foreign exchange (e.g., dealers sell EC in the first month but would not sell more than EV in the aggregate). The combination of all these curves and parts of curves in one graph is, I believe, legitimate for a short period (e.g., for the *period* of one month if the other curves represent *rates* per month).

circulation and if these sales of foreign balances decrease domestic circulation, then the "correcting" shifts of market supply and demand curves take place before the forces of private pegging are exhausted. We should examine, therefore, the extent to which purchases and sales of foreign exchange by commercial banks and dealers affect the monetary circulations of the countries.

27. If it is commercial banks that do the pegging of exchange rates, then it is obvious that their purchases immediately increase, and their sales immediately decrease monetary circulation (i.e., check deposits). The only question is whether or not their purchases of foreign balances prevent them from acquiring other assets, and whether or not their sales of foreign balances give them occasion for the acquisition of other assets. If the purchase of foreign exchange prevents the banks from making loans which they otherwise would have made, then the purchase cannot be said to cause a net expansion of monetary circulation. And if the sale of foreign exchange gives the banks occasion to acquire other assets which they otherwise would not have acquired, then the sale cannot be said to result in a net contraction of monetary circulation. Is this likely to be the case?

The answer depends on two circumstances: first, on the flexibility of the banks' ratios between reserves and deposits, and on the flexibility of their "borrowed reserves"; second, on whether foreign balances are counted among the reserves. If foreign balances are counted as reserves, the inflationary effects of their acquisition and the deflationary effects of their disposal are beyond doubt; indeed, these effects are magnified because even secondary expansions and restrictions of credit may be induced by these "changes in reserves." In the United States the law confines the concept of reserves of member banks to balances held with the Federal Reserve banks; foreign balances, therefore, are no reserve; their acquisition, by creating demand deposits, reduces the reserve ratio, and their sale, by wiping out demand deposits, raises the reserve ratio. Hence, in the United States, it is the first of the above-mentioned circumstances which determines our question.

If the ratio of reserves to deposits were absolutely constant, purchases of foreign balances by commercial banks would be at the expense of other loans and investments, unless the banks borrow from the central banks. The member banks which are "loaned up" but wish to purchase foreign balances and to hold them until prices of foreign currencies rise from their low level can do so only if they have a part of their bill-portfolio rediscounted or a part of their investment-portfolio taken over by the Reserve banks. If the banks are not "loaned up" but have a high reserve ratio (i.e., high excess reserves) and are willing to see the reserve ratio reduced, they can buy and carry foreign balances without obstacles. Hence, flexibility of the reserve ratio and flexibility of the amount of reserves are the

conditions which make for inflationary effects of foreign-exchange purchases by commercial banks.

Likewise, sales of foreign exchange by commercial banks are deflationary, if the banks are willing to see their reserve ratio (i.e., their excess
reserves) increased or if they have a part of their reserves "borrowed" and
can now repay them. If none of their reserves were borrowed and the
reserve ratio were to be kept constant, so that the banks would have to
acquire immediately other assets as soon as they sell foreign balances,
then no deflationary effects would ensue from these sales.

Looking at present-day practice we find that the reserve ratios of
member banks are sufficiently flexible to allow exchange purchases and
sales by commercial banks to have inflationary and deflationary effects.

28. If not banks but private dealers are engaged in foreign-exchange
pegging, we have to ask what funds are used by these dealers for their
purchases of foreign balances. If they use borrowed funds and arrange for
bank loans in order to purchase foreign exchange, and repay bank loans
when they sell foreign exchange, then the situation is almost the same
as described before. The banks acquire the foreign-exchange dealers' bills
instead of the foreign exchange directly. The banks' bill-portfolio rises
when the dealers buy and falls when the dealers sell foreign balances.

Had the dealers the habit of disbursing and accumulating idle balances whenever they bought and sold foreign exchange, the inflationary
and deflationary effects would be a matter of dishoarding and hoarding
(and would show through velocity, rather than volume, of circulation). If
neither idle dealers' balances nor created bank funds were available for
the dealers' purchases so that the necessary funds would have to be sought
on the open market from non-banking sources, then the inflationary effect
of their purchases would be trivial: it would be confined to the dishoarding induced by slightly increased interest rates. Likewise, the deflationary
effect of dealers' sales of foreign exchange would be confined to the hoarding induced by slightly reduced interest rates, if the dealers had no bank
funds but only private business funds borrowed for carrying their foreign
balances.

The more common practice is certainly that the dealers finance their
transactions through bank loans. Hence, again, the conclusion seems
warranted that dealers' purchases of foreign balances have the inflationary
effects, and dealers' sales of foreign balances have the deflationary effects,
which we have discussed several times; so that the effects of ordinary
transactions by foreign-exchange dealers approach the effects of the gold
movements under an orthodox gold standard.

The sharp line which many writers have drawn between the international gold standard and other monetary systems proves to be without
justification from a purely economic point of view. The time-honoured

theory of foreign exchange under the gold standard has, for example, a more appropriate application to a case of legally flexible exchanges where speculators sell foreign balances and repay debts to highly liquid banks, than it has to a case of a legally simon-pure gold standard where the central bank sells gold but allows at the same time commercial bank deposits to remain unchanged.

29. Contemporary writers on the subject have expressed the view that movements of foreign short-term bank balances "differ radically" from international gold movements as far as their effects on incomes and prices are concerned. This view is correct only if writers think of the *secondary* expansions and contractions that are invited by gold movements under the fractional reserve system: a movement of a certain amount of gold might call forth a multiple amount of bank-credit creation in the one country, and a multiple amount of bank-credit destruction in the other. We said, however, in §22 that the secondary creation and destruction of bank credit are neither necessary nor even justifiable from the point of view of international equilibrium theory. From this point of view we consider as an essential part of the mechanism only that "transfer" of purchasing power which is equivalent in amount to the international payment which gives rise to it.

If it is, thus, not expected that a certain gold flow wipes out in the one country and creates in the other country more than an equivalent amount of purchasing power, then it makes, in principle, little difference whether gold flows or whether bank balances move. To return to our example of Fig. I-4, the flow of gold is expected to reduce circulation in the paying country by $HFCE$ dollars and to increase circulation in the receiving country by HF units of its currency. Assume now that no gold is exported but that the amount HF of foreign balances is bought (by capital exporters) from domestic banks. In the paying country $HFCE$ dollars of domestic bank deposits are wiped out through this transaction. In the receiving country HF units of its currency are transferred from the idle accounts of foreign banks to the (probably) active accounts of the persons from whom the capital exporter buys securities. The amount wiped out in the one country corresponds to the amount which is "activated" in the other country. The deflationary effect in the paying country takes place, in this case, through a reduction in the volume of circulation M'; the inflationary effect in the receiving country takes place through an increase in V', the velocity of circulation.[20]

In which country the amount and in which country the velocity of

---

[20] This terminology *includes* balances due to foreign depositors as part of M' and, therefore, regards the increase in transactions as a rise in V'. If foreign deposits in domestic banks are not considered part of M', the transfer of balances from foreign to domestic depositors would be regarded as an increase in M'.

bank deposits change depends on the method of payment. One might send a check drawn on a bank in one's own country (i.e., a dollar check) and the foreign bank to which the payee sells the check may then carry an increased dollar deposit. In this case V' changes in our country while M' changes in the foreign country. On the other hand, one might buy, as in the previous example, from one's bank a draft on a foreign bank which the payee abroad deposits in his bank account. In this case M' changes in our country while V' changes in the foreign country.

To employ Fig. I-5 once more, we see that foreign bank checks in the amount of HF units of the foreign currency may be sold to our banks. Our banks thus create $HFCE$ dollars of new deposits. In the foreign country the amount of HF units of its currency is transferred from the probably active accounts of the remitters to the idle accounts of our banks which buy the foreign checks from the payees. This time, the deflationary effect in the paying country takes place through a reduction in velocity of circulation; the inflationary effect in the receiving country takes place through an increase in the volume of circulation.

30. One important difference between exchange stabilisation by central banks (or with central-bank funds) and exchange stabilisation without central-bank funds bears on the rate of interest. If central banks buy foreign exchange or gold, the reserves of member banks are increased. The same is true if an Exchange Stabilisation Fund buys foreign exchange and obtains the necessary means from the central bank, for instance, through the issue of gold certificates. The ensuing increase in excess reserves of banks and in the liquid balances of firms and individuals has the tendency to ease the money market and to lower interest rates.

If, on the other hand, commercial banks buy foreign exchange, or if dealers and speculators buy foreign exchange with funds borrowed from commercial banks or in general on the money market, the excess reserves of banks and the liquid balances of firms and individuals are reduced. The same is true if an Exchange Stabilisation Fund buys foreign exchange and obtains the necessary means by borrowing from commercial banks or on the open market, for instance, through the issue of Treasury bills. Except in the case of an infinitely elastic supply of bank credit, a tendency to stiffen the money market and to raise interest rates will result from the inflow of foreign payments.

The reverse, of course, is true for an outflow of gold or foreign exchange. If the central bank were selling gold or foreign exchange, or if an Exchange Stabilisation Fund were selling foreign exchange and using the proceeds to repay central-bank loans, the excess reserves of commercial banks and the liquid balances of firms and individuals would be reduced. But if commercial banks sell foreign exchange from their own holdings, or if dealers and speculators sell foreign exchange and use the proceeds to repay commercial-bank loans (or to place liquid funds on the money market) excess reserves are increased (or liquid balances become disposable). A tendency towards higher interest rates would follow from the former situation, a tendency towards lower interest rates may follow from the latter situation.

Thus, if no central-bank funds are engaged in exchange-stabilisation transactions, a flow of capital may lead to temporarily reduced interest rates in the country from which the capital is withdrawn, or to temporarily increased interest rates in the country to which the capital is sent. This sounds paradoxical but it is nevertheless true. If we imagine that British capitalists buy American securities, we invariably associate with this the idea that interest rates in the American markets are thereby reduced. According to our customary reasoning, the transaction involves an increased demand for American securities, hence increased security prices which are equivalent to reduced long-term interest rates. Yet this reasoning is valid (abstracting from changed expectations on the part of domestic investors) only if the increased supply of pound sterling in New York (or demand for dollars in London) leads to a purchase of the pound sterling or of gold by the American monetary authorities and to a creation of American excess reserves and liquid balances. It is different if the Exchange Stabilisation Fund, pursuing a policy of offsetting, has first to raise on the open market the dollars with which to buy the pound sterling before the British capitalist can buy American securities; or, similarly, if an American dealer or speculator has first to borrow dollars with which to take over the pound sterling, before the increased demand for securities can become effective. In these cases an increased demand for loanable funds precedes the increased demand for securities; the demand for securities is thus nothing but the (immediate) re-supply of the loanable funds raised by the buyers of foreign balances.

31. A simplified picture of this situation can be gained by the following description: a British capitalist desires to hold long-term American securities and offers London bank balances. By offering the sterling balances at a low dollar price, he makes an American dealer desire to hold London bank balances and offer his own promissory notes in the market. By offering promissory notes at a reduced price, i.e., at a higher discount— it is assumed that the supply of bank credit is not perfectly elastic—the dealer entices an American investor to hold promissory notes instead of securities and instead of idle cash. So the American investor will get the foreign-exchange dealer's promissory notes, the British capitalist will get the American securities formerly held by the American investor, and the foreign-exchange dealer will get the London balances from the British capitalist. Since the impulse to these transactions starts with the offer from the British capitalist and is continued by the offer from the foreign-

exchange dealer, the dollar prices of pound sterling and of American promissory notes have to recede. The decline in the price of promissory notes is, of course, identical with an increase in the short-term rate of interest.

In the absence of frictions, this increase in the demand for liquid funds, and the higher interest rate that goes with it, would entice the holders of long-term securities and cash balances to switch some of their securities and some of their liquid balances into holdings of short-term credit instruments. Frictions of a psychological and institutional nature, however, will often arrest any tendency towards security selling, and turn the whole impulse into dishoarding and bank-credit expansion. But inasmuch as the supply of bank loans is less than perfectly elastic the increase in short-term interest rates is sustained. Prices of long-term securities did not have to fall (or only a trifle or for only a short period) in the foregoing example, partly because of the induced dishoarding and credit creation; chiefly, however, because the possibly increased willingness to part with securities on the side of American investors, which was prompted by the attractive terms for short-term loans, was met by the increased demand for American securities by the British capitalists. If, however, the increased supply of sterling balances (or gold) had been due not to increased capital exports from Britain to the United States but to increased British commodity imports from the United States, or to any other payments from Britain to the United States, then American securities prices might have receded. The increased supply of sterling balances would have, as in the other case, led to an increased demand for American short-term funds by the buyers of the cheap sterling balances (foreign-exchange dealers, speculators, or the Exchange Stabilisation Fund) without these funds being used afterwards for the purchase of the securities offered by American investors. The funds would have gone to those who had to receive payments from the foreign remitters, for instance, to American commodity exporters.

It is thus clear that a rise in interest rates may result from a so-called favourable balance of payments if the increased supply of foreign balances (or gold) is purchased out of funds other than newly created central-bank money. Conversely, a fall in interest rates may result from a so-called adverse balance of payments if the increased demand for foreign balances (or gold) is satisfied by sales which liquidate foreign assets of individuals, firms and commercial banks instead of wiping out central-bank money.

A qualification is in order concerning the situation in which the supply of commercial-bank credit is perfectly elastic. In this situation, of course, short-term interest rates would neither fall nor rise. This would be, therefore, the intermediate case between the one where central-bank funds are created and wiped out and the other where liquid funds are employed and released when foreign balances are acquired and disposed of.

32. Organised exchange stabilisation and private pegging (based chiefly on a *belief* in the existence of a stabilisation policy) have allowed us to assume the existence of a latent supply of and latent demand for foreign exchange on the part of those who are willing to draw on, and to add to, their existing foreign balances. In the absence of any definite policy of the monetary authorities and of any definite expectations concerning such a policy, supply of and demand for foreign exchange from those who are willing to draw on, and to add to, their existing foreign balances, is absolutely indeterminate; that is to say, their supply and demand is based on ever-changing expectations which make the respective supply and demand curves shift so rapidly, erratically or unpredictably that it becomes meaningless to "assume" any such supply and demand curves even in a short-period analysis.

In the absence of any definite policy of the authorities (i.e., when the policy is indefinite even for the shortest period), the least illegitimate assumption will be that over a longer period of time nobody will want to carry an appreciably increased or decreased amount of foreign (credit or debit) balances. This assumption implies that the analysis of the foreign-exchange market is reduced again to the other (less erratic) sources of supply and demand such as commodity trade, exchange of services, regular payments, etc. "Speculation" may then at any moment result in a somewhat different exchange rate than would follow from the other factors in the market, but it cannot lead to perpetually one-sided deviations of the actual rate from the "equilibrium rate." This follows logically from our assumptions: if speculation has a persistent influence in a certain direction, then speculation is based on definite expectations and allows us to assume the shape of the respective supply or demand of foreign balances. If, on the other hand, speculation is erratic, so that none of the foreign credit balances acquired for speculative purposes are held for a long time, and none of the foreign debit balances arranged for speculative purposes are left unsettled for a long time, then speculation has no lasting net-influence on the foreign-exchange rate.

33. Expectations concerning future changes of the foreign-exchange rate shape supply and demand of those who are willing to draw on, and add to, their foreign balances (banks, dealers, speculators). But expectations as to future rate changes may enter also into the determination of supply and demand by other groups. Commodity importers will have an increased demand for foreign exchange when they expect a rise in the price of foreign currency, and a decreased demand when they expect a fall. Commodity exporters' supply of foreign exchange will decrease when a rise in the price of foreign currency is expected, and increase when a

fall is expected. These changes in supply and demand would not be due to *direct* speculation in foreign exchanges; if they were, the respective transactions would have to be included in the supply and demand of those who sell foreign balances which they have held, and buy foreign balances which they will carry. The demand for foreign exchange by commodity importers (in their capacity as commodity importers) rises because they actually intend to import more at the time being when they expect that later the imported goods would cost them more and would sell higher. In a sense they speculate in goods, not in exchange.

The importers *qua* importers do not increase their holdings of foreign balances but they increase their commodity stocks. And when they expect a fall in the price of foreign currency, they do not sell foreign balances but they diminish their commodity stocks by postponing further import orders.

An actual rise or fall in exchange rates may cause principally three types of anticipations: (1) that the exchange rates will rise or fall still further; (2) that the exchange rates will return to their former level; (3) that the exchange rates will remain at their new level. Only the last type of anticipation is fully consistent with the usual assumptions under which supply and demand curves (of final sellers and final buyers) are drawn. If a fall or rise in exchange rates arouses expectations of type (1) or (2), this is usually depicted by a shift of the supply and demand curves. Should now *every* change in the exchange rates give rise to some (un-predictable) change in expectations of type (1) and (2), then short-run analysis of the usual type would break down completely. The changes in expectations would cause the whole curves to shift as often as the rate changes; hence movements *along* the old curves (and, thus, elasticities) would become irrelevant.

Short-run analysis becomes thus impossible if rapid, erratic and un-predictable changes in expectations make almost everybody a speculator. Theoretical analysis is then more or less confined to the long period; and it loses, of course, some of its significance: its immediate applicability to currently observable facts is gone.

Changes in expectations are, by and large, eliminated as determining factors in long-period analysis. The postponement or advancing of orders by buyers, as well as the withholding or pressure-selling by sellers,[21] are supposed to cancel out in the long run. In long-period analysis the com-plications introduced by erratic changes of expectations are avoided, although several qualifications would have to be added to the statements of a long-run theory of the foreign-exchange market. We shall not ex-patiate here on these problems.

34. One of the most naïve misunderstandings in the theory of foreign

[21] These phenomena have lately become known as the "leads and lags" in foreign trade.

exchanges is the idea that the statistical balance of international payments shows the supply and demand of foreign exchange and can explain the movements of the foreign-exchange rates observed in the market. Where this idea errs can be best seen by recalling something we were taught in first-year economics.

If 125 quarts of strawberries were sold at a price of 24 cents we know that 125 quarts were demanded and 125 quarts were supplied at 24 cents, but we know neither the demand nor the supply of strawberries. If during the next period 125 quarts are sold at a price of 22 cents, we do not know whether the demand for strawberries has decreased (with a perfectly inelastic supply), or whether the supply of strawberries has increased (with a perfectly inelastic demand), or whether both a decrease in demand and an increase in supply have concurred in bringing about the result. The matter is fundamentally the same if quantities change rather than prices, or if both change. Every teacher of economics is apt to become impatient when a student confuses demand with quantity demanded, and supply with quantity supplied.

The balance of international payments can never show more than one point on the demand and supply curves; but even this is not true if one looks at the balance of payments for any given year, because the transactions during a period of a year may be the result of several changes in the supply and demand situation. And if the statistics show that imports have increased from one year to the next, this does not tell whether the increase in imports was brought about in consequence of an increase in the demand for imports, or in spite of a decrease in the demand for imports, or with an unchanged demand for imports, etc. The balance of international payments does not reveal which of the changes were "spontaneous" and which were "induced," either directly by changes in the exchange rate or more indirectly by the effects upon circulation of other items in the balance.

An attempt at analysing the foreign-exchange market with the tools and in the terminology of general price theory helps in avoiding pitfalls into which one is easily led by the often confusing terminology in which foreign-trade theory and foreign-exchange theory are usually treated.

II

Elasticity Pessimism
in International Trade

A. Overestimation of Required Elasticities: *The critical values of elasticities; The two critical assumptions; The neglect of the elasticities of supply; The supply elasticities in international trade; The start from balanced trade; The neglect of income effects* ■ B. Underestimation of Actual Elasticities: *The findings of statistical research; Statistical demand curves; Measuring aggregative elasticities; Bias inherent in the index number technique; Bias inherent in the underlying assumptions; Bias due to curve-fitting technique; Bias inherent in neglect of time lag; Questionable relevance*

For the purposes of this article, equilibrium exchange rates shall be defined as those rates which equilibrate voluntary supply and unrestricted demand for foreign exchange.[1] The establishment of such rates is often believed to be either impossible or undesirable, and those who take this position join the club of advocates of the continued use of foreign-exchange restrictions. It is convenient to distinguish three typical economic arguments for this position; they may be formulated as follows:

1. *The terms-of-trade argument:* "The present disequilibrium exchange rates and the system of exchange rationing give us much better terms of trade than we could have at equilibrium exchange rates and

---

[1] This definition is ambiguous inasmuch as "unrestricted" demand needs to be defined. In a sense, demand is always restricted, not only by the size and distribution of purchasing power, but also by a large number of institutional controls. What matters, however, for the concept of market equilibrium is essentially the absence of *discretionary* restrictions, such as allocation controls, because the concept of demand loses its usefulness if the amounts demanded depended largely on the grace of the authorities in charge.

without exchange rationing. The national income would be significantly reduced if equilibrium in the exchange markets were to be established through depreciation."

2. *The income-distribution argument:* "The present disequilibrium exchange rates and the system of exchange rationing are essential for their effects upon our national income distribution. The distribution of income would be significantly less 'equitable' if equilibrium in the exchange markets were to be established through depreciation."

3. *The perverse-elasticities argument:* "Disequilibrium exchange rates are inevitable, exchange rationing is indispensable, and equilibrium rates are unattainable, because the elasticities of demand for our imports and for our exports are too low for changes in the exchange rate to improve the market balance of payments. Equilibrium in the exchange markets cannot be established through depreciation."

The first two arguments—contending that the effects of depreciation upon the size or distribution of income would be more harmful than the effects of exchange restrictions at disequilibrium rates—obviously imply that the depreciation would have to be drastic in order to be effective. This presupposes that the elasticities of demand in international trade are relatively low. Hence, all three arguments are based on what I like to call "elasticity pessimism." *Moderate* elasticity pessimism pervades those who warn of miserable terms of trade or an intolerable distribution of income. *Hopeless* elasticity pessimism pervades those who warn of perverse elasticities making the disequilibrium in the exchange market incurable.

I shall not deal here with moderate elasticity pessimism. To prove that it is justified would not settle anything, because one should still have to prove the alleged effects upon national income. (No adequate demonstration of these effects has been presented thus far.) My aim in this essay is to deal with the more severe case of elasticity pessimism. I shall attempt to demonstrate that this pessimism is unfounded. It expresses itself, first, in a tendency to overestimate the magnitudes of the elasticities which are required if exchange depreciation is to have remedial effects and, second, in a tendency to underestimate the actual magnitudes of the elasticities.

The *required* elasticities have been overestimated because of inappropriate assumptions chosen in the basic theoretical analysis. The *actual* elasticities have been underestimated because of inappropriate techniques used in the empirical-statistical research.

A. Overestimation of Required Elasticities

The sound basis for any kind of elasticity pessimism is the probability that every supply curve for foreign exchange will over a certain range be negatively inclined.[2] It is possible, therefore, that an equilibrium in the foreign-exchange market lies in the range of negative slope of the supply curve. Thus, the amount of foreign exchange supplied would be reduced as its price is raised, that is, depreciation would yield less instead of more foreign exchange. In such a case, depreciation can have remedial effects only if the demand for foreign exchange is more responsive than the supply. For example, an existing excess demand for dollars will be reduced by depreciation of the lira if the increase in the lira price of the dollar reduces the amount of dollars demanded more than the amount of dollars supplied. Moving upward, i.e., paying more lire per dollar, within a range in which both the demand and the supply curve for dollars are negatively inclined, a dollar deficit (or excess demand for dollars) will be decreased if the supply curve is steeper than the demand curve; it will be increased if the supply curve is flatter.

What counts here are the comparative *slopes*, not the elasticities, of the two curves because, when we start from an excess demand, the elasticities do not tell the story unless we know the absolute quantities. *Only*

[2] This can be deduced from very general principles. Under given conditions (resources, technology, tastes, money) any market demand curve (for a single commodity, a bundle of commodities, or a foreign currency) is apt to be relatively elastic in its upper ranges and relatively inelastic in its lower ranges. For example, the demand for lire in terms of dollars will be relatively elastic at high dollar prices of the lira and relatively inelastic at low prices of the lira. The demand for lire in terms of dollars constitutes the supply of dollars in terms of lire. Thus we deduce that at low lira prices of the dollar the supply of dollars in terms of lire will be *positively* elastic (corresponding to the relatively elastic demand for lire), whereas at high lira prices of the dollar the supply of dollars will be *negatively* elastic (corresponding to the relatively inelastic demand for lire). The graphs in Fig. II-1 picture these relationships.

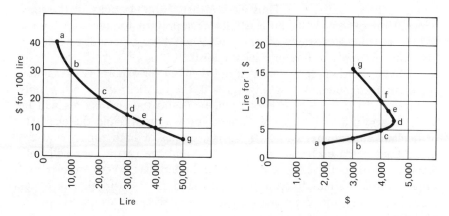

Fig. II-1. Demand for lire, by sellers of dollars, is supply of dollars, by buyers of lire

when we start from an equilibrium can the elasticities indicate the general effects of depreciation.

Depreciation is apt to affect all sources of supply and all purposes of demand for foreign exchange: not only merchandise trade, but also invisible services (tourist trade, shipping, etc.), capital services (dividends, profits from direct investments), donations (immigrants' remittances) and capital movements (private loans, securities, direct investments). Nevertheless, most analyses of the effects of changes in the exchange rate upon the market balance of payments have been confined to the responsiveness of merchandise trade. The elasticities of (domestic) demand for imports and of (foreign) demand for exports have been given the leading roles, if not the only roles, in most modern versions of the exchange-market play staged by economic theorists.

The critical values of elasticities

If the elasticity of (foreign) demand for the exports of a country is *unity* (—1.00), the amount of foreign exchange supplied by exporters will remain the same regardless of the exchange rate. In other words, the elasticity of supply of foreign exchange will be zero; that is, the supply curve will be vertical. The supply curve can have a negative slope only if the elasticity of demand for exports is numerically smaller than unity. In the extreme case, if this elasticity is *zero*, the physical exports will remain unchanged when the exchange rate changes and, with domestic prices unchanged, the domestic value of exports will be unchanged; hence, the supply curve of foreign exchange will be so shaped that it shows constant amounts of domestic money paid for the foreign exchange supplied by the exporters; that is, it will have the shape of a rectangular hyperbola, or an elasticity of minus one. Thus we see that if the elasticity of (foreign) demand for exports is 0, the elasticity of supply of foreign exchange is —1.00; and if the elasticity of (foreign) demand for exports is —1.00, the elasticity of supply of foreign exchange is 0.

Obviously, then, if the elasticity of demand for exports is —1.00 and the elasticity of demand for imports is 0, the elasticities of both supply and demand for foreign exchange will be 0 and the two curves will be vertical. And if the elasticity of demand for exports is 0 and the elasticity of demand for imports is —1.00, the elasticities of both supply and demand for foreign exchange will be —1.00 and the two curves will both slope upward to the left as rectangular hyperbolas. Were exports and imports initially equal, the supply and demand curves of foreign exchange would coincide, and depreciation could not create an excess supply of exchange.

It has become customary to generalize that the numerical values of the elasticities of demand for exports and imports must add up to *more than one* if depreciation is to create an excess supply, or reduce an excess demand, in the exchange market. Unity is regarded as the "critical value" of the sum of the elasticities. If the two elasticities add up to unity, depreciation will not affect the trade balance. If the numerical sum of the two elasticities is less than one, depreciation will have perverse effects upon trade balance and exchange market.

The two critical assumptions

The theorem of the "critical value" of the sum of the demand elasticities in international trade rests on two assumptions which must be made explicit if one is to avoid serious pitfalls.

1. The theorem assumes that the prices of all traded goods remain unchanged in the country of origin; that is, the foreign prices of imported goods and the domestic prices of exported goods are not affected by the depreciation and by the resulting changes in the volumes of imports and exports.

2. The theorem assumes that exports and imports are initially equal; that is, no import surplus, or deficit in the trade balance, exists at the time when depreciation is under consideration as a corrective policy.

No one would argue that these assumptions are realistic. Nevertheless, most economists have neglected to state the qualifications which, on account of the actual deviations from these critical assumptions, should be made regarding the critical value of the sum of the elasticities.

The neglect of the elasticities of supply

The theorem of the critical value of the demand elasticities in international trade says nothing about the elasticities of supply of the goods traded. But it is logically impossible to "neglect" the supply elasticities without making implicit assumptions about them. When an analyst, for example, assumes that a depreciation by ten per cent lowers the prices of export goods to foreigners by ten per cent, he implicitly assumes that the domestic prices remain unchanged. In postulating that these prices remain unchanged although the volume of exports is increased, he makes the implicit assumption that the elasticity of supply of these export goods is infinite. Likewise, if he assumes that the buyers of imported goods after depreciation will find their prices increased by the same percentage by which the price of foreign money is increased, the analyst postulates that the foreign prices of import goods remain unchanged despite reduced imports. Hence, he implicitly assumes that the elasticity of their supply is infinite.

It happens that the magnitudes of the supply elasticities make no difference if the demand elasticities are zero or unity. Apart from these exceptions, however, the supply elasticities are rather influential partners of the demand elasticities in the determination of the effects of depreciation upon the trade balance. In those instances in which the elasticity of demand for exports (imports) is absolutely greater than unity, the supply of foreign exchange from exports (the demand for foreign exchange for imports) will be more elastic the higher the elasticity of supply of exports (imports). Consequently, to assume infinite elasticities of supply of exports and imports is to exaggerate the curative effects of depreciation upon the trade balance in these instances. On the other hand, in instances in which the elasticity of demand for exports (imports) is absolutely smaller than unity, the elasticity of supply of foreign exchange from exports will be more negative (and the elasticity of demand for foreign exchange absolutely farther below unity) the *lower* the elasticity of supply of exports (imports). Consequently, in these instances the assumption of infinite elasticities of supply of exports must result in an underestimation of the curative effects of depreciation upon the trade balance.

The theorem of the critical value refers to demand elasticities which are numerically below unity, indeed so much so that the sum of the two elasticities is said to be unity in the borderline case between "normal" and "perverse" effects. But since this borderline case was deduced from assumptions which included infinite supply elasticities, a *correct* critical value of demand elasticities for more realistic conditions, that is, for situations with lower supply elasticities, must lie *below* unity. Even if the two demand elasticities should add up to less than unity, the effects of depreciation may still be in the direction of an improvement of the trade balance.[3]

The supply elasticities in international trade

My assertion that in the real world the elasticities of supply of exports and imports are far from infinite should be obvious. Nevertheless, what clues do we have concerning the supply elasticities prevailing in international trade?

Raw materials, agricultural as well as mineral, form a significant part of the exports or imports of many countries. That the production of these takes place under rapidly increasing costs has been among the elementary principles of economics, never disproved or even disputed. The more rapidly the production costs increase when output is forced up, the smaller will be the elasticities of supply. And, the larger the role of fixed resources in the production of any goods, the smaller the elasticity of competitive

---

[3] Assume for example that -0.3 and -0.4 are the elasticities of demand for imports and exports, respectively, and 0.3 and 0.4 are the elasticities of supply of imports and exports, respectively. Depreciation in this case would transform a zero balance of trade into a positive one, although the numerical sum of the two demand elasticities is only 0.7.

supply. The low elasticities of supply of "primary" products, particularly in the short run, have indeed become notorious, what with all sorts of price-stabilization plans advocated by national governments and international organizations. International commodity agreements have been urged upon the peoples of the world in the name of the low elasticities of supply of these primary or quasi-primary goods in international trade. Even those who doubt the merits of the schemes have no reason to doubt the contentions concerning the low elasticities of supply.

These claims cannot be made for most manufactured goods. Technological conditions may or may not make for rising cost curves, but will hardly cause *steeply* rising curves. But another important element enters here: many of the goods for which the cost curves are flat are supplied under monopolistic controls. Monopolistic sellers determine their selling prices with close attention to the elasticities of demand for their products. Where demand elasticities are low, sellers will avoid policies of price reductions. If depreciation would make the prices of a monopolistic exporter appear cheaper to foreign buyers, he would be quick to raise his prices in terms of domestic money. In other words, faced with a foreign demand of relatively low elasticity, it would be his selling prices, not his output, which would be adjusted to a changed exchange rate. And this, of course, means the same as a low elasticity of supply.[4]

The start from balanced trade

The theorem of the critical value of the demand elasticities has been formulated with regard to situations in which exports and imports are initially equal, so that, where the demand elasticities add up to the critical value, depreciation would reduce the values of exports and imports by equal amounts, leaving the balance zero. It is easily shown that matters are different if the initial situation is one of an import surplus or an excess demand for foreign exchange for imports.

A numerical example will best clarify the point. Assume that at the given exchange rate the exports of a country, call it Italy, are 100 million dollars, while its import demand is 200 million dollars; that the supply elasticities of Italy's exports as well as its imports are infinite (to choose the worst possible assumption on this score); and that the elasticity of the foreign demand for Italy's exports is only —0.4. Depreciation of the lira will improve the balance if Italy's demand for imports is of an elasticity

[4] For example, when Scotch whisky at given sterling prices would have become cheaper to U.S. buyers in consequence of the depreciation of the pound, the sellers raised the sterling prices. This was emphasized by, among others, Raymond Mikesell, in "Application of Statistically Derived Import Elasticities to Practical Problems of Foreign Trade Policy," *Econometrica*, Vol. 18 (July 1950), pp. 284–285.

numerically above —0.32. In other words, the numerical sum of the two demand elasticities has to be only 0.72 for the critical case.[5]

Needless to say, if supply elasticities of more likely magnitudes— rather than infinity—had been assumed, the resulting critical value of demand elasticities would be still smaller.

It should be mentioned that there may be cases where the total demand for foreign exchange contains considerable amounts which are perfectly inelastic with respect to exchange rates. For example, a country may have large commitments in foreign currency for the repayment of foreign loans or for reparation payments.[6] These may be the cases where trade is initially balanced or, even worse, where imports are smaller than exports. If the latter is true, our argument will operate in reverse, that is, the critical value of demand elasticities will be higher rather than lower. But a quick glance at the actual situations can tell us which is the more frequent case: in most instances in which depreciation has been under consideration in recent years, the initial position was one of an import demand in excess of exports. *The larger the excess import demand for foreign exchange relative to the value of exports, the lower will be the critical value of the sum of the demand elasticities for imports and exports.*

The neglect of income effects

A third assumption was implied in the theorem of the critical value of demand elasticities in international trade: that the national income is not altered by the changes in the exchange rates. If depreciation through its effects upon the volume of exports or upon the balance or the terms of trade should raise or lower total income, it would probably also raise or lower the demand for imports. These income effects of depreciation may be negligible in the beginning, but in the course of time, as the "multiplier mechanism" becomes operative, they may become strong enough substantially to weaken or reinforce the price effects of depreciation.

Those who fear that depreciation would so deteriorate the terms of trade as to lower the national income of the depreciating country will have to admit that the income effects of depreciation would contribute to the improvement of the trade balance. But those who minimize the

[5] The elasticity of demand for Italian exports being —0.4, a 10 per cent reduction of the foreign value of the lira will increase the physical volume of Italian exports by 4 per cent. Thus 104 per cent of the previous physical exports sold at 90 per cent of the previous dollar prices will bring 93.6 per cent of the previous dollar proceeds; export proceeds will be reduced by 6.4 per cent. If the initial import demand of 200 million dollars is to be reduced by the same absolute amount, a reduction by 3.2 per cent will do. This 3.2 per cent reduction in quantity with a roughly 10 per cent increase in price constitutes an elasticity of roughly —0.32.

[6] If commitments are fixed in terms of domestic currency the demand for foreign exchange to meet these commitments is of an elasticity of —1.0, hence, more elastic than the demand for imports is assumed to be.

changes in the terms of trade and emphasize the substitution of products of the depreciating country for products of countries whose currencies become dearer will have to admit that the income effects of the increased employment in the depreciating country, by increasing its import demand, would partially offset any remedial effects on the trade balance and might strengthen any perverse effects.

These are interesting and potentially important complications of our problem. They are probably unimportant in situations in which (a) employment in the depreciating country is so high that an increase in exports cannot raise total income, or (b) the elasticities of demand and supply are such that exports are not substantially increased, or (c) the volume of exports is too small a portion of total trade to affect income substantially or (d) the monetary authorities pursue a policy of stabilizing total money income in the country. Thus, there are enough reasons for neglecting the income effects in the discussion of the critical value of demand elasticities.

The magnitudes of the demand elasticities which are required if depreciation is to improve the foreign balance may under certain conditions be affected by the income effects of depreciation. But our conclusion that these required magnitudes have been overestimated as a result of inappropriate assumptions with regard to supply elasticities and to the initial trade balance remains essentially valid.

B. UNDERESTIMATION OF ACTUAL ELASTICITIES

For several decades the theory of international trade had included propositions concerning the elasticities of demand for exports and imports before the first attempts were made to derive quantitative estimates from statistical research. Only a few years ago the first results were published.[7] These studies prove beyond doubt the great ingenuity of the investigators.

The findings of statistical research

The data used as raw material for these estimates were the import and export statistics for the period after the first and until the second

[7] For example, J.H. Adler, "United States Import Demand During the Interwar Period," *American Economic Review*, Vol. XXXV (June 1945), pp. 418–430; R. Hinshaw, "American Prosperity and the British Balance-of-Payments Problem," *Review of Economic Statistics*, Vol. XXVII (February 1945), pp. 1–9; T.C. Chang, "International Comparison of Demand for Imports," *Review of Economic Studies*, Vol. XIII (1945–46), pp. 53–67; Chang, "The British Demand for Imports in the Inter-war Period," *Economic Journal*, Vol. LVI (June 1946), pp. 188–207; Adler, "The Postwar Demand for United States Exports," *Review of Economic Statistics*, Vol. XXVIII (February 1946), pp. 23–33; J. Tinbergen, "Some Measurements of Elasticities of Substitution," *Review of Economic Statistics*, Vol. XXVIII (August 1946), pp. 109–116; Chang, "A Statistical Note on World Demand for Exports," *Review of Economics and Statistics*, Vol. XXX (May 1948), pp. 106–116. Several other studies have been distributed in mimeographed drafts.

world war. Thus, about 20 years of foreign trade (1919–1939) were taken as the period of observation, and the trade data were compared with price indexes "observed" during the same years.

Estimates which one investigator of these data presented for the elasticities of demand for exports were −0.77 for France, −0.43 for the United States, −0.40 for the United Kingdom, −0.17 for Chile.[8] Not all findings about elasticities of demand for imports were consistent with each other. For example, one estimate of the elasticity of United States demand for imports was −0.09 while another was −0.97, more than ten times as high. There are many reasons for denying that any of the figures are acceptable for the time for which they were computed, and still more reasons for denying that they are relevant for another period.

I shall discuss some of the reasons why we must question the general validity of the elasticity estimates, and why we must regard them as underestimates. If we merely questioned the validity of the estimates, the inherent errors may have biased them in either direction. But it can be shown that the bias was predominantly toward underestimation. This critical discussion must, however, be preceded by an exposition of the general methods by which the estimates of demand elasticities were derived.

Statistical demand curves

Demand curves and demand elasticities are hypothetical constructs to which no amount of observation can give reality. A curve presupposes a series of points, whereas statistical observation can at any one moment of time furnish only one point (i.e., a quantity at a price) and never more than one point of the hypothetical curve. Reasoning that in any observed exchange a quantity must have been demanded as well as supplied at the time, one concludes that the price and quantity define a point of intersection of a demand curve and a supply curve, both of unknown shape. If statistical observation at a subsequent moment of time results in another such point, one concludes that either the demand curve or the supply curve or both have shifted. A series of observations may give many imagined "intersections" which may belong to as many different demand and supply curves, all of unknown shape. Only if we knew what we can never know, that the demand had remained unchanged over the entire period of observations, then we could interpret all changes as being due to shifts in supply and all observed points as "intersections" lying on the unchanged demand curve.

This interpretation is fundamental to the statistical derivation of demand curves. It is, of course, inconceivable that demand should remain

---

[8] T.C. Chang, *Review of Economics and Statistics*, Vol. XXX (May 1948), pp. 107 and 115.

unchanged over a long time. But by making several heroic assumptions and certain corresponding transformations of these data, the empirical investigator derives something which supposedly takes the place of an unchanged demand curve. He theorizes that the quantity demanded of any good varies chiefly with income, with the price of the good, and with the prices of other goods. Making the assumption that tastes have remained unchanged over the period of his observations (or have changed only with a "trend factor") the investigator proceeds to relate the observed quantities of the good (a) with observed income data and (b) with the observed prices of the good relative to those of all goods. The latter procedure, i.e., the deflating of the prices of the particular good for changes in the general price level, is supposed roughly to take care of the effects which changes of prices of other goods (competing as well as complementary ones) must have had upon the demand for the good in question. Regression techniques are used to separate the income effects and the price effects, and sometimes a trend effect. Changes in the population might be taken account of either by a trend factor or by dividing quantities purchased and total income by total population.[9] Changes in income distribution are duly neglected—just as are changes in taste—except if their effects show up in the trend factor. The points obtained as price effects are then connected and the curve obtained is called a "statistical demand curve."

From the slope and position of the statistical demand curve it is easy to "calculate" the elasticity of demand at a given point. The resulting estimate of the demand elasticity is, of course, subject to all the errors and biases which are inherent in the derivation of the statistical demand curve.

Measuring aggregative elasticities

Matters become very much worse if the demand curve in question refers, not to a single commodity, but to a non-homogeneous aggregate of many commodities. The concept of a demand for a bundle of commodities of changing composition is very slippery and the concept of the elasticity of that demand becomes well-nigh unmanageable.

The idea of an elasticity of demand for a heterogeneous aggregate of commodities, such as the demand for exports or imports, implies some sort of weighted average of the elasticities of demand for every single good which is actually or potentially included in the aggregate. No one has ever tried to do such a calculation for all exports and imports. The investigators, instead, have resorted to "aggregative estimates," taking indexes of total physical exports (or imports) and of average prices of export (or import) goods. This procedure, which was used in the analysis of foreign-trade statistics for the interwar years (1919–1939), added to all

---

[9] The results of these two techniques are different.

the errors and biases which are inherent in the derivation of statistical demand curves the further errors and biases which are inherent in aggregation and averaging techniques.

The deceptiveness of aggregative elasticity measurements can be quickly exposed by a mental experiment, in which we assume that we know the individual elasticities of demand for each good contained in the bundle and then try to calculate aggregative elasticity under varying circumstances.

Assume that we have imported only two goods, in equal quantities, at equal prices. Our demand for good A is relatively elastic, say —2.0; for good B relatively inelastic, say —0.5. Now the price of B falls by ten per cent while the price of A does not change. The average price reduction is five per cent; with the quantity of B increased by five per cent, an index of quantity changes will show an increase of two and one-half per cent. Thus, the aggregative elasticity of demand will be calculated to be —0.5, or equal to that of good B. The higher elasticity of A, regardless of how high it is, will not be reflected in the aggregative result.

But this is not all. Assume that the reduction in the price of B by ten per cent is accompanied by an increase in the price of A by two per cent. The price index will show a reduction of approximately four per cent. Since the quantity of A will be decreased by approximately four per cent and the quantity of B increased by five per cent, an index of quantity changes would show an increase of about one half of one per cent. This increase, compared with the four per cent decrease of the price index, would give us —0.125 as the value of the aggregative elasticity. In other words, *the elasticity of demand for the bundle of two commodities seems to be far below the elasticity of demand for any one of the commodities.*

Bias inherent in the index number technique

These are surely absurd results. One suspects that they belong to the category of exceptional freak behavior of index numbers where the effects of implicit weighting have been overlooked. The unacceptable results of the measurement of aggregative elasticity are indeed due to the effects of implicit weighting: the component individual elasticities are weighted not only for the relative values of the particular commodities in the aggregate of exports or imports, but also for their relative price variations, so that the goods which during the period of observation have the greatest variations in price will exercise the greatest influence upon the result. But this is not merely some freak behavior of an otherwise acceptable method. It is, so to speak, a congenital disability of the notion of aggregative elasticity measurements: they can indicate only what happened in one particular instance or period of observation, but have no significant application to other instances, in which the relative movements of the prices of individual goods are different.

The absurd results of our mental experiment are indicative of the errors involved in the estimates of demand elasticities for imports and exports that have been presented. Arnold Harberger has recently examined the index number techniques which were employed in the analysis of international trade figures and has proved that they implied serious errors and strong biases toward underestimation of demand elasticities.[10]

The most important of his findings may be summarized as follows:

1. When more than one commodity is imported it is statistically and even conceptually impossible to obtain an elasticity of demand for "imports," unless the prices of all imported goods move proportionally.

2. An aggregative elasticity which is useful for policy purposes is the elasticity of demand for foreign currency. This could be found by taking the value-weighted average of the elasticities of demand for all individual imported commodities, provided their prices could be taken as given to the importing country.

3. If these prices cannot be taken as so given, the individual demand elasticities must be adjusted to take account of the fact that the elasticity of foreign supply as well as the elasticity of domestic import demand are needed to determine the changes in price and quantity (and therefore in demand for foreign currency) which will result from a disturbance such as depreciation.

4. Estimates of the "elasticity of demand for imports" obtained by treating "all imports" as a single commodity and using ordinary price and quantity indices will understate the true "elasticity of demand for foreign currency" so long as the prices of imported commodities with smaller-than-average elasticities of import demand have, over the period of observation, fluctuated more than those of commodities with greater-than-average elasticities of import demand.

In other words, the data used for the calculations chiefly concerned goods whose prices underwent the greater variations and, hence, probably had low demand elasticities; the goods for which demand is likely to be more elastic were not adequately represented in the data. Where some prices rise while others fall—which easily occurs unless the observation covers a period of unretaliated currency depreciation—*the aggregative result may be entirely outside the range of dispersion of the individual elasticities.* Goods which become exportable or importable at or below certain prices, but are not exported or imported at higher prices—which implies infinite elasticities at the critical prices—are usually not included

[10] Arnold C. Harberger, "Index Number Problems in Measuring the Elasticity of Demand for Imports," a paper presented at the joint meeting of the Econometric Society and the American Statistical Association, Dec. 27, 1949. See abstract in *Econometrica*, Vol. 18 (July 1950), pp. 275–276.

in the indices and, therefore, not included in the aggregative elasticity estimates.

Bias inherent in the underlying assumptions

The bias toward underestimation of demand elasticities due to the excessive weight which goods with great price variations had in the computations, was recognized also by Guy H. Orcutt. In addition he exposed numerous errors following from the assumptions which underlie the method of deriving statistical demand curves for imports or exports and of estimating their elasticities.[11]

The basic assumption, as we have seen above, is that the demand curve, adjusted for income changes and perhaps for a trend factor, has remained unchanged for the entire period for which observations are being analyzed. Estimates based upon this assumption must be wrong if demand has in fact changed during the period. If the prices of imports have decreased but demand has also declined, elasticity estimates based on a "given" demand must be too low.

Assume that the demand for imports and the (foreign) supply of these imports are as pictured in the curves drawn in Fig. II-2. These demand and supply curves, in other words, are the "correct" curves but are, of course, unknown to man. All that the investigator "knows" is Point 1, showing the observed price-quantity position at time 1. From the trade statistics for time period 2, and in the light of subsequent observations, he now calculates Point 2 by adjusting the actually observed quantity of imports for changes in income and perhaps for a trend factor. The investigator now assumes, on the basis of the accepted methodology, that Point 2 lies on a new supply curve, S'S', but on the unchanged demand curve. That is to say, he must conclude that the demand curve is such as to pass through Points 1 and 2. In reality, demand has declined and it is not the original demand curve but a new demand curve (not drawn in Fig. II-2) which intersects with S'S' at Point 2. To the investigator the increase, KL, in the quantity demanded appears as the "response" to the reduction in price as exhibited in the movement from Point 1 to Point 2 and his estimate of the elasticity of demand will be substantially less than the actual elasticity.

Simultaneous shifts of demand and supply of imports (and exports) are not merely "possible disturbances," but are highly probable occurrences. Changes in technology, for example, are apt to change the supply conditions in certain industries simultaneously in many countries. If a country has some domestic production and some imports of a certain product, a technological change will not merely lower the supply prices

[11] Guy H. Orcutt, "Measurement of Price Elasticities in International Trade," *Review of Economics and Statistics*, Vol. XXXII (May 1950), pp. 117-132.

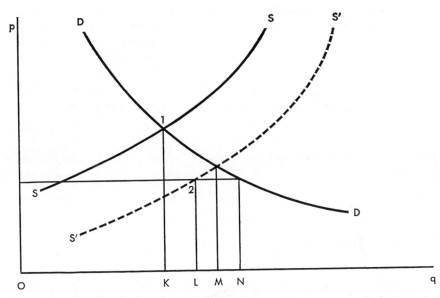

Fig. II-2. Unknown decrease in demand causes underestimation of elasticity in response to price reduction

of imports, but also those of their domestic substitutes. Hence, the demand for imports, which may be regarded as the surplus of total demand over domestic supply, is liable to fall at the same time.

One might think, at first blush, that this case of changing technology is adequately covered by using relative, rather than absolute, prices of imports. This is not so. The price reduction of a product of which some is homemade and some imported is likely to affect the index of import prices much more strongly than the general price index of the importing country. Hence, relative import prices will appear reduced, while they are actually not reduced in relation to the prices of their direct substitutes. Since the apparent reduction in import prices is not associated with that increase in the quantities imported which would have occurred without the actual reduction of the supply prices of domestic substitutes, the estimated elasticity of demand is lower than the actual elasticity.

Bias due to curve-fitting technique

A peculiar downward bias is introduced in the estimation of demand elasticity through a typical combination of errors of observation and the least-squares method of curve fitting.

"Errors of observation" in international trade statistics are less likely to occur in the quantities of goods imported than in the prices of the goods. One may, therefore, assume that the points in a scatter diagram will be both above and below the "correct" demand curve; that is, they will be scattered in a vertical direction about the curve. But this correct demand curve is unknown and a statistical demand curve will usually be derived by fitting a line so as to minimize the sums of the squares in a horizontal direction. We may see from the diagram in Fig. II-3 that the estimated demand curve will be considerably steeper than the correct one, and the estimated elasticities much lower than the actual ones.[12]

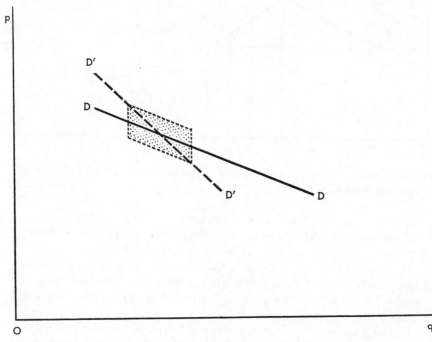

Fig. II-3. Statistical demand curve, fitted by least-square technique, is too steep

Bias inherent in neglect of time lag

All estimates of elasticities of demand for imports and exports were made from annual trade figures, usually annual averages of trade volumes and price indexes. It has sometimes been held that the problem of lags need not be serious where annual figures are used, because the most significant responses to price changes would become effective in the course of several months. This is certainly not true with regard to many long-run effects. But even strictly short-run demand curves cannot be derived from data which neglect all time lags; and the neglect of such lags results in underestimation of the elasticities of demand.

[12] Guy H. Orcutt, *op. cit*

(*a*) Trade figures for weeks or months immediately after price changes cannot well reflect the response to these price changes. A period of six or even twelve months, therefore, must include a significant interval of time during which trade was not yet affected by the new prices. Thus, the elasticity estimates will be too low.

(*b*) When price reductions are gradual, buyers will often expect further reductions and will postpone purchases. Thus, such expectations affect trade in the opposite direction from the effects of a price reduction which is regarded as the one and only change. Many of the price changes during the period for which the trade statistics were analyzed were part of continuing price movements and, therefore, must have aroused corresponding expectations. The trade figures, which were combined with annual price averages without lags, surely included these temporarily perverse reactions of trade and, consequently, falsify the actual elasticities of nonspeculative demand. The result, again, is underestimation.

(*c*) That long-run elasticities are greater than short-run elasticities is well known. For the demands for imports and exports this is true particularly for two reasons. The substitution between foreign and domestic products or materials often requires technological adjustments which are planned and made only after some time. Secondly, foreign products compete with domestic products the supply of which may be inelastic in the short run, but very elastic in the long run. The elasticity of demand for the foreign products will then likewise be very high in the long run. If a country considers depreciating its currency, it is the long-run elasticities of demand for its exports and imports which really count. The estimated elasticities derived from past trade figures without lags give a wrong picture.

Questionable relevance

We have seen several reasons why the so-called measurements of the elasticities of demand for exports and imports must have yielded estimates much below the "actual" or correct ones. The underestimation of the elasticities actually prevailing during the periods of observation was inevitably linked with the ways in which the data were used.

But let us pretend for a moment that we succeeded in measuring correctly the elasticities of demand actually prevailing at the time. Would we be justified in assuming that the values obtained would remain even roughly relevant (*a*) for later times, (*b*) for different income levels and (*c*) for different price ranges? In other words, can we claim that the estimates of elasticities at one time, with certain income levels and over certain price ranges, will be relevant for the demand fifteen or twenty years later, at very much different income levels—more than double in some countries —and for entirely different price variations?

The elasticity estimates of the past, even if they were correct, are hardly relevant to entirely different conditions. But we should not press this issue; it might lead us into undue defeatism with regard to the value of quantitative empirical research. Surely we must avoid a naive belief in the applicability of past "constants" and "coefficients" for the prediction of future economic quantities. But there is little merit in rejecting all quantitative research findings on the ground that "times change." Some quantitative relationships change rapidly and drastically, others change slowly, others again remain remarkably stable over time. We do not know enough about demand elasticities in international trade to say much about the degree to which past estimates, if correct, might be relevant in the future.

The relevance of estimates of price elasticity for different income levels is a question on which probably some significant theory might be developed. We should be able to formulate some hypothetical generalizations about the ways in which changes in the absolute and relative income levels in the countries concerned might, under specified circumstances, affect the price elasticities of demand for total imports and exports. I have not come across any literature on this problem.

The relevance of elasticity estimates for different price ranges is another unknown territory. The assumption of linear demand curves would imply that the elasticities are different from point to point, different from one range to another, different for small variations and for large. On the other hand, hyperbolic demand curves would allow us to slide along the curves with constant elasticity. Aprioristic reasoning suggests that demand curves are more elastic at higher price ranges than at lower. From this we should conclude that correct elasticity estimates for one price range could not correctly be applied to another.

III

Three Concepts of
the Balance of Payments and
the So-Called Dollar Shortage

A. The Market Balance of Payments ■ B. The Programme Balance of Payments ■ C. The Accounting Balance of Payments ■ D. Conclusions

The confusion concerning the meaning of a deficit or a disequilibrium in the balance of payments is almost as old as the study of political economy. But never before has it been so widespread; and rarely so systematically exploited. To be sure, most of the people who speak and write of the so-called dollar shortage are honestly confused. But there are probably some who know better and try to take advantage of the general confusion for political purposes if only out of patriotic motives. In any case, we have no right to abet confusion through continued equivocation. Three fundamentally different ideas are continually called by the same name. For the sake of clearer thinking they should be distinguished.

What is indiscriminately called the balance of payments may be (A.) a MARKET BALANCE, i.e., a balance of supply and demand; or (B.) a PROGRAMME BALANCE, i.e., a balance of hopes and desires; or (C.) an AC-COUNTING BALANCE, i.e., a balance of credits and debits.

The market balance of payments is a model of a given situation in the foreign-exchange market, characterised by the effective demand and supply of foreign exchange at the given exchange rate and at alternative, hypothetical rates. This is an *ex ante* concept for use in the analysis of the foreign-exchange market, with major emphasis on the effects which changes of the exchange rate might have upon the amounts of exchange effectively demanded and supplied.

The programme balance of payments is a statement of sources and uses of foreign funds, expected or planned, over a future period of one or more years, based upon the nation's capital and consumption requirements, and on a programme of meeting an excess of requirements over resources by recourse to foreign finance expected or sought. This also is an *ex ante* concept, not for analysis but for use in planning, forecasting or negotiating, with major emphasis not on what is effectively demanded, but on what is felt to be desirable with reference to some accepted standards.

The accounting balance of payments is a record of all transactions, real and financial, which have taken place over a past period of one or more years between the country's residents and residents of other countries, the record being kept in the form of double-entry bookkeeping, with each credit entry balanced by an offsetting debit entry, and vice versa. This is an *ex post* concept based on statistical information and estimates for use chiefly in the description of past developments and perhaps also in the appraisal of the present position of one nation in relation to others.

The meaning of a deficit in the balance of payments is, of course, categorically different for each of the three basic concepts. But also within each concept the meaning of a deficit is by no means clear. There may be several different deficits depending on a number of arbitrary definitions, assumptions, hypotheses, judgments, or objectives, even after one has decided whether one speaks of a market, a programme, or an accounting balance.

A. The Market Balance of Payments

In an attempt to define a dollar shortage or a deficit in the dollar balance of payments in the market sense (or supply-and-demand sense), one should be deliberately vague on certain points in order to allow for differences in assumptions and hypotheses which can be legitimately made.

A dollar deficit in a country's market balance of payments may be tentatively defined as an excess of dollar amounts effectively demanded at the given exchange rate by would-be purchasers (who are not restricted by specially adopted or discretionary government control measures) over the dollar amounts supplied at that exchange rate by would-be sellers (who are not motivated by a desire to support the exchange rate).

1. The phrase "*effectively demanded*" is to mean that the would-be buyers possess and are willing to part with the domestic money to pay for the foreign exchange. Effective demand for dollars means supply of domestic money in exchange for dollars; and excess demand for dollars

means excess supply of domestic money in the exchange market. Of course, total cash balances, bank credit outstanding and incomes are assumed to be given.

The concept of a "given" demand for dollars has several implications: (a) The case of a continuing credit expansion, of a continuous "feeding" of demand by the creation of additional bank credits or other forms of money, is ruled out.[1] (b) When an excess demand for dollars is met by sales from monetary reserves (for the sake of maintaining exchange-rate stability) these sales tend to reduce domestic circulation and, thus, the would-be buyers' ability to sustain the given demand for dollars.[2] We must understand the effective demand as that which would-be buyers of dollars can exercise before their buying power may be impaired through dollar sales out of monetary reserves. (c) When an excess demand for dollars is reduced through an increase in the price of the dollar, i.e., a depreciation of the currency, the reduction of dollar sales out of official reserves and the improvement in the foreign balance on current account may result in an increase in the domestic money supply and income level, and thus, in an increase of the demand for dollars.[3] Again, the "given" demand for dollars cannot show these repercussions of the change in the exchange rate.

In order to show the repercussions of changes in income, our working model should include, in lieu of a "given" demand for dollars, a family of demand curves with different income parameters. As long as we try to deal with a "given" demand, we have to assume that the buying power which makes this demand effective is unchanged. This assumption, I am afraid, limits the use of a market model which includes only a "given" demand curve to short-period analysis.

2. The phrase *"at the given exchange rate"* may mean any exchange rate whatever, but the excess demand for dollars would then be purely hypothetical. More often the "given" exchange rate will refer to the one

---

[1] The process of a continuing expansion would be represented by a continuing shift of the demand curve for foreign exchange upward and to the right (and of the supply curve upward and to the left). At a fixed exchange rate the excess demand for foreign exchange would continually rise, and with freely flexible rates the successive "deficits" in the market balance of payments would regularly be eliminated by continual increases in the price of the dollar.

[2] The "deflationary" effects of dollar sales out of monetary reserves would come to an end when the income flow is reduced to such a level that current savings out of received incomes are low enough to be adjusted to the reduced rate of "investment" (domestic investment minus the import balance).

[3] The existence of a continuing dollar deficit on current account at a stabilised dollar rate may be consistent (as was indicated in the preceding footnote) with stationary income equilibrium if the rate of saving has adjusted itself to the import balance. If, then, the depreciation reduces the dollar deficit, the domestic income flow must increase and, depending on the marginal propensity to import, the effective demand for dollars must also increase.

actually prevailing, at least at the outset of the imagined process. Most often it will refer to the rate fixed and maintained by the monetary authorities.[4]

3. The phrase *"not restricted by specially adopted or discretionary government control measures"* is the most delicate part of the definition; it is designed to prevent the definition from becoming unnecessarily narrow and to make it applicable to a variety of assumptions. A given demand curve for dollars assumes a large number of "underlying" conditions including the levels of income and buying power, the supply and demand conditions for all domestic and foreign products, and also the existence of governmental obstacles, incentives or prohibitions. Import tariffs, import quotas, import prohibitions, subsidies for home-made substitutes of foreign products, excise taxes on goods containing imported materials, limitations on foreign travel, and hundreds of similar governmental measures are among the factors determining a country's effective demand for dollars. To assume "absence of all government intervention" would be silly if the model is to aid in the analysis of reality. On the other hand, to assume the existence of comprehensive foreign-exchange controls (allocation controls) and to include in the effective demand for dollars only those amounts which the control authorities will actually authorise would be worse, because it would define away the very problem we are out to solve, the excess demand for dollars. On what grounds, then, should we distinguish governmental control measures that can be assumed as given among the factors determining the effective demand for dollars from other measures that cannot be so included?

The answer to this question will usually be suggested by the setting of the problem to be solved. For example, if with a given set of non-discretionary control measures the problem is to analyse the possible effects of depreciation without a change in the controls, the "given" demand will surely be on the basis of the existence of the controls. An absolutely effective prohibition of capital exports—if such a thing can exist—may exclude the demand for dollars by would-be capital exporters and reduce the relevant demand to that by importers of foreign goods and services. If the problem includes a comparative evaluation of specific (non-discretionary) control measures, the best procedure might be to work with two demand

[4] Underlying the whole market analysis is usually the notion that the size of the excess demand is a function of the exchange rate and that in all probability an exchange rate could be found at which the excess demand is zero. Nevertheless, there are theories denying the existence of an equilibrium exchange rate under certain conditions and, under other conditions, asserting that the equilibrium may be unstable. In any event, the model of the foreign-exchange market with given supply and demand functions serves equally those who believe and those who do not believe it probable that there is always an exchange rate which can equate the dollar amounts demanded and supplied.

curves, one including, the other excluding, the effects of the controls in question. If the problem is to find out whether existing restrictions which were adopted merely for the duration of an emergency can be abandoned, these restrictions will be assumed to be absent so that one may see the picture of a possible market balance or imbalance without the use of the restrictions. If controls are of a kind that can be administered only with a discretion which in turn is affected by the size of the excess demand, then the "given" demand should certainly not reflect the exercise of these controls.[5]

4. The phrase *"not motivated by a desire to support the exchange rate"* is designed to separate the sales of foreign exchange out of monetary reserves and out of foreign stabilisation loans from the sales properly regarded as the "supply" of exchange in the market in which the balance between supply and demand is being analysed.

The "market supply" is by no means confined to transactions on income account, that is, to the proceeds from sales of exported goods and services (and certain donations). It includes also all those transactions on capital account (and all those donations) which are not the result of deliberate efforts to satisfy an effective demand for foreign exchange that could not otherwise be satisfied at the given exchange rate. Long-term capital imports, that is, direct investment by foreigners and the proceeds from the sale of securities to foreigners, are unquestionable components of the market supply of foreign exchange. And there is no reason why the market supply should not also include the foreign exchange derived from official (governmental or institutional) loans for relief, rehabilitation, reconstruction, and development. Of short-term capital imports, the autonomous ones, such as funds of foreign capitalists placed in the country (whose balance of payments is being analysed) either for safekeeping or in order to profit from interest differentials are also clearly eligible for inclusion in the market supply of foreign exchange.[6] The "market supply" of dollars

[5] Ardent believers in a free economic order may have a bias towards thinking of the effective demand always as if it were as "pure" as possible, i.e., unaffected by restrictive government controls. Ardent believers in centralised planning, on the other hand, may refuse even for theoretical analysis to abstract from foreign-exchange restrictions, except in order to prove that a free market is inherently unstable and injurious to the national interest. The technique of analysis implied in the concept of the market balance dictates neither of these prejudices, although, as was said before, the logic of the conception of a demand function of determinate elasticity forbids us to include in the function the probable effects of discretionary restrictions (where the exercise of the restrictions is not restricted by any stated rules but only by the *ad hoc* rulings of the administrators).

[6] Doubtful is the inclusion of short-term capital imports of private exchange speculators. These might be either foreigners willing temporarily to increase their balances (claims) in the country, or nationals willing temporarily to reduce their foreign balances or to increase their foreign debts. They are motivated by expectations of profiting from a merely temporary weakness of the domestic currency in the exchange market. In an

includes all those dollars that come to the exchange market as effective demand for domestic money. In other words, these dollars are offered because the would-be sellers want domestic money.[7]

Excluded from the "market supply" are the dollars sold out of the gold and foreign-exchange reserves of the monetary authorities, and out of foreign stabilisation loans, and the rate-pegging purchases of domestic currency by foreign monetary authorities and international institutions such as the International Monetary Fund. These are the funds which are made available for the purpose of meeting all or part of the deficit in the market balance; they are supplied in order to support the exchange rate, not in order to get domestic currency.

5. Every supply-and-demand analysis has several *time* aspects: it pictures a situation prevailing at a particular moment of time and expected to last for a definite or indefinite period of time; it deals with quantities offered or demanded per unit of time; and it expresses the changeability of these quantities in response to changes in price with a certain time interval allowed for the adjustment. We are concerned at this point with how long the situation depicted by the market curves is expected to last. This is a time aspect of great significance in policy decisions. If an excess demand for foreign exchange is expected soon to give way to an excess supply, the problem of the "dollar shortage" is surely quite different from what it would be if no change was expected in the foreseeable future.

Disregarding day-to-day and even seasonal fluctuations, and speaking only of deficit periods long enough to constitute serious problems for monetary authorities intent upon maintaining exchange-rate stability, we may distinguish three kinds of cases: (*a*) The excess demand is judged to

---

analysis of the position of the monetary authorities, the foreign funds made available by exchange speculators might possibly be regarded as part of the market supply of foreign exchange, because this supply will relieve the pressure upon the monetary authorities and reduce the drain of official monetary reserves. From other points of view it seems preferable not to include the speculators' funds in the market supply of foreign exchange, especially since some of the consequences of these speculative transactions are very similar to those of reductions of the gold or exchange reserves of the monetary authorities. On these questions see my article on "The Theory of Foreign Exchanges," *Economica*, Vol. VI (New Series, November 1939), pp. 375–397, and Vol. VII (New Series, February 1940), pp. 23–49, especially pp. 42 ff. Reprinted in *Readings on the Theory of International Trade*, Philadelphia, Blakiston, 1949, pp. 149 ff. and in Chapter I of this Volume.

[7] Many of the comments made above regarding effective demand have analogous relevancy for the market supply. The offer of foreign exchange, for example, may be the consequence of governmental measures stimulating the exports of merchandise or prohibiting the holding of foreign balances (claims); and it may depend upon the problems at hand whether the effects of the "interventions" should be included in or excluded from the market supply. There also is again the question of changes in the level of domestic income affecting the exportability of home products and the flow from other sources of supply of foreign exchange. This either calls for a family of supply curves with different income parameters or it limits the use of a "given" supply curve to problems for which changes in income can be legitimately disregarded.

be cyclical in character, that is, associated with a particular phase of a national or international trade cycle, and hence likely to disappear in due time even without any special measures on the part of the governments concerned. (b) The excess demand is judged to be associated with structural or monetary factors expected to change before long in consequence of certain measures taken by the government or of certain developments afoot in the economy. (c) The excess demand is judged to be associated with conditions not expected to change significantly in the foreseeable future. Cases (a) and (b) are those in which the International Monetary Fund would consider sales of dollars against the currency temporarily in excess supply. In case (c) the I.M.F. would favourably consider a depreciation of the currency in excess supply.

6. There are several different *policies* for dealing with a deficit in the market balance of payments. A. The excess demand for dollars at the given exchange rate can be reduced or removed by altering the rate. The proper adjustment of the exchange rate is typically a depreciation of the domestic money, i.e., a higher price for the dollar. B. The excess demand for dollars can be satisfied at the given exchange rate through sales of gold or dollars by the national or international monetary authorities. C. The excess demand for dollars can be left unsatisfied, the short amount supplied being distributed among would-be buyers by rationing, administrative allocation or similar discretionary restrictions of foreign-exchange transactions. D. The excess demand for dollars can be reduced or removed by monetary and fiscal measures reducing the money circulation and income flow of the country. E. The excess demand for dollars can be reduced (though rarely removed) by restrictive commercial policy, thus reducing, through higher import barriers, the demand for dollars (a shift which ordinarily will imply increased domestic demand for other things including exportable goods, and thus tend to reduce the supply of dollars [8]). F. The excess demand for dollars can be reduced (though rarely removed) by persuading other countries to a more liberal commercial policy, thus increasing, through reducing their import barriers, the supply of dollars (a shift which ordinarily will imply increased domestic demand for imports and dollars [9]).

Policies E and F—import barriers and removal of export barriers—have in common with Policy D—deflation—that they are attempts to remove the gap between the supply and demand curves by shifting them

---

[8] This reservation need not be relevant where policy E is adopted after policy C has been in use for a considerable time and the particular import demand that is now eliminated by new import barriers had been in any case unsatisfied under existing exchange controls. Policy E then merely reduces the demand for imports and dollars without reducing actual imports and purchases of dollars.

[9] Where policy F is adopted on top of policy C, the new supply of dollars may merely allow some previously existing but unsatisfied import demand to be satisfied. The qualification concerning an increase in demand is then not relevant.

until they intersect at the existing exchange rate. Policy A—exchange depreciation—attempts to close the gap by movements along the existing curves towards the point where they intersect. Policy B—exchange stabilisation—attempts (by rate-pegging sales out of reserves) to fill the gap between the existing curves at the existing exchange rate. Policy C—exchange restrictions—leaves the existing curves, the existing rate and the existing gap as they are, but suspends the free market.[10]

Depreciation as well as deflation are apt to reduce real wages, the former by raising prices of imports and possibly increasing exports at the expense of home consumption, the latter by lowering money incomes in the economy. Policies A and D are unpopular for these reasons, and B and C are the monetary policies preferred by most politicians and many political economists. Since B, however, drains the foreign reserves of the country, C—restrictions—are relied upon in increasing degrees. Foreign loans strengthen the reserves for continuing policy B, but as soon as foreign loans give out, policy C becomes more stringent and the "dollar shortage" is perpetuated. This policy is rationalised by the contentions that deflation would lead to Communism, and that depreciation would under trade-union pressure become inflationary and, thus, could not eliminate the excess demand for dollars. It is true that trade-union pressure for excessive wages will lead either to unemployment or to inflation (open or repressed), and that inflation (even if repressed) results in permanent dollar shortages unless the price of the dollar is allowed to rise continually along with or ahead of wage rates. If it is politically disastrous to permit large-scale unemployment and politically impossible to outlaw disequilibrating wage increases, a policy of continual exchange depreciation might be the only alternative to a policy of permanent restrictions or abolition of the market system.[11] Needless to say, assertions about what is politically

[10] The system of "freely fluctuating exchange rates" adopts policy A as an automatic regulation of the market balance of payments. Under such a system a dollar shortage in the market sense could not last even for a quarter of an hour. Any gap between supply and demand that threatened to develop at one exchange rate would immediately be closed by the market finding a rate that would squeeze out the excess demand. Whether the rate fluctuations under such a system would be enormous or moderate would depend on various elasticities, about the size of which we know little. In all systems used in actual practice, several of the policies dealing with an excess demand for exchange are used in combination. Of the two commercial policies, F is usually a pious hope, E—import barriers—an impious fact. Of the four monetary policies, the gold standard combined policies B and D—stabilisation and deflation. Most of the systems now in use (e.g., United Kingdom) combine policies B and C—stabilisation and restrictions. Some systems (e.g., France) combine policies A, B and C—depreciation, temporary stabilisation and restrictions. In at least one case (Italy) we have recently observed a combination of all four types of monetary policy.

[11] A "temporary suspension" of the market mechanism pending certain anticipated improvements of domestic productivity and possible foreign tariff reductions would in fact turn out to be permanent. The alternative policy of countering any excessive wage increases by continual depreciation was apparently what Lord Keynes regarded as most

"disastrous" or "impossible" are matters of political opinion, the validity of which it is difficult to judge.

7. In contrast to the programme balance of payments, to be discussed presently, it makes no sense to *forecast* the market balance of payments for a future period into which the present market conditions can hardly continue—unless we believe that we know the future market conditions. The market balance of payments refers to a given exchange rate under given conditions of supply and demand. Changes in wage rates, interest rates, production costs, consumer tastes, tariffs, fiscal policy, credit policy, capital movements, etc., will alter the market conditions for foreign exchange so significantly that it is nonsense to predict the size of the excess demand for a time a year or two away. Sometimes, perhaps, one may predict that the underlying conditions are likely to change in the near future so as to reduce the gap between supply and demand of dollars that exists at the present exchange rate. Or one may deny that they are likely to change sufficiently to eliminate the gap soon. Or one may try to estimate, nay, guess, the size of depreciation that might suffice to close the gap under given conditions. But a pretence of quantitative precision in forecasts of the market balance of payments cannot be taken seriously.[12]

B. The programme balance of payments

The second concept of a balance of payments does not offer as many difficulties of definition as did the first concept. The definition of the deficit in the dollar balance of payments in the programme sense (or hopes-and-desires sense) calls merely for enough flexibility to take account of differences in judgment and in objectives.

---

feasible. See "The Objective of International Price Stability," *Economic Journal*, Vol. LIII (June–September 1943), p. 186. There is a good chance that the threat of continual depreciation will make trade unions ready to agree on schemes for wage stabilisation (or wage increases in measured steps).

[12] Some of the differences between market balances and programme balances, particularly the difference in predictability, can be clarified by an illustration from another field. The housing shortage in the market sense is sure to continue for a long time if rentals are held at the controlled levels. One may try to guess the increase in rentals sufficient to eliminate the excess demand under given supply and demand conditions. But it is impossible to forecast the amount of excess demand for next year; although we may be certain that supply conditions will not have changed considerably, demand may be completely different. For example, another round of wage increases under full employment or a reduction in the income tax might easily double the excess demand; or an increase in food prices might cut it in half. The housing shortage in the programme sense, on the other hand, can well be predicted, because the amount of dwelling space which we regard as desirable depends chiefly on the (perhaps) predictable number of families—not on their disposable incomes and on the rentals they must pay.

A dollar deficit in a country's programme balance of payments may be defined as an excess of dollar amounts needed or desired for some specified purposes (assumed to be important with reference to some accepted standards) over the dollar amounts expected to become available from regular sources.

1. The phrase *"needed or desired"* is to emphasise the contrast with the phrase "effectively demanded" that was used in the definition of the market balance of payments. The relevant magnitude in the programme balance is not the effective demand—based on the people's ability to pay —but the "requirements" computed by experts and based on what they regard as the nation's needs or desires. These needs or desires refer to the imports from abroad required to sustain certain levels of domestic consumption and capital formation.

2. The phrase *"for some specified purposes"* need not mean exact import specifications according to detailed blueprints in a comprehensively planned economy, but may refer to global figures put down as targets or forecasts in an aggregative national budget, or even to mere projections of import totals required to supplement domestic output in the achievement of certain levels of consumption and rates of development. Given these levels of consumption and rates of development, given the productive resources available in the country, and given a certain export target, the total import requirement can be deduced by addition and subtraction.

3. The phrase *"with reference to some accepted standards"* indicates that the levels of domestic consumption and the rates of domestic capital formation are, in this context, matters of political judgment. Since the programme is usually submitted in justification of governmental measures or requests, the objectives must conform to some standards widely accepted as fair and reasonable. With regard to consumption goals, the maintenance of the existing plane of living, or the return to one attained prior to an emergency, will usually be considered as a fair objective; lifting the plane of living will most easily be accepted as a reasonable objective if it can be couched in terms of public health and social security. With regard to capital accumulation, proper goals may include the reconstruction of plant worn or torn by war or other catastrophies, improvement of plant capable of securing quickly an increase in productivity such as to make the nation self-sustaining at a satisfactory living standard or any kind of development work promising to raise consumption from notoriously sub-standard levels. But it will be shown later that the "requirements," in all actual situations, are at least as much a matter of how much foreign finance appears to be obtainable as they are of how much appears to conform to "accepted standards."

4. The phrase *"expected to become available from regular sources"* is to exclude the emergency sources. The foreign finance designed to fill the dollar gap is thus separated from the dollar amounts from more regular sources upon which the programme makers are counting when they estimate the gap that remains to be filled. These, in other words, are the dollar amounts to be received as proceeds from exports of goods and services, and from loans and investments by foreign capitalists if such are safely expected. Whether dollar loans or grants firmly promised by foreign governments are included among the available dollar amounts before calculation of the deficit or, instead, are regarded as parts of the financing provided to meet the "existing" deficit is a matter of taste. There seems to be an inclination to consider foreign loans or grants for "special projects" among the ordinary "transactions supplying foreign exchange," but to put "general-purpose" loans or grants down as "compensatory official financing" sought and obtained in response to an existing deficit in the programme balance of payments.[13]

5. The programme balance of payments is always set up for a definite *period of time,* usually one year, sometimes two, three or four years. In a programme for two or more years it is customary to show declining deficits in successive years in order to emphasise the beneficial effects of the aid to be received in the first year. (This definiteness contrasts strongly with the indefinite and probably brief time period to which a given market balance of payments could refer. Every slight change in market conditions, every act of fiscal or monetary policy, might drastically change a deficit in the market balance.) Since the programme is presumably independent of the whims of the markets it is possible to plan a deficit of definite size for one or more years ahead.

6. The existing *foreign-exchange rate* is not as essential for the programme balance as it is for the market balance of payments. The amounts of dollars effectively demanded and supplied will vary if the price of dollars changes; but the amounts of dollars needed or desired for certain national purposes may be entirely independent of the price of the dollar. If the dollar becomes more expensive in terms of domestic currency, people will not be able to buy, on their given incomes, so many things for which dollars are required. But they may still need or desire these things and this is what counts for the dollar deficit in the programme balance of payments. With regard to the programme balance, the foreign-exchange rate may possibly be a factor in the effective steering of productive resources for the attainment of the production and export targets

[13] Cf. International Monetary Fund, *Balance of Payments Yearbook, 1938, 1946, 1947,* Washington, 1949, p. 10. On the inconsistencies involved in such procedures see Section C below.

set in the programme. But the more comprehensive the price and allocation controls in the economy, the less relevant will be the foreign-exchange
rates.

7. It is in the assumptions about the *level of incomes* that the difference between market balance and programme balance of payments becomes most strikingly apparent. An increase in money and real income
will most likely increase a dollar deficit in the market balance, but decrease a dollar deficit in the programme balance. In the market, the dollar
gap will be widened at a given exchange rate, because people can buy
more and, thus, more goods will be imported and fewer goods made
available for export. In the programme, the dollar gap will be narrowed,
because people produce more and, thus, fewer goods need be imported
and more goods may be made available for export.

8. Six *policies* for dealing with a deficit in the market balance of
payments were previously mentioned. Two of them, exchange depreciation and deflation, are of little relevance for the programme balance,
because relative prices are not of the essence in judging what the nation
needs, desires or can do without. The other policies remain relevant.
Import barriers and exchange restrictions are among the main instruments of implementing the programme: only for needed or desirable
imports are dollars made available. Exchange stabilisation (in the sense
of sales of dollars out of reserves of the monetary authorities) is often a
part of the programme of covering the deficit: the programme may seek
foreign loans and grants for the larger portion of the deficit, but draw on
the dollar reserves of the nation to finance the rest. In a sense, however,
one should really not speak of policies of "dealing" with a deficit in a
programme balance of payments. For this is not a deficit which first
"exists," and then is "dealt with." Instead, it is a deficit which is pro-
grammed when there is a chance to finance it. There is no sense in drawing up a programme balance with a dollar deficit when there is no hope
of finding the funds required to carry out the programme. The entire
programme is built around the potentialities of finding the foreign finance
for the deficit.[14]

9. That the dollar deficit in the programme balance of payments is
conditioned by the *financing potentialities* explains our previous remark
that the so-called standards underlying the nation's requirements are not
only flexible but, perhaps, even secondary to the appraisal of the financing
potentialities. No matter how fair and reasonable are the standards on the

[14] The staff of the International Monetary Fund recognises the planned character
of most of the dollar deficits and considers it erroneous to assume "that in some way a
deficit develops and financing must then be found for it. . . . Unless it is financed, the
deficit cannot come into being." Again, "the monetary authorities engage in compensatory financing of a deficit upon which they have deliberately decided." International
Monetary Fund, *op. cit.*, p. 23.

basis of which a country would "need" large amounts of dollars, any programme balance showing a deficit too large to be financed would quickly be revised. Thus, a realistic appraisal of how much foreign finance might possibly be obtainable (from other than "regular" sources) will be the chief determinant of the deficit. This would make the dollar shortage (in the programme sense) merely a function of the financing potentialities. In actual fact, of course, the strength of the case, resting on the validity of the standards, might influence the willingness of other nations to finance a larger deficit and, besides, matters are even more complicated than that because the authorities in most countries constantly confuse in their thinking the programme balance of payments with the market balance. It is chiefly the programme balance by which the economic benefits of a foreign loan can be judged. A loan to finance a persistent deficit in the market balance would be beneficial only if something could be gained by postponing the correction of a fundamental maladjustment of the exchange rate.

10. Apart from its use in foreign diplomacy and domestic politics the programme balance of payments is a *forecast* of future developments. The forecasting involved in the programme balance makes sense even for periods for which forecasting of a market balance would make no sense. This does not mean that the forecasting will usually be proved correct by the actual developments. Where a nation allows some degree of economic freedom and permits free enterprise to perform some of the international transactions, it may find that some things do not go according to plan, that not all targets are reached, and that the programme must be revised in several respects. Yet, even if the forecasts eventually turn out to be wrong, they often make sense at the time they are made.

As in all forecasting and programming, past experience plays a dominant role in the computation of a programme balance of payments. The figures of past imports and exports are the chief material used by the programme makers, and projections of these figures into the future, with certain revisions up or down, are their most common method. There seems to be a tendency on the part of forecasters to underestimate the pliability of the trade balance in free market economies.[15] This is prob-

---

[15] In the forty-eight years from 1867 to 1914 France had import surpluses in forty-four years, and export surpluses only in the four years (1872–75) during which she paid war tributes to Germany. Despite this example of the pliability of the trade balance, John Maynard Keynes in the discussion of the German transfer problem regarded the trade figures as "sticky." When he wrote his famous article on "The German Transfer Problem" in the *Economic Journal*, Vol. XXXIX (March 1929), pp. 1–7, he had only the 1927 trade statistics available. It showed a German import surplus of RM 2,847 million. In 1928 the import surplus was only RM 1,229 million, by 1929 the balance had changed into an export surplus of RM 36 million, and in 1930 and 1931 the export surplus reached RM 1,642 million and RM 2,872 million, respectively. In the years before 1930 the changes were chiefly increases of exports with merely small

ably so because many economists underestimate the price elasticities and income elasticities which determine the flows of goods and services in free economies. Another reason may be that they take import figures as an expression not of effective demand but rather of the needs of the nations and are loathe to programme a significant reduction in imports that would hurt. In any case, while past trade balances are of little relevance in sizing up the market balance of payments, they are important in shaping the programme balance of payments.

The *ex ante* character of the programme balance of payments is self-evident, but to the extent to which hopes are fulfilled and targets attained, the *ex post* record of international transactions may tally with the programme.

C. THE ACCOUNTING BALANCE OF PAYMENTS

The third concept of the balance of payments, the statistical record of a country's international transactions in the form of a fully balancing accounting statement, offers difficulties of definition only when it comes to define a deficit or surplus. If for all unilateral international transactions the accountants make offsetting entries on "donations" account, the only possible difference between the totals of credits and debits can be "errors and omissions," reflecting statistical deficiencies, not economic phenomena. Although everybody agrees that the accounting balance of payments "necessarily balances," many choose to present it as showing a surplus or deficit in some meaningful sense.[16]

Thus, *a dollar deficit in a country's accounting balance of payments may be defined as an excess of dollar amounts entered on the debit side of certain accounts in the annual record of its international transactions over the dollar amounts entered on the credit side of the same accounts, the accounts being selected from the full, necessarily balancing statement in order to throw light upon problems connected with market or programme balances of payments.*

---

decreases of imports; during the later years, after the onset of the world depression, the imports fell most drastically. The 1927 imports had been RM 13,801 million, the 1932 imports were RM 4,666 million. It may be said that these drastic changes in the trade balances had undesirable consequences. True enough. But this means merely that quick change may hurt, not that it is difficult to achieve; and that a forecast of a deficit based on past trade figures is in the nature of a programme, not a market balance, with the purpose of avoiding "undesirable" consequences.

[16] Cf. International Monetary Fund, *op. cit.*, "The balance of payments of a country necessarily balances. It is a system of double-entry bookkeeping under which total credits equal total debits. There can be no surplus or deficit in the balance of payments as a whole" (p. 4). Nevertheless, "the Fund's staff has endeavored to develop a concept of balance of payments surplus or deficit that would facilitate consideration of the problems of the Fund" (p. 5).

1. The phrase *"certain accounts"* serves as recognition of the fact that a complete statement of all accounts cannot possibly show a credit or debit balance, while "certain accounts" can. If these accounts, taken together, show a credit balance, the remaining accounts, taken together, must show a debit balance, and vice versa.

2. The phrase *"debit side"* stands here also for various other captions alternatively used in statements of international transactions, such as "payments," "imports," "passive," and "increase in gold or foreign assets" or "decrease in foreign debts," the latter two captions referring to gold and capital movements (provided such items are among the selected ones).

3. The phrase *"international transactions"* does not mean that every single transaction with foreigners is separately entered in the record; net changes in gold holdings and in foreign assets and debts can adequately reflect the net results of all individual transactions on gold and capital accounts.

4. The phrase *"credit side"* stands here also for various other captions alternatively used, such as "receipts," "exports," "active," and "decrease in gold or foreign assets" or "increase in foreign debt."

5. The phrase *"accounts selected"* is intended to reflect the fact that the ideas as to what is a significant selection have varied most widely. For a long time writers stressed only merchandise accounts, and up to this day many concentrate their attention on current accounts (income accounts).[17] Official donations are sometimes excluded, so that transactions on current account consist of goods, services and private donations. Others have felt that long-term capital movements (or at least private long-term capital movements) should be included among the accounts showing the significant balance.[18] This would leave movements of monetary gold and short-term capital (and perhaps official long-term capital movements) as the items offsetting or financing the surplus or deficit. There are several more possible combinations of accounts, separating private and official short-term capital movements, or using other sorts of breakdowns. A "new approach,"[19] recently developed by the International Monetary Fund in its search for a "working concept of surplus or deficit in the balance of payments,"[20] will be discussed presently.

---

[17] Cf. *Report of the ECA Mission to the United Kingdom*, London, 1948, p. 3, where the proposition that "the period from 1930 to 1938 showed a deficit in the balance of payments running at the rate of £27 million per year" refers to the "trade" balance plus "net invisibles."

[18] Cf. International Monetary Fund, *op. cit.*, p. 5, illustrating "the necessity of including private capital movements if the impact of the balance of payments on the exchange problem is to be assessed."

[19] *Ibid.*, p. 24.

[20] *Ibid.*, p. 5.

6. The phrase *"in order to throw light"* indicates the purpose, but not necessarily the result of selecting certain items of the accounting balance of payments to show a credit or debit balance. The light thrown by the balance of chosen items is more often deceptive than helpful, particularly in the analysis of the market balance of payments. Even the most careful selection of items in an accounting statement cannot indicate whether the particular transactions were "autonomous" or "induced," which is the significant thing in market analysis.[21]

7. On first thought it may appear that no difficult *time problems* are involved in the concept of a deficit in the accounting balance of payments, with all accounts recording *ex post* the transactions that have actually occurred during the year. Unfortunately, this is not so if the accounting balance is supposed to explain the situation in the foreign-exchange market. There may be, within a year, several changes, back and forth, from excess demand to excess supply of foreign exchange, that is, a succession of deficits and surpluses in the market balance of payments. But apart from this, the trade statistics of one year may contain imports or exports prepaid in the previous year or payable in the next year, in amounts not cancelling each other, so that the offsetting short-term capital movements would not reflect any "balance-of-payments pressures" in the foreign-exchange markets. Many other kinds of peculiar timing constellations may make the accounting balance absolutely irrelevant for any market balance over the year.

8. The accounting balance of payments tells nothing about the relationship between *foreign-exchange rates* and the market balance of payments.[22] Aggregative elasticity studies are absolutely unreliable.

9. The impossibility of using an accounting balance of payments as an *indication of the market balance of payments* can perhaps be better understood by imagining cases of perfect balance in the accounting

---

[21] In an analysis of the foreign-exchange market it is essential to distinguish, for example, between imports which give rise to additional demand for foreign exchange, and imports which are induced by additional supply of foreign exchange. The accounting balance of payments, regardless of the way the accounts are selected, cannot say anything about such problems. All imports are considered as representing a demand for foreign exchange.

[22] Where the exchange rates were kept stable over the years, it is, of course, not possible to learn from actual import figures anything about the exchange-rate elasticities of demand for imports. Where exchange rates changed during a year, the accounting balance of payments for the whole year cannot possibly show the effects of the rate changes. But even if we ever had a clean comparison between two periods (without overlapping anticipations or commitments), with two different exchange rates, we still could not derive the relevant elasticities, because autonomous capital movements and domestic-income levels in the two periods may have been very different. For example, while one naturally supposes that a higher price of the dollar would reduce imports into a country, a foreign loan granted to it at the time of the depreciation might enable it to import more rather than less.

balance. no matter how the accounts are selected. (E.g., assume a perfect balance of trade, a perfect balance of invisibles and no net movements of monetary gold or capital.) We still could not see from the accounting balance whether the equality of annual exports and imports was achieved (a) by a stable market balance with supply and demand unchanged during the year, (b) by a flexible adjustment of exchange rates to changing supply and demand conditions, (c) by a flexible adjustment of domestic-income levels by means of fiscal and monetary policies compensating any autonomous influences upon supply and demand for foreign exchange maintained at a stable rate (or by an orthodox gold-standard policy, which, conceivably, might do the same thing), (d) by a flexible adjustment of tariffs, subsidies and prohibitions compensating any other influences upon supply and demand for foreign exchange maintained at a stable rate, or (e) by suspending the free market, requisitioning all foreign exchange from exporters and rationing it among favoured importers. These are surely very different situations in the foreign-exchange market. Only the first of the five cases of perfect accounting balances may be described as one of a perfect market balance.

10. The thought of using an accounting balance of payments as indication or explanation of difficulties with the market balance of payments is too tempting to be given up lightly. The staff of the International Monetary Fund worked hard to solve this problem. In 1948, they reported progress [23] and, in 1949, success.[24] They admitted that the new concept that they had developed was "still in the experimental stage," and "will undoubtedly be modified" in the process of application. But they considered it "to have reached a sufficiently well-defined stage to assist in analysing problems of international exchange." [25]

The new concept, called *Compensatory Official Financing*, is provisionally defined as "the financing undertaken by the monetary authori-

[23] "It is of great importance for the Fund *to know the financial pressures on the monetary authorities* resulting from international transactions and how they are met. In the preparation of the Manual serious consideration was given to the possibility of setting up a final item . . . that would have been entitled 'Official operations to finance a deficit or surplus in the balance of payments.' The deficit or surplus would, by definition, have represented the balance of all transactions other than these official operations, and the official operations themselves would have represented *the response of the monetary authorities to the pressures arising from the balance of payments*. It was decided, however, not to set up an item of this character, because of the difficulty of determining without analysis in each particular case how certain transactions should be classified." International Monetary Fund, *Balance of Payments Manual*, Washington, 1948, p. 8. (Italics are mine.)

[24] "The staff has developed a concept of compensatory official financing . . . ," a "concept that would facilitate consideration of the problems of the Fund." International Monetary Fund, *Balance of Payments Yearbook, 1938, 1946, 1947*, Washington, 1949, pp. 4–5.

[25] *Ibid.*, p. 5.

ties to provide exchange to cover a surplus or deficit in the rest of the balance of payments." [26] It can be said of every single item, or group of items, that it covers a surplus or deficit in the rest of the balance of payments; this is in the nature of any accounting statement. Hence, what this definition apparently tries to single out is those operations which have the sole or primary purpose of providing foreign exchange in response to a situation that has arisen in the foreign-exchange market. The main criteria, therefore, are the *purpose or motive* of the operations and the *stimuli* to which they are supposed to respond. In the analysis of any particular financing operation, the analyst's decision on its purpose should depend on whether the operation would have been undertaken also "for its own sake," that is, even if there had been no excess demand for foreign exchange.[27] And the decision on the stimulus should depend on whether without the financing operation the "balance-of-payments pressures" would have resulted in some serious events in the foreign-exchange market, such as depreciation, additional restriction measures, default on governmental obligations or the like.

In applying the new concept to their statements on the "Financing of International Transactions," the staff of the Fund met with perplexing paradoxes. That they included foreign-exchange transactions of *private* commercial banks of all countries except the United States under the heading of compensatory *official* financing was probably good judgment, inasmuch as most of these banks are merely the lengthened arms of the respective monetary authorities. But the judgment concerning many intergovernmental loans and grants was so poor, I am afraid, as to deprive the new concept of most of its meaning.

U.N.R.R.A. aid, for example, was entered as compensatory financing for the recipient countries, because "it was directed to needy countries that could not make international payment for it out of their own resources." [28] That the recipient countries could not have paid for the U.N.R.R.A. supplies is certainly correct, but irrelevant for the question, because the supplies would not have been bought and, hence, would not have had to be paid for. The goods were supplied without charge, not because the countries had an excess demand for foreign exchange, but because they had an unsatisfied need for food and other necessary materials; not because there was an excess supply of local currency in the dollar market, but because people were hungry and the production lines were disrupted. If in any of the recipient countries the price of the

---

[26] *Ibid.*, p. 5.

[27] "There is a wide range of financing . . . in which it is a matter of interpretation whether or not the operations have been compensatory; the decision in these instances rests upon whether the financing was in response to general balance-of-payments pressures or whether it was for a particular project or other special purpose that would have been financed anyway for its own sake." *Ibid.*, p. 10.

[28] *Ibid.*, p. 11.

dollar had been so high, or the holdings of domestic money had been so low, that people could not afford to demand dollars, that is, if there had not been any "pressures" on the market balance of payments, this surely would not have disqualified such a country from receiving U.N.R.R.A. aid. The grants, therefore, cannot be called compensatory of any pressures in the exchange markets.

The same inconsistent application of the new concept was made in the case of E.R.P. loans and grants. Although it was recognised by the staff analysts that "project loans" are not *"compensatory* official financing" but *"special* official financing," [29] E.R.P. aid, loans as well as grants, was put down as "compensatory." The failure to observe the criteria adopted for the new concept can be appreciated by asking what were the principles of allocating the E.R.P. funds among the recipient countries. The comparative pressures in the foreign-exchange markets? the comparative excess demands for dollars? the comparative need of exchange-rate adjustments? the comparative rigour of exchange controls? None of all these. Not the pressures in the foreign-exchange markets, but the potentials for improvement in the productive use of domestic resources were fundamental guides in the allocation of loans and grants under the E.R.P. programme.[30]

11. We can now diagnose a part of the confusion in the application of the new concept. The balance-of-payments pressures which Compensatory Official Financing is supposed to relieve are, in one place, taken to refer to the market balance and, in another place, to the programme balance of payments. E.R.P. loans or grants are surely compensatory of deficits in the programme balances of the recipient countries, even if they are not compensatory of deficits in their market balances of payments. But there can be no doubt that problems of the market balance were originally what the designers of the new concept had in mind; they specifically mentioned the "use of the Fund's resources, exchange-rate adjustments and exchange controls" as the problems the consideration of which was to be facilitated by the new concept.[31]

Some of the inconsistencies in the application of the stream-lined accounting balance of payments obviously bothered the staff writers of the Fund. This is apparent from the discussion of the differences between balance-of-payments deficits in free exchange markets and in controlled

---

[29] "The development of the project, rather than the development of balance-of-payments deficits, governs disbursements under the [project] loan. A project loan may in fact be extended to a country that is enjoying a balance of payments surplus." *Ibid.,* p. 12.

[30] A critic of this statement has said that the E.R.P. dollars will always relieve the pressures in the foreign-exchange market and cover part of an existing dollar deficit in the market balance. Even this need not be true. The E.R.P. funds may be used for purposes for which there was no effective demand before the E.R.P. aid was granted.

[31] *Ibid.,* p. 5.

exchange markets. The argument runs as follows: Where the "exchange markets are free and the authorities undertake to maintain a stable rate of exchange," this undertaking *"forces"* the authorities to finance any deficit that should arise. But where the exchange markets are controlled, so that the authorities supply only as much exchange as they wish or are able to afford, they "engage in compensatory financing of a deficit upon which they have *deliberately* decided." Hence, this "planned deficit is different from the unplanned deficit of the free exchange market." But— although the staff writers had stated before that a deficit in the balance of payments can *exist* only if and in so far as it is *financed*—they nevertheless conclude that "in either case," that is, with unplanned or planned deficits, "the amount of compensatory financing is the measure of the extent to which the *existing* balance of payments has *forced* the authorities to take financial action." [32]

At the bottom of these manifest contradictions lies a neat piece of circular reasoning. Originally the idea of the staff was to call compensatory that amount of financing that was designed to provide exchange to cover a balance-of-payments deficit. Now they have ended up with measuring the balance-of-payments deficit by the amount of financing that they choose to call compensatory. This noble accounting balance is not even a distant relation of the market balance of payments. As a matter of fact, the deficit in the market sense, the excess demand for dollars, was defined away when the staff of the Fund assumed that "a country exercising an effective exchange control," by cutting down "its outpayments to whatever it finds to be the level of its international receipts," can *"eliminate the deficit."* [33] A "dollar deficit," in the sense of this peculiar way of reasoning, is then the amount of dollars made available by monetary authorities—even if the excess demand is much greater—and the amount of dollars made available by foreign governments for general purposes —even if the effective excess demand for dollars in the exchange market is larger, smaller, nil or negative.[34] This arbitrary accounting balance measures nothing but itself.

[32] *Ibid.*, p. 23. (All italics are mine.)

[33] *Ibid.*, p. 23. (Italics are mine.)

[34] The actual state of the foreign-exchange market can be judged by mental experiment: by postulating the removal of all allocation and rationing controls and asking what amounts of dollars would have to be sold or bought by the monetary authorities in order to stabilise the exchange rate, and what would happen to the exchange rate in a free market if no dollars were added to or sold out of official reserves. In some European countries the price of the dollar would surely have declined in a free exchange market if the dollars available from ERP aid had been offered for sale. This certainly does not mean that these countries do not need the aid. On the basis of the potential benefits to their economies, their need for this dollar aid—i.e., the deficit in their programme balance of payments—may be more urgent than in the case of countries with large excess demand for dollars.

D. CONCLUSIONS

Deficits in the market balance, programme balance, and accounting balance of payments mean very different things. A persistent deficit in the *market* balance of payments—an excessive amount of domestic money wanting to be exchanged into foreign money—indicates that the nation's monetary, fiscal, and wage policies (and the resulting money incomes and product prices) are incompatible with the foreign-exchange rates. A persistent deficit in the *programme* balance of payments—repeated plans to liquidate foreign assets, to attract foreign investors, to contract foreign debts, and to negotiate foreign grants—indicates that programme makers believe foreign funds could be obtained and would materially contribute to the recipient nation's development, improvement of plant, productivity of resources, and plane of living. A persistent deficit in the *accounting* balance of payments, with one of the customary selections of accounts, indicates that the nation in the past has been able to live partly on its foreign assets and/or to secure foreign loans or grants.

There is no necessary relationship between these deficits; indeed, a deficit in one of the three senses may be compatible with a simultaneous surplus in one of the other senses.[35] For example, a country with a deficit in its programme balance of payments may have a surplus in its market balance of payments. The government of that country may be anxious to obtain foreign funds for a development programme and may have succeeded in impressing a foreign mission with the urgent needs for a development loan. These needs (not satisfied out of other sources) constitute the programme deficit. But the government may have been pursuing a conservative fiscal and monetary policy, avoiding deficit spending and credit expansion. Thus, the market demand for foreign exchange would not be inflated, and the market supply at the given exchange rate may be such that the monetary authorities can make current net additions to their exchange reserves. This surplus in the market balance of payments may prevail despite the recognised deficit in the programme balance, certainly as long as the latter remains only on paper; but it may persist even after the foreign loan to cover the programme deficit has been granted, if the government—though perhaps ill-advised—continues its anti-expansionary policies and keeps national spending to a minimum. In this case the foreign funds required for the programme may be supplied in the open market before an effective market demand for them has developed.

The opposite constellation is also conceivable: a deficit in the market balance and a surplus in the programme balance of payments. Such a

[35] The following four paragraphs were written in the spring of 1958 and replace a paragraph in the version published in 1950.

surplus is of course nothing but an opinion of some planners or experts, who hold that the country, much wealthier than others, is able to save much more than others but lacks sufficient investment opportunities at home. In its own interest, they conclude, the country "ought" to have steady capital exports.[36] At the same time, however, the country may have been indulging in deficit spending and credit expansion, and/or several foreign countries may just have devalued their currencies, with the result that there exists an excess demand for foreign exchange—a deficit in the market balance of payments—in the rich country with its programme surplus.

The possibility of a deficit in the programme balance and a surplus in the accounting balance of payments is easily conceived. A country may have been paying reparations, or repaying foreign loans, or investing abroad because of political insecurity at home, and thus its balance on current account may show a surplus. Yet the experts may agree that the country is in urgent need of capital imports to bolster its development. (As, if, and when foreign capital is actually obtained and used for buying foreign goods, the accounting surplus may disappear and give place to an accounting deficit.)

A deficit in the accounting balance and a surplus in the market balance of payments may coexist in a country receiving loans and investments from abroad while abstaining from expansionary domestic monetary policies. The supply of foreign exchange, increased by the foreign funds becoming available on capital account, may be partly sold in the open market, thus depressing the price of foreign money to the lower limit tolerated by a policy of exchange stability, and partly purchased by the monetary authorities. To the extent that the foreign exchange finds sellers in the market it goes to pay for the import surplus, that is, to finance a deficit in the balance of payments on current account; to the extent that it is purchased by the monetary authorities it will be regarded as a surplus in the market balance of payments.[37]

---

[36] Distinguish the "ought" of capital exports to help other nations and the "ought" of capital exports to provide outlets for potential over-saving and to avoid underemployment at home. Only in the latter case could one speak of a "surplus" in the programme balance of payments; in the former case the capital exports would only be designed to cover deficits in the programme balances of other nations.

[37] A diagrammatical illustration of the situation described above may be helpful.

With the dollar price at the lower peg, there will be a *surplus* in the market balance of payments in the amount of MN dollars or $MNCB$ lire, and a *deficit* in the balance of payments on current account (which is the most widely used variant of the accounting balance) in the amount of JM dollars or $JMBA$ lire.

This description of a "situation" should be distinguished from a description of an "adjustment to a change," namely, from the situation in which no foreign capital had been received (and the equilibrium rate KE_1 had been "actual," not merely hypothetical) to the situation prevailing when the supply of dollars received from foreign capitalists becomes effective (with domestic income and expenditures still unchanged).

Under these circumstances, much of the current talk about dollar shortage makes little sense. A country may have a large effective demand for dollars—if the supply of domestic money is relatively large and the price of the dollar relatively low. This does not indicate the urgency of the need for any dollar aid sought to increase the productivity of the nation's resources and to improve its plane of living. And neither the urgent need nor the effective demand for dollars is indicated by accounting records reflecting past financing operations.

In the evaluation of the benefits of a loan to a nation "suffering from

In this case one would say that at the former equilibrium rate the market surplus would be KQ dollars, and that this would result in (a) a fall of the dollar rate to the lower peg, (b) a reduction in the market surplus from KQ to MN dollars, (c) a reduction in commodity exports by JK dollars, (d) an increase in commodity imports by KM dollars, and (e) an increase in exchange reserves by MN dollars.

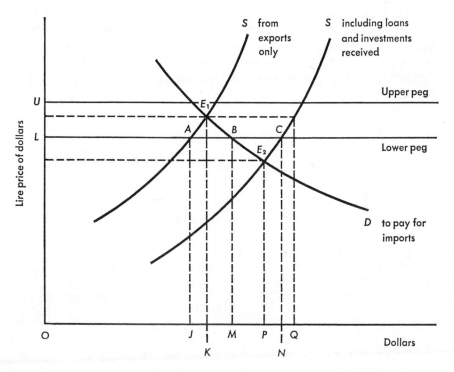

Fig. III-1. Surplus in market balance and deficit in current account due to capital imports

OU = upper peg (selling price of dollars maintained by monetary authorities);
OL = lower peg (buying price of dollars maintained by monetary authorities);
KE_1 = hypothetical equilibrium rate, if no foreign capital were received;
PE_2 = hypothetical equilibrium rate, if none of the foreign capital received were re-exported by adding it to the foreign-exchange reserve.

a dollar shortage," its programme balance of payments will be of major significance. For it will indicate what the nation intends to achieve with the aid requested, the consumption levels and the plant improvements that it visualises. The current market balance of payments of such a nation is not so significant in this respect. For if the market deficits are persistent, loans will only postpone the necessary adjustments of relative prices and exchange rates. It is for the evaluation of the usefulness of such adjustments that the deficit in the market balance of payments is most relevant. The connection between the two kinds of dollar shortages is chiefly political. It may be that the improvements in the nation's economy which are to result from the financing of the programme deficit may give its government the political security it needs for carrying out the price and rate adjustments necessarily involved in the elimination of the deficit in the market balance of payments.

In discussions of the equivocal "dollar shortage" we should insist on full identification of the concept employed. We may then discover that many of the existing differences of opinion—in the diagnosis of as well as in the therapy for concrete cases—can be easily resolved, and the rest can be reduced to questions of unknown facts or of irreconcilable political philosophy.

I V

Dollar Shortage and Disparities in the Growth of Productivity

A. Meaning and Causes of "Dollar Shortage": Monetary Policy or Structural Conditions? ■ B. Balogh Advances Hypotheses Involving Productivity Disparities, But Gives No Explanation ■ C. Haberler Provides an Explanation, Which Balogh Disregards ■ D. Williams Presents the Balogh Hypotheses, Still Without Explanation ■ E. Hicks Offers Theory, Stressing Import Substitution in Progressing Country ■ F. Hicks Applies This Theory to Account for British Experience ■ G. The Theory Implies Net Decline in Real Income, Not Merely Slower Increase ■ H. The Theory Is Really Independent of Differential Growth Rates ■ I. Need for Frequent Costly Adjustments to Disparate Growth May Suggest Policy of Trade Restrictions, But Does Not Explain Dollar Shortage ■ J. Continuing Shortage While Real Income Continually Increases Cannot Be Explained by Structural Difficulties

The debate about the dollar shortage has been going on for over ten years. The ranks of economists believing that the dollar shortage is *chronic* have been increasing, and so has the list of theories proposed to explain that "chronic" condition. One of the theories, recently propounded with great conviction, links the persistent dollar gap with *disparities in the growth of productivity* in the main trading countries.

It is to Professor J. R. Hicks and his mastery of theoretical analysis that we owe an exposition clear and lucid enough to permit critical examination.[1] But he is not the originator of the theory. He found it set

[1] J. R. Hicks, "An Inaugural Lecture," *Oxford Economic Papers*, Vol. 5 (June 1953), pp. 117–135.

93

forth by Professor John H. Williams,[2] who in turn had been anticipated by Dr. Thomas Balogh.[3] This productivity-growth-disparity theory of the dollar shortage in the versions by Balogh, Williams and Hicks will be discussed in this article.

A

A brief introductory statement of the general issues in the debate about the dollar gap may provide the necessary background for the discussion. Sir Dennis Robertson has neatly defined "dollar shortage" as

> a persistent tendency on the part of the populations of the world outside North America to spend more in that region than the sum of what they are earning in that region and what the inhabitants of that region are disposed to lend to them or invest in their borders under the play of ordinary economic motive. The symptoms of the disease are a continuous pressure on the monetary reserves of the extra-North American countries which is kept at bay partly by a series of special loans and gifts made to them by the North American countries, partly by special restrictions, imposed on themselves by themselves, prohibiting or limiting the purchase of certain classes of North American goods.[4]

A persistent tendency to overspend seems to be chiefly a matter of the will; in individuals such tendencies are treated by moral precept, friendly advice, parental discipline, threat of divorce, legal guardianship, denial of credit. For whole nations overspending is, one should think, a matter of economic policy, and policy is not unalterable. People cannot spend money that they do not have, nor buy on credit that they have not got; hence monetary policy can take care of their propensities to overspend. Governments, of course, can print their own money (except where gold coins are the only medium of exchange), or create the credit they want, and thus their propensities to overspend have to be restrained by what is called a "sound" fiscal policy.

Along such lines of reasoning, one school of thought on the dollar shortage holds that it is nothing but the result of "lax" *monetary and fiscal policies,* and that it is "chronic" only as long as these policies are con-

---

[2] John H. Williams, *Economic Stability in the Modern World* (London: Athlone Press, 1952), republished under the title *Trade not Aid: A Program for World Stability* (Cambridge, Mass.: Harvard University Press, 1954).

[3] Thomas Balogh, "The U.S. and the World Economy," *Bulletin of the Oxford Institute of Statistics,* Vol. 8 (1946); *idem,* "The United States and International Economic Equilibrium," in *Foreign Economic Policy for the United States,* ed. Seymour E. Harris (Cambridge, Mass.: Harvard University Press, 1948), pp. 446–480; *idem, The Dollar Crisis: Causes and Cure* (Oxford: Blackwell, 1950).

[4] Sir Dennis H. Robertson, *Britain in the World Economy* (London: Allen and Unwin, 1954), pp. 53–54.

tinued; the tendency of a nation to overspend can persist only because its leaders, or "popular will," resist a change in economic policies, a change which might have unpleasant, though by no means catastrophic, consequences.

For the opposite school of thought the dollar shortage is due to *structural conditions;* some members of this school hold that the dollar shortage cannot be treated by monetary and fiscal policies; others concede that it can be cured by the adoption of "classical" economic policies, but only at the expense of mass unemployment, starvation, revolution.[5]

Between these extreme points of view—one claiming that the dollar shortage can be cured by some monetary and fiscal discipline without dire consequences or indeed with substantial long-run benefits; the other claiming that the dollar shortage is basically due to unalterable structural conditions and that its "cure" through orthodox treatment would have catastrophic results—between these extreme points of view there are several shades of opinion about the relative social costs and benefits of restraining the tendency to overspend either by monetary and fiscal or by direct controls. The position of economists on these matters may be ultimately a question of social and political philosophy: of their attitudes toward economic libertarianism, interventionism, socialism, equalitarianism; but it will also depend on some issues of economic theory, especially on the acceptance or rejection of the applicability of certain models of "structural" economic conditions, conditions which supposedly obstruct, or make intolerable, the traditional mechanism of adjustment of the balance of payments and are not alterable by monetary measures.

One of these issues of economic theory is whether disparities in the rates of increase of productivity in the dollar world and the non-dollar world are apt to cause pressures, persistent or ever recurring, which would take the form of a dollar shortage not manageable by monetary measures or institutions. This is the issue before us.

[5] Cf. Balogh, *The Dollar Crisis*, pp. 136–137, and 198:

"If we disregard relative standards of life, and the possibility, indeed probability, that mass unemployment and starvation may well ensue if conscious measures are not taken to promote a more even international distribution of wealth and income, 'equilibrium' in the sense of a balance of payments is perfectly easy to produce with or without devaluation, with or without 'controls'. . . . Provided monetary demand is appropriately reduced by raising the rate of interest sufficiently and reducing Government expenditure by cutting social services and State-initiated investment, causing mass unemployment and an abrupt fall in the standard of life, external 'equilibrium' without controls could certainly be re-established."

"It would be a mistake to suppose . . . that the 'classical' methods of 'curing' the crisis will not 'work'. They will."

"A few more years of this cure", and it will be impossible to "retain the loyalty of the majority of the people for the Western social system."

B

The theory was advanced in 1946 by Dr. Balogh:

> The rise of the United States to a position unparalleled since the Roman Empire has placed the world in a dilemma unless indeed, as we shall argue below, conscious measures are taken to restore equilibrium. We either have to envisage prodigious investment activity in the United States which *increases the competitive power of that country faster than productivity rises elsewhere and thereby leads to periodic pressure abroad and probable breakdowns,* or continued depression which makes nonsense of the classical mechanism of adjustment towards a 'creditor position.' The only escape to be found from this dilemma would be that United States savings be used for foreign investment . . . or that United States business activity be maintained by social reform or 'non-productive' Government expenditures. But even in these cases—given the strong initial superiority of the United States and the aggressiveness of its managerial leadership—it is likely that *technical progress will be faster in the United States than in other countries* adhering to the 'classical' rules of the game.[6]

At other places Balogh refers, not to differential rates of progress, but rather to discrepancies in competitive power achieved. For example:

> Even after the fundamental disequilibrium in the world's balance of payments arising from the war and the slow recovery of the old world has been overcome the disequilibrium between the United States and the rest of the world is likely to persist. *This disequilibrium is due to the discrepancy in order of magnitude of the economic power of the United States and any other single country,* except perhaps the U.S.S.R. in the long run.[7]

The difference between the effects of growth as an ongoing process and the effects of power achieved by past growth may be significant, especially since productivity in a smaller and less powerful nation may conceivably increase faster than in a nation of vastly superior "economic power." Balogh did not make it clear which of the two disparities he had in mind, or whether both were supposed to have the same effects. Nor did he explain why either should have the effect he claimed for it. He apparently thought that the asserted causal relationships between growth disparities or power disparities and dollar shortage were "obvious" and would be understood without the aid of theoretical models demonstrating possible connections between assumed and inferred phenomena.

[6] Thomas Balogh, "The U.S. and the World Economy," *op. cit.*, p. 321; also, literally reproduced, in "The United States and International Economic Equilibrium," *op. cit.*, pp. 467–468. Emphasis partly supplied.

[7] Thomas Balogh, "The United States and International Economic Equilibrium," *op. cit.*, p. 476. Emphasis supplied.

C

The missing clarification and explanatory support for the growth-disparity theory was provided by one of its sharpest critics. In 1948 Professor Gottfried Haberler took a closer look at the asserted relationship between disparate changes in productivity and the dollar shortage, and he asked himself what the connections could possibly be. He came to the conclusion that

> it is possible that country B is hurt by progress in A. If, say, synthetic nitrate and rubber are developed, Chile and British Malaya *may* be permanently injured. But it is, of course, just as well possible that technological progress in A is such that it benefits B. This will be the case if progress takes place predominantly in A's export industries rather than in industries competing with B's exports, or if B can find some other lucrative exports. Obviously all sorts of things may happen and reference to the possibility or probability that progress in the United States will be faster than elsewhere is entirely irrelevant for judging the final outcome (the nature of the new equilibrium). Unfortunately, nobody can tell where future progress is likely to be concentrated, and even if we had a hint that it will be of a nature unfavourable for B it would be hard for country B to do anything about it. On the other hand, it would be easy to cite examples where in the past dire predictions to the effect, say, that the industrial countries as a whole would be placed in a difficult position by technological progress in the industrially backward countries have proved to be entirely wrong. That may be conceivably different in the future, but there is no evidence that Dr. Balogh had such long-run changes in the comparative cost situation to the detriment of some particular countries in mind when he expressed fears of the growing American superiority. In fact, he does not betray any awareness of the real issues involved.[8]

Haberler thus clearly separated the development of substitutes for imported goods from the differential rate of development in general. Balogh, however, did not take the hint. In his book on *The Dollar Crisis: Causes and Cure,* published in 1950, he did not make any use of, or reference to, Haberler's sensible suggestion. He did reply to Haberler, but only to take a whack at him for adhering to the theory of comparative

---

[8] Gottfried Haberler, "Dollar Shortage?" in *Foreign Economic Policy for the United States,* ed. Seymour E. Harris (Cambridge, Mass.: Harvard University Press, 1948), pp. 438–439. I took the liberty to reverse, in the above quotation, the notations A and B, first because the mental association of A with America as the faster-growing nation, and B with Britain, may be an aid to the reader, and secondly because it will avoid the necessity of "unlearning" the notations when we come later to review the analysis of the relations between fast-growing A and stagnant B in Hicks' statement.

advantage and neglecting the "unequal dynamic progress" and "the growing dominance and faster progress of the United States." [9]

Balogh again makes no distinctions between power, size, wealth, rapid development, industrial supremacy, monopoly position, mass production, faster increase in productivity. For example:

. . . the emergence of the United States as an *overwhelmingly dominant power* . . . reduces the chances of the restoration of a smoothly-working national economy [p. 5].

. . . the discrepancy between the *size and wealth* of the United States and any other single country has grown so enormously that producers in that country, *ceteris paribus,* acquired a considerable advantage [p. 6].

The . . . problem results from the fact that *rapid development* in the U.S. has rendered most industries in poorer and smaller countries obsolete. Insufficient attention has as yet been paid to the implications for the international competitive power of a country of its having achieved *industrial supremacy, e.g.,* of the fact that it initiates new processes of production, creates new goods in which it obtains a *monopoly position* for at least some years. Moreover, the United States based on a vast and well-protected domestic market, acquired advantages in industries in which *mass-productive methods* can be applied, *i.e.,* a growing number of the highest productivity industries [p. 8].

. . . even if there were no deflation in the U.S., other countries might easily find their currencies 'over-valued' as *productivity would rise faster* than elsewhere and wages and demand might not rise quickly enough. In any case, it is not likely that her imports would increase sufficiently with rising income, or that foreign countries will not find themselves eliminated from the most productive lines of production; thus the difference between rich and poor in the world, instead of being eliminated or diminished, would increase. If, on the other hand, deflation would supervene in the U.S., the impact on Western Europe would be even more disastrous. Thus the dollar 'shortage' might well prove to be a recurrent phenomenon involving a continuous deterioration of (at least the relative) standard of life of countries other than the U.S. [pp. 8-9].

. . . it is possible to imagine so large a *superiority in U.S. technical progress* over Europe as to turn the terms of trade sufficiently against the latter to cause an actual *fall* in the standard of life. In any case, most of Europe's efforts to raise herself might be perpetually stultified by this pressure on the terms of trade even if her standard of life did not actually fall [p. 138].[10]

It is not clear whether Balogh meant this variety of concepts to

___

[9] Thomas Balogh, *The Dollar Crisis: Causes and Cure,* pp. 230–231. This reply to Haberler is contained in an appendix, which reproduces Balogh's article "The Concept of a Dollar Shortage," *The Manchester School,* Vol. XVII (May 1949), pp. 186–201.
    [10] T. Balogh, *The Dollar Crisis.* Emphasis supplied.

constitute a series of variations of a single theme, each of them standing for one and the same causal element in a theory of the dollar shortage, or whether he meant to propose several theories, each linking a different cause with the same effect. I incline to the former interpretation of Balogh's intentions, though I do not see how they can be carried out. But I grant that there is no need to find a single cause, and I grant further that all of the different causes listed by Balogh could conceivably operate simultaneously to achieve the result—although we do not yet have the models to show how.

On the notion of the disparities in wealth, income, power, market position and continuing growth of productivity rests Balogh's conviction that the dollar shortage is chronic and should be countered by governmental planning to secure greater income equality, domestically through price and allocation controls, and internationally through discriminatory quantitative trade and exchange restrictions.

D

When Professor John H. Williams gave the Stamp Memorial Lecture in London in 1952 he gave his stamp of approval to Balogh's ideas on the causes of the persistent dollar shortage. He did not mention Balogh by name and he did not endorse his policy recommendations or warnings. For example, he declared himself "entirely on the side of a vigorous restrictive policy for countries in external deficit," with the "emphasis on general monetary and fiscal controls" rather than "direct internal controls." For, "with an intractable condition of deficient supply and excessive demand, there has been little danger of serious unemployment." [11]

But as "explanation" of the dollar shortage Williams presented Balogh's thesis with almost all its variations; thus he stated

> that there is a basic tendency toward world imbalance which, though hastened and intensified by the wars, has its roots in the *growing predominance* of the American economy; and that the succession of shorter-run disturbances is symptomatic of this deeper-seated and longer-run disequilibrating *process of change*. One important aspect of the American economy, aside from its *accelerating productivity,* is its *preponderant size* in economic terms [p. 15].

> The *great size* of the United States relative to most other Western countries, its *large home market,* its *diversified resources,* its *comparative self-sufficiency,* its *high productivity* and *rapid technological progress* have introduced a tendency away from, rather than toward, equilibrium in world trade [p. 12].

[11] Williams, *op. cit.,* p. 18.

What we need is some kind of fundamental reshaping of the world that will overcome the disequilibrating effects of American *predominance* [p. 21].

Only in two passages did Williams place the entire emphasis on productivity-growth disparities:

One of the most difficult aspects of the problem of change over time is that *progress in comparative productivities* must be regarded as a race [p. 13].

. . . over time, *if there are divergent rates of growth of productivity, the trade will be progressively less favorable to the countries less rapidly advancing in productivity*. Thus there develops a question as to how trade can be equilibrated at a tolerable level of real income [p. 14].[12]

Like Balogh, Williams apparently thought that this was self-evident. For he made no attempt to show why the divergence in productivity growth should cause trouble. He paid no attention to Haberler's suggestion that the development of substitutes for imports may be the crux of the matter, and he left the "theory" where Balogh had left it, as a contention without a reason.

E

The wanting analytical elaboration of the theory was eventually furnished by Professor Hicks in his "Inaugural Lecture" in 1953. Hicks took his text from Williams, not from Balogh. From the variety of disparities—income, wealth, power, etc.—he singled out one: the disparity in the rate of development. And, like Haberler, he recognised that the emphasis had to be placed on import-competing developments, not on development as such. But he showed in a closely reasoned argument why this had to be so.

In good classical style, Hicks distinguishes between barter effects and monetary effects. Barter effects are those which persist whatever the course of money incomes. Monetary effects are those which arise out of difficulties in the adjustment of money incomes. If a difficulty is purely monetary, people ought to find a means of doing something about it; but nothing can be done about a "real" difficulty, one inherent in a barter effect.[13]

Hicks considers two countries, A and B, which are trading together. To see what happens when productivity in A is increasing more rapidly than productivity in B, he makes the simplifying assumption that productivity is increasing only in A but remains constant in B. He analyses

[12] *Ibid.* Emphasis supplied.
[13] J. R. Hicks, *op. cit.*, p. 123.

three cases: *first,* where productivity in A is increasing uniformly, at the same rate in *all industries; second,* where productivity in A increases only in *export industries; third,* where productivity in A increases only in *industries making substitutes for imported goods.* (After Hicks is through with these three cases, including findings and applications, he adds, in a much less systematic and less analytic fashion, a fourth case, where productivity in A is increasing in industries producing export goods which compete in third markets with exports from B.)

The first case has pleasant barter effects but possibly unpleasant monetary effects for B. That the increased output of A will benefit B is almost certain because—save for very exceptional circumstances—A's demand for B's products will increase with A's income,[14] which will improve B's terms of trade. The monetary difficulties are most readily understood in terms of the classical specie-flow mechanism: with prices in A lowered—money incomes not having been raised—there will be a gold flow from B to A until prices and incomes are sufficiently raised in A and reduced in B. This good old model explains quite well how B gets some of A's supply of goods and how A gets some of B's supply of money. But nowadays all the stress is put on the deflation in B, which is feared like the devil. This purely monetary difficulty can be avoided if money income in A is sufficiently increased:

> There will . . . be some *appropriate* rate of rise in A-incomes (less, but perhaps not much less, than the rate of increase in productivity) which will keep trade between the two countries in balance, even though the level of B-incomes remains in money terms completely unchanged.[15]

While the first case holds, with the chance of monetary difficulties, a certainty of real benefits for the stagnant country, the second case is even better for that country. When the improvements are concentrated on A's export industries, and B can thus get more imports for the same money, no monetary troubles and only a real boon for B may result from this kind of development.

It is the third case which frightens Hicks, the case where the improvements are concentrated on the A-industries which compete most closely with imports from B. He calls it the case of "import-biased

---

[14] "Though it is possible to construct weird cases in which the conclusion would not follow, we can surely be confident that in practice a rise in A-incomes, with all prices constant, would cause A's demand for B-exports to *rise.*" Hicks, *op. cit.,* p. 124. The condition that all prices are constant is satisfied, in Hicks' argument, by raising money incomes in A "to the full extent of the rise in productivity." The "weird cases," in which demand for B-exports would fail to rise, presumably include the extreme assumption that many B-exports are inferior goods; they may also include the assumption that the income elasticity of demand is very low for B-exports and for import-competing A-products, but very high for goods which A had been exporting.

[15] Hicks, *op. cit.,* p. 126.

improvements," resulting, because of the reduced demand for B's exports, in both monetary difficulties and a real loss for B. The monetary difficulties can possibly be coped with, but the fall in real income in B is inevitable:

> Whatever are the monetary arrangements, whatever the course of money incomes, an improvement in A-productivity that is *import-biased* must make B worse off.[16]

F

What has been demonstrated with these three hypothetical cases? That the increase in productivity in A may be good, excellent, or bad for B, depending on whether the improvements in A are, by and large, "uniform," "export-biased," or "import-biased." But Hicks is now ready for his coup: he "assumes" that most of the progress of productivity in this century—in contrast to the nineteenth—has been of the import-biased variety; that this progress has been fastest in North America; and that this has caused a continuing dollar shortage in Britain.[17]

Hicks grants that the world picture has contained other things too: some troubles with war debts in the 1920's, with world depression and capital flight before Hitler in the 1930's, with war, war damage, and cold war in the 1940's. (The overvaluation of the pound sterling in the 1920's and the repressed and open inflations of the 1940's could also have been mentioned in this connection.) But Hicks looks for a single cause:

> A special explanation of the difficulties which were being experienced by European countries in settling their dollar debt could always be found. But the continuance of the same consequence, the same dollar shortage, as the result of these various 'causes,' has by now become very striking. That there is some general influence underlying these particular manifestations *can now no longer be doubted. It is hard to see that there is any other general force which would account for what has been happening than the disparity in growth in productivity which we have been discussing.*[18]

This complete acceptance of a general hypothesis as the explanation of concrete historical situations without presentation of evidence and without consideration of alternative hypotheses is surprising. It is even more surprising when we find that the general hypothesis does not really fit the situations in question, at least not the case of Britain during the last fifty years, to which it is supposed to apply:

[16] *Ibid.*, p. 128.

[17] There are difficulties in applying the findings of the analysis of the model countries A and B to countries of the real world. The real-world counterpart of B is sometimes the whole non-dollar world, sometimes Western Europe, sometimes Britain. This goes for Hicks' argument no less than for Williams' and Balogh's.

[18] Hicks, *op. cit.*, p. 131. Emphasis supplied.

1. The thesis of the barter effects of the import-competing improvements implies that *country B suffers a drastic deterioration of its terms of trade*. Indeed, this adverse movement in the barter terms is the quintessence of the hypothesis. Yet, the terms of trade, as Hicks fully realises, turned in Britain's favour during the 1920's and remained favourable for most of the 1930's. Hence, the theory cannot explain any "dollar shortage" in Britain in that period.[19]

2. The thesis of the monetary effects of the import-competing improvements implies that prices fall because *money incomes in country A do not rise sufficiently with the increase in productivity*. Yet, money incomes in the United States during the 1940's and the early 1950's increased faster than productivity. Hence, as Hicks would surely admit, the monetary effects of the U.S. increase in productivity during and after the war cannot have been responsible for any "dollar shortage" in Britain in that period.[20]

3. The thesis of the barter effects of the import-competing improvements implies that *per capita real income in country B suffers a net decrease*. Yet real income per capita in Britain, according to published statistics, increased during most of the time, including the period after the war in the late 1940's and the early 1950's. Hence the theory cannot explain Britain's "dollar shortage" during the period.

It is also quite likely that some other facts in the situation can be found to be inconsistent with the theory under examination. Perhaps there has not even been that disparity in the growth of productivity which is the very hub of the theory. Or, perhaps there has been no preponderance

[19] Hicks takes account of Britain's favourable terms of trade due to low prices of agricultural imports "throughout the twenties and thirties," but he holds that the advantage which "the British consumer derived" from them "masked the weakening of his own economic position." *Op. cit.*, p. 135. Perhaps so; it is quite possible that what happened to some of Britain's exports in the thirties was of lasting seriousness and its effects were only temporarily overcompensated by the cheap agricultural imports of the period. But the point is that Britain did not in fact suffer a deterioration of the terms of trade during the twenties and thirties and, therefore, that any "dollar shortage" in Britain during that time cannot be explained by the theory under examination. Hicks, however, had set out to look for a single cause of "the continuance of the same consequence, the same dollar shortage"—including the twenties and the thirties. (Incidentally, the difficulty of applying the two-country model should again be called to attention. If B is Britain, and A is America, the rest of the world is most conspicuous by its absence. As a way out, one might expand A to include the rest of the world, but then the hypothesis of a faster growth of productivity in A would surely be out of place.)

[20] This is brought out only to make sure that any *monetary* influences on the dollar situation in Britain cannot be traced to U.S. developments.

of improvements in the import-competing industries in the United States.[21] But instead of searching for evidence on these matters, I propose to elaborate now the third of the points mentioned, because the fact—that the real income of Britain has been increasing—is not contested and its inconsistency with the theory in question deserves emphasis and calls for further explanation.

G

Why should we place such heavy emphasis on a net decrease in per capita real income? Why should a theory of international equilibrium assume a crucial difference between a situation in which real income falls a little and a situation where it stays constant or increases?

Drastic reductions of real income have, at one time or other, happened to millions of families and thousands of occupations in many nations. Why should it be a calamity if the average real income of a nation decreases slightly, of a nation whose plane of living is safely above the minimum of physical subsistence? The answer which most of us, including Hicks, would give to this question is that our present institutions—collective bargaining between strong trade unions and large corporations, *plus* cost-of-living wage adjustments, *plus* full-employment policy, *plus* the elasticity of the credit supply that must go with it—are arranged not to permit reductions in real wages. If these institutions are effective, the chain of events following a downward pressure on the per capita real income of a nation may indeed be calamitous. No government will under these circumstances abstain from a policy of national overspending.[22]

Let us assume, then, that real wages are not allowed to fall; that trade unions will not accept reduced money wages and will insist on matching every increase in consumer prices with a like increase in money wage rates. Under such circumstances there will be serious trouble when the nation suffers a net loss in real income per capita. How should a nation cope with an "unavoidable" reduction in per capita real income if it is

[21] I have been assured by some who are more familiar than I am with the available data that the balance of evidence on these points is against the applicability of the theory in question.

[22] Hicks, discussing "why the devaluation of 1949 was a failure," states that "when the sterling prices of imported commodities began to rise in order to enforce a real sacrifice, wages chased after the rising prices, and the rise in wages made the devaluation largely ineffective. . . . Along that road there is no way out" (pp. 133–134). He adds in a footnote: "In a world of full employment and cost-of-living inflation, the above is the strongest objection to the devaluation 'remedy'. . . ." (Incidentally, I doubt that Hicks' dim view of the effects of the 1949 devaluation is justified. True, money wages increased in Britain by 24 per cent between 1950 and 1953. But in the same time they increased in the United States by 21 per cent. Hence, most of the devaluation effect on comparative wage levels has remained.)

"unalterably committed," by its institutions, to avoid a reduction in real wages? No such trouble arises when per capita real income is maintained or increasing. Hence, if the mentioned institutions are taken for granted, rather than as a "policy variable," [23] then the dichotomy in the theoretical model between a *net loss* in real income and merely a *retarded increase* in real income is justified.

If this assumption is accepted, the Hicks model, making the increase in productivity positive in country A and zero in B, is no longer applicable to situations in which productivity also increases in B, though at a slower rate. To be sure, import-competing improvements in A may still turn the terms of trade against B, but these barter effects need not nullify the effects of increased productivity in B. The net result may be an unchanged or increased real income in B, compatible with a system in which money wage rates must always be increased to compensate workers in full for any increases in consumer prices. Indeed, if productivity in B progresses sufficiently to leave the nation with an increased real income despite less favourable terms of trade, money wages in B may rise relative to prices without causing trade or payments difficulties, provided money incomes in A have moved up sufficiently to prevent a deflationary pressure on B.

While Hicks was quite correct in stating that his simplifying assumption facilitated the exposition, he was wrong in thinking that "it will . . . make little difference to the essence of the argument . . . if we neglect the expansion of productivity in B, and simply assume that productivity in A is increasing while that in B remains constant." [24]

Of course, the damper which the barter effects of the import-substitutions in A put on the increase in real income in B must also be a damper on trade-union ambitions in B. If money wage rates in B are pushed up to the full extent of the productivity increase in B, payments difficulties may ensue. This follows from the fact that real incomes in B cannot increase to the full extent of the increase in productivity, because some part of it will be offset by less favourable terms of trade. But payments difficulties which arise when money wages are raised faster than real income increases are fully explained by the old-fashioned "inflation theory"; it is highly confusing to attribute the difficulties to "structural developments" or "structural conditions" and, in particular, to the faster rate or special type of technological advance in the dollar area.

If, in the absence of *any* increase in productivity *anywhere*, money incomes per capita were increased in B, but increased less or not at all in

[23] That the "impossibility" of real wage reductions need not in fact be taken for granted is demonstrated by the actual reductions that have occurred in several countries. A recent example is the Netherlands, where the trade unions a few years ago agreed to accept a 5 per cent reduction in real wage rates. But perhaps these are the exceptions which confirm the rule.

[24] Hicks, *op. cit.*, pp. 123–124.

the dollar country A, every economist would expect a dollar shortage to arise in B, and he would blame it on the increase in money incomes—on "inflation." If, with increases in productivity here and there, money incomes per capita were increased in B beyond the increase in real income per capita, while the ratio of money income to real income in A increased less or not at all, the same dollar shortage would arise in B. Why in this case an economist should wish to blame some differential rates of increase in productivity for causing the dollar shortage is difficult to understand. These differential growth rates would be *neither necessary nor sufficient conditions* of the dollar shortage under the circumstances; to attribute causal significance to them is contrary to the rules of reasoning.

H

I have attempted to show (and I hope I have succeeded) that the theory of dollar shortage due to disparities in the growth of productivity does not apply to Britain "in the age in which we live." [25] In this section I shall attempt to show that—apart from the question of application—the theory is badly formulated in that it singles out an irrelevant factor and plays down the essential one.

Hicks correctly states that it is the import-biased increase in productivity, and not just any increase in productivity, that has unfavourable barter effects on the country whose exports are adversely affected. Nevertheless, he goes on talking about differential *rates* of economic progress. Yet, the *rates* of progress have little to do with his theory.

If, for example, A and B have the same rate of increase in productivity, but the increase is concentrated on A's import-competing industries and on B's export industries, B will probably suffer from both the monetary and barter effects. The terms of trade will move against B (because the elasticity of A's demand for B's exports is likely to be less than unity) even if B could continue to compete with the substitutes produced in A; but, more likely, unless the cost of transporting B-products to A, and of selling, handling, and distributing them in A, is reduced along with their production cost in B, B will lose the competitive advantage in some of its exports.

On the other hand, if the rate of improvement is twice as large in A as in B, but concentrated on A's export industries, while it is fairly uniformly distributed among all of B's industries, we should expect that B, despite the slower rate of advance, will benefit from the changes in productivity. Likewise, the rate of advance may be faster in B than in A, and the effects unfavourable to B. This would be so if the improvements in B were all in export products with very inelastic foreign demand, while A's improve-

[25] *Ibid.*, p. 130.

ments were partly in substitutes for imports and partly in new products for which an eager demand develops in B.

All this, surely, is clearly seen by Hicks. Indeed, if *we* can see it so readily, it is thanks to his useful models and the lucidity with which he has demonstrated them. Yet, we must conclude that it was an error to emphasise the rates of increase in productivity in formulating the hypothesis. What matters in this connection is not a disparity between *rates* of growth, but the *bias* or *incidence* of particular developments.

I

As productivity increases at different rates in different industries and as new products and industries emerge, the comparative advantages which countries have in the production of various goods are being altered and reshuffled all the time. In the course of this process the scope of international division of labour sometimes widens and sometimes narrows. If a country improves its capacity to make products in which it previously has had a comparative disadvantage, the composition of international trade may change, the total gains from trade may become smaller, and the volume of trade may shrink. The adjustments to the new productive opportunities may also imply a redistribution of the gains from trade—to the serious disadvantage of some countries—and may force countries to incur considerable costs of adaptation.[26]

If such changes in the array of comparative advantages should come in quick succession, one country always initiating the change, starting or increasing a production which previously had been too costly, and the other country always adjusting itself to the change, closing down or reducing a production in which it previously has had comparative advantage, the chain of losses may be exceedingly tough on the second country. And there is, of course, a good chance that a rich and strong country, with plenty of capital to invest in research and development and innovation, may come up with a string of new ventures in products that compete with the export industries of a less well-heeled and less dynamic country. It is in this sense that the faster rate of increase in productivity in the richer and more enterprising country may, if the improvements

---

[26] While the disappearance of a comparative disadvantage must needs imply that this (lucky) country loses a comparative advantage at the same time, and while the corresponding loss of a comparative advantage in the other country must needs imply that this (unfortunate) country is getting rid of a comparative disadvantage—this being a matter of sheer logic—the "lucky" country will as a rule benefit from the change, and the other country will suffer an injury. The reallocation of resources, which in the one country will be "promising investments" under the lure of profits, will in the other country be "costly reconversions" under the pressure of losses and adverse terms of trade.

happen to be competing with the exports of a weaker country, impose on the latter a heavy burden of costly and painful adjustments.

This was recognised and correctly formulated by Sir Dennis Robertson:

> What is to happen if country A is not only better endowed than country B, but if the disparity of endowment between them is continually *increasing* through the cumulative mutual interaction of capital accumulation and technological progress? It is true that at any given moment there will still be *some* distribution of function between the two countries which, if it could be instantaneously obtained, would be in the best interests of both. But the task of attaining it, and then of abandoning it almost immediately for a new one, may surpass the human capacity for adjustment in what is, *ex hypothesi*, the weaker country. Better for it, so the argument runs, to be less tightly tied in the bonds of international trade, and to make what progress it can at its own pace.[27]

The argument of the trade restrictionists is, among other things, that it is better to hold down the volume of trade because to keep it up would be too costly in terms of continuous readjustments; the argument of the trade liberalizers is that it is better to let the volume of trade be as high as the current state of comparative advantage will permit. Which of these arguments is sound cannot be decided with assurance without more knowledge about the type of technological improvements forthcoming in the countries in question. But I see no evidence supporting the notion that the improvements in the United States have been and will be breath-takingly fast compared with those in Britain and consistently of the kind damaging to Britain's exports.

But the judgment about the greater wisdom of freer or more restricted trade is one thing. It is another thing to evaluate implications for the problem of the dollar shortage. For, surely, the recognition of the costs and pains suffered by a people repeatedly forced to adjust itself to changes in production and trade initiated by its richer and fast-moving trading partner is not yet an explanation of dollar shortage. These costs and pains suffered by the people in the "slower" country do not *per se* explain why they have to spend more than they can earn or raise in the ordinary course of their business.

J

This brings us back to the theme on which we started: whether dollar shortage should be regarded as a result of economic policy or as a result of structural conditions.

[27] Sir Dennis H. Robertson, *Britain in the World Economy*, p. 58.

In a way, this question is not much different from the trivial quarrel whether a person who continually gets into financial jams does so because he is inclined to spend too much or because he earns too little. If a man has had bad luck—say, he had an accident and spent much time and money in the hospital—it would be rather cruel to explain his financial difficulties by the fact, however incontrovertible, that he was spending too much and was living beyond his means. If a man loses his job and has to change his occupation several times with substantial reductions in income, one may for a while explain his financial difficulties by his sad circumstances, but eventually one will frankly mention his failure to adjust his budget to his earnings. But if a man earns more every year and yet cannot extricate himself from his financial difficulties, one may without impropriety refuse to accept his hard-luck stories, no matter how true it is that his income is always less than it might be if it were not for this or that adverse circumstance. If his income increases slowly but surely, the obstacles which prevent him from earning much more than he does should not be presented as explanation of his being continually "broke." These obstacles are surely regrettable; they may be removable or unavoidable; they may compel him to adopt this policy or that; but they should not be given as the "cause" of his being short of funds.

I hope I will not be accused of the fallacy of thoughtlessly applying to societies what is true of individuals. I believe that in this instance the analogy of the individual short of dollars does apply to entire nations short of dollars. If a nation has a dollar shortage while its plane of living is rising, the shortage should not be explained as the consequence of structural obstacles to a faster increase in national income; it is satisfactorily explained by the economic policies adopted.

V

Equilibrium and Disequilibrium: Misplaced Concreteness and Disguised Politics

A. A Brief Review of the Uses of Equilibrium Concepts in Economics: *The major uses of equilibrium concepts in economics; The basic idea: disturbance and adjustment* ■ B. The Role of Equilibrium in Economic Analysis: *The contents and the working of a model; The four steps; Wide choice for the set of variables in equilibrium; Time and equilibrium; Definition of equilibrium* ■ C. Misplaced Concreteness and Disguised Politics: *Not an operational concept; Not the same as stability; Not a value judgment* ■ D. Equilibrium in International Trade Theory: *Consistent awareness of relativity: Joan Robinson; Built-in politics and simulated stability: Nurkse; Political criteria supported: Ellsworth and Kindleberger; Relativity and value-neutrality: Meade I; Alliance with political value judgments: Meade II; Return to value-neutrality: Meade III; Attack on persuasive definitions: Streeten; The trouble with built-in politics*

A term which has so many meanings that we never know what its users are talking about should be either dropped from the vocabulary of the scholar or "purified" of confusing connotations. Since I believe it is impossible to exclude the terms "equilibrium" and "disequilibrium" from the economist's discourse, I propose that they be subjected to a thorough cleaning job.[1] In attempting this task I shall not be concerned with the meanings of these terms in other disciplines.

[1] The ruthless criticism to which my colleague Dr. Edith Penrose subjected an earlier version of this essay is gratefully acknowledged. Thanks to her warnings, I was able to eliminate several flaws of exposition and several offences of overaggressiveness.

A. A BRIEF REVIEW OF THE USES OF EQUILIBRIUM CONCEPTS IN ECONOMICS

Economists have used the notion of equilibrium in a variety of contexts and for a variety of purposes; in proceeding from one topic to another some have failed to note transformations in the use made of it and in the meanings read into the term. Not a few who have sensed incongruities, fallacies or outright misuse turned against all "equilibrium economics," heaping abuse on any type of analysis that employed the notion.

The major uses of equilibrium concepts in economics

The most literal use of equilibrium or disequilibrium in the sense of equal or unequal weights on the two arms of a scale, without any analytical, explicatory, predictive or evaluative connotation, occurs only in connection with practically measurable quantities, such as income and expenditure in a budget, exports and imports in a trade balance, trade items and long-term capital transfers in a balance of payments. Yet even in these contexts economists have rarely been content with merely weighing the items on the two sides; they have usually wanted to connect them with other economic variables which they considered relevant for a more "inclusive" equilibrium or disequilibrium of the balance in question.

The most prevalent use of the equilibrium concept in economics is probably as a methodological device in abstract theory. Here "equilibrium" is employed in connection with "models" containing several interrelated variables; as a "useful fiction," it serves as a part of a mental experiment designed to analyse causal connections between "events" or "changes of variables."

It is a different use of the equilibrium idea when it is employed to refer to concrete economic situations: here it is supposed to characterise a historical situation as one that has lasted or will last for a relatively long time without significant change. The direct application of the concept to observed situations makes it "operational," as it were. The jump from equilibrium as a methodological device (useful fiction, purely mental construct) to equilibrium as a characterisation of a concrete historical situation (operational concept) is a big one; that many take it without noticing any strain and without noting the difference, is attributable, I shall argue, to their failure to recognise the function of the analytical concept, and is conducive to considerable confusion.

A jump in a different direction has been taken from an analytical equilibrium concept to an evaluative one. It is easy to see how it happens: the notion of equilibrium as a balance of forces acquires a connotation of "appropriateness" when the balance is thought of as one of "natural forces"; or even a connotation of "goodness" when that balance is thought of as "harmony." Once the use of equilibrium as a value judgment is condoned, the replacement of the mystical "natural" forces by "progressive" political forces appears indicated, and a variety of social goals are incorporated into the concept of equilibrium. Eventually, equilibrium comes to mean conformance with certain objectives which organised society is asked to pursue. I shall argue that such equilibrium with built-in politics often impairs the usefulness of equilibrium as a value-free analytical device.

Another evaluative equilibrium concept is used in welfare economics. In the theoretical models of the household and the firm, "equilibrium" is assumed to be sought between the various items of the plans and dispositions of the individual decision-maker so that he would find no reason to make further changes. The older welfare economists promoted this equilibrium from a methodological device (for the explanation of change) to a standard of evaluation (marking the best positions attainable); and all these equilibria became "optima" and integral parts of the maximum welfare position for the whole community. Modern welfare economists deal with the value judgments that were implicit in such a procedure, and try to bring them out into the open. Propositions about conditions under which certain "allocative and distributive equilibria" in the economy as a whole would coincide with whatever is regarded as the "highest social welfare function" are then formulated and qualified with care.

The present essay will not be concerned with welfare economics. But it will be concerned, to some extent, with the use of a value-laden equilibrium concept in positive (explicatory) economics. The chief purpose of the essay is to show the dangers to clear analysis that may arise from the failure to notice the differences between analytical, descriptive, and evaluative equilibrium concepts. As a prerequisite, we shall have to pay closer attention than has usually been given to the function of the purely analytical equilibrium concept in economic theorising.

The basic idea: disturbance and adjustment

In economic analysis some events (or changes of economic variables) are interpreted as the "adjustment" of the system to a "disturbance" consisting in some antecedent events (or changes of economic variables). Several alternative formulations are used to express this idea of adjustment to disturbance: for example, responses to an impulse, reactions or repercussions to a substantive change, effects or consequences of a cause, induced changes following an autonomous or spontaneous change, equilibration following a disequilibrating event. A conceptual scheme is constructed to establish a causal connection between two changes, or two sets of changes; this cause-and-effect relationship is understood, for purposes to be shown presently, as disequilibration-plus-equilibration, or a departure from one position of equilibrium followed by a movement toward another position of equilibrium.

The idea of equilibrium is employed in this scheme as a mental tool, a methodological device; it aids in establishing to our satisfaction a causal nexus between different events or changes. Events or changes can be imagined as well as observed; a causal connection between them can only be imagined, and the idea of equilibrium has the function, as we shall presently see, of making this connection plausible.

B. The role of equilibrium in economic analysis

After a brief discussion of the contents and working of "models" in economic analysis we shall present a four-step scheme of causal reasoning, exhibiting the strategic use of equilibria. We shall then proceed to a discussion of the relativity of equilibrium with respect to the variables selected, to the interrelations assumed, and to the adjustment time allowed. And we shall attempt a definition of equilibrium.

The contents and the working of a model

An analytic model in economics need not be "made out of algebraic functions or geometric curves or some other fancy building material."[2] It can be described entirely in plain words, unless this gets too clumsy. But no matter how it is done, the model inspector should be provided with a full specification of its contents.

The model usually contains a number of variables (e.g., prices, outputs, incomes, exports, etc.) and a number of stipulated relations between variables (e.g., quantity demanded will vary in a certain way with the price charged; aggregate imports will be some function of disposable income, etc.). Besides the relationship of identity (e.g., income is the sum of consumption and investment), there may be technological relationships (e.g., between input and output), institutional relationships (e.g., between tax payments and income), and economic behaviour relationships (e.g., between cash balances and expenditures). The model is put to work when the mental experimenter manipulates a change of an "independent" variable and "watches" how this will affect the dependent variables acting upon one another according to the assumed relationships.

[2] Fritz Machlup, *The Economics of Sellers' Competition* (Baltimore: Johns Hopkins Press, 1952), p. 5. Some of the ideas presented in the present paper were alluded to in the book.

The four steps

The following scheme illustrates the step-by-step working of a model; each step is described both in customary technical terms and in terms of catch-phrases in everyday language:

Step 1. *Initial Position:* "equilibrium," i.e., "Everything could go on as it is."

Step 2. *Disequilibrating Change:* "new datum," i.e., "Something happens."

Step 3. *Adjusting Changes:* "reactions," i.e., "Things must adjust themselves."

Step 4. *Final Position:* "new equilibrium," i.e., "The situation calls for no further adjustments."

Steps 2 and 3 may correspond to observable changes; sometimes only one of these is actually "observed" and the other merely expected to occur as consequent or to have occurred as antecedent, respectively. If both are observed in conjunction or succession the theorist will take this as a "verification" of the theory which links them in the described fashion, and he will have increased confidence in it.[3] But when the change which corresponds to Step 2 is called "disequilibrating" and a "new datum," and the changes corresponding to Step 3 are called "adjusting" and "reactions" (to the change considered "disequilibrating"), this is not based on observation; it is only an interpretation. To be plausible this interpretation requires two other steps.

In order to ascertain that the changes under Step 3 are the effects of those under Step 2 and of *nothing else,* we must make sure that there is nothing else in the picture that might be responsible for bringing about the changes under Step 3. There is only one way of doing this: we must isolate Step 2 as a possible cause of the changes under Step 3 by excluding from the model any other possible causes. This exclusion of alternative causes is accomplished by Step 1, the initial position of equilibrium, the position in which "Everything could go on as it is," without any inherent tendency to change. If we were not sure of initial "equilibrium" we could not be sure that Step 3 could not occur without Step 2, simply as the result of something already present in the initial situation. The assumption of an initial equilibrium serves to guarantee the "new datum" of Step 2 the status of being the *sole* disturbing change, the *sole* cause of anything that follows in the model (that is, of the changes interpreted as "adjustment" to, or effect of, the "disequilibrating change").

[3] Fritz Machlup, "The Problem of Verification in Economics," *Southern Economic Journal,* Vol. XXII (July 1955), pp. 1–21.

In order to ascertain that the changes under Step 3 are *all* the effects which the change under Step 2 can have in the model and that we therefore have as complete a list of adjusting changes as we care to have, we must make sure that "no further adjustments" are required by the situation. There is only one way of doing this: we must proceed with the sequence of adjusting changes until we reach a situation in which, barring another disturbance from the outside, everything could go on as it is. In other words we must proceed until we reach a "new equilibrium," a position regarded as final because no further changes appear to be required under the circumstances. The postulate of the final equilibrium serves to guarantee that the list of "adjusting changes" under Step 3 is *complete.*

In a nutshell, we have here a mental experiment in which the first and last steps, the assumption of initial and final equilibria, are methodological devices to secure that Step 2 is the sole cause and Step 3 contains the complete sequence of effects. The function of the initial equilibrium is to assure us that "nothing but 2" causes the changes under Step 3; the function of the final equilibrium is to assure us that "nothing but 3" is to be expected as an effect of the change under Step 2 (although the "completeness" of the list of effects will always be merely relative to the set of variables included in the equilibrium).

Some simple analogies exist between the pattern of mental experiments and that of laboratory experiments. Step 1, the assumption of an initial equilibrium, corresponds to the requirement of a *controlled* experiment that conditions be kept constant and the manipulated change of the selected variable thus be isolated from changes of other independent variables. Step 4, the assumption of a final equilibrium, corresponds to the requirement of the *complete* experiment that all changes be observed and noted until no further changes in dependent variables occur.

Wide choice for the set of variables in equilibrium

The economic theorist enjoys great freedom of choice in the construction of his models and in the selection of the variables included. The restraints are few and not very confining: logical consistency of the entire model, relevance of the chosen variables to the problem analysed, "understanding" of the assumed relationships among them as plausible, and applicability of the model in the sense that the events or changes assumed and deduced (as Steps 2 and 3, respectively) more or less "fit" events or changes observed or known to occur in reality. This leaves the choice of what to put into the "equilibrium" wide open. The system may contain few variables or many; it may postulate interrelationships of many different kinds; it may deliberately exclude interactions of variables which take a long time to work themselves out or, on the other hand, it may disregard regular oscillations of some variables within short intervals of time. (It is chiefly this freedom of choice which makes it often almost meaningless to declare a concrete economic situation in the real world, identified by historical time and geographic space but not specified with regard to the variables selected, as a position of equilibrium or disequilibrium.)

To realise the extent of freedom in the selection of variables that are supposed to be in equilibrium one has only to think of the simple models of "aggregative equilibrium" and of their successive extension through the inclusion of additional variables or relations. One may first recall the standard equilibrium between the three strategic aggregates, national income, consumption, and investment, linked by a simple consumption function, with investment assumed to be given. One may then recall the more complicated aggregative equilibria comprising one or more of the following relations or variables: an investment function making investment depend on income or consumption, or on absolute or relative changes in income or consumption; varying proceeds from exports and payments for imports, with the former affecting income, and with the latter dependent on income; varying government expenditures and tax revenues, dependent on income and affecting consumption (and possibly also investment); a consumption function linking consumption to various past values of income, to values of real assets, to values of cash assets; and so forth. The possible combinations of even this small number of aggregate variables and relations permit an enormous variety of equilibrium positions. Yet, all these equilibria still disregard such variables as prices, wage rates, interest rates, foreign-exchange rates, all of which are possible candidates for inclusion in the system.

The "relativity" of an "equilibrium in international trade" with regard to the relations and variables included or disregarded merits separate comment. For some problems one will choose to start from a position of balanced trade; for other problems one will choose to start from a position of a given volume of foreign investment, and hence from an "equilibrium export surplus," a surplus consistent with an equilibrium in the foreign-exchange market; and again for other problems one will choose to start from an equilibrium of income, consumption, saving and investment, with a surplus or deficit in the foreign-exchange market as part of the volume of investment consistent with the magnitudes of the other aggregates. If the system includes only these aggregates, but disregards the foreign-reserve position and bank liquidity, final equilibrium may be said to be reached with a trade deficit, the latter being equal to the excess of home investment over total saving. This final equilibrium—where no further adjustment is required of the selected variables—may involve continuing changes of neglected variables: for example, the foreign reserves may continue to dwindle towards zero and the loan portfolios of banks may go on expanding without limit.[4]

Frequently equilibrium will refer to a set of variables that fails to include some which are both relevant and significant for practical problems; such an equilibrium is sometimes denounced as a worthless or dangerous tool of analysis. To be sure, if an economist were to base policy recommendations on an analysis confined to such oversimplified equilibrium models he would be guilty of a gross lack of judgment. Yet such models may have considerable heuristic value. This value is not impaired if an important factor is left out, provided the omission is not inadvertent. Indeed, the importance of any factor can be demonstrated only by leaving it out of account and then showing the difference it makes when it is reinstated as one of the variables in the equilibrium system.

Time and equilibrium

More often than not, time is left out in the construction and operation of equilibrium models. If time is taken into account this is done in various ways, implicitly or explicitly.

In so-called period analysis, time is given two roles: it appears as an independent variable and as a subscript to other variables. In the latter role it "dates" the quantities which are linked by the lagged interrelations stipulated—where the value of a variable at one period is related to the values of the same and/or other variables at other periods. And as a separate independent variable, time (t) will determine the magnitudes which the other variables will have reached at certain points on their way to their equilibrium values and, moreover, will serve to identify final equilibrium as the position where a further increase of t will leave all other magnitudes unchanged.

In period analysis as well as in some other kinds of sequence analysis, successive positions are sometimes "temporary equilibria," regardless of whether or not the model can ever reach a final equilibrium; in other instances, however, the successive positions, although determinate, are not accurately characterised as temporary equilibria. As an example of the former type we may think of the sequence of prices and quantities sold in a model depicting the cobweb theorem. If the (timeless) demand curve is steeper than the (time-lagged) supply curve the model will not yield a final equilibrium, while the intersections of the "instantaneous supply curves" with the demand curve will each mark a point of temporary equilibrium. Every one of these equilibria is stable (in the sense that random deviations are self-correcting); it is also "final" with respect to the particular instantaneous supply curve—although it is "temporary" if the time-lagged

[4] Fritz Machlup, *International Trade and the National Income Multiplier* (Philadelphia: Blakiston, 1943; New York: Kelley, 1961), pp. 85–87, 172–173, 208.

supply curve is taken into account. Thus, one and the same position, defined by a definite set of variables of given magnitudes, will be both an equilibrium or a disequilibrium, depending on the length of time that is taken into account.[5]

In dealing with this question, the theorist has a choice between two equivalent procedures: he may either vary the maximum time interval allowed for the process of adjustment (with given time coefficients of the relations involved) or change the combination of variables making up the model. The latter is Alfred Marshall's procedure for showing the adjustments in the supply of a particular product. He distinguishes between an instantaneous market equilibrium, a short-run market equilibrium, and a long-run market equilibrium, not in terms of the time needed for the adjustments to take place, but by extending the list of dependent variables: for the first equilibrium, production is fixed; for the second, production is variable, but productive capacity is fixed; for the third, productive capacity is variable, and only the productive resources potentially available to the industry are fixed. Time itself is not a variable in the model; instead, there are three models (or sub-models) with separate equilibria; each equilibrium is "final" on its own terms, though "temporary" in terms of a model with more variables.[6]

It would be mistaken to think that an extension of the list of variables is always equivalent to a "longer-run" adjustment. The opposite may be true: the addition of variables to the set may shorten the adjustment period. Take, for example, the simple saving–investment equilibrium in a period model demonstrating the multiplier principle. If consumption is

[5] Certain equilibria in physics and chemistry are of the same type. Take the example of a simple scale (*libra*, in Latin) with two pans of different shapes but equal weight and volume, containing equal quantities of water. The equilibrium will be only temporary, since evaporation of the water will be faster from the pan with the larger open surface; there will be instantaneous equilibrium (before any water has evaporated), short-run disequilibrium (after some unequal quantities of water have evaporated), and long-run equilibrium (after all the water has evaporated from both pans). Similarly, there may be chemical equilibrium after a very small time interval but not for longer periods, depending on whether only the fast reactions or also the slow reactions are taken into account.

[6] Incidentally, no student who understands these conceptions will fall into the error of identifying a concrete situation, involving the prices paid and quantities produced in a certain country at a certain time, as a position of long-run equilibrium. All these equilibria are purely hypothetical. Never could anybody "know" that all adjustments to past events have been completed—or will ever be completed. If calendar time were substituted for the Marshallian "long run," the long-run adjustment to a decline in the demand for a product might take some thirty years or more, involving the gradual wear and tear and successive scrapping of productive capacity. Could anybody assume for the real world—what *has* to be assumed for the purpose of thinking things through—that demand and technology and all other things will remain unchanged over a period of such length? Surely, the conceptual apparatus with its final equilibrium was not intended to yield a description of an actual *situation,* but rather to ensure that full attention is given to *all the processes of change* which could be interpreted as the effects of the event or change regarded as the disequilibrating datum.

related to income received in the preceding period, and the marginal propensity to consume is high, the number of periods required to bring income close to its final equilibrium value would be enormous. This model implicitly assumes unlimited supplies of unemployed resources and of idle or newly created cash. If the model is expanded to include such variables as (limited) unemployment, wage rates, (limited) money supply, and interest rates, the equilibration of this larger set of variables will take place in a much smaller number of time periods (and, of course, the equilibrium value of income will be smaller).[7]

Just as equilibrium may by design take no account of adjustments that go beyond a certain set of variables or beyond a certain time, equilibrium may also by design overlook certain short-term oscillations or fluctuations. For example, changes in demand or production that can be interpreted as regular fluctuations—relating to different hours of the day, days of the week, seasons of the year—may be accepted as part of a stationary equilibrium (or simply disregarded if the fluctuations are irrelevant to the problem at hand), provided the "underlying conditions" remain unchanged throughout the process.[8] But oscillations and fluctuations must not be admitted as part of an "equilibrium position" unless one may assume that they can, under the rules of the model, continue in perfect periodicity, without any change in amplitude or rhythm.

Definition of equilibrium

We have not thus far attempted to formulate a definition of equilibrium, though the meaning of the term has probably become quite clear. In the light of the preceding discussion we may define *equilibrium,* in economic analysis, as *a constellation of selected interrelated variables so adjusted to one another that no inherent tendency to change prevails in the model which they constitute.* The model as well as its equilibria are, of course, mental constructions (based on abstraction and invention).

It has been suggested to me that the phrase "balance of forces" should be a part of any definition of equilibrium. I cannot accept this suggestion; "balance of forces" is simply another metaphor, perhaps a synonym but not an explanation of "equilibrium," and sadly encumbered by the reference to "forces," which is a rather mystical concept in need of a separate time-consuming cleaning job. But if it is believed that addi-

[7] There have been economists grumbling about "how anybody can speak of an *equilibrium* leaving out so many crucial variables." Such grumbles would be justified if they were directed against the choice of variables and relations, against the usefulness of the model and, especially, against policy recommendations that are based on them. But if the grumbles are about "speaking of an equilibrium" in such a case, they are methodologically unsound. Equilibrium and disequilibrium refer to whatever model you may have in mind.

[8] The technique of "disregarding" oscillations of quantities (demanded, supplied, produced) is either to reduce them to an average or to express them as rates per unit of time where the time unit embraces the whole "cycle."

tional metaphors can be helpful in defining or explaining equilibrium, then I should propose the phrase "peaceful coexistence" between selected variables of given magnitudes. Where such "peaceful coexistence" is not possible, where the selected variables are *not compatible* with one another in their given magnitudes, one or more of them will have to change, and will continue to change until they reach magnitudes that make it possible for them to live with each other as they are.

Thus, as an alternative definition of equilibrium we may propose *mutual compatibility of a selected set of interrelated variables of particular magnitudes.* Assume the set consists of variables A, B, C, and D, and that certain interrelationships among them are assumed (in the form of behaviour equations, technological, psychological or institutional relations, as well as mere definitions). If these variables are compatible in their "present" magnitudes "everything could go on as it is." Then "something happens" which increases variable C. In its new magnitude C is no longer compatible with A, B, and D, and "things must adjust themselves." Which of the variables will "give" and by how much will depend on the rules of the game, expressed in the relationships assumed among the variables. At last, the new values of the four variables may be such that they are again compatible with one another, and "the situation calls for no further adjustments."

The crux of the matter is that the addition of another variable, somehow related to one or more of the others, would change the picture. The magnitudes in which A, B, C, and D are mutually compatible when they are the only players in the game may constitute serious incompatibility when they are joined by another player, say E, of a certain size. But another addition, say F, may neutralise the "disturbing" effect of E, and A, B, C, D in their "present" magnitudes may again be compatible and "everything could go on as it is." One cannot overemphasise this *relativity* of compatibility and incompatibility regarding extra variables included in, or excluded from, the selected set. Only a complete enumeration of the variables selected and interrelations assumed makes it meaningful to assert their mutual compatibility or incompatibility, that is, the equilibrium or disequilibrium of the chosen set. And, while a *specification* of the selected variables and assumed interrelations is required for every model and every problem, the *definition* of equilibrium and disequilibrium must not narrow the freedom of choice.

C. Misplaced Concreteness and Disguised Politics

Although I recognised the existence of other equilibrium concepts in economics, I have discussed only the one designed for theoretical analysis. I strongly suspect that those who use equilibrium concepts for other purposes, such as the description of historical situations or their evaluation, believe that one and the same concept can do double or triple duty. This I challenge. My task in this section will be to show that the concept described in the previous section cannot be used for other purposes without losing much of its usefulness in analysis.

Not an operational concept

Equilibrium as a tool for theoretical analysis is not an operational concept; and attempts to develop operational counterparts to the construct have not been successful.[9] Some of the variables in a model usually have statistically operational counterparts; in rare instances all have. But even in this event the *compatibility* among the variables is always a question of the assumed interrelations and of the limitation of the model to the variables selected. The "real world" surely has infinitely more variables than any abstract economic model, and their "actual" interrelations are neither known nor, I fear, knowable (partly because they probably change unpredictably over time). It follows that the equilibrium among selected variables could not be observed even if each of the variables had an observable counterpart in the real world.

Some of the variables in a model which have observable and measurable counterparts can sometimes be arranged in sub-sets in the form of balance sheets, T-accounts or financial statements, permitting us to strike a balance between the two sides and to speak (confusingly) of an "equilibrium" or "disequilibrium" in that sub-set. For example, exports and imports can be arranged as a trade balance, or foreign-trade items and certain capital and other transfers can be arranged as an accounting balance of payments.[10] A so-called equilibrium for these items means merely equality of the sums on each side of the account, and a so-called disequilibrium means inequality of the sums. But only when this sub-set is linked with other variables—income, consumption, investment, prices, employment, wage rates, exchange rates, interest rates, foreign reserves, bank reserves, bank loans, etc.—does it become a factor in economic analysis. And only after the variables are selected and their interrelations assumed can we speak of equilibrium and disequilibrium in the sense in which these terms are used in economic analysis. Despite the operational

[9] Schumpeter once proposed a statistically discernible "neighborhood of equilibrium," with reference to cyclical fluctuations of business activity. But he always insisted on the purely fictitious and instrumental character of the equilibrium concept itself. Joseph A. Schumpeter, *Business Cycles* (New York: McGraw-Hill, 1939), pp. 68–71.

[10] For an exposition of the differences between the "accounting balance," the "market balance," and the "programme balance" of payments see Fritz Machlup, "Three Concepts of the Balance of Payments and the So-called Dollar Shortage," *Economic Journal*, Vol. LX (1950), pp. 46–68; reprinted in this volume as Chapter III.

sub-set, the model as a whole and its equilibrium are not observable, not operational; they remain mental constructions.

Perhaps similar, perhaps very different, considerations once led Per Jacobsson to make this observation on the subject: "You can no more define equilibrium in international trade than you can define a pretty girl, but you can recognise one if you meet one." [11] I like this remark for its charm and wit, but I wonder whether it hits the mark. I think I am quite competent to recognise a pretty girl, though my taste may not be the same as that of other expert observers. But I cannot recognise an equilibrium in international trade no matter how hard I look. I can define it, at least to my own satisfaction; but I cannot recognise anything in reality—in the statistical figures representing the "facts" of a "real situation"—as an equilibrium in international trade in the sense discussed, that is, as a position where "everything could go on as it is" and "the situation calls for no further adjustments" to anything that has happened.

To characterise a concrete situation "observed" in reality as one of "equilibrium" is to commit the fallacy of misplaced concreteness. At best, the observer may mean to assert that in his opinion the observed and duly identified situation corresponds to a model in his mind in which a set of selected variables determine a certain outcome, and that he finds no inherent cause of change—that is, that he believes only an outside disturbance, not in evidence at the moment, would produce a change in these variables. This, of course, is a personal judgment, meaningful only if the variables are fully enumerated and the assumptions about their interrelations are clearly stated. As matters stand, any concrete economic situation may correspond at the same time to an equilibrium of one model and a disequilibrium of another.

The use of the analytical equilibrium concept as a designation of a concrete historical situation is regarded as "misplaced concreteness," first, because of the general fallacy involved in jumping the distance between a useful fiction and particular data of observation and, second, because of the fallacy involved in forgetting the relativity of equilibrium with respect to variables and relations selected. An indefinite number of models may be found to "fit" a concrete situation in one way or another, and the choice is not dictated either by any so-called realities of life or by any conventions of the analysts.[12]

[11] Per Jacobsson, in a speech in 1949.
[12] To be sure, there are "observed" situations which invite characterisation as "disequilibria" without serious danger of confusion. For example, there will be little doubt about just what model and what variables are referred to when some gross instances of price fixing, either with unsold supplies not disposable at the official minimum price or with queues of would-be buyers lined up to get some of their demand satisfied at the ceiling price, are characterised as "market disequilibria." The implication, apparently, is that the situation could not endure were it not for the "interference." On the

The phrase "relativity of equilibrium" gives expression to the facts that any number and combination of variables may be chosen for a model, depending on the analytical or didactic habits, skills, and purposes of the economist; that the same values of variables may account both for equilibrium or disequilibrium, depending on the other variables with which they are made to keep company and on the relations assumed to prevail among them; and that different problems (perhaps concerning the same concrete situation) may call for very different models for use in analysis.

Not the same as stability

Stability in the sense of invariance over time has some connections with the notion of equilibrium which may easily lead to confusion. Since equilibrium is the position where everything is so well adjusted to everything else—in the model—that things can go on without change, this surely implies stability over time (at least until the next disturbance). And since a disturbing change must be isolated—in the model—from anything else that might require adjusting changes, this implies that "all other things remain unchanged"—particularly the interrelations assumed for the model; all in all, we presuppose the stability of a lot of things for the duration of the process that is pictured as "equilibration" in the model. With everything stable at the beginning and at the end of the imagined process, and many things stable while it goes on, the logical tie between stability and equilibrium is certainly a close one.

In addition, there is the very special meaning of "stability of equilibrium" according to which a "stable equilibrium" is distinguished from an "unstable" one depending on the presence or absence of a mechanism for the "self-correction" of random deviations from the equilibrium values of the variables involved.

However, none of these notions of stability has much to do with the stability of a price or quantity observed in actual fact. An actual price may be stable over a long time without forcing us to have it represented by an equilibrium price in the model that we may choose for explaining it. An actual price may be most unstable, jumping up and down like mad, and yet we may find it most expedient to explain these changes by means of models showing a quick succession of perfectly stable equilibria with different equilibrium prices due to a quick succession of exogenous disequilibrating changes.

We may conclude that "observed stability" and "observed instability"

---

other hand, a model that includes government price fixing, penalties for violations, unsold stocks, unsatisfied demand, etc., among its variables would show the surplus stocks or the unsatisfied demand as the "final equilibrium"—though only as "temporary equilibrium" if some lagged black-market behaviour functions are added to the list of assumptions.

should not be confused with, or attributed to, equilibrium and disequilibrium, respectively, in analytic models.

Not a value judgment

Equilibrium as used in positive economic analysis—as distinguished
from welfare economics—should not be taken as a value judgment, nor as
a reference to a "desired state of affairs." Equilibrium is not a Good
Thing, and disequilibrium is not a Bad Thing. Nor is the reverse association justified: equilibrium stands neither for the *status quo* nor for *laissez
faire*, as some dissident economists have been inclined to think.

If equilibrium analysis is employed to explain a sad situation as the
equilibrium outcome of certain conditions and events, it would be silly to
transfer our dislike of the situation to the equilibrium concept used in the
explanation. And if a sad situation is disliked and deemed intolerable, to
call it disequilibrium on that account helps neither in analysing it nor in
developing the best policy for improving it.

Of course, it is perfectly legitimate to allow our value judgments to
suggest to us the problems for analysis. If we find it desirable to secure
full employment at high wage rates we may construct models to show us
what conditions (interrelations between variables) would make full employment and high wage rates compatible with given values of the other
variables in the set; or what values these other variables would have to
attain in order to be compatible with full employment and high wage
rates with given interrelations. If we or others advocate a certain full-
employment policy we may construct models to show us what effects
could be expected, in a variety of circumstances, if various institutional
relationships were established to make interest rates, bank loans, government expenditures (or other employment-inducing variables) depend upon
changes in (absolute or relative) unemployment. But none of these
exercises, valuable and important though they are, would be aided by
incorporating our moral values or political goals into the *definition* of
equilibrium, as several economists have proposed. Some of these proposals, as we shall see in Section D, require that full employment at given
wage rates and other desirable objectives be made part of the definition
of equilibrium, so that any position in which these objectives are not
attained would always have to be called "disequilibrium."

By infusing a value judgment, a political philosophy or programme,
or a rejection of a programme or policy, into the concept of equilibrium
designed for economic analysis, the analyst commits the fallacy of implicit
evaluation or disguised politics. To choose the variables and interrelations suitable for an equilibrium analysis of problems that are dictated by
value judgments and political objectives is one thing. It is quite another
thing to insist on packaging these valuations with the definition of equi-

librium. Indeed, the analysis of the possibilities of their realisation may be impeded by such a restrictive definition.

D. Equilibrium in international trade theory

The literature on International Trade probably makes more extensive use of equilibrium concepts than any other field of economics. The pages are generously sprinkled with equilibria and disequilibria, and more often than not the writers indulge in concrete applications and also in policy advice based on some implicit hierarchy of social goals. Even some of the clearer expositors seem to have a hard time reminding themselves of their own definitions, and many a writer does not mind changing *equos* in midstream and equilibrium concepts in the middle of his *libri* (if a Latin pun may be admitted).

Consistent awareness of relativity: Joan Robinson

There are a few exceptionally consistent and methodical writers. One of them, fully aware and mindful of the relativity of equilibrium, is Joan Robinson:

> It is now obvious that there is no one rate of exchange which is the equilibrium rate corresponding to a given state of world demands and techniques. In any given situation there is an equilibrium rate corresponding to each rate of interest and level of effective demand, and any rate of exchange, within very wide limits, can be turned into the equilibrium rate by altering the rate of interest appropriately. Moreover, any rate of exchange can be made compatible with any rate of interest provided that money wages can be sufficiently altered. The notion of *the* equilibrium exchange rate is a chimera. The rate of exchange, the rate of interest, the level of effective demand and the level of money wages react upon each other like the balls in Marshall's bowl, and no one is determined unless all the rest are given.[13]

Built-in politics and simulated stability: Nurkse

Ragnar Nurkse undoubtedly knew all this, but in his now classic essay on international equilibrium he chose to disregard it.[14] Perhaps he felt strongly that he was less concerned with the niceties of abstract analysis than with the formulation of practical monetary policies (p. 4) instrumental in attaining several social objectives: "full employment" or "good

[13] Joan Robinson, "The Foreign Exchanges," *Essays in the Theory of Employment* (Oxford: Blackwell, 2nd ed., 1947). Reprinted in *Readings in the Theory of International Trade* (Philadelphia: Blakiston, 1949), p. 103.

[14] Ragnar Nurkse, "Conditions of International Monetary Equilibrium," *Essays in International Finance* (Princeton: International Finance Section, Princeton University, 1945). Reprinted in *Readings in the Theory of International Trade* (Philadelphia: Blakiston, 1949), pp. 3–34.

employment at the given wage structure" (p. 16), avoidance of inflation (p. 12), "reasonable stability of exchange rates" (p. 21), "freedom from severe exchange restrictions" (p. 21). He apparently believed that a programme of preventing "protracted departures" from "this happy state" (p. 34) could be more easily developed with the aid of a concept of equilibrium with built-in value judgments.

Thus, far from regarding the notion of *the* equilibrium exchange rate as a "chimera," Nurkse held that "there should be some more or less generally accepted notion as to what constitutes 'equilibrium' and 'dis-equilibrium' in regard to international exchange rates."[15] Since he found frequent changes in exchange rates undesirable, he made us "turn away from the imaginary system of freely fluctuating exchanges, in which the balance [of payments] is kept in equilibrium every hour or every day." He proposed that "the period which we contemplate in the definition of the equilibrium rate of exchange . . . should certainly not be less than a year" and preferably "long enough to eliminate 'cyclical' fluctuations," that is, "between five and ten years." The balance over such a period should be the "indication of equilibrium and disequilibrium." In brief, the "equilibrium rate" is the rate at which "there would be no net change in a country's reserve of international means of payments" over a period of five to ten years (pp. 6–7). But this is a *"true* equilibrium rate of ex-change" only if the balance of payments (excluding all short-term capital movements) is "kept in equilibrium" without "additional restrictions on trade" and without "depression and unemployment at home" (pp. 9–11).

Since Nurkse did not conceal his value judgments, he is not open to the charge of disguised politics; but I doubt the analytical usefulness of his evaluative equilibrium concept, and I submit that he might have avoided confusion by choosing a different term. For example, he could have spoken of the "optimum rate of exchange," the "most desirable rate of exchange," or the "full-employment rate of exchange," instead of in-voking Truth and Equilibrium by speaking of the "true equilibrium rate of exchange."

Moreover, to speak of an equilibrium over a period "long enough to permit any cyclical changes to cancel out" (p. 15) is analytically highly questionable. It virtually amounts to a confusion between equilibrium and price-stability. If it is agreed—and Nurkse does agree—that "at different levels of national income" (p. 11) or "with a different flow of foreign investment" (p. 8) the equilibrium rate of exchange would be different, is it then permissible to assume that national income (or even full-employ-ment national income) and the flow of foreign investment will remain unchanged over the period of a cycle, over five to ten years? To be sure, one can always "average" the changing rates of income and investment

15 *Ibid.,* p. 4.

over the years, but what right do we have to transfigure statistical *ex post* averages into *ex ante* norms or data to which the exchange rate should be equilibrated? If we stay on the *ex ante* level, as we should for theoretical models as well as for practical policy advice, we have no legitimate reason for assuming national incomes in the countries concerned and investment flows among them to remain even approximately unchanged over several years and, still less, for assuming that all other conditions are frozen on which "equilibrium exchange rates" would depend. Changes in technology, capital stock, labour force, industrial organisation, consumer tastes, factor prices, product prices, interest rates, bank loans, government expenditures, money stocks, and so forth would surely alter the equilibrium exchange rates frequently and significantly.[16] To assume things to remain unchanged for the duration of a particular process in an abstract model is one thing; it is quite another thing to simulate such stability for practical purposes or to make it an integral part of a concept designed for applied analysis.

Political criteria supported: Ellsworth and Kindleberger

Nurkse's notion of equilibrium in international transactions and in foreign-exchange rates has been widely accepted and elaborated upon. P. T. Ellsworth and Charles P. Kindleberger, in their excellent textbooks, adopt both the "several-years balance" as the standard for a concrete equilibrium and the social goals of satisfactory employment at satisfactory wages with moderate trade restrictions and reasonably stable prices as built-in criteria of a true (politically acceptable) equilibrium. They offer additional justifications. For example, Ellsworth writes:

> But our concept of what is desirable has modified our concept of what is normal; it is now generally agreed that we must take a broader view of equilibrium. Full employment, or at least the absence of mass unemployment, is now regarded as itself a condition of equilibrium. So likewise is the absence of an inflationary rise of prices. Hence a balance of payments which can only be balanced by means of a sharp decline in income and employment, or by a rise in income to inflationary levels, cannot be considered to be in equilibrium.[17]

The Keynesian notion of an "underemployment equilibrium" appears

[16] Under the gold standard one may picture the theoretical equilibrium rates as fluctuating, sometimes with considerable amplitude, around the gold par of exchange because expansions and contractions of bank reserves and deposits, enforced by the gold-flow mechanism and by the rules of the game, would raise and lower the equilibrium rates to the level of the gold par whenever they depart from it. *I know of no good reason why equilibrium exchange rates should remain stable unless monetary institutions and policies make them so.*

[17] P. T. Ellsworth, *The International Economy* (New York: Macmillan, 1950), p. 607.

to be rejected here, not because of any economic repercussions compelling (in an analytic model) full-employment equilibrium to be restored, but simply because unemployment is undesirable. Kindleberger, on the other hand, looks for a less normative explanation. He agrees that "large-scale unemployment . . . is compatible with a market equilibrium," but, on a wider view, "unemployment means disequilibrium, since government action to remove it is likely and will disturb the balance-of-payments position." [18] Here political repercussions are introduced into economic analysis, not through the assumption of given institutional relations (such as tax rates), but as a prediction that governments, either under political pressure or out of political conviction, will decide to do *something* to raise effective demand for products and labour. "It is suggested that, on a wider view of the social sciences, equilibrium in the balance of payments should be combined with political stability into a more generalized equilibrium." [19]

Equilibrium, to Kindleberger, becomes a political concept, partly because of the political repercussions which he predicts (without specifying them), and partly (and this is a very different matter) because to him it is a state of affairs that is "desired" and sometimes "achieved." Yet "the achievement of economic equilibrium" is contrasted with that of "other social goals, such as national political and social equilibrium or international peace." Economic equilibrium "is at best a limited objective" (p. 519). Will economists now have to agree on political philosophy and on ethical values before they can talk about equilibrium?

Relativity and value-neutrality: Meade I

J. E. Meade, in his treatise on *The Balance of Payments*, the most thorough analysis in this field, shows himself as the master of a house divided against itself. He is a strong believer in, and skilled user of, the equilibrium concept as a value-free, abstract methodological device; but he is also a persuasive advocate of the equilibrium concept as a standard of performance and a symbol for a comprehensive programme of economic policy which strives for Good Things and avoids the Bad; yet in the course of the analysis he finds it necessary to reduce the political comprehensiveness of this equilibrium concept and to break it down into separate equilibria of much smaller scope. A confrontation of these three Meades with one another will be facilitated by referring to them as

[18] Charles P. Kindleberger, *International Economics* (Homewood: Irwin, 1953), p. 412; similarly, p. 464.

[19] *Ibid.*, p. 412.—Kindleberger, like Nurkse and Ellsworth before him, is quite specific concerning the political objectives implied in his equilibrium concept. Hence, my phrase "disguised politics," used in the subtitle of this essay, does not properly characterize his procedure. His fusion of politics with economics is neither concealed nor disguised, but overt and aboveboard. (This footnote is being added because my charges have sometimes been misunderstood.)

Meade I, Meade II and Meade III, joint authors of Volume One of *The Theory of International Economic Policy*.[20]

Meade I opens the book with a resolute declaration in the Preface:

> The method employed in this volume is first to consider a number of countries in at least partial or temporary equilibrium, domestically and internationally; next to introduce some disturbing factor (which is often an act of government policy) into this equilibrium; then to consider the new partial or temporary equilibrium which the economies will attain when the direct and indirect effects of the disturbing factor have fully worked themselves out; and finally to compare the new position of equilibrium with the old [p. viii].

Meade's scheme of the equilibrium model, presented in Chapters IV and V, corresponds in almost every respect to the one proposed in this article. There is the division of the argument into the same four steps—"old position of equilibrium"; "spontaneous disturbance"; "repercussions" with "ultimate effects"; "new position of equilibrium."[21] There is also the recognition of the relativity of equilibrium regarding selected variables, but disregarding variables not included in the model. For example, Meade I allows unemployment to exist in a position of equilibrium,[22] initial or final; he allows "a new equilibrium" to be reached which "involves a deficit in [a country's] balance of payments" (p. 60) and which thus would be a disequilibrium if foreign reserves, etc., were included among the selected variables. And all these equilibria and disequilibria are "value-neutral," that is, free from political value judgments, free from connotations of good or bad, desirable or undesirable, politically acceptable or unacceptable.

Alliance with political value judgments: Meade II

Not so for Meade II, who wrote Chapter I of the book. He begins with a country "suffering" from a disequilibrium (p. 3) and he clearly identifies "balance-of-payments difficulties" with "balance-of-payments

[20] J. E. Meade, *The Theory of International Economic Policy, Volume One: The Balance of Payments* (London: Oxford University Press, 1951).

[21] "We shall confine ourselves to a comparison of the new position of equilibrium which results when some spontaneous disturbance has occurred and has had time to work out all its repercussions, with the old position of equilibrium which existed before the disturbance occurred" (*ibid.*, p. 58). The scheme is deemed necessary in order to ascertain the "ultimate effects" of the disturbance (p. 52). The only difference between Meade's scheme and mine is his inclusion of "policy changes," besides "induced changes," among the adjusting changes (pp. 42 ff.). I would treat reactions of the Government to the disequilibrating change either as part of the induced changes (though only if they follow from the assumed institutional behaviour equations) or as an additional datum (if they are not sufficiently "regular" to be subsumed among the given relations between the selected variables of the system).

[22] Meade assumes "that there is an appreciable volume of unemployment . . . to start with" (*ibid.*, p. 53). This assumption is necessary for an analysis of the "income effects" in a multiplier model.

disequilibrium" (p. 14). After showing that a country's deficit on trade items and unrequited transfers "does not necessarily represent a disequilibrium in its international position" (p. 8), he finds that its "true balance-of-payments deficit" is the "balance of autonomous trade and transfers," which "must be matched by what we have called accommodating finance." [23] But even such a "true" deficit "would be much too narrow a criterion of a disequilibrium in the balance of payments" (p. 13); to Meade a merely "potential" deficit is a sufficient criterion. For it is not the actual balance or imbalance but rather a "potential" deficit or surplus "which is the proper measure of a balance-of-payments disequilibrium" (p. 15). Such a disequilibrium without actual deficit exists if the deficit is *avoided* by resort to trade restrictions, to domestic-income deflation and unemployment, or to an adjustment in the exchange rate.

Meade II has thus adopted the political equilibrium concept proposed by Nurkse.[24] But Meade II goes on to make another distinction to the effect "that a disequilibrium of this kind may be temporary or may be more or less permanent" (p. 15). Since "it is the latter, of course, which presents the really serious problem" (p. 15), he decides that "perhaps the most basic measure of balance-of-payments disequilibrium is the country's surplus or deficit of potential and continuing payments for autonomous trade and transfers." He resolves that this is what he will mean in the rest of the book (p. 16).

Meade I might now rise and tell Meade II that a theorist is very familiar with temporary *equilibrium* but cannot understand what may be meant by permanent or enduring *dis*equilibrium—except perhaps a case of direct controls interfering with "market equilibrium." Indeed, a disequilibrium, in the theorist's model, is a constellation of variables that cannot endure if left alone, that must give rise to further change, and thus is temporary *ex hypothesi*. Meade II would have to reply that he did not mean disequilibrium in the economic theorist's sense, but instead was referring to a situation that was quite unpleasant and unfortunately could last a long time: a situation where a desired level of employment at desired wage rates could be maintained, at given foreign-exchange rates and without special trade restrictions, only with the help of accommodating capital imports (loans from abroad, forced liquidation of foreign assets, and depletion of gold and exchange reserves). If the accommodating finance cannot be secured actual balance will *inevitably* be attained, through less employment, through lower wage rates, through depreciation

[23] *Ibid.*, p. 13. For an earlier formulation of the balance-of-payments problem in terms of accommodating capital movements see Fritz Machlup, *International Trade and the National Income Multiplier*, pp. 134–135.

[24] Note, however, that what Nurkse called the "true" balance Meade calls the *potential* balance, to be regarded as the "proper" measure; "true" balance to Meade means *actual* balance, though rearranged for autonomous and accommodating items.

of the currency or through stricter trade controls. But since any and all of these equilibrations are "undesirable," Meade II would prefer to deny the attained balance the name and title of "equilibrium." [25]

Return to value-neutrality: Meade III

The sentiment and resolution of Meade II were of little avail, inasmuch as Meade III wrote most of the rest of the book. He soon found it expedient to distinguish "internal balance" and "external balance" (pp. 104 ff.), the former dealing with domestic employment (and related matters, such as price inflation and wage rates), the latter with the balance of payments (and related matters, such as trade controls and foreign-exchange rates). The full-employment standard is no longer an integral part of balance-of-payments equilibrium. For example, cases are discussed where "an inflation of domestic expenditure is needed" both to increase employment "and also to restore equilibrium to the balance of payments" (p. 115). Or, in the discussion of "conflicts between internal and external balance," the distinction of a "disequilibrium" in the balance of payments and, on the other hand, "in each national income" of the countries concerned, is consistently carried through (Chapter X). Indeed, the distinctions are quite fine, especially when Meade III separates hypothetical situations in which "the smallest element of disequilibrium," or "the least-marked element of disequilibrium," can be found either in the internal or in the external balance (p. 122).

Meade III discards also the criteria of immutable exchange rates and absence of trade restrictions from the meaning of external equilibrium. Thus, at one point he considers the possibility that the authorities of the countries "let the exchange rate between their currencies change as a means of regaining external balance without sacrificing internal balance," and the alternative possibility that they impose "direct controls over their international transactions so as to restore equilibrium to their balances of payments without disturbing their internal balance" (p. 124). And he discusses a case in which "a balance-of-payments disequilibrium is removed by means of the depreciation of the currency of the deficit country," and another case in which "the balance of payments is put into equilibrium" by price adjustments under a system of flexible wage rates (pp. 328–329). There is little doubt that Meade III had found out that the definitions developed by Meade II, reflecting a commonly shared regret over lapses from socially ideal circumstances, are not efficient tools of

[25] Similar objections to Meade's definitions were raised by Harry G. Johnson, "The Taxonomic Approach to Economic Policy," *Economic Journal*, Vol. LXI (December 1951), pp. 814–815. This review article of Meade's book, unfortunately, came to my attention only long after I had published my essay. I am now glad to have this opportunity of acknowledging that Johnson anticipated my strictures against Meade. [This footnote was added in 1963.]

economic analysis. Anxious to get on with his work, he left the political equilibrium concept behind (on pp. 13–16) and used an unpolitical one for his economic analysis.

There is still a difference to settle between Meade I and Meade III, but this is not serious. As a matter of fact, it is merely a matter of terminology. Meade I wanted "equilibrium" to be the thinking device, described in this essay, while Meade III often wanted it to refer to a balance of payments in which accommodating transactions were zero. If Meade III had spoken of deficit, surplus, and zero balances of payments, without using the word "equilibrium," he would have avoided even the appearance of a conceptual difference. But this is perhaps too much to ask. After all, one can get used to words with multiple meanings and should be able to remember that a so-called "disequilibrium in the balance of payments" means simply a surplus or deficit, which in economic analysis may figure as an initial equilibrium, an adjusting change, or a final equilibrium, depending on the problem at hand.[26]

Attack on persuasive definitions: Streeten

Philosophers of science have recently shown that some definitions, supposedly stating what something is or means, are in fact devised to persuade people to do certain things or to do things in a certain way. "Persuasive definitions" is the name characterising such definitions.[27]

Paul Streeten, in an interesting article, showed that certain definitions of balance-of-payments equilibrium fall in the category of persuasive definitions. We have seen how stable exchange rates, full employment at given wage rates, stable price levels, and unrestricted trade have been included as additional criteria in some definitions of balance-of-payments equilibrium. This expansion of criteria, according to Streeten, amounts to

[26] A reader who has successfully learned from Meade I that disequilibrium was just a step in an explanation of change might be puzzled when Meade III tells him about a type of "disequilibrium which is the most intractable" (p. 122). However, this is quickly cleared up when he is reminded that the chapter is supposed to examine alternative financial policies and their effectiveness in restoring balance-of-payments equilibrium without resort to depreciation or trade restrictions. Translated into the terms used by Meade I, the question is whether, starting from an "initial position of equilibrium" with a payments deficit financed by accommodating transfers, any measures of fiscal and monetary policy can be found which will act as a "disturbance" leading to such "repercussions" that a "new equilibrium" with a zero balance of payments will be reached, while foreign-exchange rates are unchanged and trade is not directly controlled. If the final equilibrium in any such model continues to show deficits no matter what "disturbing change" is devised by the financial authorities, then Meade III, with many practitioners in the field, calls the situation an "intractable" balance-of-payments disequilibrium, that is, one not yielding to treatment by financial policy.

[27] Cf. C. L. Stevenson, "Persuasive Definitions," *Mind*, Vol. 47 (1938), p. 331; Max Black, "The Definition of Scientific Method," *Science and Civilization* (Madison: University of Wisconsin Press, 1949), p. 69.

"begging the question"; it "conceals behind a persuasive definition value judgments not generally shared." [28]

Streeten proceeds to exemplify the dangers of persuasive definitions:

> To include, say, the presence of import restrictions in the definition of "disequilibrium" produces the convenient result that the removal of these restrictions, and devaluation or deflation, become a *necessity*, although it is hoped, presumably, that the difference between logical necessity (what follows from a definition) and political or moral necessity (what ought to be done) will remain undetected [p. 87].

It is implicitly assumed, I take it, that those who make use of a persuasive definition of equilibrium rely on the popular association of equilibrium with a Good Thing, and of disequilibrium with a Bad Thing. Thus, they hope to sell to the public the removal of import restrictions (or the adoption of full-employment policies, etc.) in the same package labelled "equilibrium."

This does not mean that the absence of import restrictions and the pursuit of fiscal and monetary policies to create a full-employment demand for goods and services are not important assumptions, perhaps indispensable ones, for the analysis of certain problems.[29] The methodological standing of these two assumptions, however, is not the same if by import restrictions we mean the use of discretionary allocation controls rather than the use of tariffs and other general rules with "predictable" impact. Discretionary controls must be excluded from many analytic models, not because we do not like them, but because we cannot predict the outcome: we would need to know the "behaviour equations" of the control authorities in order to know how they react to certain changes in the values of the variables of the model. As soon as these behaviour functions are "given," linking certain variables to others in a definite way, the controls are no longer "discretionary," and we can work with them in our equilibrium theory.

The assumption of "freedom from discretionary (theoretically unpredictable) controls" is, therefore, a necessary part of a model that includes the concept of a market equilibrium. In such a model we regularly assume certain relationships among prices, incomes, and quantities offered and demanded in the market. If some of the reactions deduced from the assumed relationships become effective only when

[28] Paul Streeten, "Elasticity Optimism and Pessimism in International Trade," *Economia Internazionale,* Vol. VII (1954), p. 87.

[29] Streeten himself assumes some sort of full-employment policy, not only explicitly, but also when he defines disequilibrium to "mean a permanent tendency to generate a deficit in the balance of payments" (p. 87). It should be clear that such a "tendency" could not persist without a continuing *policy* of offsetting, by means of loan expansions, the automatic deflationary effects of sales from exchange reserves.

licensed, and cannot materialise without special permission by an unpredictable authority, the model becomes unworkable. It is only for this reason that "market equilibrium" must postulate effectiveness of "free-market prices," and therefore absence of direct controls. Trade barriers with predictable influence on all adjusting changes are fully consistent with market equilibrium, and with any other equilibrium as well. And, incidentally, the inconsistency of the assumption of discretionary trade restrictions with an analytically workable equilibrium is no good argument against the use of such restrictions in the real world. A policy cannot be rejected merely on the ground that it does not fit into a conceptual scheme which has proved useful in analysis.

The trouble with built-in politics

The objections against persuasive definitions of equilibrium are not based on the fear that gullible people may actually be persuaded to stand up for the measures or policies "deduced" from arguments in which such an equilibrium concept is employed; the real ground for objection is that an equilibrium concept so drastically restricted by built-in political criteria becomes less useful, if not useless, in the analysis of most problems. Most problems that require analysis are such that not all the ideal conditions which are made "honorary criteria" of equilibrium can be "attained"; their analysis calls for a variety of policy variables and institutional (political) behaviour functions combined with a less circumscribed concept of equilibrium that can be used for *any* set of variables and *any* relationships among them. This statement refers chiefly to the kind of analysis in which equilibrium is thought of as the initial and final positions in an imagined process of change involving a chosen set of interrelated variables. But it holds also for an analysis in which equilibrium is thought of merely as the equality of certain (actual or potential) sums on the two sides of the account called "the balance of payments."

Take any change that would create an increase in the demand for foreign exchange, or a decrease in its supply. Whether it is a change in tastes at home or abroad, a change in the technical production possibilities anywhere, a change in fiscal or monetary policy (say, to accelerate economic development), a change in the wage structure (for example, giving higher wage rates to industrial workers), a change in the flow of investment (perhaps a greater demand for foreign investment), a reduction in the desire to hold cash, or any one of a score of similar "disequilibrating changes"—the adjusting changes will involve first an accommodating outflow of foreign reserve and eventually some of the "prohibited" movements, that is, some deviations from the built-in political requirements of "equilibrium" in the persuasive sense. For example, real wages may be reduced through higher prices of wage goods; interest rates may rise, or bank loans be curtailed, with consequent reductions in employment; foreign-exchange rates may get adjusted, etc., and the final position—the new equilibrium in the analytical sense—will be a "disequilibrium" of the balance of payments in the persuasive (or rather dissuasive) sense. Since none of the results of any of the possible adjustments would qualify for the honorific title "equilibrium," the "disequilibrium" (in the dissuasive sense) could be remedied only by a *deus ex machina:* by another disequilibrating change that happened to neutralise the first disturbance and render the unpleasant adjustments unnecessary. A virtual sabotage of economic analysis!

V I

Comments on
"The Balance of Payments"

Mechanism, Rules, and Discipline ■ The Historical-Institutional Situation ■ The Deficit in the International Accounts of the United States

In these comments I shall first discuss some semantical and "institutional" aspects of "the discipline of the balance of payments," and then I shall proceed to some ideas of my own concerning the present balance-of-payments situation of the United States.

MECHANISM, RULES, AND DISCIPLINE

Three different phrases are employed to describe in a general way the effects which movements in the balance of payments may have on the domestic monetary situation: "the balance-of-payments mechanism," "the rules of the game," and "the discipline of the balance of payments." I have noticed a tendency to use the three phrases interchangeably for the same notion, and I deplore this as a waste of words. To use different words for the same thing and have no words for other things is a wasteful allocation of linguistic resources.

Each of the three phrases can have its own meaning. The balance-of-payments *mechanism* should refer to some automatic effects, not to policy decisions. After all, this is what mechanism means: it works "mechanically," not through discretion. The automatic effects in question are upon bank reserves, an inflow of gold or foreign exchange causing bank reserves to increase, and an outflow causing them to decrease. This mechanism works even in the absence of a central bank if private banks hold gold and foreign-exchange reserves. The *rules* of the gold-standard game refer to norms for central-bank policies. To abide by the rules is to abstain from policies of offsetting, and to pursue policies of reinforcing, the effects of the balance-of-payments mechanism. A central bank obeys the rules of the game if it expands credit and buys securities when gold and foreign exchange are received and if it contracts credit and sells securities when gold and foreign reserves are lost. Now it would not be unreasonable to use the word *discipline* for the exactitude with which the rules of the game are obeyed; but it is preferable to use it instead for the stern austerity with which a nation practices anti-inflationary or deflationary policies when a balance-of-payments deficit has arisen or threatens to arise.

Thus, while the rules of the game may prescribe expansionary or contractionary policies, as the case may be, I would use the term "discipline" for only the latter. This seems sensible to me in analogy to the conduct of a private householder in spending or guarding his cash reserve. If his cash reserve is high and rising, it does not take any "discipline" to spend it. Nor, incidentally, does it take any discipline not to spend when the cash reserve is exhausted. It does take discipline to refrain from spending when the reserve is still ample but threatens to decline if a policy of ease is pursued. The "discipline" of the balance of payments, then, designates the cautious abstinence from credit expansion on the part of a monetary authority which still has plenty of reserves but has been alerted by a balance-of-payments deficit to the dangers ordinarily associated with a policy of monetary ease.

I beg your pardon if it seems pretentious for me to act as arbiter for the use of words. I am not attempting to impose my glossary upon anybody, but I would be glad if my terminological "discipline" or, if you prefer, "rules" for the economy of words were to meet with your approval.

The historical-institutional situation

May I now follow my well-known proclivities toward institutional economics and warn that one and the same theoretical model may not be suitable for different institutional arrangements. The three concepts which I have just reviewed cannot be applied to all countries at all times. When Dr. Southard [1] looked for some evidence of the "discipline" of the balance of payments in the monetary history of the United States, he might have made it clear that in the nineteenth century there were no appointed policymakers making decisions that could be regarded as either showing or lacking "discipline." We must separate in our own thinking the times

---

[1] Frank A. Southard, Jr., "United States Experience," *Journal of Finance*, Vol. 16 (May 1961), pp. 177–178.

(1) before the United States had a central-banking system, (2) after the Federal Reserve System was established but before the dollar had become a key currency, and (3) after the dollar had become reserve money for foreign banks and central banks.

In the first of these periods one can, of course, find evidence of the balance-of-payments *mechanism* at work, when private banks gained and lost gold and sterling balances. But there was no one who was supposed to obey the *rules* of the game, and no monetary authority which could feel, and make felt, the *discipline* of the balance of payments. In the second period all three concepts are applicable, but what makes it so very different from the third period is the meaning of a balance-of-payments "deficit." If this is to refer to the state of an accounting balance in which the items on current account and the autonomous capital items show an excess of payments over receipts, so that the gold stock declines and/or short-term liabilities to foreigners increase, it makes a difference whether or not foreign countries hold (and desire to hold more) dollar balances as part of their international reserves.

THE DEFICIT IN THE INTERNATIONAL ACCOUNTS OF THE UNITED STATES

If foreign countries want to build up their foreign reserves by keeping higher dollar balances in New York, only a deficit of the United States balance of payments (in the sense defined) can accommodate them. If this deficit is not large enough to meet the demand for dollar balances (the unsatisfied demand indicated, for example, by exchange restrictions on the part of the foreign authorities), some people will speak of this—to the confusion of many—as a dollar shortage or a "surplus" in the United States balance of payments (in a different sense, of course). If foreign countries are satisfied with the size of their foreign reserves but decide to switch from dollar holdings to gold holdings, the United States will suffer a reduction in its gold stock and an equal reduction in its short-term liabilities to foreigners, a movement which, however, will not be regarded as a "deficit" (in the sense defined). Of course, one may quickly alter the definition and make the ups and downs of short-term balances part of the capital balance. But then you are in semantic trouble when there is, on balance, a deficit on current account plus long-term capital account, with consequent accumulations of foreign-held dollar balances. You cannot, without the danger of an even worse confusion than there is, give the name "deficit" in some instances to an *increase* in such balances and in other instances to a *decrease* in such balances. Of course, I cannot keep you from doing so if you insist. There are those, I am afraid, who speak of a deficit first when the foreigners *acquire* dollar balances and then again when they *withdraw* them.

What a terrible semantic mess! It gets even worse when one starts using the words "equilibrium" and "disequilibrium" for this sort of thing. I shall carefully avoid using these terms to characterize any concrete situation. For we should never forget that these are purely mental constructs without empirical counterparts; one and the same situation is an equilibrium or a disequilibrium in the analyst's mind, depending on what variables he happens to include in his model and what values he gives them in his imagination. But, since no one will hold that the present state of the United States balance of payments is one that can last forever or even for another four or five years, we must use some word to express this diagnosis. Hence, I shall call it an "imbalance in our international accounts."

VII

The Mysterious Numbers Game of Balance-of-Payments Statistics

Which of the Basic Concepts of Balance of Payments? ■ Three Reasons for Revisions and New Versions ■ The U.S. Balance of Payments in 1951 ■ The Not So Stubborn Facts of History ■ The U.S. Balance of Payments in 1959 and 1960 ■ Juggling the Items between Balance and Offsets ■ Distinctions without Much Difference ■ Modern Presentations and Debates ■ The Sense of It All

Hardly anyone will be surprised when he is told that our balance of payments changes from year to year. But many may for a moment be puzzled when I say that the U.S. balance of payments for the year 1951 has changed over the years, and that the balance for 1960 will keep changing for several years. My undertaking here is to explain how "past history" is apt to change as new information becomes available, new theories are developed, and new fashions gain sway; it will be seen that statistical history or historical statistics are affected by these changes most conspicuously because alterations of numerical data are more striking than alterations in verbal exposition.

WHICH OF THE BASIC CONCEPTS OF BALANCE OF PAYMENTS?

Since I have insisted [1] that anybody who uses the words "balance of payments" without intending to confuse or to mislead ought to declare

---

[1] "Three Concepts of the Balance of Payments and the So-Called Dollar Shortage," *Economic Journal*, Vol. LX (March 1950), pp. 46, 68. See Chapter III of this volume, pp. 69, 92.

which of the basic concepts he has in mind, let me state that *accounting* balances of payments will be discussed here. There will be no reference to *program* balances of payments, and *market* balances of payments will be alluded to only briefly near the end of this essay.

A "balance" (surplus or deficit) in the accounting balance of payments is defined as the excess of the sum of selected categories of credits over the sum of selected categories of debits on the international accounts of a nation (or on the intergroup accounts of any group of people) for a particular year (or any other period of time). Where the accounts are kept on a double-entry system, so that the sum of all credits must equal the sum of all debits, the selection of categories of entries to make up the *balance* determines, obviously, the categories of entries which make up the *offsets* to the balance; and the amount of the balance must equal the amount of the offsets, with the signs reversed.[2] There are many different ways of selecting the categories of entries for the balance and the offsets and, consequently, there will be many different accounting balances of payments for any given period.

The criteria of selection of items for the balance and the offsets depend on many things, to be discussed later. The important point to keep in mind is that the criteria may depend on the circumstances of the particular time and place and on shifts of emphasis suggested by changing economic theories.

THREE REASONS FOR REVISIONS AND NEW VERSIONS

The appearance of new balance-of-payments figures for a given year in the course of subsequent years has more reasons than the one just stated. We may list altogether three reasons for the series of revisions and new versions that bewilder the uninitiated:

1. Revisions of data,
2. Reallocation of individual items to particular accounts,
3. Rearrangement of particular accounts as between balance and offsets.

Revisions of data result from new information or improved estimates becoming available. The more quickly the public wants "provisional" figures the more often will they have to be revised. If the data for 1963 are wanted as early as January or even March 1964, provisional estimates based on projections will have to take the place of estimates on the basis

---

[2] An alternative presentation, avoiding the reverse signs of the balance and the offsets, is to separate the items included in the balance from those included among the offsets by a horizontal line and to show the "total above the line" and the "total below the line" equal both in amount and in sign.

of records and reports. As the latter become available, the provisional figures are revised. Other, more drastic, revisions may be the results of new sources of information or new bases of inference discovered in later years. In any case, revisions of published data occur in most areas of economic statistics, and the balance of payments is no exception to this rule.

The other two reasons for subsequent changes in published figures are somewhat different in nature in that they represent changes of mind rather than changes of information. The allocation of an individual item to a particular account is a matter of judgment, and the arrangement of particular accounts as between balance and offsets is a matter of economic theory, or at least a matter of interpretation of observations in the light of theory.

Problems of allocation and reallocation arise not only regarding individual items but also regarding whole classes of items. As long as the accounts between which these items may be switched are part of the same group of accounts, or sub-balance, a reallocation will not affect the sub-balance. For example, when it was decided to enter imports of merchandise not at the value c.i.f. port of entry into the country but only at the value f.o.b. country of origin, this implied in many instances a reallocation of the cost of transport and insurance from merchandise account to service account. But while the debits in the trade balance were reduced and the debits in the service balance increased, the balance on goods and services remained unchanged. On the other hand, when military exports are separated from commercial exports, or altogether omitted, the credits in the balance on goods and services are reduced, but the compensating change occurs in the donations account, or unilateral transfers, where the debits due to military grants are reduced.[3]

The treatment of undistributed profits earned by foreign subsidiaries of American corporations is another such matter of judgment. One may hold that nothing is paid and nothing received, and therefore no entries should be made, as profits are earned but left in the business abroad. Or one may hold that the increased equity in the foreign corporations should be shown in the statistic, and that this increase in our foreign assets be

---

[3] If the U.S. Department of Defense sends guns, tanks, and airplanes overseas to equip its own armed forces stationed abroad, these shipments are not regarded as exports. If these same items are turned over to foreign defense organizations, one may choose between two accounting procedures. Either one holds that the American weapons and planes will serve the same purposes whether they are manned by U.S. or other NATO soldiers; in this case there is no reason for making any entry in the international accounts. Or one holds that any transfer of property from the United States to other nations ought to be shown, regardless of the purpose and of any obligations to pay; in this case one will credit the defense items shipped abroad as exports to the merchandise account and must debit the donations account for the military grants, i.e., unilateral transfers, to a foreign nation.

recorded as an outflow of long-term U.S. private capital—a debit entry on capital account—offsetting a "receipt" of reinvested earnings from U.S. capital invested abroad—a credit entry on service account. The latter technique of balance-of-payments accounting is preferred by the International Monetary Fund.

Chiefly from the different treatment of exports under military grants and of reinvested earnings of foreign subsidiaries—and partly from other differences in coverage and classification, as well as some minor revisions in the statistical data—conspicuous differences arose in the balance-of-payments figures reported by the U.S. Department of Commerce and the International Monetary Fund (though both sources use the estimates developed by the Commerce Department). This is illustrated in Table VII-1

TABLE VII-1   *Net Balances (Credits +, Debits —) on Main Accounts in the U.S. Balance of Payments, 1950, 1951, and 1952, as shown by the U.S. Department of Commerce and the International Monetary Fund (In millions of dollars)*

Net balances on main accounts	1950 Dep. of Com.	1950 IMF	1951 Dep. of Com.	1951 IMF	1952 Dep. of Com.	1952 IMF
(1) Goods and services	+2,297	+2,049	+5,164	+4,243	+4,973	+3,005
(2) Unilateral transfers	−4,601	−3,916	−4,913	−3,388	−5,043	−2,371
Sum of (1) and (2)	−2,304	−1,867	+ 251	+ 855	− 70	+ 634
(3) Capital	+ 405	+ 154	− 734	−1,272	+ 210	− 760
(4) Monetary gold	+1,743	+1,743	− 53	− 53	− 378	− 379
(5) Errors and omissions	+ 156	− 30	+ 536	+ 470	+ 238	+ 505
Sum of (3), (4), and (5)	+2,304	+1,867	− 251	− 855	+ 70	− 634

SOURCES: U.S. Department of Commerce, *Survey of Current Business*, Vol. 31, Washington, June 1951, pp. 18–19; and Vol. 33, Washington, March 1953, p. 8; International Monetary Fund, *Balance of Payments Yearbook, Vol. 8, 1950–54*, Washington, D.C., 1957, p. 211. (Because of frequent revisions the figures from Vol. 8, reproduced here, do not coincide with those published in earlier or later volumes.)

by the following summaries of the main accounts of the U.S. Balance of Payments for the years 1950, 1951, and 1952. The positive balance of goods and services was always reported lower by the I.M.F. than by the Commerce Department, because the exclusion of the military exports counted more heavily than the inclusion of the undistributed profits of foreign subsidiaries. The negative balance of unilateral transfers was lower in the I.M.F. reports because of the exclusion of the military grants. The balance on goods, services, and unilateral transfers together was more favorable (less negative or more positive) in the I.M.F. reports because of the inclusion of the undistributed profits. For the same reason the balance of capital movements was less positive or more negative in the I.M.F.

reports. The differences between the figures of "errors and omissions" given in the two columns must of course be reflected in equal differences between the other sub-balances; they are possibly due to minor revisions made by the Commerce Department after it published the data we used for Table VII-1 but before the I.M.F. had completed its tabulations. Let us note that our exhibit of discrepancies is not designed to show that one arrangement is preferable to the other, but only to show that relatively slight changes in the presentation of virtually the same data can alter the statistical picture.

Both the allocation of certain classes of items to particular accounts and the arrangement of accounts as part of the balance or of the offsets come into play in the case of transactions in long-term government securities. The decision to treat purchases of U.S. securities by foreigners as an inflow of long-term capital conflicts with the consideration that these securities may be held for only very short periods. The reconsideration involves not only a switch from long-term to short-term capital account but, for some interpreters, a switch from the balance to the offsets. But we are getting ahead of our story if we start discussing these rearrangements at this juncture. It will be more illuminating if we first recount what has happened to the balance of payments for 1951 in the course of nine or ten years.

THE U.S. BALANCE OF PAYMENTS IN 1951

The choice of 1951 was influenced only by the fact that this was a year for which at first no one doubted the existence of a substantial surplus in the U.S. balance, but which several years later was cited as one of a series of (chronic) deficits. The choice of sources or authorities cited hardly needs an explanation, but it may be mentioned that the variety of verbal expressions given to the surplus or deficit was a factor in the selection. Table VII-2 presents a collection of 20 reports on the U.S. balance of payments for 1951 which differ either in the phrases used or in the figures reported or in both.

The phrases, amounts, and signs listed in the table are reproduced from the published reports cited, either from statistical tables or from the texts, sometimes from a combination of both. The number of variations can be further increased if we add some of the phrases used for the balance of payments of later years, say 1959, and calculate the amounts by the techniques then employed. Thus, what the U.S. Treasury Department [4] in 1961 called the "Over-All Balance" and what the Commission

---

[4] Statement of Douglas Dillon, Secretary of the Treasury, in *International Payments Imbalances and Need for Strengthening International Financial Arrangements*, Hearings of the Subcommittee on International Exchange and Payments of the Joint Economic Committee, U.S. Congress, Washington, June 1961, p. 29.

TABLE VII-2   *Reports on the U.S. Balance of Payments for 1951*

Phrase used	Source	Year publ.	Surplus (+) or deficit (−) (Millions of dollars)
"Surplus in the balance of payments" ["Current account of the U.S. Balance of payments"]	1	1952	+5,029
"Deficit of the world with the United States"	2	1953	+3,686
"United States Balance, Total" ["on account of goods and services (excluding military aid exports and military expenditures), private remittances, private net direct investment and portfolio capital, and net government long-term loans"]	3	1955	+3,485
"Net surplus of goods and services requiring dollar financing" ["Measure of the insufficiency of foreign dollar earnings"]	4	1953	+3,200
"World's dollar deficit"	5	1954	+3,200
"Surplus" [offset by "Compensatory Official Financing"]	6	1952	+3,038
"Balance on goods and services, unilateral transfers other than U.S. Government grants, United States private capital, and errors and omissions" ["net outflow (−)"]	7	1954	+2,700
"Balance on goods and services and private unilateral transfers" ["excluding military end-items, but including military expenditure abroad"]	8	1954	+823
"Balance on goods and services and unilateral transfers"	9	1953	+251
"Excess of Foreign Expenditures"	10	1957	+ 99
"Excess of dollar payments over receipts" ["foreign dollar balances and gold"]	11	1961	−300
"Net surplus (+) or deficit (−)"	12	1961	−300
"Total deficit"	13	1963	−305
"Net payments position"	14	1961	−343
"Balancing items: dollar assets and gold acquired from the United States"	15	1952	−362
"Total net payments balance (deficit −)" ["U.S. overall payments balance"]	16	1959	−500
"Net balance"	17	1960	−500
"Total basic balance"	18	1963	−700
"Net balance on recorded transactions"	19	1961	−813
"Balance with the world"	20	1959	−995

NOTE: Some of the figures with rounded hundred million dollars were given in the original as billion [milliard] dollars with only one decimal place.

SOURCES:
1. Bank for International Settlements, *Twenty-Second Annual Report,* Basle, 1952, p. 20.
2. United Nations, *World Economic Report, 1951-52,* New York, p. 87.
3. United Nations, *World Economic Report, 1953-54,* New York, p. 111.
4. *Economic Report of the President,* Washington, January 1953, p. 139.

5. [Randall] Commission on Foreign Economic Policy, *Staff Papers*, Washington, February 1954, p. 15.
6. International Monetary Fund, *Balance of Payments Yearbook, Vol. 4, 1950-51*, Washington, 1952, p. 271.
7. *Economic Report of the President: Transmitted to the Congress January 28, 1954*, Washington, 1954, p. 219.
8. Organization for European Economic Co-operation, *Progress and Problems of the European Economy: Fifth Annual Report*, Paris, 1954, p. 266.
9. U.S. Department of Commerce, *Survey of Current Business*, Vol. 33, Washington, March 1953, p. 8.
10. International Monetary Fund, *Balance of Payments Yearbook, Vol. 7, 1954-55*, Washington, 1956, reissued 1957, U.S. Section, p. 9.
11. Legislative Reference Service, Library of Congress, *Gold and the United States Balance of Payments Deficit*, Committee on Foreign Affairs of the House of Representatives, 87th Congress, 1st Session, Washington, February 1961, p. 11.
12. Committee for Economic Development, *The International Position of the Dollar*, Washington, 1961, p. 33.
13. Joint Economic Committee, *The United States Balance of Payments in 1968*, Materials presented by the Brookings Institution to the Joint Economic Committee, Congress of the United States, 88th Congress, 1st Session, Washington, 1963, p. 10.
14. Federal Reserve Bank of St. Louis, *Monthly Review*, Vol. 43, St. Louis, Mo., March 1961, p. 5.
15. Bank for International Settlements, *Twenty-Second Annual Report*, Basle, 1952, p. 20.
16. Joint Economic Committee, *Staff Report on Employment, Growth, and Price Levels*, 86th Congress, 1st Session, Washington, 1959, pp. 442-443.
17. Organization for European Economic Co-operation, *Europe and the World Economy: Eleventh Annual Economic Review*, Paris, 1960, p. 125.
18. Same as source 13, p. 6.
19. Federal Reserve Bank of St. Louis, *Monthly Review*, Vol. 43, St. Louis, Mo., March 1961, p. 5.
20. Robert Triffin, "The International Monetary Position of the United States," in *Employment, Growth, and Price Levels*, Hearings before the Joint Economic Committee, 86th Congress, 1st Session, Washington, 1959, Part 9A, p. 2916.

on Money and Credit [5] in the same year called the "U.S. Payments Balance" would have been —342 million dollars in 1951; and what the Treasury called the "Basic Balance" and the Commission called the "Hard-Core Balance" would have been —710 million dollars. Perhaps the last mentioned balance is more clearly described by the Bank for International Settlements [6] in 1961 as the "Over-all balance on current and long-term capital account," which in 1951 would have been —707 million dollars.

The exhibit of published statements in Table VII-2 omitted most of the figures reported specifically for the balance of trade, the balance of

[5] Commission on Money and Credit, *Money and Credit: Their Influences on Jobs, Prices, and Growth* (Englewood Cliffs, N.J.: Prentice-Hall, 1961), p. 215.
[6] Bank for International Settlements, *Thirty-First Annual Report*, Basle, 1961, p. 112.

goods and services, and the balance of payments on current account. To include in our tabulation several reports of the latter two balances would not have been unfair, since many experts in earlier years considered them the most meaningful data to explain the "U.S. surplus responsible for the world dollar shortage." To complete the record, let us then state that the U.S. Department of Commerce [7] gave the final (revised) figures for the balance of goods and services for 1951 as $5,191 million including military aid grants and as $3,721 million excluding military aid; and that the I.M.F.[8] reported $4,243 million for the balance of goods and services including undistributed profits of foreign subsidiaries, and $3,857 million as the balance of goods and services (as above) including private donations.

The not so stubborn facts of history

The variety of figures supposedly standing for a very concrete experience, namely, the balance of payments of the United States in the year 1951, is impressive. The range is enormous: from a surplus of over $5 billion to a deficit of about $1 billion. Let us note that this is the sort of thing that so many people apparently seek when they say, "let us look at the facts"; these are the "empirical data," the "records of observation," which are taken as established facts and are to be explained with the aid of theory or, according to some, are supposed to suggest theories, or to test and verify theories. It should be understood, however, that these so-called observations, data, or facts really *presuppose* and *contain* a substantial amount of theory and that changes in the theoretical presuppositions or preconceptions may result in drastic changes of the observations, of the empirical data, of the supposedly stubborn facts.[9]

If we compare the reported figures for the 1951 balance with the years in which they were published, we can detect something of a trend: with some exceptions, the earliest publications reported the largest surpluses, later publications reported much more modest surpluses, and the most recent publications, nine or ten years after the event, reported deficits. I submit that this reflects changes of theory and that these changes of theory in turn reflect new experiences of a pre-scientific kind. In other words, the changes in the theoretical preconceptions which affected the supposedly empirical data were in turn affected by very mundane experiences, such as complaints by disappointed businessmen,

---

[7] U.S. Department of Commerce, *Balance of Payments: Statistical Supplement* [to the *Survey of Current Business*], Washington, 1958, pp. 12–13.

[8] International Monetary Fund, *Balance of Payments Yearbook, Vol. 8, 1950-54*, Washington, 1957, p. 211.

[9] For a short illustration of the concealed theoretical contents of supposed facts see Fritz Machlup, *The Political Economy of Monopoly* (Baltimore: The Johns Hopkins Press, 1952), pp. 448-454.

apologies and alibis by frustrated governments, primitive interpretations by newsmen and journalists on the basis of uninstructed theorizing by the man-in-the-street.

In the historical situation of the early 1950's many countries experienced drastic excess demand for dollars; with given or increasing supplies of domestic money and at fixed foreign-exchange rates, the amounts of dollars demanded exceeded the amounts available to the respective exchange-control authorities. The popular explanation of this phenomenon, repeated daily in the dailies all over the world, is that "payments made to foreigners exceed payments received from foreigners." If this supposed explanation is then to be supported or illustrated by statistical data, it becomes necessary to arrange the accounting balance of payments in such a way that it shows a *surplus* for the United States corresponding to the alleged deficit of the rest of the world in its transactions with the United States. Thus, the balance-of-payments theory dictates what accounting balance of payments the statistical data must show and, by appropriate juggling, are in fact made to show.

In the different historical situation of the late 1950's and early 1960's several countries found themselves faced with an excess supply of dollars. At pegged exchange rates their monetary authorities had to absorb these dollars, and some of the abundant dollar reserves were converted into gold, causing the U.S. gold reserve to decline. This evidently was the symptom of a *deficit* in the U.S. balance of payments and, of course, the statistical data had to show it. Yet, if the accounting balance of payments were arranged the way it was in the early 1950's, it would show a surplus. Hence, to accommodate the theoretical explanation of the changed situation, rearrangements of the international accounts were called for. Alas, the new arrangements applied to the records of the early 1950's transformed the previously reported surpluses into deficits. In the conflict between economic history and economic theory, history had to yield.

The various rearrangements of the accounts have by no means been unreasonable. Suspicious laymen, possibly frowning at such "statistical tricks," may be reassured that no fraud is involved here. (Of course, those "experts" who had contended in the early 1950's that the dollar shortage was due to a "chronic surplus" of the balance of payments of the United States are now greatly embarrassed—or ought to be.) The innocent "sleight of hand" by which a surplus in the balance for a given year can be transformed into a deficit for the same year requires a switch of some items from the offsets to the balance. Items in the capital accounts are most suited for the purpose. In the early reports of the balance of payments for 1951, all or most capital movements were regarded as offsets to a surplus balance, on the theory that the surplus on current account had an independent existence and the capital movements from the United

States were merely "compensating" for this surplus. (That this was very poor theory was said at the time by several critics of the myth about the "chronic dollar shortage" who knew that most of the surplus on current account was *caused*, rather than *compensated for*, by the grants and loans which the United States made to other countries.) A more correct understanding would have come to just about the contrary conclusion, namely, that the unilateral and capital transfers from this country to the rest of the world constituted a deficit balance of gifts and capital movements and that this deficit was largely, but not fully, compensated for by a surplus on current account. This classical theory, however—that the balance of goods and services can be the *balancing* factor, the offset, just as well as the factor *to-be-balanced* by offsetting international transactions—will probably never be illustrated by an appropriate arrangement of balance-of-payments statistics, since there is no way of disentangling really autonomous items from equilibrating or balancing ones. In any case, the arrangement of the early international accounts, designed to show a surplus in the United States transactions, was certainly misleading and inconsistent with good theory.

Precisely how the accounts for 1951 were "adjusted" in order to show a large surplus at first but a deficit afterwards will be explained later. At this point we are satisfied with the object lesson that the accounts *can* be juggled and *have* been juggled, and that innocent consumers of historical statistics and economic history have been taken in by the mysterious numbers game. Let us see whether the experts have reformed and are now able to present more "objective" and consistent findings; let us examine what has been reported about the United States balance of payments for the years 1959 and 1960.

THE U.S. BALANCE OF PAYMENTS IN 1959 AND 1960

The choice of the years 1959 and 1960 was influenced only by the fact that these are the most recent ones on which most of the national and international agencies have reported more than preliminary estimates. Both years have shown abundant supplies of dollars in the world markets and considerable outflows of monetary gold from the United States. But particular accounts and "sub-balances" were sufficiently different in the two years to call for different interpretations of the "balance of payments." Almost all reporting agencies had realized by now that two or more interpretations were possible, desirable, or necessary and, accordingly, they came up with new adjectives by which to modify and specify the misleadingly simple words "balance of payments."

The numerical differences in some of these better-identified balances over the two consecutive years are such that it is no longer possible to

TABLE VII-3   *Reports on the U.S. Balance of Payments for 1959 and 1960*

Phrase used	Source	Year publ.	Surplus (+) or deficit (−) (Millions of dollars) 1959	1960
"Net balance on recorded transactions"	1	1961	−4609	−2760
"Net payments position"	1	1961	−3826	−3800
"Excess of receipts or payments (−)"	2	1961	−4425	−3184
"Total net receipts or payments (−)" ["balanced by changes in holdings of gold and convertible currencies by U.S. monetary authorities and changes in liquid liabilities"]	2	1961	−3897	−3832
"Overall balance on current and long-term capital account"	3	1961	−4165	−1165
"Total balance on current, long- and short-term capital account"	3	1961	−3825	−3835
"Hard-core balance"	4	1961	−4520	−1703
"U.S. payments balance"	4	1961	−3826	−3836
"Surplus or deficit (−) on account of identified current and long-term capital transactions"	5	1961	−4348	−1872
"Over-all surplus or deficit"	5	1961	−3423	−3675
"Basic balance, deficit (−)"	6	1961	−4300	−1900
"Overall balance, deficit (−)"	6	1961	−3900	−3800
"Nation's net deficit abroad"	7	1961		−3900
"Balance on basic accounts"	8	1962	−4300	−1900
"Over-all balance (deficit −)"	8	1962	−3700	−3900
"Balance on recorded transactions" ["net receipts or net payment (−)"]	8	1962	−4271	−3281
"Overall balance"	9	1962		−3925
"Changes in holdings of gold and convertible currencies by U.S. monetary authorities and changes in U.S. liquid liabilities to foreign and international monetary authorities"	9	1962		−3564
"Basic balance"	10	1961	−4600	−1300
"Exchange-market balance"	10	1961	−2700	−3700
"Basic balance"	11	1961		− 717
"Official settlements"	11	1961		−3963
"Basic balance"	12	1962	−3900	−1300
"Official settlements"	12	1962	−2400	−4000
"Total basic balance"	13	1963	−4700	−1800
"Total deficit"	13	1963	−3743	−3881

NOTES: a. The figures for 1959 are exclusive of the incremental subscription to the International Monetary Fund in the amount of $1,375 million.

b. Some of the figures with rounded hundred million dollars were given in the original as billion [milliard] dollars with only one decimal place.

SOURCES:

1. Federal Reserve Bank of St. Louis, *Monthly Review,* Vol. 43, March 1961, p. 5.

2. U.S. Department of Commerce, *Survey of Current Business*, Vol. 41, June 1961, p. 10.
3. Bank for International Settlements, *Thirty-First Annual Report*, Basle, 1961, p. 112.
4. Commission on Money and Credit, *Money and Credit: Their Influence on Jobs, Prices, and Growth*, Englewood Cliffs, N.J., 1961, p. 215.
5. International Monetary Fund, *Annual Report for the Fiscal Year Ended April 30, 1961*, Washington, 1961, pp. 77, 81.
6. Statement of Douglas Dillon, Secretary of the Treasury, in *International Payments Imbalances and Need for Strengthening International Financial Arrangements*, Hearings of the Subcommittee on International Exchange and Payments of the Joint Economic Committee of Congress, Washington, June 1961, p. 29.
7. Federal Reserve Bank of St. Louis, *Monthly Review*, Vol. 43, October 1961, p. 10.
8. *Economic Report of the President, With the Annual Report of the Council of Economic Advisers*, Washington, January 1962, p. 149.
9. U.S. Department of Commerce, *Survey of Current Business*, Vol. 42, June 1962, p. 14.
10. Walter R. Gardner, "An Exchange-Market Analysis of the U.S. Balance of Payments," *International Monetary Fund Staff Papers*, Vol. VIII, May 1961, p. 197.
11. Robert Triffin, "The Presentation of U.S. Balance of Payments Statistics" (Table 3, "Impact of Basic Balance and Open-Market Capital upon Official Settlements"). Mimeographed paper, presented to the American Statistical Association, New York, December 1961.
12. Robert Triffin, "The Presentation of U.S. Balance of Payments Statistics: General Comments," American Statistical Association, *1961 Proceedings of the Business and Economic Statistics Section*, Washington, D.C., 1962, p. 56.
13. Joint Economic Committee, *The United States Balance of Payments in 1968*, Materials presented by the Brookings Institution to the Joint Economic Committee, Congress of the United States, 88th Congress, 1st Session, Washington, 1963, pp. 6, 10.

tabulate the reported figures in the order of their magnitudes. To list them in such an order for one year would show no order whatever for the other year. Thus we follow the simple device of listing first the official reports of various national and international agencies approximately in the order in which they were published, and then the computations of two private experts; at the end we add a report which appeared just when this essay was being sent to the printer.

The range within which the reported balances vary is much narrower than it was for the 1951 balances—perhaps because not nine or ten but only one or two years had passed since 1959 and 1960—and all of the balances are U.S. deficits; none is a surplus. For 1959 the reported deficits range from $2,400 million to $4,609 million, and for 1960 from $717 million to $4,000 million. These discrepancies are typically not between different reporting agencies but rather between differently computed and differently designated balances reported by the same agency or interpreter. (In one instance the interpreter—Triffin—changed the "basic balance" from $717 to $1,300 in a second version of the same paper. This change of mind will be explained later in this essay.)

The remarkable variations in reported balances for 1951 have been explained here by the application of later methods of interpretation to the earlier data. If we try, conversely, to apply some of the earlier methods of interpretation to the later years, we obtain almost equally drastic discrepancies. For example, the United Nations *World Economic Report* had used two slightly different arrangements of U.S. accounts for 1951, one in the 1951-52 volume, another in the 1953-54 volume (both included as Sources 2 and 3, respectively, in Table VII-2 above). If we use these same two arrangements to determine the later balances, we find that the first method gives us a U.S. deficit for 1959 in an amount of $804 million and a U.S. surplus for 1960 in an amount of $1,080 million; whereas the second method gives us surpluses for both years, $411 million for 1959 and $3,124 million in 1960.[10] Let us recall that such surpluses were once designated as "Deficits of the World with the United States." Thus, by the (now discredited) theory of the "world dollar shortage" and the statistical techniques employed in measuring it, there would have still been dollar shortage, due to surpluses in the United States balance of payments, both in 1959 and in 1960. Indeed, by one of the statistical arrangements, the U.S. surplus in 1960 would have been reported as $3,124 million—in blatant contrast to the frightening deficits, up to $3,963 million, reported for the same year.

[10] These figures are the result of the following procedures:

	1959	1960
	(Millions of dollars)	
Method used in the 1951-52 volume (publ. 1953)		
Balance on goods and services	+2146	+5590
Unilateral transfers, private	− 575	− 628
U.S. capital, net, private, direct and other, long-term and short-term	−2375	−3882
Balance	− 804	+1080
Method used in the 1953-54 volume (publ. 1955)		
Balance on goods and services	+2146	+5590
military transfers under grants, incl. in goods	+1974	+1765
military expenditures, incl. in services	−3109	−3048
Balance on goods and services excl. military items	+3281	+6873
Private remittances	− 575	− 628
Private net long-term capital, direct investment and portfolio	−2298	−2544
Government net long-term capital	+ 3	− 577
Balance	+ 411	+3124

For the methods used see United Nations, *World Economic Report 1951-52,* New York, 1953, p. 87, and *World Economic Report 1953-54,* New York, 1955, p. 111. For the data see U.S. Department of Commerce, *Survey of Current Business,* Vol. 41, Washington, June 1961, p. 12, and Vol. 42, Washington, June 1962, p. 16.

The same test could be made with similar results by using other techniques originally applied to the data of earlier years. It would be most tempting to do so with the interpretations then used by the International Monetary Fund, leading to a U.S. surplus offset by "Compensatory Official Finance." But the I.M.F. has itself discarded the use of these terms: "In order to diminish the area of subjective judgment as far as possible, the analyses in this Yearbook omit entirely the general headings 'surplus or deficit' and 'compensatory financing.'"[11] Thus, even if it were possible to apply the subjective judgment which the I.M.F. analysts might have used in recent years regarding borderline items, it would not be fair to show just how high the resulting U.S. surplus would have been for 1960 on the basis of the reasoning of earlier years.

These hypothetical 1960 surpluses should no more reassure the worriers about the present international position of the United States than the surpluses once computed for the early 1950's should have alarmed those who then refused to worry about the world situation. The only significance of the contradictory findings lies in pointing once more to their insignificance for the purposes for which they were originally presented.

JUGGLING THE ITEMS BETWEEN BALANCE AND OFFSETS

It is high time now to go on to the task of reconciling the divergent "findings." This task may be less dramatic and less entertaining than the mere exhibition of the divergencies, but it must be done if we want to understand this "mysterious numbers game." The mystery consists in acts of juggling some of the items of the complete accounting statement between a pair of boxes, called by alternative pairs of terms, such as balance and offsets, balance and compensatory finance, balance and financing items, balance and balancing items, balance and corresponding changes (in international assets and liabilities), or items above the line and below the line.

In order to save space, we may show how the large surplus of the 1951 balance can be reduced, step by step, by deducting from it another account and still another account—that is, by switching further groups of entries from the offsets to the balance, from below the line to above the line—until the balance approaches zero, becomes negative, and ends up as a fat deficit. The single steps need not be in the order in which they are taken in the following illustration. By changing the order in which accounts are moved above the line, and therefore deducted from the balance, one can obtain additional "net payments balances"; the number of possible combinations is greater than we wish to face.

[11] International Monetary Fund, *Balance of Payments Yearbook*, Vol. 5, 1952-53, Washington, 1954, p. ii.

We begin with the exports and imports of goods and services, and state that the U.S. balance of goods and services in 1951 showed a surplus of +5,191 million.

The rest of the world had to find "finance" for this. But since the foreign nations did not have to pay for U.S. military exports under grants and for other military items, one may deduct these amounts, i.e., 1,470 million

and say that the balance of goods and services exclusive of military items was only +3,721 million,

for which the world had to pay. But the U.S. provided the world with dollars through private remittances and pension payments abroad in an amount of 457 million,

so that the balance in need of settlement was only +3,264 million.

Of course, this settlement was not difficult since the U.S. Government in that year made non-military grants to foreign governments to the extent of 3,035 million,

leaving the remaining surplus in the balance of goods, services, and unilateral transfers in an amount of +229 million,

to be taken care of in one way or another. Since private U.S. capital on long term (in the form of direct and portfolio investment) moved abroad in a net amount of 965 million,

the world received really more dollars than it needed; that is, the U.S. had in fact a negative balance, a deficit, to wit, of −736 million.

The U.S. Government also made some long-term loans (in excess of repayments received on previous loans) and thus lent on long-term net 153 million,

so that the balance of goods, services, unilateral transfers, and U.S. long-term capital movements was really −889 million.

But one might also take account of the movements of private U.S. short-term capital, in an amount of 103 million

and thus change the balance to −992 million,

or perhaps also of U.S. Government short-term capital movements, which in that year reached a net amount of only 3 million,

bringing the balance to −995 million.

Let us stop here and be satisfied with the feat accomplished: in seven steps a surplus of $5,191 million was transformed into a deficit of $995 million. The accounts still left in the box labeled "Offsets" (or any of the synonyms) are chiefly foreign long-term capital, foreign short-term capital (which means U.S. liquid liabilities), monetary gold, and errors and omissions. Some of these items were taken from this box and thrown into the other, the "Balance," when the 1959 and 1960 statements were concocted.

To see the kinds of combinations that are possible with different categories of capital movements, we have to examine the customary breakdown made in the official statistics. The major distinctions used to be between U.S. and foreign capital, private and official, and long-term and short-term. These distinctions have proved to be insufficient; for example, it may be important to distinguish between private bank and private non-bank capital transactions; between government loans in dollars and those in local currencies; between portfolio investment in private securities and in government securities. Different treatment of these sub-categories is partly responsible for different findings regarding the relevant balance. For example, some balance-of-payments accountants treat all U.S. Government short-term capital transactions as part of the balance, others as offsets; others treat the dollar transactions as part of the balance but the local-currency transactions as offsets. Some of the accountants treat all movements of foreign short-term capital as offsets, others switch movements of foreign private non-bank capital into the balance, others switch bank capital transactions as well.

One item that had its traditional place below the line has in recent years been moved up above the line: "errors and omissions." This promotion was in some cases linked with the grant of a nobler title: "unrecorded transactions." With this new name it could be made clear that "unrecorded transactions" may well require settlement in the form of official monetary movements and should therefore be part of the balance rather than an offset to the balance. The occasion for this promotion arose when "errors and omissions" in the U.S. balance of payments changed from +783 million dollars in 1959 to −648 million in 1960, or in the provisional statements even to −1,040 million. There was no question that such an enormous change from one year to the next could no longer be treated as a merely statistical adjustment, but that it represented a large sum of unidentified transactions, probably capital movements,[12] on a par with those recorded under one of the accepted headings and assigned a role on the debit side of the payments balance.[13]

[12] Capital movements included in "errors and omissions" need not be clandestine operations by speculators and wary financiers, but may in no small measure be foreign-trade credits by suppliers of goods or prepayments by their customers. Movements of such "trade capital" are unrecorded, and there will be changes in "errors and omissions" whenever changes occur in the time intervals between shipment of goods and payment for them. These leads and lags may be highly significant, and it is interesting to calculate the effect which a two-week shortening of the lag of payments for imports, and an equal two-week lengthening of the lag of payments for exports, may have upon "errors and omissions." See Bent Hansen, *Foreign Trade Credits and Exchange Reserves* (Amsterdam: North-Holland Publ. Comp., 1961).

[13] There were some earlier precedents for the new placement of errors and omissions. For example, *Economic Report of the President, January 1954*, included (p. 219) a tabulation of the U.S. Balance of Payments in which errors and omissions were above

With all these complications it also became clear that not all items in the balance had the same chance of continuing long into the future in their present order of magnitude. If 1½ or 2 billion dollars in short-term funds were taken out of the country, probably in reaction to interest rate differentials or to fears of an imminent devaluation, chances are that such a flow would be reversed rather than continued. Other sub-balances, however—say, movements of merchandise, affected by such things as relative incomes, costs, and prices—have a somewhat greater chance of continuance. In consideration of these differences, the analysts found it expedient to construct at least two different payments balances and to call the one which they considered less flexible or more stubborn the "basic" or "hard-core" balance, in contrast to the more inclusive one, which includes some rather ephemeral items and is therefore more flexible and for which they chose the unimaginative, nondescriptive and vulgar name "overall balance" or "over-all balance" (depending upon the dictionary they use).

DISTINCTIONS WITHOUT MUCH DIFFERENCE

To illustrate the arbitrariness with which particular items are assigned either to the balance of payments or to the offsets (compensatory finance), I present the following imaginary brothers-case and its treatment by balance-of-payments accountants.

Two rich brothers, Peter and Paul, each own a million dollars' worth of U.S. Government securities. Peter lives in New York, Paul in Zürich. Under the influence of interest differentials, devaluation rumors about the dollar and up-valuation rumors about the German mark, both decide to sell their U.S. assets and buy German bonds. The dollar proceeds are credited to their accounts—one a domestic, the other a foreigner's deposit —at a New York bank; then both Paul and Peter sell their dollars to a German bank in Frankfurt, which credits the DM accounts of the two brothers and sells the dollars to the Deutsche Bundesbank. The latter thereby acquires additional dollar balances with the Federal Reserve Bank of New York, which it proceeds to invest in U.S. Government securities. The brothers eventually buy German bonds.

There is an initial question regarding Paul's sale of the U.S. securities and resulting acquisition of the bank balance in New York: this might be treated as an outflow of foreign long-term capital and an inflow of foreign short-term capital. We can avoid this complication by assuming that what he sold were Treasury bills, treated as short-term capital, so that this

---

the line (see above, Table VII-2, item 7). Likewise, the *Survey of Current Business* in the Balance of Payments Supplement of 1958 contained (pp. 18–19) a summary of seasonally adjusted quarterly figures in which the errors and omissions were listed with the balance rather than among the offsets.

liquidation would not require any change in the U.S. position. Deferring for the moment the purchase of the German bonds, we may focus now on the bank transactions, on the transfer of the New York bank balances—one million dollars of a domestic depositor and another million dollars of a foreign depositor—to a foreign central bank.

Peter has exported "U.S. short-term capital, private" (line No. 36 of the Commerce Department tabulation of March 1961), Paul has exported "Foreign short-term capital, private" (i.e., he has reduced "Other U.S. short-term liabilities," line No. 45), and the German central bank has imported into the United States "Foreign short-term capital, official" (i.e., it has increased "U.S. short-term liabilities to foreign banks and official institutions," line No. 44). The accounting for these transactions will depend on whether (A) all short-term capital movements are treated as offsets to the balance of payments, or (B) U.S. short-term capital movements are treated as part of the balance, while foreign short-term capital movements are treated as offsets, or (C) all private capital movements are treated as part of the balance, and only foreign official capital movements are treated as offsets. Since we have a debit entry of $1 million in line No. 36, another debit entry of $1 million in line No. 45, and a credit entry of $2 million in line No. 44, Method A, with all three items among the offsets, does not affect the balance of payments at all; Method B, with No. 36 in the balance and No. 44 and No. 45 among the offsets, creates a deficit of $1 million; and Method C, with No. 36 and No. 45 in the balance and only No. 44 among the offsets, creates a deficit of $2 million.

The last act in the play plotted in our illustration centers around the use of the German marks acquired for the purchase of German bonds. Only Peter's investment will count for any further change in the U.S. balance inasmuch as the conversion of his mark balance into long-term securities shifts U.S. short-term capital into U.S. long-term portfolio capital (line No. 35 of the Commerce Department tabulation of 1961).[14] If Method (A) has been used for the movement of bank balances, the switch into bonds now results in a $1 million deficit; if Methods (B) or (C) have been used, the switch from short into long causes no further change in the U.S. balance of payments.

Whether one of the three methods is "correct" and the others are "incorrect" can be said only after it is decided just what questions are to be answered with the help of the balance-of-payments statistic, how the situation of the time and place influences various effects attributable to

[14] As a matter of fact, this transaction, executed abroad by a foreign bank, is likely to escape the notice of our official eyes and ears: the U.S. Commerce Department receives no reports from individuals and none from foreign banks. See Walther Lederer, "Measuring the Balance of Payments," American Statistical Association, *1961 Proceedings of the Business and Economic Statistics Section*, Washington, 1962, p. 43.

the transactions involved, and what theories are considered the most relevant and applicable ones in the particular situation.

Contrast all this with the glib talk of most people about the state of or change in the balance of payments, or with the daily repeated definition offered by the Associated Press in its news reports. The contrast between expert jargon and commonsense comprehension was well expressed in the following passage by Walter R. Gardner:

> Financial writers in the press taking their cue from the government publications, are prone to speak of the balance of payments deficit as a simple case of the United States spending abroad more than it receives. They explain that the out-payments have exceeded the in-payments. And the man in the street nods his head. He knows what that is. But does he know how completely arbitrary and inconsistent is the concept of payments that must be used to arrive by this route at the official measure of the U.S. deficit? Let me give some examples. If a foreigner buys a U.S. product, his payment is, of course, recorded as such, but if he buys a U.S. security from a holder in the United States, the payment may or may not be so recorded. It all depends on what security he buys. If he buys the bond of a private company, the transaction is recognized as a payment, but not if he buys its short-term note. In the latter case, his payment is not a payment. If a U.S. resident buys a short-term note abroad, however, his payment is recognized as such. So also is his purchase of a foreign Treasury bond. But the foreigner's payment for a U.S. Treasury bond is not a payment even though his purchase of any other type of bond is. Similarly, the U.S. resident's acquisition of a deposit abroad is recorded as a payment; but the foreigner's acquisition of a deposit in the United States is not. It is obvious that this payments language is not what the man in the street thinks it is.[15]

MODERN PRESENTATIONS AND DEBATES

My agreement with Gardner's critical attitude does not extend to all of his positive and normative propositions. For he believes that there can be a "correct" presentation showing a balance which explains the past or current situation in the foreign-exchange market. Indeed he gives to this balance the name "exchange-market balance," and to its offsets the name "compensatory financing." I once tried to expound why it is not possible to give a statistical measure for what I called the "market balance of payments."[16] The main point is that we never know, except in an abstract model on the basis of purely hypothetical assumptions, which transactions are autonomous and which are compensatory.

Gardner wants to bring together

[15] Walter R. Gardner, "An Exchange-Market Analysis of the U.S. Balance of Payments," *International Monetary Fund Staff Papers*, Vol. VIII (May 1961), p. 195.
[16] See my article quoted in footnote 1, at the beginning of this essay.

the miscellany of merchandise, service, and capital transactions undertaken because of the profit to be made or because of political or other ends that are sought for reasons of their own. If this great aggregate of what might be termed autonomous transactions does not balance out, the exchange rate of the country will be pushed up or down, and the authorities must supply whatever compensatory financing is required to keep the rate from moving outside the support points. Thus we have autonomous transactions above the line matched by compensatory financing below the line. The compensatory financing may take the form of a movement of reserves, or a drawing on the International Monetary Fund, or the use of ad hoc loans or other financing for the purpose. It is only as we draw a line of this sort and group above it the autonomous transactions, and group below it the compensatory financing that comes into play only because the autonomous transactions fail to balance, that *we see what it is that is pushing the country's international exchange rate up or down and creating an exchange-market problem.*[17]

Alas, this we cannot see. We can see only what Gardner (or his deputy) has decided to put above the line and what below the line; that is, we can see which items he has *judged* to be "autonomous" and which "compensatory," but this judgment is based on his interpretation, his analysis, his theory. He presents an improved table and believes that "Each category of that table is designed to facilitate analysis." [18] But, contrary to Gardner's belief, each category and its placement in the table is the *result* of analysis. Someone else's analysis may lead to different categories and different placements in the table, even if he were trying to use his table for the same purposes that Gardner did.

One of the things which Gardner dislikes in the Commerce Department's treatment is the place of advance repayments of government loans when earlier repayment was decided upon in consideration of the balance-of-payments situation of the countries concerned. Loans by the United States to foreign governments are now generally treated—now, not ten years ago—as part of the balance of payments, indeed as part of the "basic balance" because such loans are considered a "political necessity." If the United States receives repayments of such loans, the amounts repaid are deducted—in the tabulation by the Commerce Department—from the new loans granted, so that only the excess of new loans over repayments appears in the balance. Gardner objects to this. If a repayment is made in advance of the agreed maturity because the debtor country has a "surplus" and the United States a "deficit" in the balance of payments, Gardner wants to show the repayment as a "compensatory financing" item.[19] There is nothing wrong with either treatment; it is a matter of taste. But con-

[17] Gardner, *op. cit.*, p. 196. (Emphasis supplied here.)
[18] *Ibid.*, p. 202.
[19] *Ibid.*, pp. 202-203.

sistent adherence to Gardner's procedure would call for many analogous switches, and some rather odd ones, too. Assume, for example, that the United States had first intended to make certain loans to foreign governments but then, in view of its balance-of-payments difficulties, decided to defer making these loans. Consistency with Gardnerian philosophy would require the postponement to be shown as "compensatory financing"; in other words, the intended loans would have to be entered in the balance of payments, and the postponements among the offsets. Incidentally, the inclusion of potential transactions which did not materialize because the balance-of-payments situation was too precarious is a theoretical device in good standing—James Meade proposed it [20]—but its actual use in historical statistics is not yet regarded as legitimate.

Not everything in this respect is a matter of taste; some issues are fundamental from a theoretical point of view. The terminological choice of "autonomous" and "compensatory" to characterize particular items carries an implication, or at least a connotation, of cause and effect, and this can be highly misleading. Assume—an assumption very close to the historical events of the late 1940's—that the United States made a loan to a country in dire balance-of-payments difficulties, intending to alleviate these difficulties; thanks to the loan, that country purchased from the United States imports which it otherwise could not have afforded. Gardnerian treatment would regard the loan as "compensatory finance" and the imports as "autonomous" items. In fact, however (or rather in a more appropriate interpretation of the facts), the loan caused the flow of goods: the imports were "compensatory," a consequence of the loan. Only in an exceptional case would this be otherwise: if the recipient country bowed fully to stern "balance-of-payments discipline" and did not allow the relief in its reserve position to affect either its credit policies or its import policies. The reserve position of this country would in this case be strengthened without any effects upon the country's trade balance. This is possible, but unlikely. Yet only in this case—where the loan did not affect the current balance ("basic balance")—would we be permitted to call the loan "compensatory" and the flows of goods "autonomous."

The statistical presentation proposed by Gardner uses a tripartite arrangement of the main accounts: (1) a "basic balance," consisting of "market goods and services," "direct investment," and "noncommercial transactions"; (2) an "open-market capital" balance, consisting of all private capital movements (U.S. and foreign, long-term and short-term) except direct investment, and of "net errors"; (3) the sum of the two, the "exchange-market balance," which is then offset by "compensatory financing." The innovation lies in the "open-market capital" balance, which

[20] James E. Meade, *The Balance of Payments* (London: Oxford University Press, 1951), p. 15.

contains items that others place in the basic balance as well as items that others (including the Commerce Department) place among the offsets. Gardner's criterion for the assignment of items to "open-market capital" movements is that these items "can easily shift from market to market." [21] This statistical arrangement is interesting and helpful for some purposes but not for others.

Robert Triffin adopts this innovation in his newest presentations of balance-of-payments statistics,[22] but he judiciously avoids the terms "autonomous" and "compensatory" and calls the offsets simply "official settlements." Apart from his preference for eliminating the minus signs in front of all figures for capital exports (by treating them as positive changes in the nation's stock of foreign assets [23]), his main proposal is for the preparation of a variety of tables for a variety of purposes. There is great merit in this, because it makes it clear that for different purposes different tabulations are needed. The trouble is that he proposes relatively fixed criteria for allocations to "basic balance" and "official settlements"; there is insufficient realization of, or at least insufficient emphasis on, the impossibility of obtaining reliable and permanently relevant statistical counterparts for the theoretically important economic concepts. How much is always left to the judgment of the individual interpreter is well illustrated by Triffin's change of mind regarding the "basic balance" for 1960. In the version presented in December 1961 he had computed a deficit of $717 million. He then removed from the current account an item of $228 million relating to a revaluation of foreign long-term investments in the United States, and from "basic capital exports" an item of $366 million relating to a revaluation of U.S. private investments abroad; he switched these items to "open-market capital exports." As a result, the deficit on the "basic balance" increased to $1,300 million.[24]

One highly appropriate objective in Triffin's presentation is the reconciliation of data derived from different sources and, especially, the reconciliation between flows and stocks. The statistics of transactions within a period and of asset-and-liability positions at the beginning and end of the period ought to tally, and Triffin wants tabulations that permit

[21] Ibid., p. 198. —Incidentally, it may be worth noting that, in the language of our Peter-and-Paul story above, Gardner uses Method C, calling for a negative entry in the "open-market capital" balance (and therefore in the "exchange-market balance") as Peter and Paul move their funds abroad.

[22] Robert Triffin, "The Presentation of U.S. Balance of Payments Statistics," American Statistical Association, 1961 Proceedings of the Business and Economic Statistics Section, Washington, 1962, pp. 51-57.

[23] Triffin believes that the statistics without all these minus signs would be "less misleading . . . to the layman." The layman, I am afraid, has no business using such highly technical statistics.

[24] I am indebted to Walther Lederer for figuring out just what Triffin had done to raise the deficit in the second version of his paper by almost $600 million.

cross-checking of the different sets of data. The analyses of changes in positions should relate both to the nation's total assets and liabilities and to those sub-totals which are regarded as official reserves, gross and net.

Walther Lederer, the man in charge of all the compilations and estimates that underlie the U.S. balance-of-payments statistics,[25] is fully aware of the basic issues and problems:

> The definition of surplus or deficit is a matter of analysis, and analysis may vary with the purpose for which it is made. Different types of analysis are, of course, desirable, and it is the obligation of the compilers to provide the data—as far as possible—to meet the various analytical requirements.[26]

In the arrangement he uses to present the balance-of-payments statistics, he attempts to meet chiefly one practical purpose, namely, "to measure the changes in our capability to defend the exchange value of the dollar." [27] He ought to stress that this implies his own theories about what factors are essential to this "capability" and what developments affect it favorably or adversely; and he ought to concede that others may entertain different theories. But he makes it quite clear, evidently in reply to Gardner, that his own arrangement of data "looks at past developments as they affect the future, not whether past developments have or have not exerted any pressure on the exchange value of the currency." [28] Rightly convinced that no statistical arrangement of historical data can lay open causal relationships, he repudiates any such intentions and argues that his own separation of "transactions by which changes in liquidity are measured" from "all other transactions" does "not indicate causal relationship." [29] To which he might have added, however, that the term "liquidity" is by no means unambiguous and that the concept of "change in liquidity" presupposes again some causal relationships—though perhaps the interrelations are not quite so inaccessible as those which others try to illuminate by the factitious numbers presented as "the" balance of payments.

THE SENSE OF IT ALL

After all the "debunking" that I have done in this essay, the reader has a right to ask for a statement of what is left of the elaborate attempts to present a true statistical picture of the balance of payments.

Definitely "out," relegated to the scrap heap, is the notion that there is such a thing as *"the"* balance of payments. Even if full and accurate

[25] Lederer is Chief of the Balance of Payments Division of the U.S. Department of Commerce.
[26] Walther Lederer, *op. cit.*, p. 44.
[27] *Ibid.*, p. 45.
[28] *Ibid.*
[29] *Ibid.*

information were available about each and every transaction, "the" balance would always be an arbitrary number. There are *many* ways of entering the many items into the various accounts, of organizing the accounts, of interpreting the resulting figures; and there is *no* way of arranging the data so that they can tell a true story of the causal interrelations.

It would not be fair, however, to conclude that all balance-of-payments accountants, certified or self-appointed, have been completely wrong in what they have attempted to do. There must be some sense in this mysterious numbers game; to deny it would seem presumptuous. Perhaps, after clarifying what cannot be done with balance-of-payments statistics, we can come to a less negative conclusion and show just what the sense of it all may be. In this attempt we may succeed best by restating just why the two most widely sought purposes of the accounting cannot be attained—to explain what has happened in the foreign-exchange market and, alternatively, to measure the changes in the international "liquidity" of the country concerned.

To consider the first of these purposes, assume for a moment that the monetary authorities do not intervene, either by controls and restrictions or by purchases and sales of gold or foreign exchange; in other words, assume that exchange rates are freely flexible. It is immediately clear that in this case no arrangement of the accounts can show us "what it is that is pushing the country's international exchange rate up or down"—to use Gardner's phrase. An increase in the demand for foreign goods or foreign securities will drive the prices of foreign moneys up until the amounts of foreign moneys supplied are equal to those demanded. (This, incidentally, need not imply that the equal amounts will always be larger than before; for, if the elasticity of supply for some reasons should be negative, an increase in demand for foreign moneys would result in smaller amounts supplied and demanded at increased prices.) Conversely, an increase in the supply of foreign goods and securities will push down the prices of foreign moneys until the amounts supplied and demanded are equal. (In this case the amounts are almost certain to be larger than before.) But the international accounts will merely show that the current balance, the balance of unilateral payments, and the balance of capital movements add up to zero.

In these circumstances it is not possible to see which imports have pushed up the prices of foreign money and which exports have been made only because the prices of foreign money were pushed up. Indeed, the foreign goods the demand for which reduced the exchange value of domestic money may not have been imported at all. For, needless to say, any particular increment to aggregate demand may push prices up to a level where it cannot stay in the running. Imagine an American demand arising for British steel at a time when the pound sterling is quoted at

$2.80. This demand may push the sterling rate up to $2.90, but at this rate it may no longer pay to import British steel. In this case, the potential imports that have driven up the sterling and pushed down the dollar have never become reality, and of course have never entered the balance of payments.

Under a system of pegged exchange rates, every new demand for imports would prevail and the imports would actually materialize. Let us stipulate some assumptions, the reasons for which will be explained later. Assume (1) that the dollar is not a reserve currency held by foreign monetary authorities, (2) that no country would ever consider assisting the United States in defending the value of the dollar, and (3) that the United States authorities hold pound sterling and gold as foreign reserve. Increased imports, in this case, would be paid for with sterling or gold out of the U.S. official reserve. If nothing else had changed, the loss of gold or foreign exchange could without any doubt be attributed to the recorded increase in imports. The sale of sterling or gold by the U.S. authorities would be clearly accommodating, clearly in response to the increased demand for imports, clearly designed to prevent the sterling rate from rising. It is in this case, and only in this case, that it would make sense to have all international transactions except the changes in the gold and sterling holdings of the U.S. monetary authorities put above the line as "explanation" of these changes in the official reserve. One would know, not *why* the reserves changed, but *which* foreign purchases and sales have brought about the change. This kind of balance of payments—all payments and receipts except the sales and purchases by the monetary authorities—would show which changes in payments and receipts have caused the official reserve to change—cheers, Walter Gardner!—and, at the same time, it would "measure the changes in our capability to defend the exchange value of the dollar"—cheers, Walther Lederer!

Now we drop the three stipulations. We allow the official reserves of the United States to change for reasons other than just sales and purchases of gold and foreign exchange (e.g., a foreign central bank lends its currency to the Federal Reserve Bank of New York). We allow some long-term capital transactions to be made or postponed with the intent of defending the exchange value of the dollar (e.g., a foreign government repays prematurely a debt to the U.S. Government, or a foreign government agrees to a deferment of a payment promised by the U.S. Government). And we allow the dollar to become a reserve currency so that foreign central banks are willing to accumulate dollar balances (e.g., some foreign authorities purchase dollar balances either because they are eager to hold more—"dollar shortage"—or because they are reluctantly prepared to hold more—"dollar glut"). As soon as we allow any of these things to happen, all neatness goes out of the accounting statements and none of the stated objectives can be attained. There can no longer be an arrangement of accounts that unambiguously "explains" the past events in the exchange market—sorry, Walter Gardner!—nor an arrangement that unambiguously "measures" the future capability of defending the dollar—sorry, Walther Lederer!

The complexities of a world with mutual central-bank aid, induced advancements and postponements of intergovernmental payments, and eager or reluctant accumulations of reserve-currency holdings make it impossible for us to take any arrangement of the balance of payments either as a causal explanation of the official gold and exchange transactions or as a "measure" of the change in the nation's "international liquidity" or "future capability to defend the exchange value of its currency." As regards the latter, there is no agreement on just what constitutes an increase or decrease in liquidity, and there is no doubt that liquidity can be affected by things other than the transactions included in the balance of payments.

My critical position concerning attempts to measure changes in "liquidity" is by no means unique. Most critics, though, attack not the attempts but the particular methods chosen. Some of the comments, made perhaps in a spirit of fun, may promote misunderstandings. Take the following:

> . . . If the U.S. concept of the net balance were applied to a family, the family's "total payments" would include not only its current expenses, but its expenditure on houses, stocks and bonds, and other long-term assets. And not merely its receipts from income, but any receipts from long-term borrowing to finance the purchase of these assets, would be deducted from the "total payments." Thus, a family whose only transaction consisted of buying a house for cash would have a deficit equal to the price of the house; one which financed the purchase wholly by a mortgage would have no deficit.[30]

The sarcasm involved in this analogy may make people forget the difference between a "cash position" and an "assets and liabilities position." It should be clear that the family paying cash for the new house would have vastly deteriorated its cash position, whereas the family obtaining a mortgage would have done so precisely in order to avoid the deterioration of its cash position. It would be quite misleading to argue that one should not be interested in one's cash position.

A strong argument, however, can be made in favor of another purpose of balance-of-payments accounting, once held in considerable regard but recently overshadowed by the more ambitious endeavors. This pur-

[30] *The United States Balance of Payments in 1968.* Materials presented by the Brookings Institution to the Joint Economic Committee, Congress of the United States, 88th Congress, 1st Session (Washington: 1963), p. 4.

pose could be served more successfully by a particular arrangement of the accounts, even in a world with all the complexities mentioned or alluded to. This would be an arrangement bringing out the changes in foreign assets and liabilities. It would involve a comparison of the balance on current account (including military transactions) and unilateral transactions with the balance of capital movements (private as well as official, long-term as well as short-term), gold flows, and unrecorded transactions. Such an arrangement would be relatively unambiguous, apart from "fuzzy loans," i.e., loans the repayment of which is so doubtful that they cannot be regarded as assets. The danger of a balance of payments arranged to measure changes in foreign assets and liabilities is that the layman might think that the balance was *causing* the changes in indebtedness. (Perhaps every such tabulation should be accompanied by a warning to the reader that no causal connections can be inferred from the accounts.) Such an arrangement would exclude the possibility that anybody would take this balance either for an explanation of the situation in the foreign-exchange market or for a measure of the change in the country's liquidity position. Since we cannot expect, despite all criticism, that these other objectives of balance-of-payments accounting will be abandoned, the addition of an arrangement showing the changes in indebtedness will at least, by overwhelming the public with a proliferation of balances, reduce the probability that any one of them will be regarded as the "true" balance.

■ PART TWO ■
The Effects of Devaluation

INTRODUCTION TO PART TWO

The two essays included here are not the only ones relevant to the topic to which Part Two is devoted. Chapters I and II of Part One are equally relevant. Where the devaluation of a currency is a correction of a disequilibrium-rate of exchange in the hope of restoring equilibrium in the market-balance of payments, the pertinence of the analysis offered in the first two chapters of Part One will be obvious. That analysis, of course, followed the "elasticities-approach"; that is, it rested on potential movements of relative prices. The two following essays deal with the apparent alternatives, the elasticities-approach and the income-absorption-approach, and they attempt to adjudicate conflicting claims of superiority for analyzing the effects of devaluation.

Devaluation may affect the balance of trade in several ways, of which the terms-of-trade effect is only one. That this one was found to deserve a separate essay is not explained by its relative importance but rather by its inherent theoretical difficulties. The concepts and their logical interrelations are quite involved and not easy to disentangle.

Some writers are in the habit of using the terms (currency) devaluation and depreciation interchangeably. This is unfortunate because we need both terms to describe two different notions. Devaluation is an act of government, whereas depreciation is the effect of market forces. Where exchange rates are freely flexible, depreciation will occur when the supply of foreign currencies falls or the demand for them increases. Or, where foreign-exchange restrictions are designed to maintain a disequilibrium-rate of exchange, overvaluing the currency of the country concerned, depreciation may become manifest on a "black market." The effects of devaluation, that is, of the official increase in the rates at which the monetary authorities buy and sell foreign currencies, will be different according to the proportion of foreign transactions that have been settled at black-market rates rather than at official rates. The analysis of devaluation in the two following chapters will proceed on the assumption of pegged exchange rates without foreign-exchange restrictions, so that depreciation does not precede devaluation, and devaluation represents an explicit adjustment of the peg, an increase in the official buying and selling prices for foreign currencies without any rationing or discretionary controls.

PREVIEW OF THE CHAPTERS

Chapter VIII, "Relative Prices and Aggregate Spending in the Analysis of Devaluation," after recognizing the shortcomings of the relative-prices approach, examines the aggregate-spending approach and comes to the conclusion that the latter is not a superior alternative of the former: the two are truly complementary. The disparaged "elasticities" are in fact necessary, though often tacit, assumptions behind some of the presumably independent variables in the income-absorption model.

Chapter IX, "The Terms-of-Trade Effects of Devaluation upon Real Income and the Balance of Trade," deals first with the old question whether devaluation will necessarily or most likely lead to a deterioration of the devaluing country's commodity terms of trade, but then argues that this question is of rather limited relevance for real income as well as for the trade balance, because the reallocation of productive resources which is associated with presumably "adverse" changes in the relative prices of exports and imports may be instrumental in promoting increases in real income and/or improvements in the trade position. A significant by-product of the analysis is the development of the concept of "real intake," which is a needed supplement to the well-known concepts of "real output" and "real income."

MAJOR THEMES

Among the themes deserving major emphasis is the conclusion that an analysis of devaluation is deficient if it fails to be specific about its assumptions concerning monetary policy. The effects of devaluation upon income and upon trade cannot be stated unless it is known how the monetary authorities will act and react in certain situations. Will they keep the domestic credit portfolio constant? will they offset or will they reinforce the effects of inflows and outflows of foreign reserves? will they keep constant the total reserves of commercial banks or the total money supply? will they increase domestic credit in order to stabilize the representative short-term interest rate? will they reduce the money supply in order to stabilize the price level? Without specification an analysis is impossible. Many writers fail to specify what they assume, and sometimes the unspecified (tacit) assumptions they use in different parts of their analysis are inconsistent with one another. And incidentally, some assumptions, even explicit ones, are inconsistent with the objective of devaluation, the removal or reduction of over-spending and of the consequent excess demand for foreign exchange.

Other themes worthy of repetition are those about the benefits from deteriorated terms of trade—when the more favorable terms of trade promote bad allocation and poor utilization of resources—and about the common practice of hiding under the term Y, or "income," several quite different magnitudes, such as real domestic output, real intake, and real income, although these may change by different degrees and even in different directions, especially when changes in the valuations of foreign assets and foreign debts are involved. These themes are not easy to grasp, and repeated reading of the particular sections in Chapter IX may be required before they can be fully absorbed—or rejected.

EARLIER VERSIONS AND RECORD OF CHANGES

Chapter VIII: "Relative Prices and Aggregate Spending in the Analysis of Devaluation."
Written in 1954.
Published in the *American Economic Review,* Vol. LXV (June 1955), pp. 255-278.
Japanese translation in *Chosa Geppo,* Vol. 44 (October 1955), pp. 60-74. Italian translation in Fabrizio Onida, ed., *Problemi di teoria monetaria internazionale* (Milano: Etas Kompass, 1971), Ch. 2, pp. 85-114.

CHANGES: Practically no changes from the original article; perhaps six or seven words were transposed, replaced, or inserted in the text, and an addition was made in footnote 32.

Chapter IX: "The Terms-of-Trade Effects of Devaluation upon Real Income and the Balance of Trade."
Written in 1955-1956.
Published in *Kyklos,* Vol. IX (1956), pp. 417-452.
Reproduced in Kenneth E. Boulding *et al., Segments of the Economy, 1956* (Cleveland: Allen, 1957), pp. 232-285.

CHANGES: Reproduced without changes, except for four words.

VIII

Relative Prices and Aggregate Spending in the Analysis of Devaluation

A. Deficiencies of the Relative-Prices Approach: *Given and un-changed cost conditions; Given and unchanged incomes* ▪ B. Alexander's Aggregate-Spending Approach: *The fundamental equation; Devaluation effects on income and spending; The idle-resources effect; The terms-of-trade effect; The income effects combined; Direct effects on absorption; The cash-balance effect; The income-redistribution effect; The money-illusion effect; Other direct absorption effects* ▪ C. Some Consequences of Neglecting Relative Prices: *The resource-reallocation effect; Sub-stitution effects; The terms-of-trade effect amended* ▪ D. Rea-soning from Definitional Equations: *Income and output, money terms and real terms; Trade balance in foreign or in domestic money; Causal versus ex post relations; Reversing the direction of causation* ▪ E. Implicit Shifts of Emphasis: *The role of gold and exchange reserves; The role of credit creation; Assumptions about the supply of money* ▪ F. Comparing the Two Ap-proaches: *Given and unchanged parameters; Foreign supply and demand conditions; Price elasticities in the spending approach; Conclusion*

Two approaches to the question of the effects of devaluation have been presented as alternatives, and one of them has been treated as inferior, if not absolutely inappropriate.[1] The purpose of this essay is to examine the supposedly superior approach and to give a comparative evaluation of both.

[1] S. S. Alexander, "Effects of a Devaluation on a Trade Balance," *International Monetary Fund Staff Papers*, Vol. II (April 1952), pp. 263-278.

The problem is how to analyze the probable effectiveness of a de-valuation undertaken to remove or reduce an existing excess demand for foreign exchange without the use of direct controls, when money incomes have been stable, and when no autonomous capital movements take place either before or after the devaluation. These restricting conditions serve to present the problem in splendid isolation from certain very realistic conditions—such as the presence of direct controls or of autonomous capital movements—from which abstraction must initially be made in a clean analysis.

We are not concerned here with the question whether devaluation is the "most appropriate" policy under given circumstances, or under what circumstances devaluation would be "more appropriate" than other policies. Our question is merely this: what is the best way of finding out whether devaluation will reduce the trade deficit, or what per cent of devaluation would eliminate a given trade deficit, or what size of a deficit would be eliminated by a given per cent of devaluation?

I refer to the two ways of analyzing the problem as the *relative-prices* approach and the *aggregate-spending* approach. Alexander called them the "elasticities approach" and the "income-absorption approach." [2] There are other possible names: the "supply-and-demand approach" and the "income-and-outlay approach"; or, with an allusion to doctrinal history, the "Marshallian approach" and the "Keynesian approach" to the problem.

A. Deficiencies of the relative-prices approach

The most widely used version of the relative-prices approach works with supply and demand curves for foreign exchange. The positions and shapes of these curves, and thus their elasticities at various points, are "deduced" from the supply and demand for exports and from the supply and demand for imports; and all these, in turn, are "deduced" from the supply conditions and demand conditions in all foreign and domestic markets, because every supply in foreign trade is an excess supply over domestic demand, and every demand in foreign trade is an excess demand over domestic supply.

Now the question has been raised whether one can take the shape of any of these curves as given; whether one can regard their elasticities as predetermined and use them in the solution of foreign-exchange problems. I had thought it useful to assume so,[3] and so had many others.

[2] Alexander obviously means price elasticities by the first name, since income elasticity of demand plays a main part in the second approach.

[3] Fritz Machlup, "The Theory of Foreign Exchanges," *Economica*, Vol. VI (Nov. 1939), pp. 375-397, and Vol. VII (Feb. 1940), pp. 23-49. Reprinted in *Readings in the Theory of International Trade* (Philadelphia, 1949), pp. 104-158; also as Chapter I of this volume.

Given and unchanged cost conditions

We said, for example, that the supply of exports would depend in part on "cost conditions"—as if cost conditions were something definite. But is this defensible? The cost of *one* product can be shown in a curve, other things being given and unchanged; but if other things change, the cost curve no longer stays put; if the production of many goods is to change at the same time, we cannot easily know what the cost curve for any one of them will do.[4]

In the production of a certain good, productive resources are needed; for the production of more of that good, more resources are needed. If not much is happening elsewhere, one may foretell at what prices additional resources may be available, and one may, on the basis of technological knowledge, foretell what the cost of additional output will be. But for the prices of additional resources it will make a great difference whether at the same time these resources are being released by other industries or are being demanded by them in increased amounts. It is possible that, when the production of a certain product rises, say in order to provide increased exports under the stimulus of a devaluation, the production of other goods may be cut and productive services released to the expanding export industry. But it is also possible that some other industries will increase their output under the stimulus of the same devaluation, and that they also will require more of the same productive factors; and if several industries simultaneously demand these factors, their prices will rise. Where then are our "given" cost conditions?

Given and unchanged incomes

A second argument against the relative-prices approach is the possibility of changes in incomes. The devaluation itself may have income effects: incomes may rise or fall as a result of the devaluation. But the supply and demand curves are drawn, of course, on the basis of a given buying power, a given income. Thus, these curves will not help much if we know that incomes must have changed; we have to know how income has changed and how the new curves look.

Even if we did not allow total money income to change (and we shall return to this point), there is still the possibility of significant changes in income distribution. After all, devaluation will raise the domestic prices of imported goods which may be important in the budgets of certain groups; this would alter the distribution of real income. But if income

---

[4] For an excellent exposition of the general problem of cost and supply curves, see Joan Robinson, "Rising Supply Price," *Economica*, Vol. VIII (February 1941), pp. 1-8. Reprinted in G. J. Stigler and K. E. Boulding, eds., *Readings in Price Theory* (Chicago, 1952), pp. 233-241.

distribution changes, demand is likely to change and again our curves may shift considerably.

That these arguments make it necessary to qualify and supplement the "simple" elasticity analysis had been clear to many.[5] But what Alexander suggests amounts to a repudiation of the relative-prices approach.[6] His arguments are persuasive and, with our confidence in the criticized approach shaken or destroyed, we are eager to examine the novel approach that is offered as a superior substitute.

B. ALEXANDER'S AGGREGATE-SPENDING APPROACH

The new approach to the problem of the effect of devaluation is the aggregate-spending approach, or "income-absorption" approach. While following Alexander's exposition, I shall slightly change the notations.

The fundamental equation

The *total income* of a nation can be divided or classified into *consumption* plus *investment* plus *government contribution* [7] plus *exports* minus *imports;* or

$$Y \equiv C + I + G + X - M.$$

This identity is used as the fundamental equation; it can be shortened by

[5] The income effects of devaluation have often been discussed. I wrote: "If depreciation through its effects upon the volume of exports or upon the balance or the terms of trade should raise or lower total income, it would probably also raise or lower the demand for imports. These income effects of depreciation may be negligible in the beginning, but in the course of time, as the 'multiplier mechanism' becomes operative, they may become strong enough substantially to weaken or reinforce the price effects of depreciation." "Elasticity Pessimism in International Trade," *Economia Internazionale,* Vol. III (February 1950), p. 11; reprinted as Chapter II of this volume. See also, J. J. Polak, "Discussion," *American Economic Review,* Papers and Proceedings, Vol. XLII (May 1952), pp. 180-181; A. C. Harberger, "Currency Depreciation, Income, and the Balance of Trade," *Journal of Political Economy,* Vol. LVIII (February 1950), pp. 47-60; T. Balogh and P. P. Streeten, "The Inappropriateness of Simple 'Elasticity' Concepts in the Analysis of International Trade," and "Exchange Rates and National Income," *Bulletin of the Oxford University Institute of Statistics,* Vol. XIII (March and April 1951), pp. 65-77, 101-108.

[6] ". . . the total elasticities appropriate for the analysis of the effects of a devaluation depend on the behavior of the whole economic system, and the statement that the effect of a devaluation depends on the elasticities boils down to the statement that it depends on how the economic system behaves." ". . . it is suggested that a more fruitful line of approach can be based on a concentration on the relationships of real expenditure to real income and on the relationships of both of these to the price levels, rather than on the more traditional supply and demand analysis." Alexander, *op. cit.,* pp. 264, 263.

Balogh and Streeten also rejected the "elasticities approach": ". . . we shall contend that this approach to the problem is erroneous" (*op. cit.,* p. 65). But they did not suggest an alternative one: "It is regrettable but inevitable that no single new method of analysis can be put into the place of the old approach" (*ibid.,* p. 66).

[7] This term was not included in Alexander's exposition.

merging the first three terms on the right side, that is by calling C plus I plus G by the name "absorption," [8] or A. (The expenditures of households and business and governments are the part of the national income that is being "absorbed.") The two remaining terms of the identity, X minus M, the difference between exports and imports, constitute the trade balance, signified by B. Thus, what we now have is that the *national income* is the sum of the *absorption* by the nation plus its *trade balance;* or

$$Y \equiv A + B.$$

It follows that the trade balance must always be the difference between income and absorption:

$$B \equiv Y - A.$$

The trade balance is negative when the nation absorbs more than its income. The trade balance can improve if income increases while absorption increases less or stays unchanged or falls; or if absorption decreases while income decreases less or stays unchanged.

Devaluation effects on income and spending

The question we now have to ask is to what extent devaluation can affect B, that is, the difference between income and absorption. Alexander breaks this down into three questions [9]: (1) How does devaluation affect income (Y)? (2) How does a change in income ($\triangle Y$) affect absorption (A)? (3) How does devaluation directly (that is, not via income) affect absorption (A)?

The change of the trade balance is the change in income minus the change in absorption; or

$$\triangle B \equiv \triangle Y - \triangle A.$$

The effect of devaluation upon income will show in $\triangle Y$; the effect of the change in income upon absorption, and the direct effect of devaluation upon absorption, will both show in $\triangle A$. In other words, there will be an income-induced change in A and a nonincome-induced, or directly effected, change in A. The direct effect of the devaluation upon absorption can be expressed by δA. The income-induced change in absorption can be expressed by $\alpha \triangle Y$, where α is the "marginal propensity to absorb income" (which of course will be the sum of the marginal propensities to consume, to invest, and to spend public funds).

The new symbols help to merge the devaluation effect upon income, $\triangle Y$, and the income effect upon absorption $\alpha \triangle Y$, into a single expression $(1 - \alpha) \triangle Y$, which stands for the nonabsorbed change in income. Thus,

$$\triangle B = (1 - \alpha) \triangle Y - \delta A.$$

Assume, for a moment, that income will increase as a result of de-

---

[8] This term was first used by K. E. Boulding, *Economic Analysis* (New York, rev. ed., 1948), pp. 402-428.

[9] Alexander, *Op. cit.,* p. 266.

valuation. This devaluation effect upon income and the consequent income effect upon absorption will improve the trade balance only if α is smaller than unity. But, while the marginal propensity to consume is usually smaller than unity, α, the combined marginal propensity to consume, invest, and spend publicly, may well be greater than unity. If so, $(1 - \alpha) \triangle Y$, the nonabsorbed change in income, will be negative and the trade balance will deteriorate, rather than improve, on this score. Only the direct effect on absorption can then still help matters.

Alexander states that the analysis on the basis of his model will hold in real terms as well as in money terms; he then proceeds in the belief that he talks about real income, real absorption, and real trade balance throughout.

Following the clue from the last equation, Alexander divides his subsequent discussion into two parts: the effects upon and via incomes— $(1 - \alpha) \triangle Y$—and the direct effects upon absorption—δA. He recognizes the following effects:

Effects upon and via Income [$(1 - \alpha) \Delta Y$]	Direct Effects on Absorption [δA]
	Cash-balance effect
Idle-resources effect	Income-redistribution effect
Terms-of-trade effect	Money-illusion effect
	Three other direct absorption effects

The idle-resources effect

If the devaluing country has idle resources, employment can be increased by additional consumption, investment, government expenditures, or exports. Since C and I (and tacitly, G) are assumed by Alexander to be functions of income, additional exports are the strategic factor; and additional exports are the very thing that one should expect to result from devaluation.

The increased value of foreign moneys in terms of domestic money stimulates the production of export goods; if idle resources are available, employment will increase in the export industries; as the recipients of the income increment spend it for consumption, further employment may be created in the consumers-goods industries. This process is the familiar operation of the "foreign trade multiplier." But while the multiplier, in the customary exposition, includes only induced consumption, Alexander's employment effect comprises induced spending of all kinds.

Alexander inclines to the belief that α is greater than unity, that $(1 - \alpha)$ therefore is negative, and consequently that the trade balance will become worse as a result of the income increase due to the idle-resources effect of the devaluation. If improving the trade balance is the policy objective, it would follow that the devaluing country must hope either that there will be no increase in its income and employment, or that the propensity to absorb income is less than unity—or at least that the other effects of devaluation will be in the right direction and stronger than the idle-resources effect.

The terms-of-trade effect

Alexander joins the majority of economists in the belief that de-valuation will deteriorate the terms of trade of the devaluing country. He thinks that this is so because "a country's exports are usually more specialized than its imports." [10]

If devaluation affects the terms of trade, the change in the terms of trade will affect national income and absorption. Alexander divides the terms-of-trade effects of devaluation on the balance of trade into an initial effect through price changes and a secondary effect through income-induced changes in absorption. He holds that "the normal result of a devaluation will be such deterioration of the terms of trade of the de-valuing country as to" cause an initial deterioration of its balance of payments equal to "the reduction of the country's real income associated with the deterioration of the terms of trade." [11] In other words, the initial effect will normally be an equal and simultaneous reduction (deteriora-tion) of the trade balance and of real national income. The secondary terms-of-trade effects of devaluation upon the balance of trade—the in-come-induced changes in spending—will depend on the marginal pro-pensity to absorb income. The income-induced changes in absorption may either reinforce or attenuate the initial terms-of-trade effect on the balance of trade, or may turn it in the opposite direction.

Alexander, having concluded that the *initial* terms-of-trade effects upon trade balance and upon real income are (normally) equal in direc-tion and in amount—he uses one symbol, t, for both—believes that he can find the ultimate terms-of-trade effect upon the trade balance by multiply-ing the initial effect by the marginal propensity not-to-absorb. Hence, the ultimate terms-of-trade effect upon the balance of trade would be $(1 - \alpha)t$, and thus could be positive (i.e., improving the balance) only if (since t is assumed to be negative) $1 - \alpha$ is negative, that is, if α is greater than unity.

The income effects combined

Alexander combines the two "income effects of devaluation" which he recognizes—the idle-resources effect and the terms-of-trade effect—in one expression equivalent to $(1 - \alpha) \triangle Y$. This presupposes that a

[10] *Ibid.*, p. 268.
[11] *Ibid.*, p. 269.

change in the terms of trade resulting from devaluation will affect the balance of trade only through the change in real income, and to an extent commensurate with it.

Either or both of the income effects of devaluation may be zero. The idle-resources effect on income—"presumably positive," according to Alexander—can be positive only if there are unemployed resources and if their employment is not obstructed by bottlenecks (lack of complementary factors or lack of finance). The terms-of-trade effect may be zero if devaluation does not change the terms of trade, or if the "initial" effects on the trade balance as well as the "secondary" effects through income-induced changes in spending are checked or counteracted by monetary policy.

Direct effects on absorption

Effects of devaluation upon the balance of trade which are not associated with changes in income but only with changes in the absorption of a given income, are called "direct effects on absorption." If there is no change in income, the trade balance can be increased only through a reduction in the domestic absorption of income, C, I, or G, and an equal increase in exports or reduction in imports. Such a switch from A to B, from domestic absorption to foreign-trade balance, can possibly be accomplished without transfer of productive resources or changes in production if the reduction in domestic absorption relates to imported goods or to exportable goods. Otherwise it will require a shift of production from goods and services hitherto used for C, I, or G to goods and services for X, or to goods and services substituted for M. This will involve not only adaptations in production plans but ordinarily also a transfer of productive resources between plants, firms, industries, and locations. The question is, what mechanisms are set in motion by devaluation to induce these adaptations and transfers, and what obstacles have to be overcome in the process?

A reduction in consumption and investment can, in general, lead to a reduction in employment and income just as easily as to an increase in the trade balance.[12] Whether the productive resources released from domestic C and I industries will remain idle or will be transferred to industries producing X and substitutes for M, will depend chiefly on how the economy responds to price incentives; this need not involve price reductions, because the release of the resources will have been preceded by an increase in prices of export goods and of substitutes for import goods. Moreover, the reduction in spending for C and I will have been offset by an increase in receipts for X. But the chief objective in Alexander's discussion of the "direct effects on absorption" is to examine

[12] *Ibid.*, p. 272.

whether and how devaluation may bring about the reduction in domestic spending.

The cash-balance effect

Devaluation raises the domestic prices of imports and of exports; and it will tend to raise the prices of import substitutes, of potential exports, and of intermediate goods required for their production. Thus, unless the monetary authorities restrict credit in order to force price reductions in other sectors of the economy, the price level will be somewhat increased as a result of the devaluation.

If the monetary authorities do not create more money than may be needed to purchase the foreign exchange forthcoming as a result of positive devaluation effects on the trade balance, the elevated price level will imply a reduction in the real value of total cash balances. Households and firms will attempt to build up their cash balances to the relative size they have found appropriate. They will try to do this by buying less and by selling assets and securities (debts).

Buying less in order to accumulate cash balances implies "a reduction in their real expenditures relative to their real incomes," [13] that is, a foregoing of consumption and investment. Selling assets and debt securities will depress their prices or, which is the same thing, increase interest rates. The offer of assets and debt securities at reduced prices would attract foreign buyers—which would greatly help matters—but we have excluded any autonomous capital movements from our analysis. With foreigners ruled out as buyers—because we wish to abstract from capital inflows in order to concentrate on the trade balance—and with banks ruled out as buyers—because we have excluded additional credit creation—there are only nonbank residents left as buyers, and they will overcome their liquidity preference only if the prices of securities are so attractive that it pays them to defer real investment, reduce consumption, and part with liquidity. The increased interest rates will have the effect of cutting down investment expenditures of business and consumption expenditures of households.

The income-redistribution effect

The lift in the price level that is associated with devaluation may also reduce aggregate spending from a given income by redistributing it from groups with higher to groups with lower marginal propensities to spend. Alexander mentions three kinds of shift of real income: from fixed-income recipients "to the rest of the economy," [14] from wage recipients to profit recipients, and from taxpayers to government.

[13] *Ibid.*, p. 271.
[14] *Ibid.*, p. 273.

A loss of real income which the recipients of fixed income suffer through increased prices will result in a reduction of aggregate absorption if the corresponding gain in real income accrues largely to people richer and thriftier than rentiers, fixed-salary workers, and pensioners—which is not unlikely.

A shift of real income away from wage earners will occur when wage goods are among those whose prices are raised through devaluation—which is rather common. If the shift of real income is toward profit recipients, their investment incentives may be increased by more than the consumption demand of the real-income losers is reduced. And if investment outlays increase accordingly, total absorption of income may be increased rather than reduced.

A shift from taxpayers to government would most effectively cut down aggregate spending where government expenditures are not dependent on tax revenues but are fixed in an inflexible budget not to be stepped up with a larger flow of tax receipts. Income-tax receipts would be increased where an income redistribution takes place in favor of richer people and tax rates are progressive. And income tax receipts would also be increased where total money income is allowed to increase in consequence of devaluation.[15]

The money-illusion effect

This is what Alexander has to say on the money-illusion effect:

> The money illusion may contribute a favorable effect to a devaluation if it actually leads people to pay more attention to money prices than to money incomes. If at higher prices people choose to buy and consume less *even though their money income has increased in proportion,* over and above what can be attributed to the cash balance effect, the result on the balance of payments will be favorable. But *rising money incomes and rising prices may actually operate in the opposite manner;* for example, annual savings may be calculated in money terms and may fail to rise in proportion to money incomes and prices.[16]

It should be noted that Alexander speaks here, in the italicized clauses, not of *higher* prices of foreign-trade-connected goods, but of *rising* prices and of money incomes rising in proportion.

Other direct absorption effects

Three other direct effects of devaluation upon absorption, and thus upon the trade balance, are mentioned by Alexander. One of them, which we may call the "price-expectations effect," may unfavorably affect the

---

[15] On the other hand, the revenues from specific import duties may be reduced rather than increased, and in many countries import duties are a significant portion of the budget.

[16] *Loc. cit.* Emphasis supplied.

trade balance by increasing absorption: people expecting prices to rise following the devaluation may rush out to increase their inventories.

The other two are favorable influences on the trade balance. What may be called the "high-cost-of-investment effect" consists in the discouragement which increased cost of imported investment goods may cause to investors. Investment that requires foreign equipment, to be imported at increased domestic prices, may be less attractive than it was before the devaluation and may be cut out altogether.[17]

The third effect generalizes the principle involved in the second effect to all kinds of imports: when certain goods, previously imported, become very expensive, some of the domestic buyers may give up buying these goods and may buy nothing instead. Alexander mentions this merely as a "theoretical possibility."

C. Some consequences of neglecting relative prices

My exposition of Alexander's analysis is, I hope, fair and accurate. In the first part of my critique I shall—without questioning the validity of the framework of the analysis or the merits of the procedure employed—point to some omissions and errors of reasoning which I believe can be attributed to Alexander's concentration on aggregate magnitudes and his neglect of relative prices. Although Alexander does not explicitly state that his enumeration of "income effects" and "direct absorption effects" is exhaustive, an impression is conveyed that, if not all, at least the more important ones have been covered. This, however, is not the case; we can find omissions in both categories.

The resource-reallocation effect

There are three ways in which an increase in real national income can be achieved: through fuller employment of the available productive resources; through their better utilization and more economic allocation; and through more favorable terms of trade. Only two of these possibilities are recognized in Alexander's analysis: changes in the volume of employment and in the terms of trade. Transfer of resources to different uses does play a considerable role in his analysis, but only in connection with the direct absorption effects of devaluation. That such transfer may change real national income is not mentioned and has evidently been overlooked.

In the long run, greater economy and efficiency in the use of resources have been the most important factors in the increase in the living standards of the nations. In the short run, changes in the volume of

---

[17] This seems to have been of considerable practical importance in several countries: Investment in imported labor-saving machinery, very profitable at predevaluation exchange rates, turned out to be too expensive relative to domestic labor once the exchange rates were corrected.

employment and in the terms of trade may overshadow the effects of changed resources-use upon real income; but there is no presumption for one or the other to be more important. All three kinds of changes may be effected by devaluation (and each of them may be positive or negative).

The "resource-reallocation effect" of devaluation may be especially significant when the "idle-resources effect" is negligible or zero; total employment may remain practically unchanged while the output produced may increase through a more economic or more efficient use of the resources employed. But it is also possible that both effects operate at the same time; more or fewer resources may be employed in a more or less economic way.

There are problems involved in measuring increases in real income when there are changes in the composition of output. Where the reallocation of resources implies a shift to "more valuable" products, with reductions in the output of "less valuable" products, the gain in real income can be measured only by means of a welfare index (based on market prices combined with other criteria). Even so, the principle that a reallocation of resources may increase the value of real output cannot reasonably be questioned. And where trade and production have been conducted on the basis of "unrealistic" exchange rates (overvaluing the currency) it is quite plausible that devaluation may effect a more economic use of resources with a consequent increase in real income.[18]

Substitution effects

The resource-reallocation effect has been named here as another income effect of devaluation, although in Alexander's analysis resource reallocation is treated only in connection with direct absorption effects. But all of the direct absorption effects discussed by Alexander have to do with aggregate spending, with changes in the outlay of money; if they "work" to reduce total absorption they do so owing to the failure of some income recipients to spend all of their receipts or to make all the money expenditures they would otherwise have made.[19] Perhaps the most im-

---

[18] Besides the more economic resource allocation achieved through changes in relative prices, there may be two incidental resource-economizing effects of devaluation in systems operating with direct controls: one is the saving of administrative cost by government and by business when devaluation permits some controls to be removed and others to be improved; the second is the improved efficiency under the pressure of revived competition as the industry quota arrangements implied in the bureaucratic allocation of foreign exchange and imported materials are dropped when devaluation reinstates prices in the function of resource allocation.

[19] For example, in connection with the third of the three "miscellaneous direct absorption effects" Alexander says that "when the domestic prices [of imported goods] rise, the domestic purchasers cut their expenditures on these goods but save or hoard the difference, rather than shift the expenditures to other goods." Op. cit., p. 274.

portant absorption effects are thereby disregarded: the effects of shifts in relative prices and the effects of price increases which reduce real absorption even if absorption in money terms should be unchanged or slightly increased. This reduction in real absorption may be additional to that induced by a reduction in real income, although the increased prices may reflect such a real-income reduction.

Assume, for example (in order to isolate the outcome examined here from any terms-of-trade effects), that devaluation leaves the terms of trade unchanged, lifting the domestic prices of exports and of imports by the same percentage. As imported goods are now relatively higher in price than domestic goods, substitution in consumers' plans seems inevitable; and as exportable goods are now relatively higher in price than domestic goods, substitution in producers' plans seems inevitable; transfers of productive resources will ensue. And the increased demand for import-substitutes together with the reduced supply of domestic goods from the production of which resources have been diverted cannot but cause relative price movements which are apt to reduce the real value of aggregate absorption even if total money expenditures should be somewhat higher than before.

This reduction in real absorption will be additional to that induced by a reduction in real income if some of the induced substitutions take the form of shifts between consumption and asset holding (or indebtedness) or between investment and liquidity. Let us not forget that an import surplus implies an increase in indebtedness or decrease in the holdings of securities or other liquid assets on the part of some who absorb (consume or invest). Changes in relative prices may affect the willingness of "absorbers" to run up their debts or run down their liquid asset holdings. Substitution effects may significantly influence the absorption of real income and the physical volumes of imports and exports; these are price-induced changes in absorption, not predicated on any given "propensity to absorb" or on any general price level increase.

In all four kinds of direct effects on absorption discussed by Alexander, price movements play some role. But Alexander relies little on changes in *relative* prices to bring about the required adaptations and transfers.[20] Most of the time he looks to increased or rising price *levels* to do the trick. No wonder that he is disappointed in the performance.

The terms-of-trade effect amended

The neglect of the substitution effects impairs some of Alexander's analysis of the terms-of-trade effect of devaluation. It can be shown—although only in a lengthier exposition than we can here afford—that Alexander is in error when he holds that the initial effect—before any

[20] Except in connection with the high-cost-of-investment effect.

income-induced changes in absorption take place—will "normally" be an equal and simultaneous reduction (deterioration) of the trade balance and of real national income. To be sure, these two reductions can be made equal by definition, but it would be a rather useless definition; otherwise there is nothing that would cause the initial changes in trade balance and real income to be normally equal in amount or even in direction.

The source of Alexander's error in reasoning about the terms-of-trade effect lies in the conceptual decision to treat all effects of devaluation either as effects upon and via income or as direct effects upon absorption. Since a change in the terms of trade will affect income, Alexander at once puts the terms-of-trade effect under the first heading, and fails to notice that a change in the terms of trade will also affect absorption directly, through relative-price effects.

A change in the terms of trade may be viewed as a change in the ratio of an index of export prices to an index of import prices. The effects of relative price changes are customarily (following Hicks) divided into simultaneous income effects and substitution effects. By assuming that a change in the terms of trade will "initially" affect only income but not absorption, Alexander loses sight of the substitution effects. Absorption will actually be affected through both the substitution effects and the income effects of the change in the terms of trade. Thus, Alexander's conclusion that the ultimate terms-of-trade effect upon the balance of trade would be $(1 - \alpha)t$, or equal to the income effect times the marginal propensity not-to-absorb, is wrong.[21]

D. Reasoning from definitional equations

The argument underlying the aggregate-spending approach has been developed from a "fundamental equation" which represents mere definitions. Such equations usually serve a useful purpose in aiding the organization of the analysis. But they may easily tempt an analyst into "implicit theorizing," illegitimately deducing causal relationships, and overlooking the shifting meanings of terms in different contexts. These temptations have not been successfully resisted in this instance.

Income and output, money terms and real terms

As Alexander interprets the fundamental equation (or identity), "real income . . . is equal to the output of goods and services," and the relationships expressed "hold, of course, both in real and in money terms."[22]

---

[21] A clear exposition of the rather complicated relationships involved requires considerably more space, particularly because some fundamental questions concerning the use of terms-of-trade analysis ought to be explored at the same time. I reserve these tasks for a separate essay. (See Chapter IX of this volume.)

[22] *Op. cit.*, p. 266.

While this makes good sense for a closed system, it does not for an open one, especially when the balance of trade plays a major role.

Even in a closed system there may be difficulties—due to problems of depreciation and depletion—in equating real income and output; but these difficulties can be defined away. In an open system where some output is produced for export, and imports contribute to consumption and domestic investment, output produced is not the same as real income. In order to relate output and income one would have to take account of changes in foreign assets and debts, as well as of unilateral transfers— items for which no provision is made in the equation. It is possible for employment, production, consumption, domestic investment, exports and imports, all to remain absolutely unchanged in physical terms, and for real national income nevertheless to be changed by some of the exports being sold at increased or reduced prices or given away free, or by some of the imports being bought at increased or reduced prices or received as gifts.

The conceptual difficulties implied in the possible deviations between changes in national product and national income [23] may have a significant bearing on the analysis of the effects of devaluation, especially in connection with changes in the terms of trade. What, for example, is the relevance of a "given" marginal propensity to absorb, when output and employment are affected one way, but income (with changes in foreign debts or assets) in another way? Will changes in absorption be induced by changes in employment and production or rather by changes in income that are partly due to changes in the foreign-exchange reserves?

The supposed equivalence between relationships in money and in real terms is sometimes troublesome, occasionally even meaningless. Alexander intends to "deal only with real quantities, not with money values." [24] But what is a "real" trade balance? When a country has to pay increased prices for its imports and buys a slightly reduced physical quantity of imports, what is the meaning of an improved "real" trade balance if at the same time the balance in money terms has deteriorated? Or should, perhaps, a trade balance in terms of money be translated into one in real terms by deflating the contracted foreign claims or debts by a price index? To treat exports and imports as "real quantities" makes sense; but can the difference between the two be meaningfully treated as a real (physical) quantity? [25] Can what is essentially an increase or decrease in

[23] More correctly, possible deviations between changes in the total production of goods and services and in the total amount of income earned by the members of the economy. We are not concerned here with the difference between national income and disposable income.

[24] Loc. cit.

[25] While horses and apples cannot be added, apples can be added to horses, but never subtracted from horses.

foreign claims or debts be regarded as anything but a money value, however deflated?

Trade balance in foreign or in domestic money

But this is not all. Even if the concept of a trade balance in real terms is given up, the fact remains that, as a result of devaluation, an import surplus may increase in terms of domestic money and decrease in terms of foreign money. Indeed, this is a rather probable outcome.[26] But the $\triangle B$ in the equation $\triangle B \equiv \triangle Y - \triangle A$ is expressed either as a domestic money value or as the "real" equivalent of a domestic money value. This $\triangle B$ may be negative, so that a negative B may become even more negative, while the trade balance in terms of foreign money actually improves.

If one realizes that the whole purpose of the analysis is to find out what will happen to the trade balance of a country resorting to devaluation because of a shortage of foreign currency, one may be quite disappointed about the wrong result obtained. But, serious though it may sound, the damage is easily repaired by dividing $B + \triangle B$ by the increased price of the foreign currency: the deterioration of the balance in terms of domestic money may then show an improvement in terms of foreign money. It remains true, however, that $\triangle Y - \triangle A$ will not directly give the right answer.

Causal versus ex post relations

The fundamental equation in the analysis, in the form $Y \equiv C + I + G + X - M$, is helpful in organizing an examination of the relationship among the components of aggregate spending and the foreign balance, but misleading if it is deemed to show causal (*ex ante*) rather than classificatory (*ex post*) relationships. For example, an increase in consumption expenditures may result in an increase in Y (if employment rises) or a decrease in I (if inventory is depleted) or a decrease in X (if exportable goods are domestically used) or an increase in M (if imports are purchased) or no real change at all (if prices of consumption goods rise); and there are many other more indirect possibilities and combinations— the study of which may be underemphasized by overconfident reliance on the "insight" afforded by the equation.

As a matter of fact, the equation gives very little insight into causal relationships. The merging of planned investment and unintentional inventory accumulation into one term, I, which in turn is part of A, is an example of an actually misleading "clue" suggested by the equation. Reduced consumption and reduced planned investment may sometimes

[26] See Machlup, "The Theory of Foreign Exchanges," *op. cit.*, pp. 375 ff. and *Readings*, pp. 114–122; also Chapter I of this volume, pp. 16–22.

be offset by increased unintended inventory accumulation (due to the unexpected decline in sales). This latter part of $\triangle A$ is inversely related to $\triangle Y$ as far as causal relationship is concerned; and, incidentally, the effects of devaluation upon planned inventory holdings may causally be more important than any positive relation between income and inventory investment.

The difference between causal and mere *ex post* relationships can perhaps be made clearer by asking for the meaning of the equation $\triangle Y \equiv \triangle A + \triangle B$. Obviously, if any two of these terms are given, the third can be calculated. But this is not to say that $\triangle B$ "depends" on $\triangle Y - \triangle A$ in any causal sense. To say this has no more merit than to say that $\triangle A$ "depends" on $\triangle Y - \triangle B$, or that $\triangle Y$ "depends" on $\triangle A + \triangle B$.

Yet the "income-absorption" approach does rest on such "dependence" if it proposes that an investigation of the effect of devaluation upon the trade balance should proceed by analyzing the "basic questions" of how devaluation affects both income and absorption.[27] With the same justification—or lack of justification—one might investigate the effect of devaluation upon national income by analyzing the "basic questions" of how devaluation affects both absorption and the trade balance. And an analogous procedure might be proposed for an investigation of the effects of devaluation upon consumption and investment. Such an analytical merry-go-round is entirely "in character" whenever definitional equations furnish the sole basis for inquiry into presumably causal relationships.

Reversing the direction of causation

The income-absorption approach of analyzing the effect of devaluation upon B assumes that causation goes this way: devaluation affects Y; Y affects A; devaluation affects A directly; the net changes of Y and A determine the change of B.

At one point, however, the question of a reversible process is openly raised: if devaluation affects A directly, cannot A affect Y? No doubt, it can. If absorption is reduced as a direct result of devaluation, this may cause unemployment, partly or fully offsetting a positive idle-resources effect (due to increased activity in export industries) or even resulting in a net decline in employment and output.

In the event and to the extent that the directly effected reduction in absorption causes a net decline in employment (instead of the desired transfer of resources), a sequence of secondary nonspending will cut down consumption and investment even further, depending on the propensity to absorb; and if the transfer of resources should still fail to take place, at least the purchase of imports will be reduced, with a definitely

[27] Alexander, *loc. cit.*

positive effect on the trade balance. Needless to say, no government would want to have the improvement of the trade balance take this form, but it is only fair to mention that it can happen. Analysts, however, may exclude this sequence of events by assuming that the government, pursuing a policy of full or high-level employment, will succeed in preventing a decline in employment.

E. Implicit shifts of emphasis

The income-absorption approach and the fundamental truism on which it rests may be helpful for the purpose of impressing the responsible leaders of the state as well as their economic advisers with the need "to recognize that, if the foreign balance is to be improved, the community as a whole must reduce its absorption of goods and services relative to its income." [28] At the same time the approach may be misleading in that it conceals the dependence of B (or of $Y - A$) on some key facts which can only be neglected at the risk of perilously obfuscating the policy problem.

The role of gold and exchange reserves

If no loans, investments, or repayments are received from abroad, there cannot be any negative B unless someone in the country is willing to give up foreign balances or other foreign assets. Ordinarily, the monetary authorities are the only willing sellers of foreign balances (or gold). If they do not sell, or have none to sell, the import surplus no longer exists; the real problem is not how to improve the trade balance, but whether to avoid its "automatic" improvement by the operation of "cruel" market forces—and how to make the unavoidable correction of the trade balance least painful or least harmful to the economy.

In a free market for foreign exchange—with no rate-pegging, rate-fixing, or rationing controls—there would surely evolve exchange rates at which all excess demand for imports is eliminated. One may ask *how*— by what forces and strains and stresses—this depreciation of the currency would succeed in balancing trade, but one cannot doubt that it would. A continuing import surplus, in the absence of autonomous capital imports, presupposes a policy of pegging the exchange rate by selling gold or foreign exchange; it disappears when that policy is discontinued.

The role of credit creation

If no loans, investments, or repayments are received from abroad, there cannot be any negative B unless someone in the country is using previously inactive domestic cash balances (which is not likely to go on for very long), or new currency is printed, or the banking system, with the

[28] *Ibid.,* p. 275.

active support of the monetary authorities, engages in a continuing expansion of its loans-and-securities portfolio. If this continuing supply of domestic funds is not explained, one cannot understand how "propensities to absorb" can ever lead to absorption in excess of income.

The continuing supply of new bank credit need not be a continuing net increase in the supply of money. When the monetary authorities sell foreign exchange from their reserves, the domestic money (bank deposits) that is paid for it is canceled. The expansion of the loans-and-securities portfolio of the banks merely re-creates the bank deposits canceled by the purchases of foreign balances from official reserves. To put it differently, the current credit expansion finances the current "excess absorption" by consumers and investors as well as the purchase of the foreign exchange that it requires.

Without continuing dishoarding or bank-credit expansion, the negative trade balance could not continue. Every day of excess imports would bring a further reduction in the money supply of the people and, inevitably, a decline in absorption. A persistent import surplus, in the absence of autonomous capital imports, presupposes a policy of enabling the banking system to expand credit; it disappears when that policy is discontinued.

The possibility of credit expansion, incidentally, besides being a prerequisite of the maintenance of a negative trade balance and of any deterioration of the trade balance, is also essential in other phases of the operation of Alexander's model. In particular, the working of the idle-resources effect may depend on it. While some increase in employment can usually be financed by hitherto inactive liquid funds, by and large it takes new bank money to do this job.[29]

Assumptions about the supply of money

Nothing can be said about the effects of a devaluation unless exact specifications are made regarding the supply of money and credit and the fiscal policy of the government. There seems to be a tendency in the "New Economics" tacitly to regard the supply of money as a dependent variable rather than as a policy variable. In the "very old economics,"

[29] Alexander's attempt to combine his two income effects of devaluation in one expression and to treat them alike suffers from the defect that the terms-of-trade effect on the trade balance does not operate solely via income, and moreover that "finance" is no prerequisite for it. An increase in real income produced by the idle-resources effect must be accompanied by an increase in money income and money flow; on the other hand, a change in real income produced by the terms-of-trade effect may be merely a matter of relative prices and need not be reflected in a change in money income and circulation. This difference, neglected by Alexander, may be significant and may even have its policy aspects, because inelasticity of the supply of money may be part of the monetary policy of a country, or a built-in feature of its currency system, and would largely inhibit the operation of the idle-resources effect.

where models of an unmanaged gold standard still had some applicability, the supply of money could be treated as a dependent variable. But when everybody has views on how the supply of money "ought" to be managed, and when in fact almost every government in the world does manage the supply of money, one may reasonably expect economic analysts to be explicit on this point and to state what happens under the various monetary policies which a government may choose to pursue.

On some occasions Alexander follows this good practice; for example, in discussing the cash-balance effect he first stipulates that "the money supply is inflexible." But in many places he fails to make such stipulations.[30] Indeed, he later returns to the cash-balance effect and calls it transitory because "the money supply may *respond* to the increased demand for cash balances." [31] As economists we should, I submit, make a clear distinction between a "response" explainable in economic terms (such as an increase in quantities of product supplied in consequence of increased effective demand reflected in higher prices and in greater profitability of an increased output) and a "response" explainable in political terms (such as an increase in the quantity of money—associated with increased government expenditures, reduced reserve requirements, increased open-market purchases by the central bank, etc.—either in consequence of political pressures or in anticipation of economic, social and political repercussions considered to be undesirable by the political powers). An economic response will be treated as a dependent variable; a political response should be treated as a policy variable and enumerated among the "special assumptions."

To assume tacitly, as is often done, that the money supply will "respond" to an increased demand for credit (to finance increased wage payments and increased foreign payments) may deprive an analysis, such as that of the effects of devaluation, of much of its meaning. To be sure, where the purpose of devaluation is to stimulate employment through the stimulation of exports, it will be the policy of the authorities to help supply the additional credits that are demanded. Even in this case the analyst should state what policy is assumed. But where the purpose of devaluation is to reduce or remove an excess demand for foreign money (that is, with regard to the external balance, an excess supply of domestic money), a policy of supplying the credit demanded to replace the excess demand that was squeezed out by the devaluation is not very consistent— even if it should be politically unavoidable.[32]

[30] *Op. cit.*, pp. 270, 273, although he speaks there repeatedly of "rising money incomes and rising prices."

[31] *Ibid.*, p. 274. Emphasis supplied.

[32] Even in this case a policy of devaluation may be adopted with the idea of taking advantage of lags and of gaining a breathing spell between devaluation and re-inflation. But it can hardly be repeated too often: If the chief purpose of devaluing a country's

F. COMPARING THE TWO APPROACHES

Given and unchanged parameters

The reason given for advancing the aggregate-spending approach was that its predecessor, the relative-prices approach, suffered from incurable deficiencies. The basic trouble of the latter is that it works with price elasticities which presumably are given and knowable, but actually are neither—and are even changed as a result of the very devaluation effects which they are supposed to determine.

The new approach assigns strategic importance to spending propensities. Since these spending propensities are supposed to determine the effects of devaluation upon the trade balance, the impression is created that α, the marginal propensity to absorb, is both given and knowable. Actually it is neither; indeed, we have every reason to believe that α is not stable over time and that it may change not only with the mood of the time but also momentarily according to the circumstances of the situation. Although called a "propensity" to absorb income, it contains both intentional and unintentional reactions, including unintended investment or disinvestment in inventories, which sometimes may offset the effects of intentional reactions; it comprises government expenditure (inclusive of public capital expenditure), which is not a function of income but an independent variable that can be administered in a direction opposite to that of changes in income; even in so far as it refers to private actions, it may be significantly influenced by monetary and fiscal policy; and, finally, it may be substantially changed as a result of the very devaluation the effects of which it supposedly determines.

Hence, what was said about the "elasticities approach," namely, that "the statement that the effect of a devaluation depends on the elasticities boils down to the statement that it depends on how the economic system behaves," [33] may with equal justification be said about the income-absorption relation. For, after all, the devaluation effects upon income and absorption, including the supposedly given "propensities to absorb," depend "on how the economic system behaves"—and, we may add, on how it is made to behave by monetary and fiscal policies.

From the point of view of stability over time it is hard to say which

---

currency is to remove or reduce a deficit in its balance of international payments, consistency implies a policy of monetary restraint. For, by and large, devaluation achieves its purpose by effectively reducing the foreign value of the domestic money supply and of the volume of domestic spending. A monetary policy which allows domestic spending to increase subsequently and regain its previous (presumably excessive) foreign value is clearly inconsistent with the purpose of the devaluation.

[33] *Op. cit.,* p. 264.

of the parameters are less reliable as indicators of the effects of devaluation on the trade balance—the price elasticities or the spending propensities. From the point of view of changeability in the very process the outcome of which they help determine, the spending propensities are probably less reliable than the price elasticities. And from the point of view of malleability through public policy, one probably should regard the price elasticities as the tougher factors to deal with, and the spending propensities more subject to the influence of (monetary and fiscal) policy —which means that in the last analysis not given propensities but chosen policies will determine the outcome.

Foreign supply and demand conditions

An explanation of the volume, composition, terms, and balance of trade between nations can hardly be regarded as fully convincing if it takes account of the conditions in only one of the nations concerned instead of considering all parties involved. The relative-prices approach attempts to satisfy this precept by including the supply and demand conditions in foreign markets among the determining factors. In particular the elasticities of foreign demand for the exports and of foreign supply of the imports of the devaluing country are assigned important roles.

The aggregate-spending approach makes no such provision, at least not explicitly. It attempts to deduce the devaluation effects on the trade balance solely from the effects upon national income and absorption in the devaluing country. Since the "resulting" change in the trade balance is necessarily also a change, by the same amount though with opposite sign, in the trade balance of the trading partner—perhaps the rest of the world —one wonders how this change is imposed, so to speak, on the latter, regardless of the magnitudes of their spending propensities, etc. If only the $\triangle Y$ and $\triangle A$ of the devaluing country were to determine the outcome, would this not imply that in the other countries changes in income and absorption would be "dictated" by a change in the trade balance, instead of the other way around?

Alexander's analysis is silent on this point. An enterprising builder of aggregative models might set out to construct a two-country model embodying the income-absorption relations based on the spending propensities in both countries affected by the change in foreign-exchange rates. But I am not convinced that this would be a worthwhile undertaking. It is probably more expedient to assume that "the foreign country" is the rest of the world, that the worldwide income and absorption effects of the devaluation of the one currency are so widely dispersed as to be negligible, and that therefore the elasticities of foreign demand and foreign supply are not sufficiently altered to lose their determining force on the outcome.[34] But this solution would obviously restore the elasticities approach to at least half its former role in the analysis of devaluation.

Price elasticities in the spending approach

As a matter of fact, this restoration of relative prices and price elasticities to a strategic position in the model is not left to its reconstruction by future renovators; price elasticities have been allowed to continue all along, though inconspicuously, to do their job under the new regime. Supposedly banished under the aggregate-spending approach, they have in fact played important roles in Alexander's analysis.

At some points the elasticities work behind the scene. For example, whether there can be an idle-resources effect of devaluation depends on whether the production and sale of export goods can be expanded, hence, on elasticities of domestic supply and of foreign demand; but this is not explicitly said. At other points the elasticities are clearly visible on the stage. For example, whether a direct devaluation-effect upon absorption will result in a transfer of resources or in unemployment depends on "how the economy responds to price incentives," [35] or on the "price differential between the foreign and the domestic markets" and on "the substitutability of domestic goods for imports in consumption, and of resources as between the production of domestic goods and exports." [36] At one point at least the role of price elasticities is dominant: in the terms-of-trade effect. For it is impossible to come to any conclusion concerning the effects of devaluation upon the terms of trade except on the basis of an examination of the relevant elasticities of supply and demand.

Alexander would probably deny none of this. For, although he regards aggregative analysis as "a more fruitful line of approach," to be adopted in lieu of "the more traditional supply and demand analysis," [37] he concedes that "supply and demand conditions, in the sense of partial elasticities, may be useful tools in this [income-absorption] analysis." [38] His objection is to discussions in terms of "total elasticities" and he believes that it is "total elasticities for which the conventional formulas alone are valid." [39]

[34] This suggestion was made by Michael Michaely, *Devaluation and Dual Markets under Inflation with Direct Controls,* a doctoral dissertation submitted to Johns Hopkins University, January 1955.

[35] See above p. 178.

[36] Alexander, *op. cit.*, pp. 270, 271.

[37] *Ibid.*, p. 263.

[38] *Ibid.*, p. 275.

[39] *Ibid.* These "formulas," as I have understood them, had no other purpose than to suggest qualitative (directional) relationships and quantitative possibilities. Alexander must have mistaken them for operational devices or for mere *ex post* relationships. If he means "*ex post* elasticities" when he says "total elasticities," he surely misunderstands most of those who have argued in terms of price elasticities. I, for one, have always had *ex ante* elasticities in mind.

Conclusion

The upshot of all this is that relative prices and elasticities were not really discarded in the analysis of devaluation effects; and that aggregate spending and propensities by themselves cannot possibly do the explanatory job that was assigned to them. Neither of the two "alternative" sets of tools can be spared; both are needed.

Alexander, I am afraid, has confused his readers by presenting the new approach as a substitute for the old. If clearly presented as complementary to the old, and properly amended, the new analysis can be helpful. The new tools fashioned by Alexander cannot replace the old tools of "conventional analysis"; but they can, after some substantial reshaping, increase the usefulness of the latter.

It is the habit of innovators to disparage the old ways of doing things; it is the duty of critics to appreciate the value of the new without depreciating the value of the old. In trying to pare down the exaggerated claims of the innovator they are sometimes overly critical of the new ideas. Lest I have erred in this direction, I should like to end by paying my respect to Alexander's innovating enterprise and to his contribution to the development of international-trade theory. A contribution it is, and an especially meritorious one where it gives scope to the roles of both aggregate spending and relative prices.

IX

The Terms-of-Trade Effects of Devaluation Upon Real Income and the Balance of Trade

Current Views of the Effects of Devaluation on the Terms of Trade ■ The Relevant Terms-of-Trade Concept ■ The Effects upon Income and Trade ■ Testing the "Equality Rule" ■ Income and Substitution Effects ■ Three Separate Effects on Income? ■ Illustration by Analogy ■ The Analogy Expanded ■ The Benefits from "Deteriorated Terms of Trade" ■ Real Output, Intake, and Income ■ Primary and Secondary Burden ■ Income and the Propensities to Spend ■ Appendix

Several questions concerning the effects of currency devaluation upon the terms of trade, the balance of trade, and real national income are still unsettled. In another essay I suggested that certain problems connected with the use of terms-of-trade analysis have to be explored before we can hope to clarify some of the controversial issues.[1]

CURRENT VIEWS OF THE EFFECTS OF DEVALUATION ON THE TERMS OF TRADE

There has been a remarkable change of opinion in recent years regarding the effects of devaluation on the terms of trade.

In 1945, Gottfried Haberler took it virtually for granted that devaluation would cause the terms of trade to deteriorate.[2]

[1] Fritz Machlup, "Relative Prices and Aggregate Spending in the Analysis of Devaluation," *American Economic Review*, Vol. xlv (June 1955), p. 268; reprinted as Chapter VIII of this volume.

[2] Gottfried Haberler, "The Choice of Exchange Rates after the War," *American Economic Review*, Vol. xxxv (June 1945), pp. 308, 317.

In 1947, Joan Robinson pointed out that devaluation could either improve or deteriorate the terms of trade; but since in general each country is more specialized in its production and exports than in its consumption and imports, and since with underemployment the domestic elasticity of supply of exports is likely to be high, a deterioration of the terms of trade could be avoided only in exceptional cases.[3]

In 1948, Frank D. Graham argued that relative prices of internationally traded goods would always revert to their relative opportunity costs and, therefore, devaluation would be most unlikely to have any effect on the terms of trade.[4]

In 1949, Thomas Balogh had no doubt that deterioration of the terms of trade would result from devaluation.[5]

In 1950, J. J. Polak and T. C. Chang attempted to show that devaluation could be "effective" only if it worsened the terms of trade.[6]

In 1950, Arnold C. Harberger presented several models, in one of which the terms of trade would not be affected by devaluation while in another they would deteriorate by the same percentage that the currency was devalued; in his "general model" the terms of trade would always be worsened except in (unlikely) cases of explosive instability.[7]

In 1951, Randall Hinshaw rejected the arguments and conclusions advanced by Joan Robinson and, on different lines, argued that in the short run, that is temporarily, devaluation might adversely affect the terms of trade because domestic prices of exports might be stickier than those of imports, whereas the long-run effects would be as likely to be favorable as adverse, though probably insignificant for small countries.[8]

In 1951, James Meade demonstrated that the terms of trade would more likely be deteriorated if export products and other products were highly substitutable in consumption or production, but that the terms would be improved if such substitutability were small.[9]

In 1952, Sidney Alexander reverted to the position that the "normal result" of a devaluation would be a deterioration of the terms of trade,

[3] Joan Robinson, "Beggar-My-Neighbour Remedies for Unemployment," in *Essays on the Theory of Employment*, 2nd ed. (Oxford: Blackwell, 1947); reprinted in *Readings in the Theory of International Trade* (Philadelphia: Blakiston, 1949), p. 400.

[4] Frank D. Graham, *The Theory of International Values* (Princeton: Princeton University Press, 1948), pp. 184-202, 274-283, esp. 297-300, and 343-345.

[5] T. Balogh, *The Dollar Crisis: Causes and Cure* (Oxford: Blackwell, 1949), pp. xv, xxii, 258.

[6] J. J. Polak and T. C. Chang, "Effect of Exchange Depreciation on a Country's Export Price Level," *International Monetary Fund Staff Papers*, Vol. i (1950), p. 49.

[7] Arnold C. Harberger, "Currency Depreciation, Income, and the Balance of Trade," *The Journal of Political Economy*, Vol. lviii (February 1950), pp. 56-57.

[8] Randall Hinshaw, "Currency Appreciation as an Anti-Inflationary Device," *Quarterly Journal of Economics*, Vol. 64 (November 1951), pp. 456-457.

[9] James E. Meade, *The Balance of Payments* (London: Oxford University Press, 1951), pp. 232-250.

and he proceeded to make rather curious generalizations about the impact upon the trade balance and national income.[10]

In 1952, Haberler returned with a concise argument showing that it is only in the abnormal and unlikely case in which devaluation leads to a deterioration of the trade balance that the terms of trade would necessarily be deteriorated; but in the normal case the terms of trade would be either improved or deteriorated, with no presumption either way.[11]

In 1954, Paul Streeten held that in the most probable conditions the terms of trade would be likely to turn against the devaluing country; and that they must do so whenever devaluation was taking the place of quantitative restrictions.[12]

In 1954, Kurt Rothschild argued that devaluation would lead in most cases to a deterioration of the terms of trade because price policies of oligopolistic exporters in the devaluing country would be quite different from those pursued by traders in the other countries.[13]

In 1954, Warren L. Smith confirmed the conclusion that devaluation might either improve or worsen the terms of trade, but he added that under full employment supply elasticities would be low and improved terms of trade could be expected.[14]

In 1955, George Kleiner held that only the supply elasticities of exports would be low under full employment whereas those of imports would be high, so that the terms of trade would more likely deteriorate as a result of devaluation.[15]

Also in 1955, E. Victor Morgan held that devaluation could normally be expected to effect a correction of an adverse trade balance, but that this result would of necessity involve a deterioration of the terms of trade.[16]

This brief outline of expert opinion since 1945, intended only as a

[10] Sidney S. Alexander, "Effects of a Devaluation on a Trade Balance," *International Monetary Fund Staff Papers*, Vol. II (April 1952), pp. 268-269.

[11] Gottfried Haberler, "Currency Depreciation and the Terms of Trade," in *Wirtschaftliche Entwicklung und soziale Ordnung*, ed. Lagler-Messner (Wien: Herold, 1952), pp. 149, 153-155.

[12] Paul Streeten, "Elasticity Optimism and Pessimism in International Trade," *Economia Internazionale*, Vol. III (1954), p. 5.

[13] Kurt Rothschild, "Zur Frage der Auswirkungen einer Abwertung auf die internationalen Austauschbedingungen," *Weltwirtschaftliches Archiv*, Vol. 72 (1954); in English translation "The Effects of Devaluation on the Terms of Trade," *International Economic Papers*, No. 5 (London and New York: Macmillan, 1955), pp. 174-177.

[14] Warren L. Smith, "Effects of Exchange Rate Adjustments on the Standard of Living," *American Economic Review*, Vol. XLIV (December 1954), pp. 808, 822. Mrs. Robinson had qualified her conclusions to take account of the possibility of low supply elasticities.

[15] George Kleiner, "Exchange Rate Adjustments and Living Standards: Comment," *American Economic Review*, Vol. XLV (December 1955), p. 944.

[16] E. Victor Morgan, "The Theory of Flexible Exchange Rates," *American Economic Review*, Vol. XLV (June 1955), pp. 285, 290.

representative sample, omits many more participants in the debate than it includes. Some critics of speculative theory may wonder why we do not just have a good look at the "actual facts." Empirical evidence, however, does not settle the issue. All our statistical data are the result of everything changing at the same time, so that none of the theories is disconfirmed, and none confirmed.[17]

Why, one should ask, has so much attention been given to the question? If it has been more than an intellectual exercise, the purpose was obviously to examine the probable effect of devaluation—*via* the changes in the terms of trade—upon national income. It would be interesting to know the possible reduction in national income, due to adverse changes in the terms of trade, first, because we want to know the social cost of devaluation and, secondly, because the income change might alter the effects of devaluation upon the trade balance.

The main theses of the present paper will be that

(1) even if we knew in what direction and by how much the net terms of trade will change as a result of a devaluation, this would not be enough for us to infer by how much and in what direction these changes in the terms of trade will affect real national income; and

(2) even if we knew in what direction and by how much real national income will change as a result of a change in the terms of trade due to devaluation, this would not be enough for us to infer by how much and in what direction these changes in real income will affect the balance of trade, even if the marginal propensities to spend and to import could be assumed to be known.

THE RELEVANT TERMS-OF-TRADE CONCEPT

There are different concepts of "terms of trade." Indeed the family of these concepts is rather large; its chief members are the "gross barter terms of trade," the "net" or "commodity terms of trade," the "single factor terms of trade," and the "double factor terms of trade"; some of the poorer relatives, such as the "real-cost terms of trade," the "utility terms of trade," and the "income terms of trade" are seldom met.[18] Which member of this family is referred to in our discussions?

[17] The most careful empirical inquiry into this subject is Charles P. Kindleberger's *The Terms of Trade* (New York: Wiley, 1956). Kindleberger reminds his readers of "the limitations of the analysis in these respects. Partial conclusions are handicapped by the impossibility of completely isolating the forces under analysis; conclusions of general validity are limited because of the impossibility of assigning lasting weights to the various forces" (p. 9).

[18] For definitions and explanations see Jacob Viner, *Studies in the Theory of International Trade* (New York: Harper, 1937), pp. 558-570; Gottfried Haberler, *The Theory of International Trade* (London: Hodge, 1936), pp. 159-169; D. H. Robertson, *Utility and All That* (London: Allen & Unwin, 1952), pp. 174-181; R. G. D. Allen and J. E. Ely, eds., *International Trade Statistics* (New York: Wiley, 1953), pp. 208 ff.

Devaluation is supposed to improve the balance of trade. A reduction in the physical volume of imports relative to the physical volume of exports constitutes an *adverse* change in the *gross* barter terms of trade. Hence, a devaluation will ordinarily be called successful only if the gross terms of trade are substantially deteriorated. (This is often referred to as the "primary burden" of devaluation.) The less a deficit country digs into its foreign reserves and the less it borrows abroad in order to finance imports, the "worse" are its gross barter terms. Since this may be the very object of devaluation, those who seem "alarmed" about a possible deterioration of the terms of trade as a result of devaluation must obviously mean something other than the gross terms.

Where effects of changes in productivity are involved in the analysis, the *factor* terms of trade will be most relevant. A change in the "single factor terms of trade" is a change "in the volume of imports . . . over which a unit of [domestic] productive power . . . can exercise command." [19] The simplest way to characterize this concept is to refer to changes in the import-buying power of a domestic labor hour (because labor is the productive factor of which "a unit" is the most relevant and the most easily defined). Similarly, a change in the "double factor terms of trade" might for practical purposes be seen in a change in the number of foreign labor hours indirectly purchased by one domestic labor hour through exchanging its product for the imports produced by foreign labor. Kindleberger, in search of an operational definition, defined the "double factoral terms of trade" as "the unit-value index of exports, adjusted for changes in productivity, divided by the unit-value index for imports, adjusted for changes in productivity." [20]

D. H. Robertson called the double factor terms "the most fundamental" and "the true terms of trade"; he considered them the "most relevant to discussion of relative national standards of living, or of 'equilibrium' rates of exchange." [21] But he looked to the "commodity terms of trade" as the ones "most immediately relevant to discussion of changes in the balance of payments."

There is little doubt that most writers examining what effects devaluation would have upon the terms of trade were thinking of the net terms or *commodity* terms, that is, of price changes for export goods relative to price changes for import goods. A change in the commodity terms of trade is a change in the import-buying power of a given physical export-mix. If the productivity of domestic labor is unchanged, any change in the commodity terms of trade constitutes an equal change in the single factor terms of trade. Thus, there is no need to give special

[19] D. H. Robertson, *op. cit.*, p. 174.
[20] Kindleberger, *op. cit.*, p. xix.
[21] Robertson, *op. cit.*, p. 175.

attention to the factor terms as long as productivity is assumed not to be affected by devaluation. But is such an assumption warranted?

"Productivity" is one of the fuzzier concepts in economics. As long as we mean physical efficiency of a well-defined input producing a fully specified output there is little trouble. But when we talk about productivity of resources in general in the economy (or in export industry) as a whole, index number problems involving the aggregating, averaging, and weighting of values of different products arise. When the allocation of resources and the composition of output change, there will be no clear line between "physical productivity" and "value productivity" no matter what methods of deflation for price changes are employed. "Productivity" will depend not only on the production functions (input-output ratios) in every industry but also on the allocation of resources among industries. Even when all physical production functions remain unchanged, a reallocation of given resources can alter "productivity."

If obstacles are erected which cut down the production of "more valuable" goods and force a transfer of resources to the production of "less valuable" goods, a reduction in productivity will be recorded. If existing obstacles to the movement of resources are removed, or restrictions on output or outlet are lifted, a transfer of resources to the production of "more valuable" products may take place, and an increase in productivity would then be recorded. In brief, the productivity of resources depends on how they are used.

Resource reallocation is implicitly or explicitly involved in determining the effects of devaluation on the balance of trade and on the commodity terms of trade. If it were not for substitutions in consumption and production, devaluation would change export prices and import prices by the same percentage. Only insofar as these substitutions take place will devaluation affect the commodity terms of trade. In certain circumstances (which will be discussed later) devaluation may create, aggravate, mitigate, or remedy a "malallocation" of resources and thus reduce or increase their productivity. Hence, it is not safe to assume unchanged productivity—as one does when the effects of devaluation upon national income (with unchanged total employment) are judged by its effect on the commodity terms of trade.[22]

One may formulate a general rule for the kinds of changes or events for which the commodity terms of trade are useful tools in the analysis of effects upon a nation's income. Changes or events that take place *abroad* and alter the relative prices of exports and imports, regardless of any subsequent substitutions in the use of products and resources within

[22] Of course, in the absence of any presumptions about the direction in which productivity will be affected one may have to make do with the assumption of no change, and may use the commodity terms of trade for estimating changes in real income.

the nation, will increase or reduce its income initially by an amount which is calculable with the aid of the commodity terms of trade. Subsequent adjustments in the use of products and resources will increase the initial gain or reduce the initial loss. On the other hand, changes or events taking place *within* the economy and causing changes in productivity *together* with changes in the commodity terms of trade—the extent of the change in one depending on the extent of the change in the other—will increase or reduce income by an amount not even approximately or initially calculable with the aid of the commodity terms of trade.

In other words, when a nation is *faced* with changes in relative import and export prices caused by developments abroad which do not simultaneously affect the use of domestic resources, the *commodity terms of trade* will be appropriate tools for judging the effects upon its real income. But when a nation *produces* such changes by its own actions, or when developments within the economy are causing them, then factor productivity may change together with the prices of foreign-trade goods, and the *single factor terms of trade* will be the more suitable tools for analyzing the effects on income. For, where adverse changes in the commodity terms of trade are associated with increased productivity, the factor terms of trade may be improved rather than worsened. Indeed, this was the very reason for developing the concept of single factor terms of trade. A deterioration in the commodity terms cannot ultimately determine the effects on national income of any change or measure that affects productivity.

Devaluation is such a change: it affects the commodity terms of trade along with the productivity of resources. Yet the writers who have argued about the terms-of-trade effects of devaluation have focussed on the possible changes in the commodity terms and have neglected the possible changes in factor productivity caused by the concomitant reallocation of resources.[23]

THE EFFECTS UPON INCOME AND TRADE

Among the few writers who have given explicit recognition to the terms-of-trade effects of devaluation upon income, and, through income, upon the balance of trade, is Sidney Alexander.[24] His analysis is most suggestive and deserves more than casual comment.

Alexander divided the income effects of the changes in terms of

---

[23] The question whether this gain in productivity might be obtainable by policies other than devaluation is not discussed in this paper. We are concerned only with the effects of devaluation and are urging that none be overlooked.

[24] Alexander, *loc. cit.* Among earlier writers were Arnold C. Harberger, *op. cit.*, esp. pp. 51-57; and Svend Laursen and Lloyd A. Metzler, "Flexible Exchange Rates and the Theory of Employment," *Review of Economics and Statistics*, Vol. xxxii (1950), esp. p. 297.

trade due to devaluation into "initial" and "secondary" ones. The *initial* effects, I suppose, refer to the changes in incomes of producers of exports and users of imports owing to relative *price* changes of export and import goods; the *secondary* effects arise from increased or reduced *expenditures* by those experiencing the initial income changes.

Regarding the initial terms-of-trade effects of devaluation upon income, and *via* income upon the balance of trade, Alexander advanced a few generalizations which I rejected summarily and promised to refute in a more carefully reasoned argument.[25] Alexander first discussed the possibility that devaluation would worsen the terms of trade and reduce national income but leave the trade balance unchanged. This could happen under certain conditions, for example,

> if before the devaluation the country concerned was importing twice as much as it was exporting, and if as a result of the devaluation the fall in foreign prices of exports is 2% and of imports 1%, the deficit in foreign currency would be unchanged if the physical values of imports and exports were unchanged.[26]

But Alexander continued:

> It may, however, be assumed that the normal result of a devaluation will be such a deterioration of the terms of trade of the devaluing country as to make the balance of payments deteriorate by the amount *t*. That is, *t* is the measure of the reduction of the country's real income associated with the deterioration of the terms of trade.[27]

In other words, it is contended that normally a deterioration of the terms of trade of the devaluing country will cause a reduction of its real income and an initial reduction (i.e., "deterioration") of its trade balance *by the same amount*. Alexander repeats that

> the entire deterioration, *t*, of the national income as a result of the changed terms of trade is initially a reduction in the foreign balance.[28]

It is easily possible to make this statement true by definition, but it is not possible to support it as "normally" true. Let us recall some of Alexander's terminology and denotations: "Absorption" means real expenditures for consumption and investment or what I shall propose to call the "real intake"; A stands for absorption, B for trade balance, and Y for income. Now, one may say that the reduction in national income and the "initial" reduction in the trade balance (resulting from a deterioration in the commodity terms of trade due to devaluation) must always be equal if

---

[25] *American Economic Review*, Vol. xlv (June 1955), p. 268. (See Chapter VIII, pp. 183–184.)

[26] Alexander, *loc. cit.*

[27] *Ibid.*

[28] *Ibid.*

(1) direct changes in absorption are ruled out because they are treated separately;

(2) income-induced changes in absorption are ruled out because they are not "initial"; and

(3) there are no other kinds of changes in absorption.

For it follows from $\triangle B \equiv \triangle Y - \triangle A$ that $\triangle B = \triangle Y$ when $\triangle A$ is zero.

This, however, cannot have been the meaning of the contention. Alexander granted the possibility that the trade balance would be unchanged, i.e., $\triangle B = 0$, despite an income reduction due to deteriorated terms of trade, and he held that the equality of $\triangle Y$ and the initial $\triangle B$ was only "normal." Hence, we must examine how one could come to such a conclusion and what, if anything, could be regarded as the "normal" or most probable course of events concerning the magnitudes in question.

Testing the "equality rule"

For this probe I set up a number of hypothetical test cases with varying elasticities of supply and demand, some of them yielding results broadly conforming to the "equality rule," others contradicting it most flagrantly. Then I analyzed the implications of the different assumptions to find what was the essential variation accounting for the different outcomes.

In accordance with my analytic and pedagogic propensities I used simple arithmetic in the tests, which is more time-consuming but for me more enlightening than any other technique. I shall produce two such tests in an appendix to this article; produce them, because I believe they are helpful in clarifying the issues; in the appendix, because the more sophisticated or less patient of my readers may prefer not to bother with details and especially not with clumsy arithmetic.

The first of the two tests showed the trade balance (initially) changed *pari passu* with income; real absorption was not affected initially. The second test showed the trade balance initially unchanged, while real absorption changed (initially) *pari passu* with real income. Other tests, not reproduced here, yielded all sorts of results contradicting the "equality rule," but the essential difference is sufficiently brought out in the two cases described: it all depends upon which is assumed to come first, adjustments in absorption or adjustments in the foreign balance.

Alexander's contention of "equality as a rule" presupposes that a change in the terms of trade *constitutes* a change in real income, but *normally does not cause* an immediate adjustment in real absorption, and hence will be completely reflected in an equal and simultaneous change in the trade balance. There is, however, no better reason for this presupposition than there would be for the opposite one to the effect that

"normally" the change in real income will not cause an immediate adjustment in foreign indebtedness, but will be initially matched by a change
in real absorption. There might even be some institutional grounds for the
second presupposition: if a country has no foreign reserves, or if the
authorities are unwilling to reduce them, and if foreign loans are not
forthcoming, then the adjustment of real absorption to real income cannot
help being immediate.[29]

The two opposite presuppositions are extremes, and a more appropriate one would lie somewhere between: that a reduction in real income
due to less favorable terms of trade will initially be reflected partly in
some immediate reduction in foreign reserves and partly in some immediate reduction in real absorption.

Analogues to these three presuppositions can be found in the behavior of individuals confronted with higher prices of what they buy
and/or lower prices of what they sell. On one extreme would be the
individual with a big cash balance or an unlimited charge account who,
initially completely unresponsive to the price changes, would buy exactly
the same quantities of goods and thus have the entire reduction in his real
income initially reflected in a reduction in his cash balance or increase in
his debts. On the other extreme would be the individual who, averse to
running down his cash balance or running up his debts, would spend no
more than his income even when it buys less for him.[30] Between these
extremes is the individual who, prepared to dip somewhat more deeply
into his pockets or to put a bit more on the cuff, might increase his money
expenditures relative to his income, though not to an extent that would
keep his real purchases at the former level.

The error behind the "equality rule" for income reduction and trade
balance reduction lies in the tacit assumption that real absorption will as a
rule be initially unaffected by deteriorated terms of trade. This assumption is not only contrary to fact, but it serves no good purpose as a step in
the analysis.[31]

INCOME AND SUBSTITUTION EFFECTS

The immediate initial adjustment of the trade balance to changes in
the terms of trade is not entirely an income effect in the sense of the

[29] A system of freely fluctuating exchange rates is supposed to achieve this result.

[30] Those who receive their income in kind will normally have their absorption
changed *pari passu* with their income.

[31] The opposite assumption, that the trade balance will initially be unaffected by
deteriorated terms of trade, is likewise contrary to fact under our present institutions,
but may serve a purpose in analysis, namely, to examine the effects of exchange-rate
changes under a system of freely floating rates without any "accommodating capital
movements."

Hicksian theory of the household. In the Hicksian analysis of consumer's choice the total effect of an increased buying price is interpreted as the combined effect of substitution and real-income change. For example, the decision in response to a price increase to take less of the commodity and to keep more or less money is partly a substitution between the commodity and money, partly an effect of the reduced real income upon both. If only income effects are taken into account while substitution effects are ignored, serious errors will ensue.

This is fully applicable to international trade and to aggregate absorption by the community. There are substitutions between asset holdings (or debt) and imported producer and consumer goods that occur along with, and in addition to, the income effects of changes in the terms of trade.[32] These substitution effects may significantly affect the absorption of income and the physical volumes of imports and exports; these are price-induced changes in absorption which are not included in any given "propensity to absorb."

The terms-of-trade effects on the trade balance should include these substitution effects. If one presumes with Alexander that $\triangle B = \triangle Y$, even if only "initially," the substitution effects are conjured away or at least lost sight of.

THREE SEPARATE EFFECTS ON INCOME?

In Alexander's analysis, as also in Harberger's, devaluation could affect real income in only two ways: by changing the volume of employment and by changing the commodity terms of trade. The possibility of affecting real income through a reallocation of resources was ignored. Hence I proposed to add to the "idle-resources effect" and the "terms-of-trade effect" a third one, the "resource-reallocation effect" of devaluation upon income and absorption, and thus upon the trade balance.[33]

But this analytical separation of income effects may be misleading: it may suggest that it is possible to separate them practically and perhaps to manage to avoid a negative income effect without foregoing the benefit of a positive one. Often a negative "terms-of-trade" effect is the condition of the realization of positive "idle-resources" or "resource-reallocation" effects. As was said above, the exclusive attention to the commodity terms of trade (in disregard of the single factor terms) has been associated with the failure to consider the effects of resource reallocation as a factor

[32] I should like to call attention to a very suggestive note stressing these points, by A. C. L. Day, "Relative Prices, Expenditure and the Trade Balance: A Note," *Economica*, New Series, Vol. xxi (February 1954), pp. 64-69.

[33] *American Economic Review*, Vol. xlv (June 1955), p. 265. (See Chapter VIII, p. 181.)

relevant to the end results. It can be shown that attempts to isolate, in the analysis of devaluation, changes in the commodity terms of trade and to exhibit them for separate or comparative evaluation may obstruct our understanding of the interrelationships involved.

ILLUSTRATION BY ANALOGY

The connection between changes in the terms of trade and changes in income, especially the fact that a *deterioration* of the terms of trade may be a precondition of an *increase* in income, can be illustrated by an analogy from the trade of an individual with the outside world.[34] The terms of trade of an individual are worsened when the prices of the things he sells decrease relative to the prices of the things he buys. (Individuals who can set prices of the goods or services which they offer for sale are able to change the terms of their trade—just as nations may through their wage, tax, tariff, and exchange-rate policies.)

Assume that an economist working as a free-lance writer of articles for journals and daily papers had been charging a fee of $100 for an article; he has been placing two articles a month. He discovers that he could increase the proceeds from his "exports" considerably if he reduced his fee to $50; he could place eight articles a month at this lower price, and thus raise his revenue from $200 to $400 a month. Restrained neither by considerations of prestige nor by agreement with a journalist's organization, he adopts this plan. Since the prices of his "imports"—food, clothes, entertainment, etc.—remain unchanged while the price of his exports is halved, the terms of trade of our man have deteriorated by 50%. Yet, he has little reason to deplore this deterioration, which has caused his income—at least his professional income—to double.

How would these results be analysed and evaluated in terms of the Alexander approach? The fact that our man was able to increase his professional output and income from 2 to 8 units would be treated as an "idle-resources" effect of the rate cut; the rate cut itself would be treated separately as a "terms-of-trade" effect on his income. The calculation would look as follows:

Idle-resources effect on income	
6 units at base price of $100	+$600
Terms-of-trade effect on income	
Price cut of $50 on 8 units	− 400
Net effect on income	+$200

One may prefer to calculate the value of the export increase at the new price rather than the base price, and the terms-of-trade loss of income on the old volume of exports rather than the increased volume:

<hr>

[34] I am indebted to Professor Wytze Gorter for suggesting such an analogy to me.

Idle-resources effect on income	
6 units at new price of $50	+$300
Terms-of-trade effect on income	
Price cut of $50 on 2 units	− 100
Net effect on income [35]	+$200

This sort of analytical evaluation of gain and loss is formally correct; but one may raise the objection to the procedure that it is likely to mislead many into complaining about the "unfortunate" deterioration in the terms of trade which has so drastically reduced the splendid effects of greater employment. Because of this division of credits and debits many are apt to forget that the less favorable terms of trade may be, as they were in our example, the condition of the income increase.

THE ANALOGY EXPANDED

There is another possibility, not mentioned by Alexander and not provided for by his approach; our free-lance writer may have been fully occupied at the time his literary output was small, for he may have been mending his clothes and preparing his meals. (He is a bachelor or an American husband.) With his professional income doubled, he must be and is relieved of these housekeeping chores. In other words, no idle

[35] In terms of geometric demand analysis the various magnitudes may be represented by areas in the following graph:

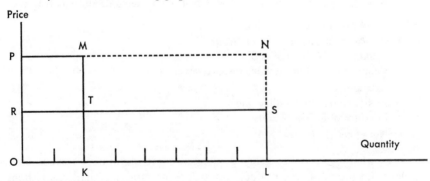

Fig. IX-1. Gains from output increase and losses from reduction in price or terms of trade

	First method	Second method
Idle-resources effect	KLNM	KLST
Terms-of-trade effect	RSNP	RTMP

The difference between the two methods lies in the addition, under the first method, of the area TSNM to both effects; the net gain is, of course, the same.

The net gain, or incremental revenue, is KLST minus RTMP, and the ratio of the idle-resources effect to the terms-of-trade effect calculated by the second method, KLST/RTMP, is the elasticity of demand.

resources were put to work to produce his increased exports; instead there was a shift of resources from "domestic" to professional use. If we have only the two items accounting for income changes—the idle-resources and the terms-of-trade effects—the calculation of the results will show only the "loss" due to the deterioration of the terms of trade; the gain from the better use of resources is kept from sight. This is clearly and definitely wrong; the "resource-reallocation" effect must be taken into account if the results are to be correctly appraised.

Assume that our model man can buy for $80 a month the services which he no longer does for himself; that is, he now imports what he previously did himself. Thus, he will find his real income increased by $120 a month (200 minus 80). A calculation dividing the net increase into gross gain and offsetting loss looks as follows:

Idle-resources effect on income		nil
Resource-reallocation effect on income		
6 units at base price of $100	+$600	
Value produced in previous resources use	− 80	
Balance		+$520
Terms-of-trade effect on income		
Price cut of $50 on 8 units		− 400
Net effect on income		+$120

Alternatively using the changed price in computing the gross gain and the base-period volume for the terms-of-trade loss, we calculate as follows:

Idle-resources effect on income		nil
Resource-reallocation effect on income		
6 units at new price of $50	+$300	
Value produced in previous resources use	− 80	
Balance		+$220
Terms-of-trade effect on income		
Price cut of $50 on 2 units		− 100
Net effect on income		+$120

Our analogy, I believe, has suggested some significant lessons concerning the terms-of-trade effects upon income, and we shall spell them out presently. But nothing has been implied concerning the effects upon the trade balance. Our plot has to be expanded further to have such implications.

Assume that our man, when he exported only $200 worth of articles, imported $250 worth of goods per month (paper, ink, etc., needed for his production, and victuals for his upkeep). Thus, he had an import surplus of $50, financed by drawing on an old savings account. When the worsened terms of trade raise his income he will step up his imports: first by the $80 worth of services needed to maintain his former consumption standards; secondly, by an amount required for investment goods used for his increased production, say $20 (for journals and books, whose amortization, however, we neglected in figuring his new income, as we also neglected any increased use of paper and typewriter ribbons); thirdly, by an amount to satisfy his propensity for increased consumption as he earns more, say $60. Thus, his imports will increase by $160 a month, or from $250 to $410. This, with his exports now at $400, will still leave an import surplus of $10, but his trade balance will have improved by $40 a month. (He could have completely balanced his budget by being a bit more modest in raising his living standard.[36])

There is no direct connection in our illustration between the (unfavorable) change in the terms of trade and the (favorable) change in the balance of trade, especially because the latter depends on the adjustment of our man's consumption to his increased income and improved liquidity position. Nor is there any direct connection between what might be regarded as the "pure" terms-of-trade effect upon income ($400 or $100, depending on the method of computation) and what might be viewed as an "initial effect on the balance of trade"—except on the preposterous assumption that our man lowered the price for his export but failed to increase its quantity (in which case he would actually have lost $100).

The net gain in income from the action which deteriorated the terms of trade—that is, from the price reduction for exported articles—was independent of the net change which took place in the trade balance. If the gain had been used entirely for increased purchases, the trade balance would not have improved; only because some of the gain was used for increased saving and greater liquidity could the trade balance improve. But the net gain, in our illustration, did depend on the high elasticities of the supply of and the demand for the exported articles: if one of these elasticities had been unity or less (for example, if our man could increase his sales only to three or four articles per month) no net gain but a net loss would have occurred. (Still, the "terms-of-trade effect" upon income calculated without taking account of an offsetting effect would have exaggerated the loss.) Finally, the net gain depended on the availability of the previously homemade services at a purchase price less than the proceeds from the increased exports. If these services could not be purchased for less than $300, there would be no gain, material or financial, from the switch of resources.

[36] In computing the net increase in income we neglected—besides the few mentioned items in the cost of production—to take account of an increase in psychic income connected with the possibly greater enjoyment of professional work compared with domestic work—though the opposite would hold for men who prefer housework to desk work. Such welfare effects of the resource reallocation cannot be considered on the same level as can changes in physical outputs and money amounts.

It should be noted that the improvement in the affairs of our model man can be attributed to the fact that his initial position was not an "optimal" one: he had been irrationally malallocating his labor resources. Some of his labor hours which could have been worth $600 in professional work (or $300 after the price reduction) were used for work that was worth only $80. Evidently, there had been no effective competition equalizing the marginal productivity of labor in different uses. If the labor employed in domestic work had been competing with the highly paid labor employed in professional work, the competition would have forced down the price at which our man offered his articles for export. Whether the implied assumption of imperfections of competition reduces or increases the value of our analogy for presumptive reasoning about international trade cannot be decided here.

One lesson, however, is clearly suggested by our analogy: we see how arbitrary it is to calculate a distinct terms-of-trade effect of an action that changes the use of resources along with the terms of trade, and how misleading it is to overlook a resource-reallocation effect when special attention is paid to the terms-of-trade effect of a measure such as the devaluation of the currency.

THE BENEFITS FROM "DETERIORATED TERMS OF TRADE"

The idea that "more adverse" commodity terms of trade may be on the whole beneficial to a nation is worth a good deal of emphasis. Of course, the deterioration of the terms of trade is not *per se* beneficial but only as a means for achieving a higher real income through increased employment or improved allocation of productive resources. But it is an unfortunate habit of mind, quite common among economists and politicians, to deplore any deterioration of the commodity terms of trade, and to recommend policies to avoid it, without examining whether it may not be a precondition for obtaining gains in employment or productivity.[37]

This is not to suggest that devaluation would necessarily worsen the commodity terms of trade—it may well improve them—or would necessarily increase productivity—it may well reduce it. While some reallocation of resources as a result of devaluation is almost unavoidable, the new allocation may be better or worse (if we may be allowed to make such a statement with the blessings of welfare economists). There is a presumption, I submit, that the reallocation will be beneficial when the currency has been seriously out of line and is devalued in order to correct its

---

[37] In a similar vein Smithies complained: ". . . changes in the net terms of trade are coming to be regarded by economists as a satisfactory and unambiguous measure of changes in gains from trade. This fashion seems to me to be offensive to theory, history, and common sense." Arthur Smithies, "Modern International Trade Theory and International Policy," *American Economic Review*, Papers and Proceedings, Vol. XLII (May 1952), p. 170.

external overvaluation relative to the prices of various products and productive services.

Another impression possibly suggested by our illustration must be dispelled to avoid misunderstandings: the resource reallocation induced by the changes in relative prices that result from devaluation does not have to involve an increase in exports. It may equally well be domestic production of import substitutes that is given a lift, and all sorts of additional substitutions in production, investment, and consumption may be engendered.

A reallocation of resources effected by currency devaluation and resulting in increased production of import substitutes and/or export goods can involve a net increase in national product

(a) if the exchange-rate adjustment permits the abolition or relaxation of direct controls and quantitative restrictions which had created (or increased) disproportions in the marginal productivities of productive services and/or discrepancies between private and social costs and benefits;

(b) if such disproportions or discrepancies due to price inflexibilities, resource immobilities, and restrictions or serious imperfections of competition are reduced in consequence of the exchange-rate adjustment;

(c) if the improvement in the trade balance checks or stops a loss (i.e., an unintended realization) of foreign assets and thus conserves them for future use with a presumably greater value for consumer welfare and/or production potential.

Even under these conditions it is difficult to prove conclusively that resource allocation will actually be "improved." The case against direct controls and for the working of the price mechanism is not convincing to everybody, and even many who on principle advocate allocation through the operation of free and competitive markets admit that there may be exceptional situations in which direct controls may operate in a more painless way. The second possibility (b), that devaluation may reduce or remove distortions in relative costs and prices, is always present, but the opposite is also possible. At first blush one may be impressed by the fact that devaluation will act like the removal of export taxes and of import subsidies—and by the presumption that taxes and subsidies distort relative prices. But devaluation may with equal justification be likened to the introduction of export subsidies and import taxes—and the presumption then would be that distortions are created rather than removed. Thus one has to establish in each particular situation that the resource allocation before devaluation is not an optimal one—owing to certain defects or restrictions in the operation of the markets—and can be improved through an adjustment of the exchange rate. (This is the possibility illustrated in our analogy.)

The third of the possible reallocation benefits, the conservation of foreign-exchange reserves, presupposes of course that devaluation has its "normal" effect of improving the trade balance. But even so, one may object to a conceptual framework under which a substitution between different assets (foreign reserve versus home investment) or a substitution between assets and consumer goods (foreign reserves versus consumption) is interpreted as a gain or loss in *income*. This objection will surely be sustained when the substitution in question is attributable to deliberate decisions to use foreign assets or incur foreign debts to obtain imports; the objection will perhaps be dismissed in situations where the authorities expressly "deplore" the loss of reserves as unintended and unfortunate if not calamitous.

The difference between these situations, which is pointed up by the distinction between autonomous and accommodating capital imports, can be elucidated by simple examples. Assume an initial situation in which no capital movements take place. Now an autonomous inflow of capital sets in, resulting either in an appreciation of the currency or in an expansion of money incomes and, in either case, in an increase in prices of domestic goods and services relative to prices of foreign-trade goods. There will be some substitution by domestic industry of foreign for domestic materials and of imported machines for domestic labor; moreover, some resources previously used for export production will be transferred to home use. This resource reallocation will be associated with a decrease in foreign assets or increase in foreign debts—which, of course, is the "realization" of the autonomous capital inflow. When the capital inflow stops, the opposite movements will take place.

In the absence of autonomous capital movements similar substitutions and resource reallocations can be induced by creating, and in the opposite direction by removing, an overvaluation of the currency *vis-à-vis* foreign currencies. For example, when money incomes are expanded at fixed foreign-exchange rates, prices of domestic goods and services are increased relative to prices of foreign-trade goods; foreign materials are substituted for domestic materials, imported machines for domestic labor, home-use production for export production. All these substitutions involve the use of foreign-exchange reserves for increased consumption and domestic investment. A devaluation of the currency may then check or stop the described substitutions, reverse the resource reallocation, and conserve foreign reserves.

On what grounds can it be said that the last of these resource reallocations is "beneficial"? If the use of resources after the domestic expansion of money incomes was an "optimum allocation" on the basis of market prices prevailing at the time, and if the use of resources after devaluation is another "optimum allocation" on the basis of post-devaluation market prices, are we justified in contending that the latter optimum is "better" than the former?

"Static" theory, where time does not count, provides no ground for such a contention; but "dynamic" theory does: where time counts, the consequences of the depletion of exchange reserves must be considered. A resource allocation which requires a continuing loss of reserves cannot be maintained in the long run. Sooner or later a reallocation will become unavoidable; it may occur through direct controls, through reductions in money incomes, through devaluation or depreciation of the currency.[38] The delay in the reallocation may in exceptional situations make for a greater real income over time, but will as a rule reduce income over time. The presumption is strong, therefore, that the long-run resource-reallocation effect of devaluation upon income will be positive even in instances in which no benefits can be claimed on the other two scores, improved productivity through the removal of direct controls and improved productivity through the removal of malallocations due to other causes. Incidentally, the three possible kinds of benefit from resource reallocation induced by devaluation are additive, and independent of one another.

REAL OUTPUT, INTAKE, AND INCOME

When in this discussion reference was made to the effects of devaluation and of consequent changes in the terms of trade upon "national income," and to effects of changes in "national income" upon imports and exports, the concept of national income was left vague. This vagueness is customary; it "covers up" the fact that there are substantial differences not only between various operational definitions, but also between several fundamental concepts usually left undistinguished. Thus, quite apart from problems of measurement, there may be differences not only in magnitude but also in direction between (1) changes in the total domestic production of finished goods and services valued at constant prices ("real domestic output"), (2) changes in the total domestic use for consumption and investment of goods and services valued at constant prices ("real intake"), and (3) changes in the total amount of income received or earned, with goods and services valued at constant prices, and with income transfers, capital earnings, and all changes in foreign assets and liabilities accounted for insofar as they arise from current transactions ("real income")—to mention only some of the simpler concepts of the large family of magnitudes related to social accounting. For our problems the triad "output," "intake," and "income" will serve important analytical purposes.

The concept of "real intake" has been familiar to us under various names. Alexander called it "real absorption"; although I do not find this

---

[38] At no point in this essay are we concerned with a comparative evaluation of these alternatives. When we discuss the effects of devaluation we do not intend to "sell" them to anyone as "better" or "less bad" than other forms of adjusting the balance of trade.

term very attractive, I have used it whenever I discussed any of Alexander's propositions. Ohlin spoke of "buying power," Viner of "value of final purchases," Haberler of the "volume of goods available for domestic use" and of "real national expenditure." [39] Some of these terms are not felicitous; "buying," "purchases," "expenditures" all disregard the possibility that some of the intake of goods or services may not be associated with expenditures but may be produced by the users themselves. Warren L. Smith employed the term "standard of living" for this concept.[40] This term, I submit, is badly misleading: if "standard of living" is not to refer, as it usually does, to consumption alone but is for some reasons expanded to include accumulation, then it is inconsistent to confine the latter to domestic investment and to exclude investment abroad. After all, we can speak of "investments" only if they promise a future return; this holds for foreign assets no less than for domestic ones. Hence, "standard of living" (if used at all in this context) should refer either to real income or to real consumption, but not to consumption plus a portion of investment. I propose the term "intake" because it is not encumbered with older connotations and is analogous in construction to its counterparts, "output" and "income."

The existence of an export balance implies that real intake is less than real domestic output; an import balance implies an excess of real intake over output, and thus the use of some foreign output in addition to total domestic output. The measurement of changes in real domestic output is complicated by the fact that imported raw materials and imported machines are used in domestic production and must conceptually and statistically be excluded from domestic output. A builder of a simple analytical model will save himself much trouble by assuming that imports consist only of finished consumers goods. In such a model, changes in real output as well as changes in real intake can be measured by the use of appropriate index-number techniques.

From the assumption that changes in real intake and changes in real output can be compared, it follows that changes in the "real balance of

[39] ". . . 'real national income' is not co-extensive with 'volume of goods available for domestic use'." Gottfried Haberler, "The Market for Foreign Exchange and the Stability of the Balance of Payments," *Kyklos*, Vol. III (1949), p. 215. See also Gottfried Haberler, "Currency Depreciation and the Terms of Trade," in *Wirtschaftliche Entwicklung und soziale Ordnung*, ed. Lagler-Messner (Wien: Herold, 1952), p. 150; and most recently Gottfried Haberler, *A Survey of International Trade Theory* (Princeton: International Finance Section, Princeton University, 1955), p. 33.

[40] ". . . we are using the term 'standard of living' as a short-hand expression for the volume of goods available for domestic use priced at the prices prevailing before the adjustment of the exchange rate." Warren L. Smith, "Effects of Exchange Rate Adjustments on the Standard of Living," *American Economic Review*, Vol. XLIV (December 1954), p. 814.—My objections to Smith's terminology do not diminish my admiration for his clear analysis and exposition.

trade" can be calculated. I mention this because I previously questioned the meaning of the notion of a change in the real balance of trade.[41] I still have some doubts about recognizing a definite "real" (physical) quantity unambiguously as "the" equivalent of a change in foreign indebtedness. In any case, I must leave it to index-number experts and national-income specialists to ascertain whether the difference between changes in real intake and in real domestic output would be an acceptable expression for a "change in the real balance of trade" and for the "real" change in indebtedness which it implies.[42]

While the difference between real output and real intake can be identified as the balance of trade, what is the difference between real output and real income? Such a difference will be found only in some specific instances: when reparations payments and gifts are counted as income of the receiving country; when certain earnings from foreign investment are included in the income of the receiving country but not deducted from the real domestic output of the paying country; when the commodity terms of trade have changed and the change is reflected partly or fully in a loss of foreign assets or an increase of foreign debts.[43]

The distinction beween real domestic output and real income is especially important "if the concept of real income is refined to reflect welfare effects resulting from induced changes in the valuation of particular goods." [44] But as we have defined a change in real income—"with goods and services valued at constant prices"—the concept is not sufficiently refined to take account of all the welfare effects of changes in resources use and product mix occurring under the stimulus of changes in relative prices. The distinction proposed here is designed to deal chiefly with the less subtle problems of changes in foreign assets and liabilities.[45]

[41] "When a country has to pay increased prices for its imports and buys a slightly reduced physical quantity of imports, what is the meaning of an improved 'real' trade balance if at the same time the balance in money terms has deteriorated? Or, should, perhaps, a trade balance in terms of money be translated into one in real terms by deflating the contracted foreign claims or debts by a price index? To treat exports and imports as 'real quantities' makes sense; but can the difference between the two be meaningfully treated as a real (physical) quantity? Can what is essentially an increase or decrease in foreign claims or debts be regarded as anything but a money value, however deflated?" *American Economic Review*, Vol. XLV (June 1955), pp. 269-270. (See Chapter VIII, pp. 185–186.)

[42] For an illustration of a problem of this sort and of possible solutions see the Appendix of this essay.

[43] Compare also Harberger who, after having distinguished between "national production" and "real consumer income," stated that "production can be used as a measure of real consumer income" only "as long as the terms of trade do not change." *Op. cit.*, p. 52.

[44] Warren L. Smith, *op. cit.*, p. 812.

[45] Haberler's distinction between "national income" and "volume of production" was chiefly designed to deal with such items as "income from foreign investment or reparation payments," gifts, foreign aid. See his *Survey*, p. 33.

For example, we can imagine a situation in which there is absolutely no change in physical output, physical intake, physical exports, and physical imports, but where the foreign prices of exports are reduced and/or the foreign prices of imports increased. A loss in foreign assets or increase in foreign debt would occur as a result. Hence, real income would be reduced although domestic output at constant prices was not changed.

A distinction between changes in real domestic output and in real income will always be implicit in attempts to separate the terms-of-trade effects of devaluation from effects *via* substitution, resource reallocation, and increased employment. Indeed, the notion of a terms-of-trade effect isolated from all other effects *implies* the idea of a change in real income without a change in real domestic output. Probably this was in the back of his mind when Alexander attempted the isolation, and in this sense alone does his rule of an equal reduction in trade balance and real income prevail—not as a "normal" equality, of course, but as a definitional one.

PRIMARY AND SECONDARY BURDEN

The loss which a devaluing country suffers if the net terms of trade are worsened as a result of devaluation is often referred to as the "secondary burden" which is imposed on the country in addition to the "primary" or "basic burden" implied in the improvement of the trade balance because of the reduction it involves in the quantities of goods available for consumption and investment in the country.

The primary burden is obviously the reduction in real intake that is unavoidable when the "real import surplus" is reduced with constant real domestic output.[46] If the secondary burden is seen as an added reduction in intake due to worsened terms of trade,[47] this second subtrahend can be identified only by first ascertaining the reduction in intake that would have taken place at constant terms of trade and then comparing this with the actual (total) reduction of intake. This is operationally impossible; moreover, domestic output may have changed in connection with the devaluation and the resulting changes in the terms of trade; and thirdly, the adverse change in the terms of trade may be reflected partly or fully in a greater loss of foreign-exchange reserves or in a greater debt to foreigners, and thus need not be reflected fully or at all in a reduction in real intake. Thus it is inappropriate to interpret both "burdens" as reductions of real intake.

A partial answer is to define only the primary burden as a reduction

[46] See Haberler, "Currency Depreciation and the Terms of Trade," *loc. cit.*

[47] "If [depreciation] worsens the terms of trade, there will be a secondary burden in terms of reduced standard of living to be added to the primary burden. . . ." Warren L. Smith, *op. cit.*, p. 808.

in real intake, and to define the secondary burden as a reduction in real income. Even this will not eliminate all conceptual and operational difficulties of giving unambiguous meanings to the two expressions; indeed only the third (probably the most serious) of the three mentioned difficulties is removed. The first difficulty, of estimating the reduction of real intake that would have taken place at constant terms of trade, will remain and prevent us from knowing the weight of the primary burden. The second difficulty will continue to interfere with the estimation of the primary burden because an increase in real output, due to increased employment or improved allocation, may avert some of the real-intake reduction; and it will interfere also with the determination of the secondary burden because an increase in output would offset some of the real-income reduction attributed to the deterioration of the terms of trade.

INCOME AND THE PROPENSITIES TO SPEND

We are now ready for the last step in this analysis: to ask how aggregate spending, imports, and the trade balance, will be affected by the changes of what was vaguely called "income."

Having realized that changes in real domestic output, intake, and income may be different in magnitude and even in direction, we must ask which change will affect consumption, investment, imports. If an analysis makes use of consumption functions, of income-induced investment, of marginal propensities to import—which is the crucial variable? Is investment a function of changes in real domestic output, real intake, or real income? Will consumption and imports be affected by changes in real output or real income?

I have no hope for a quick and simple answer. I suspect that problems of personal and functional "income" distribution and of liquid-asset holding will force themselves into the argument before much progress can be made on these questions. For it will make a difference who suffers a loss (or makes a gain) and in what form.

Take the case where devaluation leads to reduced foreign prices of exports because exporters compete vigorously for an unchangeable amount of business, the foreign demand being completely inelastic or harnessed by import quotas. Since exporters will employ unchanged quantities of resources, will produce and export an unchanged quantity of output, and will receive from the monetary authorities (including banks) an unchanged amount of domestic money in exchange for reduced amounts of foreign money, the exporters will not be affected in any way and will have no reason to alter their consumption or investment outlays. The banks, central and commercial, will have paid a higher price for foreign currency; but having paid out an unchanged amount of domestic money and thus carrying the reduced amounts of foreign balances at an unchanged total valuation in domestic money, their financial statements will not show any change. Imports, it is assumed, are all made for public investment projects, the government paying for the imports with all the foreign exchange the banks can supply and, for the rest, drawing on loans secured from foreign governments or international institutions. In brief, the unquestionable reduction in real income earned in the economy as a whole will be "noticed" chiefly by the government and some experts who record the bigger increase in foreign debt. The loss in real income in this case consists in a "mortgage on the future," and none of the present-day spenders will feel "propense" to change his outlays. Private exporters, consumers, investors, or hoarders will have unchanged money incomes and will pay unchanged prices in domestic markets. Real domestic output also is unchanged.[48]

Take another case, in which, after currency devaluation, increased physical exports fetch reduced proceeds in foreign money, for which the banks pay increased amounts of domestic money. Output at constant prices may be increased; money incomes earned by the exporters, their workers, and other owners of productive resources will likewise be increased; the balance sheets of the banks will show an increase in assets valued in domestic money, though worth less in terms of foreign money. Imports for government investment are maintained, though, because of the reduced foreign-exchange proceeds of exports, the portion financed by foreign loans is increased. Real domestic output is increased and real income decreased. The propensities to consume, to invest, and to import will in this case be based on real domestic output, not on real income (at least in the short run, before the authorities alter their fiscal and credit policies). Yet we could easily construct cases in which the opposite would hold because of a different incidence of the change in real income.

In view of these considerations we may perhaps enter a modest caveat against the propensity to treat such problems exclusively with algebraic models on the assumption that "Y is a Y is a Y is a Y."

❈   ❈   ❈

APPENDIX

The two hypothetical cases described below are designed to throw some light on the quantitative relationships between a deterioration in a devaluing country's terms of trade and its real national income; and, in particular, to test the con-

---

[48] Yet Harberger made a "fundamental assumption," for all conditions he envisaged, "that the marginal propensities to hoard, to import, and to consume home goods operate not on national production *per se* but on 'real consumer income'. . . ." *Op. cit.*, p. 52.

tention that a deterioration in the commodity terms of trade resulting from devaluation will "normally" worsen the trade balance and reduce the real income by the same amount.

Distinctions will be made between changes in the total domestic production of finished goods and services valued at constant prices ("real domestic output"), changes in the total domestic use—consumption plus home investment—of goods and services valued at constant prices ("real intake"), and changes in the total amount of real income earned, taking account of changes in foreign assets and liabilities arising from current transactions ("real income").[1]

Our assumptions will be deliberately designed to yield adverse changes in the terms of trade; indeed, the relevant elasticities in international markets will be assumed to be so unfavorable to the devaluing country that the plot is set for virtual atrocity stories.

In order to isolate the terms-of-trade effect from any idle-resources effect, we shall assume total employment to be unchanged throughout the tests. And in order to avoid the complications connected with the notion of "aggregate" or "average" elasticities of supply or demand for exports or imports of changing composition, we may assume a country with only one export good and only one import good. In order to simplify the price index problem we may assume that the import good is a finished good.

For our numerical illustrations the social accounting statement before devaluation is supposed to look as follows: Domestic consumption and investment, or "real intake," A, is 100; export, X, is 20; import, M, is 30. Thus the trade balance, B, is -10; and total output, Y, is 90. The "income equation" would be $Y = 100 + (20 - 30) = 90$.

The currency of this country is now devalued by $\frac{1}{4}$ in terms of foreign money, that is, the price of foreign money is raised by $\frac{1}{3}$ in terms of domestic money.

First Case

The supply of exports is elastic, but the foreign demand for them has an elasticity of zero. The increased domestic value of foreign money makes export orders more attractive to the vigorously competing exporters until they have bid down the foreign price so much that the domestic price is the same as before devaluation. Hence, the foreign price will be decreased by $\frac{1}{4}$. Total proceeds from exports (in unchanged physical volume) will be reduced by 25% in foreign money, and unchanged in domestic money.

The foreign supply of imports is assumed to be perfectly elastic and, therefore, available only at an unchanged foreign price. The domestic price will thus be increased by $\frac{1}{3}$. If the demand for imports is completely inelastic, an unchanged quantity will be bought for an unchanged amount of foreign money, for which 33.3% more must be paid in domestic money.

---

[1] The easiest way to visualize the difference between changes in real domestic output and in real income is to assume a case where nothing changes but the relative prices of exports and imports, all physical quantities remaining unchanged; thus domestic finished output at constant prices would be unchanged, but foreign indebtedness would be changed.

The results on the trade balance—before there are any income-induced (secondary) changes in expenditures—may be tabulated as follows:

Trade:	In physical volume	In foreign money	In domestic money
Exports:	unchanged	reduced	unchanged
Imports:	unchanged	unchanged	increased
Balance:	unchanged	deteriorated	deteriorated

There are no changes in physical production, consumption, investment, export, or import. "Real domestic output" (90) as well as "real intake" (100) are unchanged. But since less foreign money is received for the unchanged physical exports, and more domestic money paid for the unchanged physical imports, there must be changes in foreign and domestic indebtedness. The current losses of foreign balances from exchange reserves, and the current extensions of domestic bank loans will be greater than before the devaluation. In the computation of real national income the loss of foreign balances must be accounted for, though there is a problem of how this increase in the deficit is to be translated into real terms.

The domestic money value of imports is increased by $\frac{1}{3}$, that is, from 30 to 40. Since imports are included in the sum of domestic expenditures, the "income equation" now reads $Y = 110 + (20 - 40) = 90$. Income at current prices is thus unchanged; but a physically unchanged intake is now purchased with an expenditure of 110 instead of 100. This gives a general price index of 110; if we were to use it for deflating the money income of 90—though the procedure is somewhat objectionable—we would obtain a real income of 81.81. This reduction of real income by 8.19 is associated with the reduction in the trade balance by 10.

Another way of computing the change in real income would be to regard the additional loss in foreign reserves (or increase in foreign debt) as a negative item in the measurement of income without bothering with any deflator. Output measured at constant prices is unchanged at 90, but the current loss in the foreign position has increased from 10 to 20; hence, real income may be said to be reduced to 80. On this basis the reduction in real income would equal the reduction in the trade balance.[2]

Second Case

The chief differences between this and the previous case are that this time the elasticities of demand for exports and imports will not be zero, and there will be a transfer of productive resources from domestic uses to the production of exports (though no change in total employment).

If both the supply of exports and the foreign demand for them are elastic,

[2] Alternative methods, more or less sophisticated, can be suggested, and some are used in official national income estimates. One method would use different deflators for increases in liabilities to foreign creditors and for reductions in claims against foreign debtors—although the worsening of the trade balance could result in either. What is the "real value" of a current loss of exchange reserves? If the loss will have to be made up in the future, the "real" loss will depend on the prices that will prevail in the future and on the way in which the reserves will be recovered—by increased exports, reduced imports, or a combination of the two. Thus every valuation of the loss of reserves implies an anticipation of a future course of events.

there will be some increase in physical exports, some increase in their domestic price, and some decrease in their foreign price. If the elasticity of the foreign demand is smaller than unity, the proceeds in foreign money will be reduced despite the increase in physical volume of exports and the even larger increase in domestic money proceeds.

The foreign supply of imports, let us assume, is again perfectly elastic and the foreign price, therefore, unaffected by the devaluation. It follows that the domestic price must be increased by ⅓. If the elasticity of demand for imports is greater than zero, the physical quantity imported must be reduced, and the total value of imports in foreign money will be reduced by the same percentage. The total value of imports in domestic money will be increased, unchanged, or reduced according as the elasticity of domestic demand is less than unity, unity, or above unity.

The following tabulation will facilitate the comparison of the effects on the trade balance (again, before there are any secondary income-induced changes in expenditures):

Trade:	In physical volume	In foreign money	In domestic money
Exports:	increased	reduced	increased
Imports:	reduced	reduced	increased
Balance:	"improved"	+ or 0 or −	+ or 0 or −

Whether the trade balance in foreign or domestic money values is improved, unchanged, or deteriorated will depend on relative price elasticities, particularly on how much the foreign price of exports is reduced and how much the physical quantity of imports is reduced.

We shall specify our numerical assumptions with an eye to simplicity of computation: let the elasticity of supply of exports be unity, and the elasticity of foreign demand for these exports be such that their physical volume will increase by 10%; and let the elasticity of domestic demand for imports be such that the value of imports will change exactly by the same amount as the total value of exports.

A 10% increase in physical exports, with the elasticity of supply being unity, implies that the domestic price of exports has increased likewise by 10%; the total value of exports in domestic money is therefore increased by 21% (since $1.10 \times 1.10 = 1.21$). The pre-devaluation value of exports was 20; exports at constant prices will have increased (by 10%) to 22, and at current prices (by 21%) to 24.2.

Since the total value of imports is increased by the same absolute amount as the value of exports (that is, by 4.2), it must have risen from 30 to 34.2. This implies, with the domestic price of imports increased by 33⅓%, that the physical volume of imports must have decreased from 30 to 25.6 at base-period prices (because $34.2 : 1.333 = 25.6$), that is, by 4.4.

This reduction in physical imports as well as the shift of productive resources from domestic use to exports must have reduced the "real intake." The increase in physical exports from 20 to 22 must have reduced real intake by 2 (neglecting any changes in physical productivity at the margin). The reduction of physical imports was 4.4. Together, real intake must have been cut by 6.4, that is, from 100 before devaluation to 93.6, calculated at base-period prices.

What happened to national income at current prices? Exports have increased to 24.2, imports to 34.2. Domestic consumption and investment have decreased by 2, owing to the shift of resources into the export industry, and have increased by 4.2, owing to the higher payments for imports; this makes for a net increase of domestic expenditures by 2.2. The "income equation" now reads $Y = 102.2 + (24.2 - 34.2) = 92.2$.

This increase in national income at current prices involves a decrease in real income.[3] Let us indulge again in the (admittedly questionable) use of the index of prices paid for intake to deflate money income. As we have seen, the real quantity of goods and services used was cut from 100 to 93.6, but the amount of money paid for it increased from 100 to 102.2. This would give us a general price index figure of 109.2 (i.e., $102.2:93.6 \times 100$). Using this index to deflate the money income of 92.2 we obtain 84.4 as a measure of real income. Thus, income at base-period prices has declined by 5.6.

This calculation has neglected the change in the real value of the current deficit in the trade balance. To be sure, the devaluation did not affect the trade balance in the present case, but by altering the terms of trade it affected the real value of the unchanged deficit from current transactions. A given loss of foreign claims or increase in foreign debt means less in real terms when prices are higher, and more when prices are lower. Since domestic prices are higher but foreign prices are lower, the decision about the most "rational" deflator for the foreign balance is perhaps a moot question.

Perhaps the figure computed above does not correspond to what Alexander regarded as the terms-of-trade effects upon real income, particularly since our calculation included the effects of a shift of resources. But even very different methods of calculation will probably not alter the general end results of this case: a substantial reduction in real income (5.6), about the same reduction in real intake (6.4), and a zero change in the trade balance. The notion that real income and trade balance would be reduced by the same amount is flatly contradicted.

[3] Real domestic output has not changed, since the only alteration was a small transfer of production from domestic to export industries. The reduction in real income in the sense here used occurred because a drastic reduction in intake was not accompanied by any decline in the current loss of foreign assets (or increase in debt).

■ PART THREE ■
Gold and Foreign Reserves

INTRODUCTION TO PART THREE

There is a sharp hiatus between the first and second pair of essays in this group. The first two essays are specifically on gold, gold reserves, gold hoarding, gold movements, and the gold price. The other two are on foreign reserves in general, on holding all sorts of liquid assets usable for buying and paying abroad. The first two essays are chiefly "political," dealing with questions of public policy; the other two are eminently theoretical, dealing with abstract concepts and imaginary relationships potentially helpful in understanding certain problems connected with the practice of holding foreign reserves. Yet, there can be no doubt that all four essays may without any strain be joined under the heading chosen for Part Three.

PREVIEW OF THE CHAPTERS

Chapter X, "Eight Questions on Gold," attempts to give answers and, to some extent, to make forecasts from the standpoint of the United States in 1940. Critical of the increase in the price of gold in 1934, it nevertheless opposes proposals to lower it again. The chapter contains a somewhat curious appraisal of the probability that the United States would ever make use of its "over-abundant" gold stocks.

Chapter XI, "A Proposal to Reduce the Price of Gold," is another piece written on the spur of the occasion, namely, at the time of a heavy flight from the dollar into gold in the second half of 1960. Again critical of the advice that the price of gold be raised, the essay proposes the opposite course of action: modest, gradual (quarterly) reductions in the gold price, which would make the hoarding of gold a costly and foolish practice.

Chapter XII, "The Fuzzy Concepts of Liquidity, International and Domestic," protests against the replacement of clear concepts, capable of complete specification, with the vague and unspecified concept of liquidity, which tries to throw together measurable and non-measurable quantities and qualities, and to aggregate non-additive magnitudes. The concept of an international "liquidity preference" is also found to be rather useless.

Chapter XIII, "Further Reflections on the Demand for Foreign Reserves," questions the doctrine that the "needs of trade" determine any optimum amount of foreign reserves to be held by the monetary authorities of the trading nations. The desirability of holding official reserves is a function of certain aversions built into the hierarchy of economic goals: aversions to direct controls, to restrictions of credit, and to freely flexible exchange rates. The problem of the optimum amount of foreign reserve to be held by a nation is more easily analyzed by imagining that individual firms and private banks, motivated by pecuniary benefits and costs, are keeping foreign balances; the balancing of benefits and costs for centralized official reserve holding is more involved, and the idea of a "demand" for official reserves is inconsistent with the economic meaning of demand.

MAJOR THEMES

The major theme on gold is that its value is determined by political decisions of four or five governments. If they want gold to be worth $70 or $100 an ounce, they can make it worth that much simply by offering to buy it at these prices. If they want it to be worth only $30 or $20 an ounce, they can just as easily achieve these reductions simply by selling at these prices. There would not be enough private hoarders with enough marketable wealth to purchase all the gold that the United States and a few other countries could sell out of their reserves.

The usefulness of gold is largely political: it serves as a restraint on fiscal and monetary policy. If one believes that nations, freed of their golden chains, could not muster the political fortitude to avoid fiscal lavishness and excessively easy money, he should not favor the demonetization of gold. But then the idea of making gold more plentiful by drastically raising its price is patently inconsistent with the recognition of the stated role of gold in the monetary system.

The major theme on the demand for foreign reserves is that the holding of reserves involves a social cost in that the implied nonuse or deferred use of the command over foreign resources involves a sacrifice of present consumption and of the building of additional productive facilities. The only benefit of holding reserves is their eventual use in acquiring foreign goods or services at a time when they are even more valuable. The benefits, therefore, are chiefly "loss avoidance" in the future when nonforeseeable occurrences may compel wasteful economic adjustments. The analysis of the optimum amount of foreign reserve held by a nation must be in terms of equalizing the marginal benefit and marginal cost of reserve holding.

EARLIER VERSIONS AND RECORD OF CHANGES

Chapter X: "Eight Questions on Gold."
Written in 1940.
Published in *American Economic Review,* Vol. XXX (February 1941), Proceedings, pp. 30-37.
Reproduced, with extensions, in Deane Carson, ed., *Money and Finance* (New York: John Wiley, 1966), pp. 32-43.

CHANGES: (1) The introduction was rewritten in order to recall the occasion for the discussion and to give the historical setting.

(2) A few commas were inserted, and only about five words changed, in the first six sections.

(3) In the seventh section, a clause of eight words was inserted in the second sentence of the third paragraph.

(4) Footnote 1 was added.

(5) In the eighth section, four words were inserted in the last sentence of the second paragraph.

(6) The "Postscript after 23 Years" was appended.

Chapter XI: "A Proposal to Reduce the Price of Gold."
Written in 1960.
First published as a part of the article "Comments on 'The Balance of Payments' and a Proposal to Reduce the Price of Gold," *The Journal of Finance,* Vol. XVI (May 1961), pp. 189-193.

CHANGES: (1) Only the last five pages of the original paper are reproduced here, the first part being included as Chapter VI in Part One of this volume.

(2) The internal headings were supplied.

(3) No changes were made in the text, except for the insertion, here and there, of a total of seven words.

Chapter XII: "The Fuzzy Concepts of Liquidity, International and Domestic."
Written in 1961-1962.
Most of this was first published in a French version under the title "Liquidité, internationale et nationale," in *Bulletin d'Information et de Documentation, Banque Nationale de Belgique,* Vol. XXXVII (February 1962), pp. 105-116.
Flemish (Dutch) translation in *Tijdschrift voor Documentatie en Voor-*

lichting, Nationale Bank von Belgie, Vol. XXXVII (February 1962), pp. 105-116.

An English version, containing much of this chapter and a part of the next, was published under the title "Liquidity, International and Domestic: A Study of the Demand for Foreign Reserves," in *Anakoinoseis, 1962-1963* (Athens: Bibliopoleion tes Estias, 1963), pp. 29-58, and also in *Archeion, Oikonomikon kai Koinonikon Epistemon,* Vol. 44 (1964), pp. 29-58. The present English version is published here for the first time.

CHANGES: (1) The introduction and first two sections (eight paragraphs) of the French version were not used in this chapter; a new introduction was written.

(2) In the first three sections, footnotes 4, 5, 6, 8, 9, and 10 were added; and the list of "possible uses of funds" was lengthened.

(3) In the section on "Non-additive liquidity," a few sentences were inserted in the third paragraph, and the fourth paragraph is new; also footnote 11.

(4) In the section on "International Liquidity," footnote 12 was added, and a few brief clauses were inserted in the text. Footnote 13 was expanded.

(5) The section on "Liquidity Preference" was much expanded. Footnotes 15, 16, and 17 were added.

Chapter XIII: "Further Reflections on the Demand for Foreign Reserves." Written in 1961-1962.

Only the first two sections, "The Needs of Trade" and "Reserves for Contingent Liabilities," were previously published as the last sections of the French article cited as the original version of Chapter XII. Even these two sections were expanded and partly rewritten for the present volume. The rest of the chapter is published here for the first time.

X

Eight Questions on Gold

The Devaluation of the Dollar in 1933–34 ■ A Possible Reduction of the Price of Gold ■ The Costs of Large Imports of Gold ■ Gold as International Means of Payment ■ The Value of Gold ■ Domestic Circulation of Gold Coins ■ Gold and the Public Debt ■ The Value of Large Gold Reserves ■ Postscript after 23 Years

In a session on "Gold and the Monetary System" at the Annual Meeting of the American Economic Association in December 1940, Charles O. Hardy and Hans Neisser presented two papers which I was asked to discuss. Since I agreed substantially with both speakers, I decided to reshuffle some of the arguments and formulate them in a more provocative manner, to take a few questions about the gold problem which were widely discussed at the time and attempt to answer them bluntly and without scholarly caution.

Perhaps the selection of the questions will be better understood if I recall to the reader's mind that the United States in 1933 had gone off gold and in 1934 had fixed the new gold price at $35 an ounce, or almost 60 per cent above the old price. In seven years, from 1934 to 1940, the United States imported almost $15 billion worth of gold. Frank D. Graham and Charles Raymond Whittlesey were inveighing against this "golden avalanche."

At the end of 1940, when this discussion took place, World War II was in its second year in Europe, but the United States was still a noncombatant and remained so for another year.

THE DEVALUATION OF THE DOLLAR IN 1933-34

Question I: Was the devaluation of the dollar in 1933-34, that is, the raising of the price of gold by the United States, on balance a wise or an unwise policy?

A wise policy, to economists, is one which considers not only the short-run effects but also those which are more indirect and less immediate. There were probably several short-run advantages derived from the devaluation; the short-run price increase of some export articles, cotton in particular, may be admitted as such an advantage; psychological effects on business expectations were perhaps of importance at the time. But how about the more lasting consequences?

The devaluation might have been a proper measure in view of a serious gold scarcity. There was no such scarcity, says Hardy. And "the gold scarcity never was a decisive factor during the postwar era," says Neisser.

The devaluation may have prevented an embarrassing outflow of gold from the United States. But the domestic credit situation was not controlled by the gold situation, says Hardy. And he speaks, very much to the point, "of the ancient prejudice against losing gold, even under conditions where no economic purpose was served by restricting its outflow."

The devaluation was supposed to raise quickly the level of domestic commodity prices, something which was considered desirable at the time. This supposed effect was said to rest on a "statistically proven" relationship between gold and the price level. Neisser has shown that this notion is absolutely fallacious, and I believe I may state that most monetary theorists knew this at the time. To these theorists it was, therefore, no surprise that prices of nonstaple commodities failed to rise with the price of gold, but rose only later and to a much smaller extent when demand was increased gradually by other means.

The gold inflow during the first years following the devaluation may be said to have given our banks the reserve increase and thus the investing capacity needed to finance the large government expenditures. Surely, the desired increase in bank reserves could have been brought about just as well by open-market operations of the Federal Reserve banks.

What the boost of the gold price really has brought about was this: First, it shattered all attempts at world co-operation discussed at the 1933 World Economic Conference. Second, as Neisser shows, it caused a deflationary pressure upon countries then on the gold standard—a deflationary pressure to which they finally succumbed by abandoning their gold standard. And, third, it added impetus to an enormous increase in gold production, an increase which is absolutely useless, wasteful, and embarrassing. (It must be admitted, however, that the boost in gold production was due much more to British than to American gold price policies. The sterling price of gold—and this is the one which is relevant for the greatest part of world gold production—rose before 1933 by more than 45 per cent. The further increase during 1933 and 1934, which can be ascribed to the effects of the American devaluation, amounted to less than 15 per cent of the increased, or 20 per cent of the original, sterling price.[1])

Hence, with the actual motives recognized as fallacious, with other purposes achievable by better methods, and with indirect effects undesirable, we seem to be justified in stating that the devaluation was a mistake.

A POSSIBLE REDUCTION OF THE PRICE OF GOLD

Question II: Would a reduction of the gold price at this time be a wise policy?

If it is found that a certain move was a mistake, it is not always possible to repair it by moving back; moving back may often be just another mistake.

The effects of a reduction of the gold price in the United States might depend largely on whether Great Britain and other trading nations would follow suit. Hardy assumes, justifiably I believe, that they would do so. He concludes that "the principal effect of the reduction would be to impair the purchasing power of Great Britain in this country. In the short run, *more* gold might be shipped [to the United States], but the stocks available for shipment would be exhausted that much sooner."

Neisser recommends "applying a gold price policy of greater flexibility in order to secure the repatriation of American securities now in British possession: the lower our gold price the more England will be inclined to send over securities first and gold only in the second place."

I do not believe that it would be in our interest that the British finance their purchases in the United States first by selling out their security holdings and only afterwards by gold shipments. If they first unload all security holdings, an unwelcome and unnecessary pressure on our securities markets may be exerted. If they sell both their gold and their American securities simultaneously and gradually, our gold purchases create new balances for the British and our security purchases transfer existing balances to them. The British, in turn, transfer all these balances to the American producers in payment for airplanes and other matériel. By proceeding with both methods of finance at the same time, the funds newly created through the gold purchases indirectly help our public to absorb the American securities offered by the British.

It is proper at this point to mention the proposal of an import duty on gold, suggested by Professors Graham and Whittlesey. Such an import

---

[1] For this point I am indebted to Dr. Peter Drucker.

duty would create a two-price system for gold by lowering the dollar price of gold abroad without changing our official buying price. This indirect gold-price reduction through an import duty would differ from an outright reduction of our price only in optical, political, and bookkeeping respects. The effect upon foreign nations would be the same as that of an outright reduction of our gold price; for an ounce of gold they would get only $35 minus the duty.

What the gold-price reduction, outright or concealed, would mean in effect is that more gold would be needed to pay for an American airplane. With the demand for airplanes practically inelastic, gold imports would probably increase in physical amount and remain unchanged in dollar terms. And since the British gold stocks would be exhausted sooner, the problem of credits to Great Britain would arise sooner.

Hence, a reduction of the dollar price of gold at this time would mean little to us but it would definitely harm the British, whom we seem to have decided to aid. Of course, if we thus find it unwise to reduce the gold price at this time, we must be clear that the situation may change, especially when the war is over.

THE COSTS OF LARGE IMPORTS OF GOLD

Question III: Do our large imports of gold constitute a sacrifice of wealth or income?

The huge quantities of gold which we have purchased are a rather useless asset. We have neither an industrial use for them nor a monetary use in domestic circulation nor a monetary use in the sense that we may ever intend to have sufficient import surpluses to use substantial portions of the gold for international payments. If this is correct, has it not been utterly foolish to buy all this gold? Not if the gold has cost us little or nothing and if the purchase has had desirable secondary effects.

And just this is the opinion of Hardy, Neisser, and myself. We must, of course, distinguish between the budgetary or financial cost to the buyer, i.e., the U.S. Treasury, and, on the other hand, the real cost to the American public.

There is no budgetary cost to the government, at least if the purchased gold is not sterilized. And we have not permanently sterilized any gold. Neither tax receipts nor borrowed funds were employed in buying the gold, but only new bank funds created *ad hoc* through the issuance of gold certificates; hence at no cost to the government.

And, as Hardy continues, until now or until very recently there has been no real cost to the American public because what we have given in exchange for the gold has been largely commodities produced with equipment and labor which would have been unemployed otherwise. If the goods which we have exported would otherwise have remained unproduced, one cannot say that the exports constitute a sacrifice to the American public. Neisser concurs with this view, qualifying only concerning the "embodied natural resources," meaning the materials which we have taken out of the ground from exhaustible resources and used in the production of exported commodities. Both Hardy and Neisser emphasize, of course, that such costless gold purchases are confined to periods of unemployment and idle capacity.

But not only have we bought the gold at almost no cost to ourselves but we have also enjoyed a beneficial indirect effect, in the form of a contribution to our national income that has resulted indirectly from our gold purchases, even though the gold as such is of no use to us. If foreign nations use the dollars received for the gold to purchase American products, income is created in the United States. If the respending of this income creates demand for more commodities which would otherwise not be produced, further income is created. As Neisser points out, a chain of additional domestic buying is initiated by the foreign buying, which in turn is financed by our gold buying.

I suppose that Professors Graham and Whittlesey would like to object to this point. They would perhaps admit that the foreign purchases of our products have created income in the United States, but they would hold that more relief payments or more public works would have done this equally well or better.

Perhaps, but perhaps not. Would it have been politically wise to raise our government expenditures to still higher levels? Is it not better to have both exports and government spending in more palatable doses than only government spending in much more terrifying doses? We have financed commodity exports through our gold purchases, and deficit spending through our public-debt increase. Granted that the export multiplier and the government-spending multiplier may theoretically be the same, do rising export-business activity and rising government-debt figures have the same effects on business confidence and private investment? Should we neglect the fact that businessmen become paralyzed with fear when they think of the debt, whereas they nurse an old affection for gold and cheer each increase in merchandise exports? On the basis of this reasoning even Graham and Whittlesey may be persuaded to accept the thesis that our gold purchases have financed commodity exports of recent years at almost no opportunity cost to ourselves.

The results of gold purchases which have financed foreign purchases of American securities may be a different matter, because these securities may be resold to us in exchange for American products at a time when we no longer have unemployed labor and unused capacity. Indeed, as soon as some bottlenecks are reached, foreign purchases do involve real costs to us. But why should we fool ourselves with an analysis which neglects all political considerations? Are not the British purchases, even in serious bottleneck situations, of such a nature that we do not mind foregoing new 1942 model automobiles and several other things which may constitute the opportunity cost of our aid to Britain? We are in fact quite glad that the British have still some American securities—at one time acquired with the help of our gold purchases—because we have an easier political problem if we repurchase American securities than if we have to buy British government obligations.

I must guard myself against the charge of inconsistency in my answers to the first question and to this one. How can I consistently state that the raising of the gold price was, on balance, unwise but that the gold imports have had beneficial effects on the American economy? This is not inconsistent. The gold imports of the last four years were not the consequence of our devaluation. Neither the European capital flight nor the European demand for our products were, after 1936, a function of the price of gold.

Summing up, I feel justified in stating that the large gold purchases in recent years have cost us little or nothing and have made sizable contributions to our national income. Continued purchases of gold and exports of war matériel from now on do involve a larger cost, but on account of extraneous circumstances we seem to be willing to shoulder this cost for the time being.

GOLD AS INTERNATIONAL MEANS OF PAYMENT

Question IV: Are the other nations likely to abandon gold as an international means of exchange even if the United States wishes to retain it?

This question can be answered with confidence in the negative. As long as the United States is prepared to take gold at a fixed price, other nations which have access to gold will not be so foolish as to refuse to use gold in international exchange. Both Hardy and Neisser share this opinion.

Popular apprehension on this point, particularly in case of a German victory, is perhaps the result of propaganda which is attempting to create unrest and fear. Mere common sense should make us realize that any country which controls gold stocks and gold mines would be only too glad to maintain the exchange value of these assets. If anyone pictures a victorious Germany not only as possessing the remaining gold stocks of Europe but also as controlling the gold production of one or more of the British dominions, he should extend his imagination to the logical consequence of all this; namely, that the Germans will not do anything to prejudice the international acceptance of so reliable an export product. In the case of a complete German victory the question should run exactly the other way around; that is, whether the United States would be willing to continue accepting gold from a victorious Germany. Neisser does "not doubt" that in such a case we would stop.

In the case of a British victory or in the case of a survival of a sufficient number of free, trading nations, gold is likely to retain its status, in the opinions of both Neisser and Hardy. If one or more nations without access to gold prefer to do foreign trade on a barter basis, this cannot greatly affect the status of gold in the rest of the world. People are apt to confuse two different aspects of the much propagandized barter methods of foreign trade. One is that trade is controlled through government agencies rather than private business firms. The other refers to the settlement of balances. Under the barter system temporary balances remain unpaid, shown in blocked accounts in the country which has imported more, forcing the country with the export surplus either to wait patiently or to buy things which it otherwise would not care to buy or to cut down its exports. These are certainly not advantages which should tempt more countries to adopt the barter system. The authoritarian export monopoly may possibly secure advantages, but the absence of gold can hardly ever benefit a country, least of all a country that is more interested in exports than in imports but would be able to export only if it were willing to accept blocked accounts in exchange for its products. Even if some countries adopt barter agreements in foreign trade, this need not really affect the status of gold among the other nations.

The United States need not be much concerned that other nations after the war may repudiate gold as long as the United States itself does not repudiate it.

THE VALUE OF GOLD

Question V: Can gold lose its value?

Yes, if the United States decides against gold; no, if the United States continues to support it. If I may borrow a phrase from William Adams Brown, I may say that gold is perfectly safe as long as we redeem it in paper dollars or bank-deposit dollars.

There are at least three meanings in which we may be concerned with the "value of gold." Gold may lose value in terms of dollars, in terms of foreign currencies, or in terms of commodities.

The value of gold in terms of dollars depends on our government policy and nothing else; as long as our Treasury is willing to buy and sell it at $35 an ounce, gold will be worth $35 an ounce. There is nothing under the sun which should make it impossible for our government to uphold that price, although there may be many things which may make it undesirable to do so. When we feel that it is no longer desirable to maintain the price of gold we may of course lower it. Gold can lose in value in terms of dollars only through an action of our own, not through actions of foreign nations.

The value of gold in terms of foreign currencies depends on other nations. But what does it mean that gold loses in value in terms of foreign currencies? It means—if the dollar price of gold is maintained—that these foreign currencies become more and more valuable in terms of dollars; that is to say, that the foreign-exchange rates of these countries rise steadily with all the awkward deflationary pressures which this would have on their markets. We can be fairly sure that countries would not normally like to embark on such a policy. Hence, unless gold production becomes as exuberant as silver production once did, it is not likely that gold will lose value in terms of foreign currencies while we maintain its dollar value. As long as other nations feel sure that the conversion of gold into bank-deposit dollars remains possible, they will be glad to accept gold, too.

The value of gold in terms of commodities is, as long as the dollar price of gold is fixed, nothing but a matter of commodity prices. With inflationary armament and war expenditures all over the world, commodity prices are likely to rise in the next years, and in this sense the value of gold is likely to decrease. Increased gold production is only one of several and not the most powerful factor tending in this direction. Should new gold mines be discovered or new production methods be developed, the inflation through gold purchases might become very serious. Even at the present rate of gold production we may find, after the war, that the inflationary pressure is more than we like and we may find it desirable to lower the dollar price of gold. But we need not fear anything like a runaway inflation through a gold deluge. The commodity value of gold is much more a function of government spending and credit expansion than a function of the gold supply.

I suspect it is not the rise in commodity prices of which people are afraid when they ask the question whether or not gold can lose its value. What people have in mind is the $35 which an ounce of gold is now worth, or perhaps the value in terms of foreign money. In these respects, however, the United States has the decisive say and we need not worry much about outside forces.

DOMESTIC CIRCULATION OF GOLD COINS

Question VI: Would it be a good idea to readmit gold into domestic circulation?

Such a step would do no harm but it would do no good either. Gold coins in· actual circulation could never mean much in our monetary system. Even if people did prefer gold coins to $10 and $20 bills—which is more than doubtful—not much of our 21 billion dollars of gold would be absorbed by circulation, because the circulation of bills in these denominations amounts to no more than 3 billion dollars. In actual fact only a very much smaller sum would be absorbed by active circulation.

Gold hoarding might possibly absorb more. But would gold for purposes of private hoarding be very popular in times when the possibility of a reduction in the dollar price of gold is constantly under discussion? Of course, if Congress decides on new gold coinage, the people may take it as a determination to refrain from further changes in the gold content of the dollar. The present low interest rates on savings deposits and government bonds are factors favorable to the development of new gold-hoarding habits of our people.

But what is the good of such hoarding? One advantage might be that private gold hoarding would reduce the present excess reserves of our banks, something which ought to be done but can be done by other methods. Otherwise there is little that one may claim for the proposal. The prospects of possible fluctuations in the popularity of private gold hoarding would definitely be an important argument against the proposal. And there is absolutely no advantage in committing ourselves to a definitive gold price at this moment when everything is in flux and nobody knows how the world will look in a few months.

Gold and the Public Debt

Question VII: Can the United States use some of its gold to reduce the government debt?

This is only a naïve layman's question, but it pops up so frequently in discussion that it deserves an answer. When I deal with it from this forum I speak, as it were, for the galleries.

First of all, the gold in the possession of the Treasury is not at its free disposal; gold certificates have been issued against the gold; before the gold is used otherwise, the gold certificates would have to be replaced by something else: by new government debt perhaps? Increase the debt in order to decrease it?

Secondly, the present holders of the government debt—individual savers, corporations, insurance companies, and banks—are not interested in gold and would not for a moment think of holding gold coins instead of interest-bearing bonds. The gold coins paid to the present holders of government securities would be deposited and would be back at the Federal Reserve banks within twenty-four hours. The member banks' excess reserves would have grown immensely within that day. And all the newly created funds, both those of the bank customers and those of the banks themselves, would then desperately try to seek investment outlets. The savers, insurance companies, etc., could hardly be expected to hold on to their non-interest-earning bank deposits, nor could the banks afford to carry nothing but idle reserve balances in place of interest-bearing government bonds. The inflationary effect of all this would not in the least be different from that of a debt redemption through greenback issues.

Let us follow through the greenback way of paying debts in order to compare it with the "golden" way of paying debts. If the government decided to redeem its bonds with new greenbacks, there is no chance that the paper currency would be kept by the repaid bondholders. Instead it would be deposited in banks, and by the banks with the Federal Reserve banks. Excess reserves would jump sky-high and the newly created funds, both of bank customers and banks, would struggle for outlets. Knowing that the greenbacks would not stay in circulation but be exchanged for bank deposits, the Treasury could easily short-cut the whole procedure by depositing the newly issued greenbacks directly with the Federal Reserve banks and redeeming its bonds by check. Now it should be clear that it would make little difference whether the statement of the Federal Reserve banks showed new gold coins or new gold certificates or new greenbacks among its assets. In any case, excess reserves would be in dizzy height and the masses of new funds in the possession of former bondholders would start a wild, inflationary chase for earning assets. The banks would be drowned in their liquidity and would probably find themselves unable to pay salaries from their deficient earnings.

Thus the consequences of both methods of repaying government debt —using the gold or using a greenback issue—are the same and, of course, equally dangerous; but one must say that the greenback issue would be much simpler than the roundabout transactions with the gold.[2]

THE VALUE OF LARGE GOLD RESERVES

Question VIII: If the world retains gold as an international medium of exchange, will our large gold reserve be of advantage to us?

So large a reserve as the United States has can hardly ever be of any service. It can be of disservice if it is allowed to be a psycho-political temptation with regard to inflationary experiments. Otherwise the buried gold does us no harm and no good.

We shall probably never use the gold in exchange for commodity imports unless we change our attitude concerning large import surpluses. The people of the United States have too long been taught that unfavor-

---

[2] Hardly any of the U.S. government debt in 1940 was in the hands of foreign holders. The use of gold to reduce foreign debts is therefore not discussed in the text. [Added in 1963.]

able trade balances are something really unfavorable. Only in case the United States has to fight a long war or to indulge in a heavy inflation would large imports find a friendly reception. In an extended war we might be willing to buy sufficiently from South America and from India and use some of our gold to pay for the import surplus. In a serious inflation fast-rising prices might create and permit an import surplus, and in payment for this import surplus, as well as in a flight of capital, we might lose a portion of our gold stock. Apart from these (rather improbable) possibilities there is little chance at the time being that we shall use substantial parts of the gold for payments abroad.

Perhaps the possession of the vast gold stock can prove to be a valuable weapon at a future peace conference; however, we must not forget that the weakened nations after the war may have to use any credits they can get to purchase imports rather than to build up new gold reserves.

Given our attitude toward imports we seem to be justified in regarding as very unlikely that the gold which we now have will ever again leave our country. Even if the greater part of the world retains gold as the international medium of exchange and returns to some form of a gold standard, the gold to be produced in the next few years and the gold now held by other nations will probably be sufficient to take care of all international payments in the postwar period.

If this is correct then it would not be incorrect to speak most irreverently of our large monetary gold stock. One might, for example, make the drastic and cruel statement that if some 15 billion dollars of our gold stock suddenly evaporated into thin air the nation would have lost nothing.

Postscript after 23 years [3]

The forecasts made in the answer to Question VIII proved sound for some eighteen years, but turned sour after 1958. What was held to be "improbable" became a fact: the United States had occasion to "use substantial parts of the gold for payments abroad." This came about after (1) several increases in the price of gold in terms of foreign currencies, leaving some of them "undervalued" relative to the dollar, (2) substantial increases in U.S. commodity prices, tending to make the dollar overvalued relative to some other currencies, and (3) large dollar payments for foreign aid, loans, investments, and military expenditures abroad.

To reexamine old forecasts which have proved to be wrong and to reflect on the reasons for the unexpected outcome is a wholesome practice. It is more customary, though, to let the forecasts be forgotten.

[3] Postscript appended in 1963.

X I

A Proposal to Reduce the Price of Gold

Raising the Price of Gold ■ Reducing the Price of Gold ■
From Dollar Shortage to Dollar Glut ■ Our Power over the
Price of Gold ■ Effects upon Money Markets and International
Reserves

Several economists have proposed that the dollar price of gold be increased. Some of them think that this would help alleviate or remedy the
present imbalance in the international accounts of the United States. This
implies that the price of gold would not be raised equally by other
financially important countries. Others think that the price of gold should
be increased everywhere and that this would supply more international
liquidity, a desirable result if international trade is to continue growing
in the future.

RAISING THE PRICE OF GOLD

I submit that these objectives would not be served well by increases
in the price of gold and, indeed, that the proposals themselves have con-
tributed to the present imbalance. Expectations that the dollar might be
devalued inevitably result in mass decisions to switch from dollar balances into gold holdings, or at least in decisions not to build up further
dollar balances. In raising and reinforcing these expectations, the proposals have reduced the dollar liquidity preference and increased the gold
liquidity preference of the world; have therefore reduced the demand for
and increased the supply of dollars in the foreign-exchange markets and
increased the demand for and reduced the supply of gold in the gold
markets; and all this is reducing the international liquidity reserves in the
process.

I cannot blame the gold buyers and gold hoarders for acting on these expectations. The historical experience of the world has been that gold hoarders usually gained in the long run, because governments and central banks have, on thousands of occasions, increased the gold price in terms of national currencies but have almost never, if ever, reduced the official gold parity. The one-way expectation—that the price of gold can go up but cannot go down—is a destabilizing factor in the international economy. Years ago I believed, as many had taught us, that this one-way expectation, by making gold a safer store of value than money, worked on the whole as a stabilizing influence, in that it held monetary authorities to greater discipline and caution. If this was true once, it no longer is. The knowledge that gold would be demanded from the monetary authorities has not, I believe, in the last fifty years kept many governments or central banks from increasing the domestic stock of money if such an expansion was considered desirable or necessary to obtain other policy objectives. If the faith in gold does not act as an effective brake upon inflationary policies, what other purpose does it serve?

REDUCING THE PRICE OF GOLD

If the proposal I am going to make should be regarded as injudicious, or even crazy, it may harm my reputation as a political economist, but I believe it cannot harm our national interests. On the contrary, I believe that the mere discussion of my proposal may prove helpful from several points of view—e.g., as a damper on gold speculation—even if it should not be accepted as the best of all possible policies. Here, then, I beg to propose that the dollar price of gold be reduced in two, three, or more instalments. This would reverse historical experience, and those who persist in holding gold would lose money.

Before I offer explanations, let me make clear that the adoption of my proposal would presuppose negotiations, under the auspices of the International Monetary Fund, with foreign governments and central bankers, especially of the United Kingdom, France, Western Germany, and several others, and would require an act of the United States Congress, amending the Gold Reserve Act of 1934. Since I do not believe that a change in foreign-exchange rates is necessary to correct the present imbalance in our international accounts, I would assume that the British and French would reduce the price of gold in terms of sterling and francs at the same time and by the same percentage. I believe that the German mark may stand some realignment and that this could be accomplished in the least painful way by Germany's reducing the price of gold a little more than the rest of us. I assume that none of these foreign governments would want us to act unilaterally, since a reduction of the dollar price of gold without simultaneous reductions in London, Paris, and Frankfurt would imply depreciations of the sterling, the franc, and the mark in terms of dollars, which they surely would want to avoid.

As to timing and extent of the proposed reduction of the price of gold, I submit that there should be *ample advance notice* and only *moderate mark-downs*. For example, the first reduction might be by only 2 per cent, effective late in 1961 or early in 1962; the second reduction by another 2 or 3 per cent, one year after the first.[1] I do not think we should now decide to adopt a scheme of a continually dwindling value of gold— listen, ghost of Silvio Gesell—but we should leave open the possibility that further periodic reductions may be made later. (Incidentally, while advance notice of an increase in the price of gold would be foolish and harmful, advance notice of a decline is both useful and fair.)

FROM DOLLAR SHORTAGE TO DOLLAR GLUT

Now let me offer my explanations. We have gone through a transition from dollar shortage to dollar glut while the sign of the balance of payments on current plus capital account has remained the same. That is to say, we have had a balance-of-payments deficit in this sense in the very years when everybody cried his heart out over the dollar shortage. By means of this deficit we supplied, between 1950 and 1955, a net amount of almost $10 billion, or over $1½ billion a year, for reserve accumulation by the rest of the world. Despite these annual "deficits," there were many economists speaking of a chronic "surplus" in the United States balance of payments. This was sensible only in that the net supply of dollars in the foreign markets was less than was wanted and demanded for reserve accumulations in these years. By dollar *shortage* one could have meant— although few writers did—that the foreign nations wanted more than the $1½ billion a year to build up their reserves. From 1958 to 1960 our annual deficit has been over $3½ billion, and this represents a dollar *abundance* because the foreign nations *do not want that much.* Indeed, the net supply of dollars has been that high this year [1960] partly because there have been so many who were supplying dollars in the process of switching from dollars into gold. Moreover, the reason for the demand for dollars not being greater lies in the unwillingness of many foreign individuals, firms, banks, and central banks to see their dollar balances grow when a devaluation of the dollar appears imminent to them. Thus the present imbalance is, to a large extent, the consequence of the ex-

---

[1] In order to guard against the possibility that gold hoarders would sell their holdings just before the price reduction becomes effective and then repurchase at the reduced rates, it would be preferable to schedule the reductions at shorter intervals. For example, four reductions a year, of 1 per cent or three-fourths of 1 per cent each, would, with the trading costs involved, prevent hoarders from switching back and forth.

pectation that the dollar price of gold will be increased. Now an expectation that it will be reduced instead can do much to remedy the present imbalance.

The point, in short, is this: the balance-of-payments problems of a country whose short-term liabilities are the foreign reserves of other countries are different from the problems of most countries. For example, a given net supply of dollars on current and capital account constitutes a *shortage* when the demand for dollar reserves is high but an *excess supply* when the demand is low. The demand can be increased when holding dollars is made more desirable than holding gold, and this will be the case when a reduction in the dollar price of gold is expected.

OUR POWER OVER THE PRICE OF GOLD

Can we effectively determine the price of gold? If we reduce the price of gold from $35 an ounce to $34.30, will this stick—or will it be an ineffective gesture? It all depends on whether we are willing to sell any amount of gold that may be demanded at that price. If we sell without restriction and without batting an eye, the price will be fully effective— and people will stop buying gold from us. For there is no hoarder's demand for anything that he can obtain in practically unlimited quantities at a price which is sure to be lower after a while. (I am aware of the possibility that speculators will not believe our announced intentions. If we never hesitate to sell, they should learn that we really mean it.)

If the United States finds it proper, for some reason, to continue the present practice of selling gold only to central banks and treasuries, then we should arrange for some of these monetary authorities to keep the gold market always so well supplied that the price cannot rise, even for a few minutes, above our gold export point. In my opinion, the $40 episode should have been avoided, and even to allow a $36 price in London was bad management on our part.

Incidentally, the 25 per cent gold certificate reserve requirement for our Federal Reserve banks should be abolished in any case, so that the whole world will know that our gold is for sale—all of it, if anybody wants it. Of course, under these circumstances nobody will want it. On the contrary, almost everybody will want to sell his gold. In a sense, it is too bad that we should again give good dollars, and possibly good resources, for gold which will be virtually useless to us; but *noblesse oblige*. We may reduce, but probably should not destroy, the value of gold, and hence we should be willing to peg the price of gold by buying what is offered at the prices we fix. And other responsible financial centers of the West should do likewise.

As soon as it is decided that the price of gold in dollars, pounds sterling, francs, marks, etc., will be reduced, the offerings of gold will increase rapidly. The South Africans will want to sell all they can before the price reduction becomes effective. The same is true for Soviet Russia, which one can safely infer has been holding back for quite some time in the expectation of an increase in the gold price. (The proposals to increase it have got the hopes of the Russians and the South Africans up; they will be sorely disappointed, but I cannot get myself to weep tears over their disappointment.) Several central banks also will want to avoid a loss in their reserves and will, if a reduction of the gold price is announced, prefer to switch from gold into key currencies. Finally, there will be those who have switched from dollars into gold and will now switch back into dollars and other key currencies. It has been quite expensive for them to pay for storage and insurance and to forego interest on their gold holdings, but they do not mind as long as the gold price is expected to rise. But if it is to fall instead, every day of holding on to the gold would be foolish squandering. We do not know how many billion dollars' worth of gold will appear from everywhere for sale to the monetary authorities, but it will be plenty if the proposal is adopted.

Effects upon Money Markets and International Reserves

The effect upon interest rates can be quite significant. The rash of new sterling balances, dollar balances, mark balances, resulting from gold sales to the monetary authorities is apt to mean such a rapid increase in the supply of liquid funds that—if I may assume neutral effects upon business expectations—short-term rates may be reduced to levels not seen in the last two years, and long-term rates, too, may come down from their lofty heights and send ailing government securities up to par. I suspect that these side effects of the reversal of the gold-price expectations would not be considered undesirable by most of us.

One last question: How would international liquidity reserves be affected in the long run? Triffin wants an international supercentral bank to provide more liquidity. My proposal is not incompatible with the Triffin plan; indeed, it meets one of his objectives, namely, to remove the destabilizing effects of recurring flights out of key-currency reserves into gold. The advocates of gold-price increases hold, quite correctly, that an increase in the gold price would add to the reserves, first, because given stocks of gold would represent more money and, second, because new gold production would be more profitable and would therefore provide larger flows of gold. What I propose avoids the windfall profits to Soviet Russia and South Africa but would provide larger liquidity reserves by getting gold out of the hoards. It would release gold from speculative reserves to transactions reserves. Expressed differently, an *increase* in the price of gold would increase the total supply of gold, though it might also increase the speculative demand for gold; a gradual *decrease* in the price of gold would reduce the demand for gold. As the demand for gold for speculative purposes is reduced, international liquidity reserves are created both by increasing the amounts of gold available for transactions reserves and by making dollar balances and other key-currency balances more acceptable as international reserves.

I do not advance my rather unorthodox proposal as a solution to all problems concerning the imbalance in the international accounts. While I regard my proposal as more than a "gadget" or "gimmick," I do not regard it as a substitute for sound monetary and financial policies in this or any other country.

XII

The Fuzzy Concepts of Liquidity, International and Domestic

Recent discussions of the international monetary system and its proposed reinforcement or reform are largely carried on in terms of "international liquidity." Experts disagree as to whether the present system has supplied "liquidity" in insufficient, adequate, or excessive measure; whether it can provide "liquidity" in the face of shock-waves of hot-money movements; and whether it can furnish adequate "liquidity" in the long run as world production continues to grow and world trade grows even more.

In some of these contexts, "international liquidity" is obviously something measurable and comparable with other numerical magnitudes. In other contexts, however, it seems that liquidity is not a quantity but rather a quality. Thus, when the gold-exchange standard supplies large "quantities" of "international liquidity" in the form of dollar balances held as monetary reserves by the central banks of many countries, it is argued that the system's "liquidity"—evidently a quality—suffers in the process. And a "liquidity crisis" occurs when given amounts of dollar and sterling balances in the possession of foreign traders and banks are suddenly regarded as less safe and therefore "less liquid."

With this ambiguity of meaning it is possible for a system to be considered deficient in liquidity exactly because it has supplied excessive liquidity. The danger of confusion is great; in particular, it becomes difficult to ascertain the extent to which contradictory statements by different experts reflect differences in judgment or merely differences in semantics.

The same ambiguity exists with regard to "domestic liquidity." This observation has frequently been made by readers and reviewers of the Radcliffe Report on the Working of the Monetary System.[1] Several of them have asked just "what is liquidity"[2] and have embarked on textual analysis, exegesis, and criticism of the Radcliffe pronouncements on the subject. But apart from the meanings of liquidity in Radcliffian contexts, a semantic clarification of the term, with reference to both national and international monetary analysis, is overdue.

THE NEED FOR A SEMANTIC CLARIFICATION

The need for a discussion of the meaning of "liquidity" would be surprising, in view of the age of this word, were it not for the fact that economists are given to the disconcerting habit of changing their lingo. Following the vagaries of fashion, economists nowadays employ the word "liquidity" much more often, and for many more things or relations, than they used to. Once upon a time, they spoke of the liquidity of certain kinds of assets[3] and of the liquidity of particular debtors or groups of debtors, such as the commercial banks of a country. They would hardly have known then what to make of such expressions as the liquidity of an entire economy or the "international liquidity" of the entire world. Now such simple words as "quantity," "stock," or "supply," of money, reserves, or gold have apparently become too plain, too unsophisticated, for many modern experts. For, it seems, in perhaps three out of every four instances one could with good results substitute these simple old words for the term "liquidity," and, indeed, many a sentence would make better sense after such a substitution.[4] This is true in discussions both of domestic and of international monetary problems.

[1] Committee on the Working of the Monetary System, *Report* (London: H.M.'s Stationery Office, Comnd. 827, 1959).

[2] Cf. Frank W. Paish, "What *Is* This Liquidity?" *The Banker*, Vol. CIX (October 1959), pp. 590-597. For a very illuminating essay, see M. J. Artis, "Liquidity and the Attack on Quantity Theory," *Bulletin of the Oxford University Institute of Statistics*, Vol. 23 (Nov. 1961), pp. 343-366.

[3] Cf. Fritz Machlup, "The Liquidity of Short-Term Capital," *Economica*, Vol. XII (1932), pp. 271-284, where I dealt with a theoretical, not a semantic, confusion.

[4] Some writers have adopted the term "liquidity" but stated without circumlocution that they meant by it nothing but the supply of money, near-money, or credit. For example, the late Per Jacobsson said this: "By liquidity I understand the supply of credit in national currencies as needed to finance and provide the means of payment for trade and production." Per Jacobsson, "The Lessons of Experience," Supplement to IMF *International Financial News Survey*, Vol. XV (May 10, 1963), p. 170. Even more clearly defined is the term in the following statement in a Dutch bank report: "The total liquidity circulating in the economy comprises two elements; one is the money supply, or primary liquidity, while the other consists of secondary liquid assets. These include claims on banks, local authorities and the Government which are in the hands of holders other than those entities, and which can be converted in large amounts into

References to "international liquidity" are not often found in the older literature on the international monetary system. The problems, however, have always existed. The predecessors of those who now warn of an insufficiency of international liquidity used to be alarmed about an inadequate supply of gold, a maldistribution of the existing gold stocks, and the constant struggle of the central banks for the "all too narrow gold cover" (as the punsters liked to say in allusion to some bedfellows' struggle for a narrow coverlet).

THE SCARCITY OF GOLD AND THE STRUGGLE FOR THE "NARROW COVER"

The first lessons the student of the gold standard was taught by the older texts usually related to the safeguards which it provided against debasement of the currency. There was, above all, the "natural" scarcity of the monetary metal, due to the fact that its annual new supply was only a very small percentage of its total stock and could not easily be increased at will. Thus, as long as the nations of the world stuck to the "standard" and abstained from substituting other "reserve moneys" (e.g., central-bank balances) for gold, they would not be able to inflate their currencies. There was, secondly, the famous "specie-flow mechanism," with its inexorable penalties for countries which had been overindulgent in their domestic credit policies. Whenever a member country of the international gold-standard system took liberties in providing greater "ease" in its credit market, it was soon subjected to a drain of its gold reserve resulting in an automatic contraction of its domestic money supply and imposing a stern discipline on its monetary authorities.

These two features of the international gold-standard system—the scarcity of the total supply and the struggle of each separate member for a minimal part of the "narrow gold cover"—were hailed by the anti-inflationists and cursed by the anti-deflationists. By those who saw the chief merit of money in the relative stability of its value, the scarcity of gold and the penalties against lenient monetary authorities were regarded as blessings. To those, however, who saw in the expansion of monetary circulation an instrument for promoting economic growth, the restrictions which the system imposed upon domestic money creation seemed most deplorable.

None of this has really changed, only the terminology. Where our predecessors said that the scarcity of gold and the struggle for gold reserves limited the expansion of the quantity of domestic currency and

---

money at short notice without substantial expense or loss on the rate." The report then offers a statistical tabulation to show that in the Netherlands, in the first nine months of 1962, "domestic liquidity rose by Fl. 1,087 million." *Amsterdamsche Bank Quarterly Review*, No. 138, Third Quarter 1962, p. 37. Where liquidity stands for such clearly specified quantities, the use of the word in lieu of "quantity of money and near-money" is unexceptionable but quite unnecessary.

deposits, our contemporaries say that the inadequacy of world liquidity and the struggle of each country to maintain sufficient international liquidity restrict the supply of domestic liquidity. And those who fear inflation praise these limitations upon liquidity, international as well as domestic, while those who advocate attempts to accelerate growth through continuous expansion of effective demand complain about the inadequacy of liquidity. What has the new terminology got that was missing in the old?

THE MEANINGS OF LIQUIDITY

Leaving aside the (relatively clear) meaning of liquidity as the attribute (or complex of attributes) of an asset, and confining ourselves to the meanings of liquidity as a position of an individual or a group—of any size, up to a whole nation or even the whole world—we propose to interpret it, provisionally, as a "capacity to pay promptly." [5] It can be expressed as a ratio of funds disposable to funds needed over a certain period of time. But one must ask: *whose* capacity to pay *for what* and out of *what kind of sources?* And since each of these questions [6] allows for several answers, which may be combined in various ways, we shall have to face an embarrassing number of variations in the exact meaning of the term. We may also anticipate that the indefiniteness of meaning probably accounts for the popularity of the term.

Better understanding requires that we reflect on the various possibilities of answering the three questions posed. We shall begin with the possible *sources of funds,* we shall proceed next to the relevant *uses of funds,* and we shall come finally to the possible *subjects* whose capacity to pay is being referred to. In listing the possible sources, uses, and subjects of paying capacity, we shall not attempt exhaustive enumerations but only illustrative catalogues.

Possible sources of funds:
  a. Existing money balances (i.e., "cash on hand").
  b. Existing balances of money and near-money.
  c. Existing balances of money and near-money *plus* receipts from other claims [7] that can be collected promptly.

[5] For interesting comments on the gradual shift of meaning from liquidity of an *asset* to liquidity as the *possession* of liquid assets, and finally to somebody's, or some group's, liquidity *position,* comprising the actual and potential possession of assets and also the facilities to borrow relative to contingent liabilities, see H. W. Arndt, "The Concept of Liquidity in International Monetary Theory," *Review of Economic Studies,* Vol. XV (1947-48), pp. 20-26.

[6] A fourth question—to pay *what?* what kind of money?—need not be asked separately, for it is implied in the other questions. Different "moneys" are needed, depending on the particular subject and the particular purposes. This will become clear in the discussion to follow.

[7] We say "other" claims because most moneys and near-moneys are legally claims

d. Existing balances of money and near-money *plus* receipts from other claims that can be collected promptly *plus* proceeds from other assets that can be readily sold without serious (?) losses.

e. All the funds enumerated in *d, plus* such funds as can be promptly secured through borrowing on reasonable (?) terms.

f. All the funds enumerated in *d, minus* any funds needed for repaying debts due or maturing shortly.[8]

g. All the funds enumerated in *d, minus* any funds needed for repaying debts due, maturing shortly, or payable on demand.

h. All the funds enumerated in *d, minus* any funds needed for repaying debts due, maturing shortly, or payable on demand, and *minus* funds needed (?) for purchasing assets, or repurchasing debt securities outstanding, which cannot be allowed (?) to "go begging."

i. All the funds enumerated in *e, minus* funds needed for debt repayments (as in *g*).

j. All the funds enumerated in *e, minus* funds needed for repayment of debts and acquisition of assets or debt securities (as in *h*).

Some of the ten sources of funds listed are vague or indefinite, especially where subjective judgments are involved, as in the references to "serious" losses and "reasonable" terms or to "necessary" purchases of assets or debt securities which "cannot be allowed to go begging." Where the capacity to pay is that of an individual debtor, the subjectivity of the judgment is harmless or even appropriate. Where, however, the paying capacity of a group of debtors is involved, the problem of subjectivity becomes messy. To this problem we shall return when we discuss the possible *subjects* of liquidity, the possible groups of payers, but it will haunt us also when we reflect on the possible *uses* of funds. A minor difficulty will be encountered here when we find that the subtractions made in five of the sources (*f* to *j*) can alternatively be regarded as uses of funds. If they are so regarded, double counting must be avoided, that is to say, these "net sources of funds" must not be related to such uses of funds which include the same debt repayments or acquisitions of assets and debt securities.

Possible uses of funds:
1. Purchases of goods and services in the smallest tolerable (?) amounts.

---

against governments or banks. (I trust that the reader is informed that the accountant's sources-and-uses-of-funds statements include both "stocks" and "flows" of funds.)

[8] Instead of listing funds available *minus* certain requirements, as is done in items *f* to *j*, one had better treat the deductions as uses of funds. This, with a warning against double counting, is actually done later in items 5 to 7 in the list of uses. We present the alternatives because several writers on liquidity, especially international liquidity, prefer to show immediately the "net position" of the reserve holder.

2. Purchases of goods and services in the accustomed amounts.

3. Purchases of goods and services in amounts increasing at certain rates.

4. Purchases of goods and services in any amounts desired (?).

5. Payments of debts due or maturing shortly.

6. Payments of debts due or maturing shortly, *plus* debts payable on demand.

7. Payments of debts due, maturing, or callable (as in 6), *plus* purchases of assets or repurchases of debt securities outstanding, which cannot be allowed to "go begging" or are bargains too attractive to be missed.[9]

8. Purchases of goods and services as in 1, *plus* payments of debts as in 5.

9. Purchases of goods and services as in 1, *plus* payments of debts as in 6.

10. Purchases of goods and services as in 1, *plus* payments of debts and acquisitions of assets or debt securities as in 7.

11. Purchases of goods and services as in 2, *plus* payments of debts as in 5.

12. Purchases of goods and services as in 2, *plus* payments of debts as in 6.

13. Purchases of goods and services as in 2, *plus* payments of debts and acquisitions of assets or debt securities as in 7.

14-16. Purchases of goods and services as in 3, *plus* payments as in 5, 6, or 7.

17-19. Purchases of goods and services as in 4, *plus* payments as in 5, 6, or 7.

Obeying the warning against double counting in linking sources and uses of funds, we should note that, while sources *a, b, c, d,* and *e* may be combined with any of the nineteen listed uses, it would be illegitimate to combine any of the sources *f, g, h, i,* or *j* with any of the uses except 1, 2, 3, or 4. Of course, different formulations would have yielded other variations and other combinations, but our purpose here is merely to indicate by means of illustration that the number of possibilities is extremely large.

Nothing specific has been said about the period of time during which all these payments have to be made. In comparing the funds available from the various sources with the funds required for the various uses, two conventional ways come to equivalent results. Either one takes the requirements (uses) over one year and divides them by the availabilities (sources), which are in the nature of stocks on hand (and perhaps some

[9] The reader may recognize here the "speculative motive" for liquidity preference.

absolutely assured receipts [10]); or one takes these availabilities and sees for what length of time, in the absence of an ordinary income flow, they can cover payments to be made for the various uses. If the ratio of annual requirements to the (relatively) prompt availabilities is 4:1, the availabilities cover the requirements for a quarter year, or three months. But let us proceed now to the possible subjects who have funds available to pay for various uses.

Possible disposers of funds:

A. An individual household, firm, or bank.

B. A group of households, e.g., all consumers in a country.

C. A group of firms, not including financial institutions, e.g., all private firms in trade and industry in a country.

D. A group of financial institutions, e.g., all deposit banks in a country.

E. The government, including public agencies and enterprises, except the monetary authority.

F. The households *plus* the firms, excluding financial institutions, in a country.

G. The households *plus* the firms including financial intermediaries, except deposit banks, in a country.

H. The households *plus* the firms, except deposit banks, *plus* the government, except the monetary authority, of a country.

I. The households *plus* the firms *plus* the deposit banks *plus* the government, except the monetary authority, of a country.

J. The households *plus* the firms *plus* the deposit banks *plus* the government *plus* the monetary authority of a country.

K. The households *plus* the firms *plus* the deposit banks *plus* the governments *plus* the monetary authorities of a group of countries.

L. The monetary authority of a country.

M. The deposit banks *plus* the monetary authority of a country.

N. The monetary authorities of a group of countries.

O. The deposit banks *plus* the monetary authorities of a group of countries.

P. All the monetary authorities of the world.

In all instances except A and L—where the reference is to an *individual* household, firm, bank, or central bank—a troublesome question arises regarding any of the uses of funds and any of the sources of funds. The point is whether debts among members of the group and payments for intragroup purchases are to be included or "netted out." The answer will, of course, depend on the problem at hand, but a failure to ask and

---

[10] If some sources of perfectly assured receipts are added to the stock on hand, this constitutes a sort of "secondary liquidity."

answer the question can lead to serious confusion. If, for example, one wishes to examine the "liquidity" of all deposit banks in a country, it may be appropriate to exclude interbank loans and interbank deposits. Likewise, if one inquires into one country's capacity to pay for purchases from or debts to other countries, domestic purchases and domestic debts of the paying country may be irrelevant; moreover, the composition of "money balances"—source a of the paying country—is likely to be quite different from that of the money balances held by most households, firms, and banks within the country. In some cases a clear answer will be almost impossible because one "person's" money or near-money is another "person's" debt and it may not make much sense to ask for their combined liquidity, the liquidity of the two together.

NON-ADDITIVE LIQUIDITY

The liquidity of a firm, its capacity to pay promptly, can be determined as soon as one decides what sources and uses of funds should be taken into account. For example, the concept A-12-d is relatively unambiguous. It refers to the funds which a firm will need—over a given period—for purchases of goods and services in accustomed amounts and for payments of debts due, maturing, or payable on demand, and to the funds over which it can dispose in the form of balances of currency, check deposits, time deposits, accounts receivable and promptly collectible, government securities, and other assets readily salable for cash. But as soon as we ask for the aggregative liquidity of two or more firms, we run into conceptual difficulties. Should we include the purchases which one firm would make from another firm in the group? Should we include the accounts payable by one firm and receivable by another firm in the group? These questions cannot be answered in any simple manner. The capacity of the firms within the group to pay to one another is one thing; their capacity to pay to firms outside the group is another thing. To ask for their combined liquidity without specifying the intent of the question is meaningless.

It may make good sense, we have agreed, to inquire into the liquidity of the deposit banks of a country. But what can be the sense of a combined or aggregated liquidity of all households, firms, and deposit banks, all as one group, such as covered by "subject I"? Should we add the cash balances (chiefly check deposits) of the households and firms to the cash balances (chiefly central-bank funds) of the deposit banks? Should we deduct debts payable on demand, although this would virtually offset the cash balances of the depositors? Such an offset would actually be required by concept I-2-g, which prescribes that any funds needed for repaying debts due, maturing shortly, or payable on demand be subtracted from the available "liquid" funds. On the other hand, concept I-2-b would require that the bank balances of the depositors be added to the liquid assets of the banks—which would in effect amount to adding the banks' sight *liabilities* to the banks' assets. Few analysts would see much sense in such an addition. Yet we shall see later that an analogous procedure is widely accepted in calculating the "aggregate liquidity" of a group of central banks or the "international liquidity" of the free nations of the world.

We shall not in this essay make further use of our catalogue of possible meanings; its purpose—to demonstrate the multiplicity of meanings and the consequent want of clarity—has been realized. What one also discovers from the brief reflection is that a refined and specific concept of liquidity which may be appropriate in describing the position of an individual or a relatively homogeneous group is no longer appropriate for groups of heterogeneous types of cash-holders, debtors, and payors. The actions of one type of cash-holder affect the position of other types, and these effects cannot be appropriately dealt with in terms of an aggregative "liquidity" of a heterogeneous group. In particular, one must not try to aggregate non-additive items. If "money balances" consist of different things for different members of the group—say, for industrial firms, deposit banks, and central banks—the total of the "money balances" held by these different types of "subjects," let alone their combined "liquidity," does not have a definite meaning. Since the firm's cash is the bank's liability and the bank's cash is the central bank's liability, there is no point in talking about the total liquidity of the group without specifying precisely what it is supposed to include and to exclude, and what purposes it is supposed to serve. The use of technical terms is justified if they are more concise and/or more precise than the words for which they stand. The term "liquidity" is concise only at the expense of precision; it can be made precise, or even intelligible, only by a full specification of all the items that are taken into account. This, however, makes it rather useless for many kinds of discourse.

To guard against misunderstandings, it should be stated that what we need is not a *term* better than "liquidity." There is no use proposing a term if it is not clear exactly what it is to designate. A term in search of a meaning is a rather useless thing; a meaning in search of a term can easily be accommodated by imaginative word-coiners, provided the meaning is clearly and unambiguously specified. Once we know what combination of specified variables and magnitudes is highly serviceable in an analytic argument or model, we have finished forming the relevant concept, defined by the specification of its contents, and only then do we look for a name for it. The name (i.e., the term) serves as a time-saving device in oral and written discussion, since it allows us to skip the full specification of the concept whenever we have to refer to it. Needless to say, we should not borrow the term from other meanings, since this is confusing and misleading. To use the term "liquidity" for the mixed bag of things for which it is now being used violates two rules of good semantic practice: first, it involves borrowing (or stealing) a term from fairly established meanings and, secondly, it involves using the term for a nonspecified combination of ambiguous (and partly inconsistent) notions.

If analysts, in discussions of a domestic monetary situation, refuse to speak of the quantities of currency and check deposits, and insist on "looking at the whole liquidity position," [11] they evidently mean to say that other things besides currency and deposits ought to be taken into account. The term "liquidity" may help to warn the audience not to disregard "other things," but it will not help very much if these other things are not specified or, if specified, are not measurable or, if measurable, are not additive.

INTERNATIONAL LIQUIDITY

The same difficulties obtain with regard to "international liquidity." The position of an individual central bank can be discussed in terms of its capacity to meet its foreign obligations out of its disposable reserve of international means of payment plus some other funds to which it may have ready access; and there is nothing wrong with giving this capacity to pay the name "international liquidity" of that central bank. Trouble begins when several or all central banks are considered *as a group* and an evaluation is attempted of their capacity to pay one another out of their holdings of gold, convertible currencies, and foreign bank balances, or with funds obtainable through the sale of other foreign assets and through foreign borrowing. Here the problem of additive and non-additive assets and liabilities raises its ugly head. Another problem, to be discussed later, lies in the fact that contingent foreign obligations of central banks arise not only from their own foreign debts (and hardly ever from their own purchases abroad) but chiefly from purchases and debts of individuals and firms in the countries whose domestic money these central banks supply or control.

The additivity problem is essentially the same as that encountered when the "aggregate liquidity" of depositors and bankers was considered. Suppose, just for a moment, that all countries except the United States and the United Kingdom were keeping their foreign reserves in the form of dollar and sterling balances, which of course are liabilities of the United States and the United Kingdom. To count them as "international liquidity" of "all central banks taken together" is to add the foreign sight-liabilities of the United States and the United Kingdom to the monetary

[11] This phrase is used in the Radcliffe Report.

gold stock. If *all* gold were concentrated in the reserves of the United States and the United Kingdom, the so-called aggregate liquidity of the two "banker-countries" together with all the "depositor-countries" would be equivalent to the sum of the former countries' assets (gold) and their sight-liabilities (due to the depositor-countries).

To be sure, the use of the liabilities of the reserve-currency countries as foreign reserves of other central banks is precisely the "strength" as well as the "weakness" of the gold-exchange standard. Under this system the total of assets used as central-bank reserves is increased. But to designate this larger gross total of reserves as "liquidity" of the international monetary system contributes nothing to the problem—except a bit of confusion. It would be better if we admitted that the liquidities of banker-countries and depositor-countries, like the liquidities of bankers and depositors, are not additive. Whereas it is quite reasonable to include both the borrowing capacity and asset-liquidating capacity of any one central bank as part of its liquidity, the inclusion of such facilities in a notion of an "aggregate liquidity" of the international system as a whole cannot pass an examination where proper standards of logic are maintained. As one bank can borrow only what another bank lends, and can dispose only of as many assets as are bought by others, the increase in liquidity of the borrowers and sellers involves a reduction in the liquidity of the lenders and buyers.[12] This is true notwithstanding the unquestionable fact that the willingness of central banks to use their surplus reserves (as well as their own sight-liabilities) to help the deficit countries may be of utmost importance to the latter as well as to the international system as a whole.[13]

LIQUIDITY PREFERENCE, DOMESTIC AND INTERNATIONAL

Perhaps it should be noted that the concept of "liquidity preference," which has played such an important role in Keynesian and post-Keynesian monetary theory, is not preference (or demand) for liquidity in any of these complicated or sophisticated meanings. It is preference or demand for money (or for a particular kind of money), and the liquidity-prefer-

[12] The two changes are opposite but not necessarily equal, because of the different impingement of risk on the different parties involved. It is this asymmetry in the effects on the liquidity position of different countries which allows certain international arrangements—such as arrangements to borrow or to swap currencies—to have any net effects at all.

[13] In a way this inter-central-bank-lending of reserves is analogous to the inter-bank-lending in the "Federal Funds market" in the United States. I say "in a way," because the analogy is incomplete in that the Federal Funds lent and borrowed by commercial banks are deposits in the Federal Reserve banks; central banks cooperate by lending gold or deposits in other countries (as well as their own deposit-liabilities), but not deposits in a super-central bank. One might think that the market in Euro-dollars is analogous, but this is not the case, since—at least until now—only private banks, not central banks, trade in Eurodollars.

ence curve is the demand curve, intersected by the supply curve of money.[14]

If certain non-money assets are accepted as good substitutes for money for certain purposes or if certain borrowing arrangements allow people to do with lower cash balances, this involves, in Keynesian terminology, a reduction in liquidity preference—not an increase in the supply of liquidity. There is an advantage in choosing one's theoretical concepts in such a way that they have measurable, or at least quantifiable, counterparts. If liquidity preference is a demand for currency and/or deposits and is met by a supply of currency and/or deposits, the confusion caused by the infusion of non-measurable or non-additive elements is avoided.[15] An international-liquidity preference, if such a concept is to be employed, would likewise have to be a demand for a measurable and additive "international money."

If gold is the only kind of international money, the meaning of international-liquidity preference is relatively unambiguous. It is a schedule of the amounts of gold reserve a nation, a group of nations, or all nations together, will want to hold at various interest rates that could be earned by exchanging gold for foreign securities. In brief, it shows gold reserves as a function of the yield on foreign non-money assets.[16] The concept of international-liquidity preference becomes quite involved if interest-bearing dollar claims (bank balances or government securities) are international money. Assume that dollars are the *only* international money, so that international-liquidity preference refers to the holding of dollar reserves. Which interest rate, then, will be the one of which the demand for dollar reserves is supposed to be a decreasing function? Evidently *not* the interest earned from liquid dollar assets. Presumably the most relevant variable would be interest foregone by holding liquid dollar assets rather than less liquid dollar assets, that is, the interest differential between those dollar assets (bank balances, U.S. Government securities) that

[14] The Keynesian concept of liquidity preference denotes a demand curve for cash balances in terms of interest rates (or the inverse of a price index for securities) at a given level of income (that is, with income as a parameter, in order to take care of the transactions-demand for cash, a part of the total demand that varies, in the main, not with securities prices but with transactions). The older concept had been that of a demand for cash balances in terms of the value of money (or the inverse of a price index for goods and services). Where several types of money circulate and are exchangeable for one another, one may extend the theory by distinguishing separate demand (or liquidity-preference) curves for each type of money. For example, there may be a currency-liquidity preference and a deposit-liquidity preference.

[15] Whether only demand deposits or also time deposits and savings deposits ought to be included in the supply of and demand for money is a question which will have to be argued on other grounds. Bank deposits of all types are measurable and their inclusion could not be refused in the name of nonmeasurability.

[16] One may, in analogy to domestic-liquidity preference, distinguish between transactions-demand, precautionary demand, and speculative demand for gold, and assume that the first is independent of the interest rate, so that the total demand is interest-elastic only because of the other components.

are accepted as international reserve, and assets that are not so accepted. The substitute assets from which higher yields could be obtained are obviously also foreign, though not necessarily American, securities, since no part of the reserve would have to be given up for the acquisition of domestic securities.

Whether such a concept of international-liquidity preference makes much sense, analytic, didactic, or otherwise pragmatic, remains to be seen. To a large extent this would depend on institutional arrangements. For the domestic economy, liquidity preference in terms of private balances of domestic money makes sense because for many holders the substitution between liquid balances and non-money securities is a very real choice, and changes in the yield from such securities will affect this choice significantly.[17] This is not so for the official holders of international money, to wit, for the national monetary authorities. While they hold liquid dollar assets, they do not readily consider exchanging them for non-liquid foreign assets even though they might thereby obtain much higher yields. If there existed an international money market on which central banks were lending and borrowing international reserves, the interest rates obtaining in this market might affect a bank's decision either to loan out some of its reserves at higher rates or to keep "liquid" by holding on to its dollar reserves earning lower rates. In the absence of such institutional arrangements, it is hard to see what the concept of international-liquidity preference could do for us as a "tool of analysis."

The less fashionable Cambridge concept of a demand for cash balances as a function of the real value of money—the inverse of the price level—is more adaptable to international-reserve holding. Since each country holds a foreign reserve in order to pay for imports and can accumulate a reserve by collecting for exports, the prices relevant for the demand for foreign cash balances are presumably those of importable

[17] The Keynesian apparatus is really designed for a world of two assets only: money and real capital goods. Money is the asset which yields liquidity but no other returns; liquidity preference determines the demand for money as a function of the rate of return foregone. Real capital goods yield returns but lack liquidity; the marginal efficiency of capital determines the demand for these real assets as a function of the rates of return over cost. The real world, however, knows many different kinds of assets, varying in both yield and liquidity. There is a broad spectrum with a continuity of shadings between the extremes, the non-yield, perfectly liquid money assets and the high-yield, illiquid real assets. In order to deal analytically with the vast variety of assets of different yield-and-liquidity mix, it is expedient to distinguish at least two additional asset types lying between money and real assets, to construct, that is, a four-asset model with (1) *money*, (2) *near-money securities*, (3) *non-money securities*, and (4) *capital goods*. Near-money securities combine high liquidity with low yield, while non-money securities combine low liquidity with high yield. The distinction between capital goods and the non-money securities (which usually are titles to collections of real assets and to the returns they yield) is important in order to separate purely financial from real investment. The distinction between near-money and non-money securities is important in the analysis of many monetary problems. It should be noted that hardly any part of this model is of help in the analysis of international problems.

and exportable commodities. At higher prices, that is, at a lower real value of international money, more of it will be wanted for the country's foreign reserve. Any conception of this sort can show its usefulness only when the model is made to work, that is, to show what equilibrating adjustments would be generated by various kinds of disturbances. Thus, let us assume that, after an initial equilibrium of international reserves and international commodity prices, the volume of reserves is suddenly increased, say, by some international arrangement that furnishes each central bank with additional drawing rights, international balances, or gold. Unless the demand for reserves is infinitely elastic, the central banks will adjust to the excess reserves by adopting expansionary monetary policies, which will lead to increases in the effective demand for goods until the prices of international commodities have risen sufficiently to make the increased reserves just adequate. In other words, the larger volume of international money held by the central banks would eventually, through an equilibrating decline in the real value of international money, become the "equilibrium volume." The model can be used also for other "problems," for example, to demonstrate how an increase in the demand for foreign reserves that is not met by any increase in the stock of international money would compel an increase in the real value of such money—that is, an international price deflation—as an equilibrating adjustment. While all this sounds quite reasonable, it can hardly be said that the concept of the demand for international money is either indispensable or superior to other tools of analysis in this area.

Returning, despite our bad impression of its workability, to the concept of international-liquidity preference, we may pursue this idea a little further, looking for its possible implications for the case in which several kinds of international money, some carrying interest, are used simultaneously. For this case, where gold as well as interest-bearing claims in two or more foreign currencies are held in the official foreign reserves of monetary authorities, one may distinguish gold-liquidity preference, dollar-liquidity preference, sterling-liquidity preference, DM-liquidity preference, etc. One may even construct models for the quantitative determinations of these functions. Peter B. Kenen,[18] for example, proposed a function according to which the nations' willingness to hold dollar balances would depend on the interest rate paid on such balances (compared with interest rates elsewhere) and on the ratio of the U.S. gold stock to U.S. short-term dollar liabilities (or rather dollar claims of central banks).

While such models have some didactic value, I submit that aggregative functions should not be used where the described behavior is

---

[18] Peter B. Kenen, "International Liquidity and the Balance of Payments of a Reserve-Currency Country," *Quarterly Journal of Economics*, Vol. LXXIV (1960), pp. 572-586.

explained as political decision-making based, not on established rules of thumb, but on the wisdom and discretion of the authorities. It makes sense to reason in terms of an aggregative demand function which depicts the probable decisions of large numbers of individual households and firms, acting upon preferences and judgments in attempts to maximize utility or profit. It makes less or no sense, however, to reason in terms of a demand function (e.g., for dollar balances) if it is supposed to depict the probable discretionary decisions of some of the largest central banks.[19] One may perhaps speak of dollar-liquidity preference and compare its changes with those of gold-liquidity preference, but one must not go far in relying on the stability of the factors that may determine the shapes and positions of the respective curves.

Another word or two on these ideas, in a somewhat facetious vein. Closely associated with most arguments in terms of domestic-liquidity preference has been the notion of the Keynesian "liquidity trap," the infinitely elastic lower end of the curve. Some monetary politicians might well wish that there were a relevant international-liquidity preference with an analogous liquidity trap capable of absorbing any amounts of dollar claims that might be furnished by deficits in the U.S. balance of payments. How many difficulties could be avoided by such an infinitely elastic demand for dollar balances on the part of the rest of the world! (Such a "liquidity trap" for gold might be conceivable, but not for any foreign currency.)

One might think that the concept of international-liquidity preference could be of help in the analysis of the consequences of an increase in the transactions requirements possibly associated with the growth in world trade. Depicted by a shift of the curve to the right, with the stock of international money unchanged or insufficiently increased, could not the resulting increase in interest rates be read off the diagram, and the further effects—upon investment, total effective demand, income, and employment—be inferred? This question cannot be answered affirmatively once we understand that international-liquidity preference is largely politically determined and, moreover, if we realize that the increase in requirements for international transactions cash has only been assumed, not proven.

The analysis of the demand for or requirements of foreign reserves is, I conclude, not facilitated but encumbered by reasoning in terms of "international liquidity" and "international-liquidity preference." The substantive problems, however, are in urgent need of further analysis.

[19] It is not only the "political" decision-making which, because of the element of discretion, makes the concept of a genuine demand function inapplicable to the explanation of the amounts of foreign reserves wanted by central bankers. It is also the fact that they are in oligopsonistic positions in the market for reserves. It may be well to remember that demand curves are useful tools only where the would-be buyers are in purely competitive positions, and that there is no "demand curve" (as a function of price) of a group of monopsonistic or oligopsonistic buyers.

XIII

Further Reflections on the Demand for Foreign Reserves

The "Needs of Trade" ■ Reserves for Contingent Liabilities ■ Large, Small, or No Reserves ■ Private versus Official Foreign Reserves ■ External Benefits ■ Rigged Exchange Rates ■ The Demand for Foreign Reserves

This essay is a sequel to one dealing with the concepts of liquidity. Having concluded that the notions of "international liquidity" and "international-liquidity preference" contribute only to confusion, and not to a fruitful analysis of the problems involved, I felt the need for further reflections on the demand for foreign reserves. Although the supply of pronouncements on the demand for international reserves has become so abundant that it can no longer be absorbed by even the most diligent student of the monetary system, I believe that many misconceptions must be cleared up and moved out of our way before we can hope to gain better insights into the problem.

In the following attempt at clarification and analysis we shall resort to the well-tested technique of looking at the same problem from different points of view. The notion of a "demand" for, or "need" or "optimal supply" of, international money reserves will be discussed on the basis of different assumptions regarding the institutions adopted. At the outset the size of reserves will be considered under the assumption of fixed rates of exchange, which is, of course, the customary procedure. Later on, however, the size of foreign-exchange holdings, private and official, maintained under a system of freely flexible exchange rates will be considered. This may look as if the case for floating exchange rates were to be argued here, but such is not the objective of this essay. When the assumption of freely flexible exchange rates is introduced, the purpose will be strictly analytical: to look at the problem of the size of reserves in isolation from policy goals pursued under different institutions. This warning is given at this point lest the reader expect a tract on monetary policy, and it will not be repeated later lest the flow of the argument be interrupted. For the moment, and until further notice, we proceed under the assumption that most countries have adopted fixed exchange rates and intend to maintain them.

THE "NEEDS OF TRADE"

That international reserves must continually increase to take care of the secular growth of foreign trade is usually taken to be a self-evident statement, not requiring any proof. This is a different "needs of trade" theory than the one enunciated as an argument for unrestricted discounting of commercial paper. (One can imagine, though, that a novel needs-of-trade theory might be advanced in favor of an international super-central bank discounting ever-increasing volumes of commercial bills of exchange.[1])

The theory that an increased volume of international trade "requires" proportionally increased international reserves implies that there must be something like a minimum or an optimum ratio of reserves to trade (or to imports). If we inspect the available statistics, we find that these ratios have varied from year to year and from country to country, and that the variations have been large. To give a few examples, the ratio of gold reserves to imports was 5.3 per cent in the United Kingdom in 1913 and 60 per cent in France in 1928. The ratio of gold-plus-exchange reserves to imports in France was 165 per cent in 1937 and only 13 per cent in 1957; in Portugal, 21 per cent in 1928 and 187 per cent in 1954; in Switzerland, 30 per cent in 1928, 187 per cent in 1937, and 98 per cent in 1957. The ratio of aggregate gold reserves to aggregate imports of all countries (excluding the Communist Bloc) was 19 per cent in 1913, 32 per cent in 1928, 110 per cent in 1938, 55 per cent in 1948, and 35 per cent in 1957. One can surmise that some of the ratios in particular countries at certain times were uncomfortably low, but there is little empirical evidence point-

---

[1] The analogy is most suggestive. The commercial-loan or "real bill" theory took it for granted that expanding commerce "needs" an expansion of the circulating medium and that there is no danger of an overexpansion in satisfying all the demand for commercial loans that should be forthcoming in the form of "real" bills of exchange submitted for discount. If international money is needed chiefly to finance international trade, a case might be made for the creation of such money through the discounting of bills of exchange arising from international trade. The argument, like that in support of the domestic needs-of-trade theory, suffers from a confusion between need of trade and demand for capital, and from a disregard of the dependence of the demand for loans upon the rate of interest.

ing to a "right" ratio of reserves to imports either in individual countries or in all countries together. Nor do the statistical figures give any indication of the adequacy or inadequacy of the present reserves relative to imports. The ratio of official gold and foreign-exchange holdings of all countries (excluding the Communist Bloc) to their imports was 49 per cent in 1960; this was much less than the 117 per cent in 1938, but much more than the 21 per cent in 1913. Incidentally, this "drastic decline" and "sharp increase," depending on the year with which the comparison is made, teaches again the old lesson that one must not trust trends and rates of change derived from arbitrarily chosen base years.

Assuming the ratio of world reserves to world trade was "satisfactory" in some base year, on what grounds could it then be claimed that a given rate of growth in trade calls for the same rate of growth in international reserves? There are probably strong reasons for believing that the ratio of domestic-household cash balances to household expenditures is more or less stable over time. This, however, does not allow us to infer that a similarly stable relationship must also prevail between foreign reserves and imports of nations. In sectors in which clearing systems are operated, the ratio of cash balances to total transactions is most volatile. Thus, stock-market transactions can rise tenfold while brokers' bank balances rise only very slightly. I do not say that foreign trade is more similar to trade in securities than to trade in consumer goods. But we can accept the one analogy no more than the other as conclusive indication of the amounts of liquid balances "required" in foreign trade.

Another analogy, also telling against the notion that reserves should increase proportionately with foreign trade, may be found in inventory theory. There it has been shown that the need for inventories increases only as the square-root of sales.[2] This result has been applied to the transactions demand for cash in a simple model believed to be relevant for domestic money circulation.[3] The precautionary cash requirements, likewise, seem to grow only as the square root of the volume of transactions.[4] All this may fully apply to the increase of foreign-money reserves wanted or needed to sustain growth of foreign trade.

Perhaps it should be added that the growth of world trade may involve changes in the composition of trade, with either increased or reduced shares of the trade in commodities, or of countries, that are

[2] Thomson M. Whitin, *Theory of Inventory Management* (Princeton: Princeton University Press, 1953), Chapter 3.

[3] ". . . the square root formula implies that demand for cash rises less than in proportion with the volume of transactions, so that there are, in effect, economies of large scale in the use of cash." William J. Baumol, "The Transactions Demand for Cash: An Inventory Theoretic Approach," *Quarterly Journal of Economics*, Vol. LXVI (1952), pp. 550-551.

[4] *Ibid.*, p. 556. Baumol cites Edgeworth and Wicksell for earlier statements of this view.

subject to relatively greater fluctuations, seasonal and cyclical. This is another reason why the ratio of world reserves to world trade is not indicative of anything much.

Finally, one should not overlook that international payments are not always payments for goods and services. Payments on capital account, however, may either offset payments on current account or be in addition to them. In the first case the demands on foreign reserves will be diminished, in the latter increased. While the consideration of payments on capital account suggests again another reason against the assumption of a need of constant ratios of reserves to trade, we shall not at this point concern ourselves with the effects of international capital movements and of international payments or borrowing arrangements upon the size of monetary reserves.

Reserves for contingent liabilities

Neither the cash-holding practices of households, nor those of business firms or of securities brokers are closely analogous to the reserve-holding needs or practices of central banks. The chief difference lies in the fact that households, firms, and brokers need cash balances in order to pay for their own purchases (or, in the case of brokers, for purchases they agree to make for their clients), whereas central banks hold foreign reserves in order to make foreign payments for purchases not by themselves or by their clients, but by persons unknown to them. These purchasers hold domestic money and the central banks undertake to exchange it into foreign currency whenever demanded.

The "liquidity requirements" of central banks are thus for uses of funds which they do not themselves determine. Yet, the amounts of the contingent liabilities involved are not beyond the control of the central banks. By controlling the amounts of domestic money at the disposal of all the households and firms in the country, they indirectly control the amounts which the holders of domestic money can spend on purchases from abroad or in other foreign transactions. Since every unit of domestic money used for obtaining foreign exchange from the monetary authorities reduces the domestic cash balances of households and firms—unless the banking system by expanding credit replaces the balances which the households and firms have spent for foreign exchange—the authorities need not fear that their contingent liabilities (pursuant to a promise to provide all foreign exchange demanded at a fixed rate) are unlimited or even unduly large. The domestic cash balances shrink with every purchase of foreign exchange from the monetary authorities and thus the loss in foreign reserve cannot go on forever—provided the authorities follow the old "rules of the game."

In several countries, however, the new game of the rulers is opposite to the old rules of the game. Instead of allowing domestic circulation ("liquidity") to run down automatically through foreign-exchange sales to domestic money-holders (and instead of even reinforcing this automatic mechanism through the orthodox discipline of absolute credit restriction) the monetary authorities under the new game undertake to maintain effective demand (or even increase it in order to support economic growth and high employment at rising wage rates). Under such policies the contingent liabilities of the monetary authorities may indeed be unlimited and the loss of reserves perpetuated until a *deus* appears *ex machina*. For example, some strongly inflationary policies of foreign countries which are important as importers or as competing exporters may turn the trick. Of course, such "good luck" cannot be counted on and one should admit, therefore, that *no* amount of foreign reserve may be adequate for a country that indefinitely continues a policy of maintaining effective demand in the face of an excess demand for foreign currency at fixed exchange rates.

Large, small, or no reserves

Whether a country "needs" large foreign reserves, or only modest ones, or none at all, depends largely on the policies which it adopts. One may associate the various preferences in this respect with different objectives or aversions.

Assume a country has *no* foreign reserve at all. What would happen in a period of excess demand for foreign exchange? Either the nation would introduce direct controls of imports and payments or it would have to allow the prices of foreign currencies to rise. Thus, by implication, the desire for reserves implies (1) an aversion to direct controls and (2) an aversion to freely floating exchange rates. Now assume that the country does have reserves but only of *modest* size. In this case, direct controls can be avoided and an excess demand for foreign exchange can be satisfied at fixed exchange rates, provided the old rules of the gold-standard game are followed and money circulation and credit supply are allowed to contract whenever foreign currencies are sold out of reserves. *Large* reserves are needed only if such contractions are prevented by credit policies designed to maintain effective demand. In other words, the desire for large reserves implies an additional aversion, namely (3) an aversion to tighter credit and the usually associated reductions in money incomes and prices. Were it not for the offsetting credit expansions which the central banks permit when their reserves decline, the balance of payments would reverse itself quickly. But this would be in conflict with the modern objective of guaranteeing an ever-growing effective demand to support full employment at rigid or rising wage rates.

Thus, to repeat, *large* reserves are needed only if the "old-fashioned" adjustments of domestic money circulation (incomes and prices) are rejected; if freely moving exchange rates are rejected; and if direct controls of trade and payments are rejected. These rejections or aversions can be translated into a positive desire to permit any national excess-spending that may have developed to continue without restraint. The overspending, reflected in the excess demand for foreign currencies, could be stopped in three ways: by contraction of effective demand, by devaluation or unpegging of the currency, or by direct restriction on imports or payments. If none of these is allowed to come into effect, then clearly the "need" for a reserve of international money will be large, if not unlimited.

The policy of permitting a nation to spend more than its income *plus* its receipts of foreign capital and grants, and of keeping a foreign reserve to draw upon for such national overspending, is understandable if the excess demand is *temporary*. Assume, for example, that there occurs an accidental failure in some line of production, resulting in a reduced supply of exports or an increased demand for imports. To fill this gap by drawing on a foreign reserve is an efficient arrangement. It allows recourse to foreign goods and services, without forcing up the prices of foreign currencies and, consequently, the domestic prices of many exportable goods, imported goods, and substitutes for them.

In many cases, however, there is serious doubt whether the "gap" is really temporary, or even honestly expected to be temporary. When the "need" to fall back on foreign resources persists for a longer period, the arrangement is not beneficial but injurious. Only for tiding over a brief disturbance is it less costly to have and use foreign reserves and thereby avoid the repercussions by which flexible equilibrium exchange rates would affect the entire economy. But to live off foreign reserves for longer periods would be rather costly, not only because it would delay adjustments in resource allocation which eventually would prove unavoidable, but also because the maintenance of a reserve position adequate for such "enduring emergencies" imposes upon the economy a sacrifice of presumably much more productive uses of capital.[5]

It is too often overlooked that the accumulation of monetary reserves by a nation represents a formation of capital [6] that remains unproductive

[5] The word "presumably" is to be emphasized. There can be circumstances in which the presumption would not hold, particularly when the limit within which investable funds can be productively absorbed has been reached in the country concerned.

[6] A nation can accumulate foreign reserves through an export surplus—which implies diverting national product to foreign use and abstaining from taking foreign product in exchange for it—or through receiving foreign capital without using it, but keeping it as a liquid reserve instead. New methods of reserve accumulation have been proposed recently which do not involve capital formation but are the result of international credit creation by a super-central bank or by inter-central-bank arrangements.

(or almost so) in its present form and becomes productive only through its eventual use in an emergency. Until the emergency arises, the sterile (or almost sterile) foreign reserve is like an investment in accident insurance. The marginal productivity of capital invested in domestic productive facilities may be 10 or 15 per cent per annum (and even higher in some of the capital-poor nations), whereas the current yield of foreign reserves invested in liquid dollar securities or bank balances would be 1 or 2 per cent at best. The "productivity" of foreign reserves consists chiefly in the loss avoidance at the time they are used up, that is, in the prevention of those losses and damages which the nation would suffer from forced liquidation of assets and from temporary allocative adjustments that prove wasteful when subsequent readjustments have to be made. But just how high is the probability of such temporary emergencies? To be prepared for highly improbable emergencies is a luxury only the very rich can afford. For a nation to hold "unnecessarily" large foreign reserves is to forego productive domestic investment in order to be prepared for unlikely accidents. Very large foreign reserves for a relatively poor nation are like a very high fire insurance for a relatively poor family. There should be a reasonable relation between insurance premiums, risks, and income.

Perhaps a more appropriate analogy is the cash balance which everybody—household or firm—holds for precautionary motives. As far as domestic money is concerned, every business firm finds it a *necessary* investment to carry a cash balance related to its transactions needs and a *prudent* investment to carry a cash balance for precautionary and speculative purposes. The same rational considerations that firms employ in determining the size of their cash positions may be relevant for the determination of the size of the foreign reserve held by a nation.[7]

Even this effortless and painless acquisition of international fiat money would not dispose of the dilemma that the maintenance of the reserve implies a sacrifice of immediate satisfaction or earlier construction of productive facilities. (Note again the qualification regarding the limits within which investable funds can be productively absorbed per period.)

[7] There are alternative ways of looking at the problem of determining the social benefits of central reserve-holding. Instead of concentrating on the domestic resources freed and foreign resources acquired when foreign reserves are used in an emergency, one may find it important to consider and evaluate the techniques by which a monetary authority can induce the nation to make use of its accumulated reserves. If the only techniques available for this purpose are either domestic inflation or up-valuation of the currency—both encouraging imports and discouraging exports—the authorities may dislike the side-effects of these methods of inducing the use of the unnecessarily large reserves, and may prefer to hold on to the reserves even if no need for them is anticipated in the foreseeable future.

The reverse aspects of this approach to the problem may also have to be explored. One may have to take account of the benefits which a large reserve confers on a nation by allowing its monetary authorities to pursue expansionary monetary policies which could not be undertaken with smaller foreign reserves. These policies evidently

PRIVATE VERSUS OFFICIAL FOREIGN RESERVES

In the preceding sections the discussion of the size of foreign reserves has related to the holdings by monetary authorities. The "large, small, or no reserves" were the gold and foreign-exchange holdings of central banks pursuing various kinds of monetary policy, and when the discussion proceeded to the question of the "optimal" reserve of the nation it was tacitly assumed that this reserve was held by the monetary authorities. We shall now turn to a consideration of *privately* held reserves of foreign or international money.

Under most systems some private business firms would find it expedient to carry their own foreign balances. Producers importing some of their materials and exporting some of their products may find it cheaper to hold foreign exchange rather than risk buying the exchange needed for their imports at a price higher than they receive for the exchange proceeds from their exports. Private foreign balances would be especially large under a system in which the monetary authorities hold no international reserves and allow exchange rates to be determined in a free market. Of course, producing and trading firms can avoid exchange risks by hedging operations in the forward market; the cost of such hedging may in some instances be higher, in other instances lower, than the loss of interest from carrying foreign balances. If many businesses rely on hedging, it will pay others to engage in speculation, and these speculators will hold "inventories" of foreign balances. Thus, in the absence of official reserves and officially pegged exchange rates, private firms and banks will hold large foreign-exchange reserves, and the size of these reserves will be determined by private marginal-productivity considerations. In other words, the "nation" will carry a foreign-exchange reserve even if its monetary authority does not. Once this fact is recognized the relevant question to ask is whether it is, as a rule, socially beneficial to make reserve-holding a government function.

The tested approach to the analysis of a question of this sort is to inquire, in Pigovian fashion, whether the social marginal cost of reserve-holding is lower than the private marginal cost, and whether the social

---

lead to the eventual use of the reserves, but the benefits of this use—i.e., the benefits of the trade deficit induced—may be considered less important than the benefits obtained by the expansionary policy that has led to it. (Some of these problems are examined by Hang-Sheng Cheng, "A Theory of the Optimal Amount of Foreign Reserves of a Central Bank," a doctoral dissertation submitted to Princeton University in 1963.)

The difference between these approaches and the one followed in the text is not difficult to comprehend. In the text the analysis concentrates on the benefits of the future temporary trade deficit which the recourse to the large foreign reserve makes possible. The analysis suggested in this footnote adds to or deducts from these benefits the advantages or disadvantages expected to be associated with the monetary policies which induce the deficit.

marginal product of reserve-holding exceeds the private marginal product. Let us make a probing stab in this direction.

Since foreign-exchange balances are held to avoid the risk of loss from exchange-rate fluctuations, it stands to reason that risk-pooling can reduce the cost. If a thousand separate firms were holding their own foreign reserves in order to avoid risk, their total reserves would undoubtedly have to be larger than the reserves of a central pool carrying out this function for all these firms. Centralization, therefore, reduces the cost of holding reserves in amounts adequate for the purpose sought by the individual members of the pool. Does this settle the question about the comparative cost of official versus private foreign reserves? It would if centralization and government operation were the same thing—which they are not. Centralization may be only partial and need not be complete in order to fulfill its function. Just as risk-pooling in all sorts of insurance need not, in a large country, involve government operation of the insurance business but can be accomplished by a number of private insurance companies competing with one another, so can the pooling of exchange risks be accomplished by a number of private banks engaging in the foreign-exchange business for profit. Competition among several banks operated for profit can probably secure a more serious consideration of the marginal cost of reserve-holding than a central bank is likely to attempt under a beneficent management.

To put the argument more simply: If all the firms in foreign trade had to hold their own foreign reserves, the absence of pooling would surely increase the cost, because the total of reserves would be unnecessarily large. If all reserves were held in a single pool, the absence of competition would most likely increase the cost, because nothing would compel strict rationality and economy in the determination of the optimum size of reserves. But if there were, say, ten competing banks dealing in foreign exchange and holding the reserves they thought best for their business, there would probably be adequate pooling applied and adequate rationality observed in the holding of foreign reserves.

The size of the foreign reserves maintained by the private traders, jobbers, and dealers in foreign exchange would, in the absence of official reserves, depend on the marginal net returns expected from additional investment in reserves. These returns, obviously, are a function of both cost and revenue, and the revenue depends chiefly on the demand for risk-avoidance by individual business firms engaged in international transactions. Any increase in the risk of rising prices for foreign currencies would of course increase the demand for hedging and the profitability of reserve holding. Yet, complete flexibility of exchange rates would avoid the socially wasteful accumulation of foreign exchange at times when people expect that the monetary authorities might pursue a policy more expansionary than their counterparts in foreign countries, for this would immediately increase the forward exchange rates of the currencies less likely to be inflated. Under a system of pegged exchange rates and official currency reserves, speculative hoarding of foreign exchange and gold sets in, and this is likely to be a socially unproductive use of the nation's resources. With freely flexible rates and decentralized reserve-holding, the spot and forward prices of foreign currencies would anticipate the consequences of unduly expansionary fiscal and monetary policies, so that the disfunctional accumulation of reserves could be avoided.[8]

The implications of private, rather than official, foreign reserve-holding for the determination of the social optimum of the total held by the nation can, however, be analyzed more clearly if the assumption of possibly inflationary monetary policies is replaced by an assumption that the monetary authorities follow strict rules for regulating the supply of money, either limiting the total stock of money (including bank deposits) to a fixed annual rate of increase (or to a fixed amount per head of population or of the labor force) or prescribing adjustments in the stock of money to reverse any changes in a specified price index. If it were generally expected that these rules would be obeyed, the marginal productivity of exchange reserves would reflect only the probabilities of loss-and-cost avoidance in the case of short disturbances that cannot be foreseen as to time, place, and incidence but can be anticipated in actuarial fashion. In other words, the assumption of noninflationary central-bank policy allows us to rule out exchange risks arising chiefly from monetary management and to isolate the risks of exchange fluctuations arising from "real"—not merely monetary—changes and occurrences affecting international transactions. The point at issue is whether the probabilities of such changes and occurrences can be more successfully evaluated by private business firms, engaged in industry, trade, and finance, and hedging or holding foreign reserves to meet temporary emergencies, or by a governmental authority holding the bulk of the foreign reserves for the entire nation.

It may be argued that this evaluation can be made more reliably by individual firms, for what counts are not only the probabilities of the various changes or occurrences but also the estimates of their economic impacts in terms of alternative costs and losses. If each firm makes its own hedging operations in view of all the exchange risks which it faces, and if each exchange dealer makes his decisions regarding the amounts of for-

---

[8] The accumulation of reserves is called disfunctional in this case because it serves only the speculators' desire to profit from the delayed adjustment of the peg, an adjustment eventually unavoidable because of the relatively overexpansionary policy of the monetary authority.

eign balances which it seems reasonable to carry in view of his commitments and prudent expectations, the resulting determination of the aggregate foreign reserve held by the nation is apt to be optimal—with two provisos. The first proviso is that the social benefits from holding foreign reserves do not exceed the private ones; the second is that there is no great danger of exchange dealers cornering the market and rigging the exchange rates. Whether these provisos are satisfied must now be examined.

EXTERNAL BENEFITS

A temporary disturbance, we have concluded, may be more likely to cause smaller economic losses if the particular "shortages" can be met through recourse to foreign sources of supply paid with foreign currency from existing reserves than if the required products or materials can only be procured, if at all, through sacrifices of other imports or through readjustments of domestic production under the stimulus of price changes produced by exchange-rate movements made necessary by the lack of foreign reserves. The difference between the two losses is the benefit—or loss avoidance—that can be attributed to the availability of adequate reserves. The question is whether the losses avoided by firms which either hold the reserves or through their hedging operations cause others to hold them are the entire losses that are spared the economy as a whole or whether there are any third parties who also benefit (through loss avoidance) from the availability of reserves. In other words, are all the benefits internal to the firms insuring themselves against the exchange risks or are there additional external benefits?

The simplest way of getting at the main issue is to think of the losses that can be avoided through the holding of foreign reserves as the costs and losses of converting and reconverting productive plant. The owners of plant take account of all these potential costs and losses when they consider the advantages of exchange hedging or exchange holding. But some of the costs or losses of the twofold change are borne by others, for example, by the workers in the establishments affected by it. It takes only one moment's consideration to realize that business firms would act differently if they rented their machines by the day instead of owning them, and likewise, that the firms would act differently if they hired workers by the year rather than by the week, day, or hour. The losses avoidable by a firm thanks to the availability of reserves would be greater if the costs and losses of transferring and retransferring labor, or maintaining an idle work force, had to be borne by the firms concerned. Hence, the private marginal productivity of hedging and reserve holding would be higher in this case. It follows that, under conditions where labor is neither owned by the firms nor employed with annual wages, there are likely to exist external benefits not taken into account by business decisions.[9]

The same kind of reasoning is probably applicable to general inventory theory. The inventories of industrial or commercial firms are determined by optimizing—profit-maximizing or loss-minimizing—decision-making. No matter whether ordinary marginalistic principles are employed or modern game theory or electronic-computer programming to devise optimal inventory policies for the firms, only internal, not external, benefits are taken into account. Hence it might be argued that all inventories held by private business in trade and industry are apt to fall short of what would be socially optimal.[10] Should one infer from this that the government ought to take over the task of holding inventories of materials, semifinished and finished goods of all sorts in order to insure a closer approximation to the social optimum? Or, if the cost of governmental inventories of all goods were forbidding, should the government pay subsidies for private inventory-holding? Probably not, since on all halfway realistic assumptions regarding governmental efficiency the result would be much farther removed from a social optimum than would be any outcome from the unrestricted and nonsubsidized inventory practices of private enterprise.

The problem of the optimal size-determination of governmental inventories of foreign exchange is not quite so complicated as the problems would be with inventories of all sorts of goods. But has anybody ever tackled the problem, or suggested clues about possible ways of solving it? As far as I know, the problem has not even been raised, and this is not surprising since official reserves under a system of fixed exchange rates are not even supposed to be of optimal size: they are an incidental result of the market balance of payments, which in turn is an incidental result of the monetary policies of all the countries involved. Experience with freely flexible exchange rates is much too sparse for anyone to have thought of, let alone studied, the question of optimal reserve-holding. In the absence of any precepts in this regard, it would appear unwise to saddle the monetary authorities with the task of holding supplemental foreign-exchange reserves under a system of freely flexible rates.

Those who would want the monetary authorities to hold foreign exchange in order to supplement private holdings when rates are supposed

[9] We must bear in mind, as an offsetting consideration, that wage rates per hour are probably higher if labor can be hired by the hour, day, or week than they would be if labor had to be hired on annual contracts. This is so because the uncertainty and loss possibilities involved in annual contracts would reduce the private marginal productivity of labor. In other words, workers who bear the uncertainty of employment are paid for it.

[10] Conversely, if the external effects were unfavorable, the inventories held would be excessive in relation to the social optimum.

to be floating, responding to nothing but free market forces, overlook the fact that, on purely economic grounds, reserves are held only for the purpose of being eventually used. Their use—the sale of foreign currencies out of official reserves—must depress the prices of these currencies in the exchange market (or keep them from rising). If only one country intervenes in the market, while other countries stay out and leave the exchange rates alone, the operations of the intervening authority will cause no trouble. But what a mess if in the exchange between two currencies both monetary authorities in question intervene to influence the exchange rate! Assume that the authorities in one country sell the other country's currency in order to keep its rate down, while the authorities in that other country find it appropriate to sell the first country's currency at a reduced price. The exchange rate between the two currencies would in this case be inconsistent in the two markets, and *arbitrageurs* could make virtually infinite amounts of profit until one of the monetary authorities gave up or until the two authorities got together and agreed to fix the same rate. This would be a system of temporarily fixed, not freely flexible, exchange rates, and it stands to reason that authorities, having accepted flexibility as the preferred system, would sooner or later learn to stay out of the market and refrain from intervening. However, if no interventions are intended, reasons for official reserve-holding disappear.[11]

Rigged exchange rates

The second proviso has still to be dealt with: the danger that private exchange dealers, under a system of flexible rates and no official reserves, may corner the market and rig the rates. Conceivably, the largest banks dealing in foreign exchange could get together and start unloading portions of their currency holdings, or even selling short, in order to create general bearishness and to induce non-bank holders of foreign currency to sell out at still lower prices—at which the operators can cover their short sales and buy back what they had sold. Conversely, the largest op-

[11] If our earlier conclusion regarding the social benefits of reserve holding and, hence, the contention that the size of reserves privately held might be smaller than would be socially warranted, were taken more seriously, what implications would this have for official interventions in the foreign-exchange market under a system of freely flexible exchange rates? The conclusion was derived from assumptions about the social and private losses in the case of unforeseeable emergencies requiring adjustments in the allocation of real resources which would soon have to be reversed at high cost. On the basis of this argument one may claim that under a system of floating exchange rates official emergency reserves should not be used for the mitigation of day-to-day fluctuations in rates nor for meeting a demand for foreign exchange that has resulted from overexpansions of credit, but only for compensating for temporary failures in production or temporary shifts in demand. The authorities would have to use much restraint in deciding when to resort to the "emergency ration" of international money.

erators acting in concert could start accumulating larger foreign-exchange holdings, buying spot as well as forward, thereby creating a bullish attitude of the market and inducing others to speculate on a continuing rise. At sufficiently higher prices for foreign currencies the conspirators could liquidate their long positions with profit. Actions of this sort would produce disfunctional fluctuations in foreign-exchange rates. The question arises whether the monetary authorities ought to exercise a supervisory function in the market or intervene through their own "stabilizing" sales and purchases of foreign exchange.

It is difficult to evaluate the likelihood of destabilizing speculation in situations we have never experienced and can only imagine. (The few years of floating exchange rates in the 1920's, when several countries were indulging in wild inflations, and in the 1930's, when countries were trying competitive devaluations, do not hold any relevant lessons for us.) But a few general theoretical considerations may be permissible and illuminating with regard to this question. The main point to note is that the foreign-exchange market, at least as far as trade in the major currencies is concerned, is a very wide, highly competitive market; it is a market in which thousands of parties, perhaps hundreds of thousands, buy and sell every day. To be sure, the largest commercial banks would be the largest exchange dealers and might together do a substantial part of the entire business. But the market would be wide open and no single dealer would be limited by anything like a "fixed capacity" (which is what makes market shares in manufactured products less flexible). With completely free entry into the market and pure competition on the part of most buyers and sellers, it is hard to conceive of any exercise of market power by even the largest dealers acting in concert.

Similar things have been said about certain parts of the stock market —and, yet, we know of instances of "foul play" and destabilizing speculation. But certain differences between the stock market and the foreign-exchange market may be relevant in this respect. Purchases of shares of corporate stock are additions to investors' or speculators' holdings, and sales are made chiefly to reduce some investors' or speculators' holdings. In other words, the market serves mainly to transfer existing securities from one holder to another. This is not so in the foreign-exchange market; there many purchases are made by persons who need foreign balances for foreign payments, and with these payments the balances often stop being foreign exchange; likewise, many sales are made by persons who have just received balances that became foreign exchange only by being transferred to these persons. In other words, a large part of the transactions in the foreign-exchange market is not designed to transfer existing *stocks* of foreign exchange but rather to transfer a *flow* of newly emerging foreign balances to those who use them up. Of course, there are also holdings of foreign exchange shifted from one holder to another. But the large portion of the total supply that is made up of "new" foreign exchange, which did not exist the week before, and the large portion of the total demand for foreign exchange that is used for payments in which it "disappears" for good, reduce the influence upon exchange rates that can be exercised by those who want to increase or reduce their holdings.

These differences between the securities market and the foreign-exchange market may possibly be substantiated by differences in the ratios of transactions to holdings. Securities transactions per day or week are probably smaller proportions of securities holdings than foreign-exchange transactions are of private foreign-exchange holdings. If this is true, sudden decisions by financially strong parties to build up their holdings or to unload some of their holdings are apt to have greater effects on market prices of securities than of foreign exchange. This does not necessarily cause the elasticities of supply and of demand to be greater in the foreign-exchange market than in the securities market—though they probably are very much greater—but it does imply that the influence of dealers and speculators is likely to be much smaller in the foreign-exchange market.[12]

While theorizing of this sort must not be accepted as the sole basis for definitive policy recommendations, it does seem sufficiently encouraging to those who say that we need not be afraid of the big bad bear and the big bad bull in a free exchange market. Moreover, outright cornering of the market and rigging of the rates could be too easily detected for large banks to participate in such activities; and smaller operators would have too little influence to destabilize the market.[13]

THE DEMAND FOR FOREIGN RESERVES

Virtually all respectable theories of the demand for domestic money have been in real terms. Let us recall the K of the Cambridge cash-balance equation, for example in Robertson's formulation,[14] in order to realize that *real* balances and *real* income have been the main variables in the model. In discussions of the "need" for international reserves, references to *real*

[12] The size of the foreign-exchange market is often misjudged by those who believe that balance-of-payments statistics can give an impression of exchange transactions. We must bear in mind that most transactions in the foreign-exchange market do not result in entries in the accounting balance of payments. For example, capital movements, shown in the balance only as changes in the net position over the year (or quarter-year), may actually be a multiple of the net change.

[13] The question whether small-scale speculation by many individually insignificant traders would ever be likely to add up to seriously destabilizing influences on a free foreign-exchange market is controversial, but the arguments with which Friedman and others have demonstrated the small likelihood of destabilizing speculation seem convincing to me.

[14] Dennis H. Robertson, *Money* (New York: Harcourt Brace, Revised ed., 1929), Appendix A, p. 195.

balances are often missing, though when official gold and exchange reserves are measured by their ratios to imports a connection with commodity values is implicit. Still, there is insufficient realization of the possibility that supplying official foreign reserves—in amounts generous enough to give central bankers the freedom of maneuver that many deem desirable—may induce credit policies leading to rising prices with the result that the real reserves end up no higher than they were before.

Let us go back once more to the notions of a "demand for foreign reserves" under systems of fixed exchange rates, pegged by national monetary authorities. Accepting for the moment the terminological promiscuity so popular everywhere but in the loftiest ivory towers, we can find different concepts of demand for foreign reserves proposed by different experts. There is the "demand" as seen by central bankers each of whom would desire an amount of reserves adequate to allow him to pursue policies most conducive to the achievement of national employment and growth objectives without the constraints which balance-of-payments difficulties might impose in the absence of ample reserves. There is, secondly, the "demand" as seen by the political economist who wants central banks to have reserves just large enough to allow them to pursue credit policies which avoid price deflation but not so large that they can indulge in policies leading to price inflation. There is, thirdly, the "demand" as seen by a presumptive world central banker who would supply to the central banks of the nations international reserves adequate to "finance" the fastest possible increase in world trade.

In none of these propositions is the word "demand" used in the economist's sense; instead, it is used in the general sense as an expression of a peremptory wish, an urgent requirement, a strong claim. In this sense we hear it sometimes in economic discussions, say, of trade unions' demand for higher wages, of producers' demand for higher tariffs, or of taxpayers' demand for lower taxes. In the economic sense, demand refers to a series of quantities associated with a series of prices, and it always indicates someone's preparedness to acquire something in exchange for something else; hence, it involves an implied supply of a *quid pro quo* offered in return for the thing desired. In this sense we speak of the consumers' demand for butter or eggs, implying a supply of money they offer in exchange; or of the workers' demand for income, implying a supply of labor effort offered in exchange for income. It hardly needs much scrutiny to find that the three mentioned concepts of demand for foreign reserves did not imply any supply of anything offered in exchange. Good economists had better avoid the phrase when the intended reference is to political goals.

Just to see what would be meant by "demand for foreign reserves" in the strictly economic sense, let us visualize a demand curve depicting the different amounts of international or foreign money demanded for holding in reserve at various values of that money in terms of importable or exportable goods. Such a curve would in fact indicate a supply of goods, namely, the goods foregone by the nation for the sake of holding the reserve. If the prices of international commodities rise, that is, if the real value of international money falls, and the demand for reserves is of more than unitary elasticity, this means that the nation is willing to give up more goods—to export more and import less—in order to hold larger reserves. This is a meaningful conception, but only if the reserves are privately held. For only then are the decisions to acquire reserves made by those who give up alternative uses of their resources. If central bankers or governing boards make the decisions about reserve holding, they are not themselves sacrificing anything nor are they even aware of the fact that they are imposing a sacrifice upon the nation. We are back again at the problems of private reserve holding. We shall not, however, pursue them further at this point. But that our exploration has taken us again in this direction seems to indicate that these problems lie close to the main track of our inquiry and that we are not guilty of having shunted the train of our argument to a side track leading into wasteland.

■ PART FOUR ■
Reform Plans

Only a single essay forms the content of Part Four, but it is a rather long piece. It could easily have been divided into several chapters, but adherence to the form in which it was first published was felt to be preferable.

It is symptomatic of the tempo with which economic matters—conditions, institutions, policies, and plans—are changing nowadays that an essay describing current plans for reform of the international monetary system calls for a new and much enlarged edition within one year. First published in August 1962, the essay in its new form as Chapter XIV of this volume exceeds the "obsolete" version by 40 per cent in terms of words printed. The number of footnotes increased from 69 in the first published version to 105, or by 52 per cent, an increase which is accounted for, not by afterthoughts, but by new publications relevant to the subject.

New plans, or new variants of old plans, for reform of the international monetary system are being spawned at an extraordinary rate, and even if only those that deserve to be taken seriously were included in subsequent editions of this survey, its size would exhibit a growth rate envied by every growth-rate idolizer. Pronouncements—plans or comments on plans—contained in 37 new publications are discussed in the material added to my essay since its first publication.

PREVIEW OF THE CHAPTER

Chapter XIV, "Plans for Reform of the International Monetary System," begins with a description of the present system, with particular consideration of the magnitudes, composition, and distribution of international reserves and of the role played by the International Monetary Fund. This is followed by a short statement of the charges that have been leveled against the system. The main section of the chapter is devoted to descriptions of the most widely discussed reform plans, grouped in five classes: 1. extension of the gold-exchange standard, 2. mutual assistance among central banks, 3. centralization of reserves and of reserve-creation, 4. changes in the price of gold, and 5. freely flexible exchange rates. Although critical comments are not eschewed, no particular plan is endorsed in the essay, and no forecast made regarding the type of plan that may eventually be adopted.

MAJOR THEMES

A theme, rather subordinate in the essay, strikes me as pregnant from this vantage point: The attitudes of most bankers, central bankers, and national politicians with regard to the establishment of an international reserve bank sound strikingly similar to the attitudes which local bankers, city bankers, and local politicians expressed about the establishment of a national central bank in a financially developed country when it was still without a central reserve system. There was fear of loss of independence, aversion to central control, suspicion of neglect of local needs, mistrust of unbridled power, apprehension of mismanagement. In the United States the debate about the establishment of a central reserve system lasted about a hundred years, yet in the end the system was established. To say this is neither to assert that the establishment of the Federal Reserve System, or of national central banks anywhere, has been an unmixed blessing, nor to contend that the establishment of an international central bank is "in the cards." Just that the arguments are so very similar!

Since the national bankers and politicians are opposed to a system in which international reserves are centrally held and centrally created in an international institution, but are equally (if not more) opposed to a system in which no international reserves are needed and exchange rates are free to fluctuate, they favor a third system: a system in which central banks hold one another's currency as foreign reserve. Somehow they feel safer if only the *national* monetary authorities can create international reserves than if a *supranational* authority is empowered to do so. Somehow they feel that they can keep better control over reserve creation, probably because the monetary authorities of other nations, however eager they may be to incur additional liabilities which are accepted as international reserve, cannot run too far ahead of the procession. Indeed, if some of the national monetary authorities choose to go slow in the process of collective reserve creation, they can hold back the march of dimes and dollars into the reserve accounts of the world.

One other major theme, though amply voiced in the chapter previewed and also in an earlier one (Chapter XII), deserves the added emphasis of this display. It concerns the recommendation that borrowing facilities be included in the count of the world reserves. If the statistic of the aggregate reserves of all national monetary authorities taken together is designed to tell us whether reserves are adequate (though, *for what* they are to be adequate is seldom said), what should be included and what should be left out? We are urged to include, besides the net liquid assets of the national monetary authorities, also the liquid assets that are offset by liquid debts, and also all unused borrowing facilities.

Presumably, the result of this addition is supposed to indicate how free the nations may feel to increase their spending, just as the reserve position of a bank is supposed to indicate how free it may feel to extend its credit, and the cash position of a firm or a household is to indicate how freely decisions for additional expenditures may be made. It stands to reason that the statistical aggregate in question cannot serve such a purpose. This supposed measure of "international liquidity" (to use this obscurantist phrase in this context) may be likened to a measure of the reserve position of commercial banks which includes not only the *free* reserves, not only the *borrowed* excess reserves, not only the *required* reserves, but also all reserves which each bank may be *able to borrow* in an emergency. And, on the level of the private sector of an economy, it may be likened to a measure of the "liquidity position" (whatever this may mean) which includes all the unused lines of credit of all business firms and all unused charge accounts of all households.

There is a difference, I submit, between my own money in my pocket, borrowed money in my pocket, and money which I may be able to borrow. Likewise, there is a difference between *owned* reserves, *borrowed* reserves, and *borrowable* reserves (including those "borrowable" by countries which neither need nor want to borrow). To treat them all as if they were the same may serve one purpose at least: to confuse the issue.

EARLIER VERSION AND RECORD OF CHANGES

Chapter XIV: "Plans for Reform of the International Monetary System." Written in 1961-1962.

First published, under the same title, as Special Paper in International Economics, No. 3 (Princeton, N.J.: International Finance Section, Princeton University, August 1962).

Reproduced, with some deletions and some additional material, under the title "Proposals for Reform of the International Monetary System," in *Factors Affecting the United States Balance of Payments,* Materials prepared for the Subcommittee on International Exchange and Payments, Joint Economic Committee, Congress of the United States, 87th Congress, 2d Session (Washington: 1962), Part 3, pp. 209-237.

Revised edition, under the same title as the 1962 edition, published as Special Paper in International Economics, No. 3 Revised (Princeton, N.J.: International Finance Section, Princeton University, March 1964). [Chapter XIV reproduces this version with only a few additions.]

Partial reproduction in James A. Crutchfield, *et al.,* eds., *Money, Financial Institutions, and the Economy* (Englewood Cliffs, N.J.: Prentice-Hall, 1965), Selection 45, pp. 432-439.

German translation published as Kieler Vorträge, Neue Folge, No. 23 (Kiel: Universität Kiel, 1962).

Italian translation in *Bancaria,* Vol. 1962 (August and September 1962), pp. 879-900 and 1007-1020. Another Italian translation of Parts A and B in Fabrizio Onida, ed., *Problemi di teoria monetaria internazionale* (Milan: Etas Kompass, 1971), pp. 307-327.

Japanese translation in *Chosa Geppo,* Vol. 52 (February and April 1963), pp. 110-121, and 139-168.

CHANGES: (1) Section A was divided into two subsections, 1 and 2.

(2) In Subsection 1, "Foreign Reserves, Their Growth, Composition, and Distribution," the statistic on total gross reserves was brought forward by two years, to December 1962, and a new table was added to show the composition of reserves in individual countries and the distribution of reserves among countries.

(3) Subsection 2, "The International Monetary Fund," presents several pages of new material, not necessary for the knowledgeable reader but desirable for students. (In order to understand proposals which include an expansion of the scope of the I.M.F., it is necessary to be familiar with its present working.)

(4) No major additions were made to Section B; a previous footnote was made part of the text, and footnote 12 on Hawtrey's views was added.

(5) In Subsection 1 of Section C, the discussion of the multiple-reserve-currency standard was expanded by several pages dealing with the plans and pronouncements of Zolotas, Roosa, Lutz, Posthuma, and Bernstein.

(6) In Subsection 2 of Section C, the fourth and fifth paragraphs were added in order to make certain clarifying distinctions. Also footnote 37 with Hawtrey's comments was added.

(7) In Subsection 3, the additions include a paragraph and an extra sentence on the newest version of the Stamp Plan, a paragraph on the Maudling Plan, and four paragraphs (and T-Account Set 7) on an imputed extension of the Bernstein Plan. There was also added a new tabulation of the main differences between the eleven plans for creating international reserves by an international institution. Finally the last three paragraphs were added.

(8) In Subsection 4, the discussion of the Rueff and Heilperin plans was slightly modified. Additions include footnote 64 on Shannon, a paragraph on recent comments by Hahn, several paragraphs (already included in the reproduction of the essay by the Congressional committee) on the proposals by Dahlberg, by the Minority of the Joint Economic Committee, by Miyata, and by Wonnacott.

(9) Subsection 5 was enlarged by references, in footnotes 91, 97, and 99 to 102, to new publications by Meade, Sohmen, Halm, Vanek, Caves, and Johnson. Furthermore, the last paragraph, dealing with "limited flexibility," was added.

(10) A clause was inserted in the last paragraph of the "Concluding Remarks."

XIV

Plans for Reform of the International Monetary System

A. The Present System: 1. *Foreign reserves, their growth, composition, and distribution;* 2. *The International Monetary Fund* ■ B. Charges against the System: 1. *Difficulties with the balance of payments;* 2. *Inadequacy of international reserves;* 3. *Danger of collapse* ■ C. A Selection of Plans: 1. *Extension of the gold-exchange standard;* 2. *Mutual assistance among central banks;* 3. *Centralization of monetary reserves;* 4. *Increase in the price of gold;* 5. *Freely flexible exchange rates* ■ D. Concluding Remarks

There has been growing dissatisfaction with the present international monetary order or disorder. Some experts have come to regard reforms as desirable, necessary, or even urgent, and several plans for reform have been submitted. Some of these plans are radical, evidently because their proponents consider the defects and dangers of the present system too fundamental for mere patchwork to remove them. Other plans are less ambitious, probably because their proponents regard radical reforms as unnecessary or believe they are unacceptable given the conservatism of the "practical men" and their qualms about political feasibilities. It goes without saying that there must be essential differences between plans that are designed to serve different objectives, to correct different defects, or to avert different dangers.

A. The present system

In order to understand the present international monetary system, one must have some acquaintance with the working of the gold-exchange standard,[1] developments in the holdings of official reserves—their growth, composition, and distribution—and the essentials of the operation of the International Monetary Fund.

1. Foreign reserves, their growth, composition, and distribution

Most countries of the free world maintain a gold-exchange standard. Under this system, the foreign reserves of central banks and other national monetary authorities consist not only of gold but also of liquid claims against certain countries, called the key-currency or reserve-currency countries. At present these claims are composed partly of deposits in American and British banks and chiefly of American and British short-term government obligations.[2]

Since neither dollar deposits nor sterling deposits are legally redeemable in gold, some writers prefer to speak of a "currency-reserve standard" rather than a "gold-exchange standard." [3] The difference, however, is not very great, inasmuch as the U.S. Treasury does in fact sell gold at the official parity rate to foreign governments and central banks holding dollar deposits. Dollar securities can of course be readily sold and thus transformed into dollar deposits. Dollar balances of private holders can at any time be sold to their respective central banks and thus readily transformed into "official" balances. In monetary statistics, official and private dollar holdings are nevertheless stated separately, and only the official holdings are included in the "foreign reserve" of the countries concerned.

Under a worldwide pure gold standard, the foreign reserves of all countries taken together can increase only to the extent that the stock of monetary gold increases. Under the gold-exchange standard, however, the gross total of foreign reserves increases not only with the official gold stocks but also with the amounts of reserve currencies which the reserve-currency countries supply (by incurring additional current liabilities) and which other central banks are willing to hold.

Besides gold and liquid claims against key-currency countries, certain "drawing rights" on the International Monetary Fund (I.M.F.) are sometimes counted among the foreign reserves of the national monetary authorities. One must distinguish between those drawing rights which can be exercised more or less automatically—the so-called "I.M.F. gold-tranche position"—and those that can be exercised only under certain conditions —the so-called "I.M.F. credit-tranche position." An explanation of these

---

[1] It happens that my first two books dealt with the gold-exchange standard: *Die Goldkernwährung* (Halberstadt: Meyer, 1925); and *Die neuen Währungen in Europa* (Stuttgart: Enke, 1927).

[2] A few countries hold other currencies, such as French francs and West German D-Marks, as parts of their official reserves.

[3] J. Herbert Fürth, "Professor Triffin on the Problem of International Monetary Reform," *Zeitschrift für Nationalökonomie* (Winter 1961), pp. 140-147.

TABLE XIV-1   *Reserves of Central Banks and Other National Monetary Authorities of the Free World* (Billions of Dollars)

End of Year	Gold and foreign-exchange reserves							IMF Positions			Gross reserves plus IMF gold tranche [(7)+(8)]	Gross reserves plus IMF total tranche [(7)+(10)]
	Gold	Foreign-exchange reserves					Gross total [(1)+(2)]	Gold tranche	Credit tranche	Gross total [(8)+(9)]		
		Total	U.S.$	U.K.£	BIS+EPU	Others, incl. adjust-ments						
	(1)	(2)	(3)	(4)	(5)	(6)	(7)	(8)	(9)	(10)	(11)	(12)
1949	33.2	10.5	3.1	7.9	0.1	−0.5	43.7	1.7	6.2	7.9	45.3	51.5
1950	33.8	14.7	4.4	7.8	0.5	1.9	48.5	1.7	6.2	7.9	50.2	56.4
1951	33.9	15.1	4.0	8.7	0.8	1.6	49.1	1.7	6.5	8.2	50.8	57.2
1952	33.9	15.7	5.3	7.6	1.3	1.5	49.6	1.8	6.5	8.3	51.3	57.8
1953	34.4	17.2	6.0	8.1	1.5	1.5	51.5	1.9	7.1	9.0	53.4	60.6
1954	35.0	18.3	7.1	8.2	1.4	1.6	53.3	1.8	7.8	9.7	55.1	62.9
1955	35.4	18.8	7.9	8.1	1.3	1.6	54.3	1.9	7.9	9.8	56.1	64.0
1956	36.1	19.8	8.6	7.8	1.4	2.0	55.9	1.9	7.5	9.8	58.2	65.7
1957	37.3	19.0	8.3	7.2	1.5	1.9	56.3	2.3	7.2	9.5	58.6	65.8
1958	38.0	19.3	8.6	7.0	1.9	1.8	57.3	2.3	7.3	9.8	59.8	67.2
1959	37.9	19.2	9.4	7.4	0.4	1.9	57.1	3.3	12.9	16.1	60.3	73.2
1960	38.0	21.7	10.5	7.6	0.5	3.1	59.7	3.6	13.7	17.2	63.3	76.9
1961	38.9	22.4	11.1	7.6	0.6	3.0	61.2	4.2	12.8	17.0	65.4	78.2
1962	39.2	22.1	12.2	7.3	0.6	2.0	61.4	3.8	13.4	17.2	65.2	78.5
Increase 1949-62	6.1	11.6	9.1	−0.6	0.5	2.5	17.7	2.1	7.1	9.3	20.0	27.0

SOURCE: International Monetary Fund

Because of rounding, figures may not add up exactly to the given totals.

Col. (1): *Gold reserves* are only those of national monetary authorities, and are therefore exclusive of gold stocks of international monetary institutions.

Col. (2): *Exchange reserves* are foreign-exchange holdings of national monetary authorities, i.e., their deposits in the U.S.A., U.K., and a few other countries, plus credit balances with the Bank for International Settlements (B.I.S.) and the European Payments Union (E.P.U.).

Col. (3): Holdings of U.S. dollars by national monetary authorities equal liabilities of banks and the U.S. Government, to wit, (a) liabilities of the Federal Reserve Banks and other American banks to foreign monetary authorities, (b) official foreign holdings of short-term government securities and other short-term liabilities, (c) official holdings of U.S. government securities with original maturities greater than one year; all these minus U.S. liabilities to international organizations.

Col. (4): Holdings of pounds sterling by national monetary authorities equal liabilities of the U.K., to wit, (a) net holdings in sterling or Sterling Area currencies by foreign monetary authorities with banks in the U.K., (b) their holdings of British government securities, (c) funds held with the Crown Agents and Currency Boards, (d) certain intergovernment loans, (e) sterling securities issued by Commonwealth countries that are included in holders' foreign assets; all these minus U.K. liabilities to international organizations. (The net total includes some holdings by foreign individuals and corporations.)

Col. (5): Balances with the B.I.S. are B.I.S. liabilities that are counted as monetary reserves by creditor countries. E.P.U. liabilities reflect accumulated balances of E.P.U. members acquired in the course of financing trade surpluses with other members. When the E.P.U. was liquidated in 1958, remaining debtor and creditor positions were converted into bilateral claims and debts, which are not included among monetary reserves.

Col. (6): Other foreign-exchange holdings are deposits in other countries with convertible currencies. Certain divergences between claims reported by creditors and liabilities reported by debtors were included in this item.

Col. (7): This is a "gross total" in the sense that current *liabilities* of monetary authorities (or governments) to other monetary authorities are not deducted from their *assets*.

Col. (8): "I.M.F. gold-tranche position" is a member's gold subscription to the I.M.F., plus repurchases of its currency subscription, minus its net drawings or plus the I.M.F.'s net sales of its currency, plus or minus the I.M.F.'s administrative or operational expenditures or receipts in its currency. It measures the amount a member may draw from the I.M.F. more or less automatically under the Fund's gold-tranche policy.

Col. (9): "I.M.F. credit-tranche position" is the difference between members' maximum drawing potentials and their gold-tranche positions.

Col. (10): "I.M.F. total-tranche position," previously called "Gross I.M.F. position," is calculated for each member by doubling its quota and subtracting the I.M.F.'s holding of its currency. The result is a measure of the member's maximum drawing potential.

arrangements will be offered presently. At this point it suffices to understand that drawing rights are not quite the same as asset holdings, and that conditional drawing rights, or borrowing facilities, are not quite the same as unconditional drawing rights.[4]

Table XIV-1 gives foreign reserves held by the monetary authorities of the nations of the free world from 1949 to 1962, first gold holdings (column 1), then foreign-exchange holdings (columns 2 to 6), and finally I.M.F. positions (columns 8 to 10).

The increase from 1949 to 1962 in *gold* holdings amounted to $6,080 million, or 18.3 per cent, corresponding to an annual rate of increase of 1.3 per cent. The increase in *foreign-exchange* holdings amounted to $11,645 million, or 110.9 per cent, corresponding to an annual rate of increase of 5.9 per cent. It should be noted, however, that there was hardly any increase in the last two years. *Gold and foreign-exchange* holdings together increased by $17,725 million, or 40.6 per cent, corresponding to an annual rate of increase of 2.7 per cent. If we add "I.M.F. gold-tranche positions," we find that the sum of gross-reserve assets and these drawing rights increased by $19,862 million, or 43.8 per cent, corresponding to an annual rate of increase of 2.8 per cent. Finally, the sum of gross reserves and "I.M.F. total-tranche positions" increased by $26,992 million, or 52.4 per cent, corresponding to an annual rate of 3.3 per cent. This faster growth of the last magnitude reflects chiefly the increase in I.M.F. quotas from 1958 to 1959.

The composition of monetary reserves has undergone considerable change, especially notable in the relative shrinkage of the metallic nucleus of the currencies. At the end of 1949, monetary gold stocks of the nations included in Table XIV-1 had been 75.9 per cent of their gold and exchange

[4] That the difference between drawing rights and gold-and-exchange holdings is much greater than some experts like to admit is brought home by the fact that the United States did not from 1946 to 1963 exercise any of its drawing rights on the I.M.F., neither the automatic nor the conditional. Whether this reluctance of the United States to draw on the I.M.F., while giving up gold and increasing its current liabilities to foreign central banks, was reasonable or not is a matter of judgment; but the reluctance is a matter of record.

Apart from the question whether the "gross I.M.F. position" or only the "net I.M.F. position" or neither should be included among official reserves, there is also the question whether the *"gross* gold-and-exchange reserves" should be recognized as monetary reserves. The common practice of adding gold holdings and holdings of foreign bank balances and government securities without deducting current liabilities to foreign monetary authorities is questionable from some points of view. More conservative accountants actually object to the customary statistical routine of adding the "gross" reserves of the various countries. They hold that statistics of *net* reserves, where gold and foreign assets are reduced by current foreign liabilities, or at least by those in official holdings, would give a more accurate or more relevant picture of the reserve position of the countries. Most writers are satisfied with the more common usage, because the statistics of gross reserves, *supplemented* by statistics of liabilities, can furnish more information than could be learnt from the net figures alone.

reserves; at the end of 1962 they were only 63.9 per cent. Correspondingly, the portion of foreign-exchange holdings in total reserves (not counting I.M.F. positions) increased from 24.1 per cent to 36.1 per cent. Most drastic was the increase in claims against the United States: from $3,071 million at the end of 1949 to $12,176 million at the end of 1962. Claims against the United Kingdom remained almost unchanged—$7,856 million in 1949 and $7,264 million in 1962—and thus became a smaller part of total foreign-exchange holdings.

This information about the *growth* and *composition* of monetary reserves is indispensable for an understanding of the present system, but it will be helpful to have additional information about the *distribution* of reserves among the various countries. Relevant data, beginning with 1951, are presented in Table XIV-2 for the eleven financially most important countries—which together hold over 86 per cent of official gold reserves and 71 per cent of total gold-and-exchange reserves of the free world—and for four other groups of countries, which hold the rest.

TABLE XIV-2   *Gross Official Gold and Foreign Exchange Reserves, 1951, 1956, 1961, and 1962* (Billions of Dollars, End of Year)

					Composition, 1962		
	Gold and exchange reserves						Gold as
						Ex-	% of
	1951	1956	1961	1962	Gold	change	total
United States	22.9	22.1	17.1	16.2	16.1	0.1	99
United Kingdom	2.4	2.3	3.3	2.8	2.6	0.2	92
Canada	1.8	1.9	2.1	2.5	0.7	1.8	28
Japan	—	0.9	1.5	1.8	0.3	1.6	16
Belgium	1.1	1.2	1.7	1.6	1.4	0.3	84
France	0.6	1.2	2.9	3.6	2.6	1.0	72
Germany	0.5	4.1	6.5	6.4	3.7	2.8	57
Italy	0.8	1.2	3.4	3.4	2.2	1.2	65
Netherlands	0.6	1.0	1.7	1.7	1.6	0.2	91
Sweden	—	0.5	0.7	0.8	0.2	0.6	24
Switzerland	1.6	1.9	2.8	2.9	2.7	0.2	93
Total, 11 countries	32.2	38.3	43.6	43.8	33.9	9.9	77
Other Europe	2.3	2.4	4.0	4.5	1.9	2.6	42
Latin America	3.0	3.7	2.8	2.3	1.2	1.1	52
Other sterling area	7.4	7.6	7.1	7.1	1.1	6.0	15
All other countries	4.1	3.9	3.7	3.7	1.1	2.6	31
Rest of the free world	16.8	17.5	17.6	17.5	5.3	12.2	30
Total, all countries	49.1	55.9	61.2	61.4	39.2	22.1	64

NOTE: Because of rounding, figures may not add up exactly to given totals.
SOURCE: International Monetary Fund

The data in Table XIV-2 draw our immediate attention to the changes that have occurred over the eleven years from 1951 to 1962: the drastic decline in gross reserves held by the United States (to 71 per cent of its 1951 holdings [5]); the sharp increases in the reserves of Italy (to 445 per cent of its 1951 holdings), France (to 586 per cent), and Western Germany (to 1245 per cent); and the virtual absence of growth of reserves in the rest of the free world. These shifts imply substantial changes in the distribution of total gross reserves, lowering the share of the United States from 47 per cent in 1951 to 26 per cent in 1962, raising the share of France from 1 per cent to 6 per cent and the share of Germany from 1 per cent to 11 per cent. The share of the rest of the world apart from the eleven separately listed countries declined from 34 per cent in 1951 to 29 per cent in 1962. And, incidentally, the share of this "rest of the world" in total gold reserves at the end of 1962 was only 13 per cent.

Table XIV-2 reports also on the composition of gross reserves, at the end of 1962, in the eleven individual countries and in various parts of the world. As we have seen before, gold accounted for about 64 per cent of gross total reserves held by national monetary authorities, but the differences in reserve-asset preferences are most interesting. That the gold portion of the reserves of key-currency countries has been close to 100 per cent seems almost self-evident: at the end of 1962 it was 99 per cent in the United States and 92 per cent in the United Kingdom. But if the gold portion was nearly as high in some other countries also, this would seem to indicate that their monetary authorities do not put too much faith in the gold-exchange standard. The countries with the highest gold saturation are Switzerland with 93 per cent, the Netherlands with 91 per cent, Belgium with 84 per cent, and France with 72 per cent. Among the countries below the world ratio of gold to total reserves are Germany with 57 per cent, Canada with 28 per cent, Sweden with 24 per cent, and Japan with 16 per cent.

2. The International Monetary Fund

Since the International Monetary Fund has been playing an important role in the present system, and since an even greater role is being wished upon the Fund by many experts, a brief description of its present rules and policies may aid in the understanding of much that comes later. But before such a description is given, a few comments on the terminology

[5] The percentages of the 1951 holdings are calculated from the figures with two more digits reported in *International Financial Statistics* of July 1963.—With regard to the United States the decline in gross reserves (by $6,717 million) from 1951 to 1962 does not fully reflect the change in its international position. One should add the simultaneous increase in current liabilities held by other national monetary authorities in an amount of $8,162 million; this indicates a decline in net foreign reserves of $14,879 million.

commonly employed may be appreciated by some readers. (The well-informed reader may prefer to skip this section.)

The mixture of languages used in financial transactions is somewhat confusing; it may stump even the experts, since some speak and think in the jargon of the trade while others try to translate into more general language. The basic difficulty lies in the fact that an exchange of one "title" or credit instrument against another may be referred to as a sale of the one, a purchase of the other, as a loan, or as borrowing, depending on the point of view.

Some of the terminological alternatives are well known to the student of domestic-banking practices. If a commercial firm gives a commercial bank a promissory note (promising payment in 90 days) and receives in exchange a demand deposit (promising payment on demand) one may say, alternatively, that the bank "purchases" the note, "discounts" the bill, "lends" to the firm, or "creates" credit. The alternatives are even more numerous in international transactions, where the presence of at least two currencies complicates matters. If a Dutch bank gives a promissory note to a British bank and receives a sterling balance for it, the Dutch bank is alternatively said to have "sold" guilders, "purchased" sterling, or "borrowed" sterling; and the British to have "purchased" guilders, or "lent" sterling. This is still relatively simple. Sometimes, however, the economic nature of the transaction is not transparent. Assume that a foreign central bank acquires dollars; its "purchase" of dollars or "sale" of its own currency may constitute either "borrowing" dollars or "lending" its own currency; but which of the two it really is can sometimes be inferred only from the "position" of this central bank. If the Bank of Brazil "purchases" dollars and "pays" with cruzeiros, it is probably *borrowing* dollars, promising to "repurchase" the cruzeiros at some later time; but if the Bank of France "purchases" dollars and "pays" with francs, it is probably *lending* francs, expecting to "sell" the dollars again in the future. Before 1958, however, if the Bank of France "purchased" dollars from the International Monetary Fund, it was evidently borrowing dollars, not lending francs. We see that the nature of the transaction cannot be understood from the words in which it is described, unless one is well informed about the circumstances under which it occurs.

Thus, if one intends to express the economic meaning of an international financial transaction, one cannot use the trade language, or can use it only as a second language along with "academic" parlance. Most officials dealing every day with the technical aspects of their operations do not even notice that they are speaking a trade language, and many "outsiders" lack the courage to admit their less than complete comprehension. In our descriptions of international financial operations we shall usually avoid the official jargon of the trade, except when we quote or paraphrase official definitions, agreements, or rules.

The official definitions of a few terms may be supplied at this point because they were given a somewhat special meaning in the Articles of Agreement setting up the I.M.F. *Members* of the Fund are countries, represented by their governments. A member's *monetary reserves* are its *net* official holdings of gold, of convertible currencies of other members, and of the currencies of such non-members as the Fund may specify. *Official holdings* are the "central holdings," that is, the holdings of the country's treasury, central bank, stabilization fund, or similar agency, and of other institutions by agreement between the Fund and the particular government. (We shall use the term "monetary authorities" for all these official agencies.) *Currencies* include coins, paper money, bank balances, bank acceptances, and government obligations issued with a maturity not exceeding twelve months. (This is probably the greatest deviation of the official language from common usage.)

The major types of transaction with the Fund are a member's *purchases* of the currency of another member in exchange for its own currency, and its *repurchase* of its currency from the Fund with gold or convertible currencies. The member's right to purchase foreign currencies and its obligation to repurchase its own currency are related to its "quota." Apart from certain exceptions, a member's initial subscription to the Fund consists of *gold* to the extent of 25 per cent of its quota, and of its *own currency* (including its non-negotiable, non-interest-bearing obligations payable in its currency) to the extent of 75 per cent of its quota.

A member's right to purchase foreign currency from the Fund with its own currency is limited by two provisions. The Fund's holdings of a member's currency (1) should not increase by more than 25 per cent of the quota within any one year (except if the Fund's holdings of this currency at the beginning of the year were below 75 per cent of the quota or if the Fund waives this limitation, which is done with great regularity), and (2) must never increase above 200 per cent of the quota. The second provision limits a member's total net purchases of foreign exchange from the Fund to 125 per cent of the quota, spread over five years (since the payments for these purchases would raise the Fund's holdings from the original currency subscription of 75 per cent to 200 per cent of the quota). But if the member's currency has been in demand by other members, and the Fund therefore has sold some of its holdings of this currency, the member's purchasing rights are automatic and unconditional, up to the point where the Fund again holds 75 per cent of the quota in the member's currency.

These provisions explain the "I.M.F. gold-tranche position" and the "I.M.F. total-tranche position," both previously mentioned; they also explain why the former is widely regarded as eligible for addition to a country's foreign reserve, whereas the "credit-tranche position" is not. The member's right to purchase, not immediately but only later, foreign exchange with its own currency (read: with its debt certificates) but subject to an obligation to repurchase its currency (read: to repay the foreign exchange) is no more than a promise of a loan at some later time. A possibility to borrow in the future is not easily treated as a "reserve." (It is perhaps for this reason that many writers prefer the vague term "liquidity" to the more definite term "reserve.")

A member's gold-tranche position is essentially its gold subscription to the Fund, minus its net drawings, but plus any amounts of its currency subscription which it has repurchased (with convertible currencies or gold) or which the I.M.F. has sold to other members. The gold-tranche position measures the amount the member may draw from the I.M.F. more or less automatically. Yet, of all major financial countries, only Belgium includes its gold-tranche position in calculating its reserves; the United States, United Kingdom, France, Italy, and the Netherlands use only footnote references to relate certain parts of their drawing rights to their foreign position. The practice of the Netherlands Bank is perhaps the most logical of all: it calculates its "creditor position" *vis-à-vis* the Fund, measuring the amount it may draw without giving rise to a repurchase obligation.[6]

The practice of adding together the drawing rights of different countries and displaying a certain sum as a measure of "total liquidity" or "total supplementary reserves" is deceptive. A few examples may show the kind of illusions involved. Assume that a member exercises its semiautomatic drawing rights; these drawings reduce its gold-tranche position but may increase the gold-tranche position of that other member in whose currency the drawing is made; at the same time, the foreign-exchange reserves of a third country, to which the first member pays the currency of the second, will be increased. Statistical result: no change in the sum of gold-tranche positions, increase in gross foreign reserves. By a slight change in assumptions, let the first country, having exhausted its gold-tranche position, make a drawing on its credit tranche, reducing thereby the Fund's holdings of the currency of the second country below 75 per cent of that country's quota, and increasing the foreign-exchange reserves of the third country to which payment is made. Statistical result: increase in I.M.F. gold-tranche positions, decrease in I.M.F. credit-tranche positions, increase in gross foreign reserves. (The two examples are alike in their effects upon the I.M.F. total-tranche positions.) In general, the exercise of drawing rights by any country does not reduce total drawing rights,

---

[6] Such a "creditor position" exists when the Fund, having sold some of the member's currency, holds less than 75 per cent of the member's quota in that currency.

since the I.M.F. positions of the countries whose currency is drawn out increase in the process. If the deficit countries have used up all their drawing facilities, the total I.M.F. positions may show no reduction, although there can be no further drawings until some surplus countries become deficit countries. The borrowing potentials of countries that have no occasion to borrow are economically irrelevant, yet they appear in the statistics in all their "greatness."

The fact that drawings on the Fund, by increasing the foreign-exchange holdings of the countries to which payment is made, may increase the gross total of exchange reserves raises the question whether the I.M.F. under present arrangements can "create" international reserves—just as a national central bank can create reserves for its banking system. The answer is no; liabilities of the I.M.F. are not accepted as international money. Nevertheless, I.M.F. transactions do play a role in the creation of international reserves. For, in "selling" (read: lending) currencies that are used in international payments and as monetary reserves, the I.M.F. participates in the process of reserve creation by putting into circulation, as it were, currencies which had previously been created, but not yet put into circulation, by the monetary authority of a reserve-currency country at the time it made its currency subscription to the I.M.F. or purchased other currencies from the I.M.F.

A word or two may be added regarding "split monetary authorities." In some countries it is only the central bank that deals with the I.M.F.; in others it is only the treasury or a governmental exchange-stabilization fund; but in most countries operations with the Fund are divided between the central bank and a government agency. Even subscriptions to the I.M.F. have in some countries come partly from the central bank, partly from the government.[7] Such split monetary authorities do not present any practical difficulties other than of accounting and of exposition. We shall facilitate our exposition by presenting national and international monetary operations as if everywhere central banks were charged with all the monetary functions.

B. Charges against the system

Several experts, among them Per Jacobsson, late managing director of the I.M.F., and Robert Triffin, economics professor at Yale University,

---

[7] Where current transactions with the I.M.F. are executed by the treasury, it is sometimes difficult to disentangle effects upon government budget and balance of payments, since the same set of operations may finance a budget deficit and a payments deficit. If the treasury exercises its drawing rights, issuing its obligations to the I.M.F. and receiving foreign currency, it will sell the foreign currency to the central bank, receiving local currency in return; the government can thus finance a budget deficit, and the central bank can finance the deficit in the balance of payments.

have been careful to distinguish three different problems connected with the present system. To treat these problems separately is important not only for the sake of clarity but also because not all the experts share all the misgivings concerning the operation of the present system. Each of the three problems has at least two aspects calling for our attention.

1. Difficulties with the balance of payments of individual countries
   a. because of excessive deficits or insufficient surpluses [8] in the balance on current account;
   b. because of massive international movements of speculative funds.
2. Inadequacy of the growth of monetary reserves
   a. relative to the demand for "domestic liquidity" or to the "desirable" supply of domestic money;
   b. relative to the growth of foreign trade.
3. Fragility of the gold-exchange standard
   a. dangerous to key-currency countries;
   b. dangerous to countries holding large exchange reserves.

1. Difficulties with the balance of payments

Problem 1-a should perhaps be stricken from the agenda since it cannot be regarded as a defect of the present system and since the balance-of-payments problems of particular countries could not be solved or eliminated by means of any of the reform plans. Yet, some of the plans are designed to institute a system of international payments that gives countries in difficulties much more time to wait for an improvement in their balance on current account without resort to the orthodox treatment with its painful contractions of credit and effective demand. This tough remedy has become unpopular in a world more sensitive and less capable of adjusting to change. If the "old-fashioned" cure is at all accepted nowadays, one tries to postpone it as long as possible in the hope that things will get better without treatment.

There are, of course, other currency doctors, who find that such softheartedness toward patients suffering from current-account troubles is out of place and that postponement of the one reliable cure could only be harmful. As a matter of fact, some of the critics of the gold-exchange standard have stated, with a serious frown, that the acceptance of ever-increasing amounts of demand liabilities of the United States as parts of the monetary reserves of other countries postponed for almost eight years

[8] Surpluses on current account are regarded as "insufficient" when they fail to offset completely deficits in the balance of long-term capital movements and unilateral transfers. In this formulation the concept of "balance-of-payments difficulties" is confined to cases of gold and exchange *outflows*; some writers may prefer to extend the concept to include cases of heavy *inflows* of gold and foreign exchange.

substantial gold outflows from the United States and thus postponed the warning signals which such outflows would have implied. Hence, the present system is blamed for having enabled the United States to continue a credit and fiscal policy that was basically incompatible with an appropriate balance on current account.

There is obviously a serious ambivalence in the views about this problem. Some find the present system deficient because it gives countries in difficulties with their balance of payments too much time, and others because it gives them too little time, to get over their troubles. In actual fact, the system may do both at the same time, though with regard to different countries, in that it operates unequally and inequitably. It provides inadequate discipline for key-currency countries, but rather harsh discipline on other countries. Thus, the charge that the system has given too much time for adjustment to some countries (read: the United States) and too little to others is perfectly reasonable.

No ambivalence of this sort exists regarding problem 1-b, that is, regarding difficulties with the balance of payments on capital account because of hot-money movements. There is agreement on the desirability or need to improve present institutions so that they can cope more effectively with speculative capital movements.[9] Massive movements of hot money are brought about either by sudden changes in international interest-rate differentials or by rumors of imminent changes in official exchange rates. The return to convertibility and the abolition of restrictions on capital transactions have undoubtedly increased the dimensions of international hot-money movements and have thereby created difficulties with the balances of payments which perhaps cannot be managed with foreign reserves of the size now at the disposal of the monetary authorities in the countries concerned.

One may ask why the gold standard before 1914 was not exposed to shocks of this sort and could work without any special shock absorbers. The answer is simple. In the old times there never were any rumors about impending devaluations, since no country ever seriously contemplated changing the gold par of its currency. In the old times, moreover, there were no disequilibrating differentials in interest rates, or at least they were not allowed to last long, since the central banks were always trying to adjust their bank rates to the balance-of-payments situation. Under the rules of the gold-standard game, interest policy had to serve the equilibration of the balance of payments, and was not, as nowadays, subservient

---

[9] This should not be confused with problems of long-term capital movements—portfolio investment, direct investment, and foreign aid—that is, outflows of investable funds that should be reflected in the balance on current account of the investing, lending, or aiding country. (This would be part of problem 1-a, that is, difficulties due to a balance on current account that does not fully reflect the movements of long-term capital, including foreign aid.)

to employment and growth policies. Consequently, interest-rate differentials did not disturb but, on the contrary, helped maintain or restore international payments equilibrium.

This is in sharp contrast to present-day practice of some central banks, which insist on maintaining low interest rates (in order to fight unemployment) even if this leads to heavy outflows of funds.[10] A credit policy with so little regard for its external consequences is apt to aggravate widespread fears of devaluation. After all, so the apprehensive ones reason, a country which cares so little about a loss of reserves that it would not even put up with higher interest rates apparently does not care much about the maintenance of its gold parity. Under such circumstances, massive international movements of speculative funds must be expected. It may take special institutions to cope with them, chiefly by providing the means for "compensatory official financing"—that is, the foreign funds needed to meet the speculative demand—without recourse to payments restrictions and without peril to the maintenance of the fixed foreign-exchange rates.

2. Inadequacy of international reserves

The question of the adequacy, or supposed inadequacy, of the growth of monetary reserves is controversial. It has been contended, for example by Sir Roy Harrod, that reserves have grown too slowly during the last ten or twelve years. Even as early as 1952 a group of experts appointed by the United Nations reported that the total stocks of international reserves were inadequate.[11] This view was opposed by Per Jacobsson, M. W. Holtrop, Karl Blessing, and several others, who deny that either the size of reserves or their rate of increase has been inadequate. Indeed, they hold that reserves have been excessive.[12] Both factions seem willing to accept as a criterion of adequacy the influence which the reserves and their changes have upon the supply of money in the countries concerned. We have called this our problem 2-a: the question of the adequacy of reserves relative to the needs of "domestic liquidity." According to Harrod

[10] The Federal Reserve Banks, in the summer of 1960, lowered discount rates in the face of payments deficits. The reverse side of the same practice is for a central bank to insist on high interest rates (in order to fight price inflation) even if this aggravates a heavy inflow of foreign funds. The German Bundesbank did precisely this until it learned its lesson.

[11] "Our examination of existing reserves has convinced us that they are not in general adequate." Economic and Social Commission, United Nations, *Measures for International Economic Stability*, 1952. Members of the group of experts were Angell, MacDougall, Marquez, Myint, and Swan.

[12] This is also the view of Sir Ralph Hawtrey: "The defect of the International Monetary Fund has been not to provide too little liquidity but to provide too much." Sir Ralph Hawtrey, "Too Little Liquidity—or Too Much?" *The Banker*, Vol. CXII (London, November 1962), p. 712.

this influence was deflationary and responsible for an unsatisfactory rate of economic growth. Jacobsson and the central bankers, on the other hand, regarded the influence as inflationary since it permitted a general rise in the price levels of practically all countries. In view of these differences in judging the consequences of the operation of the international monetary system in the past, one cannot be very hopeful about reaching an agreement regarding the principles to be applied to the reform of the system.

The size and growth of foreign reserves relative to the needs of domestic liquidity and to the size and growth of the domestic money supply is only one of the possible criteria for judging the adequacy of the growth of gold and exchange reserves. Many experts prefer to rely on an indicator which "measures" the reserve position of the world as a whole, to wit, the numerical ratio between aggregate reserves and imports. This we have called our problem 2-b. However, the difference between the two measures of adequacy is not simply one of statistical convenience, but reflects two separate functions of monetary reserves. They are used, on the one hand, as institutional determinants of the domestic money supply and, on the other hand, as international means of payments to finance temporary deficits in the balance of payments. Hence it is quite in line with this double function of international reserves that their adequacy is judged with reference to both national circulation and international payments.

Any reduction in the ratio between international reserves and total imports indicates to some observers that the growth of gold and exchange reserves has been inadequate. This, however, presupposes, even if it is not explicitly stated, that the ratio was "just right" at the outset, or was perhaps a barely tolerable minimum. Surely, if the reserves relative to foreign trade, or total imports, had been more than adequate in the beginning,[13] a decline in this numerical ratio need not imply that the reserves have become inadequate. The total value of imports into the countries of the free world did in fact increase from $59.6 billion in 1950 to $119.1 billion in 1960. Thus, the ratio of reserves to imports fell from 81 to 50 per cent. But who can say that the 81 per cent was just right, or the bare minimum? Let us not forget that back in 1913 the ratio was only 21 per cent.

Apart from the question whether or not the ratio of reserves to imports was just right in the base year, and not unnecessarily high, there is absolutely no evidence for the contention that the need for reserves rises proportionately with foreign trade. It is true that in domestic circulation

---

[13] "Total international reserves immediately before the war were abnormally high in relation to the value of world trade." [Radcliffe] Committee on the Working of the Monetary System (London: H.M.'s Stationery Office, Cmnd. 827, 1959), p. 244, §671. The ratio of reserves to imports in 1938 was 117 per cent.

the need for cash balances on the part of householders is likely to increase approximately in proportion with consumption expenditures. On the other hand, the need for cash balances on the part of existing business firms does not usually increase proportionately with turnover. In all probability, the demand for cash balances in the economy as a whole will rise with the national product, but the increase may be smaller if the share of investment in the income increase is greater. Even within the industrial circulation of money we may expect differences in the ratio of cash to turnover, depending on the different degrees of vertical integration of industries. Besides, one may say that with an increase in the volume of transactions the demand for cash balances will increase least in those sectors of the economy in which clearing systems have developed requiring only the payment of clearing balances. It seems to me that foreign trade falls into this group and that consequently there is no theoretical support for the assertion that the need for international reserves rises in proportion with imports.[14]

Even if, on this or other grounds, one refuses to admit that the growth of international reserves relative to the growth of international trade has been inadequate during the last ten or twelve years, one may still side with the inadequacy-theorists in their pessimism for the future. The prospects for the future growth of reserves would indeed be rather dim if one could not expect the pool of reserves to be fed during the next ten years or so through continuing increases in dollar claims; and indeed further increases in the demand liabilities of the United States at the fast rate of the past years might well be unacceptable to all parties concerned. If it is agreed that the short-term indebtedness of the two key-currency countries, the United States and the United Kingdom, must not be increased substantially in the coming years and if, as a result, international reserves can grow only by means of increased supplies of monetary gold, then it is quite plausible that a real, generally recognized scarcity of reserves will develop in the course of time. To prevent such a calamity, changes in the present system are favored even by some of those experts who do not consider the past growth of reserves inadequate.

3. Danger of collapse

The consideration that the fast increase of the share of dollar claims in the total reserves of the world may be deemed unbearable for the system has brought us to the third set of problems: the fragility of the gold-exchange standard. Ever since 1950, the United States, through its

[14] Cf. the comments on this point in my article, "Liquidité internationale et nationale," *Bulletin d'Information et de Documentation*, Banque Nationale de Belgique, Vol. XXXVII (February 1962), pp. 105-116. Reproduced in a revised version as Chapter XII of this volume.

purchases, investments, loans, and aid, has put at the disposal of foreign countries more dollars than these countries have used for their purchases in the United States. In this fashion, foreign dollar claims, both of private holders and of central banks and other national monetary authorities, have increased at a fast rate. During the first seven or eight years this accumulation of the foreign-exchange reserves of various countries was welcomed by all; the demand for dollar balances was eager and the supply of dollars was therefore received with open arms. Later on, however, the accumulation of exchange reserves was continued only with formal politeness; the supply of dollars was received and added to currency reserves without great enthusiasm and merely in accordance with the customary etiquette practiced by central banks. (In other words, what was from the point of view of the United States one and the same phenomenon was elsewhere seen first as a symptom of "dollar shortage" and later as a symptom of "dollar glut.")

As the share of foreign exchange in the official reserves of the free world increased, more and more people began to doubt whether this steady excess supply of dollar liabilities could be absorbed without limit. With such doubts becoming more widespread, the willingness to accept further dollar supplies is further reduced, and fears regarding the future value of dollar exchange become increasingly serious. If then, in addition, some experts raise their voices advancing—in support of the aims of gold producers and speculators—proposals for an increase in the price of gold, the position of the dollar and the preservation of the gold-exchange standard become precarious.

The strong demand for gold for speculative purposes and hedging, especially the impatience of holders of dollar deposits and other dollar claims to exchange them into gold, then leads to a further increase in the supply of dollars in the foreign-exchange markets. Since not all central banks stand ready to increase their exchange reserves at the expense of their gold stocks, it becomes necessary for the American monetary authorities to sell gold in order to safeguard the position of the dollar. Yet, these gold losses in turn aggravate the doubts concerning the ability of the United States to defend the gold parity of the dollar in the long run, and these doubts cause private banks and public authorities to be even less willing to offer shelter to increasing amounts of dollar exchange. Hence, the more serious the fears that the gold-exchange standard will break down once again (as it did in 1931, when Great Britain went off gold), the more real becomes the danger of its actual collapse.

The consequences of such a collapse may be manifold, but most probably they would include some of the following measures and repercussions: restrictions on or termination of all sales of gold by the monetary authorities of the United States; restrictions on international payments through the introduction of foreign-exchange controls and prohibitions of capital transfers; import restrictions of all sorts; blocking of deposits of foreign nationals; the end of convertibility of most currencies, including the present key-currencies; elimination of these key-currencies from the official reserves of central banks and consequently a drastic reduction in "liquidity" everywhere; severe losses incurred by those central banks which did not match the depreciation of the key-currencies with equal devaluations of their own currencies; [15] reductions in production and employment resulting from import restrictions and export reductions. It may, of course, be possible through skillful improvisations to avoid or mitigate some of the worst consequences of the collapse of the international payments system, but it would surely be wiser not to rely on improvisations and to avert a collapse of the system through appropriate reforms. It is on the basis of this kind of argument that monetary experts have offered their plans and urge their adoption.

C. A SELECTION OF PLANS

A variety of plans have been proposed and the world will have to make a difficult choice. However, that any of the more radical innovations in the world monetary system will be adopted is far less probable than that the decision will be in favor of a policy of "muddling through," with only small repairs to the worst cracks and breaks in the old structure. One must not hold it against the "practical men" and politicians if they resist more ambitious innovations since, after all, the arguments and favorite notions of the scholars diverge so widely. To help us survey the plans proposed, we shall begin with a simple classification which also includes alternatives that represent more nearly a continuation than a reform of the present system. Our classification distinguishes five types of different solutions, but the possibility of combining any two, despite all their differences, yields a considerably larger number of choices.

1. Extension of the gold-exchange standard
   a. with continuing increase of dollar and sterling reserves;
   b. with adoption of additional key-currencies.
2. Mutual assistance among central banks
   a. with safeguards against expansive credit and fiscal policy;
   b. with expansion of domestic credit and expenditures.
3. Centralization of monetary reserves and reserve creation
   a. with overdraft facilities available to deficit countries;
   b. with autonomous reserve creation by the world central bank;
   c. with finance of aid to underdeveloped countries.
4. Increase in the price of gold

---

[15] The losses which The Netherlands Bank suffered as a result of the depreciation of the pound sterling in 1931 exceeded the Bank's entire capital.

a. with the gold-exchange standard continued;
b. with the gold-exchange standard abolished.
5. Freely flexible exchange rates
a. in order to make internal monetary policies more independent;
b. because internal monetary policies are too independent.

1. Extension of the gold-exchange standard

It may be doubtful that, in view of all its defécts and deficiencies, imaginary or real, the present system can long endure in its present form —but it is not impossible. The system may prove to be viable even without special measures for its reinforcement. If the "practical people" continue to resist all more extensive plans for reform, muddling through will be the only practical possibility. This may lead to an unhappy ending but, again, with some luck things may come out all right. It is conceivable that confidence in the dollar and in the pound sterling will be fully restored; that the constant predictions of an increase in the price of gold will no longer be taken seriously; that the further increase in demand liabilities of the United States will not exceed the willingness of other central banks to accept them as part of their reserves; that the monetary authorities of countries still suffering from an excess demand for dollars for foreign payments will at last become healthy enough to afford the acquisition of dollar balances for purposes of accumulating a foreign reserve; and, finally, that the growth of the foreign reserves of the free world through new gold production, gold dishoarding, and through the said increase in dollar balances will be fully adequate to meet the world's need for reserves. It takes some optimism, however, for one to count on all these conditions of a happy ending actually to materialize.

Alternative 1-b would put the gold-exchange standard on a broader base. Some of the strong currencies—for example, the German mark, French franc, and Swiss franc—might be recognized and adopted as additional key-currencies, in that other monetary authorities would get used to holding demand deposits in the new key-currency countries. To be sure, it would be rather anomalous for reserves to be held in currencies that are needed only rarely for current transactions. If, however, trade or capital transactions with countries with convertible currencies are sufficiently frequent so that good use can be found for balances in these currencies for transactions purposes, there should be no obstacle to the inclusion of such deposits in the official monetary reserves. Just as a large firm may have accounts with several banks or in several cities, so the central bank of a country may hold in its official reserve the currencies of several other countries. Of course, a necessary condition for this extension of the reserve portfolio is that none of the several potential key-currencies be regarded as weak or soft.

The recognition of additional key-currencies means not only that the monetary authorities of third countries hold reserves in the form of several foreign currencies, but also that the present two key-currency countries hold some of their reserves in currencies of the new key-currency countries. It may seem odd that the Federal Reserve Bank of New York should hold balances in Frankfurt while at the same time the German Bundesbank holds balances in New York. This almost looks like financial kite-flying, since the mutual establishment of credit balances by way of mutual lending creates assets in the form of official reserves without any effort, expense, abstinence, or saving on the part of any of the countries concerned.

It is important to understand how, under such a "multiple-currency-reserve system," official reserves will be affected by international payments. (T-Account Set 1 may be helpful in clarifying the effects of payments upon reserves under various circumstances.) If payments are made from one country to another in the currency of a third country, then, and only then, will the effect be precisely as under the full gold standard: the paying country will lose reserves and the receiving country will gain reserves, total monetary reserves remaining unchanged. In a key-currency

---

T-ACCOUNT SET 1   *International Payments in a Multiple-Currency-Reserve System*

Assumptions:
  (1) There are four reserve currencies, the U.S. dollar ($), the pound sterling (£), the French franc (Fr), and the West German mark (DM).
  (2) The central banks, executing and receiving payments, do not pursue any particular portfolio policy regarding their foreign-exchange holdings but leave the composition of their reserves to the accident of the individual choices made by the payers when they decide what form their payments are to take. That is to say, the central banks accumulate the currencies which they receive in payment, and pay out the currencies which the clients order.
  (3) All exchange rates equal 100, so that in converting one currency into another we are spared the effort of calculating the equivalent.

First Example: Payments from the United States to Brazil, in U.S. Dollars

United States			Brazil		
Foreign	Domestic deposits	−100	Foreign		Domestic deposits	+100
exchange	Foreigners' deposits		exchange		
£	United Kingdom		$	+100	
Fr	France		£		
DM	Germany		Fr		
	Other (Brazil)	+100	DM		

RESULT: The monetary reserve in the United States is unchanged, the monetary reserve in Brazil is increased.

Second Example: Payments from the United States to Brazil, in DM

United States			Germany		
Foreign	Domestic deposits	−100	Foreign	Domestic deposits	
exchange	Foreigners' deposits		exchange	Foreigners' deposits	
£	United Kingdom		$	United States	−100
Fr	France		£	United Kingdom	
DM −100	Germany		Fr	France	
	Other			Other (Brazil)	+100

Brazil			
Foreign		Domestic deposits	+100
exchange			
$			
£			
Fr			
DM	+100		

RESULT: The monetary reserve in the United States is decreased, the monetary reserve in Brazil is increased.

Third Example: Payments from the United States to Germany, in U.S. Dollars

United States			Germany		
Foreign	Domestic deposits	−100	Foreign	Domestic deposits	+100
exchange	Foreigners' deposits		exchange	Foreigners' deposits	
£	United Kingdom		$ +100	United States	
Fr	France		£	United Kingdom	
DM	Germany	+100	Fr	France	
	Other			Other	

RESULT: The monetary reserve in the United States is unchanged, the monetary reserve in Germany is increased.

Fourth Example: Payments from the United States to Germany, in DM

United States			Germany		
Foreign	Domestic deposits	−100	Foreign	Domestic deposits	+100
exchange	Foreigners' deposits		exchange	United States	
£	United Kingdom		$	United Kingdom	−100
Fr	France		£	France	
DM −100	Germany		Fr	Other	
	Other				

RESULT: The monetary reserve in the United States is decreased, the monetary reserve in Germany is unchanged.

country the monetary reserve will not change when payments are made or received in its own currency. Hence, total reserves of all countries combined will increase when payments are made from a key-currency country in its own currency; conversely, total reserves will decrease when payments are received by a key-currency country in its own currency.

Of course, the monetary authority of a key-currency country will hardly leave it entirely to the whims or habits of bank clients to determine how the amount and composition of its foreign-exchange reserve are to change. Convertible currencies can be exchanged one for the other, and key-currency countries may at any time use their deposits in other key-currency countries to reduce their own obligations. Any such compensation of claims against liabilities destroys monetary reserves in the same way that the establishment of credit balances in key-currency countries creates monetary reserves. It would be quite likely that the central banks of key-currency countries would, in close cooperation, take advantage of these possibilities to create and destroy monetary reserves.

An explicit proposal for broadening the gold-exchange standard was made by Xenophon Zolotas, Governor of the Bank of Greece, who recommended that the present "reserve countries should build up sufficient balances of major, convertible currencies to be used as 'masse de manoeuvre' in the foreign exchange market and to serve as the first line of defense of the key currencies." [16] Zolotas called the new system the "multi-currency international standard." Two features of the Zolotas Plan are noteworthy. First and foremost, every country whose currency is used in the foreign reserves of other central banks and treasuries should provide a "gold guarantee"—not necessarily an obligation to redeem the currency in gold, but a gold clause protecting foreign monetary authorities against losses from devaluation. Secondly, preferential treatment regarding interest rates and taxation should be accorded to official foreign depositors of short-term balances. These provisions are designed to make it more attractive for central banks to hold large portions of their reserves in the form of foreign claims rather than in gold.

First steps toward the establishment of a multiple-currency-reserve system were announced in May 1962 by Robert V. Roosa, Under Secretary of the U.S. Treasury, and by the Federal Reserve Bank of New York.[17] In connection with certain forward-exchange transactions the United States had started to hold various foreign currencies as part of its foreign reserve.

[16] Xenophon Zolotas, *Towards a Reinforced Gold Exchange Standard* (Bank of Greece, Papers and Lectures, No. 7, Athens, 1961), p. 11.

[17] Robert V. Roosa, "The Beginning of a New Policy," Remarks at the Monetary Conference of the American Bankers Association, Rome, Italy, May 17, 1962. Reprinted in *Factors Affecting the United States Balance of Payments*, Subcommittee on International Exchange and Payments, Joint Economic Committee, 87th Congress, 2d Session, Part 5 (Washington, 1962), pp. 327-332.

For example, the Federal Reserve Bank of New York had paid $50 million to the dollar account of the Bank of England in New York against a corresponding payment by the Bank of England of nearly £18 million to the sterling account of the New York Bank in London; and a similar arrangement had been made with the Banque de France. These reciprocal arrangements were designed to provide "forward cover" to both parties.

In addition, Roosa intimated that during any temporary or persistent surplus in the overall balance of payments, the United States would not reduce its liabilities to foreign monetary authorities—which would lower the total of international reserves—but would instead acquire foreign currencies. These currencies would be added to the reserves of the United States, so that total reserves would increase. Thus it would be possible, in principle, to make world reserves increase both as a result of a U.S. deficit and as a result of a U.S. surplus. Payments *from* the United States, in the case of a deficit, could increase the dollar holdings of the recipient countries; payments *to* the United States, in the case of a surplus, could increase the foreign-currency holdings of the United States. Alternatively, the United States, after having accumulated sufficient exchange reserves, could decide to meet temporary deficits by using some of these holdings, thereby avoiding an increase in liabilities or an outflow of gold. During 1962 arrangements for bilateral "swing credits" or "swaps" through mutual holdings of currencies were concluded by the United States with France, England, the Netherlands, Belgium, Canada, Switzerland, and Western Germany.[18]

The Roosa Plan encompasses "more or less continuous holdings by the United States of some moderate amounts of the convertible exchange of various leading countries." This is regarded as "a means of further economizing on gold reserves." The "net effect . . . would be to multilateralize a part of the role performed now by the two key currencies, within a framework that would place great stress on still further cooperation among monetary authorities. . . ."[19] In actual fact, and somewhat in contradiction to Roosa's contention, the system resulting from the currency swaps would be a network of bilateral, not multilateral, arrangements.

The Roosa Plan for multiple-currency reserves does not include any "gold guarantees." Indeed, Roosa rejects guarantees of compensation for losses in the event of devaluation as unnecessary, cumbersome, harmful,

[18] Charles A. Coombs, "Treasury and Federal Reserve Foreign Exchange Operations," *Monthly Review of the Federal Reserve Bank of New York*, October 1962, p. 137; reprinted in *Factors Affecting the United States Balance of Payments*, Subcommittee on International Exchange and Payments, Joint Economic Committee, 87th Congress, 2d Session, Part 5 (Washington, 1962), p. 364.

[19] Robert V. Roosa, *op. cit.*, p. 331.

and worthless.[20] He believes that confidence in the dollar as a reserve currency must be beyond suspicion and need not, and cannot, be bolstered by gold guarantees. But he expects a good deal from the proposed "reciprocal holdings of currencies." In the future, "the new arrangements also are capable of providing for a steady growth in the monetary reserves needed to service the trade requirements of an expanding world." And "whether or not there is a corresponding increase in the supply of gold in the world's monetary reserves, additional increases in the supply of dollars can rest upon an accumulation by the United States of incremental amounts of the currencies of other leading countries. These other currencies, while not equally capable of serving the multitude of functions required of a reserve currency, can, as the United States acquires holdings of them, be brought into a further mutual sharing of some of the responsibilities which the international reserve system must itself carry." [21]

A distinction should be made between "currency swaps" (the reciprocal holding of currencies) and "stand-by-credit swaps" (or simply "stand-by swaps," that is, reciprocal credit facilities on a stand-by basis). Practical differences may be seen in accounting procedures, balance-sheet effects, and timing. In the case of a currency swap, each of the participating central banks credits the account of the other at the time the arrangement is made, and the foreign-exchange holdings of both banks are "visibly" increased. In the case of a stand-by swap, mutual drawing facilities are granted, but nothing happens until one of the banks actually exercises its drawing rights. As a rule it will only do so, not to increase its reserves, but to change the form of its current liabilities, for example, to repurchase some of its own currency offered in the spot or forward-exchange market abroad.[22] Since the multiple-currency-reserve system is concerned with the *holding* of foreign reserves, stand-by swaps are really of a different nature, coming under the heading of plans of type 2, for mutual assistance among central banks.

[20] Robert V. Roosa, "Assuring the Free World's Liquidity," *Business Review, Supplement,* Federal Reserve Bank of Philadelphia, September 1962, pp. 5-7; reprinted in *Factors Affecting the United States Balance of Payments,* Subcommittee on International Exchange and Payments, Joint Economic Committee, 87th Congress, 2d Session, Part 5 (Washington, 1962), pp. 343-346.

[21] *Ibid.,* pp. 11 and 12, or p. 350, respectively.

[22] By January 1963, the Federal Reserve Bank of New York had contracted for reciprocal stand-by credits with the central banks of eleven countries and with the Bank for International Settlements in a total amount of $1,050 million. Total drawings under these swap arrangements exceeded $600 million between March 1962 and February 1963, but the net debtor position of the Federal Reserve Bank of New York was less than $100 million by the end of February 1963. See Charles A. Coombs, "Treasury and Federal Reserve Foreign Exchange Operations," *Federal Reserve Bank of New York, Monthly Review,* Vol. 45 (March 1963), pp. 39-45.—The largest stand-by-credit swap was arranged in May 1963, in an amount of $500 million, between the United Kingdom and the United States.

Even before Roosa's "Beginning of a New Policy," Friedrich Lutz, professor at the University of Zurich, had come out with an endorsement of the "multiple-currency standard" as the second-best reform of the international monetary system (the best, in his judgment—freely flexible exchange rates—apparently being unacceptable to the bankers of t⎁e world). Lutz distinguishes the multiple-currency standard—where "every country is prepared to hold its international reserves in other foreign currencies besides dollars" and "America too is ready to hold foreign exchange balances" [23]—from the "multiple-currency standard *with gold*," and contrasts both with the present system of "two key-currencies and gold." He believes that the distribution of reserves among several currencies would make the system less sensitive to crises of confidence. Moreover, "since the volume of international reserves must increase as world trade increases, it follows that national currencies would be bound to form in the future an ever-growing proportion of total international reserves. This would mean that a system in which there were only one or two key-currency countries could not survive in the longer run. America's dollar liabilities to other countries could not grow to a multiple of the American gold stock without undermining confidence in the dollar. The other countries would eventually insist on taking gold instead of accumulating additional dollar balances, and a very real shortage of international reserves would some day develop" (p. 66). Such a calamity could be averted by "the adoption of the practice of keeping international reserves in several national currencies" (p. 73).

The Lutz Plan says nothing about gold guarantees or gold clauses, but it does "require that all of the reserve-currency countries should be ready . . . always to surrender gold to the monetary authorities of other countries on request." [24] That such requests might wreck the system and would therefore have to be limited by close international "cooperation" is not mentioned by Lutz, though he probably regarded it as self-evident.

The advocacy of the multiple-currency standard represents, in a way, a strange reversal in the history of thought on international monetary economics. Students of monetary economics remember the Bimetallism debate. When both gold and silver were international money, convertible into each other at a fixed rate, there was periodic trouble. Depending on the relative scarcity or abundance, people were always rushing from one money into the other. Experience taught eventually that safety lies in

[23] Friedrich A. Lutz, *The Problem of International Economic Equilibrium*, Professor Dr. F. de Vries Lectures (Amsterdam: North-Holland Publishing Comp., 1962), p. 63.

[24] *Ibid.*, p. 66. For a more recent statement of these proposals, see Friedrich A. Lutz, *The Problem of International Liquidity and the Multiple-Currency Standard*, Essays in International Finance, No. 41 (Princeton: International Finance Section, 1963).

having only *one* international money. Yet, the world is now blessed with three international moneys: gold, dollars, and pounds sterling. There are periodic rushes, sometimes from sterling into dollars, sometimes from dollars into gold. This is to be expected since dollars, pounds, and gold are produced in quantities determined without regard to the ratios in which, at fixed rates of exchange, the world may wish to hold them. If three international moneys, supplied from sources independent of one another, are convertible into each other at fixed rates, Gresham's Law will operate and the scarcest of the moneys will go into hoards. Now some experts, instead of seeking safety in a return to a single international money, hope to find safety in larger numbers and urge that there be six or eight international moneys! Such a system, however, with fixed exchange rates between the different moneys, can work only if all the issuers of these moneys observe strict discipline in keeping their currencies scarce.

Even this may not be enough. Assume that different central banks maintain different ratios in their reserve holdings; country A holds 40% gold, 30% dollars, 10% sterling, 10% francs, and 10% D-mark, while country B holds 60% gold, 20% dollars, and 20% francs. Any temporary flow of funds from A to B would change the demand for the various reserve moneys and, consequently, make some scarce and others abundant. Or assume that general elections are coming up in one of the reserve-currency countries, with one of the contending parties promising to pursue an expansionary monetary policy. The resulting expectations may start hot-money movements out of this and into the other reserve currencies and into gold.

To cope with difficulties of this sort, it was proposed that the most important monetary authorities should undertake to hold gold and foreign currencies in fixed proportions.[25] This, according to press reports, was one of the provisions of the first Posthuma Plan, discussed in the summer and fall of 1962 in the Monetary Committee of the European Economic Community and among the central bankers of the Basle Club. Posthuma is a director of the Netherlands Bank. This plan was not published, and the reports about it may be less than accurate. If it is true that it provided for an upper limit of 60 per cent for the gold portion of official foreign reserves, with the other 40 per cent of gross reserves to be held in foreign currencies, the plan would go far to banish the danger of any shortage of international reserves for many years to come. (At present the gold portion of the gross reserves of the eleven countries listed in Table XIV-2

---

[25] John H. Williamson holds that such formal commitments (of fixed and standard-ized gold-and-currency mix) are probably essential if the multiple key-currency proposal is to increase "liquidity." John H. Williamson, "Liquidity and the Multiple Key Currency Proposal," *The American Economic Review*, Vol. LIII (June 1963), pp. 430-431.

is 77 per cent. The reduction in the gold ratio would imply an increase of the currency reserves by some $11 billions.) And if a "currency bundle" of a fixed composition is to be held by each of the central banks, the danger of a flight from one currency into another would be substantially reduced. Of course, each participating country would have to give the other countries a gold-value and exchange-value guarantee for its currency. The holding of reserves in a fixed gold-and-currency mix has been referred to as the essence of a "composite standard." [26]

In a newer version [27] of the Posthuma Plan the emphasis is not on fixed proportions in which the various currencies are to be *held* in official reserves, but rather on fixed proportions in which countries have to meet deficits in their payments balance to other countries. The member countries of the O.E.C.D. (Organization for Economic Cooperation and Development) should by agreement fix these proportions for several years to come; for example, any deficit would have to be paid 3 parts in gold, 2 parts in foreign exchange, and 2 parts in the paying country's own currency. In other words, each country would agree to accept the liabilities of the deficit country for $\frac{2}{7}$ of any payments due, and to take another $\frac{2}{7}$ in other currencies; only $\frac{3}{7}$, or less than 43 per cent, would be received in gold.

The number of currencies accepted as official reserve would be equal to the number of parties to the agreement, each giving an exchange-value guarantee for its currency in the official holdings of the other countries. The significant difference between this system and a system with only two, or a few, key currencies, would be that, according to Posthuma, "all countries would be treated in the same way." No longer would one reserve-currency country be able to pay by increasing its liabilities, while other countries found their gross reserves reduced with every payment they made. By implication, all countries would be in the same measure under the traditional "discipline" imposed by losses of gross reserves; the losses, however, would be lightened for all, since every country would be able to cover a part of its deficit with its own liabilities. The addition of these liabilities to the gross reserves of the monetary surplus countries would, of course, provide more or less regular increases to the monetary reserves of the free world.

The basic idea of the Posthuma Plan was endorsed by and incorporated into the Bernstein Plan of 1963. Bernstein, formerly Director of Research and Statistics at the International Monetary Fund, prefers, how-

[26] Edward M. Bernstein, in *Outlook for United States Balance of Payments*, Hearings before the Subcommittee on International Exchange and Payments, Joint Economic Committee, Congress of the United States, 87th Congress, 2d Session, December 12, 13, and 14, 1962 (Washington: 1963), p. 208.
[27] S. Posthuma, "The International Monetary System," *Banca Nazionale del Lavoro Quarterly Review*, No. 66 (September 1963), pp. 239-261.

ever, to keep the number of reserve currencies to eleven—the currencies of the United States, Canada, United Kingdom, Japan, Belgium, France, Germany, Italy, the Netherlands, Sweden, and Switzerland—and he proposes an agreement "among the eleven countries to standardize the composition of their holdings of gold and foreign exchange and their use in international settlements with each other." [28] The best way to accomplish this is, according to Bernstein, "to establish a Reserve Unit, equivalent to a gold dollar, consisting of a stated proportion of each of the eleven currencies. Thus, a reserve unit might consist of about 50¢ in U.S. currency and lesser amounts in sterling, French francs, marks, lire, Canadian dollars, yen, guilders, etc. The proportion of the reserve unit consisting of each currency would be agreed on the basis of its present role as a reserve currency and its importance in international trade and investment. Some consideration should be given to the total reserves of a country, but not to their present composition."

Any country holding gold would undertake to hold also a minimum amount of reserve units. "The ultimate objective would be for each country to hold reserve units amounting to at least one half of its gold reserves." In order to avoid an excessive upsurge in monetary reserves, "the plan would have to be put into effect by stages. Initially, for example, about $3.5 billion of reserve units could be created and countries would be obligated to hold a minimum of one reserve unit for each $9 of reserves they hold in gold" (p. 6).

To create the reserve units each participating country would deposit its own currency with the International Monetary Fund in an amount "equal to its *pro rata* share of the reserve units to be created. . . . In return each country would be given a credit on the books of the Trustee denominated in reserve units." (Bernstein calls the Fund a "Trustee" and thereby avoids some such term as "International Reserve Bank.") "Thus, the Trustee would hold $3.5 billion in the currencies of the eleven participating countries and they, in turn, would hold $3.5 billion in reserve units" (p. 7). All currencies held by the Fund would be guaranteed against exchange depreciation. The countries would be "obligated to convert balances of their currencies, when held by the monetary authorities of the other countries, in gold and reserve units" in precise proportions, initially 90 per cent in gold and 10 per cent in reserve units, but later (when the proportion of reserve units to gold is eventually increased to the ultimate ratio) two thirds in gold and one third in reserve units. Two features distinguish the Bernstein Plan of 1963 from other multiple-currency-reserve systems. One, the countries would hold the foreign currencies not directly, in their own portfolio, but indirectly, in the form of reserve-unit

[28] Edward M. Bernstein, "A Practical Proposal for International Monetary Reserves," Model, Roland & Co. *Quarterly Review,* Fourth Quarter 1963, p. 6.

credit balances in a central reserve pool; second, the reserve-currency mix would be standardized and not subject to changes at the discretion of the separate monetary authorities. These provisions would safeguard the system against sudden switches from one reserve currency into another or into gold.

If, under the multiple-currency-reserve plans à la Zolotas, Roosa, or Lutz, a system with five or six key-currencies should develop or, under the Posthuma Plan, the system should have as many as 15 or 20 separate reserve currencies, there is one necessary condition for things to develop successfully along these lines: there must be a large measure of confidence in the credit and fiscal policies of the reserve-currency countries. After all, the willingness of a central bank to allow its monetary reserves to grow by an accumulation of claims against a particular country implies its willingness to grant increasing amounts of "credit" to the central bank of that country. A central bank that increases its holdings of a foreign currency is in effect making a loan to the central bank issuing that currency. This could not be expected if there were serious misgivings about the policies pursued by the "borrowing" central bank, especially if there were fears that it intended to continue an "unsound" policy despite ever-mounting indebtedness. Thus, in the last analysis, a development of type 1-b converges upon the basic idea of the alternatives of type 2. The reverse need not be true. Although the extension of the gold-exchange standard in the manner just described would involve mutual assistance by central banks, most of the plans for mutual assistance among central banks are entirely independent of any recognition of additional key-currencies. Indeed, the most widely discussed plans of type 2 take it for granted that the dollar and the pound sterling remain the only reserve currencies.[29]

2. Mutual assistance among central banks

The simplest and most common way in which one central bank may extend credit to another would be for the helping bank to purchase the currency of the bank in need of help and to continue to hold the acquired foreign exchange for the time being. This can be done either without any previous arrangements or on the basis of stand-by agreements. The transaction itself is not one between the "lender" and the "borrower," since the obligations of the borrower are offered for sale by

[29] That different features of a plan qualify it for more than one type or category need not indicate that our classification is inadequate. The Bernstein Plan of 1963, providing for an extension of the gold-exchange standard to include eleven reserve currencies, for mutual assistance among central banks in various forms, and for a degree of centralization of monetary reserves, falls into three categories. Needless to say, every classification is arbitrary, and different analysts may choose to emphasize different aspects.

third persons, and since the bank which acquires these obligations makes its payment to the seller rather than to the implicit borrower, the obligated bank.

Other kinds of assistance do involve direct transactions between the lending and the borrowing central banks. For example, the lending bank may put at the disposal of the borrowing bank gold or claims against (i.e., currencies of) third countries and thereby reduce its own assets; or, alternatively, it may supply claims against itself, and thereby increase its liabilities. Finally, there is the possibility of an intermediary, such as the International Monetary Fund, stepping in between the lending and the borrowing central bank. All of this may be on the basis of *ad hoc* agreement or of stand-by agreements, providing for credits or drawing rights upon demand.

Distinctions may also be made according to what the lending bank lends (or parts with) and what it receives for its portfolio. It may lend (1) gold, (2) foreign exchange, that is, currency of a third country, or (3) its own currency, that is, its own sight-liabilities. In exchange, it may receive for its portfolio (a) currency of the country in need of help, (b) medium-term or long-term obligations of the borrowing country, payable in gold or in the currency of a third country, (c) medium-term or long-term obligations of the borrowing country, payable in the latter country's currency, (d) medium-term or long-term obligations of the borrowing country, payable in the currency of the lending country, or (e) obligations of an intermediary institution, such as the I.M.F.

The combination (3a) can quickly be recognized as the "simplest and most common way" described in the first sentence of this subsection: the purchase by the helping bank of the currency in excessive supply. Combination (3c) is exemplified by the lending country's purchases of U.S. government securities. Combination (3d) is illustrated by several arrangements reported in 1962 and 1963, under which the United States borrowed, for example, German marks against special U.S. bonds denominated in German marks, with maturities up to two years.[30] (The operations themselves can take so many different forms that it may be helpful to inspect some of the ten alternatives shown in T-Account Set 2.)

Of the various forms which the support action may take, those most favored by international bankers call for loans to the I.M.F. by central banks of surplus countries in their own currency, enabling the Fund to sell these currencies to the monetary authority of the deficit country, which pays with its own liabilities (and a promise to repurchase these liabilities as soon as possible). The purpose of this support action is to

---

[30] Some of these borrowings were actually not between central banks but rather between treasury departments. For example, the U.S. Treasury borrowed German marks from the treasury of Western Germany.

T-ACCOUNT SET 2   *Alternative Forms of Support of One Central Bank by Another*

Assumptions:

(1) The Deutsche Bundesbank (D.B.B.) is to act in support of the pound sterling.
(2) In examples 1 and 2, the D.B.B. purchases pounds sterling offered in the market; in examples 3 to 6, it makes a loan to the United Kingdom (U.K.); and in examples 7 to 10, it makes a loan to the International Monetary Fund (I.M.F.) to supply the funds to the U.K.
(3) In examples 6 and 10, the U.K. uses the new funds to reduce its demand liabilities to (or its short-term debt held by) the D.B.B.

Example 1. The D.B.B. purchases pounds sterling from German nationals.

D.B.B.

Foreign exchange £	+100	Domestic deposits	+100

Example 2. The D.B.B. purchases pounds sterling from foreign nationals.

D.B.B.

Foreign exchange £	+100	Foreigners' deposits	+100

Example 3. The D.B.B. makes a loan of gold to the U.K.

D.B.B.

Gold	−100		
Loan to U.K.	+100		

Example 4. The D.B.B. makes a loan of dollars to the U.K.

D.B.B.

Foreign exchange $	−100		
Loan to U.K.	+100		

Example 5. The D.B.B. makes a loan of D-Mark to the U.K.

D.B.B.

Loan to U.K.	+100	Foreigners' deposits	+100

Example 6. The D.B.B. makes a loan of D-Mark to the U.K., which the U.K. immediately uses to repay some of its demand liabilities held by the D.B.B.

D.B.B.

Foreign exchange £	−100		
Loan to U.K.	+100		

Example 7. The D.B.B. makes a loan of gold to the I.M.F., and the I.M.F. sells the gold to the U.K. against pounds sterling.

D.B.B.

Gold	−100		
Loan to I.M.F.	+100		

Example 8. The D.B.B. makes a loan of dollars to the I.M.F., and the I.M.F. sells the dollars to the U.K. against pounds sterling.

D.B.B.

Foreign exchange			
$	−100		
Loan to I.M.F.	+100		

Example 9. The D.B.B. makes a loan of D-Mark to the I.M.F., and the I.M.F. sells the D-Mark to the U.K. against pounds sterling.

D.B.B.

Loan to I.M.F.	+100	Foreigners' deposits	
		U.K.	+100

Example 10. The D.B.B. makes a loan of D-Mark to the I.M.F.; the I.M.F. sells the D-Mark to the U.K. against pounds sterling; and the U.K. uses the D-Mark immediately to repay some of its demand liabilities held by the D.B.B.

D.B.B.

Foreign exchange			
£	−100		
Loan to I.M.F.	+100		

provide compensatory finance to a country suffering from a massive outflow of short-term capital. (Examples 9 and 10 in T-Account Set 2 illustrate this case.)

This is the kind of action recommended in proposals made by Xenophon Zolotas,[31] Edward M. Bernstein,[32] and Per Jacobsson.[33] All

[31] Xenophon Zolotas, in International Monetary Fund, *Summary Proceedings of the Twelfth Annual Meeting of the Board of Governors,* 1957, p. 42; *idem,* in International Monetary Fund, *Summary Proceedings of the Thirteenth Annual Meeting of the Board of Governors,* 1958, p. 91; *idem,* "A Proposal for Expanding the Role of the International Monetary Fund" (mimeographed, February 24, 1961); *idem, The Problem of the International Monetary Liquidity* (Bank of Greece, Papers and Lectures, No. 6, Athens: 1961); *idem, Towards a Reinforced Gold Exchange Standard* (Bank of Greece, Papers and Lectures, No. 7, Athens: 1961).

[32] Edward M. Bernstein, *International Effects of U.S. Economic Policy,* Joint Economic Committee, United States Congress, 86th Congress, 2d Session, Study Paper No. 16 (Washington: 1960), pp. 85-86; *idem,* "The Adequacy of United States Gold Reserves," *American Economic Review,* Papers and Proceedings, Vol. LI (1961), pp. 439-446; *idem,* "The Problem of International Monetary Reserves," Statement in *International Payments Imbalances and Need for Strengthening International Financial Arrangements,* Hearings before the Subcommittee on International Exchange and Pay-

these proposals provide that the most important industrial nations with balance-of-payments surpluses make loans to the I.M.F., enabling it to place the acquired funds at the disposal of the monetary authorities of important industrial nations suffering from outflows of short-term capital. These plans differ from one another merely in technical details. (This is not to say that technical details may not be important.) For example, under the Bernstein Plan the central banks in trouble could with relative certainty count on the availability of I.M.F. support, whereas under the Jacobsson Plan—which represents a compromise with the more orthodox points of view of central bankers in continental Europe—the lending banks would have to approve of the intended I.M.F. action in each case.[34] All these plans are designed to reinforce the gold-exchange standard against the onslaught of hot-money movements. Their common feature is that the I.M.F. would borrow from the central banks in the countries receiving capital inflows and would make the borrowed funds available to the central banks suffering from the capital outflows.

The role of the I.M.F. in these interventions is that of an intermediary and guarantor, not that of a bank of issue or of a commercial bank engaged in the creation of credit. A real bank (in the economic sense of the word) would not have to start looking for lenders (depositors); it would purchase long-term obligations in the open market or acquire short-term obligations by granting loans, and in the process would create its own deposit liabilities which would serve their holders as means of payment and transactions-cash balances. Under the proposed arrangements, however, the I.M.F. is to borrow liquid international means of payment in the form of demand liabilities of central banks in strong positions and pass them on to the central banks battered by the hot-money storm.[35]

The way in which the support action proposed in the Zolotas, Bernstein, and Jacobsson Plans compensates for the results of a short-term capital movement is demonstrated in T-Account Set 3. First the results of

---

ments, Joint Economic Committee, United States Congress [87th Congress, 1st Session] (Washington: May 1961), pp. 107-137.

[33] Per Jacobsson, quoted in "Fund Report at ECOSOC," *International Financial News Survey*, International Monetary Fund, Vol. XIII, No. 16 (April 28, 1961), pp. 124-126; *idem*, in International Monetary Fund, *Summary Proceedings of the Sixteenth Annual Meeting of the Board of Governors*, 1961, pp. 27-29, 157-158.

[34] See "General Arrangements to Borrow," Paragraph 7, and "Letter from Mr. Baumgartner, Minister of Finance, France, to Mr. Dillon, Secretary of the Treasury, United States," points C and D, reproduced in *International Financial News Survey*, International Monetary Fund, Supplement, Vol. XIV (January 12, 1962).

[35] The difference between credit creation and credit transfer is demonstrated in T-Account Set 8 on pp. 337–338.—It should be noted that Zolotas proposed also a multiple-currency-reserve system (see p. 303) and that Bernstein later formulated his proposals in a way that could easily be extended to comprise central reserve creation (see p. 334).

an assumed outflow of funds from the United States to Germany are shown: a flight from the dollar on the part of private holders of American balances forces the Deutsche Bundesbank (D.B.B.) to purchase all dollars offered for sale. Then it is shown how the actions under the loan arrangement with the I.M.F. undo most of what the capital outflow has done: the dollar holdings of the D.B.B., accumulated as a result of the hot-money movement, are gone, replaced by a nonnegotiable claim against the I.M.F., and the demand liabilities of the United States to the D.B.B. are replaced by a U.S. debt to the I.M.F. Both the lending and the borrowing countries may be satisfied with these transformations of assets and liabilities. The lending country will have secured a gold guaranty for a part of its excessive holdings of foreign exchange, and the borrowing country will have a part of its excessive sight liabilities funded, that is, replaced by a debt of deferred maturity.

T-ACCOUNT SET 3   *Short-Term Capital Movement and Compensating Support Action*

Assumptions:
   (1) An outflow of short-term capital occurs from the United States; one-half of the funds withdrawn are owned by U.S. nationals, one-fourth by German nationals, one-fourth by other foreigners.
   (2) All these dollars are offered to German banks; the Deutsche Bundesbank (D.B.B.), intent upon maintaining the fixed exchange rate, purchases the dollars.
   (3) The United States wishes to draw German mark (DM) from the International Monetary Fund (I.M.F.) in order to reduce its demand liabilities to the D.B.B.
   (4) The I.M.F. calls on the D.B.B. for a loan under the credit arrangement; the D.B.B. lends DM to the I.M.F. and receives a nonnegotiable instrument evidencing the Fund's indebtedness.
   (5) The I.M.F. sells (read: lends) the DM to the United States.
   (6) The United States uses the acquired DM to reduce (buy back) its liabilities to the D.B.B.

   RESULTS OF ASSUMPTIONS *(1) and (2):* Hot-money movement from United States to Germany.

United States			Germany			
	Domestic deposits	−50	Foreign exchange $	+100	Domestic deposits	+25
	Foreigners' deposits, private	−50			Foreigners' deposits, private (U.S.)	+50
	Foreigners' deposits, official (D.B.B.)	+100			private (others)	+25

RESULTS OF ASSUMPTIONS *(4) to (6):* D.B.B. loan to I.M.F. in order to support U.S. position.

I.M.F.

Claim against U.S.	+100	Debt to D.B.B.	+100

United States				Germany			
Foreigners' deposits, official (D.B.B.)	−100		Foreign exchange $	−100			
Debt to I.M.F.	+100		Claim against I.M.F.	+100			

COMBINED RESULTS: The U.S. official liabilities to Germany (i.e., the D.B.B.'s holdings of dollars) are unchanged, because the increase resulting from the capital movement was compensated for by the support action.

The purposes for which, and the conditions on which, the loans under the "arrangements to borrow" are to be made invite comment of a more general nature. For they reflect a remarkable change in official thinking from the time of Bretton Woods to the present. International loans, then, were designed to help countries in balance-of-payments difficulties *not* caused by capital movements, let alone short-term capital movements. And the main idea, then, was that central banks assisted by international loans might be spared painful adjustments through "deflationary" methods. Under the present plans, the international loans are specifically designed to help countries in difficulties arising from short-term capital outflows. And the main idea is to keep an eye on the aided countries to see that they do not pursue "unsound" policies, which evidently means that they do not indulge in policies of undue monetary expansion. What are the theoretical considerations behind these changes? Can a strong case be made for international loans designed to compensate for the results of hot-money movements?

The chief argument is that international support to monetary authorities suffering an outflow of short-term capital is likely to achieve its purpose, whereas similar support in the case of balance-of-payments difficulties due to an unsatisfactory state of the balance of goods and services is often doomed to failure. The better prospects of success with the hot-money trouble than with the "basic-balance" trouble lie in the different sources of funds going abroad and the different urge to domestic credit expansion in the two situations.

Domestic funds seeking foreign exchange to pay for purchases and investments abroad come out of transactions cash balances, that is, balances actively engaged in the industrial circulation and the domestic income flow. Any net outflow of funds from this "circuit flow" reduces the effective demand for domestic products and services, and the monetary authorities take it to be their duty to replace the leaked-out funds through newly created ones. As the importers buy foreign exchange and pay the banks for it, domestic deposits in active circulation are destroyed; only an expansion of credit, through loans or open-market purchases, can make up for the contraction, and the pressures in favor of a credit expansion are hard to resist. However, by maintaining effective demand at the level at which domestic prices and incomes produce an excess demand for imports and investments abroad, the monetary authorities perpetuate the deficit in the market balance of payments at the given exchange rate. They continually feed, through their credit expansion, the excess demand for foreign currencies and must then satisfy this demand out of their monetary reserves. Assistance by foreign or international institutions can replace losses of monetary reserves. But, as this is apt to encourage the monetary authorities to continue their policy of "offsetting" [36] the effects which the balance-of-payments mechanism has upon domestic circulation, the deficit is likely to become "fundamental"—that is, curable only through devaluation of the currency.[37]

This is not so when the deficit in the foreign-exchange market is due

[36] In a way, the practice of re-creating through credit expansion the domestic money destroyed through official sales of gold or foreign money upsets an almost axiomatic truth: that he who spends some of his money has less of it left. If Mr. A. buys something from Mr. B. and pays for it, A's money balance is reduced; and if a large group of A's buy from a large group of B's, paying them in money, the amount of money held by the A's should be expected to be down from what it was before. Yet, if a nation A buys from a nation B and pays for its purchases, complaints are raised about any reduction in the money stocks available in A and claims are made to bring them up to the former level, so that effective demand in A may be maintained. This is evidently a case of "eating one's cake and having it too." Should now the national policy of maintaining effective demand in the face of a deficit in foreign payments, known as "offsetting," be systematically matched by an international policy of maintaining the deficit country's monetary reserves by replacing the outflows through international support action? To do this would no doubt be possible. Just as a central bank in a country that consumes and invests more than its national income can, with a policy of maintaining effective demand, always re-create the domestic cash balances that are destroyed by payments abroad, so the foreign central banks could always, with a policy of international assistance, re-create the net reserves of the troubled central bank that were depleted by its foreign payments. (This suggests a touching fairy tale in which a warmhearted shopkeeper visits his customers every night to return to them the money he has taken in during the day from their purchases, so as to make sure that next morning they will have enough money for new purchases.)

[37] Pertinent statements by Sir Ralph Hawtrey deserve to be quoted at this point: "A reserve should be relied on only to cover temporary deficits in the balance of payments, that is to say, those caused by an excess spending that can be brought to an end by a suitable restriction of demand. Liquidity is no solution for the chronic weakness due to the over-valuation of a money unit." And "to rely on increasing liquidity in a case of fundamental disequilibrium is like trusting to baling instead of stopping a leak." Sir Ralph Hawtrey, "Too Little Liquidity—or Too Much?" *The Banker*, Vol. CXII (London, November 1962), pp. 711, 712.

to a speculative outflow of short-term capital. Domestic funds seeking foreign exchange for speculative purposes come, initially at least, out of cash balances held for precautionary and speculative motives. These balances are not actively engaged in the industrial circulation and in the domestic income flow. Their use for purchases of foreign exchange does not reduce the effective demand for domestic products and services, and hence the pressures upon the monetary authorities to replace the diminished stock of money will be less powerful. Of course, there will be repercussions upon the active circulation of money and upon aggregate demand. One of these repercussions may be through interest rates and the availability of credit. Speculative buyers of foreign exchange will also use funds other than their own speculative cash balances. They will sell government securities and they will use all the bank credit they can get. Still, the initial impact upon effective demand will be smaller than in the case of "basic-balance" trouble. Thus the monetary authorities may show greater resistance to the pleas for easier money. As they refuse to feed the excess demand for foreign exchange with expanded credit, and as the speculative cash balances become depleted, the deficit in the foreign-exchange market is likely to decline. It may still last longer than the monetary authorities can stand; the size of the inactive cash balances, reinforced by some switches from transactions cash and by some help from commercial banks, may overtax the gold and exchange reserves of the authorities and their ability to stand further increases in demand liabilities to foreign holders. Yet, it is precisely this situation for which the international arrangements to borrow are designed. As the drain on the monetary reserves is alleviated by the international support action, and as the increase in demand liabilities to foreign banks is transformed into deferred liabilities to the I.M.F., the speculators' nerves are calmed. With the return of confidence in the authorities' capacity to maintain the stability of the currency, and with the progressive depletion of speculative cash balances, the outflow of short-term capital comes to an end, and may even be succeeded by a reverse flow.

It may be helpful to summarize the argument. The danger that a central bank in trouble will use international assistance for an extension of its credit will be much smaller if only hot-money movements are the cause of its difficulties. This is so because the outflow of speculative funds need not be associated with a reduction in effective demand for goods and services and consequently the monetary authorities may not feel compelled to act in support of effective demand. On the other hand, payments for imports or for long-term investment abroad are financed from cash balances held for transactions purposes and hence from funds taking part in the normal circuit flow. One must expect, therefore, that monetary authorities intent upon maintaining effective demand would be pressured or feel duty-bound to embark on a compensatory expansion of credit. This difference is a sufficient explanation for the fact that foreign central banks are willing to offer their loans only to compensate for speculative hot-money movements, and even in these cases wish to insist that their support actions not be made ineffective through "unsound" policies in the deficit countries.

3. Centralization of monetary reserves

Just as the establishment of a national central bank can multiply the capacity of a country's banking system to create domestic money, so the establishment of a world central bank can multiply the capacity of the world monetary system to create international reserves and to make the individual central banks shock-proof. No wonder, then, that the centralization of central-bank reserves appears to many as the best solution of the monetary problems of our time, and to some as an inevitable development in the course of time.

The Keynes Plan [38] for the establishment of an international Clearing Union and the Triffin Plan [39] for the extension of the I.M.F. into an international central-reserve bank [40] are the best known of the proposals along such lines. Practical men and politicians are usually averse to plans of this sort, but there have been remarkable exceptions. Thus, in 1957 Sir Oliver Franks, President of the Board of Lloyds Bank, recommended that the I.M.F. be gradually transformed into a super-central bank.[41] It was almost sensational when, in 1961, Harold Macmillan, the British

[38] *Proposals for an International Clearing Union.* Presented by the Chancellor of the Exchequer to Parliament by Command of His Majesty, April 1943. (London: H.M.'s Stationery Office, Cmd. 6437.)

[39] Robert Triffin, "Tomorrow's Convertibility: Aims and Means of International Policy," *Banca Nazionale del Lavoro Quarterly Review*, No. 49 (June 1959), pp. 131-200; *idem*, "Statement," in *Employment, Growth, and Price Levels*, Hearings before the Joint Economic Committee, Congress of the United States, 86th Congress, First Session, Part 9A (Washington: 1959), pp. 2905-2954; *idem, Gold and the Dollar Crisis* (New Haven: Yale University Press, 1960); *idem*, "Le Crépuscule de l'Etalon de Change-Or," in *Comptes Rendus des Travaux de la Société Royale d'Economie Politique de Belgique*, No. 272 (1960); *idem*, "After the Gold Exchange Standard," *Weltwirtschaftliches Archiv*, Band 87 (1961), pp. 188-207.

[40] Triffin himself denies that his plan would establish a super-central bank or world central bank. He argues that the I.M.F., though with new functions under his plan, would still lack control over and responsibility for "national monetary issue functions." (*Weltwirtschaftliches Archiv, op. cit.*, p. 200.) Triffin to the contrary, the criterion of a central bank should be found in the centralization of both reserves and reserve creation.

[41] "At present, the credit-creating powers of that institution [the I.M.F.] are rigidly limited by the size of quotas; nor would an all-round increase in quotas be a suitable remedy for the situation we have in mind. There might be general advantage for the world, however, if the Fund could move in the direction of becoming a super-central bank." Sir Oliver Franks, "Statement by the Chairman," in *Report and Accounts 1957*, Lloyds Bank Limited, January 1958, p. 20.

Prime Minister, declared himself a supporter of this idea.[42] (Oddly enough, a few months later, at the annual meeting of the I.M.F., the representatives of the United Kingdom failed to give even the slightest support to developments in this direction.) Among economists there are many who regard these proposals as premature but certain of eventual acceptance. A few economists go so far as to regard them as the only real solution.[43]

We shall describe here only those parts of the Keynes Plan which we regard as particularly important for purposes of comparison with several other plans of this type. Under the Keynes Plan, the deposit liabilities of the Clearing Union are expressed in terms of a new international currency unit, called Bancor, with a fixed (though not inalterably fixed) equivalent in gold. Redemption of deposits in gold is not obligatory and depositors—the central banks of the member countries—can use their balances only for transfers to the accounts of other central banks. With the exception of some foreign-currency holdings of members of a "currency group" (for example, the Sterling Area), central banks should not be permitted to hold foreign currencies as part of their reserves. Thus, monetary reserves should consist only of gold and bancor. Bancor deposits with the Clearing Union can be established or increased in two ways: first, through the sale of gold to the Clearing Union and, secondly, through the use of overdraft facilities by central banks that suffer a deficit in their international balance of payments in excess of the credit balances on their bancor accounts. Since a credit of the Clearing Union to a central bank overdrawing its account can be used only for payments to other central banks, it creates new bancor credit balances.

The par values of all currencies are fixed, but can be altered when surpluses or deficits in the balance of payments become chronic. Each country is assigned a quota which determines the upper limits for its

[42] "Just as each individual country painfully acquired a central banking system, so there ought—ideally—to be a central banking system for all the countries of the Free World.

"All sorts of remedies are being suggested. The main difficulty about many of them is what I might call the mental hurdles which they present. It is normal to think of money as something painfully acquired; a dollar represents so many drops of sweat or so many ulcers. There seems to be something immoral in increasing the credit base by mutual agreement. It is done often enough in our internal economies; but the extension to the international field is hard to swallow. All the same, I repeat, expanding trade needs expanding money.

"The needs of our time demand a new attitude . . . An old fashioned or doctrinaire approach is not good enough. We must use the energy and abundance of our free enterprise system to transform our economic life. Above all, we must try to jump —even the older ones among us—the mental hurdles." Sir Harold Macmillan, Address at the Massachusetts Institute of Technology, April 7, 1961.

[43] "It is clear that a solution of the international payments problem by the introduction of a common currency, or by some sort of advanced clearing system, is the only real and final answer." Erik Ambjörn, "International Payments and the I.M.F.," *Skandinaviska Banken Quarterly Review,* Vol. 42 (July 1961), p. 72.

debit balances with the Clearing Union. The quotas are fixed by reference to the sum of each country's exports and imports (the average over the last three to five years). A charge of one per cent per annum shall be paid by a member if its debit balance exceeds one-fourth of its quota and a charge of two per cent if its debit balance exceeds one-half of its quota. Not only bancor borrowers, however, but also creditors, are subject to charges. For a credit balance in excess of one-half of its quota an overly liquid central bank must pay a charge of one per cent.

Central banks can escape these charges not only by pursuing domestic credit policies designed to reverse the balance in their international payments and thus to reduce their credit or debit balances on their bancor accounts—the debtor banks by contracting credit, the creditor banks by expanding—but they can also escape the charges by mutual bancor loans. Central banks with excessive credit balances on their bancor accounts can lend some of their bancor reserves to central banks with debit balances. A brisk credit market in bancor reserves would be likely to develop, a market limited to central banks lending and borrowing from one another. (Such a market for central-bank reserves would have its prototype in the "federal-funds market" of New York, in which American commercial banks lend and borrow legal reserves in the form of deposits with the Federal Reserve Banks.) This particular feature of the Keynes Plan really belongs to our category 2, the plans for mutual assistance among central banks. There are, however, important differences between Keynes' credit market for international reserves, on the one hand, and the stand-by credits under the Bernstein Plan or under the Jacobsson arrangements. In the first place, these stand-by arrangements provide for assistance only in emergency situations (such as speculative capital flows), whereas the credit market for international reserves would be an institution functioning day after day. Secondly, the loans under the I.M.F. arrangements are in the currencies of the lending countries, whereas they are in bancor deposits under the Keynes Plan. Thirdly, the debts of the central banks that arise from I.M.F. loans are medium-term obligations, in contrast with the day-to-day loans in the market for borrowed reserves under the Keynes Plan.[44] Fourthly, the loans under the I.M.F. arrangements are a last resort of the central banks in trouble (apart from the introduction of payments restric-

[44] The idea of a regular international credit market for monetary reserves deserves more attention than it has been given thus far, entirely apart from any plan for the centralization of reserves. Just as business firms can operate with much more modest cash balances if they are always able to borrow on short term, and just as commercial banks can operate with much lower reserves if they have ready access to a lively money market, so central banks could work with smaller monetary reserves if they could at any time turn to an international credit market and secure the needed international means of payment. The velocity of circulation of the monetary reserves would be larger; that is to say, the ratio of needed reserves to the value of foreign trade would be smaller.

tions or the abandonment of fixed exchange rates), whereas the credit market for bancor deposits would be merely a small portion of a rich program of provisions liberally bestowing upon central banks munificent drawing rights upon the Clearing Union.

What distinguishes the Keynes Plan most significantly from later proposals for centralization of monetary reserves is that it provides for only two means of asset acquisition and deposit creation by the Clearing Union, namely, gold and overdrafts. Each overdraft by a central bank creates bancor deposits for other central banks and thus creates new monetary

---

T-ACCOUNT SET 4   *Keynes Plan: Reserve Creation through Loans to Central Banks*

Assumptions:
   (1) Some countries with deficits in their balances of payments but insufficient credit balances with the Clearing Union make use of the overdraft facilities.
   (2) In overdrawing their accounts with the Clearing Union through making transfers to other countries, the drawing (borrowing) central banks will have created debit balances on their accounts and additional credit balances on the accounts of the receiving countries.
   (3) The credit balances with the Clearing Union constitute monetary reserves of the member countries.

Clearing Union

Overdrafts by central banks		Deposits of central banks	
	+100		+100

---

reserves. (This is demonstrated in T-Account Set 4.) However, as soon as the central banks in debt to the Clearing Union succeed in removing their payments deficits and in reversing the flows of foreign payments, the overdrafts will be paid off and the central-bank reserves that had been created by their use will be destroyed in the process. Since the rules of the Clearing Union are supposed to induce the monetary authorities of all countries to avoid both excessive indebtedness and excessive credit balances, and since it in the members' interest to be neither in debt nor overly liquid, nothing would be more natural than that all would do their best to see that overdrafts were paid off as soon as possible. It follows from this that one could not count on a steady growth of bancor deposits from year to year.[45]

There is, thus, no active policy of reserve creation on the part of the

[45] Sir Dennis Robertson realized this long ago, when he wrote: "It is arguable that the proudest day in the life of the Manager of the Clearing Union would be that on which, as a result of the smooth functioning of the correctives set in motion by the Plan, there were *no* holders of international money—on which he was able to show a balance sheet with zero on both sides of the account." D. H. Robertson, "The Post-war Monetary Plans," *Economic Journal*, Vol. LIII (1943), p. 359.

Clearing Union. Whatever fiduciary bancor creation there is would result from clearing balances in international payments that are in excess of a member's bancor balance. Payments which a country with a credit balance on its bancor account made to another country with a credit balance would give rise merely to transfers from one account to another with no change in the sum total of reserves. Payments which a country without a credit balance—or even with a debit balance—would make to a country with a credit balance—or at least without a debit balance—would create new reserves as a credit entry is made on the account of the receiving country. Conversely, total reserves would be reduced whenever payments were made from a country with a deposit to a country with a debit balance. Payments between countries with debit balances on their bancor accounts would have no effect upon the size of total indebtedness and total reserves.

There is one provision in the Keynes Plan which could contribute to a secular growth of monetary reserves. It calls for periodic increases in the quotas of the member countries as their foreign trade increases. These quotas, it will be remembered, determine the drawing rights of the member countries. The fact, however, that a central bank has access to overdraft facilities that increase from year to year does not mean that the bank will actually take advantage of such facilities. Just as some of the largest business firms never borrow from the banks, no matter how cordially the banks invite them to use their credit facilities, and just as some commercial banks consistently refrain from making use of discount facilities extended by their central banks, so it is to be expected that some of the central banks will always be so conservative and restrained in their credit policy that they would never—at least never for long—have to overdraw their accounts with the Clearing Union. It may not matter to them how high the limits are for their purely hypothetical drawing rights. Raising the lines of credit for someone who does not wish to borrow has no effect. To be sure, there are, and will always be, some less conservative monetary authorities which—driven by political pressures or by their own convictions—pursue decisively expansive credit policies and thereby cause their balances of payments to show chronic deficits. Only insofar as these countries were prepared to see their indebtedness to the Clearing Union increase year after year could one, as a result of such prodigality, expect the monetary reserves of the world to increase in the long run.

This last remark may call for a qualification, for there is an important interdependence between internal and international money creation. Domestic credit expansion would, under the Keynes Plan, lead to international credit expansion inasmuch as the domestic credits would give rise to deficits in the balance of payments and, eventually, to the use of the overdraft facilities of the Clearing Union. This international credit expansion in turn would give rise to further internal credit expansions inasmuch as the increase in monetary reserves would automatically increase the domestic reserve positions of commercial banks and would also reduce the reticence of the central banks whose monetary reserves have increased. Thus there are, after all, some forces of long-term expansion in operation and one cannot deny that the Keynes Plan makes it possible for monetary reserves to undergo a secular growth. It remains true, nevertheless, that such growth would not be guaranteed under the plan. The plan does not even give the management of the Clearing Union any prerogative or any instrument to achieve the formation of monetary reserves in case all central-bank managers are conservative and prevent balance-of-payments deficits and debts to the Clearing Union—in ever-increasing amounts—from arising or from lasting any length of time.

The Triffin Plan would work in a very different manner in this respect. It, too, provides for overdraft facilities for central banks, but in addition it gives the management of the expanded International Monetary Fund (X.I.M.F.[46]) a prerogative to initiate the creation of monetary reserves by means of an aggressive credit and open-market policy. Triffin provides for these open-market transactions by the expanded I.M.F. probably because he has concluded that one may not count on the central banks' demand for I.M.F. loans being of just the right magnitude to bring about the "optimal" supply of monetary reserves. Hence, the Triffin Plan enables the management of the I.M.F. to take the initiative and increase or reduce the deposits of the central banks with the I.M.F. through purchases and sales of securities in the open market. If the I.M.F. recognizes a need for secular growth of monetary reserves, its open-market purchases will exceed its open-market sales; and with the increasing securities portfolio of the X.I.M.F. the reserves of the central banks held at this "central bank of central banks" will increase. (The creation of reserves by the X.I.M.F. is pictured in T-Account Set 5.)

In order to appease those of his critics who fear his plan to be inflationary, Triffin is ready to propose an upper limit for the annual rate of increase of monetary reserves, something like 3, 4, or 5 per cent per year. Unwilling to accept an annual rate of growth mechanically fixed at a particular percentage, he thinks of the mentioned numbers merely as an upper limit, and not as a minimum, of annual reserve creation. In any case, the Triffin Plan rests on the conviction that the world's need for monetary reserves rises, over the decades, faster than the gold stocks of the monetary authorities can increase. The centralization of reserves which Triffin

[46] The abbreviation X.I.M.F., meaning not "ex-I.M.F." but "expanded I.M.F.," was introduced by Altman. See Oscar L. Altman, "Professor Triffin on International Liquidity and the Role of the Fund," *International Monetary Fund Staff Papers*, Vol. VIII (May 1961), p. 156.

T-ACCOUNT SET 5   *Triffin Plan: Reserve Creation through Purchase of Securities*

Assumptions:

    (1) An expanded International Monetary Fund (X.I.M.F.), whose deposit liabilities are part of the member countries' monetary reserves, purchases securities in the open market.

    (2) The seller of the securities deposits the X.I.M.F. cashier's check with his bank; this bank deposits it with its central bank; and this central bank deposits it on its account with the X.I.M.F.

    (3) The increased credit balances with the X.I.M.F. constitute increased monetary reserves of the member countries.

X.I.M.F.

Securities		Deposits	
purchased in open market	+100	of central banks	+100

recommends is designed to secure an adequate rate of growth of monetary reserves without exposing the nations to the dangers inherent in the maintenance and expansion of the gold-exchange standard.

In its original version the Triffin Plan requires each member country to hold at least one-fifth of its monetary reserves in the form of deposits with the I.M.F. These balances would bear interest. The central banks would acquire I.M.F. balances initially by depositing gold or foreign exchange. They would receive a guaranty for the value of foreign currencies deposited, and any balances acquired through the deposit of gold or dollars should be redeemable in gold (provided the balances that a central bank retained after any conversion into gold would still be at least 20 per cent of its entire monetary reserve). The fragility of the present gold-exchange standard is overcome in that the holders of dollars and pounds sterling will—when the reform becomes effective—exchange these currencies against convertible I.M.F. deposits and in that the I.M.F. will treat the claims it thereby acquires against the U.S. and U.K. governments as long-term debts repayable in small annual installments, rather than as sight liabilities of these two countries.

Implied in this and similar plans is the fact that the centralization of monetary reserves permits a gradual reduction of the part which gold plays in the growing monetary reserves of the world without exposing the system to the danger of collapse. If the monetary reserves of the world are to grow faster than the monetary gold stocks, evidently the share of gold in these reserves must become smaller and smaller. So long as a few key-currencies are used as a substitute for gold reserves, as is the case under the gold-exchange standard, there will be the danger of a speculative run on the banks of the key-currency countries. This danger is eliminated if deposits with the super-central bank serve as monetary reserves.

On this score, the Triffin Plan is only a variant of the Keynes Plan. It is the difference in the methods of reserve creation which, as we have indicated, distinguishes the two plans, despite their superficial or fundamental similarities in other respects.

Many who have compared the two plans regard the Keynes Plan as more inflationary than the Triffin Plan. At best, this is correct only in the short run: if, for example—as immediately after the world war—many countries in desperate need of capital pursue domestic credit policies that compel them to make full use of all overdraft facilities afforded by the Keynes Plan. In the long run, however, the Keynes Plan provides less possibilities of expansion than the Triffin Plan. Keynes, apparently, was more oriented toward the short run than the long—a bent of mind which he explicitly admitted in other connections. Probably he was not greatly impressed with the "danger" of too slow a long-term growth of monetary reserves.

A different method of expanding the I.M.F. was proposed by Maxwell Stamp.[47] His plan does not really provide for a centralization of monetary reserves but it does expand the I.M.F. into an institution creating international reserves. Consequently, the Stamp Plan had best be discussed together with the plans of type 3. Stamp proposes that the I.M.F. issue, within a year, certificates in the amount of $3 billion for distribution to the governments of less developed countries. The central banks of countries willing to accept these certificates in payment for exports and to use them as monetary reserves would actually receive them when the underdeveloped countries made their purchases. There would be no need to make the certificates redeemable in gold if only they were accepted in payment by all or most member countries of the I.M.F. and could be used for payments to other member countries.

"The Stamp Plan–1962 Version" removes some of the most frequently voiced objections to the original plan: "it sets limits both to what the Fund can create in the way of credit and to the amount of Fund paper which any individual country can be asked to absorb." [48] The amount of credit to start with is only $2 billion; the certificates are to be given to the International Development Association as a loan for fifty years, with interest charges according to what I.D.A. would receive from the underdeveloped countries; advanced countries in balance-of-payments surplus, or very

---

[47] Maxwell Stamp, "The Fund and the Future," *Lloyds Bank Review* (1958), pp. 1-20; *idem*, "Changes in the World's Payments System," *Moorgate and Wall Street* (Spring 1961), pp. 3-22. In his second article, the author describes two plans which he calls Plan A and Plan B. The latter recommends a system of stand-by credits rather similar to the arrangements proposed by Bernstein and Jacobsson. We shall discuss here only Plan A, and this only will be meant when we refer to the "Stamp Plan."

[48] Maxwell Stamp, "The Stamp Plan–1962 Version," *Moorgate and Wall Street* (Autumn 1962), pp. 5-17.

fully employed, may "opt out" as primary exporters to the poor countries and need accept the certificates from other monetary authorities only up to a total amount equal to their quotas.

From the point of view of the I.M.F., the issuance of certificates constitutes a creation of money different from that provided under the Triffin Plan in two respects: first, regarding the speed of the reserve creation, and, secondly, regarding the quality of the assets acquired. The securities which the X.I.M.F., under the Triffin Plan, is to acquire in the open market would be highly salable obligations of financially strong governments or international organizations, such as the International Bank for Reconstruction and Development. The assets which the X.I.M.F. would acquire under the Stamp Plan through the certificates issued to underdeveloped countries would be obligations of financially weak governments which probably would not be salable and possibly would never be paid off or, alternatively, 50-year bonds of the I.D.A., which might not be very salable either. (A transaction under the Stamp Plan is pictured in T-Account Set 6.)

T-ACCOUNT SET 6   *Stamp Plan: Reserve Creation through Aid of Development*

Assumptions:
  (1) An expanded International Monetary Fund (X.I.M.F.) is authorized to issue Certificates which are accepted in payment by member countries and form part of their monetary reserves.
  (2) These transferable Certificates are distributed, through an international agency, to governments of underdeveloped countries.
  (3) These governments purchase imports from other countries and pay for them with the X.I.M.F. Certificates.
  (4) The Certificates, received in payment for the exports, are now additional monetary reserves of member countries.

X.I.M.F.

Debts of underdeveloped countries (or I.D.A.)		Certificates (reserves of central banks)	
	+100		+100

Whereas the open-market purchases of the X.I.M.F. under the Triffin Plan could always be reversed by subsequent open-market sales, there is no reversibility in the case of development loans. Gilt-edged securities can always be sold if it turns out that reserves have been created at too fast a pace or that loans to particular central banks ought to take the place of securities holdings in the portfolio of the X.I.M.F. No such flexibility exists under the Stamp Plan. On the other hand, under this plan the creation of reserves would not only contribute to the "liquidity" of the central banks of the free world but would also be part of a scheme to aid poor countries. The weight of this argument can perhaps be tested by applying it to the principles of national credit creation. How would we react to the proposal that our central banks, instead of creating money through discounts and advances to commercial banks in good standing or through purchases of shiftable government securities, should give their newly issued money to the poor widows and orphans in the land?

The methods of reserve creation under the three plans thus far discussed are sufficiently far apart in the spectrum of alternatives to show some essential contrasts. The chief difference lies in the "ideal type" of assets which the international credit institution—whether Clearing Union, Fund, or World Central Bank—acquires in the process of creating additional reserves. Under the Keynes Plan, it acquires *debts from overdrafts by central banks* whose balances have been depleted and whose deficits in the international balance of payments force them to make use of their drawing rights. Under the Triffin Plan, it acquires *negotiable securities traded on the largest exchanges* and easily disposable without loss. And under the Stamp Plan, it (indirectly) acquires *nonsalable obligations of poor governments* of underdeveloped countries. The reserves created (à la Keynes) through overdrafts may not prove to be durable, since they may disappear as soon as the debtor countries pay off their debit balances. The reserves created (à la Triffin) through open-market purchases are as durable as the management desires, but it is not certain that they will always increase effective demand to the full extent; the sellers of the securities may choose to keep their proceeds idle instead of spending them, and the central banks of the countries in which the sellers reside may choose to sterilize the increased reserves instead of using them to expand credit. The reserves created (à la Stamp) through the finance of aid to underdeveloped countries are both durable and certain to cause an increase in the demand for goods and services, since the underdeveloped countries are likely to spend every cent they can get and are unlikely to repay the loans soon, if at all. (In the original version of his plan, Stamp explicitly mentioned the possibility of nonrepayable aid, that is, donations.)

These strong contrasts show up only because, in our construction of models for purposes of analysis, we have singled out for emphasis particular characteristics of the three plans. This probably exaggerates the differences that would emerge if the plans were carried out in practice. After all, the Triffin Plan does include the possibility of overdrafts by the central banks of deficit countries and thus it includes the *modus operandi* of the Keynes Plan; similarly, the Triffin Plan could be used for the finance of development aid, just like the Stamp Plan, by the simple means of concentrating the open-market purchases of the X.I.M.F. upon obligations of the I.B.R.D. Exaggeration of differences, however, is usually a better device than minimization of differences if one attempts to understand the possible and the most probable effects of measures or institutions.

There are other plans for reserve creation through an international institution—such as the X.I.M.F.—but most of them can be treated as variants of the three plans discussed. The Day Plan [49] is a direct descendant of the Keynes Plan. Day, who teaches at the London School of Economics, submitted his proposal to the Radcliffe Committee, which gave it an official endorsement.[50] It differs from the original Triffin Plan chiefly in that it eschews a provision which has been most offensive to many bankers and politicians, namely the requirement for central banks to hold one-fifth of their reserves in the form of balances with the X.I.M.F. If these deposits carry interest and are freely transferable, one may count on the central banks being willing to hold balances on their X.I.M.F. accounts for transactions purposes and as part of their monetary reserves. Triffin has accepted this modification of his plan,[51] though he would prefer the reserve requirement until the central banks have become used to holding X.I.M.F. balances.

Voluntary rather than required reserves in the form of X.I.M.F. deposits are also provided for in the proposal by James Angell, of Columbia University.[52] Of course, the member countries would have to commit themselves to accept X.I.M.F. deposits in payment from other member countries. Such a requirement to accept these deposits would suffice to make them into international means of payment and to induce the central banks to hold a part of their reserves in this form. According to the Angell Plan—which, incidentally, explicitly recognizes the X.I.M.F. as the central bank of central banks—the role of gold in the international monetary system would be fundamentally changed. No longer should central banks be required to pay one another or the X.I.M.F. in gold, no

[49] A. C. L. Day, "Memorandum of Evidence," [Radcliffe] *Committee on the Working of the Monetary System*, Principal Memoranda of Evidence, Vol. 3 (London: H.M.'s Stationery Office, 1960), p. 75.

[50] *Committee on the Working of the Monetary System*, Report (London: H.M.'s Stationery Office, Cmnd. 827, 1959), Chapter VIII, p. 241, §660, and pp. 247-248, §678.—The report contains the following statement: "We see great merit as a long-term objective in Mr. Day's . . . proposal for a transformation of the International Monetary Fund . . . into an international central bank, with its own unit of account, free to accept deposit liabilities or extend overdraft facilities to the central banks of member countries" (p. 248).

[51] Robert Triffin, "The International Monetary Crisis: Diagnosis, Palliatives, and Solutions" in *Quarterly Review and Investment Survey*, Model, Roland and Stone (New York: First Quarter 1961), p. 6.

[52] James W. Angell, "The Reorganization of the International Monetary System: An Alternative Proposal," *The Economic Journal*, Vol. LXXI (December 1961), pp. 691-708.

longer should they demand payments in gold, and no longer should they be permitted to sell gold to private parties or to central banks not members of the Fund. Deposits with the X.I.M.F. would have a fixed equivalent in gold but would not be redeemable in gold. The X.I.M.F. and the member countries could sell gold to one another, but only at their mutual convenience.

The creation of monetary reserves by means of creation of new deposits with the X.I.M.F. takes place, under the Angell Plan, through the acquisition by the Fund of two types of assets: (1) gold, especially when it is offered for sale by a member country, and (2) demand liabilities of the member central banks (that is, national currencies). These demand liabilities may be acquired by the Fund (a) directly from the central banks owing them or (b) indirectly from other central banks owning them. Purchases of such national currencies and payment for them in deposit liabilities of the X.I.M.F. represent, of course, loans to central banks. In this respect, the Angell Plan is a variant of the Keynes Plan. It differs from the Keynes Plan by providing for much narrower limits both for credit expansion by the Fund and for debt expansion by the individual central banks. Angell proposes three limitations to expansion: first, a limit on the increments to total currency holdings by the Fund (for example, 10 per cent during the first two years); second, a limit on increments in the Fund's holdings of a particular currency (perhaps 20 per cent); and third, a limit on a country's liabilities *vis-à-vis* the Fund relative to the reserve ratio of its central bank (for example, it might be provided that a central bank whose X.I.M.F. balance exceeds 30 per cent of its total demand liabilities should use this excess to reduce by repurchase the Fund's holdings of its currency). The X.I.M.F. would have at its disposal several instruments by which it could compel the monetary authorities of member countries to reduce excessive debts to the Fund.

Let us note three other provisions of the Angell Plan which differentiate it from the Keynes, Triffin, and Stamp Plans. First, it contains special provisions concerning balance-of-payments difficulties of countries exporting primary products if and insofar as these difficulties are caused by fluctuations in their export prices. Secondly, the Angell Plan, in sharp contrast with the Stamp Plan, prohibits long-term loans to underdeveloped countries. Thirdly, in contrast with the Triffin Plan, it includes no provision for secular growth of monetary reserves. According to Angell, there is no evidence that an increase in the volume of foreign trade would cause increasing clearing balances and thus require increasing foreign reserves.

The next four plans to be listed in category 3 were all presented by Sir Roy Harrod, of Oxford University. What we really call the Harrod Plan, the only one he supports with full conviction, involves an increase in the price of gold and will be discussed in the next section. However, faced with great resistance to this, his favorite plan, Harrod made several proposals for centralized creation of international money.[53] All four proposals, designated by Harrod as Plans A, B, C, and D, aim at the same objective: to supply the monetary authorities of all countries so adequately with reserves that they would be relieved of their constant worries about the maintenance of a balanced payments position and would not be restrained in realizing their goals of national credit creation.

The central banks would be able to sit back and calmly watch their reserves run down over the years and not feel compelled to raise interest rates or impose import controls or devalue the currency. Of course, they would need massive reserves if they are to be able to sit it out until the balance of payments reverses itself, apparently by some lucky accident. Harrod holds that, in view of the unequal distribution of world monetary reserves, the total reserves should be approximately equal to the total annual imports of the world, or approximately $120 billion at the present time. Since the gold and foreign-exchange reserves of the monetary authorities of the free world (not counting their I.M.F. drawing rights) amount to approximately $60 billion, Harrod proposes that another $60 billion of reserves be newly created.

Under Harrod Plan A, the I.M.F.—or should we again say X.I.M.F.? —would create a new international means of payment, the I.M.F. unit. Initially, a total of $60 billion in these I.M.F. units would be credited to the accounts of the member countries, apportioned in relation to their share in total imports. Their present claims or drawing rights vis-à-vis the I.M.F. would be added and their present debts deducted. Additional credits would be entered on the I.M.F. accounts of the member countries to the extent of some $3 billion a year. None of these credits—neither the initial nor the subsequent ones—needs ever be repaid: they represent grants rather than loans. (Perhaps we should designate them one-time dowries plus permanent alimonies.) The I.M.F. deposits would not be redeemable in gold but could be freely used in payment among the central banks of all member countries and converted into other currencies at fixed exchange rates.

Harrod Plan B does not create I.M.F. units but assigns to all member banks drawing rights expressed in terms of national currencies. The drawings, however, are to be made by checks in terms of other currencies, the conversions made at fixed exchange rates. (The drawing rights assigned to the countries would correspond in amount to those furnished by the grants under Plan A.) Each central bank can draw checks on the I.M.F. and use

[53] Sir Roy Harrod, *Alternative Methods for Increasing International Liquidity* (Brussels: European League for Economic Cooperation, 1961). An abbreviated German version was published as an article, "Möglichkeiten zur Erhöhung der Liquidität," *Aussenwirtschaft*, 16. Jahrgang (June 1961), pp. 155-172.

them to pay its debts in any currency or to buy the currency of any member country. The central banks of member countries deposit the checks received on their I.M.F. accounts. The I.M.F. balances would not be redeemable in gold, nor would they carry interest. Nor would there be any interest charges on debit balances with the Fund, because obligations to pay interest and/or to repay overdrafts might restrain members from using their drawing rights freely. The I.M.F. would cover its expenses out of modest spreads between exchange rates in converting currencies.

Harrod Plan C would create new monetary reserves, not through grants to members of the I.M.F. nor through nonrepayable overdrafts, but rather through the Fund's open-market purchases of government obligations. Plan C differs from the Triffin Plan—which also creates reserves through open-market purchases—in several details (for example, in that I.M.F. balances would carry no interest and would not be redeemable in gold, regardless of the origin of the balances) but the chief difference is the magnitude of the proposed operations. Harrod's estimates of the liquidity requirements of the world are very much higher than Triffin's.

Under Harrod Plan D, the I.M.F. would create monetary reserves in the process of financing buffer stocks of primary commodities. An International Buffer Stock Authority would purchase primary commodities at support prices and pay for them with checks on the I.M.F. Should the financial needs for the acquisition of these buffer stocks not be sufficient to create enough monetary reserves to meet the needs for international liquidity, then the I.M.F. would have to use additional methods of reserve creation, for example, open-market purchases of securities as under Plan C. All of Harrod's proposals are marked by largesse which goes back to his views regarding the needs and supply of money.

In September 1962, Reginald Maudling, Chancellor of the Exchequer of the United Kingdom, made some (not very specific) proposals,[54] which quickly became known as the Maudling Plan. One clear provision of the Plan is that surplus countries acquiring the currencies of deficit countries (in an attempt to support them) may deposit these new balances with a newly established "mutual currency account" of the I.M.F., receiving in exchange I.M.F. certificates of indebtedness. These I.M.F. certificates (or deposits) are guaranteed at their original gold value, bear minimal interest, and can be used for payments to other monetary authorities when the country holding them develops a deficit position. To the extent of these

[54] Address of the Rt. Hon. Reginald Maudling at the Annual Meeting of the Board of Governors. See International Monetary Fund, *Summary Proceedings of the Seventeenth Annual Meeting of the Board of Governors, September 1962* (Washington, D.C., 1962), pp. 61-68, esp. pp. 67-68.

new currency deposits, the I.M.F.—or its "mutual currency account"—would be an international monetary authority issuing a new internationally acceptable reserve currency, in exchange for national currencies. These I.M.F. deposits would be preferred by most central banks to dollar or sterling balances, because I.M.F. liabilities carry an automatic gold-value guarantee, while this is rarely so in the case of the liabilities of the United States or the United Kingdom. (In November 1962, the United Kingdom limited its effective dollar guarantee for its sterling liabilities to 5 per cent of the official holdings of the members of the European Monetary Agreement.) With regard to the type of asset acquired and the method of reserve creation, the Maudling Plan comes closest to the Keynes Plan of 1943 and to certain aspects of the Triffin and Angell plans.

An extension of the Bernstein Plan of December 1962 deserves to be placed among the proposals for centralization of international reserves and reserve creation, although it de-emphasizes the amendments that might make his Plan appear more radical than his earlier proposals.[55] He recommends "three steps": (1) that countries should regard not only their "gold tranche" but also their "credit tranche," hence their entire drawing rights with the I.M.F., as parts of their gross reserves; (2) that these drawing rights should be less conditional than they are now, in particular, that countries should be able to draw on their quotas without prior approval of the I.M.F.; and (3) that countries should draw on the I.M.F. "as a matter of course whenever they use their own reserves," that is, even in small amounts and at frequent intervals, so that drawings on the quotas would be seen as normal occurrences, not as indications of weakness.[56]

These three steps would not by themselves establish a central banking institution capable of creating new reserves, even if the proposals were practicable, which in their present form they are not. For it is not feasible, under existing accounting rules, to treat drawing rights as genuine reserves. No bank or central bank can regard anything but unconditionally available liquid *assets* as its reserve. Not even the "gold tranche" at the I.M.F. is so regarded by most central banks, but this at least is a real asset. The credit tranche, however, is not an asset and cannot be made into an asset, except by means of a separate step, alluded to by Bernstein only in an oral extension of his statement. This step would be to transform the potential credit into an actual credit, that is, into a deposit liability of the I.M.F.[57] For, after all, ability to borrow is not the same thing as "cash on

[55] Edward M. Bernstein, "Statement," in Outlook for United States Balance of Payments, Hearings before the Subcommittee on International Exchange and Payments, Joint Economic Committee, Congress of the United States, 87th Congress, 2d Session, December 12, 13, and 14, 1962 (Washington: 1963), pp. 205-218 and 221-240.

[56] Ibid., p. 218.

[57] Bernstein still "would not call them deposits," though he proposes that "these quotas are transferred from one country to another as they are used" (p. 234).

hand," and the accountant cannot treat it as such. Only by transforming the quotas into cash on hand, that is, into deposits with the I.M.F., can they become genuine reserves.

If Bernstein were willing to take this step, he would secure the creation of reserves, though only in a once-for-all fashion. Yet another step would be needed to achieve long-term growth of reserves, a step which Bernstein seems willing to recommend: periodic increases in the countries' quotas (read: I.M.F. deposits). His first recommendation along such lines provides for quota increases either whenever necessary or every five years (p. 234), but under some pressure he seems prepared to propose that the quotas (read: I.M.F. deposits) be increased annually or gradually and steadily (pp. 237, 238).

With these amendments, the (imputed) Bernstein 1962 Plan would extend the I.M.F. into an X.I.M.F., and mere borrowing rights into organized reserve creation.[58] Against what kinds of assets would these X.I.M.F. deposits be created? Against sight-liabilities ("currency") issued by the central banks. Thus, the X.I.M.F. would create international reserves by regular periodic advances to central banks in predetermined amounts —a procedure not very different from that described in Harrod Plan A, except that Bernstein does not indicate in what currency the X.I.M.F. deposits should be expressed. This is quite in line with Bernstein's thinking, since he really wants only borrowing rights and not deposits. (A transaction under the extended Bernstein 1962 Plan is pictured in T-Account Set 7.)

We have mentioned several times how far apart are the different views regarding the need for secular growth of monetary reserves. The extremes are represented by Harrod and Angell: the former wants to manufacture $3 billion a year, whereas the latter does not think any annual increase will be needed. In this respect a proposal by A. C. L. Day is interesting.[59] He proposes that each central bank be asked every year "whether it regarded any net change in its reserves over the year as permanent, or as merely temporary and therefore to be corrected subsequently." The algebraic sum of all changes in reserves that are regarded as permanent, minus the year's gold production, "would be the amount of the net new

[58] ". . . the reserves would be created by mutual credit. You would be giving credit not to one borrower, but everybody would get simultaneously a mutual credit. And this would be a permanent mutual credit" (p. 236). In all fairness it should be noted that Bernstein disclaims any notion that he has "extended" his plan, and he emphatically denies, in a letter to me, that anything he has proposed "would convert the Fund into a central bank."

[59] A. C. L. Day, "The World's Payments System," in *International Payments Imbalances and Need for Strengthening International Financial Arrangements*, Hearings before the Subcommittee on International Exchange and Payments, Joint Economic Committee, Congress of the United States, 87th Congress, 1st Session (Washington: 1961), pp. 325-330, esp. p. 330.

T-ACCOUNT SET 7   *Extended Bernstein Plan: Reserve Creation through Periodic Credits to Central Banks*

Assumptions:
  (1) An expanded International Monetary Fund (X.I.M.F.) transforms the potential drawing rights (quotas) of central banks into actual deposits, by crediting the central banks' current accounts, and debiting their "quota accounts" for the same amounts.
  (2) The central banks' balances on their current deposit accounts with the X.I.M.F. are freely transferable among central banks and are considered as part of their international reserves.
  (3) Since quotas are periodically increased but never reduced, X.I.M.F. advances under this procedure need not be repaid by the central banks.
  (4) The national central bank whose balance-sheet entries are shown below receives 5 per cent of the increment in total quotas.

X.I.M.F.

Quota accounts (liabilities) of central banks	+100	Deposits of central banks	+100

One Central Bank

Deposit with X.I.M.F.	+5	Quota liability to X.I.M.F.	+5

international creation of money that would be regarded as justifiable in the following year." The I.M.F. is to put this amount of international reserves at the disposal of the central banks by making loans to poor countries, possibly by purchasing long-term bonds of the World Bank. In this fashion, according to Day, "the supply of international money would be determined by the amount which countries wished voluntarily to hold."

What all these plans, beginning with the Keynes Plan and including all other prototypes and variants, have in common is that an international financial institution is charged with the function of creating—through the acquisition of claims or other assets (or fictitious assets)—additional deposit liabilities that would be accepted by the central banks as part of their monetary reserves. Table XIV-3 affords a convenient overview by listing the eleven plans of type 3 discussed in this section, indicating for each what kinds of asset are to be acquired, and on what occasion, by the reserve-creating international monetary authority. The list does not mention such relatively unimportant matters as what should be the form or name of the liability of the international institution—deposit balances or certificates, denominated in bancor or in dollars—or whether the institution should be an expanded International Monetary Fund or a new "International Reserve Bank" or an "International Clearing Union."

TABLE XIV-3 *Plans for Creation of International Reserves by an International Monetary Authority: Types of Asset Acquired and Occasion of Acquisition*

Plan	Types of Asset Acquired	Time or Occasion of Acquisition
Keynes 1943	1. New liabilities of central banks of deficit countries 2. Gold	1. When a country incurs a clearing deficit larger than its balance on deposit 2. When offered
Stamp A 1958	New debts of governments of less developed countries or of International Development Agency	Immediately and whenever judged to be desirable
Triffin 1959	1. New liabilities of central banks of deficit countries 2. Government securities traded in open markets 3. Liabilities of central banks and governments of U.S. and U.K. now held as reserves 4. Gold	1. When a country incurs a deficit larger than its reserve balance 2. Whenever judged to be desirable 3. Immediately 4. When countries deposit it
Harrod A 1961	Nonrepayable debts of central banks of all countries in fixed amounts	Immediately and annually
Harrod B 1961	Nonrepayable debts of central banks of deficit countries	When central banks make use of drawing rights
Harrod C 1961	Government securities traded in open markets	Whenever judged to be desirable
Harrod D 1961	Debts of Buffer Stock Authority for purposes of price supports of primary commodities	When buffer stocks are purchased
Day 1961	Debts of poor countries or bonds of World Bank	When central banks indicate permanent increase in desired reserves
Angell 1962	1. New liabilities of central banks of deficit countries 2. Liabilities of central banks now held as reserves	1. When offered by these or other central banks 2. When offered by central banks holding them
Maudling 1962	Liabilities of central banks of deficit countries held by other central banks	When offered by other central banks which acquired them in order to support them
Bernstein ext. 1962	Liabilities of central banks of all countries	Transforming present I.M.F. "credit tranche" and subsequent periodic quota increases

It is by this function of creating new international reserves that the plans of type 3 can be distinguished from those of type 2, which provide for reserves to be borrowed or transformed, but not newly created, by a central institution. To the extent that the I.M.F. plays a role under plans of type 2, that role is one of an intermediary and guarantor.

Those familiar with the theory of money and banking know of the fundamental distinction commonly made between the creation of additional credits and the process of merely passing credit on from lender to borrower. The outward appearances of the two kinds of transaction are often so similar that many observers, looking chiefly at the legal, accounting, or statistical effects, overlook the economic difference. Only in extreme cases are the outward appearances different enough to impress themselves upon the less theoretically inclined observer. In the strict model of *credit transfer*, the I.M.F. *sells* its long-term or medium-term obligations and acquires in exchange "liquid" funds in the form of deposit liabilities of the central banks of surplus countries, funds which it then proceeds to lend (or sell) to the central banks of the deficit countries. In the strict model of *credit creation*, the X.I.M.F. *purchases* long-term or medium-term obligations and gives in exchange "liquid" funds in the form of its own additional deposit liabilities, which become additional monetary reserves of the countries whose residents sold the obligations. (A schematic presentation of the difference is given in T-Account Set 8.)

T-ACCOUNT SET 8   *Credit Transfer versus Credit Creation by the Fund*

Assumptions:
- (1) In order to contrast credit transfer and credit creation most sharply, two strict models will be constructed, one of the International Monetary Fund (I.M.F.) incapable of providing funds beyond the amounts of national currencies put at its disposal, the other of an expanded International Monetary Fund (X.I.M.F.) capable of creating funds through the purchase of assets with its own deposit liabilities which are accepted by member countries as part of their monetary reserves.
- (2) In each model the sequence of actions will be described and the results, depending on the probable use of the funds, indicated.

STRICT MODEL OF CREDIT TRANSFER BY THE I.M.F.

First Act: The I.M.F. issues (or sells) its medium-term instruments of indebtedness to the central bank of a surplus country. The I.M.F. is now equipped with (borrowed or acquired) liquid funds (foreign currency) to be passed on to a client in need.

Surplus Country

I.M.F. securities	+100	Deposit liabilities	+100

I.M.F.

Deposits in surplus country	+100	Debt to surplus country	+100

STRICT MODEL OF CREDIT TRANSFER—CONTINUED

Second Act: The I.M.F. lends (or sells) the liquid funds (foreign currency) to the central bank of a deficit country, in exchange for a medium-term promise to repay (or repurchase its domestic currency).

I.M.F.

Deposit in surplus country	−100		
Loan to deficit country	+100		

Deficit Country

Deposit in surplus country	+100	Debt to I.M.F.	+100

Third Act: What happens afterwards depends on the use the deficit country makes of the foreign funds put at its disposal. (a) If it uses them to buy imports from the surplus country, then the new deposit liabilities created by the surplus country during the first act will enter the active money flow in the surplus country. (b) If the deficit country uses the funds for paying for imports from third countries, then the deposit liabilities of the surplus country become part of the monetary reserves of the third countries (at least temporarily). (c) If the deficit country uses the funds to repay existing demand liabilities to the surplus country, then the deposit liabilities of the surplus country created during the first act disappear, together with its existing claims against the deficit country. This is the result which, as a rule, is intended by the entire scheme.

STRICT MODEL OF CREDIT CREATION BY THE X.I.M.F.

First Act: The X.I.M.F. purchases medium-term obligations and pays for them with its own newly created deposit liabilities. We assume, for the purpose of this illustration, that half of the debts acquired by the X.I.M.F. consist of securities sold by private banks in the surplus country, the other half of securities sold by the central bank of the deficit country. (Regardless of this assumption, the reserves of the central banks are increased by the full value of securities purchased by the X.I.M.F.)

X.I.M.F.

Securities	+100	Deposit liabilities	+100

Surplus Country

Deposit with X.I.M.F.	+50	Deposit liabilities (domestic)	+50

Deficit Country

Deposit with X.I.M.F.	+50		
Securities	−50		

Second Act: What happens afterwards depends on what the sellers of the securities will do with the proceeds and what use the central banks will make of their increased reserves.

It can be demonstrated that under certain conditions credit transfer and credit creation have the same effects. Such conditions, however, are not very likely to be present in the world of today, and it would serve little purpose to consider them here. By and large, an increase in the liquidity position through easier access to, or availability of, credit is not as effective as an increase in the liquidity position through actual possession of surplus cash balances; in their effects upon credit and fiscal policy, borrowed reserves are not quite the same as fully disposable reserves.[60]

To characterize the I.M.F. under present arrangements and under plans of type 2 as a mere intermediary, rather than as a creator, of international reserves is not to say that the reserves transferred by the I.M.F. are not "created by ink." Of course they are; but they are created by the central banks whose currencies are acceptable as international reserve assets, as these banks make their currency subscriptions to the Fund or as they issue their currency to the Fund in payment for currencies of other countries.

From a slightly different point of view, the polarity conceived between pure transfer and pure creation of reserves is less satisfactory than a tripartition which recognizes a middle position. Pure transfer is at one end; its criterion is that no additional reserve assets result from the transactions in question; if any country ends up with more assets, another must have less: the totals of gross as well as net reserves remain unchanged. Pure creation of reserves is at the other end; its criterion is that not only the gross reserves but also the net reserves of all national monetary authorities taken together are increased as a result. Midway between pure transfer and pure creation lie the processes by which gross reserves, but *not* net reserves, of the countries are increased; the total of reserve assets held by national monetary authorities is increased but their combined current liabilities (to other national monetary authorities) are increased too.

Some of the reformers reject any plans that involve pure creation of reserves; others, however, hold that this is the only kind of plan that will work in the long run.

---

[60] Dr. Sterie T. Beza suggests to me that the difference in effectiveness of available credit, on the one hand, and actual credit balances on the other, could be compensated for by adjusting the "dosage" accordingly. Thus, if the former is only half as effective as the latter, one could still achieve the same results by making the line of credit twice as high as the amount of newly created balances would be. I accept this suggestion, but submit that, in actual fact, the availability of credit through credit transfer has much narrower limits than has the possibility of credit creation. In other words, transferred reserves are hard to get, yet it would take larger amounts of them to achieve a given purpose; created reserves can be had in unlimited amounts, though relatively small amounts of them would do the job.

4. Increase in the price of gold

The fourth method of augmenting international "liquidity" is fundamentally different from the first three, all of which are somehow connected with borrowing and debt. In the case of the continuation and extension of the gold-exchange standard, additional debts of key-currency countries become new monetary reserves for other countries. In the case of mutual assistance among central banks, the central banks of surplus countries are willing to accept increasing debts of deficit countries and, if the I.M.F. acts as an intermediary, an exchange of roles takes place whereby the Fund assumes the part of creditor of the deficit countries and of debtor to the surplus countries. The same is true in the case of the centralization of monetary reserves, but in addition new reserves are produced through credit expansion creating deposit liabilities of the international central credit institution.

All this is different in the case of reserve creation through an increase in the price of gold. If, for example, the price of gold is doubled, an ounce of gold will be worth $70 rather than only $35 and, as long as money supply, commodity prices, and trade volume have not yet increased, the ratio between the monetary gold stock and all those magnitudes with which it is usually compared will be doubled too. There may also be an increase in the annual increments to the gold stocks of the free world through new gold production (and perhaps also through sales from the stocks of the U.S.S.R. and other holders of gold). Without any physical increase in the annual supply of gold, the annual increase in terms of dollar or other currencies would be twice as high as now; with a physical increase in gold production, its money value would be higher still (and the same is true for sales from Russia and from non-monetary gold stocks). Assuming, for example (though it is not likely), that a doubling of the price were to cause a 50 per cent increase in the physical quantity of gold supplied, the money value of the quantity annually supplied would increase by 200 per cent, which would mean a tripling of the value of the annual increment to the gold reserves of the free world.

The two effects of an increase in the price of gold—the up-valuing of the existing gold stocks in the monetary reserves and the increase in the annual additions to these gold stocks—should be kept apart in theory as well as in policy. For it would be possible, in principle, to refrain from using the up-valuation of the existing gold reserves as the basis for an increase in the supply of money and credit, whereas the purchase of new gold at an increased price would automatically result in a faster increase in the supply of money. The "capital gain" through the revaluation of the existing gold stocks can be sterilized. It can be blocked, or declared a profit not subject to distribution, so that the higher valuation of the monetary gold stocks would not necessarily lead to an increase in the issue of banknotes or in the amounts of deposit liabilities. (How the balance sheet of a typical central bank would be affected by a revaluation of its gold reserve is shown in T-Account Set 9.)

T-ACCOUNT SET 9   *Reserve Creation through Revaluation of Gold Stocks*

Assumptions:
   (1) A central bank holds one-half of its monetary reserve in the form of gold, the other half in the form of foreign exchange.
   (2) The price of gold is doubled.
   (3) The book value of the gold reserve is written up accordingly and the capital accounts are credited with the amount of the gain.
   (4) No distribution of the capital gain is contemplated.
   (5) The balance sheet of the bank with its main items is shown before and after the revaluation of the gold.

Before the Revaluation of Gold

Central Bank

Gold	100	Notes	100
Foreign exchange	100	Deposits	300
Loans and securities	200		
	400		400

After the Revaluation of Gold

Central Bank

Gold	200	Notes	100
Foreign exchange	100	Deposits	300
Loans and securities	200	Capital gain	100
	500		500

Different techniques may be used to prevent the distribution of the capital gain. The statute or decree increasing the price of gold may provide, for example, that the capital gain has to be turned over to the treasury in the form of one-half of the physical gold stock and that the treasury will not be permitted to sell this gold. (In this case, the balance sheet of the central bank would look the same before and after, except that in terms of physical weight half the quantity of gold would have the value of 100 monetary units.) The technique used by the United States in 1934 to sterilize its gold profits was slightly different. The Federal Reserve Banks (as also all private holders of gold) were required to sell their gold stocks to the Treasury at the old price, and the Treasury paid for them with gold certificates, which took the place of the previous gold stocks among the assets of the Federal Reserve Banks. The Treasury now owned all the gold, and its value at the increased price exceeded the value of the gold certificates by the percentage of the revaluation. (The largest part of the free gold—not needed to cover the gold certificates—was later used by the U.S. Treasury to pay its first subscription to the I.M.F.)

The proposals advanced in recent years for an increase in the price of gold have not been specific and have been more or less silent on the use or sterilization of the gains from revaluation. To be sure, it is one of the chief arguments in favor of an increase in the price of gold that a doubling in the money value of the gold stocks would allow the key-currency countries to repay, in part or in full, their demand liabilities to the countries holding foreign-exchange reserves. The "net liquidity" of all central banks concerned would be increased as a result, either through the elimination or reduction of foreign liabilities or through the substitution of "honest" gold for the supposedly dubious foreign-exchange reserves or, in some instances, through a net increase in total reserves. (The effects of the revaluation upon different central banks holding reserves of different composition are shown in T-Account Set 10.)

If the United States were to use the entire appreciation of its monetary gold stocks to repay foreign obligations, the amount of its monetary reserve would remain unchanged; its "net position," of course, would be enormously improved. (Incidentally, its balance of payments on current account would also be somewhat improved, inasmuch as the interest payments on the repaid foreign debts would be saved.) In a country that has held its monetary reserve entirely in the form of foreign exchange, the total value of the reserve, net as well as gross, would remain unchanged despite the doubling in the price of gold, the only difference being that its foreign-exchange holdings would have been transformed into gold (not earning any interest). In a country that has held its reserve entirely in gold, the monetary reserve would be exactly twice what it was before. A country that has held one-half of its reserve in gold and the other half in foreign exchange would come out with a net gain of 50 per cent and a corresponding increase in its monetary reserve. (In view of this unequal distribution of gains one cannot suppress a comment on the central banks' attitudes in this respect: If central banks had taken the repeated forecasts of an increase in the price of gold seriously, and were selfish enough to have their reserve position improved in the process, they would have tried to convert all their foreign-exchange holdings into gold and the present international monetary system would have long since collapsed.)

Even if, after an increase in the price of gold, none of the countries were to pay out in money the capital gains made through the appreciation of gold reserves (and if, therefore, the flow of funds and expenditures were nowhere directly increased as a result of the appreciation), one could hardly count on all central banks leaving their improved liquidity and increased reserve ratios completely unused. To some protagonists of the increase in the price of gold, for example to Sir Roy Harrod,[61] the im-

T-ACCOUNT SET 10   *Gold Revaluation: Capital Gains and Composition of Reserves*

Assumptions:

    (1) In order to show the effects of a worldwide increase in the price of gold, the "typical" movements on the accounts of four different countries, holding reserves of different composition, will be shown.

    (2) Before the revaluation of gold the United States has a reserve of 100 monetary units, and the other three countries have each a reserve of 10 monetary units.

    (3) The monetary reserves of the United States and of Country A consist entirely of gold; the reserve of Country B, entirely of dollars; and the reserve of Country C, half of gold and half of dollars.

    (4) The price of gold is doubled everywhere.

    (5) The United States uses the increment in the value of its gold stock to repay its foreign obligations to central banks, that is, to redeem their dollar holdings in gold.

Results of Revaluation of Gold

United States				Country A			
Gold	+100	Gain	+100	Gold	+10	Gain	+10

Country B				Country C			
				Gold	+5	Gain	+5

Results of Redemption of Dollars in Gold

United States				Country A			
Gold	−100	Foreign deposits	−100				

Country B				Country C			
Gold	+10			Gold	+5		
Dollars	−10			Dollars	−5		

Combined Results: No capital gain accrues to Country B, and only a moderate gain to Country C. The United States, with the largest gain, has its foreign liabilities paid off. Country A has the largest increase in gross reserves.

---

[61] Sir Roy F. Harrod, "Imbalance of International Payments," *International Monetary Fund Staff Papers*, Vol. III (April 1953), pp. 1-46, esp. pp. 1-5; *idem*, "Plan for Restoration of Full Gold Convertibility of the Dollar Together with a Revision of the Gold Content of the Dollar," *Gold Reserve Act Amendments*, Hearings before a Subcommittee of the Committee on Banking and Currency, U.S. Senate, 83rd Congress, 2d Session (Washington, March 30, 1954), pp. 129-138; *idem*, "The Role of Gold Today," *The South African Journal of Economics*, Vol. XXVI (March 1958), pp. 3-13; *idem*, "Europe and the Money Muddle," *Economic Journal*, Vol. LXVIII (September 1958), p. 538; *idem*, "Why the Dollar Price of Gold Must Rise," *Optima*, Vol. 8 (September 1958), pp. 120-127; *idem*, "World Recession and the United States," *International Affairs*, Vol. XXXIV (London, October 1958), pp. 452-453; *idem*, "A Rejoinder to Mr. Katzen," *The South African Journal of Economics*, Vol. XXVII (March 1959), pp. 16-22; *idem*, "World Monetary Liquidity," *The Irish Banking Review* (March 1959), pp. 20-25; *idem*, "Memorandum of Evidence," [Radcliffe] *Com-*

provement in the reserve position of the various nations appears desirable precisely for the reason that their monetary authorities would be more readily inclined to resort to credit expansions in pursuance of full-employment and growth policies. Advocates of the increase in the price of gold whose attitude in this respect is quite different would have to propose sterilization measures designed to prevent such credit expansions. Oddly enough, no such measures were proposed in some of the writings of Jacques Rueff,[62] the noted and influential French economist, and Michael Heilperin,[63] professor of the Geneva Institute for Advanced International Studies, two anti-inflationist advocates of an increase in the price of gold. Their recommendations did not include provisions on the strength of which monetary authorities could effectively resist the strong pressures and temptations to pursue easy-money policies after their gold reserves had all of a sudden jumped to twice their former size. Of course, if the United States were to use its entire gain from the gold-price jump for redeeming its liquid dollar liabilities, this problem might be reduced or removed as far as the United States is concerned; but the problem would remain for several other countries.

The increase in the annual accretion to the monetary gold stocks due to an increase in the price of gold is what all advocates of these plans regard as a most desirable effect of the measure. In particular, they expect this increased annual accretion to take the place of the present annual increase in American demand liabilities, which ever since 1951 has been the source of supply of "needed" monetary reserves to the free world.

---

mittee on the Working of the Monetary System, Principal Memoranda of Evidence, Vol. 3 (London: H.M.'s Stationery Office, 1960), pp. 115-116; idem, "Gold: The American Dilemma," The Director (London), Vol. XIII (December 1960), pp. 486-487; idem, "Postwar Maladjustments," Topical Comment (London, 1961), pp. 13-16 and 56-60; idem, "A Plan for Increasing Liquidity: A Critique," Economica, New Ser., Vol. XXVIII (May 1961), pp. 195-202.

[62] Jacques Rueff, "The West Is Risking a Credit Collapse," Fortune, Vol. LXIV (July 1961), pp. 126-127, 262, 267-268. See also a series of articles in the Neue Zürcher Zeitung, June 26, 27, and 28, 1961 and in Le Monde (Paris) and The Times (London), June 27, 28, and 29, 1961. Rueff is not very explicit regarding the need for the increase in the price of gold, probably because he does not want to disturb the lay reader and does not wish to incite another rush of gold speculation. He leaves it to the informed reader to infer from the arguments presented that the proposal for an increase in the price of gold is a logical necessity.

[63] Michael A. Heilperin, "Monetary Reform in an Atlantic Setting," International Payments Imbalances and Need for Strengthening International Payments Arrangements, Hearings before the Subcommittee on International Exchange and Payments, Joint Economic Committee, U.S. Congress, 87th Congress, 1st Session (Washington: 1961), pp. 331-340; idem, "L'aube d'un nouvel étalon-or," Comptes rendus des travaux de la Société Royale d'Economie Politique de Belgique, No. 277 (February 1961); idem, "Pläne für eine Reform des Internationalen Währungsfonds," Wirtschaftsberichte der Creditanstalt-Bankverein, Vienna, 13. Jahrg. (September 1961), pp. 38-43; idem, "The Case for Going Back to Gold," Fortune, September 1962, pp. 108-110, 144, 146, 151, 152, 154, and 159.

From 1952 to 1962, the gold stock of the national monetary authorities has increased by $530 million a year on the average, and the dollar-exchange reserves have increased by almost $700 million a year on the average. If now the annual increment through new gold were to double in value, a further increase in dollar holdings could be dispensed with. If the accretion of new gold should increase also in physical quantity and therefore be more than doubled, perhaps even tripled, in terms of money, then no one would have to worry any longer about the adequacy of the growth of monetary reserves.

The future supply of monetary reserves would no longer depend on additional dollar debts, and the existing dollar and pound sterling liabilities could be eliminated from the monetary reserves at a single stroke—these are the chief advantages Rueff and Heilperin expect from an increase in the price of gold. Their objective, in other words, is the abolition of the gold-exchange standard and a return to the full gold standard in the sense that gold alone would serve the central banks as cover and reserve. The revaluation of the old gold would enable the key-currency countries to repurchase the present foreign-exchange holdings of the other countries, and the increase in the annual supply of new gold would enable the world to do without future accumulations of foreign exchange as monetary reserves. The immediate goal of abolishing the gold-exchange standard would be to avert the danger of its collapse; Heilperin's ultimate aim is "the full rehabilitation of gold in the international monetary system."

In this regard one may recognize a parallelism between the Triffin and Angell plans, on the one hand, and the Rueff and Heilperin plans, on the other: All four are based on serious doubts regarding the viability of the gold-exchange standard and on the consequent desire to eliminate foreign exchange from the monetary reserves as quickly as possible. According to Triffin and Angell, the foreign-exchange holdings would be converted into I.M.F. deposits; according to Rueff and Heilperin, they would be converted into gold obtained through the revaluation of the gold stocks.

Abolition of the gold-exchange standard is no part of the Harrod Plan. To give up the use of sterling deposits as monetary reserve of other countries would be an unnecessary sacrifice, according to Harrod. (A sacrifice for the United Kingdom or for the other countries? Probably for both.) Harrod, therefore, recommends that the gold-exchange standard be preserved. Under his plan, the increase in the price of gold should not serve to replace foreign-exchange holdings by increased gold holdings but rather to supplement them. This is in conformance with Harrod's conviction that under the present system the world will suffer in the future and has suffered in the past from a serious lack of liquidity and that the long-existing scarcity in the supply of money and credit could and should be relieved by the up-valuation of gold.[64]

What kind of assumptions are made by the advocates of an increase in the gold price concerning the demand for gold for purposes of private hoarding and speculation? We know Harrod's views on this point. He expects that, after the increase in the price, gold will flow out of private hoards into official reserves. This expectation seems perfectly justified. The question is, however, how long could one expect such flows to continue? Can one reasonably assume that the hoarders, the speculators, and their wise advisors will believe this up-valuation of gold to be the definitive one, the ultimate one? Would such a belief not contradict all experience? The proposed official increase in the price of gold would be only the second such step for the United States—the first since 1934; for Great Britain, however, this would be the third revaluation—the first since 1949; and for France, the seventh—the first since 1958. For some countries it would be the tenth or twelfth official increase in the price of gold within the memory of its older people.[65] If now a worldwide increase in the price of gold were to be effected for the sake of an improvement in international "liquidity," would it then not be all too probable that all the smart people —as well as the outsmarted ones—would expect a repetition of this measure every few years? In view of the speed in which these days, with the interdependence between wage-push and demand-pull, any inflationary potential actually materializes, one can hardly doubt that in due course voices would be raised to claim that the gold reserves, though increased through the revaluation, have again become inadequate relative to inflated trade figures. Such claims would be made at least by some of the adherents of a policy of permanent stimulation of effective demand (and probably also by those who savor capital gains on gold-mine shares). It goes without saying that discussions of this sort would give rise to renewed speculation and hoarding of gold.[66]

Under these circumstances, one must seriously question whether an increase in the price of gold would result in a reduction in the long-run demand for gold by private hoarders. The opposite is more likely. What is more important, however, is that the short-run demand for gold by

[64] Among the advocates of an increase in the price of gold we should mention Ian Shannon, *The Economic Functions of Gold* (Melbourne: F. W. Cheshire, 1962).

[65] Cf. Franz Pick, *Gold: How and Where to Buy and Hold It* (New York: Pick's World Currency Report, 1961). Dr. Pick's "Currency Cemetery" contains a list of more than 200 devaluations in the period 1949-1961. Within these thirteen years there were eight devaluations in Argentina, nine each in Chile and Indonesia, and fourteen each in Brazil and South Korea.

[66] Compare the comments of the Radcliffe *Report* on the undesirable consequences of an increase in the price of gold. *Committee on the Working of the Monetary System, Report* (London: H.M.'s Stationery Office, Cmnd. 827, 1959), p. 246, §674.

private hoarders would probably be subject to substantial fluctuations and might lead to the type of massive movements of hot money experienced during the second half of 1960. Since anyone who speculates for a rise in the gold price can always gain but never lose (apart from interest and other carrying charges), this one-sided speculation may assume ever larger dimensions. To change this situation, the present writer, at the end of 1960, presented the Machlup Plan for gradual and periodic reductions in the official gold price.[67] If the leading monetary authorities of the free world were to reduce, over a period of several years, the price of gold by, say, ¾ or 1 per cent every three months, one could expect that several billion dollars' worth of gold would be dehoarded and offered for sale to the monetary authorities. In order to secure "credibility" for such a program, it would of course be necessary for the monetary authorities to be prepared at all times to sell gold out of their reserves in unlimited quantities at the reduced prices. As soon as the speculators were convinced that they could buy all the gold they wanted, and at a reduced price if they waited a while, they would be transformed from buyers into sellers. After all, any amount of gold they sold they could buy back within a few weeks at a lower price; and, undoubtedly, they would want to postpone such repurchase if they knew that another reduction was imminent.

It would not be necessary to continue the periodic reductions in the price of gold year-in, year-out (except if the monetary authorities were to decide upon a demonetization of gold). The chief objective would be to make it perfectly clear all around that gold hoarders could lose money. If capital losses were just as likely as capital gains, then gold would no longer be the object of hoarding and speculation for a rise in price. In particular, it would always be possible to avert a run on the reserves of the present key-currency countries and to force a retreat of the speculative forces if the monetary authorities were prepared cold-bloodedly to announce another reduction of the gold price. If there should be another crisis of confidence about the future of the dollar, before the gold-exchange standard is either reinforced or abolished by adoption of one of the other plans, the Machlup Plan may yet prove to be an expedient makeshift.

A plan for the reduction of the price of gold can always be made the subject of public discussion without harm of any kind, since such discussion could only calm the speculative fever. This is very different in the case of plans for an increase in the price of gold. Their public discussion is always likely to incite speculation and possible runs on the banks, causing serious injury to the credit market and the monetary system.

[67] Fritz Machlup, "Comments on the Balance of Payments and a Proposal to Reduce the Price of Gold," *The Journal of Finance,* Vol. XVI (1961), pp. 186-193. See Chapter XI of this volume.

Discussion of plans for an increase in the price of gold may generate the danger of a bad *deflation,* with banks closing their windows, or altogether collapsing, and restrictions imposed on national and international payments. The actual *execution* of plans for the up-valuation of gold reserves may generate the danger of a bad *inflation* with lavish extensions of credit. In addition to all this, the up-valuation would have various highly undesirable effects. For example, there would be unjust rewards for speculators and embarrassing penalties for those who have given credence to the assurances about the stability of the dollar and pound sterling and who by their trust have several times averted the collapse of the present system. Finally, the up-valuation of gold would cause completely arbitrary international transfers of income in favor of gold-producing countries, such as South Africa and Soviet Russia. These aspects may be largely political, but they make the plans for gold revaluation still less palatable than they would be solely on account of their economic consequences.

Strong arguments against an increase in the price of gold and in favor of a reduction in the buying price, or alternatively, in favor of fluctuating gold prices were presented by L. Albert Hahn,[68] noted German or ex-German economist. He scoffs at the present system of protecting gold speculators against the risk of loss, for "nothing calms speculation so effectively as losses." He recommends reducing "the price the Central Banks pay for gold offered by private individuals and on the London market . . . Even a small reduction of the buying price might work miracles." Hahn presents several alternative proposals: (1) that central banks stop selling gold to "hoarders and speculators" and also stop buying from them; (2) that central banks sell gold only to other central banks; (3) that private ownership of gold be forbidden in all countries, as it has been in the United States. The reduction of the buying price of gold seems to be the proposal regarded as the most effective by Hahn.

Another proposal for a reduction of the price of gold has recently been made by Arthur O. Dahlberg, of New York.[69] The Dahlberg Plan "to reduce gradually by 2 per cent per year the U.S. Treasury's purchase price of gold" has other objectives than merely to end the speculation against the dollar and the preference for hoarding gold. The chief objective pursued is to "make money move," that is, to discourage the holding of inactive cash balances (bank deposits) and to increase the velocity of circulation. In previous years Dahlberg had recommended for this purpose that a tax of 2 per cent annually be levied on bank deposits and currency. As a substitute for this plan he now proposes to achieve what

---

[68] L. Albert Hahn, "Anachronism of the Gold Price Controversy," *The Commercial and Financial Chronicle,* March 7, 1963.

[69] Arthur O. Dahlberg, *Reduce the Price of Gold and Make Money Move* (New York: John de Graff, Inc., 1962).

has been called "dwindling money" by legislating "that all depositors may demand gold for their deposits, and all commercial banks must offer to pay off in gold their demand obligations to depositors." [70] Since the price of gold is to be lowered by 2 per cent per year, he expects banks to debit all accounts with a carrying charge of 2 per cent a year, "in line with the falling value of the proffered gold." [71] In order to prevent people from switching into bank notes and other currency, Dahlberg presents various schemes by which currency too can become subject to periodic depreciation. All these proposals are not pertinent to our subject, the reform of the *international* monetary system. The Dahlberg Plan apparently seized upon the idea of the gradual reduction of the price of gold because it could be linked with his pet idea of money that slowly depreciates and will therefore not be used by hoarders as a store of value.

An alternative plan to discourage speculation in gold against the dollar was contained in the minority views on the annual report of the Joint Economic Committee of the U.S. Congress.[72] The Joint Committee minority plan does not contemplate reductions in the U.S. purchase price of gold but rather elimination of the U.S. guarantee to purchase "gold from foreigners at $35 an ounce or at any other predetermined price." If the United States refuses to purchase gold—and if other monetary authorities will not buy it either—the price of gold in the world market may fall much below $35, and this would introduce "a new element of heavy risk in speculative operations." According to the minority views, the "termination of the guarantee to buy at a fixed price would be likely to sharply reduce such speculation and, at the same time, stimulate a return of sizable amounts of gold to the United States."

The reasoning behind this argument is correct, provided other monetary authorities join with the U.S. Congress in a declaration which makes their intentions to refuse gold purchases at $35 an ounce generally credible. If there is serious doubt that gold can always be sold to governmental and monetary authorities, the speculator's risk of loss from holding gold may be much greater than under a plan of gradual reductions of the official price. (The free-market price of gold may drop by 10 or 20 per cent, not just 2 or 3 per cent.) But will hoarders and speculators have these doubts? That the U.S. and other governments no longer guarantee to buy gold means neither that governments will in fact refuse to buy gold nor that people will believe such intentions. The practical difference between this termination of guaranteed purchase, according to the minority plan,

---

[70] *Ibid.*, p. 17.

[71] *Ibid.*, p. 18.

[72] *Annual Report of the Joint Economic Committee*, Congress of the United States, on the January 1962 Economic Report of the President, with Minority and Other Views, 87th Congress, 2d Session (Washington, 1962), p. 125.

and the periodic reductions of the selling and purchase price of gold, according to the Machlup Plan, lies precisely in the credibility of the official announcements. The price reductions cannot be disbelieved if the authorities actually offer to sell unlimited quantities of gold at the announced price.

Two recent proposals for gold price increases purport to avoid most of the disadvantages of the gold-price-raising plans discussed. The authors, Kiyojo Miyata [73] of Japan and Paul Wonnacott [74] of the United States, arrived independently, but by the same train of reasoning, at the plan to increase the price of gold gradually by about 2 per cent a year. The main features of the plan are that there must be no uncertainty about the future price of gold, that the magnitudes and dates of the price increases must be announced in advance, and that the annual percentage increase must be less than the interest rates in the money markets. In the absence of uncertainty there will be no speculation against the dollar, and with the gold appreciation less than the interest rate there will be no gain in gold hoarding, but rather a definite carrying cost. (In order to avoid even small jumps in the gold price, the increases may be quarterly or monthly. Alternatively, there might be a spread of about 2 per cent between the official buying and selling prices of gold.) After the fear of currency devaluation in an indefinite future by indefinite proportions is eliminated, people will stop hoarding gold and start dehoarding. At least this is what Miyata and Wonnacott expect. The advantages of gold revaluation—annual increases in international reserves apart from the annual sales of new gold to the monetary authorities—can therefore be had without the disadvantages and dangers that are associated with the plans for substantial price adjustments.

This plan deserves consideration, especially if pressures for gold revaluation increase in force, if the resistance to increasing the international reserves by other methods remains unyielding, and if there is agreement that larger reserves are really needed.

5. Freely flexible exchange rates

We now come to the fifth method for "solving" the problems of the present international monetary system. Just as the fourth method was seen in sharp contrast with the first three, the fifth is fundamentally different from the other four. The extension of the gold-exchange standard, mutual assistance among central banks, centralization of reserves and of reserve

[73] Kiyojo Miyata, "A Proposal To Increase the Price of Gold," *Banking* (Osaka), No. 176 (1962) [in Japanese].

[74] Paul Wonnacott, "A Suggestion for the Revaluation of Gold," *The Journal of Finance,* Vol. XVIII (March 1963), pp. 49-55.

creation, and finally the increase in the price of gold—all these plans were designed to serve the same objective, namely, to increase "international liquidity" so-called. The introduction of freely flexible exchange rates, on the other hand, would relieve the central banks once and for all of any functions in the international payments system and would remove any requirement to hold reserves for foreign payments. This is so because equality of receipts and disbursements would be secured through the free adjustment of foreign-exchange rates to the supply-and-demand situation of the moment.

Gold and exchange reserves are needed only if exchange rates are not permitted to move to the level that would equilibrate the market at the moment. There is always a price at which the quantities supplied and demanded are equal, though this price may be subject to fluctuations from day to day. If exchange rates have to be maintained at fixed levels, then surpluses and deficits will necessarily occur and must be compensated for by the monetary authorities through their purchases or sales of gold or foreign exchange at the fixed prices. In order to be able to meet more enduring deficits (that is, in order to meet a prolonged excess demand for foreign exchange) at fixed exchange rates, the monetary authorities need gold or exchange reserves. Deficits in the balance of payments would usually be short-lived if the central bank were to permit a reduction in the country's effective demand, that is to say, if it did not allow credit expansion to replace that part of the domestic money that had disappeared from circulation when it was paid to the banks by the purchasers of foreign exchange. If, however, effective demand is maintained at its level in spite of the payments to foreign countries, then the deficit (that is, the excess demand) in the foreign-exchange market can be of long, or indeed indefinite, duration. Without fortuitous change or deliberate adjustment, even the largest monetary reserves would eventually be exhausted.

Under such circumstances it is questionable whether a system of fixed exchange rates is at all tenable and, if not, which system is to be preferred, eventually adjustable rates or freely flexible rates. Strictly speaking, this does not exhaust all possibilities: free flexibility can, for example, be confined to a predetermined spread; or it may be restrained by official compensatory transactions in the foreign-exchange market if the monetary authorities believe they should avoid "unnecessary" or "excessive" fluctuations in the rates. Such systems of "freely flexible exchange rates with reservations" are widely regarded as more practical and more acceptable than perfectly free rates. For one can hardly expect monetary authorities to abstain under all circumstances from interfering in the market through their own sales or purchases. Yet, the differences between entirely free and predominantly free exchange rates may be disregarded in the present discussion.[75] We shall confine ourselves here to a comparison between the three main types: fixed, occasionally adjustable, and freely flexible exchange rates.

Fixed, nonadjustable exchange rates are possible only if the following prerequisites are met: 1. *Pegging operations.*—The monetary authorities have to sell and to buy foreign exchange in any quantity at the fixed prices; that is, they must be prepared to see their exchange holdings grow without limit when there is an excess supply, and dwindle without restraint when there is an excess demand. 2. *Domestic circulation.*—The monetary authorities have to expand or contract domestic circulation according to the balance-of-payments situation; that is, they must be prepared to eliminate an excess supply of foreign exchange by creation of domestic money and through the associated increase in domestic prices and incomes, and to eliminate an excess demand for foreign exchange by destruction of domestic money and through the associated reduction in domestic prices and incomes. 3. *Foreign-payments restrictions.*—The monetary authorities may for a limited period compensate for some omissions or imperfections in the first two requirements by imposing restrictions on international payments, that is, by prohibiting or restricting certain international transactions that contribute to an excess supply or excess demand in the foreign-exchange market.

These prerequisites are usually not fulfilled nowadays. Especially the second requirement—the preparedness to inflate or deflate for the sake of exchange stability—is rarely satisfied. Most monetary authorities refuse to match an inflation that is going on abroad; they prefer to stem the inflow of foreign exchange by an up-valuation of their currency. Likewise, they refuse to submit to a deflation that may be prescribed by the state of the balance of payments; they prefer to cope with a continuing outflow of foreign exchange by resorting to a devaluation of their currency. Thus, it appears that foreign-exchange rates "fixed until further notice" are the closest approximation to the former ideal of irrevocably fixed exchange rates.

For an evaluation of the system of occasionally adjustable exchange rates—the system with adjustable peg, as it is sometimes called—it will be necessary to find out just what the conditions are under which monetary authorities decide that an alteration in exchange rates would be appropriate. Under the provisions of the I.M.F., exchange rates should be ad-

---

[75] Probably the most important difference is that even moderate purchases and sales of foreign exchange by independently acting monetary authorities of different countries are apt to lead to mutually incompatible exchange rates between the same currencies. Unless the monetary authorities are in continuous accord with one another —agreeing on the supposedly free market rate, which they must act in concert to obtain or maintain—their interventions in the foreign-exchange markets will result in inconsistent rates, providing juicy profits to exchange arbitrageurs.

justed only in the case of "fundamental disequilibrium." The diagnosis of fundamental disequilibrium is, however, largely a matter of judgment, and ordinarily the views of experts in this regard are rather divergent.[76] By and large, a disequilibrium is regarded as fundamental if in the country concerned the prices of goods and services relative to the prices prevailing in the countries with which it trades are out of line with the fixed exchange rates between the particular currencies. The trouble is that this condition cannot be ascertained through statistical observation of relative prices and that the actual existence of substantial excess supply or excess demand in the exchange market appears to be the ultimate criterion of disequilibrium. If such a disequilibrium has existed for a very long time and the diagnostician has little hope that it can be removed without inflation or deflation of price and income levels, then he decides to call it "fundamental."

The comparative advantages or costs of the system of occasionally adjustable exchange rates—of exchange rates fixed until further notice —can be judged only after a few questions are raised and answered. (1) How probable is it that a "fundamental disequilibrium" in the balance of payments will emerge in a country that pursues conservative credit and fiscal policies, that is, how probable that lasting changes—to which the external value of the currency must be adjusted—will occur in the net commodity-terms of trade, originating either from non-monetary changes within the country or from any changes abroad? (2) How probable is it that a "fundamental disequilibrium" in the balance of payments will emerge in a country that pursues credit and fiscal policies subservient to full-employment and growth policies? (3) What are the most probable reactions of speculative capital to disturbances in the balance of payments in a country where there is a regular practice of adjusting exchange rates that are regarded to be out of line?

In answering the first question, let us first take into account those disturbances of equilibrium which originate from non-monetary changes within the country, that is to say, alterations in the supply-and-demand situation that stem from technical progress, from changes in tastes, from shifts in the supply of labor or capital, or from any other changes of non-

[76] I have argued elsewhere—"Equilibrium and Disequilibrium: Misplaced Concreteness and Disguised Politics," *Economic Journal*, Vol. LXVIII (1958), pp. 1-24; reprinted in this volume as Chapter V—that we ought to avoid designating a concrete historical situation as one of "equilibrium" or "disequilibrium," and should confine the use of these concepts to theoretical analysis, where all the variables can be fully specified in regard to which a certain position is or is not liable to undergo an adjusting change. I am violating this sound rule in this paper (1) in order to save the space that would be needed for a more satisfactory formulation and (2) because the frame of reference is relatively clear, since I speak of disequilibrium only in the sense of an excess demand (or excess supply) for foreign exchange at a given exchange rate at given prices, incomes, interest rates, money supply, and employment.

monetary character. (Many authors speak in this connection of "struc-tural" [77] changes and risk thereby awkward misunderstandings.) These sorts of disturbances of equilibrium—or, more correctly, changes to which in a theoretical model we assign the role of "cause" of other changes—are surely not infrequent, but their effects upon the balance of payments prob-ably go in different directions and largely neutralize each other. Fixed exchange rates are almost never "equilibrium exchange rates" either in the sense of the monetary situation or in the sense of short-term supply and demand in the foreign-exchange market; the "deviations from equilib-rium," however, are usually not too large and are likely to offset each other in the long run. Even those changes that can be attributed to economic growth are no more likely to go one way than another in their effects upon the balance of payments. There is no truth in the notion that an economy with a fast growth of productivity will tend to have surpluses in its bal-ance of payments, and that a more slowly growing economy will tend to have deficits.[78] The exact opposites, that is, deficits for the faster growing economy and surpluses for the slow one, are equally probable, because the effects of differential rates of growth depend on several factors; in conjunction with all other influences, one may expect that the effects upon the balance of payments will by and large be neutral. In short, there is no great likelihood that changes in the "real" economic magnitudes, in the non-monetary data of the economy, will cause large fundamental dis-equilibria in the balance of payments. (To mention one exception, how-ever, the drastic changes associated with reconstruction after a war, result-ing in an exceedingly fast increase in the industrial capacity of a country, may have caused a fundamental disequilibrium. I am thinking of the case of Western Germany.)

The danger of a fundamental disequilibrium originating abroad from the monetary policy of other countries is quite serious. If the countries most important in world trade indulge in continuing price inflation, a nation attempting to avoid inflation, or at least not matching the rate of foreign inflation, will be exposed to a continuing flood of foreign exchange. Such a disequilibrium—in the form of a permanent excess supply of for-eign exchange—is fundamental inasmuch as it can be removed ultimately only through domestic inflation at a rate approximately matching the foreign one or through an up-valuation of the currency.

The second question refers to countries pursuing full-employment

[77] See my article "Structure and Structural Change: Weaselwords and Jargon," *Zeitschrift für Nationalökonomie,* Vol. XVIII (1958), pp. 280-298; reprinted in Fritz Machlup, *Essays on Economic Semantics* (Englewood Cliffs, N.J.: Prentice-Hall, 1963), pp. 73-96.

[78] See my article "Dollar Shortage and Disparities in the Growth of Productivity," *Scottish Journal of Political Economy,* Vol. I (1954), pp. 250-267; reprinted in this volume as Chapter IV.

and growth objectives by means of expansionary credit and fiscal policies. If the monetary authorities of these countries attribute every lapse from full employment and every retardation of economic growth to an inadequacy of effective demand, and accordingly proceed to treat the supposed deficiency with injections of new money, then the additional buying power created in this fashion will cause a chronic ebb of foreign exchange. To remove this fundamental disequilibrium—in the form of a permanent excess demand for foreign exchange—devaluation will be the ultimate prescription.

The third question suggests a rather obvious answer. If it is generally known that the official exchange rates will be adjusted whenever a fundamental disequilibrium has developed, speculative capital will move from countries where foreign exchange is scarce to countries where foreign exchange is in plentiful supply. This must be expected since owners of liquid funds will wish to avoid the capital losses from holding a currency likely to be devalued and will not want to pass up opportunities for capital gains from holding a currency likely to be up-valued. The longer the time for which the adjustment of "unrealistic" exchange rates is postponed the greater will be the nervousness of hedgers and speculators; and, since the short-run gains from the expected changes in exchange rates will look far more attractive than the returns on productive investment, ever-increasing amounts of investable funds will be transformed into speculative funds. Inventory policies of industrial firms, especially stocks of imported or exportable materials and products, as well as production and shipping schedules will be increasingly affected by anticipations of the official changes in exchange rates. In short, exchange speculation will no longer be confined to liquid funds but will spill over to all economic decision-making in production and trade.

That all this is apt to cause damage to the economy can hardly be doubted. The only open questions concern the size of the damage attributable to the postponement of the exchange-rate adjustment and the length of the "optimal" period of putting off the decision to adjust the peg. Once it has become clear that a "disequilibrium" in a definite direction is developing and that an adjustment of the exchange rate may eventually prove inevitable, what advantage can be seen in postponing the adjustment for a long time, or indeed what sense can there be in postponing it at all, even for a brief period? Why should occasional or periodic adjustments be better than daily adjustments, that is, freely flexible exchange rates?

These more or less rhetorical questions reflect the ways of reasoning by some of the economists who in recent years have become advocates of freely flexible exchange rates. It would not be appropriate to speak in this connection of definite plans named after their authors, inasmuch as most of the writers in this group have only dealt with the major principles involved and not with the practical aspects of a system of freely flexible exchange rates. Perhaps they have thought it unnecessary to go into any details since the system was so very simple—no more being involved than that monetary authorities stay out of the foreign-exchange market, neither selling nor buying nor interfering through direct controls. Alternatively, the supporters of free exchanges may have been thinking that it is still too early to discuss details, that the basic principles should first be clarified.

In an enumeration of the best-known economists who have declared themselves as favoring freely flexible exchange rates, in principle or under certain conditions, the following names should not be missing: Frank D. Graham,[79] Charles R. Whittlesey,[80] Lloyd W. Mints,[81] Roger Dehem,[82] Milton Friedman,[83] Alfred Bosshardt,[84] Hans Bachmann,[85] John Burr Williams,[86] Erik Lundberg,[87] Friedrich A. Lutz,[88] Gottfried Haberler,[89]

[79] Frank D. Graham and Charles R. Whittlesey, "Fluctuating Exchange Rates, Foreign Trade, and the Price Level," *American Economic Review*, Vol. XXIV (1934), pp. 401-416; Frank D. Graham, *The Cause and Cure of "Dollar Shortage,"* Essays in International Finance, No. 10 (Princeton: International Finance Section, 1949); reprinted in part in William R. Allen and Clark L. Allen (Editors), *Foreign Trade and Finance* (New York: Macmillan, 1959), pp. 124-133.

[80] Charles R. Whittlesey, *International Monetary Issues* (New York: McGraw-Hill, 1937).

[81] Lloyd W. Mints, *Monetary Policy for a Competitive Society* (New York: Macmillan, 1950), esp. Chapter 5.

[82] Roger Dehem, "Exchange Rate Policy: Experience and Theory Reconsidered," *Economia Internazionale*, Vol. V (August 1952), pp. 559-578.

[83] Milton Friedman, "The Case for Flexible Exchange Rates," *Essays in Positive Economics* (Chicago: University of Chicago Press, 1953), pp. 157-201; reprinted in part in William R. Allen and Clark L. Allen (Editors), *Foreign Trade and Finance* (New York: Macmillan, 1959), pp. 313-347.

[84] Alfred Bosshardt, "Von der Stabilität zur Flexibilität der Wechselkurse," in V. Wagner and F. Marbach (Editors), *Wirtschaftstheorie und Wirtschaftspolitik*. Festschrift für Alfred Amonn (Bern, 1953), pp. 201-223.

[85] Hans Bachmann, "Das Postulat flexibler Wechselkurse," *Aussenwirtschaft*, Vol. 8 (December 1953), pp. 258 ff.

[86] John Burr Williams, *International Trade under Flexible Exchange Rates* (Amsterdam: North-Holland Publ. Comp., 1954).

[87] Erik Lundberg, "The Dilemma of Exchange Rate Policy," *Skandinaviska Banken Quarterly Review*, Vol. XXXV (1954), pp. 90-96.

[88] Friedrich A. Lutz, "The Case for Flexible Exchange Rates," *Banca Nazionale del Lavoro Quarterly Review*, Vol. 7, No. 31 (December 1954), pp. 175-185; *idem*, "Das Problem der Konvertibilität europäischer Währungen," *Ordo*, Bd. 6 (1954), pp. 79-131; *idem*, "Das Problem der internationalen Währungsordnung," *Ordo*, Bd. 10 (1958), pp. 133-147; *idem*, *International Payments and Monetary Policy in the World Today*. Wicksell Lectures 1961 (Stockholm: Almquist & Wiksell, 1961), p. 23; *idem*, *The Problem of International Economic Equilibrium*. De Vries Lectures (Amsterdam: North-Holland Publ. Comp., 1961).

[89] Gottfried Haberler, *Currency Convertibility* (Washington: American Enterprise Association, 1954); *idem*, "Konvertibilität der Währungen," in Albert Hunold (editor), *Die Konvertibilität der europäischen Währungen* (Erlenbach-Zürich u Stuttgart, 1954), pp. 15-59.

Emil Korner,[90] James E. Meade,[91] W. M. Scammell,[92] Alfred Amonn,[93] L. Albert Hahn,[94] Emil Küng,[95] Hanns-Joachim Rüstow,[96] Egon Sohmen,[97] Fritz W. Meyer,[98] George N. Halm,[99] Jaroslav Vanek,[100] Richard

[90] Emil Korner, "Freier Wechselkurs und richtiges Geld, die Heilmittel für jedes Aussenhandelsdefizit," *Schmollers Jahrbuch für Gesetzgebung, Verwaltung und Volkswirtschaft*, Vol. LXXV (1955), pp. 303-322.

[91] James E. Meade, "The Case for Variable Exchange Rates," *Three Banks Review*, No. 27 (September 1955), pp. 3-27; idem, "The Future of International Trade and Payments," *Three Banks Review*, No. 50 (June 1961), pp. 15-38; idem, "The Future of International Payments" in *Factors Affecting the United States Balance of Payments*, Subcommittee on International Exchange and Payments, Joint Economic Committee, Congress of the United States, 87th Congress, 2d Session, Part 3 (Washington: 1962), pp. 241-252.

[92] W. M. Scammell, *International Monetary Policy* (London: Macmillan, 1957), esp. pp. 82-108.

[93] Alfred Amonn, "Abwertung und Aufwertung oder freie Wechselkursbildung?" in: Erwin v. Beckerath, Fritz W. Meyer and Alfred Müller-Armack (Editors), *Wirtschaftsfragen der freien Welt*. Festschrift für Ludwig Erhard. (Frankfurt a.M.: Knapp, 1957), pp. 568 ff.

[94] L. Albert Hahn, *Autonome Konjunktur-Politik und Wechselkurs-Stabilität* (Frankfurt a.M.: Knapp, 1957); reprinted in L. Albert Hahn, *Geld und Kredit* (Frankfurt a.M.: Knapp, 1960), pp. 93-130; idem, "Monetäre Integration—Illusion oder Realität," in Wilhelm Meinhold (Editor), *Internationale Währungs- und Finanzpolitik* (Berlin: Duncker & Humblot, 1961), pp. 99-123.

[95] Emil Küng, *Zahlungsbilanzpolitik* (Zürich: Polygraphischer Verlag, und Tübingen: Mohr-Siebeck, 1959), esp. pp. 532-594.—Küng recommends freely flexible exchange rates only under certain conditions, which however are presently to be found in most countries.

[96] Hanns-Joachim Rüstow, "Die Problematik stabiler Wechselkurse," in *Probleme des Zahlungsbilanz-Ausgleichs* (Beihefte der Konjunkturpolitik, Berlin, 1959).

[97] Egon Sohmen, *Flexible Exchange Rates* (Chicago: University of Chicago Press, 1961); idem, *International Monetary Problems and the Foreign Exchanges*, Special Papers in International Economics, No. 4 (Princeton, N.J.: International Finance Section, Princeton University, 1963).

[98] Fritz W. Meyer, "Wechselkurse," *Handwörterbuch der Sozialwissenschaften*, Bd. 11 (Stuttgart, Tübingen, and Göttingen, 1961), pp. 571-585.

[99] George N. Halm, "Fixed or Flexible Exchange Rates?" in *Factors Affecting the United States Balance of Payments*, Subcommittee on International Exchange and Payments, Joint Economic Committee, Congress of the United States, 87th Congress, 2d Session, Part 4 (Washington: 1962), pp. 253-266; idem, "Feste oder flexible Wechselkurse?" *Kyklos*, Vol. XVI (1963), pp. 28-46; idem, "Statement," in *Outlook for United States Balance of Payments*, Hearings before the Subcommittee on International Exchange and Payments, Joint Economic Committee, Congress of the United States, 87th Congress, 2d Session, December 12, 13, and 14, 1962 (Washington: 1963), pp. 179-181.

[100] Jaroslav Vanek, *The Balance of Payments, Level of Economic Activity and the Value of Currency: Theory and Some Recent Experiences* (Geneva: Librairie E. Droz, 1962); idem, "Overvaluation of the Dollar: Causes, Effects, and Remedies," in *Factors Affecting the United States Balance of Payments*, Subcommittee on International Exchange and Payments, Joint Economic Committee, Congress of the United States, 87th Congress, 2d Session, Part 4 (Washington: 1962), pp. 267-285; idem, "Statement," in *Outlook for United States Balance of Payments*, Hearings before the Subcommittee on International Exchange and Payments, Joint Economic Committee, Congress of the United States, 87th Congress, 2d Session, December 12, 13, and 14, 1962 (Washington: 1963), pp. 177-179.

Caves,[101] Harry G. Johnson.[102] But these are by no means all the advocates of the system and their arguments in its support are not the same. Some of them, for example, do not question the superiority of fixed over fluctuating exchange rates provided that the absence of direct controls in foreign-exchange dealings, foreign trade, and foreign payments is guaranteed unconditionally. If, however, fixed (or temporarily fixed) exchange rates are secured by restrictions and direct controls, and if monetary authorities are inclined or induced to stick to official exchange rates that have become quite unrealistic and can be maintained only with foreign-exchange controls, then the ranking of systems is reversed and freely flexible exchange rates are given preference over fixed ones.

Almost all representatives of this way of thinking recognize that a fully autonomous monetary policy is incompatible with the maintenance of fixed exchange rates. But we must distinguish those who *recommend* an autonomous monetary policy—a credit policy independent of the balance of payments—from those who do *not* recommend it but regard it as a given and unalterable fact with which realistic observers should reckon. Members of the first group are convinced that the rate of employment and the rate of growth can be increased or supported by expansionary credit and fiscal policies. This is why they favor an autonomous monetary policy with freely flexible exchange rates. Members of the other group question the theory that injections of additional purchasing power can secure higher rates of employment and faster rates of growth in the long run, but they know that the most influential men in charge of the economic policies of certain nations believe in this theory and will not refrain from applying it. Application of this theory, however, implies autonomy of monetary policy—a policy supposedly in the service of "internal balance" —and therefore long-run incompatibility of fixed exchange rates. Hence, even nonbelievers in the blessings of independent monetary policies regard freely flexible exchange rates as the best way out of the dilemma.[103]

---

[101] Richard Caves, "Statement," in *Outlook for United States Balance of Payments*, Hearings before the Subcommittee on International Exchange and Payments, Joint Economic Committee, Congress of the United States, 87th Congress, 2d Session, December 12, 13, and 14, 1962 (Washington: 1963), pp. 174-177, also pp. 192-193, and 197.

[102] Harry G. Johnson, "International Liquidity: Problems and Plans," *Malayan Economic Review*, Vol. VII (1962), pp. 1-19, esp. 6-7; *idem*, "Statement," in *Outlook for United States Balance of Payments*, Hearings before the Subcommittee on International Exchange and Payments, Joint Economic Committee, Congress of the United States, 87th Congress, 2d Session, December 12, 13, and 14, 1962 (Washington: 1963), pp. 219-221, also 233; *idem*, "Equilibrium under Fixed Exchanges," *American Economic Review*, Vol. LIII (May 1963), Papers and Proceedings, pp. 112-119.

[103] Besides the two groups mentioned, there is a third one, consisting of those economists who believe neither in "accelerated growth through money creation" nor in "international coordination of monetary policies," but have different reasons for advocating freely flexible exchange rates.

A strong argument in opposition to flexible exchange rates is based on the fear that the resistance to credit inflation may be weakened under such a system. This possibility should certainly be taken into account. The most essential and most difficult task of a central banker is to prevent inflation. Overindulgence in easy-money policies is apt to lead to a loss of reserves if exchange rates are pegged, and to a loss in the foreign market value of the currency if exchange rates are free to move. Which of the two is the greater embarrassment to the central banker and, thus, will stiffen his backbone in resisting the incessant political pressures for maintaining easy money?

Some economists hold that, once flexible exchange rates become the accepted practice or institution, currency depreciation will lose most of its terror, and all bars to inflation will be down. Other economists are convinced that, if fixed exchange rates are held sacrosanct, the fear of continuing or complete depletion of foreign reserves induces not abstinence from easy-money policies but adoption of exchange restrictions. And there is widespread agreement that, if inflation is bad and restrictions are evil, the combination of the two is cancerous. Is it likely, however, that economists will agree on an "indifference curve" between rates of inflation and degrees of direct controls; that they will agree on, for example, just what degree of inflation might be acceptable as a price to pay for complete absence of direct restrictions of imports and payments? Assume our judgment of the heads, the hearts, the backbones, and the guts of the monetary managers of a country leads us to expect that under a regime of fixed exchange rates they would hold the rate of price inflation down to 3 per cent a year and would check the resulting drain on gold and exchange reserves by prohibiting certain capital outflows and adopting certain quantitative restrictions on imports; whereas the same managers under a regime of perfectly free exchanges would allow the rate of inflation to rise to 6 per cent a year. Which outcome would be preferable? It would be hard to obtain agreement on the *value judgment* on the basis of which this question could be answered. And of course even the question presupposes that there can be agreement on the *probability judgment* concerning the central bankers' differential propensities to inflate under various conditions.[104]

If *all* central bankers were determined and strong enough to avoid inflation under any circumstances, the difference between fixed and float-

---

[104] The judgments in question are even more complicated, because the attitudes of the central bankers and treasury officials who run the show for the time being may be less important than the attitudes of those who are likely to replace them when they are dismissed. Convinced and consistent anti-inflationists may possibly be kicked out precisely because of their conservatism, and be succeeded by men more willing to compromise. This probability must be taken into account when the "differential propensities to inflate" under various conditions are judged.

ing exchange rates would not be too great. For, in the absence of inflation, floating rates would be fairly stable. "Exchange-rate stability without pegging" might become the major policy objective of the monetary authorities. But if some of the central bankers were less determined and permitted monetary expansion at a faster rate than others, a stabilization policy would run into difficulties. A country adhering to a policy of exchange-rate stability would then have to match the credit expansion of the major trading countries, just as in a system of pegged exchange rates foreign inflations would be imported through balance-of-payments surpluses. Even the advocates of pegged rates must call for periodic adjustments of the peg if they wish to hold the line against inflation while foreign nations indulge in satisfying their people's chronic preference for ever-more liquidity through easy money.

The chief and most frequently mentioned argument of the opponents of exchange-rate flexibility concerns the risks of foreign trade under fluctuating exchange rates. Reference to the possibility of hedging on better-developed forward markets does not completely answer this objection; more telling is the reference to the probability that the risks of exchange *restrictions* imposed to "protect" fixed exchange rates may be greater than the risks of exchange *fluctuations* in free markets, and that the effects of restrictions may weigh more heavily than the cost of hedging against the risk of fluctuations.

The advocate of fixed exchange rates points to the great benefits which domestic trade derives from the national unity of the currency, from its universal acceptability at par, the par-collection of bank checks in all cities and different parts of the country, and the certainty that this will not be changed in the future. Then he infers that fixed exchange rates confer similar benefits to international trade. A correct reply would not deny this inference, but would point to an essential difference between intranational and international monetary arrangements—the same difference, incidentally, which prevents those economists who unconditionally advocate adoption of freely flexible exchange rates among different countries from advocating flexible exchange rates also among the different districts or provinces within a country. The difference is that nations claim, and districts or provinces do not claim, "sovereignty" in credit policy.

A uniform currency in a country is possible only as long as no part of the country has autonomy in the creation of money. If particular provinces or districts undertook to support regional growth or full employment by enlarging effective demand through regional credit creation, the national unity of the currency could not long be maintained. There could not be a uniform D-mark for Western Germany if, say, Schleswig-Holstein claimed the prerogative of printing D-mark to finance public-works projects. The United States could not for long keep a uniform dollar if, say, Mississippi and Kentucky started autonomous credit and fiscal policies to accelerate their economic growth by printing greenbacks and creating bank credit. The preconditions for the maintenance of fixed exchange rates among different countries and for the maintenance of a uniform currency for the different parts of one country are essentially the same, to wit, that no country and no part of a country is independent in the manufacture of money.

It is really not necessary to take a firm position in the controversy and come out either on the side of fixed exchange rates or on the side of freely flexible exchange rates. It may suffice to insist on consistency and to have it understood that fixed exchange rates can be maintained only among countries which pursue monetary policies coordinated with one another, rather than policies independently designed to obtain "internal balance" regardless of external effects. This means that countries which are not prepared to subordinate their monetary policy to the requirements of external balance should accept flexible exchange rates.

The incompatibility of expansionary full-employment and growth policies with fixed exchange rates is recognized by several central bankers. They stress that economic growth and full employment can be obtained better, if not only, by other means than expansion of bank credit and budgets. They are tactful enough not always to repudiate the politicians' commitments to monetary and fiscal measures for full employment and accelerated growth; but they are forthright in giving priority to the task of safeguarding the stability of the currency and in accepting the balance of payments rather than the employment rate or growth rate as the ultimate guide to their credit policies. From such a position one may consistently take a firm stand against the unpegging of exchange rates and in favor of the maintenance of the fixed-exchange standard. Those, however, who are prepared to put the money-creating power of the banking system at the disposal of full-employment and growth policies regardless of the state of the balance of payments cannot in all consistency oppose exchange-rate flexibility.

Yet, it may be too narrow to trust nothing but logical consistency and well-thought-out economic programs; there may be some sense in placing confidence in the outcome of a series of inconsistent pragmatic improvisations. It is possible, for example, that monetary authorities, despite repeated declarations and assurances to the effect that their policy shall first and foremost serve the full-employment and faster-growth objectives proclaimed in political platforms, will cast aside these goals in the interest of external stability of their currencies when, after serious losses of monetary reserves, it becomes manifest "what's up." In other words, independence and autonomy of monetary policy are sometimes unceremoniously dispensed with when things get really hot. This is why some economists who admit that independent credit policies are incompatible with fixed exchange rates, and who know the strength of the nations' propensity to be independent, have nevertheless remained faithful advocates of fixed exchange rates. Such faith—resting on the hope that the independence of monetary policy will be given up eventually—perhaps reflects less realism than it is credited with, considering the large number of devaluations in the last 15 years.

It is neither necessary nor probable that there will be in the foreseeable future a formal decision to adopt an international monetary order for the entire free world. There are, however, regional groups of countries that are linked also through a common monetary ideology; these countries may well agree on certain monetary arrangements. If, for example, the members of the European Economic Community are agreed on the principle that their credit and fiscal policies should be coordinated so that through concerted central-bank action a high degree of conformity can be achieved in the supply of money, then stability of exchange rates among these countries can be secured without serious trouble. On the other hand, if no such parallelism in monetary policy can be achieved between a conformist group of countries and countries that refuse to conform, it would be unreasonable to count on fixed exchange rates being maintained in the long run between the conformist countries and those that "go it alone." Rather than wait until a fundamental disequilibrium emerges and forces countries into delayed adjustments of their exchange rates, it might be better for all parties concerned if the external values of the autonomously managed currencies could remain flexible. Fixed exchange rates among countries with coordinated monetary policies, and freely flexible rates among countries pursuing autonomous policies—this appears to be the maxim consistent with the theorems of monetary economics.

Theorists often complain about the conservatism of practical men who are quick to reject the theorists' proposals as impractical. Sometimes these proposals are impractical only because the "practical" men are unwilling to consider them seriously. Sometimes however the theorists overlook or disregard circumstances, customs, practices, or incidental problems, which seem to be important to the practical man. In the case of the proposal for unpegged exchange rates several unsolved questions must be expected to arouse misgivings on the part of the practical banker; they will have to be dealt with and shown to have satisfactory answers before one may hope to see the objections withdrawn.

Whereas central banks with very small foreign reserves may find it relatively easy to remove the peg holding their exchange rates, especially when faced with balance-of-payments difficulties at the exchange rates hitherto fixed, a central bank possessing a large reserve—be it in the form of gold or foreign exchange—may find it very hard to justify a decision to unpeg the exchange rate. The decision would be difficult both in a surplus and in a deficit position of the market balance of payments.

In a *deficit* position, why should the monetary authorities refuse to sell from their abundant reserves? Why should they remove the peg and let the prices of foreign currencies and of gold rise to the levels at which current demand is reduced to the flow of current supply? Why should they allow their large reserves to remain unused, locked up, and unavailable to those who have an effective demand for them? In a *surplus* position the authorities may have a somewhat better case for the removal of the peg. For they may argue against a further accumulation of foreign reserves with its normally inflationary effects upon the economy. On the other hand, will not the refusal to purchase any more gold or foreign exchange depress drastically the prices of foreign currencies and produce cries of anguish on the part of exporters receiving smaller proceeds and of producers competing with cheaper imports? And how should the central bank justify the write-down of the book value of its foreign reserve and how can it account for this severe capital loss?

One possible answer to these questions is that the possession of large gold and foreign-exchange holdings is not an appropriate position for a country to start a system of exchange-rate flexibility. If this really is the answer, the proponents of the system will have to furnish prescriptions for central banks concerning the best methods of reducing their foreign reserves in preparation for U-day, the day of unpegging. The key-currency countries are special cases calling for special prescriptions. Let us assume, contrary to fact and only for the sake of the argument, that the monetary authorities in the reserve-currency countries would like to get rid of their heavy responsibilities and that they have decided that the abolition of fixed exchange rates would be a good way of doing so. Could they as honest bankers disappoint the confidence of their depositors, refuse to sell gold and allow the foreign values of their currencies to drop? Could they ever take the initiative in a drive to exchange flexibility if this were taken as a breach of explicit or implied promises?

To raise these questions is not necessarily to doubt that they permit of reasonable answers, but only to draw attention to the need for discussion. Speculating about the possible lines which one of the answers could take, one might suggest that the legal and moral obligations of reserve-currency countries could be fulfilled out of their existing gold holdings if all foreign creditors were given an option to receive gold at the present gold parity. Indeed, such a procedure, to the extent that the option would be exercised, could relieve the reserve-currency countries of sterile gold hoards as well as of interest-bearing foreign debt. After all, after a general unpegging of the gold price and of the exchange rates, there would be no special reason for any of the monetary authorities to hold on to gold stocks.

This realization raises another question which demands study, namely, the question of the future of gold under a system of freely flexible exchange rates. The refusal of the most important monetary authorities to purchase gold, and their unrestrained desire to sell off all their gold holdings, could easily destroy the value of gold overnight. Only their concerted effort to support the price of gold by holding on to it, by refraining from throwing it onto the market for whatever price it may fetch, can avoid transforming—for some time—the "precious metal" into a virtual "non-valeur." For there simply would not be enough private buyers and enough liquid funds to absorb, within a short time and at anything near the present price, all the gold now used as monetary reserves.

These remarks may sound strange to ears used to continual whispers that the price of gold *may* be raised and to periodic shouts that it *ought* to be raised. Bankers, inclined to regard as practical only what is not too much in contradiction with political interests, may find it ridiculous to have gold referred to as a potential non-valeur. Whether it will ever come to the demonetization of gold depends on which ideology will win. In a world in which the discipline of the gold standard is felt chiefly as a nuisance, and monetary management is regarded primarily as an instrument of national growth-and-employment policy, not even the most inventive representatives of vested interests will be able to maintain the myth that the demonetization of gold is "impractical." [105]

At the moment, however, the verdict of "impracticality" cannot be appealed to a higher court of political judgment. If it is suspected that a system of flexible exchange rates may weaken or subvert the people's faith in the monetary role of gold, the system will be opposed with fanatic fervor. This places its advocates on the horns of a dilemma. Either they must build into their plans a solid program to safeguard the value of gold or they must resign themselves to the fate that their plans will continue to be scorned as the utterly impractical notions of inexperienced theorists not taken seriously by "anybody."

One way to obtain recognition of the economic advantages of exchange-rate flexibility might be to abstain from all allusions to such radical ideas as unlimited flexibility, complete withdrawal of monetary authorities from foreign-exchange markets, cutting loose from gold, or similarly subversive notions. Instead, one might propose merely a widening of the spread between gold-export and gold-import points, allowing

[105] Perhaps the present author can reassure the friends of gold that he himself has been an old and faithful advocate of the orthodox gold standard in the purity described by the most obsolete textbook. He would still vote for a 100 per cent pure gold standard, where gold is really a "standard," not merely a price-supported commodity.

exchange rates to move, say, five per cent up and five per cent down from the official gold par of exchange. This "flexibility within limits"—with possible strong interventions in the exchange markets by monetary authorities defending the lower and the upper limits of the foreign values of their currencies through sales and purchases, respectively—may be acceptable to both the practical men and the reformers. Limited flexibility within a broad band, such as the proposed margin of ten per cent, might give sufficient leeway for the operation of an adjustment mechanism that works more via relative prices than via domestic incomes. The problems of defending the limit rates and, in some situations, of changing them would still involve many of the difficulties now inherent in the system of the adjustable peg. Yet, the advocates of freely flexible exchange rates may consider limited flexibility a sufficient advantage to justify the provisional sacrifice of the rest of their program.

D. CONCLUDING REMARKS

We have reached the end of our survey. If it perhaps has failed to describe and discuss *all* of the plans for reform of the international monetary system which have been presented in recent years, at least the most widely discussed plans have been included in our review. In addition, in exploring the preconditions of adopting these plans, the ways in which they might work if adopted, and the most probable consequences to be expected from their operation, we have made enough general statements applicable to the explanation and evaluation of other plans not treated here.

The author has abstained—or at least tried to restrain himself—from making blunt value judgments. If nothing else, he has avoided calling any of the plans impossible, absurd, or foolish. On the other hand, he has not concealed either his acceptance or his rejection of certain theories and presuppositions. Some readers may be disappointed that the author has not come out in favor of any one particular plan. There is, however, a good reason for such reticence or caution. An intelligent choice would have to depend on many conditions, and one cannot ascertain whether and to what extent they are fulfilled. What under certain circumstances would appear as the best solution may under other circumstances be hopelessly wrong. In economic policy decisions much depends on how they fit in with other measures adopted and objectives accepted. Monetary policy, credit and fiscal policy, commercial policy, wage policy, investment policy, growth policy, employment policy, counter-cyclical policy, etc., etc., are so closely related to one another that it would not be possible to formulate a rational policy concerning the international monetary system irrespective of all other areas of economic policy.

Policies regarding the international monetary system must take account of the measures and intentions of the governments of a multitude of nations. The theories entertained by influential monetary experts will, of course, be important, but what is really decisive in the relevant considerations are the notions, the beliefs, the courage, and the powers of persuasion of central bankers, ministers of finance, and other leaders of economic policy in the major countries. Consequently, one cannot possibly expect that there will be one particular plan among all plans for the international monetary system that may be singled out and proclaimed as "the best" under any set of conditions.

To say this is not to make a virtue of indecision. Sooner or later, and more likely sooner than later, the reform of the present system will have to be taken up seriously. The stop-gap solution initiated at the Vienna meeting of the I.M.F. and formalized in the "General Arrangements to Borrow," and the bilateral credit-swap arrangements between the United States and several other countries, may tide us over the worst difficulties for some time, possibly even for several years. To be sure, we should never expect a solution that is really definitive, but perhaps we may hope for one that can dispel for a longer time the apprehensions, nervousness, and fears of collapse.

■ PART FIVE ■

Capital Movements and the Transfer Problem

When a rough outline of this book was shown to a fellow economist, he questioned the wisdom of including my essays on the transfer problem, a "dead issue" of only historical interest. As is so often the case with questioning attitudes, this challenge to my judgment has proved very fruitful. It prompted me to do more work, historical as well as theoretical, and to write two new essays in addition to my three earlier statements.

Far from being a dead issue, the transfer problem is alive and kicking; indeed, it is one of the most troublesome economic problems of our days, though it is now seldom discussed under that name; but its name is not important—it has had several aliases in history. Now, if competent economists have failed to recognize that the balance-of-payments problem of the United States at the present time (1963) is essentially a problem of adjusting the balance on current account to the heavy payments obligations for foreign aid, military expenditures, and investments abroad—in short, a transfer problem—it was evidently important that someone take pen in hand and attempt clarification.

In order to sharpen the historical perspective I am placing at the beginning of the sequence my new essay on the four biggest transfer stories of modern times. This may help toward a better understanding of the old adage that history repeats itself, though usually not without variations. The British payments in the Napoleonic wars, the French payments after the Franco-Prussian war, the German payments after World War I, and the United States payments after World War II—with all the differences in economic institutions, conditions, and relative magnitudes—have one thing in common: the problem of the real transfer.

The two essays which follow the first one in this group are the most "dated" ones in the entire collection. The first of the two, written in 1928, was specifically addressed to the problems of German reparations and Schacht's objections to Germany's foreign long-term borrowing. The second, published in 1930, was part of a discussion in the journals, in which Keynes, Ohlin, Rueff, and Haberler were among the protagonists. My decision to include my two early essays was influenced chiefly by my conviction that much can be learned from observing the development of economic reasoning over time under the influence of historical experience and contemporary theory formation. Reading the old essays along with the new ones may bring into view some significant changes of emphasis as well as of theorizing; and to observe these changes may be worth the cost of some repetition among and within the essays. By judicious cutting of the old essays I have tried to reduce some of the repetitiveness.

The fourth essay in this sequence, first published in 1943 as a section in a book, is the application of the income-multiplier theorem to the transfer problem. Another new essay, written in 1963, attempts, besides semantic clarifications, an exposition of the transfer mechanism under conditions of economic growth. The new vistas that are opening up on the old problem should invite the interest of other analysts and induce them to do more work on it.

The sixth essay is another selection from my 1943 book. I found it worth reproducing because this statement on the causal and logical relationships between capital movements and trade balance is not sufficiently accessible, being a small part of a monograph on the multiplier; and I believe, somewhat immodestly, that it ought to be more accessible because the literature has not furnished a newer statement to take its place. Since the errors of reasoning which are examined and clarified in this essay have been hardy enough to reappear in print with great regularity, it seems appropriate to make the antidote more easily available.

The seventh and last essay was added in the second edition of this volume. It contains a theoretical and quantitative analysis of the deteriorating payments position of the United States during the 1960's in terms of a never-closed transfer gap.

PREVIEW OF THE CHAPTERS

Chapter XV, "The Transfer Problem: Theme and Four Variations," is an historical sketch comparing British, French, German, and American confrontations with the problem of large foreign payments obligations. The size of the payments is in each case compared with estimates of the national income and of the volume of foreign trade of the paying nation. The ratios, presumably indicative of the magnitude of the "problem," are ranked, with rather surprising results.

Chapter XVI, "Foreign Debts, Reparations, and the Transfer Problem," is a critique of Schacht's arguments, in 1927, against the acceptance by Germany of large foreign loans on the ground that their repayment, together with reparations, would jeopardize the stability of the currency. The essay presents models of the transfer mechanism by which the receipt of foreign loans "automatically" creates an import surplus and the repayment of loans (and the payment of reparations) "automatically" creates an export surplus.

Chapter XVII, "Transfer and Price Effects," is a brief rejoinder, prompted by contentions that the successful solution of the budgetary problem does not guarantee the solution of the transfer problem. The argument of the essay runs chiefly in terms of deflationary price reductions being capable of overcoming all obstacles to the transfer, though possibly endangering the continued extraction of domestic funds out of the income stream.

Chapter XVIII, "The Transfer Problem: Income Effects and Price Effects," applies the multiplier technique to the analysis of the income effects of such a contraction of primary disbursements (home investment) as is implied in an honest solution of the budgetary problem. Without the support of price movements, and with positive marginal propensities to save and to import, income effects alone will not, as a rule, be sufficient to bring about the transfer of all the funds extracted out of the flow of domestic investment. Only through a combination of income and price effects can the full adjustment of the trade balance be brought about.

Chapter XIX, "The Transfer Problem Revisited," has three objectives: first, to inquire into the question of a clean conceptual separation between the budgetary and the transfer problem; second, to provide a semantic analysis of the very different things meant by the catch-all "transfer difficulties"; and third, to present algebraic models to analyze transfer possibilities under conditions of economic growth and, in particular, to determine the budgetary requirements which the paying country has to fulfill in order to accomplish its obligations while the receiving country expands its investment outlays at various rates.

Chapter XX, "Capital Movements and Trade Balance," examines the question of whether capital movements determine the trade balance or the trade balance determines the flow of capital. Both these relationships are "true" depending on the definition of "capital movements." *Autonomous* movements of long-term capital will, with great probability, effect a flow of goods in the same direction; whereas *net* capital movements, comprising both autonomous and induced flows, will be the logical correlative of the trade balance (with due account taken of gold flows). Thus, one proposition is *true*, stating a causal relationship, the other is a *truism*, stating a tautology. The causal analysis is supported by descriptions of all sorts of "spontaneous" transactions.

Chapter XXI, "The Transfer Gap of the United States," measures the annual changes, from 1950 to 1967, of real transfers, financial transfers, and the transfer gap of the United States. The failure of adjustment processes to close the gap is attributed to monetary and fiscal policies; reducing the exchange value of the dollar is seen as the only solution.

MAJOR THEMES

A theme running through all essays on the transfer problem concerns the meaning of the assumption that "the budgetary problem is solved." If it means that the money which is to be converted for payments abroad has been "extracted" *from* the pockets of the people in the paying country, this presupposes that the money has neither been put *into* these pockets with the assistance of bank credit extension nor that it is being put *back* into these pockets by banks or government lightening the burden of the tax or debt payers. In other words, solving the budgetary problem implies reducing the consumption or investment outlays in the paying country.

The same theme recurs in the general theory of capital movements. Here, no less than in the case of unilateral transfers, the crucial question is whether there is a contraction in the paying country and an expansion in the receiving country. The answer will depend on the circumstances of the particular case as well as on financial institutions and monetary policies.

The extent to which price effects and income effects share the work of adjusting the trade balance to the flow of capital and unilateral payments is of importance: income effects may involve unemployment, price effects may involve a worsening of the terms of trade for the paying country. The "secondary" burden due to adverse changes in relative prices will surely be smaller than that due to unemployment at inflexible prices.

The themes connected with transfer under conditions of economic growth will not be included in this cursory review. They should be sought out in the essay in which they occur.

EARLIER VERSIONS AND RECORD OF CHANGES

Chapter XV: "The Transfer Problem: Theme and Four Variations."
Written in 1962.
First published in a German version under the title "Das Transferproblem: Thema und vier Variationen," in *Ordo*, Vol. XIV (1963), pp. 139-167. The English version, unchanged in content, is published for the first time in this volume.

Chapter XVI: "Foreign Debts, Reparations, and the Transfer Problem." Written in 1928 in a German version.
First published under the title "Währung und Auslandsverschuldung: Bemerkungen zur Diskussion zwischen Schacht und seinen Kritikern," in *Mitteilungen des Verbandes österreichischer Banken und Bankiers*, Vol. X (September 1928), pp. 194-208.

The English version is published here for the first time.

CHANGES: (1) All headings were added. The translation is rather free and avoids some of the aggressiveness of the German original.

(2) The introduction was not changed.

(3) The section on "The Facts" was shortened by a few sentences, without omitting anything of substance.

(4) The section on "The Concern for the Future" was not changed in substance, though perhaps the tone of the English translation is less apodictic than that of the German version.

(5) The content of the section on "The Supposed Explanation of the Alarm" was left unchanged.

(6) In the section "A Sequence Model," the previously tacit assumption, that changes in cash balances and buying power would always induce changes in spending, was made explicit in the fourth paragraph. The seventh paragraph was expanded to make the exposition clearer, as was also the eleventh, where the difference between a single payment and a series of payments was pointed out. On the other hand, a lengthy footnote in the German version was omitted in the present chapter.

(7) Models A and B differ from the original version only by speaking of "incomes and prices" where it originally read only "prices," and of "exports and imports" where it originally listed only one of the trade directions. Explanations in the earlier text had, however, indicated that the wider meanings were intended.

(8) The sections on "Money Supply and Trade Balance" and on "The Transfer of Reparations" were left substantially unchanged.

(9) The section "Objections and Qualifications" differs from the 1928 version chiefly in tone, but partly also in content. The drift of the argument was maintained, but the exposition altered. The essay now ends on a note different from the concluding chords of the original article.

Chapter XVII: "Transfer and Price Effects."
Written in 1929 in a German version.
First published under the title "Transfer und Preisbewegung" in the *Zeitschrift für Nationalökonomie*, Vol. I (1930), pp. 555-560.
The English version is published here for the first time.

CHANGES: (1) Some of the headings were added. The translation is rather free and avoids some of the aggressiveness of the German original.

(2) The translation, without changing anything of substance, attempts to tone down the argument: to reduce it from an attitude of cocksureness to one of judging "reasonable" probabilities. This is particularly true of the section on "The Loss of Money and the Loss of Goods."

(3) The "Postscript after 35 Years" was added.

Chapter XVIII: "The Transfer Problem: Income Effects and Price Effects."
Written in 1942.
First published in Fritz Machlup, *International Trade and the National Income Multiplier* (Philadelphia: Blakiston, 1943. Third printing, New York: Kelley, 1961), as part of Chapter IX, pp. 178-187.
   CHANGES: (1) Only a few words were changed in the introductory paragraph and in the section now headed "The Assumptions," except for the list of notations which had to be expanded (since most notations had been introduced earlier in the book).
   (2) In the last section, a sentence referring to another chapter of the book on the multiplier was expanded.
   (3) A few footnote references and, particularly, footnote 13 were added.

Chapter XIX: "The Transfer Problem Revisited."
Written in 1963.
Not previously published.

Chapter XX: "Capital Movements and Trade Balance."
Written in 1942.
First published in Fritz Machlup, *International Trade and the National Income Multiplier* (Philadelphia: Blakiston, 1943. Third printing, New York: Kelley, 1961), as Chapter VIII.
   CHANGES: (1) Apart from a few words changed, inserted, deleted, or transposed, no changes were made in the first four sections.
   (2) In the section on "Types of Autonomous Capital Movements" an explanatory sentence was added at the end of the second paragraph; and the second paragraph before the last was expanded. "Britain" and "British" were substituted for "England" and "English."

Chapter XXI: "The Transfer Gap of the United States."
Written in 1968.
First published in *Banca Nazionale del Lavoro Quarterly Review*, No. 86 (September 1968), pp. 195-238.
Italian translation in *Moneta e Credito*, Vol. XXII (June 1969), pp. 149-193.
   CHANGES: The "Postscript after Eight Years" was appended.

XV

The Transfer Problem:
Theme and Four Variations

Variation I: *Britain,* 1793–1816 ■ Variation II: *France,* 1871–
1875 ■ Variation III: *Germany,* 1924–1932 ■ Variation IV:
United States, 1950–1963 ■ Coda: *Comparison* ■ Finale:
Qualifications

If a country undertakes to make very large payments abroad—for military
expeditions, subsidies, war indemnities, foreign aid, loans, or investments
—the question arises whether it will thereby exhaust its reserves of gold
and foreign currencies (or, in the absence of disposable reserves, have its
own currency depreciated without a definite limit) or whether its trade
balance will adjust itself to the flow of capital and unilateral payments and
thus produce the international means of payment with which the foreign
commitments can be met. This, in a nutshell, is the transfer problem.

The historically most conspicuous appearances of the transfer problem will be compared in this paper, not in exhaustive detail but in rough
sketches drawn with sweeping strokes of a thick brush.[1] The comparisons,
to be meaningful, must not be confined to the magnitudes of the foreign
commitments; the relative burden on the paying country has to be judged
by sizing it up as a ratio to some relevant "aggregates" of the time. I
propose to compare the foreign remittances with national-income estimates and with foreign-trade statistics. The former comparison may aid us
in sizing up the *budgetary* problem: in a narrow sense, as a fiscal problem
of raising sufficient tax revenues, and in a wider sense, as the problem of
reducing the domestic intake out of a given national income. The latter

[1] The sketching artist acknowledges the competent research assistance of Leon
P. Sydor.

comparison may help in sizing up the *real transfer* problem: the problem of increasing exports and/or reducing imports in order to have the trade balance adjusted to the remittances abroad.

VARIATION I: BRITAIN, 1793-1816

During the Napoleonic wars, between 1793 and 1815, Britain had to maintain armies on the continent of Europe, grant subsidies and loans to allies and prospective allies, and make various payments to foreign diplomatic agents. (See Table XV-1.) The annual payments for the armies fluctuated between £100,000 (in 1804) and £17,900,000 (in 1813), and

TABLE XV-1   *British Foreign War Expenditures, 1793-1816* (In Millions of Pounds)

Year	British armies in Europe	Subsidies, loans, and payments to foreign states and agents	Total
1793	.6	.8	1.4
1794	2.3	3.0	5.3
1795	4.4	5.1	9.5
1796	1.0	3.4	4.4
1797	.2	1.4	1.6
1798	.2	.2	.4
1799	1.3	2.1	3.4
1800	1.1	3.4	4.5
1801	1.7	2.2	3.9
1802	.6	.8	1.4
1803	.2	.1	.3
1804	.1	.6	.7
1805	.8	1.9	2.7
1806	.7	1.1	1.8
1807	1.7	.9	2.6
1808	3.9	2.8	6.7
1809	5.6	2.7	8.3
1810	6.8	2.3	9.1
1811	11.6	2.2	13.8
1812	13.0	1.8	14.8
1813	17.9	8.2	26.1
1814	15.5	6.8	22.3
1815	7.0	4.9	11.9
1816	1.3	1.6	2.9
Total	99.5	60.3	159.8

SOURCE: Norman J. Silberling, "Financial and Monetary Policy of Great Britain during the Napoleonic Wars," *Quarterly Journal of Economics,* Vol. XXXVIII (February 1924), pp. 214-233.

totaled £99,500,000 over the 24 years from 1793 to 1816. The subsidies, loans, and other payments to foreign states and diplomatic agents fluctuated between £100,000 (in 1803) and £8,200,000 (in 1813), and totaled £60,300,000 over the whole period. On both accounts together, Britain paid out £159,800,000 in 24 years, or an average of £6.66 million per year.

All that we have under the name of national-income statistics for the United Kingdom within the period under consideration are estimates for two years, one for "circa 1800" in an amount of £297 million, the other for "circa 1812" in an amount of £405 million.[2] Since this was an inflationary period, the drastic increase is somewhat deceptive; but, of course, the foreign payments are also stated in current pounds sterling, so that the ratios of payments to national income are sufficiently indicative of the relative burden. We have the choice, however, of comparing the average payment of the 24-year period (£6.66 million) with the average of the two national-income estimates (£351 million)—which gives us 1.9 per cent— or comparing the average payment of the period 1793-1805 (£3.04 million) with the 1800 income estimate (£297 million)—i.e., 1.0 per cent—and the average payment of the period 1806-1816 (£10.94 million) with the 1812 income estimate (£405 million)—i.e., 2.7 per cent.

Foreign-trade statistics of the period were originally in a form hardly usable, because physical volumes were entered at fixed prices; but they were later recomputed with current prices.[3] Since we are dealing here with a rather long period, and since foreign payments were so much smaller during the first half than during the second half of the period, we shall compute separate ratios for the years up to and after 1805. Our trade statistics, incidentally, begin only with 1796, which complicates the comparisons presented in Table XV-2.

The ratios computed in Table XV-2 convey relevant impressions about the relation between the amounts to be transferred abroad and the values of merchandise exports, imports, and total foreign trade; but the trade figures do not indicate to what extent the transfer was actually accomplished through adjustments of the trade balance. We do not have any comprehensive balance-of-payments statistics to show just how Britain financed her unilateral payments as well as her considerable import surpluses. Only for three years between 1796 and 1816 did adjusted British trade statistics show export surpluses. These years, 1797, 1802, and 1816, did not coincide with the years of the largest unilateral payments but rather followed them with considerable lags. It stands to reason that

---

[2] Phyllis Deane, "Contemporary Estimates of National Income in the First Half of the Nineteenth Century," *Economic History Review*, Vol. VIII (April 1956), pp. 339-354.

[3] Albert H. Imlah, *Economic Elements in the Pax Britannica* (Cambridge, Mass.: Harvard University Press, 1958), p. 37.

TABLE XV-2   *Britain's Foreign Trade, 1796-1816, Compared with Unilateral Foreign Payments*

	1793-1805	1796-1805	1806-1816
1. Exports (average per year)		£ 47.31 million	£ 54.54 million
2. Imports (average per year)		53.24 "	62.98 "
3. Trade volume (average per year)		£ 100.55 million	£ 117.52 million
4. Foreign payments (average per year)	£ 3.04 million	£ 2.33 million	£ 10.94 million
5. Payments/exports	6.4%	4.9%	20.1%
6. Payments/imports	5.7%	4.4%	17.4%
7. Payments/trade volume	3.0%	2.3%	9.3%

NOTE: Since trade figures for 1793-1795 are not available, average annual foreign payments in the period 1793-1805 are compared, in the first column, with the average trade figures of the period 1796-1805.

SOURCES: For foreign trade, Imlah, *op. cit.*; for foreign payments, Silberling, *op. cit.*

gold exports, capital reimports, and foreign borrowing, besides receipts from invisible exports—for services and income from foreign investments—must have financed the import surpluses and the unilateral payments for the wars on the continent. In the absence of information on these items, we cannot say (1) to what extent a real transfer was not called for (the unilateral outpayments being financed by foreign borrowing and by repatriation of British capital) and (2) to what extent such a transfer was actually achieved by the import surplus being reduced below the amount that would just have offset the invisible exports.[4]

The absence of notorious "transfer difficulties" does not mean that the pinch caused by what is now called a payments imbalance was not seriously felt. Indeed, the problem was intensively discussed at the time and there were those who attributed the depreciation of the pound [5] entirely

[4] A few of the experts of the period asked themselves these very questions. One of them referred to the likelihood of "some . . . international transfers of capital" offsetting the "unfavorable balance" due to the extraordinary remittances. John Hill, *An Inquiry into the Causes of the Present High Price of Gold in England* (1810), pp. 8-9. Another explained that "we are borrowing money [abroad] to carry on our foreign expenditure, at a high rate of interest." J. C. Herries, *A Review of the Controversy Respecting the High Price of Bullion* (1811), pp. 43-44. Both these references are from Jacob Viner, *Studies in the Theory of International Trade* (New York: Harper, 1937), p. 146.

[5] The depreciation of the pound, measured by the high price of gold bullion, reached its "peak" in 1813, when the unofficial price of gold was 36.4 per cent above par. The price of silver fluctuated not quite parallel with that of gold but its peak exceeded the prewar level by approximately the same percentage. The exchange rates of the French franc and the Hamburg banco had their highs in 1811, at 39.1 per cent and 44.0 per cent above their respective pars. Commodity prices were highest in 1814, being 98 per cent above the 1790 level. See Ralph G. Hawtrey, *Currency and Credit* (London: Longmans, 3rd ed., 1927), p. 335.

to the heavy remittances abroad. Others, however, attributed it solely to the excessive quantity of banknotes and held that the unilateral payments would not have caused the pound to depreciate in its foreign value had it not been for its "overabundance." [6] The theoretical analysis of this first transfer story by the economists of the period was "classical" in every respect, particularly in the sense that it laid the foundation for all the future discussions of the transfer mechanism. One difference, however, should be noted: from 1797 on, the year when Britain suspended the gold standard, the exchange rates were floating, not pegged. The next three transfer stories to be recounted are either in a setting of fixed gold pars of exchange or of stable exchange rates. [7]

VARIATION II: FRANCE, 1871-1875

Under the peace treaty of Frankfurt, which in 1871 concluded the Franco-Prussian War, France was committed to pay victorious Prussia five billion francs as indemnities. Including interest the amount was even higher, but the transfer of the Alsatian railways to Prussia was counted as payment in kind so that the balance to be settled was just about five billion. France agreed to pay this sum before March 1, 1875, but succeeded in raising most of it through two domestic bond issues in 1871 and 1872 and in completing all her payments before the end of 1873. Of the actual payments Fr.742 million were in gold, silver, and (German and French) bank notes, and Fr.4,248 million were in foreign bills of exchange (Fr.2,799 million German and Fr.1,449 million non-German) bought in London, Paris, Brussels, Amsterdam, Hamburg, Berlin, and Frankfurt. [8]

---

[6] The most consistent expositors of the latter view were John Wheatley and David Ricardo, who held that unilateral payments could be accomplished through trade-balance adjustments even without any changes in prices and exchange rates. The "anti-bullionists" blamed the depreciation entirely on the balance of payments and denied that there had been an over-issue of paper currency. Most of the "bullionists" were willing to admit that the depreciation of the pound during the restriction period (1797-1819) was due both to excessive note issues and to extraordinary foreign remittances. See Viner, *op. cit.*, pp. 119-148.

[7] In France, redemption in gold was suspended from August 1870 to December 1877, but, except for 1871, the "depreciation" of the franc was minimal, rarely more than one per cent below the gold par.

[8] The most authoritative account of the French indemnity payments is in the report of Léon Say, French Minister of Finance, to the National Assembly in August 1874. *Journal Officiel de la République Française*, Sixième année (Versailles, 1874), Annexe no. 2704 (Séance du 5 août 1874), 2 décembre 1874, pp. 7919-7930, entitled "Rapport fait au nom de la commission du budget de 1875 sur le payement de l'indemnité de guerre et sur les opérations de change qui en ont été la conséquence, par M. Léon Say, membre de l'Assemblée nationale." The report was reprinted in Léon Say, *Les finances de la France sous la troisième république*, Tome 1 (Paris: 1898).

The literature on the French payments is large, but most of it is based on Say's report. See, e.g., Jean Figard, *Lendemains financiers d'une guerre: Léon Say, Ministre*

Large amounts of the French bonds, though issued in Paris, were purchased by foreigners. It was estimated that Fr.300 million of the 1871 loan and Fr.2,288 million of the 1872 loan were subscribed from abroad, and that the largest portions of the foreign subscription were 33 per cent from Germany, 28 per cent from Belgium, and 23 per cent from Britain.[9] In addition, large amounts of foreign securities, such as Italian consols and Austrian railroad bonds, which French savers had acquired before the war, were sold to foreign capitalists in the years 1871 to 1873. To the extent of these inflows of foreign long-term capital, the problem of the real transfer was postponed for the time being. The postponement was probably not for long, for it is known that most of the French bonds sold to foreigners were repatriated—purchased by French savers—in subsequent years.[10]

The weight of the burden upon the French economy shall again be judged by comparing the foreign payments with national income and foreign trade of the time. According to available estimates,[11] French national income was Fr.19,400 million in 1859, Fr.22,200 million in 1872, and Fr.26,400 million in 1882. Since the indemnity payments were completed within less than three years, the national-income estimate for 1872 is fully relevant. The question, however, is whether we should assume that the burden was borne in two, three, or more years, that is, whether we should take one-half, one-third, or less of the total indemnity as the pertinent sum for computing the burden relative to annual income and trade figures. Since the bond issues of 1871 and 1872 raised most of the needed funds, it would seem that one-half of the payment ought to be compared with a year's national income, though this view disregards the inflows of foreign capital. On the other hand, we shall see that the real transfer abroad, in the form of export surpluses, was spread over four years, 1872 to 1875, and from this point of view it would seem more reasonable to use one-third, if not one-fourth, of the total payments as a measure of the real burden. The exact total paid in money was Fr.4,991 million. One-half of it (Fr.2,495 million) is 11.2 per cent of the 1872 national income (Fr.22,200 million); one-third of the payment (Fr.1,664 million) is 7.5 per cent.

For the comparison with foreign trade we must choose between statistics at "official values" and statistics at "corrected values." The offi-

des Finances après 1870-71 (Paris, 1915); Horace Handley O'Farrell, The Franco-German War Indemnity and Its Economic Results (London: Harrison, 1913).

[9] Michael G. Mulhall, The Progress of the World since the Beginning of the Nineteenth Century (London: Edward Stanford, 2nd ed. 1880), p. 262.

[10] Harold G. Moulton and Constantine E. McGuire, Germany's Capacity to Pay (New York: McGraw-Hill, 1923), p. 228.

[11] François Perroux, "Prise de Vues sur la Croissance de l'Economie Française, 1780-1950," in Income and Wealth, Series V, ed. Simon Kuznets (London: Bowes & Bowes, 1955), pp. 41-78.

cial valuations were questioned by French critics and found to be somewhat too low; the corrected series had import values raised by 3 per cent
and export values raised by 10 per cent.[12] In Table XV-3 both series are
presented for the years 1867 to 1875.

The official figures have a special charm for our study in that they
show import surpluses in every year before 1872, and export surpluses in
the four years from 1872 to 1875. Since after 1875 the trade balance reverted back to import surpluses, this statistical evidence can be used as a
splendid illustration of the trade adjustment to unilateral payments flows.[13]

TABLE XV-3   *French Foreign Trade, 1867-1875* (In Millions of Francs)

	Official values			Corrected values		
Year	Exports	Imports	Trade balance	Exports	Imports	Trade balance
1867	2,826	3,027	−201	3,109	3,118	− 9
1868	2,790	3,304	−514	3,069	3,403	−334
1869	3,075	3,153	− 78	3,382	3,248	134
1870	2,802	2,867	− 65	3,082	2,953	129
1871	2,873	3,567	−694	3,160	3,674	−514
1872	3,763	3,570	192	4,138	3,677	461
1873	3,787	3,555	232	4,166	3,662	504
1874	3,701	3,508	193	4,071	3,613	458
1875	3,873	3,537	336	4,260	3,643	617

SOURCES: Official values from Direction Générale des Douanes, *Tableaux
Généraux du Commerce.* Corrected values from Cameron, *op. cit.*

The trade balances at corrected values show such fluctuations from year
to year as to make it preferable, for purposes of our comparison, to use
averages over two periods: 1867-1871, the five years prior to the transfer,
and 1872-1875, the four years during which the transfer was accomplished.

To appraise the size of the adjustment which the nation had to accomplish in its foreign trade if the entire amount of the unilateral payment
were to be transferred in the form of merchandise, we compare the
average annual indemnity payment (one-half, one-third, and one-fourth,
depending on what one chooses to regard as the relevant distribution of
the total burden over time) with the pre-1871 and the post-1871 average
annual exports, imports, and total trade values. The ratios can be read off

[12] The corrections were made by René Pupin, *Richesse Privée et Finances Fran-
çaises* (Paris, 1919) and used by Rondo E. Cameron, *France and the Economic Development of Europe* (Princeton, N.J.: Princeton University Press, 1961), p. 523.
[13] It was in fact so used by Jacques Rueff, "Mr. Keynes' Views on the Transfer
Problem: A Criticism," *Economic Journal,* Vol. XXXIX (1929), pp. 388-399.

lines 8, 9, and 10 of Table XV-4. The burden looks exceedingly heavy, especially if one regards the payments as accomplished within two years and compares them with the lower trade volume that existed before the payments started: 38.7 per cent of foreign trade. But even if the lowest of all ratios is taken into account—the 16.0 per cent which one-fourth of the total indemnity payments represents of the increased trade volume during the period of the "real transfer"—the task looks strenuous enough.

TABLE XV-4   *French Foreign Trade, 1867-1875, Compared with Indemnity Payments*

	1867-1871			1872-1875		
1. Exports (average per year)	Fr.3,160 million			Fr.4,159 million		
2. Imports (average per year)	3,279 "			3,649 "		
3. Trade volume (average per year)	Fr.6,439 million			Fr.7,808 million		
4. Trade balance (average per year)	Fr.−119 million			Fr.+510 million		
5. Indemnity (one-half)	—			Fr.2,495 million		
6. Indemnity (one-third)	—			1,664 "		
7. Indemnity (one-fourth)	—			1,248 "		
	(5)	(6)	(7)	(5)	(6)	(7)
8. Indemnity/exports	79.0%	52.7%	39.5%	60.0%	40.0%	30.0%
9. Indemnity/imports	76.1%	50.7%	38.1%	68.4%	45.6%	34.2%
10. Indemnity/trade volume	38.7%	25.9%	19.4%	32.0%	21.3%	16.0%

Of course, only a part of the indemnity payments was transferred in the form of merchandise. The change from an average import surplus of Fr.119 million to an average export surplus of Fr.510 million, together Fr.629 million per year, represents a real transfer in an amount of Fr.2,516 million over four years. This is only a little over one-half the total indemnity payments. The rest, as we have seen, was paid temporarily through gold and currency exports, imports of foreign capital, backflows of French capital from abroad, etc., and its real transfer was probably accomplished later through invisible exports, chiefly capital services.

VARIATION III: GERMANY, 1924-1932

The Treaty of Versailles in 1919, after World War I, imposed upon defeated Germany the obligation to pay reparations to the victorious nations. The amounts to be paid were not immediately fixed. Under the Dawes Plan of 1924 a schedule of annual payments of increasing magnitude was agreed upon, but revised in 1929 by the Young Plan. There is no agreement about the amounts of reparations paid before 1924, because they consisted chiefly of direct deliveries of material, equipment, and fixed assets, the values of which were set at relatively low figures by the governments of the recipient countries but at very high figures by Germany. Reparations in kind continued after 1924 at mutually agreed values, but payments in foreign currency assumed increasing proportions. When the world depression became stifling and world trade was drastically restricted, a suspension of international debt payments was agreed upon under the Hoover Moratorium of 1931. The German reparations, which under the Young Plan should have continued until 1988, were officially stopped in June 1932. (Table XV-5 presents the statistics of payments from 1925 to 1932.)

TABLE XV-5   *German Reparations Payments, 1925-1932* (In Millions of Reichsmarks)

Year	Payments in RM for deliveries in kind	Payments in RM for armies of occupation	Payments in foreign currencies	Total
1924-25	414	208	271	893
1925-26	658	102	416	1,176
1926-27	617	82	683	1,382
1927-28	725	71	943	1,739
1928-29	985	49	1,419	2,453
1929-30	515	32	728	1,275
1930-31	464		921	1,385
1931-32*	214		747	961
1924-32				11,264

* Apart from the amounts shown for this period the Bank for International Settlements reported that it collected from Germany RM 172 million between April and June 1932. It is not clear what part, if any, of this amount was transferred before the suspension of payments.

SOURCES: For 1924-30, S. Parker Gilbert, *Final Report of the Agent General for Reparations Payments* (Berlin, May 20, 1930), Exhibit XIII, p. 519; and pp. 244-248.

For 1930-32, Bank for International Settlements, *First Annual Report, Second Annual Report,* and *Third Annual Report,* Annex VIa, Annex Va, and pp. 28-29, respectively.

The obligation to pay reparations in foreign currencies had been met without great difficulties between 1925 and 1927, and to some extent even until 1929, because large amounts of foreign (chiefly American) loans were received by Germany during those years. In some years the loans provided more dollars to Germany than were needed to pay for reparations, and the excess could be used to incur large import surpluses. Only after 1929 did reparations payments exceed capital imports—and two years later reparations as well as debt payments were stopped. Hence an actual transfer problem arose only when the inflow of foreign capital was declining and reparations payments in foreign currencies were increasing. If the entire period 1924-1932 is considered, Germany may be regarded as a net-receiving, not a net-remitting country. Nonetheless, in theoretical and political discussions the German transfer problem loomed large, perhaps for the very reason that the receipt of foreign capital had created import surpluses which seemed incongruous for a nation obliged to make large unilateral payments. Indeed, some authorities regarded these import surpluses as proofs of Germany's incapacity to pay reparations.

The discussion of Germany's capacity to pay—to raise the necessary funds domestically and to convert the collected funds into foreign currencies—was joined by a large number of well-known economists. In retrospect we are amazed when we apply our usual measures to gauge the weight of the burden imposed upon Germany: it was much lighter than that borne by France after 1871. In 1925, Germany paid RM 414 million through deliveries in kind, RM 208 million in domestic currency for the allied armies of occupation, and RM 271 million in foreign currencies.[14] The total of RM 893 million was 1.6 per cent of the national income of Germany in 1925, estimated at RM 57,000 million.[15] In 1929, the year in which German reparations payments reached their peak, they amounted to RM 2,453 million. In that year Germany's national income was RM 71,000 million (at current prices). Thus, the relative burden was 3.5 per cent in 1929. Over the eight years 1925-1932 German payments, including those made in German currency for deliveries in kind and for armies of occupation, totaled RM 11,264 million; without the payments for the armies—which in the view of some ought not to be included among reparations payments and which apparently raise no problem of transfer— the eight-year total was RM 10,720 million. The average annual payment, therefore, was RM 1,408 million (or RM 1,340 million excluding occupation cost). We have three national-income estimates for the period: RM 57,000 million for 1925, RM 71,000 million for 1929, and RM 41,000 million for 1932. If the arithmetic average of these three years—which include the first, the last, and the peak year of the period—may be taken as the annual average for the eight years, we find it to be RM 56,333 million; and the average annual burden was 2.5 per cent including occupation cost (or 2.4 per cent excluding occupation cost).

For the evaluation of the real transfer problem the Reichsmark payments for the occupying troops will be excluded, but reparations in the form of deliveries in kind will be included both among payments and among exports. This is in some ways inconsistent. One may object to the inclusion of reparations in kind, on the ground that the goods so deliv-

[14] S. Parker Gilbert, "Final Report of the Agent General for Reparation Payments, May 21, 1930," in The Execution of the Experts Plan, Fifth Annuity Year and Transition Period, Vol. I (Berlin, 1930), p. 246.

[15] Walther G. Hoffman and J. Heinz Müller, Das deutsche Volkseinkommen, 1851-1957 (Tübingen: Mohr-Siebeck, 1959), p. 56.

ered would not have been exported otherwise and, therefore, did not constitute an encroachment on commercial exports. Yet there were, among other things, large deliveries of coal, which could just as well have been exported through normal trade channels. The coal deliveries, moreover, may have diminished the capacity of other industries to compete in export markets. Some of the other deliveries in kind may have involved goods produced with the help of imported materials and may thus have constituted a burden on the trade balance. One may, on the other hand, object to the exclusion of the Reichsmark payments for the armies of occupation, on the ground that these payments may have led to purchases of goods imported, or produced with imported components, or exportable. Yet, payments to a German army stationed in Germany would have caused very similar purchases, but would never have been regarded as contributing to the transfer problem; the foreign troops in Germany took the place of German troops, and the fact that German soldiers were replaced by foreign soldiers and thus released for industrial employment can be taken as an alleviation of the transfer problem rather than as an aggravation. Hence, our conclusions regarding the treatment of these items may be taken as justified.

Some statistical discrepancies in our comparisons may arise from the fact that foreign-trade data are for calendar years whereas reparations payments are given for "annuity years" (ending in August), and probably also from differences in timing between government payments for deliveries in kind and their actual execution. By lumping several years together we may minimize such discrepancies and, moreover, separate the period during which foreign loans were received in large amounts from the later period in which such inflows occurred in one year only. The data for two four-year periods, 1925-1928 and 1929-1932, are presented in Table XV-6.

TABLE XV-6   *German Foreign Trade, 1925-1932, Compared with Reparations Payments*

	1925-1928	1929-1932
1. Exports* (average per year)	RM 10,840 million	RM 10,214 million
2. Imports (average per year)	12,224 "	8,808 "
3. Trade volume (average per year)	RM 23,064 million	RM 19,022 million
4. Trade balance (average per year)	RM −1,384 million	RM +1,406 million
5. Reparations payments** (average per year)	RM 1,182 million	RM 1,498 million
6. Reparations/exports	10.9%	14.7%
7. Reparations/imports	9.7%	17.0%
8. Reparations/trade volume	5.1%	7.9%

    * Includes deliveries for reparations in kind.
    ** Includes deliveries in kind, but excludes payments for occupation troops.
    SOURCES: See Table XV-5 and XV-7.

In the first period no "real" transfer took place, evidently because Germany received much more foreign capital than she paid for reparations. For this period, therefore, the ratio of reparations to foreign trade, 5.1 per cent, is not relevant except as an indication of the trade adjustment to be faced when no more capital was to be received from abroad and a real transfer of reparations payments had to be accomplished. In the second period, 1929-1932, the real transfer in the form of an export surplus was just about equal to the reparations payments; the payments were 7.9 per cent of the total value of foreign trade. This is a relatively modest ratio, much less than any such ratio descriptive of the French indemnity payments after 1871. It is hard to understand why some economists in the late 1920's made such a fuss about the supposed severity of the German transfer problem. The remarkable speed with which the German trade balance adjusted itself to the termination of capital inflows and to the net payments of reparations can be seen more clearly from annual data as presented in Table XV-7.

TABLE XV-7   *German Foreign Trade, Annual Data, 1925-1932* (In Millions of Reichsmarks)

| | Exports | | | | |
| | | Reparations | | | |
Year	Commercial	in kind	Total	Imports	Balance
1925	8,930	492	9,422	11,744	−2,322
1926	9,930	631	10,561	9,701	+ 860
1927	10,375	579	10,954	13,801	−2,847
1928	11,757	663	12,420	13,650	−1,230
1929	12,664	819	13,483	13,447	+ 36
1930	11,328	707	12,035	10,393	+1,642
1931	9,211	388	9,599	6,727	+2,872
1932	5,677	62	5,739	4,667	+1,072

SOURCE: *Statistisches Jahrbuch für das Deutsche Reich.*

No precise year-by-year data of foreign capital inflows are available, but statistical compilations of German bond issues floated abroad have been published. From the middle of 1924 until the end of 1927 foreign long-term capital in an amount of RM 5,500 million was received,[16] and the receipts of short-term funds were estimated to have been approximately of the same magnitude. Thus, there is no mystery about the causes of the German import surpluses in that period. The subsequent change from an import surplus in an amount of RM 2,847 million in 1927 to an approximately even balance in 1929 and to an export surplus of RM 2,872

[16] Robert R. Kuczynski, *American Loans to Germany* (New York: Macmillan, 1927); *idem, Deutsche Anleihen im Ausland 1924 bis 1927* (Berlin: Verlag der Finanzpolitischen Korrespondenz, 1928).

million in 1931 represents so perfectly the kind of adjustment depicted by the theoretical model that one may be tempted to think the figures are "assumed" instead of taken from statistical records.[17]

VARIATION IV: UNITED STATES, 1950-1963

Immediately after the military operations of World War II had been terminated, the United States embarked upon an unprecedented course of action: to assist both the exhausted allies and the defeated enemies and, later on, also the underdeveloped neutrals with generous grants and loans of funds. Governmental remittances were made for relief and rehabilitation, for reconstruction and development, for military and economic aid of various sorts, and for military expenditures abroad; in addition there were private remittances and investments abroad in increasing amounts. Table XV-8 supplies the statistics of all these unilateral payments and long-term capital movements to foreign countries in the years 1949 to 1961.

During this period, annual government remittances varied between $4.9 billion and $8.9 billion; private remittances between $0.9 billion and $4.6 billion; and the totals between $6.6 billion and $12.3 billion. In the customary breakdown of the statistics of international payments these disbursements appear partly on current account (military expenditures and deliveries under military grants), partly on donations account (military grants, foreign-aid grants, and private unilateral remittances), and partly on capital account (loans and investments, governmental and private). All of the payments, however, are somehow derived from the national income of the remitting country, and most of them may give rise to problems of trade adjustment. Hence, we shall again attempt to gauge the significance of the sums of foreign payments by comparing them with the national income and foreign trade of the country. A few brief observations, however, seem to be in order in connection with the statistical data presented in Tables XV-8 and XV-9.

(1) Deliveries of goods under military transfers do not as a rule require trade adjustments in the ordinary sense of the word. We shall nevertheless include them just as we included deliveries in kind when we discussed the German reparations problem. The deliveries must, of course, be included both among the remittances—Column 4 of Table XV-8—and among the exports—Column 3 of Table XV-9.

---

[17] Perhaps it should be noted that Keynes, when he warned that Germany could not do without the large import surplus, knew only the data of 1927, and thus was unaware of the fact that, at the very time he wrote his famous article on the transfer problem, in 1929, the import surplus had already disappeared.

TABLE XV-8   *United States Foreign Remittances, 1949-1961* (In Billions of Dollars)

	Government					Private			
	Non-military		Military			Capital Portfolio and direct invest-ment abroad (net)*	Unilat-eral remit-tances abroad (net)	Private Total	Grand Total
Year	Foreign aid and grants	Foreign loans & invest-ments (net)	Expen-ditures abroad	Grants of goods and services	Govern-ment Total				
	(1)	(2)	(3)	(4)	(5)	(6)	(7)	(8)	(9)
1949	5.1	0.7	0.6	0.2	6.6	0.6	0.5	1.1	7.7
1950	3.6	0.2	0.6	0.5	4.9	1.3	0.4	1.7	6.6
1951	3.1	0.2	1.3	1.4	6.0	1.1	0.4	1.5	7.5
1952	2.1	0.4	2.0	2.6	7.1	1.2	0.4	1.6	8.7
1953	2.0	0.2	2.5	4.2	8.9	0.4	0.5	0.9	9.8
1954	1.8	0.1	2.6	3.4	7.9	1.6	0.5	2.1	10.0
1955	2.0	0.3	2.8	2.6	7.7	1.2	0.5	1.7	9.4
1956	1.9	0.6	3.0	2.6	8.1	3.0	0.5	3.5	11.6
1957	1.8	1.0	3.2	2.4	8.4	3.2	0.5	3.7	12.1
1958	1.8	1.0	3.4	2.3	8.5	2.8	0.5	3.3	11.8
1959	1.8	0.4	3.1	2.0	7.3	2.4	0.6	3.0	10.3
1960	1.9	1.1	3.0	1.8	7.8	3.9	0.6	4.5	12.3
1961	2.1	1.0	2.9	1.5	7.5	4.0	0.6	4.6	12.1

* Excluding reinvested earnings of foreign subsidiaries.
SOURCE: U.S. Department of Commerce, *Survey of Current Business.*

(2) Present-day statistics provide adequate information on both vis-ible and invisible trade, that is, goods and services. The service balance will, therefore, be shown in Table XV-9. Since, however, in the earlier transfer stories, British, French, and German, only merchandise trade was compared with foreign remittances, we shall for the sake of consist-ency also confine the present comparison to merchandise movements. The only exception is Column 3 of Table XV-9, because for military transfers the figures are furnished for goods and services together (the services probably forming only a small part).

(3) Private American investments abroad, as shown in Column 6 of Table XV-8, are exclusive of reinvested earnings of foreign subsidiaries of American firms. The undistributed profits are likewise omitted in Col-umns 8 and 9 of Table XV-9. The exclusion seems justified because these capital returns and investments do not give rise to either remittances or merchandise movements.

TABLE XV-9 United States National Income, Foreign Trade and Payments, 1949-1961 (In Billions of Dollars)

Year	National income	Exports (excl. military)	Net transfers under military grants	Total exports	Imports	Foreign trade: goods and services				Foreign payments total (from Table 8)	Excess of payments over current surplus
						Trade volume	Trade balance	Service balance *	Balance of goods and services		
	(1)	(2)	(3)	(4)	(5)	(6)	(7)	(8)	(9)	(10)	(11)
1949	217.7	12.1	0.2	12.3	6.9	19.2	5.4	1.5	6.9	7.7	-0.8
1950	241.9	10.1	0.5	10.6	9.1	19.7	1.5	1.3	2.8	6.6	-3.8
1951	279.3	14.1	1.4	15.5	11.2	26.7	4.3	2.0	6.3	7.5	-1.2
1952	292.2	13.3	2.6	15.9	10.8	26.7	5.1	1.8	6.9	8.7	-1.8
1953	305.6	12.3	4.2	16.5	11.0	27.5	5.5	1.7	7.2	9.8	-2.6
1954	301.8	12.8	3.4	16.2	10.4	26.6	5.8	2.0	7.8	10.0	-2.2
1955	330.2	14.3	2.6	16.9	11.5	28.4	5.4	2.2	7.6	9.4	-1.8
1956	350.8	17.4	2.6	20.0	12.8	32.8	7.2	2.3	9.5	11.6	-2.1
1957	366.9	19.4	2.4	21.8	13.3	35.1	8.5	2.8	11.3	12.1	-0.8
1958	367.4	16.3	2.3	18.6	12.9	31.5	5.7	2.3	8.0	11.8	-3.8
1959	400.5	16.3	2.0	18.3	15.3	33.6	3.0	2.3	5.3	10.3	-5.0
1960	415.5	19.4	1.8	21.2	14.7	35.9	6.5	2.3	8.8	12.3	-3.5
1961	427.8	19.9	1.5	21.4	14.5	35.9	6.9	2.8	9.7	12.1	-2.4

* The receipts for services are exclusive of undistributed profits of foreign subsidiaries (which are excluded also from foreign payments), and the payments for services are exclusive of military expenditures (which are included, instead, among foreign payments in column 10).

SOURCE: U.S. Department of Commerce, Survey of Current Business.

The ratios of foreign payments to national income, exports, imports, and trade volumes are given in Table XV-10 for each year from 1949 to 1961. The ratios to national income vary roughly from 2½ to 3½ per cent. It is worth noting that in 1949, when payments were the highest relative to national income, they were on the low side in absolute amount; payments were much higher in 1959, when they were lowest in relation to national income. Over the entire period of 13 years, the average national income was $330.6 billion, the average of foreign payments was $10.0 billion, the ratio therefore 3.02 per cent. If we omit 1949 and divide the other 12 years into two equal periods, we find that for 1950 to 1955 average national income was $291.8 billion and average foreign payments were $8.7 billion, the ratio therefore 2.98 per cent; and for 1956-1961 average national income was $388.2 billion, average foreign payments were $11.7 billion, and the ratio was 3.01 per cent.

TABLE XV-10   *Ratios of United States Foreign Payments to National Income, Exports, Imports, and Trade Volume, 1949-1961* (In per cent)

| Year | Ratio of foreign payments to | | | |
	National income	Exports	Imports	Trade volume
1949	3.5	62.6	111.6	40.1
1950	2.7	62.3	72.5	33.5
1951	2.7	48.4	67.0	28.1
1952	3.0	54.7	80.6	32.6
1953	3.2	59.4	89.1	35.6
1954	3.3	61.7	96.2	37.6
1955	2.8	55.6	81.7	33.1
1956	3.3	58.0	90.6	35.4
1957	3.3	55.5	91.0	34.5
1958	3.2	63.4	91.5	37.5
1959	2.6	56.3	67.3	30.7
1960	3.0	58.0	83.7	34.3
1961	2.8	56.5	83.4	33.7

The ratio of foreign payments to exports varied between 48.4 and 63.4 per cent; the ratio to imports between 67.0 and 111.6 per cent; and the ratio to the trade volume between 28.1 and 40.1 per cent. For the entire period the ratio of payments to the trade volume was 34.2 per cent; for 1950 to 1955 it was 33.6 per cent, and for 1956 to 1961 it was 34.3 per cent. These ratios are very high indeed in comparison with those found in the previously presented accounts of transfer cases, especially that of the German reparations. Summaries of all four transfer stories will facilitate such comparisons, but before we are ready for this task we must discuss the peculiar experience of the United States regarding the transfer of its foreign remittances.

The experience was peculiar in that the United States had absolutely no transfer problem from 1946 to 1949, and was unaware of its transfer problem for another eight years, until 1958. Thus for twelve years of heavy foreign remittances no "transfer difficulties" were felt. In the first four years, export surpluses exceeded or approximately equaled the foreign payments made by the United States. These export surpluses arose without any deflationary policies or spending contractions on the part of the remitting country; they were called forth by the extraordinary export demand for American goods on the part of the receiving countries. Many writers attributed this flow of goods to the needs of the war-torn and exhausted economies of Europe; not needs, however, but only demand can direct flows of goods and services, and the effective demand for imports was created by generous monetary expansions in the importing countries. Thus, the paying country did not have to restrict its own demand for its output—as it is required in the customary model of the transfer mechanism—because the other countries engaged in inflationary increases of their money circulations.

After a few years, several countries began to bring their houses into order, either by adjusting their exchange rates to the expanded money circulation or by checking the rate of monetary expansion. The United States, however, increased its foreign remittances and still failed to contract domestic spending. Hence, the export surpluses began to fall short of the foreign payments and have continued to do so ever since. But the "deficit" of the United States payments balance remained undetected for several years, because the supply of dollars in the world markets was absorbed in the monetary reserves of the central banks of the rehabilitated, recovered, and vigorously growing countries of Western Europe. The dollar shortage of the early postwar years, an excess demand for dollars to pay for imports to Europe, was thus replaced by another type of dollar shortage, a demand for dollars to build up the foreign-exchange reserves of monetary authorities. This situation could not go on forever: as the United States, by its continuing remittances in excess of its trade balances, created dollar liabilities year-in year-out, the time had to come when the central banks of Western European countries had accumulated all the dollar reserves they wanted. And as the further supply of dollars was no longer absorbed with eagerness but only out of courtesy and friendly accommodation on the part of the different central banks, dollar shortage had given place to dollar glut. The excess supply of dollars—of short-term liabilities by the United States—became apparent in 1958, when some holders of dollar reserves began converting them into gold.

Thus, after some twelve years of extraordinarily large foreign remittances, transfer difficulties had arisen—but almost no one recognized them as such. All sorts of diagnoses were made: that the United States had pursued unsound monetary and fiscal policies, that it had allowed wage rates and labor cost to be pushed up excessively, that monopolistic corporations had tried to make inordinately high profits, that industry had priced itself out of the market, that the growth of the economy was too slow relative to that of other countries, that the dollar was overvalued and a fundamental disequilibrium had developed. There is, of course, much truth in some of the diagnoses: in particular, it is true that in some countries, Italy for example, industrial exports had become cheaper because labor productivity had increased faster than wage rates; and it is true that in other countries, France for example, industrial exports had become cheaper because devaluation of the currency had reduced labor cost in terms of foreign money. But these are not sufficient explanations of the situation in the United States; had it not been for the large foreign remittances, there would not have been any difficulties. We have only to note that commercial exports from the United States were as high in 1960 as they had ever been, and in 1961 were at record height (see Column 2 of Table XV-9); and that the balance of goods and services in 1961 was the second highest on record (see Column 9 of Table XV-9). Hence, apart from the bad year 1959, the "gap" cannot be attributed to a deterioration of the competitive position of American industry.[18] If one points to the fact that the excess of payments over the trade balance has been larger since 1958 than it had been before, one should also point to the fact that the payments, on donations and on U.S. capital accounts, have likewise been larger than in most of the earlier years. Thus, the difficulties are primarily those connected with the transfer problem.[19]

[18] The years 1956 and 1957 showed exceptionally high exports, largely because of the Suez crisis in Europe. Compared with 1955 and earlier years, U.S. exports in 1958 and 1959 do not look bad. It was chiefly the rise in imports that caused the larger "gaps" in these years.

[19] The statistics presented above may to some extent exaggerate the size of the transfer problem because of the inclusion of all "transfers under military grants." These deliveries in kind often relate to goods that would never have been exported commercially and therefore cannot be held to encumber the trade adjustment. If these deliveries are of goods not currently produced but, say, of old stocks of arms and equipment no longer needed by the U.S. armed forces, they do not even encroach upon resources available for the production of export goods or of import substitutes. Objections may also be raised against the inclusion of "tied loans" to the extent that they create their own offsets in the form of additional exports. In these instances, however, it would be practically impossible to ascertain which exports were, and which were not, involved in the tying provisions and whether those that were had not aggravated the transfer problem through the employment of productive resources otherwise available for increases in exports or reductions in imports. Undoubtedly, the inclusion of all these grants and loans among foreign payments is more defensible than their exclusion in whole or in part would be, and this on general grounds, not only on

Our earlier promise, to undertake a systematic comparison of the four transfer stories narrated in this essay, will now be fulfilled. Table XV-11 presents summaries of the four cases in the form of ratios of the foreign remittances to national income and to foreign-trade volume. These ratios are given for single years or for periods of years.

A few reminders will perhaps be helpful. In two instances, Britain and Germany, it was found preferable to break the entire period of extraordinary remittances into two sub-periods as far as the ratios to trade volume are concerned. In the case of France, three alternative periods are presented because the payments were made so fast that it is not clear whether they should be presumed to have been accomplished within two, three, or four years. In the case of the United States it hardly matters whether the focus is on single years, short periods, or the whole period: the ratios are surprisingly similar.

In comparing the four cases, one astonishing finding is that the burden on the economy of the paying country was in several respects least heavy in the case of Germany. The reparations payments from 1924 to 1932 were only 2.5 per cent of national income. This is less than the British wartime remittances from 1806 to 1816, which were 2.7 per cent of national income; it is less than the United States postwar payments, which were 3.0 per cent of national income, no matter whether we look at 1949 to 1961, 1950 to 1955, or 1956 to 1961; and it is much less than the French indemnity payments, which were between 5.6 and 11.2 per cent, depending on what payments period is assumed to be relevant. The German reparations payments were, depending on the period, 5.1, 6.4, and 7.9 per cent of the trade volume. This is less than the British war payments from 1806 to 1816, which were 9.3 per cent of the trade volume; and it is much less than were either the French indemnity payments or the United States postwar payments in relation to foreign-trade volume.

---

grounds of consistency with the previous transfer stories, particularly the German reparations in kind.

For the benefit of those who are nevertheless troubled by the apparent exaggeration of the transfer difficulties through the inclusion of government grants and foreign aid, let us point to the fact that the share of these items in the total payments has been declining. As another look at Table XV-8 will corroborate, military grants have declined absolutely as well as relatively. In 1953, they were $4.2 billion, or 43 per cent of total foreign payments; in 1961, they were only $1.5 billion, or 12.5 per cent of the total. Foreign aid and grants, nonmilitary and military together, have similarly declined: in 1951, they were $4.5 billion, or 60 per cent of the total; in 1953, $6.2 billion, or 63 per cent; in 1958, $4.1 billion, or 36 per cent; and in 1961, $3.6 billion, or 30 per cent. Since it is chiefly in recent years that the transfer difficulties have become troublesome, one need not fear that the statistical picture has been distorted by the inclusion of tied transfers.

TABLE XV-11   *Ratios of Foreign Payments to National Income and Foreign-Trade Volume, Britain 1793-1816, France 1872-1875, Germany 1924-1932, and United States, 1949-1961*

| | | Ratio of foreign payments to | |
		National income	Foreign-trade volume
Britain	1793-1816	1.9%	
	1793-1805	1.0%	3.0%
	1796-1805		2.3%
	1806-1816	2.7%	9.3%
France	1872-1875	5.6%	16.0%
	1872-1874	7.5%	21.3%
	1872-1873	11.2%	32.0%
Germany	1924-1932	2.5%	6.4%
	1925	1.6%	
	1929	3.5%	
	1925-1928		5.1%
	1928-1932		7.9%
United States	1949-1961	3.0%	34.2%
	1949	3.5%	40.1%
	1951	2.7%	28.1%
	1958	3.2%	37.5%
	1959	2.6%	30.7%
	1950-1955	3.0%	33.6%
	1956-1961	3.0%	34.3%

Another highly astonishing finding is that the burden of foreign payments is so very heavy in the case of the United States. In relation to national income, the French paid more, but this was a one-time effort, made and accomplished in a short time; the United States has shouldered its burden for about sixteen years so far and seems prepared to carry much of it, if not all, for many more years. In relation to foreign-trade volume the payments by the United States—some 33 or 34 per cent—are heavier than anything undertaken by any of the other countries. This should give us a good deal to think about the size of the task required if the payments are to continue in the present magnitude and ultimately must be matched by export surpluses achieved through an adjustment in the trade balance. No country has faced a transfer problem of such gravity. Yet, this does not mean that it cannot be solved.[20]

[20] It may be quite inappropriate in a partly historical, partly theoretical analysis to venture a prognosis. But the author is willing to take the risk, both of making this improper digression and of being proved wrong by future events. Thus, he boldly advances the prognosis that the transfer difficulties of the United States will be solved through three, or perhaps four, developments: first, through price inflations in the countries of Western Europe, in the sense that their price-creep has been and will be faster than that in the United States and will allow the U.S. export surplus to increase; second, through reductions in the amounts of foreign payments by the United States, chiefly on government account; third, through a demand for dollar balances in the

FINALE: QUALIFICATIONS

Some comments on the theory behind the comparisons seem desirable. Concerning the relevance of the ratio of foreign payments to national income as an indication of the relative burden, at least two qualifications should be made. First, a given percentage burden may weigh more heavily on small incomes than on larger ones. Hence, relatively low ratios of remittances to national income need not indicate at the end of the eighteenth century the same "light" burden which they would mean in the twentieth century; and the relatively high ratios of payments to national income in the United States at present may, in view of high per capita incomes, be regarded as entirely tolerable. Secondly, to the extent that parts of the foreign payments are effected, not out of current income, but through borrowing from abroad or through the use of gold stocks and liquidation of foreign assets, the reduction of "domestic intake" is deferred. In this case the ratio of payments to national income does not mean the same thing; it gives an exaggerated impression of the immediate "pinch" on domestic consumption and investment.

The relevance of the ratio of foreign payments to foreign trade rests on the probability that a given absolute amount of adjustment in the trade balance can be the more easily achieved the larger the volume of trade has been. This does not imply, however, that equal ratios of foreign payments to foreign trade indicate equal ease or equal difficulty in achieving the required adjustment of the trade balance. To achieve a given percentage increase in the value of exports may be easy in some countries, difficult in others, depending, for example, on the elasticities of foreign demand for their exports.[21] Likewise, a given percentage reduction in the

---

foreign reserves of countries which cannot yet, but will in the future, afford to build up their monetary reserves. There may be added a fourth remedial development in the form of an agreement among the major monetary authorities of the world to the effect that they reduce the gold portion and increase the foreign-exchange portion of their foreign reserves—but there is little enthusiasm for such a solution at the present time. I stated the first two parts of this prognosis in an article on "Dollar-Pessimismus und Goldspekulation," in the *Frankfurter Allgemeine Zeitung*, November 10, 1962. The third part is contained on p. 13 of my *Plans for Reform of the International Monetary System* (Princeton University, International Finance Section, 1962), reproduced as Chapter XIV of this volume. The fourth possibility was suggested by the discussion of the Posthuma Plan. (On the Posthuma Plan, see Chapter XIV of this volume.)

[21] It has been suggested to me that the ratio to world trade may be a more relevant indication of the difficulty of adjustment, because the elasticity of foreign demand for a nation's exports may tend to be smaller the greater the nation's share in world trade. Thus, if the ratio of foreign payments to the country's foreign trade is weighted by the ratio of its trade to world trade, the country's trade volume cancels out and what remains is the ratio of payments to world trade. I have rejected this suggestion for several reasons, chiefly because one must not infer the elasticity of demand for exports from just one factor, the nation's share in world exports.

value of imports can be more easily achieved in some countries than in others.[22]

This is no doubt both true and significant. But many other factors can be enumerated which are also likely to affect the comparative difficulties of the transfer of foreign payments. The point is that of all the relevant factors very few can be ascertained and measured. The two which I have proposed for purposes of comparison have the merit of being measurable as well as relevant.

[22] Whereas a small elasticity of foreign demand would make it more difficult for a country to expand the value of its exports, a small elasticity of foreign supply would make it easier to reduce the value of imports, because import prices would fall and physical imports need not decline so much. Those who want to "infer" the ease of adjustment from the share of the country's foreign trade in total world trade are now faced with obverse effects upon export expansion and import reduction, one being more difficult, the other easier, under the elasticity conditions "inferred" from the relative shares in world trade.

XVI

Foreign Debts, Reparations, and the Transfer Problem

The Facts ■ The Concern for the Future ■ The Supposed
Explanation of the Alarm ■ A Sequence Model ■ Money
Supply and Trade Balance ■ The Transfer of Reparations ■
Objections and Qualifications

The discussion touched off by Schacht's pronouncements [1] on foreign
debts, reparations, and the stability of the currency has now been going
on for almost a year [1928]. Schacht's thesis can be divided into a statement of facts, an expression of alarm, and an explanatory argument. In a
nutshell, it says
  (1) that during the last few years Germany has obtained foreign
      loans of unprecedented magnitude and has put a large part of the
      funds to unproductive uses;
  (2) that this is extremely unsound and should cause serious concern
      for the future; and
  (3) that the cause of future trouble lies in the transfer problem—a
      shortage of foreign exchange—liable to arise when the loans
      become due, which will place the German currency in jeopardy.
Anticipating the results of our considerations, we may say
  (1) that the statement of facts is incontestable,
  (2) that the expression of alarm is justified, but
  (3) that the explanatory argument, based on a faulty though widely
      held monetary theory, must be rejected.
In discussing the point of view taken by Schacht (and, incidentally,

---

[1] Hjalmar Schacht, *Eigene oder geborgte Währung?* (Leipzig: Quelle, 1927).
[Schacht was President of the Deutsche Reichsbank.]

also by Parker Gilbert, the Reparations Agent, and numerous other well-known persons) we shall proceed in the order indicated above.

THE FACTS

From the middle of 1924 until the end of 1927, Germany contracted 5.5 billion Reichsmarks' worth of long-term foreign debts and almost the same amount of short-term debts. These figures, at the very core of the Schacht controversy, have been verified for at least the long-term debts. Robert Kuczynski in his study of foreign loans to Germany arrived at a figure of 1,238 million dollars (or 5.2 billion Reichsmarks) for the amount of long-term, publicly placed debts alone.[2]

Before the War [1914], Germany was a capital-exporting country. One may compare former capital exports with present capital imports in order to put the magnitude of the latter in perspective. According to the generally concurring estimates of Moulton, Eulenburg, and Fisk, Germany had increased its foreign assets by not quite 2 billion dollars during the 20-year period from 1893 to 1913. During the 3½-year period from the middle of 1924 to 1927, the reverse capital movement amounted to some 10 billion Reichsmarks, or about 2.4 billion dollars. Thus: 2 billion dollars in 20 years, compared with 2.4 billion in 3½ years.

So much for the magnitude of the borrowing. What about the charge that these foreign loans have to a large extent been used unproductively? Schacht thinks that the unproductive use of the foreign loans can be inferred from the fact that primarily "raw materials and foodstuffs" have been imported, "only a small part of which is processed to be re-exported, whereas the largest portion is evidently used to increase domestic consumption."[3] By this argument, the importation of a machine would be recognized as productive, but if the machine were produced domestically and a carload of flour imported instead, this import would be regarded as unproductive, or mere consumption. Walter Eucken,[4] along with several others, has rejected this conclusion, though the fallacy of the notion had been shown more than a hundred years ago by Smith and Ricardo.

To the extent that foreign loans were obtained by private industry we may assume that they were used productively. The private entrepreneur, committed to pay interest and repay the principal, has surely made his calculations and concluded that there will be a net return on his in-

---

[2] Robert R. Kuczynski, *American Loans to Germany* (New York: Macmillan, 1927); *idem, Deutsche Anleihen im Ausland 1924 bis 1927* (Berlin: Verlag der Finanz-politischen Korrespondenz, 1928). The first work covered only 1924 to 1926, the German book included 1927.

[3] Schacht, *op. cit.,* p. 9.

[4] Walter Eucken, "Auslandsanleihen," *Magazin der Wirtschaft,* Vol. IV (26, Jan. 1928), pp. 120-124.

vestments. Schacht also emphasizes this point and observes: "There is a great difference between the indebtedness of government and the indebtedness of a private firm in that the private entrepreneur risks his own skin while government administrators risk the skins of the taxpayers." [5]

As a look at the following table shows, government has no small share in the present total of Germany's foreign indebtedness.

TABLE XVI-1   *Long-Term Loans to Germany, Publicly Offered in Foreign Countries, 1924 to 1927*

	Million dollars	Million Reichsmarks
German Republic	230	966
States	156	655
Provinces, counties, cities, etc.	105	441
Public utility corporations	162	681
Public credit and savings institutions	174	731
Religious and welfare organizations	26	109
Government and nonprofit organizations	853	3583
Industrial corporations	306	1285
Commercial companies	79	332
Private enterprise	385	1617
Total	1238	5200

SOURCE: Robert R. Kuczynski, *American Loans to Germany* (New York, 1927), p. 35, revised in Robert R. Kuczynski, *Deutsche Anleihen im Ausland 1924 bis 1927* (Berlin, 1928), p. 18.

NOTE: The loans listed above do not include those privately placed with foreign banks, insurance companies, mortgage companies, etc.

Large portions of the amounts borrowed by financial institutions were probably reloaned to public utilities and other government enterprises.[6] In any case, the proportion of funds taken up by profit-seeking borrowers is fairly small. Considerations of profitability have clearly been pushed aside by considerations of socio-economic productivity. This is well characterized by official statements incorporated in loan prospectuses, and repeated by various governmental spokesmen, to the effect that public investment in newly established educational institutions, religious institutions, sport halls, and athletic facilities will have real productivity —high returns for the national economy—through the resulting promotion of the intellectual, moral, and physical development of the people. These ringing words and well-meaning conceptions may conceal serious misuse

[5] Schacht, *op. cit.*, p. 20.
[6] Most, or perhaps all, public utilities in Germany are owned and operated by local government.

of public funds. Productivity evidenced by profitability is mundane but unequivocal. Since the bulk of the foreign loans which Germany has obtained has gone to nonprofit organizations, one may reasonably suspect that the returns on the investments financed by these funds will be largely intangible and nonpecuniary.

According to the directives of the German Advisory Council,[7] a capital investment should be regarded as productive only if it pays for itself, that is, if it returns enough to pay the interest and to repay the principal. Certainly, by this criterion only the smaller part of the funds obtained were used productively. Even the construction of bridges, highways, harbors, and canals does not usually fall in this category, for such projects are ordinarily not set up in such a way that they can out of their own returns guarantee the service of the debts incurred.

These conclusions would not be altered even if some public institutions were able to show that they spent the proceeds of the foreign loans on unquestionably profitable projects. For when states, provinces, and municipalities obtain foreign loans, they free parts of their regular revenues and other funds, which can then be spent for uses that cannot be regarded as profitable. If without outside funds various appropriations could not have been made, or could have been made only in more modest amounts,—and one can hardly doubt that this is so and, indeed, the Reparations Agent [8] has commented to the same effect—then the contention that foreign loans are being used unproductively seems to be justified.

The concern for the future

That the borrowing has been extravagant and the uses of the funds unproductive are charges that seem to be well-founded and to have aroused great concern and loud protest. Before we examine the reasons Schacht gives for his concern and protest, let us ask what kind of misgivings and apprehensions would be justified by a well-reasoned consideration of the established facts.

The most unpleasant aspect of borrowing is usually the commitment to repay. Profitable enterprises, whether private or public, have ordinarily no grave problems in meeting this obligation. This is not so in the case of unprofitable enterprise, and there will be a difference between private and public. When the time comes to repay the loan, if incomes are insufficient to permit repayment, a private firm can defer its problem—by secur-

---

[7] The Advisory Council was established in 1925 to rule on the appropriateness of certain types of foreign loans applied for by various government departments and agencies.

[8] *Die Reparationsleistungen im zweiten Teil des dritten Planjahres, Report of the Agent-General of December 10, 1927* (Berlin, 1928), p. 105.

ing an extension of the loan or by obtaining credit from other sources— or liquidate some of its capital. If these courses of action do not yield adequate funds, the repayment cannot and will not be made, and the creditor loses his money. In the case of a government enterprise, on the other hand, the funds needed for paying interest and repaying the principal are obtained through taxation. The larger the amounts to be repaid the more severe must be the taxes.

The tax haul effected in order to permit the payment of foreign debts is real and definitive: it seizes returns wherever there are returns, it reduces incomes and purchasing power, it may destroy the profitability of many private enterprises and result in capital consumption and capital loss. At this stage, the public parks and churches, the well-lit streets and highways, the modernized and smokeless railroad trains, the sport arenas and the swimming pools would be a weak consolation to the faltering economy. Undoubtedly, the future taxpayers, and indeed the entire suffering population, would find that they were paying too high a price for the public amenities and facilities.

It is quite possible, of course, that national income will have increased sufficiently for the economy to bear these future drains without serious difficulties. A wealthy and prosperous economy could and would afford all these public installations without any worries and pay for them out of its regular tax revenues. But a time of extreme capital shortage, when the economy must borrow even its indispensable working capital, is not the right time to sink money into luxurious installations that cannot pay for themselves. To spend freely and lavishly, to act in a cavalier fashion with the money of others, on the assumption that we shall be prosperous fifteen years from now and have no trouble repaying the loans—this surely is not a responsible attitude.

All this has little or nothing to do with currency and the transfer problem, though it may be highly relevant for another aspect of the reparations problem. For, after all, a nation whose capacity to produce and to raise taxes will be strained to the limit for reparations payments ought to avoid any extravagances that may be costly in the future. The nation throws all caution to the winds when it allows luxury installations to be constructed with borrowed money and without any consideration of future returns.

THE SUPPOSED EXPLANATION OF THE ALARM

It is on grounds very different from those just stated that Schacht and many politicians and journalists object to the excessive foreign loans and their unprofitable uses. They base their objections on arguments founded on what they think is monetary theory.

On the basis of their particular monetary theory, Schacht and others are in constant fear of what may happen to the balance of payments. Again and again they complain that "our efforts to equilibrate our balance of payments are jeopardized by constant uncertainty," [9] and any such jeopardy to the equilibrium of the balance of payments means for them a threat to the stability of the currency.

In the present context there are three debit items in the balance of payments that are held to be particularly dangerous and which, if working together, may spell ruin: Germany's need for imports; the transfer of reparations payments; the repayment of foreign loans. If the first two of these items have already caused concern for the future and the third item is now added, the outlook is more than alarming.

Several variants exist of the so-called balance-of-payments theory. In early times, under the gold-coin standard, some people were afraid that a deficit in the balance of payments could deprive the country of all the gold coins in circulation, so that one day the nation would be left without any currency at all. Later versions of the balance-of-payments theory made people fear for the maintenance of the gold-bullion and gold-exchange standard. A deficit in the balance of payments, they thought, would create such a heavy demand for foreign exchange that the stability of foreign-exchange rates could not be maintained.

Both these versions of the theory fail to take account of the so-called balance-of-payments mechanism. The working of this mechanism causes the domestic circulation of money to decline when gold leaves the country or when foreign exchange is sold out of the reserves held by the central bank; and as the monetary circulation declines, the demand for foreign goods and foreign currency declines. (As the domestic money that is paid in purchasing foreign exchange from the banks and from the central bank disappears from circulation, prices and incomes are depressed, and the excess demand for foreign exchange comes to a halt.) Schacht knows this; indeed this is the very point of his argument: he is disturbed by the decrease in domestic circulation, fearing that the money supply will be inadequate for the national economy.

This view is surprising, coming from the vigorous and resolute central banker who engineered the severe restriction of German money circulation in the spring of 1924—and thereby saved the German currency. Yet Schacht is quite eloquent on the issue; at one point he states as follows: "the concept of a 'monetary system' [Währung] comprises something more than mere stability of the value of issued bank notes in terms of gold; it comprises also the necessity of supplying the national economy with an *adequate amount of means of payment* of stable value." [10]

[9] Schacht, *op. cit.*, p. 2.
[10] Schacht, *op. cit.*, p. 1.

One who long preceded Schacht in the history of monetary theory, a man by the name of David Ricardo, had a different view on the subject. This is what he said: "The issuers of paper money should regulate their issues solely by the price of bullion, and never by the quantity of their paper in circulation. The quantity can never be too great nor too little, while it preserves the same value as the standard." [11]

Schacht, however, pronounces with emphasis: "Since the Reichsbank recognizes that it has the responsibility for maintaining an adequate circulation of means of payment of stable value, it cannot tolerate that just anybody in Germany can at his own discretion add to the increase of our foreign financial commitments." [12] This "dialogue" between Schacht and Ricardo shows that the two monetary experts are separated not just by a century but also by a wide gulf between their ways of thinking. Inasmuch as Schacht is concerned about "undesirable" variations in the supply of domestic money, whereas in actual fact such variations play an important role in the course of international payments and transfers, we must examine just what that role is and exactly how important it is.

A SEQUENCE MODEL

A model or sequence analysis of the processes involved in international capital movements is sketched out below. Model A depicts the receipt of a foreign loan, Model B the repayment. While the terms used reflect modern circumstances, the model follows the simple schematic presentation which Ricardo gave us in his pamphlet on the price of bullion. All we have to do to modernize Ricardo's analysis is to speak of "foreign funds," "foreign currency," or "foreign exchange" instead of "specie." Since, to make it shorter, we present the model in a very sketchy outline form, some additional comments are required.

The terms chosen are not quite descriptive of the transactions taking place in the real world; they must not be taken literally. For example, when we speak of a "flow of foreign funds," we must not imagine that dollar notes or coins are actually shipped from or to the United States. All that happens is that entries are made in the dollar account of German borrowers or German exporters, that is, these persons are credited on their New York accounts. Conversely, when German importers or debtors make payments in dollars, what happens is that certain dollar balances are reduced. That foreign exchange—in particular, dollars—can be sold to or

---

[11] David Ricardo, *Proposals for an Economical and Secure Currency* (London: Murray, 1816); reprinted in *Works of David Ricardo*, ed. Piero Sraffa (Cambridge: University Press, 1951), Vol. IV, p. 64.—Ricardo meant that the issuers should not use their discretion concerning the adequacy of the quantity in circulation.

[12] Schacht, *op. cit.*, p. 18.

purchased from the central bank at approximately fixed exchange rates is the characteristic of the gold-exchange standard, the monetary system of our time. In maintaining convertibility, the central bank must exchange domestic money into foreign money and vice versa. If in entry No. 2 of Model A the dollar balances received by the borrower are exchanged for German marks, this corresponds to the usual course of events. It would be a mere coincidence if the borrower were at the same time an importer of American goods.

To be sure, foreign-exchange transactions are normally carried out in the open market, that is, between the individual customer and some commercial bank—and not, therefore, directly with the central bank. However, this is irrelevant for our purposes. The central bank comes in to take care of the excess supply or excess demand that may occur in the market at the official exchange rate and it does so by buying or selling the amount of foreign exchange that cannot be cleared in the market. Thus, in the last analysis it is the central bank that buys or sells the dollar balances arising in the course of the processes described and, through its purchases or sales, increases or reduces the quantity of domestic money in circulation, a step which is of crucial importance in the sequence of events.

Another simplification is made when in entry No. 5 of Model A an increase in incomes and prices is listed as the direct consequence of the increase in domestic money supply. It should be understood that certain actions are tacitly implied in this sequence, in particular, that the borrowers who receive marks in exchange for their dollars use these cash balances for domestic disbursements. It is only through spending these cash balances that incomes are created and prices of goods and services increased.

In the last column of the model, the effects upon imports and exports of goods and services are shown. In limiting the effects upon the current account of the balance of payments, we are disregarding the effects upon private capital movements, for example, through sales and purchases of securities. Such securities are, as a rule, highly exportable commodities, especially sensitive to changes in prices; and the money market may be even more responsive to changes in the domestic money supply. The effects of changes in the domestic money flow may be reflected most rapidly and with the smallest amount of friction in movements of short-term capital under the stimulus of slight changes in the short-term rate of interest. Yet, we choose to disregard all reactions through equilibrating private-capital movements and to place all the emphasis on the movements of goods and services, because the former are only intermediate steps in the sequence of events, whereas the latter have finality.

In describing these effects upon imports and exports of goods and

MODEL A   *Sequence Analysis of the Processes Involved in an Inflow of Capital: Receipt of a Foreign Loan*

	Flow of foreign funds	Sales and purchases of foreign exchange	Changes in domestic money circulation	Changes in domestic incomes and prices	Exports and imports of goods and services
1.	Foreign loan is arranged and dollar balances are received;				
2.		the dollars are sold to the central bank,			
3.		which issues marks to pay for them;			
4.			this increases domestic circulation;		
5.				incomes and prices increase;	
6.					this stimulates imports (and restrains exports);
7.		to pay for the imports, dollars are bought from the central bank,			
8.		which receives marks in exchange;			
9.			this again reduces domestic circulation;		
10.				incomes and prices decrease again;	
11.	the dollar remittances for the imports use up the dollar balances.				

services, we are stressing (in Model A) the stimulation of imports and add the check on exports only in parentheses. Our purpose here is to make the emergence of imports more conspicuous because it is an *import* surplus which can be regarded as the ultimate reflection of the receipt of foreign loans.

MODEL B   *Sequence Analysis of the Processes Involved in an Outflow of Capital: Repayment of a Foreign Loan*

	Flow of foreign funds	Sales and purchases of foreign exchange	Changes in domestic money circulation	Changes in domestic incomes and prices	Exports and imports of goods and services
1.		Marks are accumulated to buy dollars when payment falls due;			
2.			this reduces domestic circulation;		
3.				incomes and prices decrease;	
4.					this stimulates exports (and restrains imports);
5.	in payment for exports, dollar balances are received;				
6.		the dollars are sold to the central bank,			
7.		which issues marks to pay for them;			
8.			this again increases domestic circulation;		
9.				incomes and prices increase again;	
10.		the accumulated marks are used to buy dollars for loan repayment;			
11.	the dollar remittances for loan repayment use up the dollar balances.				

The two models show the sequences of events involved in the receipt of repayment of a *single* loan; thus there is only one payment in each case, not a series of payments. Regarding these "single-shot" models, we find that in all but the last of the five columns every movement has its counter-movement, every change is offset later by a change in the opposite direction. Thus the flow of foreign funds is countered by a back-flow (entries 1 and 11 in Model A, 5 and 11 in Model B); the exchange trans-actions of the central bank are offset by opposite operations at a later point (2 and 7 in Model A, and 6 and 10 in Model B); the changes in the domestic money supply are reversed before long (4 and 9 in Model A, 2 and 8 in Model B); and the movements of domestic incomes and prices are undone as a consequence of the reversal of the changes in circulation (5 and 10 in Model A, 3 and 9 in Model B). The movement of goods and services is the only one that is definitive, not offset or reversed by any counter-movement. The increase in imports (Model A) is the real and ultimate result of the receipt of the foreign loan, and the increase in exports (Model B) is the real and ultimate result of its repayment. (These commodity movements are, of course, only one-time events reflecting the one-time flow of funds. They are "ultimate" in the sense that the com-modities are received or given up for good, not that they continue forever; the import or export surpluses are temporary just as money supply, in-come, and prices are only temporarily increased or reduced.)

Although an increase in imports (and/or reduction of exports) is the ultimate result of the receipt of foreign loans, it is important to observe that it is by no means necessary that either the foreign lenders or the domestic borrowers have such a result in mind; no one connected with the arrangement, remittance, or receipt of the loans needs to have any thought of a movement of goods into the country receiving foreign loans. This change in the trade balance is the automatic end-effect which the au-tonomous capital movement produces through the increased supply of foreign exchange to the central bank and the resulting increase in domestic money circulation. The movement of foreign exchange can be regarded as the *intermediate step,* the change in domestic money circulation as the *motor-force,* and the movement of goods as the *ultimate result* of the capital transfer.

In the process of repayment of foreign loans the sequence of events would be exactly analogous to that in the process of receipt where gold was the medium of payment, both domestic and international. One and the same model would suffice to show payments in either direction. Under the gold-exchange standard, however, the model showing the process of receiving the loan (Model A) would apply to the process of repaying it only if the mark had the same status in international payments as the dollar. This assumption is not permissible if the foreign loans cannot be repaid in marks but must be repaid in dollars. Hence we need Model B to show how dollars become available for loan repayments even when no dollar balances are available at the outset.

For the sequence sketched in Model B we assume therefore—to make the solution of the problem as hard as possible—that Germany has no gold and no exchange reserve out of which repayments of foreign loans can be made. Under this assumption it is necessary to put the motor-force of the process, the automatic contraction of domestic circulation, at the beginning of the sequence of events. This contraction is neither a *deus ex machina* nor the product of a deliberately restrictive monetary policy; [13] it is brought about by individual debtors spontaneously preparing to repay their loans. In order to have their money ready on the day payment is due, they must for some time have limited their expenditures and accumulated a balance. This is how the reduction in domestic circulation and effective demand is brought about, a reduction which in turn causes the decrease in prices and incomes and the increase in exports of commodities (and securities). Thus, the preparation for repaying the loans automatically brings forth the foreign exchange with which to make the payments.

Let us recall that only *one* repayment, not a series of repayments, is shown in Model B. This explains why it displays the pairs of movement and counter-movement—the mutually offsetting changes in dollar flows, central-bank transactions, domestic circulation, and domestic incomes and prices. Only one of the changes is not offset: the goods that have gone out are not coming back; they reflect the "real" repayment of the loan. In a model sequence involving a *series* of repayments—for example, where loans were to be paid off in installments, or where different loans fell due successively, period after period—phases 1 to 6 of the second payment would coincide with phases 7 to 11 of the first payment, phases 1 to 6 of the third payment with phases 7 to 11 of the second, and so forth. As a result, the counter-movements in dollar flow, central-bank transactions, money supply, and income- and price-levels would be deferred until the entire series of repayments were coming to an end. In other words, domestic money circulation would stay down, and incomes and prices would remain at their reduced levels, during the whole period of loan repayment; and the export surplus would not be a one-time affair but would continue throughout that time.

The same remarks, *mutatis mutandis*, apply to the receipt of a series of loans. That is to say, domestic money circulation, incomes, and prices would remain at the higher levels, and the import surplus would continue, during the entire period of capital inflow.

[13] I should like to emphasize this point very strongly because my model has been criticized for its failure to include a "restriction of credit" among the assumptions. It is not necessary, however, to assume that the central bank institutes a restrictive policy; it suffices to assume that an expansion of credit is avoided. Since we are talking of an *automatic* contraction, one inherent in the system, no explicit assumption about the absence of an offsetting expansion of credit is required.

MONEY SUPPLY AND TRADE BALANCE

The role of the dollar as the medium, and therefore the intermediate step in the process of capital transfer, is usually correctly evaluated. After all, the inflows and outflows of dollars are too clearly visible to be missed. It is less well understood that in this process the dollar flow has the function of transmitting purchasing power. This transfer of purchasing power is crucial for any credit transaction. More often overlooked than recognized is the fact that the foreign loan, from the point of view of the economy as a whole, is actually utilized only when this purchasing power is exercised and results in an import of real goods. To repeat: the movement of goods is the sum and substance of the movement of capital. Receiving loans means more imports; repaying loans means more exports, with the movements of goods not a precondition but instead a consequence.

This is completely missed and misunderstood by all those economists who consider themselves certified balance-of-payments accountants but naively believe that one can project a balance of payments into the future or infer from the present state what the future state of the balance of payments will be. They all stare, as if hypnotized, at the large import surplus of today [1928], without which, they believe, the German economy cannot live. And then they raise the rhetorical question how, with such a deficit in the balance of payments, the nation can be expected to pay debts or reparations. Needless to say, if one takes the import surplus that has actually resulted from the receipt of foreign loans as given and unalterable, one can come to no other conclusion but that the repayment of the loans or the payment of reparations will be impossible. Only a handful of economists have seen the logical snare. The fallacy of the autonomy or independence of the balance of trade constitutes the fundamental defect in the naive balance-of-payments theory.

We have pointed to the flow of dollars as the intermediate step; to the movement of goods as the ultimate result; and to the change in domestic circulation as the motor-force of the international movement of capital. Domestic circulation is first expanded and then retracted in the course of the receipt of foreign loans. Conversely, effective circulation is first contracted and then again restored in the course of the repayment of foreign loans. But between the up and down in the domestic money flow lies the increase in imports; and between the down and up lies the increase in exports. It is through the motor-force of changes in domestic money circulation that the international flow of dollars is transformed into an international movement of goods. Under the present monetary system, the change in domestic money circulation is a necessary condition for the real consummation of foreign loans and loan repayments.

Under a different monetary system—a system with flexible foreign-exchange rates—changes in the exchange rates would take the place of changes in circulation. Incidentally, within the narrow limits of the fixed gold points, this also holds true for fixed exchange rates. Within these limits, changes in exchange rates act as the motor-force in that they make domestic prices higher or lower in terms of foreign currency. Insofar as this narrowly limited flexibility of rates is insufficient, the transfer process can work only by means of changes in domestic circulation. Those who believe in the maintenance of the gold standard or of stability of exchange rates should conscientiously eschew anything that may obstruct these important changes in circulation. Any such obstructions impede or render impossible the real use of foreign loans, in the one case, and their repayment, in the other.

This again has been misunderstood, particularly by Schacht. He dislikes the increase in circulation and regards it as inflation, and he dislikes the decrease in circulation and regards it as deflation. Changes in circulation in accordance with the currency principle have been similarly opposed in several countries engaged in the reform of their currencies. In Austria, for example, Dr. Spitzmüller, President of the central bank, condemned as "inflationary" the practice of the National Bank in 1924 of purchasing at fixed exchange rates all foreign currencies received through foreign loans. It was overlooked that such an increase in circulation differs from an ordinary inflation of credit and currency in that the real resources of foreign countries—a supply of foreign goods—stand behind the addition to the domestic supply of money.

How serious Schacht's opposition is to foreign-induced monetary expansion can be seen not only from his pronouncements but also from the policy of the German Reichsbank during recent years. In contrast to Ricardo's precept that central-bank management should refrain from passing judgment concerning the adequacy or inadequacy of domestic circulation so long as the gold par of exchange is maintained, Schacht has evidently made his computations and arrived at the judgment that the German money supply is large enough and ought not to be increased as a result of that "undesirable" inflow of foreign exchange. At one time he threatens to reduce domestic credit in order to offset any increase in circulation through the inflow of foreign currency.[14] At another time he tries to assert his control over the money market by competing with foreign loans through reducing the discount rate and increasing domestic credit.[15]

What are the implications of these measures? If the central bank,

[14] Schacht, *op. cit.*, p. 12. See also *Die Stabilisierung der Mark* (Stuttgart: Deutsche Verlags-Anstalt, 1927), p. 176.

[15] This was in fact the policy of the Reichsbank in the first half of 1923. See below.

instead of following the currency principle and of acting as an exchange-stabilization fund in the way shown in our model, reduces domestic credit to offset the effects of the increase in its foreign-exchange holdings, it prevents an increase in domestic circulation, incomes, and prices, and hence the increase in imports. In other words, it prevents the economy from obtaining the goods which foreign countries make available to it through their loans. The dollars, for example, instead of being used for buying goods from abroad, remain idle in the central bank's reserve. Then, of course, President Schacht can say, as he did on October 21, 1926, before the Committee on Inquiry (*Enqueteausschuss*): "We have no need for these reserves."

The second kind of counter-measure is more dangerous. If Schacht, in the name of fighting an "inflation" induced by foreign loans, promotes domestic credit creation, and thus tries to fight foreign-induced expansion by home-induced expansion, only one outcome can be expected: the effects upon domestic prices and incomes, the increased inducements to import from abroad, remain the same as in the case of foreign loans received and foreign exchange purchased by the central bank, but there will soon be difficulties in paying for the increased imports since people will demand from the central bank the foreign exchange the inflow of which has been warded off as a supposedly superfluous addition to reserves. The actual policy of the Reichsbank can serve here as the best illustration. Early in 1927 it undertook to discourage foreign loans and seek "closer contact" with the German money market by reducing the discount rate from 6 per cent to 5 per cent, after the previously existing preferential tax treatment for foreign lenders had already been abolished. Within five months the Reichsbank succeeded in increasing its domestic loans by 1,000 million Reichsmarks. During the same time it lost 1,000 million Reichsmarks worth of foreign exchange, with the result that the reserves fell below 40 per cent of circulation (account being taken of the Renten-banknotes in circulation). This development came to an end on the Black Friday of May 13, 1927, followed by the reinstitution of preferential tax treatment for foreign loans and, on June 10, by an increase in the discount rate.

A third form of sabotage against functional changes in domestic circulation is merely the counterpart of the first type of "offsetting" operation, but it is probably the most serious of all: sabotage of the contraction in circulation which ought to function as a motor-force in the process of repaying the foreign loans. This is "where we came in," as we set out to state Schacht's argument. Schacht is opposed to any decrease in domestic circulation, because it leads to "an insufficient supply of circulating media in our economy." [16] However, as we have seen, the will to repay foreign

---

[16] Schacht, *Eigene oder geborgte Währung*, p. 18.

loans must be reflected in a restraint on the part of the debt payer in using his purchasing power for other things, and hence in a decline in effective circulation. If one opposes this decline in domestic circulation, he opposes also getting hold of the needed foreign exchange. A policy of preventing a reduction in circulation is a policy of preventing the transfer. Any squeamishness about all this is out of place. Willingness to pay back the loans, which expresses itself in the self-denying withholding of purchasing power by those who have to make the payments, brings forth the foreign exchange needed for the transfer. Any central-bank policy motivated by sympathy for the suffering debt payers and by desire to create easier money can only disturb and impede the process.[17]

That the foreign exchange needed for the transfer has to be obtained through an increase of exports or a reduction of imports is generally realized. But most people fail to comprehend the interdependence of things, in particular, how the balance of trade can change from the present import surplus to an export surplus. Once we understand the working of our model, we accept it as evident that this change, the increased exports and/or reduced imports, will come about as a result of the preparations for making the foreign payments. Of course, only he who has the means can pay; he can prepare for payment only such amounts as he can obtain through reducing his expenditures or increasing his receipts, since the preparation for payment must involve a withholding of purchasing power. But if a soft-hearted central-bank policy undertakes to replace by domestic credit expansion[18] the purchasing power withheld, then the effective circulation and the cash balances of would-be buyers are not reduced and there will be no pressure upon incomes or prices, no tightening of the money market, no increase in exports, no reduction in imports—and no transfer.

THE TRANSFER OF REPARATIONS

It is interesting to note that the Dawes Plan provides for precisely this kind of sabotage of the transfer—moved evidently by pity for the people suffering a reduction in buying power. If not impeded, the transfer of reparations is accomplished by a process very similar to that involved in the transfer of loan repayments. This is shown in the model

[17] It is often said that central banks are unable to deny the increasing demands for bank credit when the time comes to repay foreign loans. This is a matter of policy. The central banks must avoid offsetting the decline of their foreign-exchange holdings by increases in their portfolio of domestic loans.

[18] As the money market gets tighter in the course of these events, greater demands will be made on the central bank's discount window if its bank rate is left unchanged. Bank managers must have enough backbone to leave unsatisfied any demand for credit that exceeds the previous volume of credit outstanding.

sequence presented below (Model C) for a single payment of reparations. The economy prepares for the payment by imposing taxes and depositing the tax revenues to the account of the Reparations Agent. Those who have paid the taxes are left with less money to make purchases of all sorts; active cash balances and effective circulation in the economy are reduced. As a result, disposable incomes and prices will be depressed, interest rates will be higher, foreign buyers for domestic products and domestic securities are attracted, and domestic purchases of foreign products and foreign securities are reduced. The end effect is that the foreign exchange will be forthcoming with which the Transfer Committee can make the reparations payment.

If, however, the Dawes Plan provides that funds deposited to the account of the Reparations Agent should, as soon as they exceed a certain amount, be reloaned to the German economy, it actually holds up the execution of the transfer. For, when the accumulated money balances are loaned to German borrowers, the decline in effective circulation is nullified and there will be no reduction of effective demand, no pressure on domestic prices, no tightening of the money market, no increase in exports, no decline in imports, and hence the foreign exchange needed for the transfer will not be forthcoming.

As long as the Reichsmark equivalent of the reparations payment can be collected through severe taxation of the German economy and as long as the funds so raised are blocked and kept out of effective circulation, the transfer will be possible. The motor-force of the process, the cancellation of domestic purchasing power, brings about the ultimate result, the increase in exports; and the medium for the foreign payment, the foreign exchange, is thereby procured "automatically," as it were. In other words, the transfer problem is solved once the budgetary problem—the problem of raising the domestic funds without resort to credit creation—is solved.

OBJECTIONS AND QUALIFICATIONS

This proposition, perhaps a little too apodictic in its formulation, is subject to a major objection by those who are inclined to reject it, and subject to cautious qualification by those who accept it. The reference is to the effect of trade barriers. The pure theory of automatic transfer (of amounts raised by cutting domestic spending) may be inapplicable in a real world addicted to protective tariffs, where the export surplus required to produce foreign exchange is prevented from emerging through import barriers raised by foreign countries.

The objection is serious and its implications are widely accepted as implacable and definitive. Parker Gilbert, the Reparations Agent, discussing the limitations of Germany's capacity to transfer reparations, declares:

MODEL C   *Sequence Analysis of the Process Involved in the Payment of Reparations*

	Flow of foreign funds	Sales and purchases of foreign exchange	Changes in domestic money circulation	Changes in domestic incomes and prices	Exports and imports of goods and services
1.		Taxes are collected and deposited on blocked accounts;			
2.			this reduces domestic circulation;		
3.				incomes and prices decrease;	
4.					this stimulates exports (and restrains imports);
5.	in payment for exports, dollar balances are received;				
6.		the dollars are sold to the central bank,			
7.		which issues marks to pay for them;			
8.			this again increases domestic circulation;		
9.				incomes and prices increase again;	
10.		the accumulated marks are used to buy dollars for reparations payments;			
11.	the dollar remittances for reparations payments use up the dollar balances.				

"To the extent that German exports are hindered by obstacles interposed from without, other countries must bear the responsibility" for restricting the possibilities of transfer.[19] The same point has been made by Keynes, Snowden, Stamp, and others, including, of course, many German writers and especially those who adhere to the balance-of-payments theory. But also those who accept the theorem of the automatic transfer of funds collected and withheld from domestic spending emphasize that the demands for reparations and the demands for protective tariffs in the recipient countries are incompatible.

Dr. Hans Simon, for example, attributes the existence of a transfer problem "solely" to the absence of free trade.[20] He recommends that loans from abroad be taken only for enterprises whose productive activities will eventually result in exports which foreign countries are prepared to buy and which, therefore, will provide the foreign exchange needed for loan repayments. Dr. Walter Sulzbach proposes a compromise to the effect that the amounts to be transferred be brought into relation with the tariff rates of the recipient countries. A formula should be sought under which the Reparations Agent each year would be allowed to transfer only a certain maximum amount determined in inverse proportion to the level of import duties.[21]

Certain tacit assumptions underlie these statements: it is assumed either that continual price deflation in the paying country is institutionally impossible, or that the import tariffs of all other countries are continually raised enough to offset any reductions of German export prices. These assumptions may well be warranted but should be made explicit.[22]

Let us first reexamine how things work out if wages and prices are flexible and if exports are not prevented from expanding; next we shall assume that effective tariff barriers prevent additional exports; and finally we shall drop the assumption of wage and price flexibility. We may again start from the sequence analysis presented in Model C but must bear in mind that, instead of the *single* payment considered in this model, we are now concerned with a continuing *series* of payments, that is, with new tax payments every period and thus with a new set of repercussions starting every period.

[19] S. Parker Gilbert, Agent General for Reparations Payments, in a "Memorandum for the German Government," dated October 20, 1927 and reproduced in *Report of the Agent General for Reparation Payments* (Berlin, December 10, 1927), p. 205.

[20] Hans Simon, "Bemerkungen über den Zusammenhang von Reparationen, Auslandsanleihen, Währungs-und Konjunkturpolitik," *Bank-Archiv*, Vol. XXVII, No. 6, (December 1927), p. 90.

[21] Walter Sulzbach, "Zum Transfer-Problem," *Der Deutsche Volkswirt*, June 17, 1927.

[22] This paragraph and the remaining ones of this essay replace a longer exposition in the original [1928] version, which, based on an assumption of perfect price and wage flexibility, presented the problem in an unduly contentious way.

As we have seen before, in a continuing series of payments the phases 1 to 6 of any installment coincide with phases 7 to 11 of a preceding installment, with the result that the deflationary effects of further tax collection will neutralize the reflationary effects of any export increase. Hence, domestic money circulation, incomes, and prices, all reduced by the preparation for paying the *first* installment of the reparations, will remain at the reduced level, and exports, if not fenced off by other countries, will continue at the increased level period after period.

How will the course of events be changed by the imposition of effective tariff increases in all foreign countries? Assume that every reduction in German export prices will be met by an equal increase in all foreign import tariffs. Obviously, in this case, the phases 4 to 11 of the model sequence cannot materialize, and the preparation for the first payment cannot produce the foreign exchange needed for the transfer, except insofar as German imports decline. The collections of the next period will generate another contraction of the money circulation and a further reduction of incomes and prices (phases 1 to 3) but, with another increase in all tariffs preventing any additional exports, the reflationary repercussions of such exports will again be omitted. Thus, every subsequent tax collection will have deflationary effects not offset by reflationary export increases. As long as the increases in foreign tariffs keep pace with the German price deflation caused by the continuing tax collections, the transfer will be limited to the size of such export surpluses as can be created through reductions in German imports.

Under the assumption of perfect wage and price flexibility, the unwillingness of foreign countries to accept additional German goods no matter how cheaply they are offered would, of course, frustrate the transfer of reparations, but there need be no reduction of real income produced by Germany. What is not exported—to pay for reparations—remains available to the German economy, though at ever-decreasing prices. German money wages would fall lower and lower, but real wages would be unaffected, since commodity prices would fall correspondingly. Now, as we drop the assumption of wage and price flexibility, we see a very different picture. For, in this case, the preparations for reparations payments, the tax collections deposited on blocked accounts, must lead to unemployment and reduced production. This, strangely enough, may improve the possibility of transferring some of the collected funds, because imports are liable to fall drastically. An impoverished people cannot help cutting down on their purchases from abroad. But even more important will be another consequence: the collection of funds for reparations payments would be impaired and may become impossible. In other words, the budgetary problem, soluble at full employment, may become insoluble under the circumstances.

Even apart from unemployment and reduced production, resulting from the combination of heavy taxes, wage rate inflexibility, and foreign import restrictions, the budgetary problem of the paying nation may become acute in another way. If the obstreperous tariff policies abroad prevent German exports from expanding, while the German money supply is allowed to run down mercilessly and German prices are depressed to lower and lower levels, a spread develops between the internal and external value of the Reichsmark, and it grows wider from day to day. With the reparations fixed in gold and the dollar fixed in Reichsmark, while the internal value—the commodity value—of the Reichsmark continually increases, the tax burden must become increasingly severe. Eventually the real tax burden becomes intolerable, and the further collection of taxes for reparations becomes impossible.

This analysis has led us to a surprising result in that it has shown that the failure to solve the transfer problem is apt to lead to a failure to cope with the budgetary problem,—provided the latter is defined as the collection of tax funds in the full amount of the obligations for reparations without the aid of any bank-credit expansion (or of any loans from funds earmarked for reparations). This reverses significantly the usual statements about the relationship between the budgetary problem and the transfer problem, whether they say that the solution of the former does *not* guarantee a solution of the latter, or whether they say that it *does*. I now submit that the successful raising of the domestic funds will as a rule lead to the possibility of transferring them but, where this is not so, the impossibility of transfer will eventually inhibit the further raising of the domestic funds. Thus, the two are, after all, closely linked with each other: either both problems are solved or neither.

XVII

Transfer and Price Effects

A Limiting Case ∎ Four Propositions: *The required reduction of prices; The low elasticities of demand for export goods; The required reduction of wages; The double burden upon incomes* ∎ The Loss of Money and the Loss of Goods ∎ Commodity Value of Reparations and the Terms of Trade ∎ Postscript after 33 Years

In his article under the same title, Haberler [1] comments on several points I made in my essay on the transfer problem.[2] I tried there to offer a schematic exposition of the processes in the international transfer of capital. I must admit that I am one of those who, despite Marshall's warning, sometimes attempt to compress a complicated problem (such as the transfer problem) into a "short statement" at the risk of furnishing a "fragment." Now I want to reexamine my fragmentary statement and see to what extent it was misleading.

A LIMITING CASE

I denied, in essence, that there is a transfer problem separate from and independent of the budgetary problem; Haberler recognizes that a transfer problem may remain even after the budgetary problem is solved. This may suggest that there are significant differences of opinion between Haberler and me. Fortunately, this is not the case, and Haberler's careful

[1] Gottfried Haberler, "Transfer und Preisbewegung," *Zeitschrift für Nationalökonomie*, Vol. I (1930), pp. 547-554.

[2] Fritz Machlup, "Währung und Auslandsverschuldung," *Mitteilungen des Verbandes österreichischer Banken und Bankiers,* Vol. X (1928), pp. 195-208; reproduced in a revised English version as Chapter XVI in this volume.

way of expression averts any danger of my rushing into a battle against windmills. As a matter of fact, the only difference between us is that I failed to consider an imaginatively constructed "limiting case" which does pose a well-nigh insoluble transfer problem. It is the special case of a country with a single export good, the foreign demand for which has an elasticity of one or less than one.

Such a country would have to have some additional and rather subtle characteristics. A good, after all, is not inherently, not by its nature, an export good; it may be *not* exportable today but exportable tomorrow. The limiting case, however, must not permit this. It must either presuppose that the consumption habits of the people in the particular country are completely different from those of all other peoples in the world or, a little more simply, stipulate a complete embargo on all potential exports except the one privileged export article with the unfortunate elasticity. In addition to the embargo on exports, there must be a ban on foreign tourists coming to this particular country, so that the possibility of invisible exports is also excluded. Now even I must admit that this unfortunate country could not escape a transfer crisis.

As a thorough scholar striving for completeness and precision, Haberler deals with this limiting case, put forth by Keynes; but, unlike Keynes, he repeatedly emphasizes how extremely inprobable it is that such conditions would ever exist. Yet, since he agrees with Keynes that actual conditions may *approach* the limiting case (although he does not believe that even this applies to the situation existing in Germany today), we shall attempt to reappraise objections directed against the transfer optimists.

Four propositions

Even after the assumptions described above as unlikely are dropped, the following circumstances, stressed in Keynes' theory,[3] remain to be considered:

1. that prices of export goods in the paying country would have to drop very sharply in order to bring about an increase in exports;

2. that even large price reductions may, because of the low demand elasticities ascribed to the export articles, lead only to an increase in the physical volume of exports but not to the required increase in the foreign value of the export surplus;

3. that the required reductions in export prices may hardly be practicable since they would presuppose substantial reductions in costs, especially reductions in wage rates; and

4. that the required pressure on wages and prices cannot be expected

[3] In the article cited in footnote 9.

as an automatic consequence of the collection of taxes for reparations, but must be accomplished by means of additional reductions in real income.

These four propositions will now be examined in turn.

The required reduction of prices

One school of thought (Wheatley [4]–Ricardo [5]–Ohlin [6]) denies that prices must fall; another school of thought (Thornton [7]–Mill [8]–Keynes [9]) holds that a reduction of prices is indispensable for the transfer to be accomplished. This conflict can be decided by pointing to another "limiting case," which is easily conceivable: the case in which the contraction of purchasing power in the paying country and the expansion of purchasing power in the receiving country result in decreases and increases, respectively, in the demand for the same goods.

Haberler overestimates, in my opinion, the distance of such an assumption from conditions prevalent in reality when he holds that this limiting case, so favorable for the automatic solution of the transfer problem, is almost equally improbable as the Keynesian limiting case, under which transfer becomes impossible. It does not strain one's imagination to suppose that the goods given up as "least important" by consumers in the paying country, that is, the goods which buyers with reduced disposable incomes can no longer afford to buy, are of the same kind as the goods which buyers with increased incomes can now afford to buy. I do not think it is at all essential that these goods have previously been export commodities, though this, for some reason, is usually assumed. They may just as well have been import commodities, or commodities which previously have not entered into foreign trade.

[4] John Wheatley, *Remarks on Currency and Commerce* (London: Cadell and Davies, 1803), pp. 52-57; *An Essay on the Theory of Money and Principles of Commerce* (London: Cadell and Davies, 1807), Vol. I, pp. 64-71, Vol. II, pp. 134-135; *Report on the Reports of the Bank Committees* (Shrewsbury: Eddowes, 1819), pp. 20-29.

[5] David Ricardo, *The High Price of Bullion, A Proof of the Depreciation of Bank Notes* (London: Murray, 1810; 4th ed., 1811); reprinted in *The Works of David Ricardo*, ed. by J. M. McCulloch (London: Murray, 1846), pp. 268-269 and 291 ff.

[6] Bertil Ohlin, "The Reparations Problem," *Economic Journal*, Vol. XXXIX (June 1929), pp. 172-178; reprinted in American Economic Association, *Readings in the Theory of International Trade* (Philadelphia: Blakiston, 1949), pp. 170-178.

[7] Henry Thornton, *An Inquiry into the Nature and Effects of the Paper Credit of Great Britain* (London: Hatchard, 1802), pp. 131-132.

[8] John Stuart Mill, "On the Laws of Interchange Between Nations," in his *Essays on Some Unsettled Questions of Political Economy* (London: 1844), reprinted by the London School of Economics (1948), pp. 1-46; *Principles of Political Economy* (First edition 1848, Ashley edition, London: Longmans, 1926), Book III, Chapter XXI, pp. 619-628.

[9] John Maynard Keynes, "The German Transfer Problem," *Economic Journal*, Vol. XXXIX (March 1929), pp. 1-7; reprinted in American Economic Association, *Readings in the Theory of International Trade* (Philadelphia: Blakiston, 1949), pp. 161-169.

It should be admitted, nevertheless, that in the most likely situations price changes will be needed to bring about an export surplus, and indeed the emphasis in the model analysis presented in my previous essay was upon the price effects.

The low elasticities of demand for export goods

It is good practice to think through a problem from all possible suppositions and assumptions; but it is important to ask how probable it is that the factual assumptions, the consequences of which are analyzed, will actually prevail in the real world. As Haberler shows, it is altogether improbable that a country exporting a large variety of goods will ever find the demand for a considerable part of its "actual and potential export commodities" to be of elasticities of one or less than one. Haberler also observes, very much to the point, that for the demand curve to have this property is even more unlikely in the case of a country competing with other export nations in the world market, than it might be in the case of a country exporting goods as the sole producer in the world. We must not, moreover, overlook that, as Ohlin stresses, the demand functions of the receiving countries, as a result of their increased buying power, undergo significant shifts, which make the elasticities of the previous demand quite irrelevant. It is precisely these shifts of the demand curves which, in the most favorable case discussed above, may create the opportunity for additional exports without the necessity of a reduction of export prices.

The required reduction of wages

To the extent that the improvement on the merchandise balance *cannot* be achieved through an increase in the foreign demand for exports from the paying country or through a decrease in this country's demand for imports, but has to be brought about the hard way, that is, through reductions of export prices and (more than proportionate) increases in export quantities, reductions of production cost will indeed be required. Except for certain shapes of the cost curves (which are conceivable, though it is hardly permissible to assume they are prevalent) the required reductions of costs cannot, by and large, be expected without wage reductions. The transfer optimists are in full agreement with the transfer pessimists that there is a need for wages (that is, in Keynes' words, for the "gold-rates of efficiency wages") in the paying country to lag behind those of other countries. The transfer optimists, however, take the view that extracting the domestic funds for foreign payments—the pressure implied in the taxation for reparations—will automatically tend to depress wages. Thus, the lowering of incomes, including wage incomes, is not, as others believe, any particular action or measure that must be taken in order to increase exports and effect the transfer, but is rather the direct consequence of the budgetary operations, the collection of taxes.

The double burden upon incomes

That the taxes which extract the funds for reparations payments out of the pockets of the people represent a burden on income and, consequently, a forced decrease in expenditures, is recognized by Keynes. He maintains, however, that for the transfer to be effected an extra burden, a second reduction in real income independent of the first, will be required. Only this additional pressure can create the export surplus. (That Keynes has the "first" and "second" reductions of income in reverse order is irrelevant.) He does not specify in what way, apart from the collection of taxes, real wages are to be cut a second time. Apparently he sees no easily practicable way and, for that reason, doubts altogether that the transfer will be possible. Haberler suggests that the additional pressure to achieve the transfer might come from a (possibly necessary) credit restriction by the central bank. He thus shares Keynes' view that the pressure on income from raising the funds for reparations does not automatically create the possibility of their transfer; and that, therefore, a "second" pressure or additional burden may be required.

I thought I succeeded in showing in my previous essay that this was not so. Perhaps I should attempt to present my argument with greater clarity.

The loss of money and the loss of goods

It is argued that despite the collection of taxes for reparations and the consequent reduction of domestic effective demand the transfer may be impossible because the export surplus that would provide the required foreign exchange cannot be produced. In order to make this statement more plausible and, at the same time, to resolve a further problem, we shall make the assumption that a general increase in all foreign tariffs prevents the increase in exports. In order to exclude other ways of obtaining the foreign exchange needed for the transfer, we shall assume further that there are no securities, long-term or short-term, which foreign capitalists may want to purchase and, finally, that imports cannot decline —either because there have not been any or because both price elasticities and income elasticities of demand for imports are zero. Thus, by excluding reductions in commodity imports and increases in capital imports, and by assuming increases in foreign tariffs, we have set up the worst imaginable conditions for our problem.

Reparations are not paid in one shot but rather in a series of installments, recurring period after period. Assume that the collection of domestic funds for the first installment has been successful and the Reichsmarks raised have been deposited and earmarked for transfer. The consequent reduction in domestic money incomes—buying power, money circulation, or disposable liquid balances (depending on which terminology you may prefer)—depresses prices; but, owing to the increase in foreign tariffs, the domestic price reduction fails to induce additional exports and, thus, to produce foreign exchange. Hence, despite the solution of the budgetary problem, despite the tax burden and the downward pressure upon prices, the transfer of the first installment has been frustrated.

What is usually overlooked, however, is that this burden, in the absence of an increase in exports, is only a loss of money income, not of real income (provided wage rates are sufficiently flexible). The country has not suffered a loss of real resources, but only a contraction in its money circulation. A deflation may of course be most unpleasant, but need not cause any losses in production if wages and prices are not sticky. Hence, there is no real burden, no real curtailment of domestic consumption and investment, so long as there is no increase in exports. The reduced money incomes can purchase at reduced prices an undiminished real output.

Is it perhaps at this point that some deliberate measure must be taken to force a "second" cut-back in income? No indeed. Without any special policy or new action, the raising of domestic funds goes on and on the next pay day, when income taxes are withheld, and on the next date when other taxes are due, the same process—with another contraction of money circulation and another decrease in prices—is repeated. Can we assume that the whole world will raise tariff walls every few weeks in order to offset the deflation of money circulation and prices that comes with each payment of reparation taxes? To assume this would not be reasonable; the continuing siphoning out of domestic buying power through periodic collection of taxes and the blocking of the tax revenues for reparations payments constitute a kind of "dumping" [10] for which no ordinary policy of tariff raising can be a match. And, let us bear in mind, it is only with the eventual increase in exports—only when the so-called improvement in the balance of trade is achieved—that the "first" *real* burden is imposed on the *real* income of the paying country. A "second" burden, an "additional" curtailment of German real incomes, is not necessary; the eventual successful transfer is the "first" sacrifice of real resources and, when it comes about, it will still be the consequence of nothing but the extraction of domestic funds for reparations payments, not of any other government measures. [11]

[10] This is "dumping" only in a loose, though widely used, sense. It is not dumping in the strict sense of setting export prices lower than prices for domestic sales.

[11] Perhaps we should restate the assumptions on which these conclusions are based: (a) perfect flexibility of wage rates and prices, (b) absence of domestic credit expansion to aid the payment of the taxes, (c) absence of domestic credit expansion to offset the contraction of money circulation, (d) absence of domestic loans from the funds accumulated on the accounts of the Reparations Agent. [Added in 1963.]

COMMODITY VALUE OF REPARATIONS AND THE TERMS OF TRADE

Because of the retardation of the transfer, because of the fact that sharp increases in foreign tariffs have to be overcome by an even sharper deflation of domestic prices, a significant relationship is altered: although the external value (exchange rate) of the Reichsmark has remained unchanged, its internal value (commodity value) has increased. The lag of the transfer behind the raising of the domestic funds, caused by the mischievous increase in foreign tariffs, forces the paying nation to pay the fixed *money* reparations by means of increased *real* reparations. Thus the burden of the reparations, fixed in terms of gold or dollars, becomes heavier in real terms; it may even become unbearable, and thus may jeopardize the possibility of continuing to collect the required taxes.

The difference between Keynes' view and the one set forth here is perhaps not so great as it may appear at first blush. There is some kinship between the notion of a "worsening of the terms of trade" for the paying country and my concept of "increased reparations in real terms"; and thus it is possible that the controversy about the transfer problem is due partly to terminological misunderstandings. Terminological variances are indicated by the fact that Haberler sees the danger of "transfer difficulties" at one point in wage disputes, at another point in budget difficulties, but also uses the term "transfer loss," evidently the same as my increase in reparations in real terms, interchangeably with "transfer difficulties." All these meanings of "transfer difficulties" are quite different from the most common one: since "transfer" means, to most people, the conversion of the accumulated domestic money into foreign currency, "transfer difficulties" should logically be understood as a lack of the foreign exchange needed for the conversion.

The majority of transfer pessimists expect the transfer crisis to appear in the form of a shortage of foreign exchange. I do not assume that this is what Keynes had in mind. We should ask of him, and of the other theorists who support his thesis, a clean distinction and clarification of the concepts involved. Otherwise it is possible for the devotees of the most primitive misunderstandings to appeal successfully to the authority of the best minds in economic theory.

POSTSCRIPT AFTER 35 YEARS

The terminological clarification asked for in this brief essay has never been provided, although the theoretical analysis of the transfer problem has been greatly advanced in the intervening years. I shall undertake the semantic task and add a few other reflections in a separate essay, entitled "The Transfer Problem Revisited" (Chapter XIX).

At this point, however, I admit to some embarrassment about the excessive orthodoxy in my analysis of the transfer problem in 1928 and 1930. Not that the assumption of perfect flexibility of wage rates is *per se* inappropriate or indefensible; but to assert propositions inferred from this assumption as apodictic verities with immediate applicability to a concrete historical situation, or even to policy recommendations, is surely illegitimate. A few of my transgressions along these lines have been omitted or mitigated in my translation for the present volume, but I have allowed enough of them to stand in order to avoid false pretensions regarding my performance of earlier years. By too much retouching, stressing the correct predictions or anticipations, and glossing over the wrong ones, a "reproduction" of old writings may give an exaggerated impression of the writer's wisdom or prescience. There is more justification for reproducing old articles in order to show the development of ideas over time than there is to establish priorities or prove precocity.

My failure, 35 years ago, to recognize the problems of price and income deflation was quite typical of many, perhaps most, economists of the period who had observed the ravages of inflation but had no firsthand experience of the evils of deflation. Since, moreover, the received system of economic theory had been based on the assumption of competitive markets, in which prices always moved to equilibrate supply and demand, a condition of irreducible or pressure-resistant wage rates appeared as an anomaly not calling for an extensive remodeling of economic theory. This may explain, though not excuse, my disregard, in 1928 and 1930, of most of the real-income losses that may be associated with deflation.

XVIII

The Transfer Problem:
Income Effects and Price Effects

The Assumptions ■ The Transferable Portion of the Levy without Price Effects ■ Alternative Routes from Here On

The transfer problem is, in briefest form, the following: If a country
is capable of raising, out of the given domestic income flow, the funds
needed for the payments to foreign nations, will the transfer of these
funds be trammeled or precluded sooner or later by a lack of foreign
exchange?

THE ASSUMPTIONS

The problem, unfortunately, was not quite so clearly formulated in
the beginning. The presupposition, that the funds are raised in the paying
country so as to reduce disbursements for consumption and home investment, was not always explicitly stated. Undoubtedly, if no reduction of
primary disbursements and incomes were brought about in the paying
country, and no increase in disbursements in the receiving countries
either, then the transfer problem would be hopeless from the beginning.
If the fulfillment of the obligations to foreign nations is taken seriously at
all, then the successful reduction of domestic purchasing power must be
an unshakeable postulate.

On the other hand, the expansion of disbursements and incomes in
the receiving countries cannot be relied upon. Hence, if one wishes to
analyze the problem first on the basis of the least favorable assumptions,
he will have to assume that disbursements in the receiving countries
remain unchanged, while disbursements in the paying country are reduced
by the full amount of the fixed obligations.

The next question then is how much of an adjustment of the trade balance can be expected under the assumed circumstances to result from income effects alone. The paying country probably has some stock of gold or foreign exchange to start with. But for a continuous transfer, to be maintained period after period, year after year, only an export surplus can provide the necessary foreign exchange.[1] In general, the export surplus can be created through income effects, price effects, and exchange-rate effects.[2] Exchange-rate effects are definitely ruled out as incompatable with the postulate of stable currencies. Price effects are provisionally ruled out, that is, stable prices are assumed, so that we can isolate the income effects and thereby see what portion of the "levy" can be produced in foreign funds without any change in the net barter terms of trade.

By the term "the levy" we designate the reduction of disbursements for consumption and home investment in the paying country, a reduction which is assumed to be equal to the imposed obligations to foreign nations. For the sake of simplicity we shall assume that it is a reduction in domestic investment in country A, and shall denote it by $-I_A$. In the receiving country, B, home investment, as we have decided before, is unchanged: $I_B = 0$. No third country exists in our model. There will be four crucial parameters in the story: the marginal propensities to save, s_A and s_B, and the marginal propensities to import, m_A and m_B. Changes in incomes, relative to the base period, that is, before any levy is raised, will be denoted by Y_A and Y_B; and the ultimate changes (when the adjustments are completed) by $Y_{A,\infty}$ and $Y_{B,\infty}$.

Now, given $-I_A$, s_A, m_A, s_B, and m_B, what will be the ratio between the eventually resulting change in the trade balance, $m_B Y_{B,\infty} - m_A Y_{A,\infty}$, and the levy, $-I_A$?

THE TRANSFERABLE PORTION OF THE LEVY WITHOUT PRICE EFFECTS

We may use the formulas (41) and (42) developed for the home-investment multipliers involving two countries.[3] Taking into account that $I_B = 0$, we may write

[1] An inflow of loans and investments from abroad may take the place of an export surplus. In the case of Germany this actually happened. The Germans received more foreign loans than they paid reparations.

[2] Besides these three, there may be a primary investment effect. Reduced investments in the paying country may involve a reduced import demand for investment (construction) purposes; increased investments in the receiving country may involve an increased import demand for investment (construction) purposes. The former result leads to reduced imports, the latter to increased exports of the paying country. Although we choose to rule out these primary investment effects upon foreign trade in our analysis, they still operate in reality.

[3] Fritz Machlup, *International Trade and the National Income Multiplier* (1st ed., Philadelphia: Blakiston, 1943; 3rd printing, New York: Augustus M. Kelley, 1961), pp. 175-176.

$$(46) \qquad Y_{A,\,\infty} = I_A \frac{s_B + m_B}{(s_A + m_A)\,(s_B + m_B) - m_A m_B},$$

and

$$(47) \qquad Y_{B,\,\infty} = I_A \frac{m_A}{(s_A + m_A)\,(s_B + m_B) - m_A m_B}.$$

Hence, the eventual export surplus of A,

$$(48) \qquad m_B Y_{B,\,\infty} - m_A Y_{A,\,\infty} = I_A \frac{-s_B m_A}{(s_A + m_A)\,(s_B + m_B) - m_A m_B}.$$

For the portion which the export surplus is of the levy we obtain

$$(49) \qquad \frac{m_B Y_{B,\,\infty} - m_A Y_{A,\,\infty}}{-I_A} = \frac{s_B m_A}{s_A s_B + s_A m_B + s_B m_A}.$$

In this fraction the denominator exceeds the numerator by $s_A(s_B + m_B)$. If m_B is the marginal propensity of the rest of the world to import from country A, then it will surely be negligible. Thus, it is $s_A s_B$ which reduces the transfer possibilities created through income effects.

If s_A, the marginal propensity to save in the paying country is zero, the denominator becomes equal to the numerator, and an export surplus equal to the levy will develop. In plain words this means: if the decline in income does not lead to an induced reduction in savings in the paying country, then income will continue to decline until a sufficient export surplus is created (in spite of somewhat declining exports) [4] simply through induced reduction of imports.

Nobody will contend that this is a very hopeful or desirable state of affairs. Yet, one must insist that in this case the transfer problem is "solved" completely, in that one hundred per cent of the "levy" becomes available in foreign exchange derived from an induced export surplus. In actual fact, however, this solution of the transfer problem would possibly be identical with a breakdown of the budgetary problem of "internal collection." That is to say, it would become impossible to raise by means of taxation the necessary funds to meet the obligations; domestic funds would be lacking, not foreign exchange. The national income—money income being a perfect measure of real income since all prices are by assumption unchanged—might be so much reduced that the required funds could no longer be extracted from the impoverished population. Those who denied the existence of an independent transfer problem

---

[4] If m_B is zero, exports remain at their level. But if m_B is anything above zero, the reduction in foreign income, which follows from the diminished imports of the paying country, must somewhat reduce foreign purchases from the paying country.

would, in this case, be vindicated: the transfer problem would be "automatically" solved to the same extent to which the budgetary problem could be solved.

So much about the case where s_A is zero. If the marginal propensity to save is not zero in the paying country, so that induced reductions in saving arrest the decline in income, then only less than one hundred per cent of the levy can be produced in foreign means of payment with unchanged terms of trade. The ratio of the induced export surplus to the levy will depend (assuming that m_B is negligible) on the magnitude of $s_A s_B$ in relation to the magnitude of $s_B m_A$, or, that is, on the relative sizes of s_A and m_A. The larger m_A in relation to s_A, the greater the portion of the levy which becomes available in foreign funds. If s_A and m_A are equal, one half the levy becomes transferable without resort to gold stocks and without the need of price changes.

To express it somewhat more exactly, we may state that, if the marginal propensity of the rest of the world to import from country A is negligible, i.e., if $m_B = 0$, formula (49) becomes

$$(50) \qquad \frac{m_B Y_{B,\,\infty} - m_A Y_{A,\,\infty}}{-I_A} = \frac{s_B m_A}{s_A s_B + s_B m_A},$$

which is equal to $\dfrac{m_A}{s_A + m_A}$ or $\dfrac{1}{\dfrac{s_A}{m_A} + 1}$.

The common sense of it is this: The export surplus without price changes (and without foreign income expansion) can be created only through a fall in imports. Hence, the greater the marginal propensity to import, the greater will be the transferable portion of the levy. The greater the marginal propensity to save, the smaller will be the transferable portion of the levy, but the smaller will be also the secondary decline in income that results from the levy, i.e., from the reduction in primary disbursements.

Alternative routes from here on

Although this is about all that multiplier analysis has to contribute to the setting of the transfer problem of unilateral payments, it would hardly be excusable to leave the subject at this point, without any send-off or suggestions as to where to go from here.

It is a matter of taste whether we drop first the assumption that prices remain unchanged or whether we choose as our next step to allow foreign disbursements to increase. The one alternative would add price effects—changes in the terms of trade—to the income effects operating in the paying country, but would not yet allow changes in demand in the receiving country. The other alternative would add income effects in the receiving country to those in the paying country, but would not yet allow changes in relative prices and their effects on trade.[5]

If the second alternative is preferred, we need merely refer to some cases of my Model X, showing the effects of inverse changes in investments in two countries.[6] Tables X-a, X-b, X-d, and X-f would all be possible variations of the transfer case, with fully effective levy in the paying country and either full or only part-way expansion of disbursements in the receiving country. The transferable portion of the levy was 75 per cent and over, in the first three of the four cases, but only some 42 per cent in the case described in Table X-f. In no case did the export surplus which could be achieved merely through income effects reach the full amount of the levy.[7] Only in case IX-a was a one-hundred per cent transfer possible, because of zero marginal propensities to save.[8]

If one follows the first alternative rather than the second, and looks into price effects while leaving primary disbursements in the receiving country unchanged, he is more in line with our original intention to analyze the problem on the basis of the least favorable assumptions.

Changes in prices are fairly certain to occur when incomes change. About the likelihood and the extent of such price changes I may refer to the chapter entitled "Apologies and Confessions" of my book on the multiplier,[9] in which I explain why multiplier theory would be useless if direct applicability were required of it. At this point we simply take it for granted that in our case of an income reduction—both primary and

[5] Readers versed in the literature of the field will recognize in the choice between the alternatives the main issues of the transfer controversy of the late 1920's and early 1930's. It was Lord Keynes who concentrated on the price effects and refused to consider income effects in the receiving country.—J. M. Keynes, "The German Transfer Problem," *Economic Journal*, Vol. 39 (1929), p. 1; "A Rejoinder," *ibid.*, p. 179; "A Reply," *ibid.*, p. 404. It was Professor Ohlin who concentrated on the income effects in both countries and minimized the price effects.—Bertil Ohlin, "Transfer Difficulties, Real and Imagined," *Economic Journal*, Vol. 39 (1929), p. 172; "Mr. Keynes' Views on the Transfer Problem," *ibid.*, p. 400

[6] Fritz Machlup, *op. cit.*, pp. 160-171. The tables referred to in the next sentences are also on the cited pages.

[7] If there are primary investment effects, e.g., if the receiving country buys from the paying country equipment or materials needed for increased investment, the final export surplus will be greater, although the income effects will of course be smaller.

[8] Lloyd A. Metzler demonstrates cases where full transfer is achieved merely through income effects in spite of positive saving propensities. But Metzler reaches his conclusions only by assuming a marginal propensity to invest which raises the marginal propensity to spend to a figure equal to or in excess of 1. In other words, the marginal propensity to invest which Metzler assumes in the particular cases offsets or overcompensates the marginal propensity to save. See Lloyd A. Metzler, "The Transfer Problem Reconsidered," *The Journal of Political Economy*, Vol. L (1942), pp. 397-414.

[9] *International Trade and the National Income Multiplier*, especially pp. 202-211.

secondary (and also tertiary if the banking system restricts credit when its reserves dwindle [10])—prices are liable to fall. The effects of this price fall may be felt in exports or imports or in both. For some reason, the effects upon exports are usually, in discussions of the problem, given much more attention than the effects upon imports.

The price effects upon exports are discussed in terms of the elasticity of foreign demand for the products and services of the paying country. Should this elasticity be less than unity—with foreign incomes assumed not to be expanded—the total value of exports would fall rather than rise in consequence of the price reductions. This "possibility" was the quintessence of the pessimistic transfer theories of Lord Keynes and his followers. The degree of probability that the foreign demand for the products of the paying country should, in actual fact, fail to be elastic was not examined with sufficient care. This probability, as I have pointed out elsewhere, is not great. Firstly, one must consider that of the various exports of the paying country not all are likely to be a large share of the world supply of the goods in question; thus, even if the total demand for certain goods is inelastic, the demand for the particular product of one country in competition with the same (similar) products of all other countries is apt to be elastic, perhaps even *very* elastic. Secondly, one must bear in mind that not only actual export articles but also potential export articles count when the possibilities of an increase of exports are scanned; the elasticity of foreign demand for a good of which nothing has been exported hitherto, may be "infinity"—that is to say, a small price reduction may make the good exportable.

So much concerning price-induced exports. What about the probability of a price-induced fall in imports? The prices of import articles are not changed, for it was assumed that no expansion of foreign incomes occurs. The reduction of imports through the domestic fall of incomes has already been fully accounted for. But there is yet another force reducing the domestic demand for imports: price reductions of domestic goods. We know that large groups of goods (groups—rather than particular goods) are always competing, not complementary, with one another.[11] Thus, that the mass of domestic goods and services is competing with the mass of imported ones is undoubted. Therefore, if prices of domestic goods and services fall, substitutions of domestic for foreign goods will

[10] It has become customary to call the reserve-induced expansion or contraction of bank credit the "secondary" expansion or contraction. See, among others, Jacob Viner, *Studies in the Theory of International Trade* (New York: Harper, 1937), p. 395. However, since we have used the term secondary for those income changes which arise in connection with the re-spending (failure to spend) consequent upon the increase (decrease) of primary disbursements, we must demote the bank-induced changes in disbursements and income to the rank of tertiary changes.

[11] J. R. Hicks, *Value and Capital* (Oxford, 1939), p. 50.

take place. At the changed relative prices, the total (and average) propensity to import cannot remain at its former level, that is to say, we must expect a price-induced fall in imports on top of the income-induced fall in imports.

Of course, incomes will not fall as much as they would in the absence of price changes. For, after all, the sequence of income reductions and the eventual income level depend, among other things, upon the development of foreign trade. If price-induced improvements of the trade balance appear in the picture, the fall in incomes will be stopped at an earlier point. This means also that the income-induced fall in imports, if accompanied by a price-induced fall in imports, will not be as heavy as it would be without price changes. But the two together will certainly be much heavier than one alone. Hence, with the fall in domestic prices, the arising export surplus will be greater, and the income decline smaller, than was shown before in my Model X. If all three factors—income-induced fall in imports, price-induced fall in imports, and price-induced increase in exports—are pulling together, it is not impossible that one-hundred per cent of the levy can be transferred without too much of a secondary income contraction in the paying country.

Should now also the conditions abroad be less adverse than was assumed, in that expansions of primary disbursements in the receiving countries take place, then there is still less ground for a "pessimistic" transfer theory. With income expansions abroad, a foreign-induced increase in exports will join the other three factors which have just been named as the forces combining in the creation of an export surplus for the paying country. Should price effects in the income-expanding, receiving countries also join in, so that the price-induced improvements of the trade balance of the paying country can become that much greater, any remaining reason for transfer pessimism will be displaced by very comforting thoughts. It may become quite possible that the ultimate income reduction in the paying country is less than the levy—see, for instance, Table X-d [12]—and at the same time, the export surplus, with the aid of price effects, equal to, or above, the levy. And if the price changes are of a peculiar type,[13] the barter terms of trade may be improved rather than deteriorated.

This is not the place to expatiate on these points. We leave the subject

---

[12] Machlup, *op. cit.*, p. 166.

[13] Haberler pointed out, as early as 1930, that the commodity terms of trade of the paying country may be improved as a result of the payments. This would happen if the reduced buying power of the people in the paying country resulted chiefly in a reduction of their demand for imports, while the increase in buying power of the people in the receiving country resulted chiefly in an increase in their demand for the products of the paying country. See Gottfried Haberler, "Transfer und Preisbewegung," *Zeitschrift für Nationalökonomie*, Vol. I (1930), pp. 547 ff.

with the conclusions that there is no *a priori* reason for believing the transfer problem to be a very grave or even insoluble one; that an expansion of primary disbursements in the receiving countries can do much to remove or ease all transfer difficulties; and that flexibility of prices, and particularly of costs, can greatly alleviate the squeeze in the paying country.

XIX

The Transfer Problem Revisited

A Restatement of the Problem ▪ A Semantic Analysis ▪
Transfer under Conditions of Growth ▪ Leave-taking

A murderer returns to the scene of his crime; a sentimentalist revisits the places in which he has experienced great happiness; and a scholar goes back to problems he has worked on in the past—and finds there is more work to do. Criminal, sentimentalist, or scholar, I feel compelled once more to deal with the transfer problem, after my "classical" pieces of 1928 and 1930, my "modern" model of 1943, and my historical essay of 1963. That the problem is not out of date should be clear to all who have observed the transfer problem of the United States in recent years.

I shall begin with another restatement of the problem, which, hopefully, will allow us to rise from a state of primitive confusion to "confusion on a higher level." I shall then proceed to a semantic analysis, a task I called for in my 1930 essay (Chapter XVII of this volume). And I shall conclude with suggestions of expansions of the existing models to equip them for incorporation of assumptions regarding economic growth.

A RESTATEMENT OF THE PROBLEM

If country A is supposed to pay to country B an amount of x dollars per period—as debt repayment, reparations payment, grant, loan, or investment—and accordingly reduces its domestic disbursements by this amount, may one confidently expect that its trade balance will become more positive (less negative) by x dollars and provide the foreign exchange needed for the payment? This looks like a straightforward statement of the transfer problem. But as soon as we start asking a few pertinent questions, matters become blurred.

433

What assumptions are appropriate concerning primary disbursements [1] in the receiving country? Can an expansion of disbursements in B take the place of a contraction in A? May we legitimately speak of a transfer problem if disbursements in A are not reduced by x dollars, but only by less, or not at all, or are even increased? Can one properly say that the budgetary problem in A has been solved if tax payments have been facilitated by credit expansion, or if a contraction of the money supply has been offset by bank credit? If government lacks the courage or the callousness to insist on the reduction of effective demand in the paying country, is this a transfer problem or a budgetary problem? Is it an economic or a political problem?

Any answers to these questions will depend partly on terminological decisions and will therefore be arbitrary to some degree. Strictly speaking, we have no right and no reason to expect an improvement of A's trade balance that will permit the required transfer if there is neither an increase in disbursements in B nor a decrease in disbursements in A. In a way, one may find it a little disingenuous to speak of a transfer problem when A, the paying country, has no intention to cut its domestic spending by the amount it is obligated to pay to B. Under certain conditions, particularly in the context of economic growth, one may relent and grant that a "smaller than otherwise warranted" expansion of domestic disbursements may be equivalent to an absolute curtailment of domestic disbursements in the absence of growth.

As a matter of fact, all historical situations in which "transfer problems" arose were characterized by expansions, not contractions, of domestic demand—although the theoretical discussions always started from the assumption that the domestic funds set aside for transfer had been successfully "extracted out of the pockets of the people" (as Keynes put it). Thus, from the very beginning, the theory of the transfer and the identification of historical transfer problems were at odds with each other, and many writers were lacking in candor when they were diagnosing "transfer difficulties," although the budgetary problem had not been solved and no solution had even been attempted. (The possible reconciliation through explicit references to economic growth did not occur to any of the earlier writers on the subject.)

The budgetary problem—the domestic stinting, which is a test of the genuine willingness to make the foreign payment—is often difficult to solve. In the case of governmental payments (foreign loans, grants,

---

[1] Positive primary disbursements are new additions to the income stream, in contrast to secondary disbursements by income recipients who re-spend some or all that they have received. Secondary disbursements are assumed to be "induced" by changes in income, according to the marginal propensity to consume. Primary disbursements are "autonomous" changes in investment or consumption, though usually they are thought of only as investments. Negative primary disbursements are autonomous reductions in investment or consumption.

reparations, debt payments) it involves an increase in taxes or a reduction of public expenditures; and in the case of business payments (direct investments abroad, repayments of debts to foreign creditors) it involves a reduction in domestic outlays for plant, inventory, dividends, or wages. In both cases the inclination to resort to borrowing new funds from the banking system is strong; but to the extent that monetary expansion helps in the "extraction" of the domestic funds, the budgetary problem has not really been solved. Since the demand for bank credit will "naturally" increase when taxes are raised or debts have to be paid, and since meeting this demand would imply failure to extract the money out of the income stream of the economy, the refusal of bank loans becomes part of the solution of the budgetary problem. Bankers and banking experts, however, may understandably balk at the suggestion that the discount rate be raised, or bank credit more strictly rationed, in order to help solve the "budgetary" problem of making foreign payments.

The budgetary problem is especially serious in periods of unemployment, because unemployment is apt to be aggravated by a decline in domestic spending. Political resistance to cutting domestic spending (increasing taxes, restricting credit, raising interest rates, etc.) may become too strong to be overcome. To insist that this is a "transfer difficulty" is not consistent with the distinction made between problems of collecting domestic funds and problems of converting them into foreign exchange. To insist, on the other hand, that difficulties in reducing domestic spending should *not* be regarded as a transfer problem is to enforce terminological discipline, but need not imply a moral or political judgment that sterner methods of monetary and fiscal policy be pursued. If the cry "we cannot pay" is answered with "you have not tried," the answer need not be interpreted as an admonition to try harder.

Even if it is agreed that difficulties in curtailing domestic demand are not transfer difficulties—since a transfer problem in the strict sense cannot exist before the domestic stinting has become a reality—there is still a question of diagnosing just where the difficulties lie. It is one thing if it is *economically* impossible to raise the domestic funds—say, because higher tax rates fail to bring in higher tax revenues, new taxes reduce the receipts from old taxes, debtors become bankrupt. It is another thing if it is *politically* impossible to raise the funds—say, because the government is ousted, revenue officers refuse to enforce the law, a revolution occurs. And it is again another thing if the *government decides* not to try raising the funds—say, because political or economic consequences are regarded as intolerable. All these distinctions are relevant, but they are rarely made. Most frequently the discussion is fudged with other questions, some of which may more legitimately come under the heading "transfer problem."

In some circumstances one can draw a clear line: the budgetary problem refers to difficulties in adjusting domestic spending to the requirements of foreign obligations, whereas the transfer problem refers to difficulties in adjusting production and trade to an accomplished reduction in domestic demand in such a way that an increase in exports and/or a decrease in imports produce the foreign exchange for converting the accumulated funds. But circumstances may be different, and it may be possible for the transfer problem to be solved before the budgetary problem is solved. This may be the case, for example, if an expansion of effective demand takes place abroad which suffices to "pull in" the goods and services of the paying country and which thus provides it with the foreign exchange to make the payments. The unpleasant or painful process by which a contraction in the paying country "pushes out" the goods and services is thus replaced by the painless or pleasant process of a foreign inflation "pulling them in." Since this possibility exists, and the transfer problem *can* be solved without budgetary exertions and restrictions, it has become even more tempting to complain of transfer difficulties when the lucky foreign expansions fail to emerge. Admittedly, the solution to the payments problem through monetary expansion abroad, rather than through contraction in the paying country, is much more in line with present-day economic institutions and ideas.

Another way of having the transfer problem solved without prior attempts to solve the budgetary problem is through increases in efficiency in production which allow reductions in costs and prices in the paying country. Assuming that technology advances and efficiency improves every year in most industrial countries, the problem for the paying country becomes a question of keeping wage rates from rising as fast as average productivity increases. Even this would be of no avail if the same policy were successfully pursued in most other countries; what the paying country really needs is that its production costs fall relatively to costs abroad. Some additional conditions, though, must be fulfilled if such changes in cost relations are to be sufficient to produce the required improvement of the trade balance. But again, the possibility that the transfer problem is solved in this fashion tempts some writers to speak of transfer difficulties when this possibility does not materialize, because, for example, wage rates in the paying country or productivity in foreign countries rise too fast.

A SEMANTIC ANALYSIS

Proceeding now to my assignment in semantics, I shall attempt to sketch out some of the principal differences between the various things meant, among different people or in different contexts, by the words *transfer difficulties, transfer losses, transfer burdens, transfer crises.* I distinguish, in my taxonomic catalogue, three main categories of meaning, which can be subdivided in various ways.

1. *Shortage of foreign exchange needed for the transfer:* What is meant, simply, is that there will not be enough foreign exchange available to perform the transfer. Various shades of this meaning are distinguishable.

a. *Unavailability of foreign exchange:* The lack of foreign exchange is unavoidable and the transfer, therefore, impossible.

b. *Partial and conditional availability of foreign exchange:* Given the general behavior patterns—"structural parameters," in modern jargon— particular fiscal and monetary policies can secure such adjustments in the balance of trade as will provide foreign exchange to meet larger or smaller portions of the transfer obligations. For conditions in which no price effects and only income effects operate in the adjustment mechanism, quantitative relationships between changes in primary disbursements (for domestic investment and consumption), total national income, and the balance of trade have been derived.

If primary disbursements abroad (as well as prices, wages, exchange rates) are unchanged and the behavior patterns (propensities to save and to import) are "normal and stable," the reduction in national income of the paying country will exceed (by the multiplier) the curtailment of its primary disbursements, and the increase in the trade balance will fall short of it. The reduction in national income may be treated as "transfer loss"—see 3, c, (3) on p. 440; but the fact that the increase in the trade balance will be only a portion of the curtailment of domestic disbursements may be treated as a "partial availability of foreign exchange." Depending on the analyst's taste, he may express the shortfall of the transfer as a ratio to the curtailment of disbursements or, to show the predicament at its worst, as a ratio to the ultimate reduction of national income.[2]

Alternatively, it may be asked how large a curtailment of disbursements would produce precisely that increase in the trade balance that suffices to meet the payments obligations. In this case, the needed foreign exchange would be produced in full, but only with "difficulties," which may be measured by the relative "excess curtailment" of disbursements or, still more impressive, by the relative income reduction associated with the desired change in the trade balance.[3] Considerations of this sort cavalierly abstract from all price adjustments and have therefore limited

[2] If ΔI is the curtailment in primary disbursements, ΔB the resulting improvement in the trade balance, and ΔY the ultimate reduction of national income, one may express the shortfall of the transfer by $\Delta B/\Delta I$, $(\Delta I - \Delta B)/\Delta I$, or $\Delta B/\Delta Y$.

[3] If the expression is supposed to assume a *higher* numerical value for *greater* "difficulties," one may propose $\Delta I/\Delta B$, $(\Delta I - \Delta B)/\Delta B$, or $\Delta Y/\Delta B$. It should be noted that ΔB is the positive improvement of the trade balance in the full amount of the required transfer, whereas ΔI and ΔY are negative.

applicability. But, at least, they specify what is meant by the terms employed.

2. *Political difficulties in executing policies consistent with the transfer:* The distinction between political and economic difficulties is often disparaged as artificial and arbitrary. It is important, however, to separate "economic" effects—that is, changes in prices, incomes, employment, etc.—from "political" ones, such as the outcome of an election, a vote of nonconfidence, the resignation of a cabinet, the dismissal of a minister, demonstrations by street mobs, stones thrown at the police force, the shooting of a public figure, etc. It is for fear of political difficulties that policies consistent with, or even prerequisite for, the transfer of funds to meet foreign obligations are sometimes eschewed by the men in charge.

3. *Economic sacrifices and losses of real income or intake associated with the transfer:* These are the various curtailments of real income and intake which are variously referred to as "burdens," "losses," etc. My distinction between *income* and *intake* is essential because unrequited exports associated with unilateral transfers, such as reparations payments, are not as such reductions of national income—since production for export is a part of the national product—but only curtailments of the intake, that is, of what is available for domestic investment and consumption.[4] Other transfer-related losses, however, cut into both national income and domestic intake. The following classification will be helpful.

a. *Primary burden:* This is the reduction in domestic intake resulting from the induced increase in exports and decrease in imports of goods and services, valued at prices prevailing *before* the collection and the transfer of funds. The price effects of the budgetary operations (e.g., tax policies) or of any monetary policies pursued in connection with the transfer (e.g., credit policies) may change the weight of the burden and should be distinguished from the "primary" burden of the foreign obligation.

b. *Price effects:* The price effects, sometimes referred to as "secondary burden," are of two kinds, which are easily confused with each other.

(1) *Terms-of-trade effects:* Transfer-connected changes in prices of exported and imported goods and services may change the commodity terms of trade of the paying country. If the terms of trade deteriorate, that is, if export prices fall in relation to import prices, this represents a loss of real national income and can be interpreted as an extra burden upon the paying country. The terms of trade may, however, improve as a result of

[4] For a more thorough discussion of the concept of domestic intake, see my essay on "The Terms-of-Trade Effects of Devaluation upon Real Income and the Balance of Trade," reproduced as Chapter IX of this volume.

the foreign payments—for example, if the decline of demand in the paying country is especially heavy with respect to imported goods, and the increase in demand in the receiving country favors products of the paying country. In such a case, the terms-of-trade effects are favorable and the "secondary burden" on this account will be negative.

(2) *Price-deflation effects on fixed obligations:* If prices in the paying country are reduced as a result of the deflation normally connected with the extraction of funds for payments abroad, whereas the foreign obligations are fixed in terms of money, the commodity equivalent of the payments is increased. The "secondary burden" imposed on the paying country by the increase in the real value of its foreign obligations is independent of any change in the commodity terms of trade. Even if the commodity terms of trade remain unchanged or are improved, the effect of price deflation upon the real value of the fixed obligations may still increase their weight. Assume that import prices fall proportionately more heavily than export prices, so that the terms of trade improve and the national income of the paying country benefits from this change; price deflation will still aggravate the burden of the obligations. The "real reparations," as I said in 1928, will have become heavier.

c. *Output losses:* None of the losses to real income or intake thus far mentioned in this list was a loss of output due to failure to use available inputs to the full extent or in an optimal fashion. Such losses, however, are liable to occur in the course of the deflationary process normally connected with unilateral payments to foreign countries—unless all prices, including those of labor, are perfectly flexible, which they never are. Depending partly on the degree of flexibility, there may be three types of output losses in connection with the deflation caused by extracting funds to be transferred.

(1) *Transitional unemployment and work stoppages:* Even if wage rates are not rigid, their downward adjustment may take time. In some instances, wages will come down only after unemployment has shown clearly that labor is in excess supply; in other instances, disputes about adjustments of collective wage agreements will be associated with strikes and lock-outs and, hence, with men-days idle because of work stoppages.

(2) *Transitional misallocation of resources:* Even if wage rates and commodity prices are not rigid, this adjustment to reductions in demand will not be equally fast in all industries. In some industries, prices fall as soon as demand declines; in others, however, production is curtailed first and it takes considerable time until prices are adjusted. Differences in the speed of adjustment must, even if no substantial under-employment develops, result in resource allocations which cannot be optimal from a long-run point of view. Hence, there will be a temporary loss of real national income because of an inferior composition of output.

(3) *Long-term unemployment:* If wage rates in broad sectors of the economy resist the downward pressures exerted by the reduction of domestic demand, deflation will take the form of long-term unemployment. Some writers will blame this unemployment, and the consequent loss of output, on the absence of competition in the labor market, rather than on the attempt to make large payments to foreign countries. But we are not concerned with determining who is to be blamed, but rather what are the relevant causes and effects. *Given* the downward rigidity of wage rates, the deflation connected with the collection of funds to be transferred is apt to result in long-term unemployment.

It is interesting to note the remarkable career which the last of the transfer losses shown in this list has had in academic economics. In the beginning it was completely absent from the analyses of the transfer problem; then it was recognized as a possible qualification, at best as a "friction" in the normal process; later it was advanced to the role of a significant factor in the process; and finally it was assigned the leading role. This final recasting of the transfer model took place when the "income approach" had gained preference over "price economics," and most events came to be analyzed on the basis of a set of rather peculiar assumptions, namely, fixed wage rates, fixed prices, fixed interest rates, fixed exchange rates. If these assumptions are sustained, the only possible adjustments are those of output and employment, and the transfer problem becomes one of the relationships between the induced change in the trade balance and the associated change in real income. An analysis of this type was presented in my book on *International Trade and the National Income Multiplier* and is reproduced in Chapter XVIII of the present volume.

In our catalogue of meanings, we have distinguished, besides "shortage of foreign exchange" and besides "political difficulties," six types of economic loss: primary burden, terms-of-trade losses, losses through increases in the real value of the fixed obligations, transitional unemployment, transitional misallocations, and long-term unemployment. If these different types of economic loss are no longer scrambled together as "transfer difficulties," analysts of the transfer problem will begin to understand one another.

Transfer under conditions of growth

We have noted the peculiar contrast between the economist's definition of the transfer problem and his historical identifications of transfer difficulties. Rarely in history, if ever, have absolute contractions in money supply and effective demand occurred in countries preparing to meet foreign obligations. Yet, the definition, designed to separate transfer and budgetary problems, has imposed the condition of an absolute contraction in the paying country by speaking of the problem of converting the funds *extracted*. This discrepancy suggests that the models explaining the transfer mechanism be reconstructed to display *relative*, rather than absolute, contractions—relative not only to the increase in primary disbursements in foreign countries, but relative also to the rate of growth of real resources and total output in the paying country.

The problem of transfer under conditions of growth is not essentially different from that of transfer between stationary economies. In both cases, the problem is to ascertain the "warranted" rate of primary disbursements in the paying country; that is, that rate which, given the rate of primary disbursements abroad and given the countries' propensities to save and to import, is apt to create the desired increase in its balance of trade. For the case without growth, and assuming the absence of price effects, I furnished the algebraic apparatus in my multiplier analysis. It may be helpful to reformulate it slightly at this point before we consider the case with growth in both countries. For the sake of brevity, we shall omit the lengthy though highly illuminating period analysis, and jump over all transitional adjustments directly to the "ultimate" values of all variables in the model.

Wanted is the "warranted" increase in primary disbursements in the paying country, that is, I_A (changes in domestic investment and consumption outlays not induced by changes in income). Given are I_B, the actual increase in primary disbursements in the receiving country; T, the amount to be transferred each period; s_A and s_B, the marginal propensities to save, and m_A and m_B, the marginal propensities to import, in the two countries. We express the warranted I_A as a ratio q of the actual I_B, that is,

(1) $$I_A = q \, I_B.$$

The condition which makes q the warranted ratio is, of course, that an export surplus will develop in A of the size T, the amount which A is obligated to transfer per period. There will be increased exports from A (induced by Y_B, the increased income in B), reaching [5] a magnitude of $m_B Y_B$. There will also be increased imports in A (induced by Y_A, its own

---

[5] To simplify the notations we omit two symbols: Δ and ∞. Since every variable is a change over the amount in the base period, a Δ might precede every term; moreover, since equilibrium—though gradually approached over time—would be "reached" only after an infinite length of time, the values for Y ought to be indicated by $Y_{\to \infty}$. The reader will surely prefer the shorter expressions without prefixes and additional subscripts, but he should bear in mind what they signify.

A more discriminating notation would also use some symbols—bars, dots, or hats—to distinguish the "warranted" increase in primary disbursements in country A, here denoted simply by I_A, from the "actual" increase in primary disbursements in country B, here denoted by I_B. Both printer and reader will, I suppose, prefer not to have the equations further encumbered.

increased income) reaching a magnitude of $m_A Y_A$. Since, eventually, the induced exports are supposed to exceed the induced imports by an amount T, this requirement may be expressed by the following equation:

$$(2) \qquad m_B Y_B = m_A Y_A + T.$$

Two more equations will express the equilibrium conditions in the two countries. Since incomes will go on changing as long as induced savings exceed or fall short of the sum of the changes in home investment and trade balance, equilibrium presupposes the following two equalities:

$$(3) \qquad I_A + T = s_A Y_A,$$

and

$$(4) \qquad I_B - T = s_B Y_B.$$

To obtain a clearer perspective and to display a "causal ordering"[6] of these relationships, we rewrite the system of equations as follows:

$$(3a) \qquad I_A - s_A Y_A \qquad\qquad\quad - T,$$
$$(2a) \qquad\qquad - m_A Y_A + m_B Y_B = \quad + T,$$
$$(4a) \qquad\qquad\qquad\qquad s_B Y_B = I_B - T.$$

What we have here is a recursive system of three linear equations with three unknowns: I_A, Y_A, and Y_B. They are so arranged that the lowest row contains only one unknown, Y_B; once this equation is solved and the value of Y_B substituted into the equation in the second row, the latter can be solved for Y_A; now the equation of the top row can be solved for I_A by substituting the value of Y_A obtained from the equation in the second row.[7] The resulting formula for I_A is as follows:

$$(5) \qquad I_A = \frac{s_A m_B I_B - T\,(s_A s_B + m_A s_B + s_A m_B)}{m_A s_B}.$$

The ratio q of the warranted I_A to the actual I_B is, therefore,

[6] For an exposition of the concept of "causal ordering," see Herbert A. Simon, "Causal Ordering and Identifiability," in *Studies in Econometric Method*, edited by William C. Hood and Tjalling C. Koopmans, Cowles Commission Monograph No. 14 (New York: Wiley, 1953), pp. 49-74.

[7] With this ordering, the matrix of the coefficients is such that all principal diagonal elements are non-zero and all elements to their left are zero; thus we have a "nonsingular triangular matrix," which permits of particularly easy schemes of reduction. In the first draft of this essay I had used high-school algebra with numerous awkward substitutions, just as I had done in my book published in 1943. Harold Kuhn then showed me how much more elegantly such solutions can be reached by matrix algebra. In my second draft, I blithely replaced my sequence of algebraic substitutions with the neat matrix and determinant furnished by Kuhn. Hang-Sheng Cheng subsequently showed me the still simpler method used by Herbert Simon for causally ordered structures. Finally I profited from discussion with Hourmouzis G. Georgiadis. My gratitude to Kuhn, Cheng, and Georgiadis is, I am sure, shared by the reader.

$$(6) \quad q = \frac{I_A}{I_B} = \frac{s_A m_B}{m_A s_B} - \left(\frac{s_A m_B}{m_A s_B} + \frac{s_A}{m_A} + 1\right)\frac{T}{I_B}.$$

This is not a pretty formula, but it tells us how q is determined. It is a function of all six given values and—on the reasonable assumption that T is sufficiently smaller than I_B—q will be larger the smaller are m_A, s_B, and T, and the larger are m_B, s_A, I_B. All of this should be intuitively obvious. Expressed in words, the warranted increase in domestic disbursements in the paying country will be larger if its transfer obligation is small, its import propensity low, and its propensity to save is high; and, furthermore, if the other country increases its spending by large amounts, has a high propensity to import, and a low propensity to save.

Before we proceed, we may consider a few special cases. Let us ask first what would happen if s_A were zero. From equation (3a) we can see immediately that, in this case, I_A would be equal to $-T$, which is to say, that the warranted change of primary disbursements in A would be negative and numerically equal to the amount to be transferred; no matter how high primary disbursements in B should be raised, the reduction in primary disbursements in A must be of magnitude T if a transfer of T is to be made possible.

This result is self-evident on the basis of purely verbal reasoning. If the marginal propensity to save is zero in the paying country, so that there will be no induced saving or dissaving however much income may change, equilibrium requires that the export surplus (needed for the transfer) is exactly offset by a reduction in primary disbursements. This does not mean that the size of investment expansion in Country B has no effect upon A. It does, through the income increase in B, affect A's exports, which in turn increases A's income, which in turn affects A's imports. But the eventual increase in A's imports will fall short of the eventual increase in A's exports by precisely A's reduction in primary disbursements. If A's marginal propensity to save is not quite zero, but close to it, the warranted change in disbursements may still be negative; it becomes zero, and eventually positive, as s_A assumes higher values. One may suggest the generalization that a country which has heavy foreign obligations and a low propensity to save must—in the absence of relative price changes—refrain from expanding its home investment, and may have to curtail it; for its increase in income it must rely on expansion abroad and on the increase in exports that is induced by such foreign outlays and incomes.

What happens if s_B or m_A becomes zero? Actually, our algebraic model becomes indeterminate in either case. But equation (4) tells us that, with $s_B = 0$, $I_B = T$; this means that I_B is no longer "given" as a policy variable which the receiving country may be free to set at will, but it must be made equal to T. In other words, the receiving country must increase its primary disbursements exactly by T if the trade balance is to be no larger and no smaller than the required transfer; and, in this case, I_A becomes independent of I_B. If $m_A = 0$, equation (2) tells us, $m_B Y_B$ must be equal to T; hence, again, the responsibility for achieving the transfer will be on the receiving country. At given prices, no change in incomes in the paying country can induce any change in imports; only an increase in exports can achieve the transfer. I_B, therefore, cannot be independently "given" but, as can be seen from equations (2) and (4), must be made equal to $(s_B + m_B)Y_B$; that is to say, it must be so adjusted that sufficient income is generated to induce enough purchases by the receiving country from the paying country to effect the transfer; and again I_A is independent of I_B.

Now we may consider the case in which both countries have increasing amounts of real resources available and, therefore, can increase their primary disbursements and their total incomes every period. Assume that Country B, realizing its full growth potential, increases its disbursements, I_B, by a given rate every period. At what rate will then the paying country be permitted to increase its primary disbursements without running into trouble, that is, without reducing its export surplus below the amount T, which it is obligated to transfer every period?

In the language of the differential calculus, we approach this question by differentiating equation (5) with respect to I_B, which gives us immediately

$$(7) \qquad \frac{dI_A}{dI_B} = \frac{s_A m_B}{m_A s_B}.$$

If we wish to transform the ratio of absolute changes in disbursements into a ratio of relative changes, we may multiply both sides of (7) by I_B/I_A:

$$(8) \qquad \frac{dI_A/I_A}{dI_B/I_B} = \frac{I_B}{I_A} \frac{s_A m_B}{m_A s_B} = \frac{1}{q} \frac{s_A m_B}{m_A s_B}.$$

Again, the results are not surprising to one who allows his intuitive reasoning to run ahead of his mathematical operations. At first blush, though, he may wonder at the absence of T from the last formula. Yet, it ought to be clear that the relative size of T is already implied in the magnitude of q and has no business making a second appearance. The warranted rate of increase of the warranted rate of domestic disbursements will be larger the smaller are q, s_B, and m_A, and the larger are s_A, and m_B. It is worth noting that the propensities, which have already had their influence upon q, reassert their importance by influencing, in the same direction, the rate at which the paying country may raise its disbursements as the other country continues to grow.

Still another implication is worth noting: the warranted rate at which the paying country may increase its domestic disbursements without jeopardizing its export surplus is definitely limited by the realized growth potential of the receiving country. In other words, if the rate of increase of available real resources happens to be greater in the paying country than the rate of expansion commensurate with that in the receiving country, and if all price effects are ruled out, the paying country cannot expand as fast as its own resources would permit, without running into transfer troubles. The warranted expansion in A is tied to the actual expansion in B in the way indicated, as long as the assumptions of fixed wage rates, prices, and exchange rates are maintained.

The expansion in the paying country is even more severely limited if its growth potential falls short of what we have called the warranted rate which is dependent on the realized growth in the receiving country. This is because an attempt to grow faster than the supply of resources permits would be inconsistent with the assumption of fixed wage rates and prices; in a model that promises any degree of correspondence with observable facts, the assumption of price stability would have to be dropped in this case, and the inflationary process would soon reduce or wipe out the export surplus needed for the transfer.

In a world in which wages and prices can only rise but never fall, the case of transfer obligations of one growing economy to another has, if our reasoning has been correct, very special properties:

(1) It may not be necessary for the paying country, in order to accomplish the transfer, to effect an absolute curtailment of its domestic disbursements; indeed, it may increase them period after period and nevertheless achieve and maintain an export surplus sufficient to furnish the required foreign exchange.

(2) The rate of domestic disbursements and the rate of their increase are limited, if the export surplus is to be maintained, by the supply of real resources; if domestic spending increases faster than the supply of resources, price inflation results and the required export surplus cannot be maintained.

(3) The rate of domestic disbursements and the rate of their increase are also limited, if the export surplus is to be maintained, by the realized growth in the receiving country, with which these rates are linked in definite relationships determined by the relative saving and importing propensities in both countries as well as by the relative size of the transfer obligation.[8] It may happen that this limit imposed from the outside is narrower than that imposed by the own growth potential of the paying country; if domestic spending is allowed to increase faster than at the

[8] The size is relative to the increase in primary disbursements in the receiving country.

warranted rate, and if relative price reductions cannot be effected, the required export surplus cannot be maintained.

In the growth case, as in the stationary case before, it is worth reflecting on the fact that the warranted rate of increase in domestic spending in the paying country will no longer be affected by what happens abroad if either s_A or m_B becomes zero. In this case, $\dfrac{dI_A/I_A}{dI_B/I_B}$ becomes likewise zero. In plain English, no matter how fast the receiving country expands and grows, the paying country continues to labor under the constraints which we have spelled out for these conditions.[9]

LEAVE-TAKING

I am breaking off my visit rather abruptly, I must not stay longer. I have the feeling that—though I have straightened out a few things on the semantic side—I leave the subject in a rather disorderly state. Others, I trust, will clear up any mess that I have made by my new diggings.

One final thought, again on the matter of definition. After all my emphasis on strictness in the use of the word "transfer" as the conversion of domestic funds extracted, without aids or refunds, out of the income stream of the paying country, I have apparently ended up with models of transfer without previous budgetary contraction. My defense is that I have not neglected the budgetary problem, not regarded it as solved when it was not. I have, instead, treated the budgetary problem by re-phrasing the question to read: just what degree of budgetary restraint will secure the successful transfer of the full amount of the obligation? I believe that this formulation implies the solution of the problem of extracting the required funds.

---

[9] It is interesting to note the contrast with regard to the limiting cases in which one of the propensities becomes zero. If either s_A or m_B becomes zero, the responsibility for adjusting its policy variables so that the transfer can be achieved will rest entirely on the paying country. If, on the other hand, either s_B or m_A becomes zero, the entire responsibility will be that of the receiving country.

XX

Capital Movements and Trade Balance

Induced or "Accommodating" Capital Exports ■ Spontaneous Capital Exports ■ Net Capital Export ■ Cause or Effect ■ Types of Autonomous Capital Movements ■ Primary Disbursements in the Capital-Exporting Country ■ Primary Disbursements in the Capital-Importing Country ■ Reasonable Assumptions

The analysis of changes in capital items is much more complicated than the analysis of current-item changes in the balance of payments. The mere mechanisms as such are not easy to understand; the problems of causation are perplexing.

If the handy pair of adjectives, autonomous and induced, are applied to international transactions on capital account, that is, to changes in the balance of indebtedness, one should note that the meaning of these adjectives cannot here be the same as in connection with transactions on current account. We had best define autonomous capital movements as those transactions on capital account which are not in response to any other change in the balance of payments. For reasons which will become clear only later, we shall want to know in the case of autonomous capital movements where the initiative for the transaction originates. That is to say, we shall have to ask whether an autonomous capital export from A to B was spontaneous lending on the part of A capitalists or spontaneous borrowing on the part of B borrowers; only in rare cases is the initiative divided and the transaction based on simultaneous and deliberate decisions of both parties. With regard to the "induced" capital transactions we must bear in mind that the "induced" does not have here the specific meaning of "directly induced by a change in income" that it has in connection with imports.

There is a significant difference between items on capital account and items on current account, which must be brought out before we proceed. Many "entries" in the international balance of payments under the heading of capital movements are merely the reverse side, the rear aspect, so to speak, of a transaction which is entered as a separate item on the other side of the ledger. To ascribe causal significance (such as affecting foreign-exchange markets or money circulation or income flow) to both entries would in many cases be erroneous. To bring out this aspect, it is convenient to use the adjective "induced" for those capital transactions which are merely "responses" rather than "forces" in the markets of foreign and domestic funds.[1]

INDUCED OR "ACCOMMODATING" CAPITAL EXPORTS

If, for example, an exporter in country A sells B-funds, which he receives in payment for his increased exports, to the banking system of A, and the banking system of A decides to hold the B-balances, the records of the international balance of payments will show the merchandise export on the credit side and the foreign lending (which is implied in the banking system's increased holdings of claims against foreigners) on the debit side.[2] This foreign lending counter-balances the merchandise export in a bookkeeping sense but not in the sense of neutralizing its effects.[3] The

[1] Ragnar Nurkse, *Internationale Kapitalbewegungen* (Vienna: Springer, 1935), p. 225, defines "induced capital movements" as those which result from changes in other items in the balance of payments. Carl Iversen, *Aspects of the Theory of International Capital Movements* (London: Oxford University Press, 1935), pp. 453, 465, *et al.*, has obviously the same things in mind when he speaks of "short-term equalizing capital movements." The "equilibrating capital movements" in the terminology of Charles Poor Kindleberger, *International Short-term Capital Movements* (New York: Columbia University Press, 1937), p. 7, are somewhat less inclusive. He defines them as "those resulting directly from changes in other items in the balance of payments," which leaves those resulting less directly as separate categories. See below, footnote 6.

[2] Increased holdings of deposits in foreign banks, together with increased holdings of foreign bills of exchange or other short-term claims against foreigners, are listed among the "short-term capital exports" (short-term foreign lending), that is, as debit entries, in the international balance of payments. It may be preferable to separate *explicit* foreign lending, such as the holding of additional foreign bills of exchange, from the *implicit* foreign lending which consists merely in holding larger deposits in foreign banks. Viner, for instance, does not include changes in foreign bank balances when he speaks of foreign lending or borrowing, or even of "net" foreign lending or borrowing. See Jacob Viner, *Studies in the Theory of International Trade* (New York: Harper, 1937), pp. 423-425. Most contemporary writers, however, follow the procedure of Keynes in that all increments in balances held abroad are included in "foreign lending." See J. M. Keynes, *A Treatise on Money* (London: Macmillan, 1930), Vol. I, pp. 131-132 and 161-166.

[3] This explains two of the various meanings of "balance of payments." In the one sense, the balance of payments must always "balance"; credit and debit entries can never be unequal. In the other sense, the balance of payments is called "favorable" if a credit item, though counter-balanced by a debit item, is not neutralized in its effects on exchange rates, circulation or income flow.

statement that the export creates income is true only because somebody, e.g., the banking system, is willing to acquire foreign claims (or gold) and to release the domestic funds needed to finance the production of the export goods. Thus, this foreign lending (or gold purchase) must not be considered as a separate force, but rather as a response to, or perhaps an integral part of, the force exerted by the increase in exports.

The willingness on the part of banks or foreign-exchange dealers to acquire and hold foreign balances is usually dependent on the existence of a system of organized exchange-rate stabilization, such as the gold standard in one of its several forms or the operation of an exchange stabilization fund.[4] The assumption of stable foreign-exchange rates—an assumption maintained throughout our argument—implies the existence of an organization (central bank, stabilization fund, or a group of leading commercial banks) which is always prepared to buy any amounts offered, or to sell any amounts demanded, of foreign balances (or gold)—possibly at price pairs with only modest spreads between buying and selling quotations. By increasing its holdings of foreign claims and balances the banking system engages in foreign lending ("capital export") and, simultaneously (except in the case of deliberate offsetting operations), in an expansion of the domestic circulation. *Vice versa*, by reducing its holdings of foreign balances the banking system performs a "capital import" and (save for offsetting) a contraction of the domestic circulation.

If nobody were willing to increase his holdings of foreign balances (or gold), foreign-exchange rates could not remain stable and no income would be created through exports. Exporters would have to dispose of foreign funds to those who have immediate use for them, that is, to importers. Increased exports would merely lead to a reduction of the price of foreign money low enough to induce an importer to use it for an increase in imports. Hence, an exchange-rate-induced increase in imports would immediately offset the autonomous increase in exports.[5]

The statement that an increase in exports or decrease in imports

[4] For a brief discussion of various systems of organized exchange-rate pegging, ranging from uncoordinated actions of foreign-exchange speculators to the most dignified forms of the gold standard, see my article on "The Theory of Foreign Exchanges," Part II, *Economica*, Vol. 7 (New Series), 1940, pp. 37-39; reproduced as Chapter I of this volume.

[5] If the expression "favorable balance of payments" is used in the sense of a credit balance on current account (i.e., a net export surplus in merchandise and services) the situation referred to in the text would not constitute a "favorable balance of payments." If this ambiguous expression is used, however, to describe situations on the foreign-exchange market which involve, in a system of pegged foreign-exchange rates, an increase in the banks' or fund's holdings of foreign balances and gold; or, in a system of flexible foreign-exchange rates, a decline in the price of foreign exchange, then the "finding" is different. The situation referred to in the text, where imports and exports balance completely, would then still be considered as a favorable balance of payments, because the export was the autonomous change and the import only induced by a reduction in the rates of foreign exchange.

creates income presupposes, therefore, the existence of some degree of exchange-rate pegging; it implies the preparedness to accommodate the exporters who offer foreign claims or balances by taking these assets off their hands and holding them for the time being. This "induced" foreign lending may perhaps be characterized as "accommodating" lending. Behind this foreign lending is *not a spontaneous demand for foreign claims or securities* but rather a latent preparedness to accommodate those who come to dispose of foreign balances. In rare cases, and for a short while only, the exporters themselves may hold the foreign claims and finance the exports (the production of the export articles) out of idle funds (dishoarding) or by borrowing from banks. More often, however, speculators and, most often, the banking system (including exchange stabilization funds) will be making the accommodating foreign loans.

"Accommodating" should not mean here that it is done out of sheer kindness or as a service to customers. The "accommodating" purchases or sales of foreign bills and balances are profitable for speculators, dealers, banks, and even monetary authorities. All except the monetary authorities engage in these transactions strictly for business reasons. We may distinguish according to the underlying motives three types of "accommodating" foreign lending. (*a*) Banks or capitalists buy the foreign balances in order to hold foreign interest-bearing claims (or securities). They are attracted by a differential between foreign and domestic interest rates (or relative yields), a differential which is created by or connected with the increased supply of foreign bills or balances. (*b*) Banks or foreign-exchange dealers buy the foreign balances in order to hold them until later when their rates in the foreign-exchange market are expected to be a few points higher (i.e., near the upper of the stable pair of prices). They can anticipate this price differential because of a slight downward pressure upon the current buying rates, which, at the time, is being exerted by the increased supply of foreign balances. (Motives (*a*) and (*b*) are often working together and, in the case of bills, are really inseparable.[6]) (*c*) Exchange stabilization funds or central banks buy the foreign balances in order to prevent foreign-exchange rates from falling. They may either hold the foreign balances until the market turns or convert them into gold.

[6] See Viner, *op. cit.*, p. 404. Kindleberger, *op. cit.*, pp. 8-9, calls movements motivated by (*a*) "income short-term capital movements" and those motivated by (*b*) "speculative short-term capital movements." But these two of Kindleberger's categories include more than our "induced" or "accommodating" capital movements; for, obviously, expectations concerning interest or exchange-rate differentials may be due also to things other than changes in the balance of payments. Only to the extent that the interest (or security price) and exchange-rate differentials are caused by other changes in the balance of payments, are Kindleberger's "income short-term capital movements" and "speculative short-term capital movements" part of what we call here "induced" (or "accommodating") capital movements.

SPONTANEOUS CAPITAL EXPORTS

An entirely different matter is spontaneous foreign lending. *Here it is the demand for foreign balances and securities which undergoes a change* and calls for equilibrating adjustments. Now, in all systems which provide for some sort of stability of foreign-exchange rates, a spontaneous change (positive or negative) in foreign lending, that is, a spontaneous export or import of capital, is likely to be "met" by accommodating changes of opposite direction.[7] An increased demand for holding foreign assets is met by a latent supply, in that speculators or the banking system stand ready to part with the foreign balances which are newly demanded; *vice versa,* a decreased demand for holding foreign assets (i.e., a supply of foreign assets) is met by a latent demand for foreign balances, in that speculators or the banking system are prepared to acquire and hold the foreign balances which are offered. But it would be wrong to suppose that this counter-balancing of spontaneous changes by accommodating changes in foreign lending will as a rule neutralize the former ones with respect to their effects on circulation and income flow. In certain cases the accommodating capital movements do neutralize the spontaneous ones, but in other cases they do not.

Scrutiny of this problem will throw light upon an old controversial issue, an issue which bears some resemblance to the question of which came first, the chicken or the egg. The question of whether capital movements lead the trade balances, or trade balances direct the capital movements, has given rise to much discussion and it was somewhat bewildering that experts should arrive at opposite answers. The classical view was that capital movements were the cause and trade balances the effect.[8] The opposite tenet is that the trade balance is the cause and capital movements the effect.[9] And there is also the compromise view that

---

[7] Cf. Iversen, *op. cit.,* p. 465: ". . . the long-term real capital movement . . . is temporarily offset by a short-term equalizing capital transfer in the opposite direction."

[8] For references to the writings of Hume, Thornton, Wheatley, Ricardo, Longfield, Torrens, Joplin, J. S. Mill, Cairnes, Bastable, and Nicholson, see Viner, *op. cit.,* pp. 292-304. Among modern representatives of this view are Taussig, Wicksell, von Mises, Cassel, Angell, Ohlin, Iversen, and many others. With some qualifications Haberler may also be counted among the adherents of this view. Angell, commenting on the case of Canada from 1900-1913, stated that the change in the balance of trade followed the capital movements with a time lag "that runs up to a year in length." James W. Angell, *The Theory of International Prices* (Cambridge, Mass.: Harvard University Press, 1926), p. 411.

[9] This view was more prevalent first in Germany. Today, however, the outstanding representative of this theory is Keynes, and, hence, it is now widely held. Keynes opposed the theory of the adjustment of trade balances to capital movements on the ground that foreign trade was not easily adjustable; one must not apply, he said, "the theory of liquids to what is, if not a solid, at least a sticky mass with strong internal resistances." And he states: "Historically, the volume of foreign investment has tended,

"there is no apparent *a priori* reason why the dependence should not be as much in one direction as the other." [10] We shall see that certain patterns of thinking seem to enforce a one-way dependence only, to the exclusion of any possibility of "the other" dependence, and yet, we shall find that these apparently contradictory patterns of thinking are reasonably acceptable and reconcilable.

Now, returning to the question from which we departed, what are the decisive points in the problem of the neutralization of spontaneous capital movements? Reasoning in terms of a spontaneous change in the domestic demand for foreign assets, we find that everything will depend on whether this change is at the expense (or in favor) of (a) idle funds, (b) bank debts, (c) domestic investment, or (d) consumption. In the first two of these cases the spontaneous change in foreign lending may in fact not merely be balanced but also neutralized by the opposite accommodating change in foreign lending. In the last two cases, however, the balancing is not neutralizing. More concrete language may help to make this clear.

Let us assume a spontaneous increase in foreign lending: individuals or firms wish to acquire foreign claims or foreign securities. They buy them and pay for them (a) by reducing their liquid balances with domestic banks, or (b) by increasing their debts to domestic banks. (The situation is no different if they finance themselves by selling domestic securities which are bought by the banks or by somebody who thereby reduces his liquid balances or increases his bank debts.) In case (a) the banking system sells foreign balances to the individuals and firms who demand them, and finds its deposit liabilities reduced through the withdrawal (cancellation) of funds which have been inactive anyway. (Expressed in the widely used symbols of Irving Fisher's equation of exchange, M' is reduced, V' increased, $M'V'$ unchanged.) In case (b) the banking system, as in (a), gives foreign funds to those who demand them, but, this time, not against a reduction in deposits but against an increase in credit outstanding. (Circulation, volume, or velocity, is not affected at all.) In both cases, in (a) as well as in (b), the domestic money flow is unaltered.[11]

While, customarily, one still speaks of an "unfavorable balance of

---

I think, to adjust itself—at least to a certain extent—to the balance of trade, rather than the other way round, the former being the sensitive and the latter the insensitive factor." J. M. Keynes, "The German Transfer Problem," *Economic Journal*, Vol. 39 (1929), p. 6.

[10] Viner, *op. cit.*, p. 364. But Viner continues (p. 365): "Examination of such data as are readily available strongly confirms, however, the orthodox doctrine . . . that major long-term capital movements have . . . mainly been 'disturbing' rather than 'equilibrating' in nature." Disturbing means here the same as autonomous, or being the cause; equilibrating means the same as induced, or being the effect.

[11] Of course, the story is not complete. The switch in foreign balances or other assets may have effects on investment or consumption expenditures abroad; and repercussions through foreign trade—foreign-induced exports—may then be felt at home.

payments," in neither of these cases does a change in foreign-exchange rates (beyond the few points compatible with "stability") or in the domestic money flow take place; all shocks are absorbed by the banking system. But the same preparedness of the banking system will not prevent an effect upon the income flow if the adverse balance of payments is associated, as it would be in cases (c) and (d) respectively, with changes in domestic investment or consumption. The spontaneous increase in demand for foreign assets—whether it is motivated by especially attractive yield expectations or whether it is a flight of capital [12]—may reduce domestic investment and consumption, either in that the buyers of the foreign assets themselves cut down their other disbursements or that they raise the needed funds in such a way as to cause others to reduce their investment and consumption expenditures.[13] Thus, in cases (c) and (d), the balancing of the spontaneous capital exports by accommodating capital imports does not neutralize the former; primary disbursements are reduced and the income flow will ebb.

NET CAPITAL EXPORT

Now it is a matter of taste how one chooses to treat the further adjustments from this point on. One may prefer to start with a fresh breath and regard the reductions in home investment and consumption as autonomous changes which, through a lowering of incomes, result in an induced fall in imports, hence, in an export surplus. Or one may prefer not to lose sight of the autonomous foreign lending from which things have started and which may have been associated not only with reduced investment and consumption at home but also with increased investment and consumption abroad. But in any case one may insist that up to this point there has not yet occurred any *net* lending; for, we must remember, the spontaneous increase in foreign lending was balanced by an accommodating decrease in foreign lending when the banking system gave up foreign balances out of its own holdings (or possibly out of new borrowings abroad which it arranged for *ad hoc*) and turned them over to those who had felt the spontaneous desire to make foreign loans or investments.[14] Only later, when reduced home investment and consumption are cutting incomes in the "lending" country, and increased home investment and consumption are raising incomes in the "borrowing" country, will the

---

[12] I have dealt with the problems of capital flight in a German article, "Die Theorie der Kapitalflucht," *Weltwirtschaftliches Archiv*, Vol. 36 (1932), pp. 512-529.

[13] For example, a failure to renew short-term loans to firms or consumers may force the debtors to reduce their expenditures drastically.

[14] As I mentioned before, Viner does not include changes in the banks' foreign bank balances in his "net foreign lending" or "net foreign borrowing." In trying to interpret the Keynesian position, I am, of course, using the Keynesian concept of net foreign lending.

"lending" country experience both a home-induced fall in imports and a foreign-induced rise in exports. This favorable trade balance will, at least in part, replace the foreign holdings with which the banking system has first parted. That is to say, the banking system, which had accommodatingly performed negative foreign lending as it gave its balances to those who spontaneously performed positive foreign lending, will now acquire the foreign balances which exporters (with their business increased) cannot sell (at stable exchange rates) to importers (with their business reduced); thus, the banking system will now accommodatingly engage in positive foreign lending. This means that it is, after all, the improved trade balance which, by reversing the direction of *accommodating* capital exports, permits the *spontaneous* capital exports, or a part of them, to become *net* capital exports.

One can now understand why some writers prefer to place all the emphasis on the adjustment of the net capital flow to the trade balance: because this so-called adjustment is a certainty, whereas the adjustment of the trade balance to the spontaneous capital exports is only a probability. There is nothing which assures equality between spontaneous capital exports and the changes in investment and consumption expenditures; nor is there any equality between the changes in these expenditures and the improvement in the trade balance. Therefore, important as the relationship may be for the explanation of reality, the quantitative relationship between spontaneous capital export and improved trade balance is rather uncertain. On the other hand, the net capital export (together with a possible gold inflow) is necessarily equal to the improvement of the trade balance. This equality follows directly from the definitions of the items involved; the statement cannot be wrong; but whether this statement is very useful in the explanation of actual phenomena is another matter.[15]

CAUSE OR EFFECT

We should not quarrel about tastes. One way of exposition, more nearly neo-classical in character, has the advantage of tracing the whole

---

[15] The logical difference between the two statements about capital movements and trade balance should be noted. The one which says that the trade balance adjusts itself to the capital movements—read: *spontaneous* capital movements—expresses a mere probability; this statement remains in the realm of *causality*. The other, which says that the capital movements—read: *net* capital movements—adjust themselves to the trade balance, expresses an absolute certainty; thus this statement belongs to the realm of *tautology*. Only if one were willing to change the second statement so that it would refer no longer to net capital flows but instead to certain types of capital flows, for instance long-term capital movements, would the statement change its logical character and become one about cause and effect; its probability value, however, would be definitely inferior to that of the opposite proposition. (Cf. Viner's remark quoted in footnote 10 above.)

sequence of events from the autonomous movement of capital, via the reactions of the monetary system, to the trade balance. The other way has the advantage of reducing the whole network to the simplicity of the investment-and-consumption scheme. Since, as we have seen, spontaneous foreign lending becomes net foreign lending only if it affects, in at least one of the countries concerned, the disbursements for home investment and consumption, it is justifiable to start from there. But starting from there, that is from the changes in investment and consumption, one cannot help seeing all movements of capital only as induced ones, effected by the income-induced changes in the trade balance. These changes in the trade balance are simply those shown by the theory of the home-investment multiplier. Expressed in a few catchwords, the train of thought is then the following:

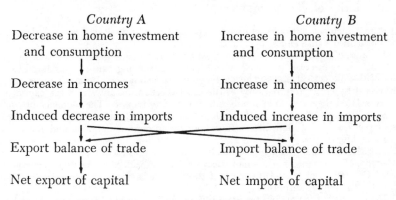

Country A	*Country B*
Decrease in home investment and consumption	Increase in home investment and consumption
Decrease in incomes	Increase in incomes
Induced decrease in imports	Induced increase in imports
Export balance of trade	Import balance of trade
Net export of capital	Net import of capital

This may no longer look like a theory of the effects of spontaneous capital exports—which apparently have taken place "before the curtain rose"—but it is a perfectly acceptable and convenient pattern of reasoning.

I believe that our discussion has disposed of some of the seemingly irreconcilable differences in this chicken-or-egg controversy between the "neo-classical" and "neo-mercantilist" schools of thought. In both types of analysis the changes in disbursements for investment and consumption in one or both countries and the concomitant changes in incomes, are essential steps. The change in the trade balance may be attributed with equal justification either to the changes in incomes or, tracing it back one or two steps further, to the spontaneous demand for foreign assets on the part of capitalists in the lending country (that is, to that change in demand from which changed disbursements and incomes have originated). The capital export may be detected with equal reasonableness either in the *spontaneous* demand for foreign assets or in the accommodating foreign lending which consists in acquiring the foreign balances derived from the export surplus and which accounts for the eventual *net* balance of increase over decrease in the holdings of foreign claims. And, of course, if the words "capital movements" stand for *net* capital movements including all changes in foreign bank balances,[16] then one can always maintain and "prove" (with a reservation concerning gold flows) that capital movements "result" from the trade balance (or, more correctly, from the balance of current items). On the other hand, if the words "capital movements" stand for *long-term* capital movements, then one must say that all the alternative patterns of thinking make it perfectly plausible that the trade balance can adjust itself to a capital flow which precedes it. Whether the capital movement, in the long-term sense, will in reality more often lead or follow the trade balance, becomes again a real question. This question cannot be decided merely by implicit theorizing; but the evidence presented by careful investigators points to the more frequent priority of capital movements.[17]

[16] This includes not only interbank deposits but also debit and credit balances of A-nationals in B-banks and of B-nationals in A-banks.

[17] Viner, after a painstaking examination of the available data, takes Canada from 1900-1913 as an example of a case where foreign borrowing can be considered as the cause of the import surpluses. The evidence is fully convincing and whatever doubts were raised by critics referred only to the exact mechanisms by which the capital imports translated themselves eventually into commodity imports. The sequence of events was probably something like the following: Flotation of Canadian issues in London— Use of parts of the sterling proceeds to pay for interest obligations and for certain imports of investment goods—Sale of rest of the sterling balances to Canadian banks —Use of the Canadian bank funds (received in exchange) for investment expenditures in Canada—Expansion of Canadian incomes (and advances in relative prices)—Increased Canadian imports—Utilization of the foreign balances of Canadian banks for paying for the import surplus.

Nonetheless, it is possible to argue differently. As Harold M. Somers has pointed out to me, one may attribute the fact that Canadian issues were floated in Britain rather than in Canada to an institutional factor, namely the excellence of the London capital market compared with the Canadian. If Canadian banks had initially acquired the new issues, the sequence would have been different, with the imports leading and the foreign borrowing trailing. For example: Flotation of new issues in Canada, acquired by Canadian banks—Use of the (thereby created) Canadian bank funds for investment expenditures in Canada—Expansion of Canadian incomes (and advances in relative prices)—Increased Canadian imports—Demand for foreign balances to pay for the import surplus—Drain on Canadian bank reserves—In order to replenish their reserves Canadian banks sell in the London market the bonds out of their portfolio.

The end effects of both sequences are the same. In neither of the two cases could import surpluses continue for a long time were it not for the British purchases of Canadian bonds. Yet the initiative to sell the bonds in Britain is of a different character in the second sequence: it can be said in this case that the sales are forced upon the Canadians by their unfavorable trade balance. This time the foreign borrowing has not led but followed the import surplus.

Viner does not rule out interpretations of this sort. He says himself, with reference to the Canadian experience: "From the data . . . it is possible to argue that at times at least the import surpluses resulted from original secondary expansion, and that the borrowings were engaged in to obtain the foreign funds necessary to liquidate trade balances already incurred and to restore reserves encroached upon in paying for past debit trade balances." (*Op. cit.*, p. 429.) In general "there was a variable time-lag between borrowings abroad and economic transfer, with the recorded, or long-term,

The theory of the effects of autonomous capital movements upon trade balances and national incomes may be conveniently divided into two parts. First comes an analysis of the effects of the spontaneous capital transactions upon aggregate disbursements for home investment and consumption in the countries concerned. Second comes the analysis of the effects of changes in investment and consumption upon trade balances and incomes. The first was characterized above as the story that takes place before the curtain rises over the drama of the second analysis, a drama, incidentally, which can be produced with the technique of the home-investment multiplier (applied, of course, to at least two countries at the same time). Even if one is chiefly concerned with the part that can be treated with the multiplier technique, it seems appropriate to gain some insight into the "antecedent actions." How does the spontaneous capital flow affect primary disbursements in the countries concerned?

The answer will depend on several circumstances, usually described in terms of liquidity positions and investment opportunities, but it depends also to a considerable extent on the type of transactions which constitute the capital outflow or inflow. To analyze the "several circumstances" would involve almost the whole theory of investment; we cannot undertake such an enterprise here. But to get some idea about the influence which the nature of the international capital transactions may have upon the rate of domestic disbursements is a possible task. It calls for distinguishing among a few rather fundamental types of autonomous capital movements. Such an attempt to classify them according to their nature and the character and locus of the initiative from which they originate may be helpful, although it cannot be claimed that the principle of classification is sound for all purposes or that our list is complete in any respect. (The point of going into the question of initiative and spontaneity is pretty much the same as that of inquiring whether in a commodity market an increase in the quantity sold is due to an increase in demand or an increase in supply. By and large, therefore, the distinction between spontaneous and non-spontaneous autonomous capital movements corresponds to the theoretically significant distinction between shifts of curves and movements along curves.)

Every *autonomous* capital export of one country is, by definition, an autonomous capital import of another country. (Autonomous, we re-

---

borrowings usually but not always preceding the economic transfer chronologically." (*Op. cit.*, p. 431.)

Viner mentions New Zealand after 1919 as an example of a case where a loss of exports can be regarded as the cause of borrowing from abroad. (*Op. cit.*, p. 365.)

peat, does not mean here "not induced by any changes in income" but means instead "not in response to other changes in the international balance of payments.") But an autonomous capital movement need not be *spontaneous* on the part of both the lending and the borrowing country; that is to say, the initiative may be that of only one of the two parties. We shall find in our classification cases of strictly one-sided spontaneity, but also some of joint spontaneity, so that cases listed once for the capital exporting and again for the capital importing country may be merely two aspects of an identical transaction. In such cases the supply of funds (demand for assets) by the exporting country and the demand for funds (supply of assets) by the importing country can both be regarded as increased.

The classification which is offered here is designed to maintain symmetry.[18] But one should bear in mind that most items have more than one possible opposite. One pair of opposites, for example, is "lending" and "borrowing"; but "lending" and "collecting" is another. It is the second type of opposites which underlies the symmetry design of our classification.

Spontaneous Capital Exports

(1) Increased demand for holding foreign assets [19] involving *"direct investment" abroad* under the control of the capital exporter.

(2) Increased demand for holding foreign assets involving *"direct lending" to borrowers abroad* (with direct contact between lender and borrower but without "control" of one over the other).

(3) Increased demand for holding foreign assets resulting in *acquisition of old foreign securities* or other assets, without significant contacts with foreign sellers or debtors.

(4) Increased demand for holding foreign assets resulting in *subscriptions to new issues of foreign securities.*

(5) Increased demand for holding domestic assets hitherto held in foreign hands resulting in *"repatriation" of domestic securities* or other assets.

(6) Increased demand to reduce one's own debts to foreign creditors, effected in (premature) *debt repayments to foreigners.*

(7) Fulfillment of foreign obligations (at maturity) and *unilateral payments to foreign countries,* such as indemnities, reparations, etc.

[18] For the sake of symmetry, separations which suggested themselves for the list of spontaneous capital exports were made also in the list of spontaneous capital imports or *vice versa,* even if they might serve there no useful purpose.

[19] "Foreign Assets" include claims against foreigners, foreign securities (bonds and shares), rights and other sorts of property abroad.

Spontaneous Capital Imports

(8) Decreased demand for holding foreign assets involving *sale or liquidation of direct investment abroad.*

(9) Decreased demand for holding foreign assets involving recall or *non-renewal of direct loans to foreign debtors.*

(10) Decreased demand for holding foreign assets resulting in the supply and *realization of foreign securities* or other assets by domestic holders, without significant contacts with foreign buyers.

(11) Increased supply of domestic assets for sale in foreign markets, including *flotations of new issues abroad.*

(12) Increased supply of domestic assets to foreign investors, including *receipt of "direct investments" from abroad.*

(13) Increased demand for foreign loanable funds resulting in *direct borrowing from foreigners.*

(14) Collection of foreign obligations (at maturity) and receipts of *unilateral payments from foreign countries,* such as indemnities, reparations, etc.

The matter of "autonomous but not spontaneous" capital exports or imports can now be made clearer by reference to examples from these lists. The spontaneous capital export of type (3), taking the form of securities purchases by capitalists of the capital exporting country, is not likely also to be spontaneous from the point of view of the capital importing country. It is of course conceivable that an increased demand for foreign securities of type (3) is exactly matched by an increased supply of securities of the other country, say of type (11); but this would be a sheer coincidence. It is much more likely that the sales of securities by the capital importing country are merely responses to an increase in prices offered. The sellers of the securities may not even know who acquires their former holdings. Their sale of securities, since it is actually a sale to foreigners, constitutes an autonomous long-term capital import, but it is *not a spontaneous capital import;* [20] that is, behind it is not any increase in the demand for funds. Instead, there is an increase in the amount of funds demanded in response to the reduced price of funds (that is, in response to the increased price of securities). An example of autonomous but *not spontaneous capital exports* may be found in the combination of a spontaneous capital import, say of type (10), with a response on the part

[20] And it is not an induced capital import either. On the contrary, the induced (accommodating) capital flow which will accompany the transaction will be a capital export from this country, because its banking system will be building up reserves in foreign balances as it acquires the proceeds from the securities sales. This is not to deny that securities transactions can be also induced (accommodating) as was pointed out on p. 450.

of capitalists in the capital-exporting country. They purchase the securities, not because they have an increased demand for them, as in capital export of type (5), but rather because the amount demanded increases in response to the lower price of the securities offered.

An example of two-sided initiative, joint spontaneity between the lending and the borrowing countries, may be found in case (1) of the list, the counterpart of which, from the point of view of the capital importing country, is type (12). Likewise, types (2) and (13) may be the two aspects of an identical transaction, seen from the two countries in question. And, surely, (7) and (14) are merely two aspects of the same thing, because if obligations are fulfilled at appointed dates the initiative must be regarded as common to debtor and creditor. It is probably safe to say that, in our times of "security capitalism," one-sided spontaneity is more frequent than joint spontaneity.

The chances that capital movements will affect the levels of consumption and home investment in the capital exporting and in the capital importing country are quite uneven in the various types of movements. In general, subject to qualifications, it seems that any such effects on domestic disbursements are most likely to arise in the country in which a spontaneous capital import takes place. The case of "direct investments" undertaken in a foreign country is the one most likely linked up with increased disbursements in that country. In most other cases the shocks originating from the capital movements may be partly (or even completely) absorbed by flexible monetary mechanisms without much impact on primary disbursements.

PRIMARY DISBURSEMENTS IN THE CAPITAL-EXPORTING COUNTRY

Looking first into possible effects upon primary *consumption* expenditures, we begin with the unilateral payments [cases (7) and (14)]. If it is government funds (e.g., indemnity payments) that are transferred abroad and if these funds are being raised through taxation borne by lower-income classes, restrictive effects on consumption are certain to be felt. But if the government raises the funds through borrowing, no primary restriction of domestic consumption need arise. (In the receiving country the effects will depend on the use that is made of the received funds. Their use for government expenditures does not yet assure *increased* government expenditures; the received funds may serve merely to continue an unchanged level of expenditures with a reduced level of domestic borrowings. If the received funds are used to compensate for tax reductions, increased consumption may result, but probably only if the taxes which are reduced were borne by lower-income groups.)

Effects on primary consumption expenditures in the case of private capital transactions are not likely. Perhaps if the "capital exporter" raises the funds he needs for the acquisition of foreign claims or securities by "calling in" domestic loans outstanding, an encroachment upon primary consumption is possible. If the spontaneous export of capital is so "urgent"—as it is likely to be only in the case of a flight of capital—that not only domestic loans are seriously restricted but also the capitalists' propensity to save rises sharply, then a substantial fall of primary consumption will be associated with the rise in the demand for foreign assets. (In the receiving country there is nothing which would produce a symmetrical increase in primary consumption expenditures.)

The qualifying word "primary" (by which statements about "consumption expenditures" have been modified here all the way through) is quite essential. For even if consumption is not directly affected by the inflow or outflow of capital, changes in investments in one or both of the countries concerned will, through changes in incomes, result in secondary (induced) increases or decreases of consumption expenditures.

That changes in domestic *investment* are associated with changes in the domestic demand for holding foreign assets or with increased borrowing or taxation for government payments abroad is probable but not certain. If the acquisition of foreign assets for some reason appears more attractive, it may well take the place of home investment. Thus, in all spontaneous capital export cases home investment may be encroached upon. However, in times of easy money, a large part of the funds for the acquisition of foreign assets will probably come from liquid reserves and new bank credits; to the extent that this takes place without a stiffening of the interest rate, the level of current home investment will not be reduced.[21] Liquidity reserves are not inexhaustible, of course; so one may assume that sooner or later, if the process has started from a saving-investment equilibrium and if the new demand for foreign assets is maintained, this demand must be satisfied at the expense of domestic investment. But this is not necessary at all. If, while the first installments of the spontaneous foreign lending are met out of liquidity reserves, investments begin to increase in the receiving country, expanding income in the latter will induce commodity purchases from the lending country. And these new exports will do two things in the capital exporting country. One is that the reserve position of the banking system, possibly weakened through the spontaneous capital outflow (or, that is, accommodating capital import in which they had to engage), is relieved through the foreign proceeds from the commodity exports. The other is that the new exports generate income which results in induced saving. And this increased saving can assist in feeding further installments of the spontane-

[21] We are faced here with our cases (*a*) and (*b*) of the four ways of financing foreign lending, referred to above on p. 452.

ous capital outflow without encroachment upon the given level of home investment.

The likelihood that the capital movements of types (1)–(6), which are all spontaneous from the point of view of the lending country, actually will raise current investment in the receiving country is not equally great in all cases. The probability is greatest in type (1), the counterpart of which is listed as type (12). Surely this case of "direct investment" implies that the transferred funds are also disbursed dollar for dollar, since the investment is under the direct supervision of the capitalists of the lending country; the disbursement of the funds in the receiving country, except to the extent that machines are transferred in kind or other equipment is brought in from abroad, is almost part and parcel of the international transaction. A qualification may be needed concerning that part of the direct investment which goes into purchases of real property and other not newly constructed or produced assets, and thus does not represent additional primary disbursement. In the case of "direct foreign lending" and "direct foreign borrowing" [types (2) and (13)], when the initiative for the capital movement is as much on the side of the borrower as it is on the side of the lender, it would likewise be rather exceptional if the recipient did not make use of the borrowed funds. But we must not forget the possibility that the direct foreign borrowing may be merely a refunding transaction, which would release loanable funds to the money market of the receiving country but would not directly contribute to current investment.

If interest rates were flexible, and if liquidity preferences (the demand for money balances for "speculative motives") were not too elastic, and if the marginal efficiencies of capital were sufficiently elastic, one might say that immediate investment by the first recipients of funds from abroad was not essential at all. For, if the increased supply of loanable funds succeeded in lowering interest rates without much raising the inactive liquid balances, the use of large portions of the funds for real investment would be assured. (It would even "necessarily follow" from all these assumptions.) But the "if's" are too many and too unlikely to be realized.

Thus, if the capital import is merely the reflection of foreign demands for securities [type (3)] without any direct contacts between the capitalists of the "lending" country and the recipients of the funds in the "borrowing" country, the effects are indeed uncertain. Sellers of the securities which are acquired by the capitalists of the lending country may decide to hold liquid balances in the place of the sold assets and nobody may be induced to embark on real investment ventures. Or the banking system may absorb the entire shifts between types of foreign indebtedness with no more real change than an increased willingness to make loans (in the receiving country) if such were demanded. Hence, the autonomous capital movement may completely fail to call forth an increase of investment in the "borrowing" country.[22]

One way in which foreign purchases of securities may translate themselves into increased primary disbursements in the capital importing country is through reactions of the stock exchanges. There is a certain probability that the stock markets react favorably to the increased foreign purchases, and that higher stock prices call forth new issues for new real investment and, through the stimulus of capital gains, also increased consumption.[23] Little can be said about the degree of probability or about the magnitudes involved. The resulting additional investment and consumption may be anything between zero and a multiple of the autonomous capital inflow; that they may be just equal to it is one among an infinite number of possibilities.

Little needs to be added concerning the cases where the securities sales are spontaneous in the capital importing country. The chance that spontaneous realizations of foreign assets [type (10)] will be associated with increased home investment is greater than in the cases of non-spontaneous securities sales, although it will still depend on the conditions of the money and capital markets. (But now it is the effects upon the disbursements in the capital exporting country which are all in the dark. Those, in the capital exporting country, who are induced to take over—repatriate—the securities which are spontaneously sold by holders in the capital importing country, will rarely do so at the expense of current home investment, though this would not be inconceivable.) In the case of new securities issues in foreign markets [type (11)] the association with increased home investment in the capital-importing country is fairly clear. (However, in the capital-exporting country the easy credit conditions which attract the new flotations are possibly the result of such a degree of liquidity that little or no inroads on home investment in the capital-exporting country need take place.)

---

[22] It may be well to remember that all mentioned capital movements are not yet *net* movements; the "borrowing" country is not yet net-borrowing. Hence, if no changes in investments are achieved, incomes and trade balances do not change either and all autonomous increases in the foreign indebtedness of the "borrowing" country must be continuously offset by accommodating decreases in its foreign indebtedness. For instance, while security holders sell out to foreigners and hold domestic bank balances, the banking system holds increased amounts of foreign balances ("outside reserve").

[23] See my book *The Stock Market, Credit, and Capital Formation* (London: Hodge, and New York: Macmillan, 1940), pp. 107 ff., 159, 316 ff., *et al.*

REASONABLE ASSUMPTIONS

The foregoing account of the probable effects of autonomous capital movements upon primary disbursements was designed merely to permit a tentative and very general orientation and to give an idea about the reasonableness of certain assumptions for the next steps in the analysis of income and trade. I am aware that I have neglected or unduly minimized the operations of various auxiliary mechanisms—money markets, securities markets, foreign-exchange markets, commodities markets—which can be instrumental in bringing about some closer adjustments between capital transactions and primary disbursements. But a more intensive study could be fruitful only if problems of *timing* were included, timing in the sense of the order in and the lag with which actions take place, and also in the sense of the phase of the business cycle during which these actions occur. This is far too big a problem to tackle at this point.

XXI

The Transfer Gap of the United States

A. The Chronic Deficit: *Alternative Hypotheses; Tautological Inflation* ▪ B. The Theoretical and Statistical Concepts: *Net Real Transfers; Net Financial Transfers; The Transfer Gap* ▪ C. The Statistics, 1950-1967: *Real Transfers, 1950-1967; Financial Transfers, 1950-1967; The Transfer Gap, 1950-1967; The Parallel Changes in Real and Financial Transfers; Regression Analysis* ▪ D. Explanations and Implications: *Theoretical Explanations; A Paradox and Its Solution; The Off-Year, 1967; The Transfer Correlation and Its Policy Implications* ▪ E. The Normal Value of Financial Transfers: *Normal Capital Exports; Capital Exports, 1950-1967; Europe's Need for American Capital; Military Expenditures Abroad and Net Financial Transfers; the Required Net Real Transfers; Exchange-Rate Adjustment*

Several years ago I attempted a reinterpretation of the payments deficit of the United States: I suggested that it could most appropriately be explained as a transfer problem. The United States was making financial transfers to foreign countries—military expenditures, government loans, private loans, and direct investment—in amounts which for various reasons it was unable to match with real transfers, that is, with an excess of exports over imports of goods and services. I have argued and defended this explanation in several articles and books.[1]

On at least two occasions—in 1962 and 1963—I offered this hypothesis together with the optimistic prediction that the transfer problem

---

[1] "Pessimismo del dollaro e oro", *Rivista Internazionale di Science Economiche e Commrciali*, Vol. IX (1962), pp. 1108-1119; "Das Transfer-problem: Thema und vier Variationen", *Ordo*, Vol. XIV (1963), pp. 139-167; *International Payments, Debts, and Gold* (New York: Scribner's, 1964), pp. 386-395;

would eventually be solved by monetary expansion in surplus countries, with their rates of price inflation exceeding that of the United States. This prediction has gone sour. But the failure of my prediction does not compromise my hypothesis, especially since it is rather clear why the prediction has failed to come true. The United States, after it had been pursuing a cautious policy of stabilizing the price level for several years, embarked in 1963 on a policy of monetary and fiscal expansion designed to reduce unemployment and accelerate the rate of economic growth. At the same time, the countries with the largest payments surpluses undertook to decelerate their rates of inflation. I am not blaming any of the governments for their policy decisions, though it seems fair to say that all countries went too far in their zeal to do the right thing: the United States overindulged in fiscal ease and the Europeans jammed their monetary brakes too tight. I mention this only to explain why I was wrong when I counted on differential rates of inflation to solve the transfer problem of the United States. That problem, after a few years of attenuation, has again aggravated and is now as serious as it ever was.

My aim in this paper is to restate my hypothesis, to offer additional support for it by means of statistical illustration, and to point out why I regard the official prescriptions for removing the payments imbalance quite useless, or worse than useless. Realizing, however, that several alternative explanations of the imbalance have been proposed, I think I should first state my reasons for preferring my own hypothesis.

A. THE CHRONIC DEFICIT

There are many ways to define and measure a deficit in the balance of payments. By several definitions, the deficit of the United States started in 1950 and is still very much in evidence. The character of the deficit has changed over the years; for example, during the earlier years it was possible for many to speak of dollar shortage whereas for the last eight or ten years the talk is of a dollar glut. Some interpreters even now protest against the designation of the payments position of the United States as a genuine deficit. Perhaps, then, it would be more judicious to say exactly what kind of statistical arrangement of data is referred to when one says that the payments deficit has lasted now for 18 years. The most widely quoted figures are those published by the U.S. Department of Commerce under the name of "balance on liquidity basis". The deficit in this sense is measured by the decrease in official reserve assets of the United States plus the increase in liquid liabilities to all foreigners.

Involuntary Foreign Lending (Stockholm: Almqvist & Wiksell, 1965), pp. 51-57; *The 1968 Economic Report of the President*, Hearings before the Joint Economic Committee, Congress of the United States, 90th Congress, 2nd Session, Part 2 (Washington, February 1968), pp. 399-416.

The statistics of the balance of payments have exhibited deficits so defined in 17 out of the last 18 years.[2] For these deficits several explanations have been offered.

Alternative hypotheses

My own explanation is that the large financial transfers of the United States were° not quite matched by its export surpluses because, in the absence of sufficient expansion of demand, incomes, and prices in other countries, only painful doses of deflation in the United States or an unwanted reduction in the exchange rate of the dollar could secure the reductions in relative incomes and prices that would be needed to raise the export surplus to the required size. This diagnosis, together with a number of factors which I shall later discuss in detail, does not allow of any optimistic expectations regarding the elimination of the deficit in the foreseeable future.

Other explanations lead to different conclusions. I shall select seven alternative hypotheses for a brief review; they permit or imply an optimistic diagnosis—either that the trouble is not alarming or that it will soon disappear. I shall state each hypothesis in a single sentence and add another sentence to indicate why I reject it.

Hypothesis No. 1: The persistent statistical deficit is not a symptom of disequilibrium, but only a reflection of financial intermediation by American banks to accommodate liquidity-loving savers and investors in foreign countries; everything will be all right as soon as foreign monetary authorities begin to see the light and will consent to accumulate dollars in ever-increasing amounts.—The answer is that the foreign authorities will not accept this interpretation of our deficit, even if we should be willing to accept it (which I am not).

Hypothesis No. 2: The sequence of deficits in the payments balance has been due to a variety of strokes of bad luck, ranging from delays in the introduction of compact automobiles and strikes in strategic industries to sudden upsurges of direct investments abroad; the series of unlucky accidents will eventually come to an end, and balance will be restored all by itself.—The answer is that hard-luck stories cannot be believed after 18 years of deficit.

Hypothesis No. 3: The deficit in the last few years has been the result of unduly lax fiscal policy; the tax increase and budget cut of 1968 will stop the inflation and restore external balance.—The answer is that the removal of the budget deficit was badly needed to prevent the pay-

[2] Even the one exceptional surplus, in 1957, the year after the Suez crisis, would turn into a deficit if "Errors and Omissions" were put "below the line," that is, treated as a financing item rather than an unrecorded long-term capital inflow.

ments deficit from getting worse; but such a disinflationary policy is not sufficient to remove the payments deficit unless the surplus countries indulge in inflationary policies—which they have no intention of doing and which they, with the exception of France, may be able to avoid.

Hypothesis No. 4: The deficit in the last three years may be attributed to the wage-price spiral turning faster in the United States than in the surplus countries; as soon as the United States succeeds in slowing down the cost-push inflation, its payments position will improve rapidly. —The answer is that the surplus countries are no less anxious to hold down the cost push and (except France) may even be more successful than the United States.

Hypothesis No. 5: The deficit has been due to excessive monetary expansion keeping interest rates unduly low and allowing a high rate of domestic investment as well as huge investments abroad; the Federal Reserve Banks have terminated this policy and one may expect the increased tightness of credit in the United States to improve both its current and its capital balance.—The answer is that the interest differentials in the past reflected, most of the time, the richer flow of savings in the United States, rather than an inflation of credit, and that the present tightness in the United States will not be allowed to continue once the stern fiscal policy, which has at last been adopted, becomes effective.

Hypothesis No. 6: The new balance-of-payments program, announced by President Johnson in January 1968, will reduce the payments deficit by 2.5 billion dollars, which goes far to restore external balance. —The answer is that a reduction of outpayments by $2.5 billion will not achieve a reduction of the deficit by a similar amount, and whatever reduction can be achieved by this program will at best be temporary, since temporary restrictions are unlikely to produce lasting results.

Hypothesis No. 7: The present payments deficit is to a large extent attributable to the direct and indirect effects of the war in Viet Nam; as soon as the war is terminated, the reduction of military expenditures abroad and the reduction of imports due to defense expenditures at home will remove most or perhaps all of the present payments deficit.—The answer is that foreign-aid expenditures may (and should) take the place of military expenditures abroad, and expenditures in the war on poverty should (and will) take the place of defense spending at home; but even if some savings in foreign outlays can be made, the feedback effects upon our exports may be considerable, so that it would be unrealistic to expect restoration of the external balance from an end of the war.

Tautological inflation

At least three of the alternative hypotheses listed explain the deficit by pointing to inflation: to excessive fiscal ease leading to a budget deficit, with domestic overspending (demand pull) resulting in higher imports and lower exports; to wage-price spirals (cost push) resulting in prices not competitive enough to produce an adequate export surplus; or to an easy-money policy of the Federal Reserve raising aggregate demand and inducing capital to go abroad. Inflation hypotheses to explain the American payments deficit have been most popular abroad, because they have fitted the complaint about "imported inflation" often repeated in surplus countries. Yet, these hypotheses are unsatisfactory in that they point to the wrong "variables" as the chief causal factors and perhaps also suggest the wrong policies as remedial factors.

I must admit, however, that my rejection of the inflation argument—the thesis that the payments deficit of the United States can be attributed to its excessive monetary expansion—is vulnerable in at least two respects. First, one cannot deny the existence of at least three inflationary periods in the United States during the last 18 years: a demand pull during the Korean War (1950-53), a cost push in the late 50's (1956-58), and again a demand pull in recent years (1965-68); each of these no doubt aggravated the transfer problem. Secondly, some highly respected economists deem it not altogether foolish to hold that *every* payments deficit is "due" to excessive demand in the deficit country, since if aggregate demand were much smaller there would be no deficit.

This second proposition amounts to a near-tautology. A payments deficit of a country can be defined as an excess supply of the country's currency in the foreign-exchange market, and it stands to reason that this excess supply can be removed if the total supply of the currency is "sufficiently" reduced. If a "sufficient" dose of deflation can remove the payments deficit, may one not hold the failure to deflate to be the "cause" of the deficit? This would be a defensible position but, though not "absolutely foolish", not very enlightening. To attribute the *emergence* of a payments deficit to an excessive increase in the supply of money and in total spending makes good sense; but to attribute the *persistence* of a payments deficit, which may or may not have arisen from excessive money creation or spending, to a nondecrease in the supply of money and in spending is not good analytic practice.

Incidentally, even if the thesis of "tautological inflation" as an explanation of each and every payments deficit is unsound on logical grounds, it is not inconsistent with the transfer hypothesis, that is, with the position which attributes the payments deficit of the United States to its failure to solve its transfer problem. For, as almost all economists concerned with this subject have stressed, the transfer problem lies in the capacity or incapacity of the economy to produce an export surplus of a size sufficient to meet its transfer commitments *although* the amounts to be transferred have been successfully syphoned out of the income stream of the economy. If its "money flows" have not been appropriately reduced, then one can hardly be surprised if the real transfer, the increase in net exports of goods and services, cannot be accomplished. This failure is therefore "explained" by the insufficient extraction of income or money or buying power from the "pockets" of the people in the country that has undertaken the large foreign commitments.

Whether these are government commitments for reparations, military expenditures, or foreign aid, or private capital movements to foreign lands makes little difference. The amounts transferred must have been taken away from domestic disbursements if one is to expect flows of goods and services to match the outflow of funds. (In lucky circumstances, overexpansions abroad may take the place of the retrenchment of domestic spending.)

It would be easy to show that at no time were net reductions made in aggregate domestic spending in the United States. Hence, it could be said with apparent conviction that the failure to make these cuts was equivalent to inflation of domestic demand. Again, this proposition is not very helpful. One must not forget that transfer theory was formulated in largely static terms, not with reference to growing economies. Under conditions of economic growth, one need not assume domestic spending to be cut absolutely when funds are sent abroad, but only to be increased at a reduced rate. It is hard to know, however, what the warranted rate of increase of domestic disbursements would be when foreign payments have to be made while the economies concerned, the paying as well as the receiving countries, continue their normal growth.[3]

We know from traditional transfer theory that a reduction of domestic disbursements by the exact amount of the financial transfers may not be sufficient to achieve real transfers of the same magnitude. Under certain conditions an extra dose of spending reduction, with the multiple dose of income deflation, would be needed to close the transfer gap at fixed exchange rates. While one could hold that the failure to reduce the rate of increase of domestic spending by an amount commensurate to the outflow of funds constitutes an act of quasi-inflationary behavior, one cannot reasonably take the existence of any transfer gap as an indication of culpable overexpansion. It may be possible to close a transfer gap by deflationary policies; but the failure to pursue such policies cannot in sound analysis be regarded as inflationary policy. In this sense, "tautological inflation" is no better as explanation of a transfer gap than it is of any other type of deficit in the balance of payments.

---

[3] To my knowledge, the only analysis of the problem appears in my essay "The Transfers Problem Revisited", in this volume, pp. 433–446.

B. The theoretical and statistical concepts

For an attempt to provide a statistical test or illustration of the thesis that the payments deficits of the United States can be explained as "transfer gaps", we need a set of statistical concepts that approximately correspond to the theoretical constructs used in transfer theory. We can never expect that available statistical records will provide precisely what would be needed. Sometimes, however, relatively innocuous manipulations with, or rearrangements of, the statistical data will furnish acceptable substitutes for what would qualify as suitable counterparts for the constructs of theory.

For our present purpose we need, before all, the statistical counterparts for Net Real Transfers, Net Financial Transfers, and the Transfer Gap.

Net Real Transfers

For a statistical computation of the flows of goods and services that may be regarded as "real transfers" one cannot simply accept either the balance on current account or the balance of goods and services. The current account includes purely financial transfers, and some of the services that are usually shown among exports and imports cannot be regarded as real transfers in the sense of the relevant theory.

The current account includes unilateral transfers to foreign countries. Since the capital account comprises only those financial transfers which change the country's claims on and liabilities to foreign countries, it is quite correct that unilateral transfers, such as donations and pensions, are shown in the current account. For our purposes, however, private remittances and government pension payments to residents of other countries, and government grants, military or otherwise, to foreign countries must be regarded as financial transfers.

If exports of goods and services under military grants are excluded from the statistics of exports, and the grants equally excluded from the statistics of unilateral transfers, one avoids an exaggerated impression of the co-variation between real and financial flows. The inclusion of transfers in kind on both sides of the balance of payments might increase the regression coefficient in the function linking the two variables and thus might give exaggerated statistical support to the theory that the real flows are influenced by independenly determined financial flows. We decide, therefore, that we shall omit from our computations the military grants as well as the exports of goods and services under these grants.[4]

---

[4] One might think that for the same reasons "tied loans" and the sales tied to them ought to be excluded from the current and capital accounts, respectively. However, there is the possibility, and indeed a strong suspicion, that many of these sales would have been made in any case, so that an increase

Military expenditures abroad are usually reported as imports of foreign services. This is not appropriate for our purposes. If we want to examine the "feedback effects" of military expenditures—for example, the increase in exports that come about as an indirect result of increases in the foreign expenditures of the United States—we must treat the military expenditures as financial transfers. We shall, therefore, omit them from the statistics of imports and relegate them to the statistics of financial outflows.

Earnings from capital are usually reported in the balance of goods and services: the income on investments abroad is regarded as payment for a "capital service" sold to foreign countries. This is unsatisfactory for a test of transfer theory. According to that theory one should expect that real flows are induced by the flow of monetary returns from capital invested. Hence, the earnings of dividends and interest will be shown here as financial transfers; whether these purely financial flows do or do not generate real flows in the same direction is precisely what is to be tested.

To make these rearrangements of the customary presentation of balance-of-payments statistics is not to question the soundness of international convention. These statistics have to serve many different purposes and an arrangement most suitable for one purpose may be quite unsuitable for another. Our present purpose requires rearrangements that can help reported magnitudes to become approximate counterparts of the abstract concepts of a theoretical model constructed for a particular explanatory task. Whether certain transactions change the investment position, indebtedness, or liquidity of the country is not relevant to the transfer problem. But whether certain changes in the international movement of goods and services can be explained as the results of changes in the movement of funds, this is what matters in the assignment before us.

Transfer theory assumes that the flows of goods and services will be reshaped through income effects and substitution effects emanating from changes in incomes and prices which, in turn, are engendered by changes in the flows of funds, especially by changes in domestic spending due to financial receipts and payments from and to foreign countries. It follows that, for a statistical test or illustration of transfer theory, we want the balance of goods and services to consist chiefly of such items as are sold and bought out of incomes and at market prices, or at least under conditions that allow income elasticities and price elasticities of supply and demand to come into play.

It should be clear that military expenditures change primarily when

---

in sales under tied loans would be a decrease in regular sales. It is therefore advisable to leave both the loans and the sales in the respective accounts.

the general staff so decides, and this decision is not greatly affected by relative incomes and relative prices at home and abroad. Earnings from capital may be related to changes in aggregate income, but changes in relative incomes and prices at home and abroad will hardly be among the major factors affecting the payment of dividends and interest. Thus, the relegation of these transactions from their customary places in the balance of goods and services to the balance of financial transactions should be accepted as a reasonable rearrangement.

Net Financial Transfers

Besides the two items relegated from service account to the account of financial flows, the latter is composed of unilateral transfers and capital movements.

Unilateral transfers consist of private remittances, payments of government pensions, and government grants. In order to save space, private remittances and government pensions can be merged, both being rather stable or slowly increasing amounts. A merger of government grants and government loans to foreign countries suggests itself because for the problem at hand it makes little difference whether any repayments can be expected in a distant future. With regard to claims by foreign governments and to flows of private capital the problems are more complicated and some decisions about what to include and what to exclude have to be made. We must warn at the outset that these decisions will inevitably be somewhat arbitrary.

One might presume that movements of long-term capital may reasonably be regarded as autonomous, whereas short-term flows may be treated as induced by other changes in the balance of payments. Such a presumption, however, would be quite wrong, particularly for recent years when (sometimes in order to improve the appearance of the statistical balance of payments) maturities of government securities and bank deposits were doctored to make what was essentially short-term capital be covered by the operational definition of long-term capital. On the other hand, there are liquid dollar holdings of foreigners which, in spite of their legal and institutional form (permitting immediate withdrawal on demand), are to some extent quasi-permanent from an economic point of view. Thus, the distinction between short and long term, if judged by the terms of the contract, is not acceptable as a proxy for the distinction between autonomous and accommodating.[5] One should attempt to keep the category of financial transfers strictly apart from the category of so-called "financ-

---

[5] I coined the term "accommodating capital movements" in 1941 and defined it in my book *International Trade and the National Income Multiplier* (Philadelphia, 1943, reprinted New York: Augustus Kelley, 1961), p. 134.

ing items", that is, from financial transactions designed to absorb an oversupply of (or meet an excess demand for) dollars in the foreign-exchange market. It would be nice to produce a clean account of the financial transactions that are likely to influence the flow of goods and services rather than be influenced by it.

This, unfortunately, cannot be done. The available statistics of the balance of payments do not provide the necessary distinctions and separations. One is always tempted to follow the easiest route and accept what is furnished ready-made, without alterations. The official statistics of the U.S. Department of Commerce treat all movements of American capital as autonomous, that is to say, changes even in short-term foreign assets held by residents of the United States (including banks) are shown "above the line", not as financing items reflecting other transactions on current or capital account. On the other hand, for movements of foreign capital some finer distinctions are made and certain types are shown as items financing the deficit of the overall balance. However, the distinctions are rather tenuous and certainly not relevant for our purposes.

In my first attempt to support my transfer hypothesis with statistical data[6] I decided to include in the account of financial transfers all movements of American capital and none of foreign capital. The decision to include all "Private U.S. capital, net"—short or long-term, banks or nonbanks—among financial tranfers to foreign countries was probably less objectionable than the decision to exclude all movements of foreign capital. In a second attempt (not published) I followed the procedure of the U.S. Department of Commerce and included "nonliquid" claims by foreign holders, but excluded "liquid" claims. The trouble with this procedure is that the "nonliquid" assets held by foreigners comprise also the long-term government securities and the long-term deposits in American banks that are held by foreign official agencies and private banks. Yet, changes in the size of these holdings cannot be regarded as autonomous; they are largely accommodating, induced by conditions in the foreign-exchange market. Hence, they have no place in our account of independently determined financial flows.

On the other hand, it is surely incorrect to regard all changes in the size of liquid, near-liquid, and pseudo-nonliquid dollar assets as accommodating capital movements. Different motives for holding such assets are probably associated with different implications of changes in their size. The case of official holders, chiefly central banks, may be unambiguous, but for private holders, chiefly trading firms and commercial banks, we ought to distinguish several reasons for increases in dollar holdings:

---

[6] See p. 415 of my statement before the Joint Economic Committee of the Congress, cited in footnote 1 on the first page of this article.

1) Foreign traders may want to hold larger transactions balances because the turnover in their foreign business (dollars collected and paid) is increasing. 2) Foreign commercial banks may need larger transactions balances because the turnover in their foreign-exchange business (dollars purchased and sold) is increasing. 3) Foreign commercial banks may wish to hold more dollar assets in response to more attractive interest-rate differentials or spot-forward rate margins; they may acquire the dollars by buying them (in the market or from their own central bank), by borrowing them, or by lending to American institutions. 4) Foreign commercial banks may extend more loans to American borrowers at the initiative of the latter. Increases in dollar claims, arising from 3) and 4) are evidently temporary financing, unlikely to go on for very long and even likely to be reversed rather soon. On the other hand, increases in dollar claims arising from 1) and 2) are sustainable; they are flows that can go on year after year, associated with the growth in world trade. These increases in liquid dollar holdings would qualify for inclusion in autonomous financial transfers.

Alas, the international capital accounts cannot be disentangled. Perhaps one could use sophisticated econometric techniques to separate changes in foreign dollar holdings "explained" by growth in world trade from changes "explained" by nongrowth factors; or changes dependent on the *volume* of international transactions from changes dependent on the *balance* of international transactions. The former would be eligible, the latter ineligible for inclusion in the account of financial transfers as autonomous foreign capital flows into the United States. I have not undertaken any such separation and have decided to exclude all changes in assets, short-term or long-term, that are held by foreign official agencies or are liabilities of the U.S. Government or of American banks. I have included only three types of transactions: direct investment in the United States, changes in holdings of American securities other than Treasury issues, and other long-term foreign liabilities of private nonbank residents of the United States. The restriction to these three items in the foreign-capital account will become most significant in the last few years, especially in 1966 and 1967, when American banks reported increases in long-term liabilities to foreigners (time deposits and certificates of deposits) of almost 1 billion each year,—amounts which I do not recognize as autonomous capital inflows.

The Transfer Gap

The amount by which Net Real Transfers fall short of Net Financial Transfers is the Transfer Gap. As I have said before, the operational concepts used in statistical records, estimates, and compilations do not fully correspond to the theoretical constructs used in the abstract models. We have just seen how difficult it is to separate financial transactions into those that can be regarded as autonomous transfers and those that are merely accommodating, induced by imbalances and financing the gap.

The differences between the statistical transfer gap and the statistical liquidity deficit were alluded to in the preceding section. The chief items accounting for these differences are: 1) errors and omissions, which I do not treat as autonomous financial transfers,[7] but which official statistics treat as unrecorded transactions requiring financing (that is, increases or reductions of reserve assets or liquid liabilities); 2) changes in foreign long-term liabilities of American banks and in short-term liabilities of nonbank residents, both of which for the official statistics are "above the line" (that is, not among the financing items) but which I exclude from autonomous transfers; and 3) changes in foreign liabilities of the U.S. Government other than marketable or convertible Treasury obligations, changes which I again exclude from autonomous transfers while official statistics abide by the accepted definitional criterion of non-liquidity.

We should also note a difference between the statistical and the theoretical transfer gap. The latter must distinguish between an inherited deficit, due to any kind of past disturbance (including unclosed transfer gaps) and new changes in the balance of payments due to new financial transfers. No such separation can be made for statistical transfer gaps. In theory one can start from an equilibrium position with a zero deficit; can then introduce financial transfers, bringing forth real transfers of somewhat smaller magnitude and leaving a transfer gap of a certain amount in a particular period; then introduce additional financial transfers, which again produce real transfers and perhaps another gap, while the effects of the earlier remittances are causing still further changes in the real flows, perhaps reducing the gap remaining from the earlier adjustment process. Thus, an old transfer gap and a superimposed, new transfer gap can be analytically separated. Empirical research is rather helpless regarding such possibilities; if a transfer gap is calculated for a particular year, there is no way of saying how much of it can be attributed to a lack of adjustment to past events and how much to increased financial transfers of the current year. Regression analysis of the year-to-year data, with or without lag, may serve as a weak substitute for the unlimited possibilities of the manipulations on a model in which all parameters and coefficients are fixed by the analyst's decision.

---

[7] "Errors and Omissions" may include wrong valuations in commodity trade, unrecorded services, changes in leads and lags in payments for exports and imports, and unrecorded transactions in short-term or long-term capital. Only the latter would qualify for inclusion as autonomous financial transfers, but their share in Errors and Omissions is probably negligible.

The most embarrassing vexation in this business is our inability to know which part of a statistical transfer gap is really attributable to un-manageable transfers and which part to entirely different causes. For example, a payments deficit may have arisen for reasons unrelated to financial transfers—say, a rate of income-and-price inflation faster than in other countries, or some shifts in demand—but at the same time finan-cial transfers were made which in the absence of the other disturbances would be fully matched by real transfers. Statistics, nevertheless, will ex-hibit a "transfer gap". The only saving grace in this connection may be the length of the time series: if deficits persist for a time long enough to make regression analysis meaningful, regressions of real transfers on financial transfers may indicate how much of the changes in the former can be satisfactorily "explained" by the latter, and whether a great deal is missed by disregarding all other factors in the picture.

C. THE STATISTICS, 1950-1967

We are now sufficiently, or perhaps excessively, prepared to look at the statistical series. All the data for the international transactions of the United States are taken from the *Survey of Current Business*, Vol. 48, No. 6 (June 1968) published by the U.S. Department of Commerce. For the Gross National Product (GNP) series, included in order to allow rele-vant comparisons, earlier issues were consulted. All figures are in current dollars, not corrected for price changes. It is partly for this reason that comparisons with GNP are needed. For example, the transfer gap may look much bigger in 1967, with $4.8 billion, than it was in 1950, with $3.6 billion. Yet, the gap was only 0.6 per cent of GNP in 1967, but 1.3 per cent in 1950.

The figures shown in Table 1 are in billions of dollars, the figures in Table 2 are percentages of GNP.

Real Transfers, 1950-1967

Exports of goods and services increased from $12.2 billion in 1950 to $38.9 billion in 1967, not counting exports under military grants and earnings from capital. The increase, by 219 per cent, was due to some extent to higher prices—the unit value of exported merchandise increased by 34 per cent during the 18 years—but chiefly to larger quantities. Of the 17 changes from year to year, only three (in 1952, 1953, and 1958) were decreases, the other 14 years were increases. The compounded an-nual rate of increase over the period was 7.1 per cent for the total value of exports of goods and services.

Imports of goods and services increased from $11.1 billion in 1950 to $34.4 billion in 1967, not counting military expenditures abroad and

GROSS NATIONAL PRODUCT, REAL AND FINANCIAL TRANSFE

(In billi

	1950	1951	1952	1953	1954	1955	1956
1. Gross National Product . .	284.8	328.4	345.5	364.6	364.8	398.0	419
Goods and Services							
2. Exports, excl. earnings from capital	12.2	16.9	16.2	15.0	15.5	17.4	20
3. Imports, excl. military expenditures and excl. earnings from capital	11.1	13.4	13.3	13.5	12.9	14.4	16
4. Net Real Transfers [2-3] .	1.1	3.5	2.9	1.5	2.6	3.0	4
Autonomous Financial Transactions							
5. Military expenditures abroad	0.6	1.3	2.1	2.6	2.6	2.9	2.
6. Remittances and pensions .	0.5	0.5	0.6	0.6	0.6	0.6	0.
7. U.S. Government grants and loans, net	3.6	3.2	2.4	2.1	1.6	2.2	2.
8. Private U.S. capital, net . .	1.3	1.0	1.2	0.4	1.6	1.3	3.
9. Sum of transfers to foreign countries	6.0	6.0	6.3	5.7	6.4	7.0	9.
10. Earnings from capital, net .	3.2	1.5	1.4	1.5	1.8	2.0	2.
11. Foreign long-term capital net, excl. gov't securities and bank debts	0.1	0.2	0.2	0.2	0.3	0.4	0.
12. Sum of transfers from abroad	1.3	1.7	1.6	1.7	2.1	2.4	2.
13. Net Financ. Transfers [9-12]	4.7	4.3	4.7	4.0	4.3	4.6	6.
Payments Deficits							
14. Transfer Gap [13-4] . . .	3.6	0.8	1.8	2.5	1.7	1.6	1.
15. Liquidity Deficit	3.5	0.0	1.2	2.2	1.5	1.2	1.
Annual Changes							
16. Net Real Transfers [4] . .		+ 2.4	− 0.6	− 1.4	+ 1.1	+ 0.4	+ 1.8
17. Net Financial Transfers [13]		− 0.4	+ 0.4	− 0.7	+ 0.3	+ 0.3	+ 1.
18. Transfer Gap [14]		− 2.8	+ 1.0	+ 0.7	− 0.8	− 0.1	0.0

TABLE I

...D PAYMENTS DEFICITS OF THE UNITED STATES 1950-1967

...dollars)

1957	1958	1959	1960	1961	1962	1963	1964	1965	1966	1967
441.1	447.3	483.7	503.7	520.1	560.3	590.5	632.4	683.9	743.3	785.0
23.7	20.2	20.5	23.9	24.7	25.9	27.8	31.7	33.3	36.9	38.9
16.9	16.8	19.4	19.2	19.1	21.1	22.3	24.3	27.6	32.3	34.4
6.8	3.4	1.1	4.7	5.6	4.8	5.5	7.4	5.7	4.6	4.5
3.2	3.4	3.1	3.1	3.0	3.1	3.0	2.9	2.9	3.7	4.3
0.7	0.7	0.8	0.7	0.7	0.8	0.9	0.9	1.0	1.0	1.3
2.6	2.6	2.0	2.8	2.8	3.0	3.6	3.6	3.4	3.4	4.2
3.6	2.9	2.4	3.9	4.2	3.4	4.5	6.6	3.8	4.3	5.5
10.1	9.6	8.3	10.5	10.7	10.3	12.0	14.0	11.1	12.4	15.3
2.2	2.2	2.2	2.3	3.0	3.3	3.3	4.0	4.2	4.2	4.6
0.4	0.1	0.7	0.4	0.4	0.3	0.3	− 0.1	− 0.3	1.2	1.4
2.6	2.3	2.9	2.7	3.4	3.6	3.6	3.9	3.9	5.4	6.0
7.5	7.3	5.4	7.8	7.3	6.7	8.4	10.1	7.2	7.0	9.3
0.7	3.9	4.3	3.1	1.7	1.9	2.9	2.7	1.5	2.4	4.8
− 0.6	3.4	3.9	3.9	2.4	2.2	2.7	2.8	1.3	1.4	3.6
+ 2.0	− 3.4	− 2.3	+ 3.6	+ 0.9	− 0.8	+ 0.7	+ 1.9	− 1.7	− 1.1	− 0.1
+ 1.1	− 0.2	− 1.9	+ 2.4	− 0.5	− 0.6	+ 1.7	+ 1.7	− 2.9	− 0.2	+ 2.3
− 0.9	+ 3.2	+ 0.4	− 1.2	− 1.4	+ 0.2	+ 1.0	− 0.2	− 1.2	+ 0.9	+ 2.4

REAL AND FINANCIAL TRANSFERS AND PAYMENTS DEFICIT AS PERCENTA(

	1950	1951	1952	1953	1954	1955	195(
1. Gross National Product . .	100.0	100.0	100.0	100.0	100.0	100.0	100.
2. Exports, excluding earnings from capital	4.3	5.1	4.7	4.1	4.2	4.4	5.
3. Imports, excluding military expenditures and earnings from capi al	3.9	4.1	3.8	3.7	3.5	3.6	3.
4. Net Real Transfers	0.4	1.1	0.8	0.4	0.7	0.8	1.
5. Military expenditures abroad	0.2	0.4	0.6	0.7	0.7	0.7	0.
7. U.S. Government, grants and capital, net	1.3	1.0	0.7	0.6	0.4	0.6	0.
8. Private U.S. capital, net . .	0.5	0.3	0.3	0.1	0.4	0.3	0.
9. Sum of transfers to foreign countries	2.1	1.8	1.8	1.5	1.8	1.8	2.
10. Earnings from capital, net .	0.4	0.5	0.4	0.4	0.5	0.5	0.
13. Net Financial Transfers . .	1.7	1.3	1.4	1.1	1.2	1.2	1.
14. Transfer Gap	1.3	0.2	0.5	0.7	0.5	0.4	0.

earnings from foreign capital placed in the United States. The increase, by 210 per cent, was due to a small extent to higher prices—the unit value of imported merchandise increased by 15 per cent—but chiefly to larger quantities. Of the 17 annual changes, five (in 1952, 1954, 1958, 1960, and 1961) were decreases, the other 12 were increases. The compounded annual rate of increase over the period was 6.9 per cent for the total value of imports of goods and services.

The net export surplus, here called Net Real Transfers, varied between $1.1 billion (in 1950 and also in 1959) and $7.4 billion (in 1964). It exceeded $5 billion in five years (1957, 1961, 1963, 1964, and 1965). Of the 17 annual changes, nine were increases, and eight decreases.

A glance at Table 2 reveals considerable stability of exports and imports as percentages of GNP. Exports (excluding earnings from capital) varied only between 4.1 and 5.3 per cent of GNP, imports (excluding military expenditures) between 3.5 and 4.4 per cent. (It is noteworthy that the two highest "import propensities" occurred in the last two years.) The export surplus (Net Real Transfers) varied between 0.2 and 1.5 per

GROSS NATIONAL PRODUCT OF THE UNITED STATES, 1950-1967

957	1958	1959	1960	1961	1962	1963	1964	1965	1966	1967
00.0	100.0	100.0	100.0	100.0	100.0	100.0	100.0	100.0	100.0	100.0
5.3	4.5	4.2	4.7	4.7	4.6	4.7	5.0	4.9	5.0	5.0
3.8	3.8	4.0	3.8	3.7	3.8	3.8	3.8	4.0	4.3	4.4
1.5	0.8	0.2	0.9	1.1	0.9	0.9	1.2	0.8	0.6	0.6
0.7	0.8	0.6	0.6	0.6	0.6	0.5	0.5	0.4	0.5	0.6
0.6	0.6	0.4	0.6	0.5	0.5	0.6	0.6	0.5	0.5	0.5
0.8	0.6	0.5	0.8	0.8	0.6	0.8	1.0	0.6	0.6	0.7
2.3	2.1	1.7	2.1	2.1	1.8	2.0	2.2	1.6	1.7	1.9
0.5	0.5	0.5	0.5	0.6	0.6	0.6	0.6	0.6	0.6	0.6
1.7	1.6	1.1	1.5	1.4	1.2	1.4	1.6	1.1	0.9	1.2
0.2	0.9	0.9	0.6	0.3	0.3	0.5	0.4	0.2	0.3	0.6

cent of GNP. While these are minute fractions of GNP, their variability is impressive: the high figure is more than seven times the low.

Financial Transfers, 1950-1967

The largest items in the category of financial transfers to foreign countries are military expenditures, U.S. Government grants and loans, and private capital exports. Over the years these three items changed ranks in relative size: government grants held top rank only in the early years (1950-52), were then overtaken by military expenditures, and finally (beginning in 1956) by private capital exports. (Private capital exports would not be in first place if the returns on this capital, the earnings of foreign dividends and interest payments, were deducted. These earnings are not shown in Table 1; only net earnings from capital, those received minus those paid, are entered as transfers received from foreign countries.) The annual averages of these three transfers for the entire period of 18 years were quite similar: $3.1 billion of private capital, $2.9 billion of government grants and loans, and $2.8 billion of military expenditures. The sum of transfers to foreign countries (disregarding earnings from capital and inflows of foreign capital) increased from $6.0 billion in 1950 to $15.3 billion in 1967.

Net earnings from capital, that is, the excess of returns received on American capital placed abroad over those paid on foreign capital placed in the United States, increased from $1.2 billion in 1950 to $4.6 billion in 1967. The increase reflects the investment position of the United States, steadily improving as a result of the cumulative exports of American capital.

Inflows of foreign private long-term capital—comprising only the three types I have chosen to include—were relatively insignificant in most of the years until 1966, when they suddenly assumed importance. They had been between $0.1 and $0.4 billion in twelve of the 14 years from 1950 to 1963, and even negative, indicating withdrawals, in 1964 and 1965. The upsurge in 1966 and 1967, to $1.2 and $1.4 billion, respectively, is surprising, especially since it was not accompanied, as one might suspect, by a decline in liquid or short-time claims of private nonbank foreigners. On the contrary these claims increased at the same time, as did also the dollar holdings of foreign commercial banks and official agencies.

I should perhaps repeat the warning that some portion of the increases in liquid dollar holdings by private foreigners, banks as well as others, would in the nature of things qualify as autonomous, not accommodating, capital inflows. Only because I was unable to find an easy way of measuring or estimating the magnitudes of these inflows did I feel compelled to exclude them. The exclusion does not, however, vitiate the conclusions which I shall draw from the present analysis.

Net Financial Transfers, as computed from the six items included in Table 1, varied between $4.0 billion (in 1953) and $10.1 billion (in 1964). They stayed at $4.7 billion or below until 1955, were between $5.4 and $7.8 billion in the years from 1956 to 1962 and again in 1965 and 1966, and reached higher levels in three years, 1963, 1966, and 1967, when they amounted to $8.4, $10.1 and $9.3 billion, respectively.

It is usually overlooked that the large increases in financial transfers reckoned in dollars did *not* constitute increases relative to GNP. As we see in Table 2, the year in which the highest fraction of GNP was committed to transfers to foreign countries was 1950, the very first year of the period. At 1.7 per cent, this fraction was equalled only once, in 1957, and never surpassed in any of the other years. The lowest percentage figure is recorded for 1966, the only year when net transfers fell below 1 per cent of GNP. The apparently heavy transfer commitments of 1967 were, at 1.2 per cent of GNP, really quite modest; in only four of the 18 years were the net financial transfers below that figure.

Analogous comparisons for the individual items are also illuminating. The "extravagant" military expenditures in 1967, which shocked the observers at home and abroad, were only 0.55 per cent of GNP less than they had been in eleven of the other 17 years.[8] The "lavish" amount of government grants and loans to foreign countries in 1967, which aroused the anger of American businessmen and politicians, was only 0.54 per cent of GNP, again less than they had been in eleven of the other 17 years.[8] And private capital exports in 1967 were 0.7 per cent of GNP, less than they had been in six of the other 17 years (8). If the earnings from private capital invested or lent abroad ($6.2 billion in 1967) are set against new capital outflows of the year, it can be seen that all of these outflows, and even more, was paid for out of the returns on past investment.

The Transfer Gap, 1950-1967

Computed in current dollars, the Transfer Gap, in the 18 years shown in Table 1, varied between $0.7 billion and $4.8 billion. The low was in 1957, the year following the Suez crisis, the high in 1967, the year of the monetary overexpansion associated with the escalation of the war in Viet Nam. In only two years was the gap less than $1 billion and in only two years was it more than $4 billion. In the remaining 14 years it varied between $1.5 billion (in 1965) and $3.9 billion (in 1959). Its average size over the entire 18 years was $2.4 billion.

These variations of the transfer gap are very small in comparison with GNP and with the volume of foreign trade. The invariance of the gap is especially remarkable if we omit the last year of the series. From 1950 to 1966, GNP increased from $284.8 billion to $743.3 billion, and the trade volume (exports plus imports) increased from $23.3 billion to $69.2 billion; yet the transfer gap was $3.6 billion in 1950 and only $2.4 in 1966. There was no tendency for the gap to become narrower; indeed, in 1967 it was wider than ever. However, one cannot help being impressed by the stubbornness and apparent intractability of that relatively small shortfall of the export surplus. With the huge increases in GNP and in the volume of foreign trade, why should it have been impossible to squeeze or switch another two or three billion dollars worth of goods and services out of domestic and into foreign use?

In Table 1, the officially reported deficits on liquidity balance are shown immediately below the transfer gaps. For several years, the discrepancies between the two magnitudes are conspicuous enough to arouse curiosity and call for explanation. In 14 years the transfer gap

---

[8] In order to make these comparisons, calculations had to be carried out to two decimal places. Table 2 shows the percentages only to one decimal place.

exceeded the liquidity deficit, in the other four years the opposite relationship prevailed. The transfer gap is the larger of the two magnitudes whenever inflows of foreign long-term capital are recorded that we exclude from item No. 11 of Table 1, such as foreign purchases, private or official, of U.S. Government bonds (or other Treasury securities of maturities over 12 months) or foreign long-term loans, private or official, to American banks (for example, in the form of time deposits) and/or when errors and omissions are entered with a positive sign and treated in effect as unrecorded receipts.[9]

These unrecorded receipts, excluded from the figures entered in Table 1, were chiefly responsible for the transfer gap exceeding the liquidity deficit in every year before 1960. In that year, errors and omissions changed their sign from positive to negative and thus became unrecorded payments or outflows. In the last two years, 1966 and 1967, it was chiefly the increase in foreign official holdings of medium-term U.S. Government securities and of time deposits or certificates of deposits in American banks that made the liquidity deficit appear smaller than the transfer gap.[10]

From what has been said before, it should be clear that the transfer gaps were minute fractions of GNP. (See Table 2). Only in 1950 was the gap above 1 per cent. In the other 17 years the percentages varied between 0.2 and 0.9; this high figure was reached in two years, 1958 and 1959. The gaps in 1965 and 1966 were only 0.2 and 0.3 per cent, and the alarming gap in 1967 was not higher than 0.6 per cent of GNP. I point to these relative mini-gaps not in order to skirt the issue: the problem of adjustment. On the contrary, I believe that a full realization of the proportions involved may help us understand what can and what cannot be expected to contribute to the solution of the problem.

The parallel changes in Real and Financial Transfers

In every one of the 18 years did Net Real Transfers fall short of Net Financial Transfers, but the 17 changes of the two magnitudes from one year to the next were ordinarily in the same direction. Financial trans-

---

[9] In 1957, when the balance of payments on liquidity basis showed the only surplus in all 18 years, this was the result of errors and omissions of record height: $1.2 billion for eceipts from unrecorded transactions.

[10] The liquidity deficits in 1966 and 1967 would have been much bigger if "foreign official agencies", chiefly central banks, had not chosen to invest large amounts in "long-term time deposits or certificates of deposit" in American banks. Such holdings had been small in earlier years, but in 1966 and 1967 they increased by $793 million and $1,040 million, respectively. Had these amounts been in the usual form of "liquid liabilities", the liquidity deficits would have been that much bigger.

fers increased in nine years and real transfers increased in seven of these years; financial transfers decreased in eight years and real transfers decreased in six of these years. (In two of the four years in which real transfers did not move in the same direction as financial transfers—1951 and 1961—the gap was narrowing.)

The parallelism in these movements indicates, in my opinion, that the trade balance was surely not sticky or inflexible and that the adjustment mechanism was at work throughout the period, even if the adjustments of the export surplus were not of the size required to close the transfer gap. In several years, the change in real transfers matched the change in financial transfers closely; for example, the increases in 1956 were matched precisely—both were $1.8 billion—and the increases in 1955 and 1964 were more than matched, as net real transfers increased slightly more than net financial transfers. At least once, the matching was accomplished over two years: reductions of net financial transfers by $3.1 billion in 1965 and 1966 were accompanied by reductions in real transfers by $2.8 billion, in the same two years.

To expect complete matching in single years would be to suppose that the adjustment process works without any lags and without any slippage. To entertain such a supposition would be unreasonable. However, be this as it may, the parallelism of changes observed over the period is impressive. If we disregard the first two years and omit also the last year, and thus look at the series only from 1952 to 1966, we find that in 13 out of 14 years the changes were in the same direction. This does not, of course, prove that the changes in real transfers were determined or influenced by changes in financial transfers, but the hypothesis of such an influence is surely consistent with the statistical record. The reverse hypothesis, posing an influence of the real flows upon nonaccommodating financial flows, would lack theoretical plausibility. There is no theory that would explain or predict that military expenditures, government grants, direct investment, and portfolio investment in long-term foreign securities depend on, and will rise and fall with, changes in the export surplus.

Regression analysis

The preceding argument, based on simple parallelisms and covariations of statistical magnitudes, is probably too primitive, since more respected techniques are at our disposal. We shall regress Net Real Transfers on Net Financial Transfers.[11]

Using the numbers from Table 1, and letting y denote Net Real

[11] I am indebted to my colleague, Professor Wallace E. Oates, for doing the computations for me.

Transfers and x denote Net Financial Transfers, regression of y on x for all 18 observations yields the equation

$$y = -1.14 + 0.80 \ x. \qquad R^2 = 0.64.$$
$$(1.1) \quad (5.3)$$

The numbers in parentheses under the parameters are the T-statistics; they indicate that the coefficient of the x-variable is highly significant at a 99 per cent level of confidence, whereas the constant term is not significantly different from zero at a 95 per cent level of confidence. The coefficient of determination, $R^2 = 0.64$, indicates that 64 per cent of all changes in Net Real Transfers are statistically explained by changes in Net Financial Transfers.

It is apparent that the observation for 1967 lies well off the regression line fitted through the other 17 observations. Using only these 17 observations, from 1950 to 1966, the regression equation becomes

$$y = -1.74 + 0.92 \ x. \qquad R^2 = 0.71.$$
$$(1.8) \quad (6.0)$$

As before, the coefficient of the x-variable is highly significant, whereas the constant term is not (at a 95 per cent level of confidence) significantly different from zero. The coefficient of determination, $R^2 = .71$, is higher than for the first equation.

With the coefficient of the x-variable, 0.92, not significantly different from unity, this equation would support the hypothesis that any increase (or decrease) in financial transfers would be accompanied by almost the same increase (or decrease) in real transfers.

The observation for 1967 is sadly out of line; something must have happened to prevent the adjustment of real transfers to the large increase in financial transfers in that year. Few economists would be at a loss to explain the misbehavior of real transfers in 1967. We reserve our comments for later. But we should report here that, had exports and imports behaved in conformance with the regression equation for the previous 17 years, Net Real Transfers in 1967 should have been $6.8 billion instead of the $4.5 billion actually achieved.

D. EXPLANATIONS AND IMPLICATIONS

The results of the regression analysis are surprising. Not even the greatest transfer optimists would have expected to see a regression coefficient as high as that—except perhaps Professor Albert Hahn, the proponent of the "boomerang theory", which holds that, as all boomerangs come back, each and every manipulation of financial transfers will be fully reflected in changes of the trade balance and, hence, leave the balance of payments unchanged.

The fact that, according to our equation, an average of 92 per cent of all changes in the Net Financial Transfers of the United States between 1950 and 1966 was reflected by changes in its Net Real Transfers to foreign countries calls for some theoretical explanations. Moreover, if we believe what we have seen, we must not disregard its political implications. For it means that all policy recommendations by official experts, American and European, and all policy measures adopted by the U.S. Government to remove or reduce the payments deficit by checking and controlling financial outflows have been patently wrong.

Theoretical explanations

In my testimony before the Economic Committee of the U.S. Congress, in February 1968, I made the following presentation:

> "There are two extreme positions concerning the effectiveness of such a corrective measure. At one end is the opinion that a reduction of a financial transfer, say by $1 billion will leave all other items in the payments balance unchanged and merely reduce the financing item that is, reduce the loss of gold or the increase in liquid foreign liabilities.
> "At the opposite end is the opinion that a reduction in financial transfers by $1 billion will reduce the export surplus by the same amount and hence will leave the deficit, and the need to finance it, unchanged.
> "I propose to regard the first theory as naive and the second as over-sophisticated; both are wrong. The truth lies in the middle, and whether it comes closer to the naive or to the over-sophisticated theory will depend on circumstances."

I then proceeded to a brief exposition of the circumstances that might determine the outcome. I first discussed the possibility that restrictions on a particular form of financial transfer may lead to offsetting changes in other items within the capital account. For example, a cut in capital exports to Europe may result in an increase in American capital flows to Canada, in a reduction of European investments in the United States, or in withdrawals of European capital from the United States. Substitutions of permitted for prohibited transactions could thus make the imposed controls ineffective. As a next step in the exposition, I assumed that the controls would be effective and actually reduce Net Financial Transfers. The extent to which this reduction would or would not be reflected in a parallel reduction in Net Real Transfers would depend on the effects upon aggregate spending at home and abroad and on the effects which the changes in spending would have upon incomes, prices, imports, and exports in the countries concerned.

The desired objective of the imposition of restrictions on financial transfers is, of course, to remove the deficit. This objective can be achieved only if the export surplus does not decline *pari passu* with the amount of financial transfers. Now, what are the conditions for "independence" of the export surplus from the financial outflow? Just what circumstances would have to prevail for Net Real Transfers to be unaffected by a reduction in Net Financial Transfers? Assume that, because of restrictions imposed, investments planned by an American firm in Europe are either indefinitely postponed or fully financed by funds raised in European markets. To leave aggregate spending in the United States unaffected, it would be necessary that the American firm decide that its own funds which it had planned to use for its European investments will not be touched. In other words, the firm must refrain from using any of these funds for any other purpose and must build up an idle cash position, not needed and not wanted for anything. To leave aggregate spending in Europe unaffected, it would be necessary that some Europeans can find hitherto idle cash or can persuade their banks to extend new credits enabling them to make outlays in the same amounts as would have been made with the funds of the American firm. Assuming the American firm goes ahead with its plans but finances them with European funds, total spending in Europe can be unaffected only if these European funds would have remained idle in the absence of the borrowing by the American firm.

These are rather strong conditions, not likely to be realized. If they are not realized, then aggregate demand will be affected by the restrictions on capital. There will be more spending in the United States, resulting in larger imports and in reduced efforts to seek export outlets for American products. And there will be less spending in Europe, with the result that imports will be less than they would be otherwise and the export business will be pushed more vigorously. Hence, the restrictions on capital exports from the United States are likely to lead to reductions of the American export surplus on goods and services. The next question is what conditions would have to prevail to cause this impact to be 100 per cent.

Accepted transfer theory, based on income effects alone, does not support the expectation of a 1:1 relation between changes in financial and real transfers. Even if domestic spending in the United States is increased by precisely the amount of funds which the restrictions prevent from going abroad, and even if spending in Europe is reduced exactly by the amount of funds prevented from coming from the United States, income effects, reinforced by multiplier effects, cannot produce complete adjustment of the trade balance to the change in the capital balance. They cannot, at least, as long as the marginal propensities to save and to import are within the most likely ranges. Income effects alone can account at best for trade adjustment of somewhere between 40 and 70 per cent of the effected changes in financial transfers. There is no reason, however, to rely on income effects alone.

Several other factors, besides income effects, may play important roles. 1) So-called "direct effects" of changes in financial transfers may affect purchases from abroad—that is, the recipients of the foreign funds may immediately use them for buying imports, and the reduction in the availability of foreign funds may inhibit such purchases. 2) Price effects of changes in aggregate spending may redirect the flows of goods and services to conform to the changes in the financial flows. (According to one strand of the classical tradition, price effects should be regarded as more important than income effects.) 3) Induced changes in investment —accelerator effects—may greatly reinforce the income effects, that is to say, domestic investments may change in a parallel fashion with the domestic disbursements affected by increases or reductions of financial transfers. (If the marginal propensity to invest equals the marginal propensity to save, changes in real transfers will completely match all changes in financial transfers.) 4) Monetary policies of the countries may reinforce the automatic effects of changes in financial transfers. For example, the country confronted with increasing financial outflows may restrain domestic spending by tightening credit; countries receiving increased capital inflows may allow the secondary credit expansions to occur which the banks would be induced to undertake; in the opposite case, of reductions in financial transfers, the country with reduced outflows may exercise less restraint, and the country with reduced inflows, more restraint in monetary policy, with the normal effects on the flows of goods and services.[12]

Any one of these four factors may cause, or contribute to, full matching of changes in financial flows by parallel changes in real flows. It is difficult to diagnose the conditions actually prevailing and thus to predict the actual outcome at any particular time. Yet, the existence of conditions making for full matching is by no means so unlikely as to cause great surprise at the observations of the 17 years, 1950 to 1966.

A paradox and its solution

There remains a big puzzle, however. If the conditions actually were such that changes in financial transfers from 1950 to 1966 were so

[12] For a more detailed explanation of all these factors see above, pp. 425–432, and 440–446.

promptly matched by parallel changes in real transfers, why then did the transfer gap fail to close or even to get any narrower? (The average gap of the last four years, 1963-1966, was $2.4 billion; the average of the 17 years, 1950-1966, was $2.3 billion; the average of the last five, six, and seven years varied between $2.2 and $2.3 billion.) It seems strange that the "transfer mechanism" should work perfectly for increases and reductions of remittances but not at all for the initial or chronic gap. This is a paradox that cries for an explanation.

Analogies are sometimes helpful, and I can think of several. Foremost among them is the idea of automatic governors, regulators, balancers, robot controls, servomechanisms, or feedback systems, designed to adjust speed rotation, flow level, temperature, pressure, charge, load, voltage, and many other things, working well and accurately—but set at a wrong point, say, two or three notches below the desired magnitude. Alas, this analogy does not tell us why the balance-of-payments or the transfer gap should be automatically controlled by an adjustment mechanism which holds the deficit consistently to $2.3 billion. Why should the mechanism work so well in stabilizing the gap or deficit around this value—forcing the flow of goods and services to change consistently with the flow of funds—but fail to work in reducing the deficit to zero?

The answer may lie in the interference of some "manual controls" with the automatic ones, or of more or less discretionary policies with the undesigned reflexes and reactions or general rules of thumb that are behind the so-called automatic system. Perhaps the payments deficit oscillated with so narrow deviations around a central value because monetary and fiscal policies became circumspect and restrictive whenever the deficit increased beyond the accustomed level, and became more relaxed and more liberal whenever the payments position showed signs of improvement.

In order to attempt some checking of this hunch—I hesitate to call it a "test" of a "hypothesis", because my attempt is too superficial to deserve these names—I looked into the record of behavior of three monetary variables which are determined or influenced by the monetary authorities of the United States: Federal Reserve Credit, Member Bank Reserves, and Total Money Stock. In view of concurrent developments, which may modify the effectiveness of these variables, the amounts of Federal Reserve Credit (holdings of loans and Government securities) and of Member Bank Reserves (held in Federal Reserve Banks) had been adjusted to take account of changes in reserve requirements, and the series of Total Money Stock (demand deposits at all commercial banks, currency outside banks, foreign demand balances at Federal Reserve Banks, and time deposits at commercial banks, without interbank deposits and deposits of the U.S. Government) was taken to include what is sometimes called quasi-money.[13] I then compared the annual changes of these three variables with the payments position of the United States in the same years. Some of the findings merit report and comment.

1. After the first large deficit, in 1950, there was between 1951 and 1957 only one very bad year, 1953, with a liquidity deficit of $2.2 billion. The Federal Reserve Banks engaged in considerable offsetting (by expanding its loans and investments) but did so with sufficient restraint to keep Member Bank Reserves down to a rate of increase of only 0.7 per cent, the lowest rate between 1950 and 1955.

2. The years 1958, 1959, and 1960 were the worst sequence of record deficits: $3.4, $3.9, and again $3.9 billion. (The transfer gaps in my computation were even higher.) The reaction of the Federal Reserve System was very late but drastic. In 1960, Federal Reserve Credit was reduced absolutely, the rate of increase becoming —0.6 per cent, and Member Bank Reserves likewise fell absolutely, the rate of increase becoming —0.5 per cent. Neither of these things was done before or after 1960 in the entire period from 1950 to 1967. Total Money Stock increased by only 0.1 per cent, the lowest annual increase in the 17 years.

3. After four years of relatively high deficits between 1961 and 1964 ($2.7 billion in 1963 and $2.8 billion in 1964), 1965 brought relief, with a deficit of only $1.3. The monetary authorities took quick advantage by increasing Federal Reserve Credit by 12 per cent in that year—the highest rate of increase in the 17-year period—and thereby allowing Member Bank Reserves to increase by 5 per cent—the highest rate between 1951 and 1966. Total Money Stock, likewise, increased in 1965 by the record rate for the period, 8.9 per cent.

The three episodes are consistent with the suspicion that some of the more drastic actions of the monetary authorities between 1950 and 1966 served to keep the payments deficits within bounds. The policies of 1953 and 1960 were clearly designed to halt expansion or force contraction of domestic credit and aggregate spending; the policy of 1965 was an extraordinary push toward monetary expansion, at a time when the payments deficit was reduced but far from disappearing.

It is the third episode that suggests an explanation of a "lower limit" to the deficit. If expansionary forces are allowed free rein as soon as the payments position becomes slightly less embarrassing, this is analogous to setting the automatic governor or regulator of the servomechanic

---

[13] The source for the series used was *Triangles of U.S. Economic Data,* published periodically by the Federal Reserve Bank of St. Louis.

system at a nonzero point. This is not to say that there has been a deliberate attempt to prevent restoration of external balance. Far from it; the goal of external balance has, at least since 1960, been one of the "top priorities" of the country's economic objectives—but only one among several. The goals of full employment and faster growth, various targets in the wars on domestic poverty and on hostile foreign powers, and a few other aims, all these compete for first rank in public policy. At a particular moment the government's prime concern will be with that objective which to attain it has most spectacularly failed; but its concern will be diverted to some competing objective long before full success in the previous effort has been achieved. If monetary expansion is thought to be a medicine against unemployment and sluggish growth, though it is toxic with regard to the external payments position, an improvement of that position will entice the authorities to take the toxic medicine long before the payments deficit is cured.

The suggested solution of the paradox rests on a political, not an economic hypothesis; but this should cause no surprise, since all governmental decisions, in the economic area no less than in others, are political. Again, no criticism is implied, for it can hardly be otherwise. One cannot even complain about the weakness, inconsistency, unreliability, or shortsightedness of government, for one may in full rationality argue that the attainment of a chosen end may, after an honest try, appear too costly; if too much of what is also badly wanted, say, a high rate of employment, has to be sacrificed in order to gain complete removal of the payments deficit by means of monetary policy, one must understand the tergiversation on the part of monetary authorities. It is not possible to be consistent in the use of an instrument that is supposed to serve several different objectives at once. In brief, if deflation of credit, money, incomes, prices, and employment is needed to remove the external deficit of the nation, the deficit will not be removed.

The off-year, 1967

While excuses can be made for the monetary authorities' failure to get rid of the payments deficit by means of deflation, the monetary and fiscal behavior of the off-year, 1967, cannot thus be defended. The statistical observations for that year have been found to be far off the regression line fitted for the period 1950 to 1966. The examination of the monetary record yields some data that illuminate the strange behavior of the variables of our main concern in this study.

Perhaps it should first be recalled that the liquidity deficit of 1966 was low enough to tempt the policy makers into continuing a policy of fiscal and monetary ease. They should have been told, however, that

conscious window-dressing and inappropriate consistency in the application of inflexible definitions of liquidity (such as classifying near-liquid
liabilities as nonliquid) understated the liquidity deficit in a most misleading or deceptive way. (Note that the Transfer Gap in 1966 was $2.4
billion while the liquidity deficit was reported at $1.4 billion.) Whether
misled by the supposedly modest payments deficit of 1966 or by other
delusions, the Congress and the monetary authorities chose to combine
a large budget deficit with a large credit expansion in 1967. While the
Congress delayed an urgently needed tax increase, the monetary authorities increased Federal Reserve Credit by 9.3 per cent over the year
before and thereby increased total Member Bank Reserves by 5.6 per
cent, the highest annual increase in 16 years. Total Money Stock, as a
result, increased by 8 per cent, the second-highest rate in the same
period.

Not surprisingly, the deficit of 1967 was a whopper. The seriously
understated liquidity deficit was "only" $3.6 billion, but the Transfer
Gap was $4.8 billion, the biggest ever.

Having designated 1967 as the "off-year", I should warn that this
does not mean to imply a suggestion that 1968 will be back in line. The
increase in taxes, the cuts in the budget, and the slow-down in money
creation probably came too late to halt the price and income inflation and
improve the payments position in 1968. The deficit on capital account may
be lower than in previous years, but the surplus on goods and services
will probably be much lower too. The inflation has surely had its effects
on real transfers, raising the demand for imports and reducing the supply
of exports.

Had there been many more years like 1967 in the series of post-war
payments deficits, I would not have taken the time to defend the hypothesis that a transfer problem was the source of the troubles. Monetary
overexpansion would have been a perfectly good explanation. But 1967
was the exception, not the rule. Even for that year, one can hardly attribute the entire deficit or gap to inflationary policy. Of the statistical Transfer Gap of 1967—$4.8 billion—one could, on the basis of our regression
equation, attribute about one-half to fiscal-monetary inflation and the
other half to the chronic transfer difficulty which, at unchanged exchange
rates, only net deflation could have overcome.

The transfer correlation and its policy implications

If it is correct to regard 1967 (and probably 1968) as exceptional
and to assume that, after the inflationary policy of the United States
is stopped, things will revert to the pattern observed between 1950
and 1966, important policy implications should be recognized. For, if
changes in Net Financial Transfers are almost fully matched by changes

in Net Real Transfers, expectations that restrictions on capital outflows and/or reductions in military expenditures abroad will close the Transfer Gap will necessarily be disappointed.

A strong alliance of official, academic, and self-appointed experts has insisted that the payments deficit of the United States can be and will be removed by drastic reduction in remittances to foreign countries. The official experts want to restrict the outflow of private capital, academic experts want to cut or stop military expenditures abroad, and many experts from business and finance want to reduce foreign-aid outlays. I submit that all three groups are wrong if they believe that the reductions which they favor would reduce the payments deficit by even approximately similar amounts. Indeed, if the observed correlation still holds, the exports surplus would decline *pari passu* with the financial outflows, and the gap would be practically unchanged. If the financial transfers were cut to the size of the normal Transfer Gap, the export surplus might disappear altogether—and the gap might survive.

The implication of all this should be clear: the balance-of-payments program pursued by the United States Government, and applauded by the governments of the surplus countries, is useless for the purpose for which it is designed, and injurious to several other matters of considerable economic and political importance.

E. THE NORMAL VOLUME OF FINANCIAL TRANSFERS

The argument in the preceding section was that attempts to correct the payments deficit by restricting financial outflows are misdirected and futile, because a reduction in Net Financial Transfers will cause Net Real Transfers to be reduced, rather than the Transfer Gap. In the remaining part of this paper, however, we shall, for the sake of another argument, assume that the attempt to correct the deficit by restrictions of financial outflow may, after all, be successful in achieving their purpose, that is, in closing the gap by cutting Net Financial Transfers down to the level of Net Real Transfers, a level not simultaneously lowered in the process.

This assumption is not meant to be a retreat from a carefully developed position, but only a device to exhibit another error in the reasoning of the advocates of restriction. They usually overlook that temporary measures have only temporary effects and cannot produce or promote adjustment to long-run forces. I shall argue that the financial transfers to foreign countries have not been abnormally high; that they cannot be expected to be substantially lower in the long run as fractions of GNP and must therefore be expected to increase in dollar volume; and that voluntary or mandatory controls and restrictions, however effective they may be for a few years, cannot reduce the "normal" volume of financial transfers in the long run.

Normal capital exports

For many observers the idea of a "normal" volume of capital exports seems to be difficult to accept. The same persons, economists or laymen, who like to talk about all sorts of things as being "structural" or "structurally determined" believe that governments could and should give the flow of capital just about any magnitude or direction they like. Exports or imports of commodities are recognized among the "sticky aggregates", in physical volume, in total value, or in relation to national income or GNP, and many "propensities" are accepted as relatively stable and not easily shaped by government edicts—but not international capital movements, and not propensities to lend or invest abroad. These, apparently, can be made to be what the political powers may prefer them to be or, at least, they can be cut down to any size that the powers approve.

I do not like the words "structure" and "structural", because they are more often misused than used with clear and honest meanings. But when they refer to certain relationships that are not easily altered or influenced and have inherent stability or resilience, the terms are used legitimately. If these terms are applied to such things as ratios of imports to national income (average or marginal, at given relative prices), then I submit that we can with not much less justification speak of a structural level of capital movements among countries with different income per head and different capital endowment.

The United States has more capital per head, more capital per worker, and also a greater supply of new savings per head and per worker than any other country in the world. This relative abundance makes it more than likely that the marginal efficiency of new investment will as a rule be lower in the United States than elsewhere (or would be lower if capital outflows were restricted). This state of affairs implies that, in the absence of prohibitive risks and obstacles, long-term capital will normally flow from the United States to other countries. It is possible, of course, that, for one reason or another, investment opportunities in the United States will at times be more promising or attractive than elsewhere, but—assuming peace and order—such periods will be only relatively brief. The same technological or organizational developments that may at certain times make new investment particularly attractive in American industries will soon thereafter create similar investment opportunities abroad and restore the conditions for capital exports from the United States. One must reckon with this tendency as a persistent force for many years to come.

Capital movements from countries where the supply of new savings is larger to countries where it is smaller, relative to the available supply of human and natural resources, are beneficial to both the exporting and the receiving countries. Some governments do not see it this way, for example, when they have sectional rather than national or international interests at heart, when they are motivated by meta-economic feelings such as national pride, or when, in choosing between the long view and the short, they impatiently adopt the latter. For the international community, there can be no doubt, general welfare calls for a distribution of the total supply of capital in such a way that the marginal social returns are equalized in all uses everywhere—and this implies capital exports from the country where the sources of new savings are, relative to other resources, the richest.

Acceptance of this proposition does not include specification of any particular order of magnitude or of any particular selection of recipient countries. To speak of the latter problem first, if countries are ranked by supply of new savings per head, nothing can be said a priori about whether those of rank Nos. 2, 3, or 4 will be net suppliers of capital funds or net recipients. Since capital is conveyed in various forms and at various terms, it is quite likely that a country will both import and export capital, receiving direct investment by foreign firms and making direct investment abroad, selling securities, equity as well as debt, to foreign buyers and buying securities from foreign sellers. Thus, even if countries with a large domestic supply of capital may be net exporters, their receiving foreign capital in large amounts would be neither uneconomic nor irrational in any sense.

Again, nothing can be said a priori about the size of net capital exports. One can, at best, examine the historical records and speculate on whether the observed magnitudes and ratios have been the results of accident, of temporary circumstances, or of conditions likely to prevail in the future. Several choices have to be made about the data: should we be more interested in fractions of GNP or in dollar amounts; in the sum of private and governmental capital or in private capital alone; in American capital alone or in the net balance on capital account, American and foreign; in capital exports including reinvestments of earnings from capital lent or invested in the past or in exports of "new" capital, not counting reinvestments of profits, dividends, and interest? On all four questions I decide in favor of the first alternative. I propose to look at ratios to GNP, because dollar volumes alone can hardly give us a long-run norm in a context of growth. I propose to look at the sum of governmental (grants and loans) and private capital (loans and investments), because all these financial resources supposedly come from the same source, the U.S. national income. I propose to focus only on

American capital, and to disregard imports of foreign capital, chiefly because these imports amounted to very little until 1966, and the very small figures were rather unstable (even becoming negative in two years). Finally I propose, though rather half-heartedly, for reasons to be explained later, to include reinvestments of earnings.

Capital exports, 1950-1967

From 1950 to 1967, foreign grants and loans by the U.S. Government varied between 0.4 and 1.3 per cent of GNP; only in the first two years, 1950 and 1951, did they exceed 1 per cent, and the average over the 18 years was 0.54 per cent.

In the same period, foreign long-term loans and investments by private Americans varied between 0.1 and 1.0 per cent of GNP; only in four years, 1951 to 1954, did they fall short of 0.5 per cent, and the average over the 18 years was 0.7.

Together, capital exports, governmental and private, varied between 0.7 and 1.8 per cent of GNP; only in four years (1953 to 1955 and in 1959) were they below 1 per cent; in another five years (1950, 1957, 1960, 1963, and 1964) they were 1.4 per cent or higher; and the average over the 18 years was 1.2 per cent of GNP.

During the last five years of the period capital exports were restricted, first through the imposition of the Interest Equalization Tax in 1964, then through the introduction in 1965 of voluntary restraints upon loans and direct investments. Although the imposition of mandatory controls early in 1968 may indicate that the previous programs did not do all that the Government hoped to achieve, we were told in repeated statements by the Secretary of the Treasury that the tax on the purchase of foreign securities and the voluntary controls on foreign loans by banks and on loans and investments by large corporations were effective in reducing exports of American capital. Total capital exports, private and official, were only 1.1, 1.1, and 1.2 per cent of GNP in 1965, 1966, and 1967, whereas they had been 1.6 per cent in 1964 and almost 1.4 per cent on the average from 1960 to 1964. One may argue that the capital exports in the early 1960's were abnormally large because this was a period of widening horizons for American corporations, many of whom discovered for the first time the opportunities of foreign investment, especially the new opportunities behind the tariff wall of the European Economic Community. However, though these particular opportunities may be getting exhausted, we should not regard them as so unique and *sui generis* that we could not expect them to be replaced by other attractive outlets in Europe or elsewhere.

If we accepted 1.4 per cent of GNP as the norm for unrestricted capital exports of the United States, we would tacitly accept rather niggardly allocation for aid to developing countries. There has been wide agreement on a simple rule of thumb: the rich nations should be prepared to give 1 per cent of their gross national product for the economic development of poor countries. (This rule has recently been restated by UNCTAD, the United Nations Conference on Trade and Development, with the interpretation that this target indicates the amount the developing countries ought to have left for their use after paying interest and amortization of principal in servicing their old debts.) The United States has averaged only one-half of the target aid and the Congress seems unwilling to continue even this much. If appropriations in future years become more generous and get closer to the target, perhaps in order to emulate the much larger appropriations made by France, Germany, and the Netherlands, we should see normal capital exports to both developing and developed countries exceed 1.5 per cent of GNP.

The notion that the normal rate of capital exports ought not to be financed out of earnings from capital exported in prior years, but to constitute net additions to the resources available to the receiving countries, seems reasonable though unrealistic. On that basis, that is net of earnings received from past loans and investments, private capital exports would have been negative in eleven of the last 18 years, including the last three, 1965 to 1967.[14] Since accumulated investment grows continually, dividend and interest payments increase from year to year and first overtake and eventually dwarf the flow of "new" capital. The idea that a rich economy shares its supply of current domestic savings with less affluent economies implies that new outside resources will be made available to these economies. When earnings from past foreign investment exceed current capital exports, the flow of additional resources from the rich country appears to be negative. If it is to remain positive, the rate of capital exports including reinvestment out of earnings must increase over the years—until the supply of current savings (relative to other resources) in the countries that hitherto imported capital catches up with that of the rich country.

This proposition, if it is considered plausible, is not an argument for grants, merely nominal interest rates, or continually deferred repayment of loans to developing nations. It is at best an argument for rising targets for aid counted in the conventional way. It may even be countered by an economic argument: if the capital of prior years has been put to good uses, productively invested, the returns on this capital are really part of the resources of the countries that supplied the capital. It is therefore inappropriate to say that the countries that received the capital use

---

[14] Calculated from balance-of-payments statistics, *Survey of Current Business*, June 1968.

their own resources to service their debts or to repatriate profits and principal. There is, however, no use arguing to whom the returns of capital properly "belong", to the user or the supplier. The demand that the capital exports from more affluent to less affluent countries be increasing fractions of GNP does not depend on the answer to that question.

Europe's need for American capital

The preceding discussion related chiefly to the capital exports of the richest and the capital imports of the poorest countries. There is, however, a very different question, relating to the highly developed countries of Europe, which "structurally" are probably net exporters of capital but have been "flooded" with American capital. Can it be argued that these capital imports are structurally determined? If not, would not the "normal" outflow of capital from the United States be much smaller?

Several collateral circumstances complicate the answers. There is the temporary attractiveness of direct investment in the European Economic Community in view of the customs union with its protective tariffs against products from outside. There is the "management gap" between European and American industries, which may operate as attraction for capital in joint supply with managerial talent. Perhaps these and similar factors account for the entire flow of funds and no more permanent and fundamental reasons exist for the flow of American capital to Europe. Moreover, the inflow of capital funds from the United States has not been accompanied by a transfer of real resources, but to a large extent only by an accumulation of liquid dollar balances. The fact that there has not been real but only a paper transfer suggests to some that Europe had no need for the American funds. A "structural" theory pronounces on relationships in real terms; if no real transfers have taken place and no real resources, therefore, been received, does this not prove that the capital was not really needed?

Such an inference would not be logically sound. From the existence of a Transfer Gap it does not follow that the large financial transfers had no economic function. That the real transfers were not achieved proves only that the adjustment policies of the countries concerned were inadequate. The international flow of goods is directed by international income and price differentials and these differentials can be changed by policies affecting aggregate demand and exchange rates. The richest country can "pull in" real resources from the poorest countries if it expands effective demand vigorously enough; the poorest countries can "push out" real resources to the richest if they deflate enough. Such movements would indicate neither that the rich needed the resources, nor that the poor did not need them.

The question may be differently interpreted. Since Europe did not "miss" the real resources which it failed to receive, but apparently had all it wanted, it evidently did not need them. Perhaps the word "need" confuses the issue, because it suggests a lack or want of something. The point, however, is whether or not the transfer of real resources could improve their optimal allocation. A country with a given endowment of resources and a given supply of current savings, may have a relative abundance or a relative scarcity of capital, depending on conditions elsewhere. An increase in the supply of capital abroad may change a relative abundance into a relative scarcity of capital in a country in which nothing at all has changed.[15] In this sense, it does not depend on Europe alone whether it "needs" more capital. As long as marginal yields are greater than zero, all countries could do with more than they have.

Military expenditures abroad and Net Financial Transfers

The series of foreign military expenditures of the United States, expressed as percentages of GNP, shows considerable stability. Apart from the first year of the period covered, 1950, the deviations from the average, 0.57 per cent, were small; the low was 0.4 per cent, the high 0.8 per cent, and in 14 of the 18 years the percentages were 0.5, 0.6 and 0.7.

It does not follow that this has to continue for many more years. Public opinion in the United States is becoming increasingly opposed to the country's role as "policeman of the world". One cannot expect that the swing from foreign intervention to isolationism will be complete, but there is a prospect of reductions in the share of GNP going to military expenditures abroad.

Several experts entertain high hopes regarding the relief for the balance of payments with the end of the war in Viet Nam. I believe these hopes are exaggerated. What I hope and expect is that destruction will give way to rebuilding, and that this change will reduce military expenditures and increase foreign aid. Raising the appropriations to foreign aid and lifting the restrictions on private capital exports may easily take up all that can be saved on military expenditures.

It is possible that in the future foreign long-term capital will come to the United States to a much larger extent than it has in the past. There may be increasing attractions both in direct and in portfolio investment. One had better not count on such developments, however. In any case, the order of magnitude of such capital imports is not likely to be such

---

[15] Few persons in the United States may admit that the country "needs" more immigration. Yet, as long as labor could earn more in the United States than elsewhere, labor is "scarce" in the United States.

as to call for a significant modification of Net Financial Transfers from the United States.

My conclusion is that we must reckon with a long-term norm for Net Financial Transfers of at least 1.5 per cent of GNP, and probably higher.

The required Net Real Transfers

The Transfer Gap must be closed soon, and there is only one way of doing this safely: by increasing Net Real Transfers to the level of Net Financial Transfers. For, even if one assumes that the latter can be reduced by means of government restrictions, no one can expect that such restrictions can be maintained and enforced permanently in an essentially free society or that temporary restrictions can have permanent effects, reducing normal outflows to a lower level. If there is something like a normal level of Net Financial Transfers, attempts to reduce them temporarily by temporary restrictions cannot reasonably be regarded as "adjustment measures". Such measures may at best suppress the imbalance, but cannot remove it.

Real adjustment thus requires raising the level of Real Net Transfers of the United States to 1.5 per cent of GNP, and perhaps higher. With a GNP of about $870 billion expected for 1968, the required surplus on goods and services included among "real transfers" would be some $13 billion, and thus, a huge Transfer Gap must be expected this year. Projecting (not predicting) the increase of GNP at a compounded annual rate of 7 or 8 per cent—one-half real, one-half in price inflation—we may put for the year 1970 GNP at around $1,000 billion and the required Net Real Transfers at about $15 billion. That this would call for very substantial changes in the foreign-trade performance of the United States can best be realized by comparing the targets with the actually achieved figures of recent years: they were $4.6 and $4.5 billion in 1966 and 1967, and they may be even lower in 1968.

Many readers will probably be shocked by my ambitious targets. Yet, my ambition is by no means mercantilist in character; it is only an honest attempt to spell out the meaning of what virtually every economist and politician demands, namely, adjustment to achieve balance in international payments.

Looking at previous years, the Net Real Transfers of the United States have only five times in the 18 years reached or exceeded 1.1 per cent of GNP and have only once, in the exceptional year of 1957, reached the required 1.5 per cent. Thus a "big push" will be needed to do normally what has been achieved only once, thanks to fortuitous circumstances.

No one should think, however, that it would be impossible to achieve the required increase in the export surplus. The statistical Transfer Gap of 1967 was $4.5 billion. About one-half of it was attributable to an inflationary expansion in the United States, accompanied by exceptional slack in the demand from Germany and other European countries. Our estimate of the genuine Transfer Gap was between $2.3 and $2.5 billion. Once the European countries reach higher levels of effective demand and the United States succeeds in disinflating, the Transfer Gap should be reduced to its chronic level. The present volume of foreign trade of the United States is about $73 billion. An improvement in the balance of goods and services by $2.5 billion would be only 3.4 per cent of the trade volume. To be on the safe side, the improvement target ought to be 4 per cent of the trade volume, in addition to the improvements that should come from adjustments of aggregate demand in the United States and abroad. If the price elasticities of supply and demand in the foreign trade of the United States are within the ranges calculated by econometric techniques, a reduction of the external value of the dollar by four per cent would do the trick.

Econometricians recently have calculated the price elasticity of foreign demand for American exports to be greater than 3, and the elasticity of American demand for imports to be greater than unity. With all due reservations regarding the accuracy of such findings and the stability of the estimated coefficients, it seems safe to assume that a 4 per cent reduction in the exchange rate of the dollar would accomplish a combined change in exports and imports of at least 4 per cent, chiefly an increase in exports. It goes without saying that this need not mean more American products sold to Europe; with a complex multilateral-trade pattern, it would be naive to ask in advance which countries would buy what American goods at reduced prices.

Exchange-rate adjustment

A unilateral reduction in the exchange value of the dollar is impracticable, partly because of its (still uncut) link with gold, partly because the rate for the dollar can never be less than what other countries are willing to pay for it. The proposal that countries with payments surpluses raise the exchange rates of their currencies is impracticable, partly because their governments are unwilling to act deliberately to reduce the competiveness of their industries, partly because they can never be sure if the appreciation is not too little or too much and whether it would not prove completely wrong within a year or two. Just imagine France would have reacted to her supposedly persistent payments surplus by an appreciation of the franc, just before the enormous cost push of the summer of 1968. This French episode has taught us a lesson.

The point of it all is that a small adjustment of the exchange rate of the dollar can achieve without too much pain what a deflation in the

United States could accomplish only with almost unbearable suffering. A deflation that could push extra quantities of American goods into export markets and empty American pockets sufficiently to reduce the demand for imports, together enough to close the chronic Transfer Gap, would be intolerable. But how can the required adjustment of exchange rates be managed?

My prescription is for a widening of the margin of permissible deviations from par values—the so-called band proposal. Under the present rules of the Fund, deviations of exchange rates in the free markets are limited to 1 per cent of parity in each direction. This limitation ought to be changed to permit wider deviations, perhaps 5 per cent up and down. Variations of exchange rates of this order of magnitude would allow the adjustment mechanism to operate on the international flows of goods and services. No government would have to take unpopular action; supply and demand would be allowed to determine exchange rates within the fixed limits; and any variations within these limits would reverse themselves when conditions change.

This is not the place to furnish details for my prescription, to evaluate the arguments of its opponents, or to examine how the very serious obstacles in the way to its acceptance can be overcome. The chief aim of this article was to explain the persistence of the Transfer Gap and to indicate what kind of measures can, and what kind of measures cannot, be helpful in closing it.

Postscript after Eight Years[1]

With the hindsight at our disposal in 1976 we might be inclined to say that I was not sufficiently pessimistic in 1968 in my diagnosis and prognosis and, hence, not sufficiently radical in the therapy proposed. A strong case, however, can be made justifying my judgment on the basis of the statistical data available and the political attitudes prevailing at the time. I did correctly point to the deterioration of the external 'position of the United States; I noted the excessive monetary expansion of 1965 and the resulting large payments deficit of 1967; I observed that "the increase in taxes, the cuts in the budget, and the slow-down in money creation probably came too late to halt the price and income inflation and improve the payments position in 1968"; and I made the stark pronouncement that "real adjustment" required "raising the level of Real Net Transfers" to some $15 billion in 1970.

In 1967 I had recommended that the United States cut the link between dollar and gold in order to repair the overvaluation of the dollar without resorting to deflationary policies; and early in 1968 I had warned that the United States had only the choice of taking this "drastic action . . . now or two or three years from now."[2] Since the Government could not be persuaded to take this action in 1968—it took it precisely three years later—there was not much it could do to make the needed adjustment. As I wrote in the essay here republished, "A unilateral reduction in the exchange value of the dollar is impracticable, partly because of its (still uncut) link with gold, partly because the rate for the dollar can never be less than what other countries are willing to pay for it." In these cir-

1. Postscript appended in 1976.
2. Fritz Machlup, *Remaking the International Monetary System: The Rio Agreement and Beyond* (Baltimore: The Johns Hopkins Press, 1968), p. 121.

cumstances a widening of the band of permissible fluctuations around par values appeared to be the only makeshift available. I thought that a depreciation of the dollar by 4 per cent "would do the trick." This may well have been true in 1968. Three years later, in 1971, it was no longer true, and more substantial changes in the exchange rates became unavoidable.

INDEX

Accommodating capital movements, see Capital movements
Accounting balance, 3–4, 70, 82–88, 138, 141–166, 274 n
Adler, John H., 59 n
Alexander, Sidney S., 171–172, 174–194, 196, 201–204, 206–207, 213–214, 216, 222
Allen, Clark Lee, 5, 356 n
Allen, Roy G. D., 5, 198 n
Allen, William R., 5, 356 n
Altman, Oscar L., 324
Ambjörn, Erik, 320 n
Amonn, Alfred, 357
Angell, James W., 295 n, 329–330, 333, 335, 336, 345, 451 n
Arbitrage, in commodities, 12; in foreign exchange, 8, 272, 352 n; in gold, 28–37
Amdt, Heinz, W., 248 n
Artis, M. J., 246 n
Autonomous capital movements, see Capital movements
Autonomous change, in causal analysis, 112; induced versus, 50, 84, 129 n, 447–448; in foreign trade, 11–12, 50, 449; in investment and consumption, 434 n, 441–446
Autonomous items in payments balance, 50, 84, 130 n, 160–161

Bachmann, Hans, 356
Balance of payments, adjustment, 11, 16, 21–22, 30–33, 35–39, 149, 160, 264, 293–295, 316, 466, 486–490, 501–503; basic, 145, 146, 150, 151, 156, 159–161, 316–319; concepts of, 69–92, 141, 448 n; deficit and deflation, 31, 37, 71 n, 75–77, 189, 316, 401–402, 409, 415–416, 422–424, 425, 467–468, 493, 502–503; difficulties, 52–55, 76, 84–86, 105, 129, 275, 293–295, 316–319, 354, 362–363, 401–402, 465–470; discipline,

136–138, 160, 264, 294, 308; "favorable," 35, 47, 449 n; forecasts, 3–4, 69–70, 74–82, 393–394 n, 408; mechanism, 27–50, 101, 127 n, 136–138, 188–189, 247, 263–264, 293, 317, 352, 365, 401–416, 437, 449–450, 490, 503; offsets to, 83, 141, 148–149, 153–161, 448; statistics, 140–166, 274 n, 376, 388, 467, 471–486; United States, 138, 140–166, 241, 259, 388, 390–393, 465–503
Balance of trade, capital flow affecting, 20–22, 25–26, 30–33, 38–39, 149, 160, 402–408, 411, 447–464; devaluation affecting, 51–68, 171–194, 201–205, 212, 467; diagrams showing, 11–12, 16, 20–22, 29–31, 35–39, 40–41; "favorable," 22, 23; fluid or sticky, 81–82, 386 n, 451 n; initial equilibrium of, 55, 57–58; in real terms, 176, 185–186, 214–216; invisible items affecting, 22–25; is income minus absorption, 175; unilateral transfers and, 375, 380, 385, 388, 393, 426–432, 434, 436–446, 468, 471–473, 483, 500
Balogh, Thomas, 8 n, 93, 94, 95 n, 96, 97, 98–99, 102 n, 174 n, 196
Barn proposal, 364–365, 503
Barter effects, 100–103, 105, 106
Bastable, Charles F., 451 n
Baumgartner, Wilfrid, 314 n
Baumol, William J., 262 n
Beckerath, Erwin von, 357 n
Benefits and costs, of foreign reserves, 265–276
Bernstein, Edward M., 281, 308–310, 313–314, 321, 333–336
Beza, Sterie T., 339 n
Bimetallism, 306
Black, Max, 132 n
Black market, 123 n, 168
Blessing, Karl, 295
Boomerang theory, 486–487